# THE SOJOURNERS

## Life on the American Homefront During World War II

A novelized memoir of American life as witnessed by a young boy who grew up during the World War II era and the Cold War '50's.

By

R. Allen Pender

© 2002 by R. Allen Pender. All rights reserved.

No part of this book may be reproduced, stored in a retrieval system, or transmitted by any means, electronic, mechanical, photocopying, recording, or otherwise, without written permission from the author.

ISBN: 0-7596-8913-X

This book is printed on acid free paper.

This book is dedicated to my parents, grand parents, aunts and uncles and all those of their generations, the plain people who weathered the Great Depression and the winds of a World War. Without them there would be no story and possibly no nation. They were truly members of a great generation who left us the legacy of an indomitable American spirit sustained by their faith in God and the God given freedom and institutions of this Nation.

# INTRODUCTION

A few years ago, my granddaughter Amanda was doing a school assignment. A part of her research required that she interview her grandparents to determine such things as the national origin and the dates and places of birth of her ancestors. Another part of the assignment required her to ask about the participation of her ancestors in any historical events.

Her questions were simple enough. I knew some of my family history back to my great-great-grand parents and I had spent a great deal of time in my early life with my great- grand-mothers, so it didn't take too long to fill one side of a lined sheet of paper with the names and vital statistics of her ancestors; at least those dating back some seven generations. But, something was missing. A name with a birth date and a date of death separated by a dash doesn't tell the whole story. The dash line between birth and death represents a life time. That person had a personality and lived through a period of world history that dictated where they lived and what type of work they did.

Unfortunately, the generations preceding that of my grandparents did not have the technology to record and document their period of history. Photographs came into vogue during the later portion of my grandparent's lifetime. Black and white photos were common place during my mother's generation. I have plenty of photographs from that period. However, the inanimate images captured on film still do not convey the nature or personality of the subjects.

I had the unique opportunity of entering this world as it was in the grip of the Great Depression. This timing provided me with a platform to witness some of the most significant events of the twentieth century and quite possibly of all humanity.

In order to answer my grand daughter's question regarding our participation in historical events I have written this story about a people whose lives were forever altered by an event that occurred on December 7, 1941.

The Japanese attack on Peal Harbor brought the United States into a World War against the Axis powers, Germany, Japan and Italy. The attack on the American bases in the Hawaiian Islands was treated as just as severe as if the attack was on mainland United States. Today it would be. Even though it is off shore, the Hawaiian Islands are now one of our American States.

Practically overnight our Nation went into a War mode and I was able to witness possibly the greatest mobilization in the history of the modern world. This sometimes sleepy relaxed country, separated from the rest of the world by two oceans, was now caught between an Axis war machine intent on dominating and subjugating the world.

The threat to our homeland united the American people as never before. We had great pride in our country and great faith in our God. Individually and collectively we were prepared to make the sacrifices necessary to insure the sovereignty of our country and preserve our way of life.

It wasn't easy. Forced by circumstances beyond their control, families were disjointed, uprooted and replanted in new surroundings totally different from the historical home places their families enjoyed for generations. The people of this nation had to learn new occupations and to live in a war time economy. They had to assimilate into a new society composed of people of different ethnic and racial backgrounds. Everyone had to live and work together to defeat the common foe. This would be done, while each element of society tried to maintain some part of its traditional culture.

This story about the middle part of the twentieth century depicts one family's struggle to maintain their character despite the changes imposed by a world at war and a society struggling to adjust to the changes dictated by this era.

The impact of a war time America had a lasting effect on those who lived through that era. With the advent of the atomic age and the Cold War; a part of our society forgot the Spiritual source of this nation's strength as they charged ahead to get a part of the "good life" before an atomic conflagration destroyed the world. In prosperity they had forgotten their faith and ignored God.

This story, though fictional, depicts actual places and incidents as it reconstructs the lives of the characters that lived through this era. After more than fifty years, two elderly men, former boyhood neighbors meet to reminisce about those times. The meeting triggers a flood of memories where people, that were once part of the scene, become more than names. They take on personalities and without out realizing it at the time, their words and behavior have an impact that extends well beyond their lifetime. These men come full circle when they return to the old neighborhood where the missing element of their lives is revealed in the telling of the story.

The final words of this story were written on September 10, 2001. The next day September 11, 2001 became the Second Day of Infamy to be witnessed by this writer. I pray to God it will be the last.

R. Allen Pender

# TABLE OF CONTENTS

| | | |
|---|---|---|
| Chapter 1 | The Meeting | 1 |
| Chapter 2 | The Day of Infamy | 6 |
| Chapter 3 | Rally 'Round the Flag Boys | 18 |
| Chapter 4 | Attack on the Home Front | 24 |
| Chapter 5 | Moving to the Front | 29 |
| Chapter 6 | The Journey to a Strange Land | 32 |
| Chapter 7 | The High Mark of the Confederacy | 39 |
| Chapter 8 | A Walk Through the Neighborhood | 44 |
| Chapter 9 | Who Shot out the Street Light? | 47 |
| Chapter 10 | New Kid in the Class | 51 |
| Chapter 11 | The Intimidator | 57 |
| Chapter 12 | Showdown on the Basketball Court | 63 |
| Chapter 13 | Springtime in the Neighborhood | 73 |
| Chapter 14 | Decoration Day | 80 |
| Chapter 15 | The Summer of '42 | 84 |
| Chapter 16 | Mr. Seymour's Camp | 91 |
| Chapter 17 | Misty Smell of Moonshine | 106 |
| Chapter 18 | Of Urban Indians and a Raccoon Tale | 119 |
| Chapter 19 | Grampa's Rock and the Start of a New Tradition | 129 |
| Chapter 20 | Peaches, Pears, Preserves and Bears | 143 |
| Chapter 21 | Grampa's Lake – Epilog | 158 |
| Chapter 22 | Battles on the Homefront | 163 |
| Chapter 23 | The Outskirts | 175 |
| Chapter 24 | What Ever Happened to Leroy Ravioli? | 189 |
| Chapter 25 | Jerking The Bells at Saint Mary's | 198 |

| Chapter 26 | Revenge on the Dentist | 207 |
| --- | --- | --- |
| Chapter 27 | Breakout at the Slaughter House | 216 |
| Chapter 28 | The Counter Spies | 224 |
| Chapter 29 | Junior High School | 233 |
| Chapter 30 | The End and the Beginning | 240 |
| Chapter 31 | Return of the Automobiles | 246 |
| Chapter 32 | Christmas Surprise | 256 |
| Chapter 33 | Knaves of the Open Road | 266 |
| Chapter 34 | The Island in the Sun | 273 |
| Chapter 35 | The Mechanic | 301 |
| Chapter 36 | The Great Race | 315 |
| Chapter 37 | The '37 Chevy | 334 |
| Chapter 38 | The New House | 346 |
| Chapter 39 | Play Ball | 353 |
| Chapter 40 | High Jinx on the Road | 367 |
| Chapter 41 | A New Adventure | 379 |
| Chapter 42 | Completing the Walk | 402 |
| Chapter 43 | All Aboard for Newark | 407 |
| Chapter 44 | The Welcome Home Parade | 416 |
| Chapter 45 | The Answer | 432 |

# CHAPTER 1

# THE MEETING

My aunt Josephine approached me as I was moving towards the open casket.

"Richard, a man came here earlier looking for you. He said that he hadn't seen you in over fifty years. He left his card, and wants you to call him." With that said, she handed me the card.

"Thanks, Aunt Jo," I said.

The card was a Police Courtesy Card, signed by John Moccia, Deputy Chief of the Newark, N.J. Police Department.

John Moccia is a name from almost a lifetime ago. We were neighbors in an eight family building in Elizabeth, N.J. during the World War II years. It is both pleasant and odd that someone from the past would contact me at this moment. I have spent this past Easter weekend thinking about and remembering the moments I had shared with my Uncle Billy over the past sixty five years. He died during surgery Good Friday morning and now rests in this casket at the age of eighty-three.

My Uncle Jack, who is my senior by eleven years, comes to my side as I stand alone at the casket. After we hug each other in a brotherly embrace, he says, "Richard, our buddy is gone. Didn't we all have some great times together? We are the only two left in the family now."

Despite the fact that the funeral home was full of relatives, including cousins and nieces and nephews, Jack was right. We are now the only two remaining people in our family who share the memories and personal experiences of a bygone era in the history of our family and country.

"By God, Jack, I don't think this younger generation could know, or understand half the things we did, or why we did them."

The younger generation is only concerned with the here and now. They are oblivious to the routes that were taken to place them in the present time and place.

As a Nation slowly recovering from the "Great Depression," America was suddenly thrust into World War II. This catastrophic event set in motion an internal migration within this country that created new towns and expanded cities inhabited by people like us; People Forced to Move. The mobilization for the War effort brought people from every region and walk of life together. We shared a common cause and eventually shared our regional cultures, and recipes. We brought a bit of our past with us and planted it in a new location.

*R. Allen Pender*

With the merging of regional dialects and habits, we created a small subculture unique to a one square mile area in a semi rural section at the boundary of our adopted city, Elizabeth, New Jersey.

This is where I met John Moccia and many others, during that period.

As we grew, we saw this country emerge victorious and become the preeminent world power. Then, just as fast as we had come together to support the war effort, we separated in the post-war years.

When the War era ended, people again had to adjust their lives to a changed world. War time industries were being converted to peacetime use and technology spawned during the war was being used to help establish new industries. For many families, previous roots had been severed and new and different roots were beginning to take hold. Opportunities in employment and housing became available to a public which had been restrained by a depression and a war. The twenty year period, between 1930 and 1950 was actually a rearrangement of American life. The changes in technology, consumer goods, employment and educational opportunities vaulted us in new directions.

Those of us, who grew up in the 30's and 40's and matured in the 50's, can look now at a world so foreign from the one we originally entered. While the advances in technology and the improvement in the standard of living have surpassed anything we could have imagined sixty years ago, the old values, the base upon which our civilization is built, have been seriously eroded. Our children and grandchildren are now facing the challenges of the new century. Their life experiences are or will be so different when compared to those which me and my peers were exposed. For the most part, we of my generation have been remiss in our duty to educate our children in the history and values of their ancestors. We have forgotten our past and our duty.

A few days after my uncle's funeral, I placed a call to John Moccia, who we used to call "Chicky."

The phone was answered with a sharp "Hello, Deputy Chief Moccia."

"Hello, yourself, Deputy Chief, Chicky."

"I detect a southern inflection in your voice, is this Richard A?"

"It is, and I was pleased to get your card. How are you? I'm sorry I didn't get to see you at the funeral home."

"R.A., when I saw your uncle's death notice in the paper; I called my son and told him something inside me was urging me to go to the funeral parlor to find you. My son never believed any of the stories I told them about the War Years in Elizabeth, or about the southern neighbors who made every day a circus."

"Well, we sure made the best of some hard times."

"Listen, when can we get together for lunch? I'm retiring from the Police force next month and I'm on my terminal leave now. Is there any place near the old neighborhood where we could meet?"

"Sure. Remember Cotton's Gin Mill? It's now a bar and restaurant. I'm flexible, so the choice is yours."

"How about this Friday at noon?"

"I can make that."

"Great!"

"Chick, it's been good talkin' to you. And I'll see you Friday."

"OK, R.A., see you Friday."

It is about a thirty mile drive from my home to the old neighborhood in Elizabeth. I had allowed myself some extra time so I could drive around the area and locate some of our old haunts. Needless to say, the past fifty years have changed the character of the area considerably from the way it was in the days of our youth. I parked my car and stood out in front of "Carl's Tavern", which in our day was "Cotton's Gin Mill." The lunch time crowd was arriving and I was scrutinizing everybody over sixty for some recognizable features. It was five minutes to twelve, so I figured that I would stand here for ten more minutes and then I would go inside. Possibly Chicky was early, and already inside. In which case, I could ask the bartender to page him.

That wasn't going to be necessary, as I noticed the stocky man now coming down the street break into a wide grin.

"You old cotton picker, you haven't changed a bit. I could recognize you anywhere in a New York minute."

"I'll have to credit that ability to your police training, Chick and not to any state of preservation nature may have bestowed on my body. And, say, you look like you gained a few pounds since I saw you last."

Rubbing the top of his head he said, "And lost a few hairs along the way… Let's get inside and see if we can get a table."

With the forwardness that is developed during the lifetime of being a police officer, Chicky introduced himself to the bartender and asked for the quietest table in the house. Immediately a waitress escorted us to a table in the back room.

"I see that badge even carries weight over here."

"Sure, these guys always like another courtesy card, and they never know how you're connected locally."

For the next ten minutes or so we brought each other up to speed as we drank O'Doule's make believe beer. No details, just the normal statistics. Like; how many kids and grand children we each had. We provided a brief history of where we lived, our occupations, military service, education and finally, our plans for the retirement years.

Then Chick said, "I wish we had some way to document those times. I want my sons to finally hear someone corroborate my stories. They find it hard to believe that we had such adventures during that time."

"The easiest way is to write it all down. I started some research with my Uncle Billy, before he died. I wanted to write about the changes in automobile racing from his and my time to the present. So, why not document our time during World War II, it will be interesting to see where it leads."

"Could you do that?"

"I never wrote a book. But, I have written many reports and technical papers during my career. So, why not? I have the time now."

"You know, I remember your uncle and your grandfather. I remember your telling me that your uncle was a race driver, but most of it I dismissed at that time. When I saw that obituary in the newspaper and then all the memorabilia at the funeral parlor, I knew it was true. Here was a man, in the Racing Hall of Fame, a real true champion, with all the credentials, and I remember him as just as your uncle, like anybody's uncle. I remember your grandfather taking us to all kinds of places. We always went into these factories by the boiler room door and came out with a sample of what ever was made in these plants. In one boiler room they even made beer. Nobody ever believed me when I told them we went to a brewery in a hospital."

"Oh, yes! My grandfather could always find a way to combine work and pleasure. He was never tied down by any formalities."

"But, you know Richard; we did things together every day for about five years. I couldn't wait to wake up in the morning to see what adventure was going to take place that day. And suddenly around 1947... BAM!! Everyone started to move away."

"Well, most folks had put their lives on hold during the War Years and I guess it took a little while for them to catch their breath, and finally get on with their lives."

"That's true. But, we entered a whole new scene. My parents were concerned with getting us a house and a car... and seeing that we finished school and started a career. And that's what I did."

"I think everybody did more or less the same thing."

"Richard, you had a great high school baseball career. I used to follow your games in the Newark News. I always thought you would make it to the Big leagues. How come you didn't pursue that career?"

"I got side tracked by a few things, and suddenly I was too old and had been away from the game to long, so I had to move in a different direction."

"The Korean War, Right?"

"That was one thing. Then gettin' married, going to school, raising kids and never finding the right career field that suited my temperament and interest. I flitted about quite a bit."

"I was on the straight and narrow. Two years as an MP in Germany, then home to become a Newark cop for the rest of my life. Each year I hated the job more and more, and now I can finally leave it. I haven't really been able to enjoy life as I thought it would be. Maybe, now I can find out what I really want to do and have a simple uncomplicated life, without the pressure. I was taught that if you followed certain rules and did certain things you would have a happy fulfilled life. It's not so."

"I pursued that same quest. However, I applied the oft quoted "Yogi" Berra euphemism in my journey, "when you come to a fork in the road, take it." I came to a lot of forks in the road and more often than not took the wrong fork.

Moses and the tribes of Israel wandered in the wilderness for forty years. I did them ten better, until I finally took the correct fork. I believe God was watching me at all times and finally at the last fork and at the right moment, He placed a sign for the right road. And, now I'm really fulfilled and richly blessed."

"It sounds like you had a pretty wild time over the last fifty years, R.A."

"Not really wild. But, interesting. Sort'a like ridein' a roller coaster. Lots of ups and lots of downs; all real fast. A tremendous lesson about life."

"Well, you were always the adventurous type. Your family was always doing something different from the rest of us. They had a different attitude about things. I could never put my finger on it. Maybe, it was something about where they came from… I don't know."

"It took me a lot of years to find that answer, and once I did, I found the key to understanding, fulfillment and peace."

The waitress arrived with our lunch and two more O'Doules.

As we sat eating, my mind drifted back many decades, as I prepared for the inevitable question that would be asked, in response to my last statement.

## CHAPTER 2

## THE DAY OF INFAMY

Sunday wasn't my favorite day of the week.

The "Sabbath Laws" were respected with a few minor exceptions. Stores that sold newspapers and Sunday baked goods were open for a very short duration. And the movie theater wouldn't open till late afternoon.

The "Sabbath Laws" or "Blue Laws", as they were called in various areas, were actually Laws made to respect the Christian Sabbath, Sunday, The Lords Day.

You must remember, this was the 1930's in America. There weren't any shopping malls. The super market food stores had yet to appear on the scene. We did not have the highway and road networks that we now use to scoot from place to place with relative ease. We also didn't have the language synonymous with the road system. Words like commuter, gridlock, tailgating, rubbernecking and jug handle, had yet to be coined. Almost all cars were black and covered with dust. Each make was unique with identifiable characteristics and didn't resemble the gumball colored assortment of cars named after animals and birds now running up and down the road.

The quality of the road surfaces ranged from a form of paved surface on U.S. highways to a tar and gravel surface on State and County roads, then to just plain natural dirt on local roads. Once each year an application of waste oil was spread over the dirt to keep the dust down. It was an effective way to dispose unwanted waste oil. Environmentalists had not yet been born, so there were no protests to stop this practice. Thinking back now, I can't remember ever hearing about anyone getting sick or dying from the ingestion of an oiled road. I guess we just didn't eat roads back then.

Ruts and holes preceded radar as a natural way to control speed, especial if your mother-in-law was in the back seat with the kids, wearing her Sunday hat and holding pot of beans. More grandmothers arrived at their destinations looking like they had a three day binge on a roller coaster. Pity the poor lady, especially if she had false teeth. "Hang on Grandma, seat belts will be invented in thirty years."

Every car carried a tire repair kit and a hand operated tire pump. A fifty mile Sunday excursion would usually require at least one tire repair stop. If the weather was bad, or you needed to go to the bathroom, you would probably encounter two more flats.

*THE SOJOURNERS*
*Life on the American Homefront During World War II*

The tire situation was so universal that it was the most widely used and accepted excuse for any situation. Today people have to rely on exotic excuses, which can easily be verified by news and traffic reports. For us the story was simple. "Had a flat tire."

Nobody was ever kidnapped by an alien space ship. UFO's and aliens from outer space had not been invented yet. The only space ships were the German Zeppelins, which were lighter than air aircraft, somewhat like the Goodyear Blimp, except much larger. They made trips from Germany to the United States. Their era came to a fast end in 1937 when the hydrogen gas that held them aloft ignited inside the Zeppelin Hindenburg as it was about to land in Lakehurst, New Jersey…so much for the myth about the superiority of German engineering.

About one in five families had a telephone, and most of them were on a party line. "Call waiting," meant that you had to wait until one of the parties on your line had finished their call before you could use your phone. There wasn't any "caller I.D.", but your operator generally knew who was on the phone and who was calling. If you called for information, your operator could do that and also give you all the local news. Every time a phone rang a person answered. If no one answered, it meant they weren't in. All you had to do was ask the operator and she could tell you where they went.

Today we have answer machines and voice mail. Answer machines say, "We're not in to take your call." Of course we know that. The phone wasn't answered. And, the answer machine doesn't say if and when we should call again. Most businesses have voice mail. Not only does voice mail tell you where you are calling, which you knew in the first place, but by pressing an assortment of numbers on your phone you can find out who is not in to take your call. It appears to me that people don't go to work any more. Voice mail calls them to let them know who called, and then another machine sends you a letter requesting more information.

We didn't know how well off we were with "Betty the Operator."

Television was still in the future. Radio was still rather primitive. Live broadcasts coast to coast were not possible yet. If you wanted to listen to a baseball game the sports announcer would read a Teletype account of the game over the radio. The announcer would ad lib the action of the game for the radio audience, without knowing if such action was really taking place. Our President in the eighty's, Ronald Regan, was one of these announcers, and he didn't' do a bad job in the White House either.

Progress was coming. In 1937 you could get a radio and a heater in a new car. Prior to that, you had to have an "automobile robe" if you rode in the car in winter. This "automobile robe was a big heavy blanket kept in the car to cover everyone, but the driver.

The windshields of the car were defrosted by a hose coming from the engine compartment to a duct below the windshield. If your car engine was worn and had blow-by, the inside of the car would soon be like the inside of a smokehouse. "So open the windows and get under the automobile robe."

As I previously stated, Sunday wasn't my favorite day. Not that Sunday's were so bad. They really weren't. I just didn't like the Sunday dress code.

Depending upon the season, we would wear shirts and ties with short pants and high socks, or *knickers* and high socks to school.

If you never wore knickers, you have been denied the experience of a lifetime. Knickers were sort of like baseball pants in that they were baggy and had an elastic band sewn into the bottom of the pant leg, which that grabbed the wearer's leg just below the knee. High socks were worn up to the knee and tucked under the band of the knicker. These things were made of wool and came in the most God awful drab colors you could imagine. The high socks were no better, being in ugly shades and patterns of brown, dark green and dark blue. If you ever see a photograph displaying someone wearing knickers, the person in the picture has a scowl on his face. That is very easy to understand if you ever wore knickers.

A lot of men in my generation are now suffering back problems. I attribute a great deal of this problem to knickers. Boyish movements tended to cause the high socks to sneak out from under the knicker and move by gravity and centrifugal force towards the ankle. The young man involved, would in the course of his movement try to pull up his sock and reestablish its position under the knicker. This was a chronic condition and made the human body move in directions for which it wasn't designed. It was most serious in the running mode since two of the ugly socks could be falling at the same time.

I don't know who invented knickers. I think it had to have been somebody who was a Communist, or a spy for one of the Fascist countries. I saw pictures and heard talk about the German Nationalist movement in this country. These supporters of the new German regime would have big meetings called *Bunds*, where they dressed in brown uniforms with pants that looked like knickers. Remember, these were the same people who designed and built the Zeppelin that blew up.

I seriously believe that the Zeppelin was bringing in another load of knickers, to distract and demoralize us. A Nation that is constantly pulling up fallen socks is able to concentrate on little else.

Right after school, we would race home and change into our bib overalls. The only child I ever see wearing this garment now is the cartoon character, Dennis the Menace.

Bib overalls were great. They were extremely functional.

By tying a piece of string around the legs of the trousers at the ankles, an effective shopping bag was created. A boy could then have both hands free to climb a tree; fruit trees in particular.

As most fruit trees belonged to someone else, speed, agility and deception were required to quickly pick and load your hoard and escape from the premises before the owner knew you were there. The ill gotten gains were picked and dropped into the overalls. Both hands were free to make a speedy exit and the contraband was smuggled across the property line.

When it was necessary to escape from the bib overalls, the straps coming over the shoulder could be unbuttoned at the bib, or simply peeled off the shoulder. The loose fitting overalls would then just drop to the ground. This was an important feature. Being boys, we couldn't interrupt our missions to run home to go to the bathroom, so we became experts at a subject I would later learn was called, "field sanitation" by the Army.

Brooks, ponds, and even big puddles, had a magnetic effect on our youthful spirits. Naturally, we couldn't just wade into these water resources in our clothes. Bib overalls could soak up a lot of water. Wet clothes would blow the cover of our mission. So, to keep our mothers "on a need to know basis", we could quickly shed our clothing thinking nobody would be the wiser. I don't think my mother ever caught on to the game. However, I heard her say to my father on several occasions, "Joe, what is going on outside? You better close the windows; this house smells like a swamp."

On Sunday we wore "goin' to Church clothes." Again it was a shirt and tie and either short pants with high socks, or knickers that your Grandmother, or some other well meaning individual purchased with your best interests in mind. Added to this get-up was a little cap that had a short brim and a fuzzy button in the center of the cap.

This was the uniform of the day for Sunday. It could not be taken off until bed time Sunday night. This was the "LAW."

My father worked for a local newspaper. He was a printer by trade and along the way he learned the English language, grammar and spelling included, better than anyone I have ever met. Daddy would take the calls from reporters and as they were talking, he would be composing a news story in hot lead on his Linotype machine.

My father worked six days a week. He was a slender man never weighing more than one hundred and sixty pounds, but he sure could gobble up a Sunday breakfast.

Fried ham steak, eggs sunny side up and fried grits was the normal Sunday breakfast before going to Church. Fried grits was and is still one of my favorites. My mother would cook the grits on Saturday and when they were of the right consistency; that was when the grits were softly boiling and bubbles like little volcanoes would be breaking the surface, with a soft "blup-blup-blup" sound. Momma would then pour the grits into bread pans and set them to cool. On Sunday, my mother would turn over the bread pan and out would fall a loaf of grits.

The grit loaf would be cut into slices one quarter inch thick. The slices would then be dipped into beaten egg, rolled in cracker crumbs and fried in bacon fat over medium heat until browned.

I liked to pour syrup over my grits. Other people like gravy on theirs, but either way it is Good Eattin'.

All scrubbed and well fed, we got dressed in our Sunday best. My mother would tie my necktie, and as usual, she pulled so tight on that thing that I thought my eyes would pop out. Who invented ties anyhow? I know it was imposed upon us by some foreign power.

I saw them, in the movies. Englishmen, like Ronald Coleman and David Niven always wore ties. But, you never caught Gene Autry or Tom Mix wearing a tie. Somebody put a tie on Tarzan one time and he got so mad that he dove off the George Washington Bridge into the Hudson River. I never saw a tie on Tarzan after that.

The ties we wore to school were different from Sunday ties. You didn't have to tie them. They came from the five and ten cent store already tied. They were attached to an elastic band which you just slipped over your head and under your shirt collar.

As compared to English ties, these ties had some function. If some other kid was bothering you, all you had to do was jerk his tie down and swiftly let go. "Whoop", the knot would hit him in the throat and the confrontation either dissolved, or a rapid get away could be executed.

I'm pretty sure these ties were an American invention.

Finally we would get into my father's 1935 Ford two door sedan for the trip to Church.

God said we had to go to Church on Sunday. So we went. A lot of other people went too. All of these people knew who was supposed to be at Church. And, if you weren't there a lot of questions were asked.

"We missed your family last week, was there any problem?"

"Well, we had two flat tires Sunday mornin'.

Since every car had a spare tire, you had to invoke the two flat excuse for missing Church.

Kids from the first grade and up had to sit in special section with their grade group.

My mother would give me five cents to put into the Sunday collection plate. And, away I would go to join my associates in mayhem.

The first ritual of the day would be a hat fight. We would take our little hats off and chase each other around trying to smack someone with the fuzzy knob of our hat. A direct hit on the neck or face would leave a red mark. The rules were simple, the kid with the most red marks lost. This game would last until a supervising adult arrived. We would then be reprimanded and lectured on the rules of behavior while we were in God's House.

We were lined up and marched to our appointed pew. Hat fighting was now replaced by quiet nudging. Usually the kid who had the largest red marks on his face started it. Then he would either slam his elbow into the side of the boy on either side, or give a sideways kick to the ankle of each boy next to him. This action would be passed back and forth across the pew until someone made a noise and stirred the adult into action. That boy was the loser.

At our young age we were not theologically astute.

I knew from a very early age that there was a God. My mother taught me that. She would say;

"You better be good, 'because God is watching you."

"If you make faces like that; God is gonna freeze your face that way forever."

Or, "God is gonna punish you for what you did."

When I did do something bad, my mother would always find out.

"How do you know I did that, Ma?" I would ask.

"A little bird told me," she would reply.

I had a pretty good idea of the system God used.

God had a lot of Parrots. When he saw me do something bad, He would dispatch one of these Parrots to tell my mother.

He would also send this Parrot to tell my father that I should be punished. When my father came home from work he always knew when I had been bad, and I'd get spanked.

Besides watching me all the time and telling my mother about my behavior, God had some good points. He had a Son, who was born on Christmas. To celebrate this occasion, God had an employee named Santa Claus; deliver us presents on His Son's birthday. God's son was named Jesus. Jesus got very sick. But, on Easter He miraculously rose. God was so happy that He had this rabbit come around and give us colored eggs and candy.

God is really good. When I figure how bad I was most of the time and He still gave me presents; I think He likes kids.

No doubt God is very smart. He had a very efficient communication system even before the telephone was invented.

God was very mysterious. Sort of like the giraffe my mother used to say would get me in the bath tub.

"Get out of that tub before a draff comes in." She would holler.

I would get out of the tub and look out the bathroom window and say, "Ma, there's no giraffe outside the window." Why would she think a giraffe would want to come into our bathroom? I had been all over the area by my house and never saw one giraffe. And now when I take a bath, some giraffe is gonna come all the way from Africa to my house just to peek in the window. That's plain silly.

We went to visit God every Sunday. He had His house, the Church. But, He was never home.

When we went to see my Grandmothers on Sunday, she was home, else we wouldn't go.

The people in the Church would sing songs and say prayers to get God to come out and say, "Hello." But, He never did.

The Preacher would then get up and give a message from God, and that seemed to satisfy every body. Because the next thing that you saw were these men in blue suits passing plates to get our nickels. And from the look on their faces they knew when you had a nickel and they wanted it.

I would try counting the number of kids in Church and figure at five cents per head, how many PEPSI'S God and His Son would drink in a week.

"Pepsi Cola hits the spot, twelve full ounces that's a lot. Twice as much for a nickel too, Pepsi Cola is the drink for you."

In our religious instruction we would hear stories about people that had beards and wore dresses and sandals. These people got into all kinds of trouble with God and other folks. No doubt it was the dresses and sandals that caused them these problems. It reminded me of the *knicker* problem.

I could relate to some aspects of these stories. But I couldn't understand much more. The songs and prayers really confounded me, so I just sort of lip synced every thing with exuberance and not a sound ever came from my mouth.

After Church we would go home and get prepared to visit my Grandparents.

My mother was the oldest child in her family. My two uncles and two aunts lived with my grand parents. I had two great grandmothers, who also lived there.

My father was the youngest in his family. My grandmother lived with my father's older brother, my Uncle Bill and his wife, Aunt Hazel.

My mother's parents were maybe ten years older than my father's brother, so the ages of my aunts and uncles on my mother's side closely paralleled the ages of my cousins on my father's side.

It appeared to me that we spent equal time with both sides of the family. Where ever we went for Sunday dinner was fine with me. Either place had amenities suitable for my activities.

Behind my Uncle Bill's house were peach trees that produced big juicy peaches. I could eat those peaches right off the tree or bring them into the house and my Grandmother would clean them, cut them up and serve them to me in cream.

Beyond the peach trees were woods and a small crick (stream). An old railroad spur ran through the woods to where I do not know. But, along the rail line black berries grew in profusion. I liked this spot and am sure Indians once lived here because it was such a good place.

Once a year a Carnival would come and setup in an open space beyond the tree line on the other side of the railroad tracks.

Twice each night a man called "THE HUMAN CANNON BALL" would be shot out of huge cannon with a trajectory that sent him above the tree line. I had these times down perfectly and would break off any activity to race up to my cousin Billy's attic bedroom and catch a glimpse of "Mr. Cannon Ball" as he soared above the trees.

My three female cousins, Betty, Jean and Margie, would always laugh and shout, "Look out, here comes Richard A, its Mr. Cannon Ball Time."

In my young mind, I think I envied "Mr. Cannon Ball's" ability to escape the force of gravity and soar free, even if only for a moment.

The ladies, Grandma, Mom, Aunt Hazel and Aunt Ruth along with my cousins Betty, Jean, Margie and Barbara would wash the dishes and clean-up the kitchen while the menfolk went to the porch to discuss the topics of the day.

My cousin Billy wasn't around in the warm months. In 1938 he signed a contract to play baseball in the Cleveland Indians organization. His career had progressed quite well and my uncle felt from the reports he had that Billy had a good opportunity to make the parent team in 1942.

My busy day would end as light became dusk and the fireflies started their evening dance. I would chase them all over creation and capture as many as I could in a glass jar, only to release them as the time approached to go home.

My mother's parents, Gramps and Gramma lived in a big house. There was a barn in the back were my Uncle Billy and his friends built and fixed race cars. Deep into the rear yard was a huge garden.

Gramps made a lot of money as a developer and manufacturer of the lead acid storage battery. His trade name was EVER-READY. As the story goes, he lost it all as the "Depression" gripped the country and the world. He was forced to sell his trade name to Union Carbide, and that name continues today.

I didn't know it at the time, but a bank had foreclosed on the property and because of the depressed times they couldn't find any buyers, so the family continued to live there.

Gramps was into a new business. He had developed chemical compounds to treat the water and fuel in power plants. Soot O, Sludge O and Scale O, were the product names, and Gramps traveled all over to sell them.

Gramps and Gramma always presented the appearance of prosperity. I guess it was leftover from the days when they were wealthy. I never saw my grandfather in anything but a shirt and tie, vest and suit coat. On Sundays Granma looked like a high society lady, with the latest millinery creation and a fur wrap. They really stood out in a crowd.

My grandparents had colored help that lived in the Servants Quarters.

Sam and Millie had been employed by my grandparents in the prosperous days before the "Depression." When Gramps could no longer afford to pay them, an arrangement was made whereby they would stay and perform certain chores for their room and board. It appeared to work out well and I was the beneficiary of their affection.

Things were starting to turn around for Gramps, and by 1939 he purchased a brand new Chevrolet.

My parents had built-in baby sitters. Many times they would drop me off on Saturday and I wouldn't see them 'till Sunday dinner.

I was treated like a little King. In fact, my great-grand mothers called me "the Bonnie Prince" and my grandfather would introduce me as "The Crown Prince." And I was treated like royalty.

There were so many things to do and people to it with, that there was little opportunity to get in trouble.

When my Uncle Billy had to go on an errand, he would plop me behind him on his Indian Motorcycle and away we would go. And nobody cared if I got dirty.

He and his racing associates would put me into the seat of a sprint car or midget racer and I would operate the various controls as they made adjustments.

In the afternoon Gramps would take me to a small dairy and we would milk cows and then bring the fresh warm milk home. Gramma and Millie would the set about doin' what you do with milk to make cream and ice cream and sweet butter. Gramps knew where to get anything and got it in abundance.

Food was never lacking. My grandfather knew every tenant farmer in five counties and he knew when every crop was due to come in. For a little cash money he bought great volumes of raw produce, chickens, hog parts and beef parts.

Harvest time meant "cannin' time" for my grandmother. She was the boss of this operation and everyone in the family participated.

Mammy Millie was in charge of vegetables and she would have me shuck bushel baskets full of lima beans, peas, beans and corn.

Together we would wash and sort potatoes, yams, cabbage, carrots, beets cukes, peaches, pears and any other stuff my grandfather brought home.

The ladies in the family would be in the big kitchen preparing all this food to go into Mason Jars that were set into large pots of boiling water.

By September the whole process would be completed and the jars would be set on shelves in the cellar. There was enough food for all of us to draw on through the coming winter. My joy was in the peach cake my mother would make in winter, it was worth the summer work.

Sunday and Holiday dinners at my grandparents were nothing short of spectacular. It wasn't unusual to have thirty people for a Sunday dinner. Christmas and Thanksgiving were something else. Gramps and my aunts and uncles invited their friends, plus our immediate family, plus our extended family, plus folks who were shirt tail relatives and everybody came.

My grandfather would often say, "We're millionaires without money."

By the standards of today, we would have been classified below the poverty line. There wasn't any welfare, relief, food stamps, or S.S.I., for us to lean on. We were independent, relying only on God to provide our needs. The proof was available, if anybody looked at our larder.

My grandparents were generous to a fault. They felt they were rich. They had a home, a family, food, and a passion for life.

Any person in need of food, shelter, clothing and understanding fellowship was welcome at their home. Jesus said, "What ever you do for the least of these, you do for Me." Gramps and Gramma lived that verse without any qualifications. And our family was blessed.

1941 was a bumper crop year. Things were starting to look up. Gramps business was going well and he told us at Thanksgiving that the Bank had agreed to renegotiate the mortgage on the property and the land and home should be ours again in the coming year.

Uncle Billy had won several Auto racing championships during the past few years and now he and his racers were preparing to head for Texas, Arizona and California in quest of the AAA Championship.

My cousin Billy was called by the Cleveland Indians to report for Spring training as a candidate for the left field position in the "Big Show."

I had a baby sister born in 1940. My parents had saved some money over the last couple years and they made the down payment on the contract for a piece of land to build their own home.

We lived in a rented house within town limits. We were looking forward to having more space and land to farm. Every Tarheel is a farmer first and some other occupation second.

I was going to be nine years old in March of 1942. I would be eligible to play baseball in the "Boys League." They used real white baseballs, not the taped up things my friends and I played with. They had a real field instead of a cow pasture. And every body got a new hat. I could hardly wait for March to come.

All things considered, my life was really good. The only things I really needed were a motor scooter, a B-B gun and a left handed baseball mitt. With those items my life would be perfect.

I lived a Tom Sawyer-Huckleberry Finn lifestyle, much to my mother's consternation. However, my grandmother always came to my defense.

"Now leave him alone. He's just a growing boy." She would always say. Gramma knew how to treat boys, after all she had three of her own, Gramps, Billy and Jack — my role models.

"Leave them alone and they'll come home waggin' their tails behind them." She would chant.

Sunday, December 7, 1941 was a typical Northeastern North Carolina autumn day. It was sunny and light jacket cool.

Big doin's were going on at Gramma's.

Uncle Billy and his racing buddies were going to leave tomorrow on their tour through the Southwest to California. Everybody and I mean everybody was coming to eat and see them off.

The freshly painted, shiny race cars were lined up outside the barn. Tables had been setup under the trees in the side yard, and under direction of my grandmother, women were scurrying about getting the necessary items for this grand feast. I helped by staying out of the way.

All meals at our home started with thanks and praise to the Lord, and any person who wanted could add their own feelings to the prayer. Sometimes I thought we would never get to eat.

This was one of those days. With all the race drivers in attendance, prayers were offered for their safety and safe return.

Likewise, the race drivers offered prayers of thanksgiving for the hospitality afforded them. Everybody offered prayers and thanks to the Lord for all sorts of things. Finally we ate.

It was quite a party. Great food and great fellowship.

Sometime in the early evening, my Uncle Jack's friend, Charles, rushed in.

"Pop, turn on the radio, the President is coming on. The Japs have bombed Pearl Harbor."

"Charlie, you're crazy."

"No, I'm serious. It happened."

Somebody turned on the radio in the parlor and all the men went in and stood around. I sat on the floor about two feet from the radio.

The radio crackled to life and the announcer said," It has been confirmed that at 7:55 AM. Pacific Time, carrier based aircraft of the Imperial Japanese Navy have attacked the American Fleet at Pearl Harbor. We are awaiting a message to be delivered by President Roosevelt."

I sat looking at the amber dial of the radio, half expecting these Japanese airplanes to fly into my grandmother's parlor.

Gramps stood, with one hand leaning on the radio. Others just looked quietly at the radio. Not a word was spoken.

President Roosevelt finally came on the air and announced that a state of war now existed between the United States and Japan. He would be presenting a resolution of war to Congress against all the Axis powers, Germany, Japan and Italy. The President then asked us to pray with him for the success of our Nation.

I heard some sobbing as the ladies filed in during the President's speech. But, by the steely looks in the eyes of the men, I knew a fight was commin'.

Gramps finally spoke,:
"There's no such red in budding rose,
in falling leaves or in sparkling wine.
There's no such white in April blossoms,
in crescent moons or in mountain snows.
There's no such blue in women's eyes,
in ocean depths and heaven's dome.
There's no such pageantry in clustering stars,
in streaming lights, in all the spectrums of the sea and skies.
In the name of our country
and as a token of love,
I present you with our flag.
May you ever love and defend it."
The marching orders had been given.
December 7, 1941, "A date that will live in infamy."
Franklin D. Roosevelt,
President of the United States of America

## CHAPTER 3

## RALLY 'ROUND THE FLAG BOYS

In the 1950's Hollywood released a movie called "TORA, TORA, TORA." This movie depicted the Japanese planning and executing the attack on Pearl Harbor.

How true the dialog between the Japanese leaders was, as depicted in the film, was Hollywood's guess. At one point in the movie the Japanese Squadron Leader returns to the aircraft carrier and reports to Admiral Yamamoto.

"Sir, the attack was successful; we have destroyed the American fleet. We have defeated the Americans."

To which Admiral Yamamoto replies, "I am afraid the only success we have had is to wake a sleeping giant."

If Admiral Yamamoto had actually said those words, it was the understatement of the century.

The sleeping giant was wide awake, fully dressed and puttin' on new boots to stomp the Axis powers.

My great grandmother Deering simply and eloquently expressed the indignation we all felt.

"Those sneaky, heathen Japanese, who attacked us on The Lord's Day, will burn in the fires of Hell."

"We came on wooden ships to this Land God gave us, and we built a Country. No sneaky Japs or Nazis are gonna' take it. We won't allow it and God will see to that."

Of course Grandma didn't come here on a wooden ship, but our ancestors did. We had fierce pride and faith in our Nation. We were Americans from day one.

Sure, we had separated from the Union eighty years ago and fought bitterly over our regional differences. Many of those scars still remain, and many of the wrongs have not been righted. But that was a fight between Americans. Just as a family in conflict will unite to fight an interloper, we Americans, South and North have always united against a common foe.

Upon the signing of The Declaration of Independence, Benjamin Franklin remarked, "A new race of people has been created, called the Americans Race."

Mr. Franklin hit the nail right on the head.

Despite our diversity as individuals, we were all Americans first and foremost.

Yes indeed, Admiral Yamamoto, the sleeping giant was on the move and comin' after you.

Mr. great-grand mother Deering's words were not some sort of idle bravado. She had lived through the War Between the States. She had seen this country immersed in the Spanish-American War and World War I, and both times we rose victoriously. She also knew the high price which had to be paid.

Grandma loved "Gone with the Wind." She probably saw that movie more than any other living person.

When I was about four years old, she bought me crayons and a "Gone with the Wind" coloring book. Like any four year old, I had my own ideas on how to color. Grandma wouldn't give me any peace. She would stand over me and supervise my coloring.

"No young man; Scarlet's dress is this color here, and Rhett's coat or Ashley's coat is this color here. Now, do it right."

The dialog would continue on like that, until I finally asked, "Grandma did you know Scarlet O'Hara?"

"Why of course, you little scallywag, I knew them all. I even saw Mr. Lincoln once."

Scarlet O'Hara, Rhett Butler, and all the other characters in "Gone with the Wind" were fictitious. But, Grandma knew people like them. She was in fact one of those people.

Grandma came from a privileged family that had lost every thing as a result of "The War." Everything that is, except dignity and the courage to persevere.

Her branch of our family tree, which included Cyrus McCormick, came here to farm the land as free men. They left England, the motherland in wooden ships, not knowing exactly where they were going and what fate awaited them. After arriving on the shores of this wilderness across the ocean, they began a new life and a grand adventure in a new land. They helped to lay the foundations upon which the succeeding generations would build a nation spanning the continent between two oceans. A nation of free and independent people governed by a system of Law as set forth in The Bible by God, The Almighty Sovereign of the Universe.

No wonder Grandma was proud. No wonder we all are proud and ready to defend what our generations helped to build.

I sure hope Grandma only saw Mr. Lincoln, and didn't say anything out of line in his presence.

My grandfather's mother Grandma Morisey, the other half of the great-grandmother duo was a petite quiet woman. She had a tough life, and she constantly gave praise and thanks to God for even the smallest crumb that came her way.

Since the news broke, Grandma was praying for Japs and Nazis. She was asking God to send the Holy Spirit to the Japs and Germans so they might be redeemed by the Blood of the Lamb and enter the Kingdom of God through Jesus Christ.

If God listened to anybody, He listened to Grandma. She never sought anything for herself.

My Great-grand father died at the age of thirty five, and Grandma was left with my grandfather, age five and two older sisters.

Grandma was a well educated young woman. But, she could only find work as a domestic. My grandfather never went to school. He went to work with his mother and usually was assigned to kitchen duty. Their earnings were pooled to sustain the family.

Obviously, she taught Gramps how to read. His education came from books and life experiences, and he was conversant on any subject.

I cannot begin to comprehend the hard type of life they had at that time. She was a woman of faith, and God watched over her and provided for her. She never walked alone.

She made stories from the Bible and history come alive for me. Grandma was a blessing. I am sure Grandma's prayers would be instrumental in the success of the war effort.

Every one quietly left my Grandparent's house that Sunday night.

My mother and father did not even speak on the ride home.

I broke the silence with, "there won't be any school tomorrow, will there, Ma?"

"Why not?"

"Well we gotta git busy to fight those Japs."

"You go to school, and leave the war to us", answered my father.

I wasn't privy to any adult conversations, but starting Monday a lot of talk was goin' on.

I was busy. I had my own little War Room where I was preparing plans for the defense of our town. I had a Map of the World and I was figuring the directions from which the enemy might come. And we were goin' to be ready.

Right now I only had five kids, including me, in my regiment. The problem was; two had to be home by 5 o'clock and two could only come on Saturday. We would be in real trouble if the battle were anytime except Saturday, after breakfast.

I thought about recruiting some colored kids for my regiment, but after the problems I had last baseball season, I figured I better hold off until this war really heats up.

The Government was having no such problems.

*THE SOJOURNERS*
*Life on the American Homefront During World War II*

Daddy came home from work Monday evenin', and told us Uncle Bill and my cousin Billy had enlisted in the Navy that morning.

Uncle Bill had prior service. As a boy he was working on a freighter ship carrying coal. When the United States entered World War I, all American ships were assigned to the U. S. Navy. So Uncle Bill was in effect a prior serviceman of World War I.

England had entered war against Germany in 1939, and France followed shortly thereafter. Because of this situation, American men had to register for the Draft, meaning they would be called for military service if and when the occasion arose.

In these early days of the war, men were enlisting before the draft notices were sent out. A few men had gotten the draft call as early as 1940 when the Government wanted to slowly build up military strength. But, the Japanese hit us before that was accomplished.

Canada was part of the British Empire and many Americans had gone up there to join the fight against the Germans. At that time the United States was aiding the British with supplies in their war against Nazi Germany and many in this country felt that it was a European war and didn't involve us.

The German leader was a funny looking guy, named Adolf Hitler. He had his hair combed down over his eyes and had a little twitchy black mustache. He walked like a chicken and was always sticking out his arm like he was practicing to be a traffic cop. It always seemed odd to me that a country would pick a leader who looked and acted like Charlie Chaplin. But then these were the same people that filled that Zeppelin with hydrogen. I guess they were prone to making mistakes.

While Hitler was taking over Europe, the Japanese were taking over the Far East.

I didn't know much about the Japanese, or the Germans for that matter. All I knew was what I saw in the Newsreel at the movies.

My mother had cousins who were in the Diplomatic Service stationed in Japan at one point in their career. They sent us a movie film some time back. This silent film showed some big city in Japan that was filled with Japanese people standing shoulder to shoulder waving flags at their Emperor, Mr. Hirohito, who was sitting on a white horse.

The film then shifted to a city in China. The next thing we saw were Japanese airplanes flying over this city and dropping bombs. Buildings were falling, people were being hurt and things were burning. It was pure horror and that was the vision that came to my mind as I listened to the radio announcer report on the attack at Pearl Harbor. The attack in the film was Shanghi, China in 1937.

*R. Allen Pender*

My mother liked Japanese art, and we had paintings and figurines in our home. My mother's cousins, George and Hugh had gone to sea as merchant seamen in the early 1930's. Each time they returned home they brought things from foreign lands. We had carved ivory elephants from India, water color paintings and little hand painted figurines from Japan, and pressed butterfly coffee tables from French Indo China. I even had a little speedboat from Hong Kong that had its own steam engine and ran on lighter fluid.

Everything Japanese was now packed and sealed in boxes.

It was also unlikely that George and Hugh would be returning to that part of the world. Since 1940 they had been serving aboard ships that were bringing supplies to England under the "lend lease program." They were already in the war.

Hitler and the Japanese had designs to conquer the world. I don't know how they planned to split the pie. They also had a third minor partner, a fellow named Mussolini from Italy. I think they promised him the world wide franchise for Pizza parlors.

This odd lot of funny looking characters appeared more suited to a Three Stooges' Movie, or a comic strip, rather than world conquest. We would soon learn they weren't funny. They were insane.

These people were power hungry and had no concern for human life. Any means justified their end. The only thing that stood in their way of world conquest was us, the United States.

An American unit called "The Flying Tigers" was already fighting in China under the Chinese Flag. Americans could be found in the British armed services. And now Americans by the millions were leaving home and hearth to prevent the destruction of our country by these war lords from Europe and Asia.

We would normally be preparing for Christmas at this time of the year, but the war put a damper on the season.

Our town had a small business district. The shopping area was about one city block in size with a small park on the end fronting the River. The town had strung lighted decorations across the street and had a big lighted Christmas tree in the park by the river.

The annual Christmas parade was always held on the first Saturday in December. For a small town, it was a great affair.

The local businesses would set out tables on the side walk and provide cookies, popcorn, coffee, tea, and apple cider. Just about every one in town was there. Those that weren't watching were in the parade.

Suddenly the decorations were lit and you could hear the High School band start up. And then from around the corner came the parade. By big city standards this wasn't a large sophisticated parade. There were a few floats built on either farm wagons or the back of flat trucks. Some wagons were pulled by horses and some by farm tractors. The live nativity scene from the Baptist Church was always on a wagon pulled by mule. Cotton boles were attached to some floats to simulate snow.

The people in the parade were waving to every one they knew and folks were passing drinks and cookies out to the parade performers. Mary and Joseph were eating popcorn. I guess they needed energy after their long trip to Bethlehem in the cotton snow.

The parade finished at the Christmas tree in the park. After a short speech by some town official, the band started to play and everyone joined in singing as the tree lights came on.

When the crowd began disbursing, I would drag my parents to see the store windows that displayed my choices of a Christmas gift.

Their answer was always the same. "Well, we'll see."

We were depression kids, so we weren't used to getting a lot of gifts, or expensive gifts.

Sprinkled with soap flakes and illuminated by the colored lights hanging across the street, anything from a penknife to a fishing pole looked wondrous in the store window displays. Those lights blocked out the night sky and created a sanctuary of warmth and peace apart from the dark world surrounding us.

The lights did not come on Monday, December 8, and would not come on again for a long time. Our sanctuary was invaded by the darkness and our peace was destroyed.

# CHAPTER 4

# ATTACK ON THE HOME FRONT

Every two weeks I would walk with my mother to a real estate office near the beginning of Broad Street. My mother would pay the man in the office a couple of dollars toward the down payment on the land we were buying.

The building next to the real estate office was Clayton's Store. This store was the forerunner of today's convenience stores. It had a gasoline pump outside and a Dr. Pepper vending box on the porch. Inside he sold newspapers, tobacco, some groceries, farm produce, candy, ice cream, bait, ammunition and sundry articles, including "white lightnin'." I could get five Tootsie Rolls for a penny or an ice cream cone for five cents.

A week or so before Christmas, Mom and I walked down to pay the real estate man. I had a penny just burning a hole in my pocket and I was thinking of filling that pocket with Tootsie Rolls.

When my mother went into the real estate office, I made a dash for Clayton's.

I mounted the porch in one jump and stopped short. The store windows were covered with paper on the inside and a handwritten sign in the door window said, "Store Closed, Gone to War."

I was really mad. The Japs and Nazis made us shut off the Christmas lights and now they attacked me in my sweet tooth.

Clayton must have left on the Bus.

A big bus had started coming to town every Monday. It would stop in front of Henry's Drug Store, where a small group of people were waiting. When the bus stopped, only the young men in the waiting group boarded the bus. Inside the bus were more young men. As the bus pulled away, the people left by the drug store waved ... and some cried.

These men were going to war.

At my age I couldn't really comprehend the size of The United States. But, I could envision buses all over this country, where men were being picked up on Mondays to go to war.

My recollection of Christmas, 1941 could be compared to a non holiday. The mood was somber, not joyful and festive as in previous years.

There were empty seats at my grandmother's dining table, and even the Christmas tree had lost its sparkle.

In the weeks to come, we would be joining the Monday morning group at the drug store. Next week my Uncle Bill and Cousin Billy would be going off to the

Navy. The following week, my Uncle Billy and Uncle Jack would be going to the Army Air Force.

The barn had been cleaned out. The race cars and the tools were gone. The only thing left was some paint overspray on the barn walls.

Sam and Millie were packed up. They were leaving for Detroit. They had relatives there and jobs were available in defense work.

My father had tried to join the Army, but he got turned down. Daddy was deaf in one ear due to a boyhood illness and he couldn't get in the service. He had a cousin, a captain in the local horse calvary, who tried to pull every string he knew to get Daddy accepted. But, nothing worked.

My mother's sister, Eileen had recently gotten married to a fellow named Ed, who worked for the Standard Oil Company. He worked in a little laboratory at a local bulk storage depot. The company just notified him to move to their Linden New Jersey refinery.

My Aunt Hazel and her three daughters were going to move to Baltimore. She had her mother and brother up there. Her brother worked for the railroad and had a house big enough for every body. My grand mother was going to move in with my Aunt Ruth and Cousin Barbara.

It sure looked like all the bases were covered. Gramps, Daddy and me would remain here and tend to the homestead, so everyone had a place when they returned.

Now, came the curveballs.

Gramps had an offer to sell his boiler water treatment products to a chemical company in Newark, N. J. He would also go to work for this company and be based in Newark, N. J.

Aunt Hazel's brother was transferred by the railroad to a place called Rahway, N.J., and we couldn't even find it on the map. The railroad people must be very nice, because when he told them his sister and her family were coming to live with him till the war was over, they got him a big house in Rahway, N.J. and said Aunt Hazel could come and send her furniture and everything on a train.

Aunt Ruth was a divorcee, and sharp as a fox. She heard about the job opportunities up north, so she made a deal with Aunt Hazel that would allow her and Grandma to move with their stuff on the train to Rahway, N.J.

In very short order these moves began to take place.

If we weren't going to the drug store to see somebody off on the bus, we were packing boxes and loading trucks for somebody to move away.

The little world I knew, no longer existed. My family had been ripped apart without a shot having ever been fired.

Even at school faces would disappear, as other families were going through the same turmoil. Some teachers even disappeared.

My hate for the Japs and Germans was growing stronger every day.

I went on strike. Never again would I wear knickers. If my mother made me wear knickers to school, I would simply play hookey. After getting caught a few times by the truant officer, I won my point.

There was a war on. Nobody could fight a war wearing knickers. We had to have clothes that were militarily functional. Clean blue jeans were now permitted, provided you wore a shirt and tie.

Each day after school I went to Headquarters.

We had dug a hole in the ground at a soft rise near the tree line at the far side of our cow pasture ball field. Using scrap wood, we constructed a three foot high building over the hole. Inside we had a wood stove made from a five gallon can. A piece of straight galvanized pipe was set into the top of the can to serve as a flue. A piece was cut out of the side of the can for a fire box door and then that piece was attached to a metal bracket bolted to the can, so we could close the opening.

Headquarters was stocked with cans of water, cocoa mix and Kool-Aid.

We piled up pieces of turf around the wood sides of the building and dug an arc of fox holes out in front of Headquarters.

Our first task was to secure weapons. We made slingshots. A crotch of a hardwood tree branch was used for the frame. Old inner tubes were cut into strips and tied around each of the crotch ends after a piece of leather, usually a shoe tongue, was slit and slid over the inner tube strip. The branch part of the crotch was the handle and the projectile was loaded into the leather pocket.

We used stones, gravel, acorns, or any other small round objects for target practice. For the real battle, we're going to use marbles. We went all over collecting marbles from people and had a good supply on hand.

We built a big slingshot in the crotch of a tree. It took three boys to load and pull back the inner tubes, but that sucker could shoot a mud clod or a big stone out past the fox holes.

We studied the enemy.

"How do we know who were fightin', Richard", asked David.

"Well, I heard tell that the Germans have square heads. So any body who comes a long wearin' brown knickers, has a head like a box of dog biscuits and don't say the password like we do is a German."

"Japs are real little with big teeth and eye glasses. And my Uncle Billy tol' me that they made their airplanes from our junk cars. So, iffin you see an ole Ford with wings flyin' round, it's a Jap.

"What password, you talkin' 'bout?"

"Hot Dog and Lollipops."

"Germans will say," frankfooter", and Japs will say," Rorripop."

We were ready for the attack whenever it came. Each man had three sling shots and we were good shots. We took target practice every day. We could load and shoot on the run and had the big sling shot zeroed in on second base. If those Japs and Nazis knew about us, they would steer clear of this place.

We ended training at supper time and each of us went home to scan the night skies for enemy aircraft.

At school we had air raid drills. The Teacher would herd us into the hallway and we would sit there 'till they said "All Clear." We would then go back to our classroom and pickup where we left off. Now, I wondered, if it was a real attack would we go back to our class room after the "all clear", or would go home? I sure wouldn't want to be in this school if Germans and Japs were around. I had other plans.

Our country needed all the help it could get.

Hitler's armies were storming all over Europe and Africa. German submarines were sinking ships in the Atlantic Ocean, right off our coast. I heard people from the Outer Banks tell of seeing the glow of burning ships at sea.

During those early months of the war, the enemy was running all over us. And it seemed like they were heading this way.

The Japs were spreading across the Pacific, like peanut butter. They had invaded the Philippines and the small American Army there was fighting tooth and nail to keep them at bay.

Things looked bleak. Every day we expected a German submarine to appear in our river.

This war was getting real bad. My whole family was gone. The only remaining people were Daddy, Mom, me and my little sister Joyce Alice.

And now the Germans and Japs hit us another blow.

Daddy worked for local daily newspaper. Newspapers depend on advertising for revenue, and these days there wasn't much to advertise. Also, there was a shortage of paper to print the newspaper. So, the people that owned the newspaper decided to stop making a daily newspaper and only print a paper once a week.

Daddy and the other men were to be laid off in two weeks.

My Dad was a member of the International Printers Union and the Newspaper Guild. He had always worked for the local newspaper. But newspaper men and southern newspapermen in particular, were not known to stay in one place a long time. Most of these men were drawn by an ambition to work in the big city newspapers. During his time, my father got to know many of these itinerant people.

Dad's immediate reaction was to contact people he knew around the country. He felt secure in knowing that his Union membership gave him the ability to claim any job opening on any newspaper.

Unfortunately, newspapers around the country were in the same fix as our local paper.

*R. Allen Pender*

If Hollywood was ever looking for the model southern newspaper man, Daddy was it. He was a slender; six foot tall, light haired man. Each day he wore a white short sleeve shirt and a bow tie. Out in public he wore a tan straw fedora hat with a feather in the band. Going back and forth to work he always wore a seersucker jacket, even on the hottest day.

My father had a seventh grade education. He started as a "printer's devil" when he was twelve years old. A "printer's devil" was a "gofer" for the print shop. He'd go fer coffee, go fer lunch, go fer copy, sweep the floors and put the type back in the cases.

I once asked him how he became a newspaper man.

He told me his Uncle Henry, was a newspaper man and had worked in the greatest newspapers in this country. Uncle Henry would send him copies of the papers he worked on and when he came on his infrequent visits, he would regale my father with stories of the cities where he had been working and of the people he had met. Uncle Henry knew the famous lawman, Bat Masterson, who was the sports editor of the New York Telegram. Naturally his stories intrigued my father. So much so, that when Daddy decided to quit school and go to work, Uncle Henry made the arrangements for him to become an apprentice, "a printer's devil."

Some years later I asked my Aunt Ruth where Uncle Henry sat on our family tree.

She said, "Oh, that Will Porter, he was your granddaddy's cousin. He bedeviled your father with all his stories. He was a newspaper writer and he made up the name Henry 'cause he got drunk and in trouble so many times. I reckon he got chased all over this country before he ended up in New York."

I guess ole Uncle Henry was quite a story teller, and quite a writer.

My father served his apprenticeship which took eight years. During that time he studied all aspects of the English language in addition to learning the skills of a printer and nuances of the newspaper business.

My father was a quiet methodical man, who paid his dues to his profession for over twenty years and now some foreign enemy has caused him to be severed from his identity.

# CHAPTER 5

# MOVING TO THE FRONT

Naturally, I wasn't privy to all the conversations between my mother and father. I only knew what I overheard, and most times it didn't make any sense. I had no comprehension of what it took to support a family, even in the best of times. I always thought things came sort of automatic. A person grew up and then this job appeared for him, so he could get married and have kids. There was no effort and everything just happened.

Sarcastically, my father would say, "Sure, I have a hole in the ground out back, where I just reach in and pull up dollar bills."

I looked for that hole many times, and never found it. I was now starting to rapidly learn about reality.

The Bible says, "to eat, you must work."

It made me reflect back to those "canning days" in the hot summer. We worked in the summer to eat in the winter.

My father was now going to be out of work and there wasn't much chance of finding a job in our area that would pay him enough to keep a family. Although my father was employed during the Depression, my mother and father had been able to save little money. Other members of family didn't have steady jobs, so my parents would help out as the needs arose. And now, if something didn't happen soon, we would be the ones in need.

One Friday my mother and I had supper alone. She said Daddy would be home later because he was going to a funeral.

"Who died," I asked?

"The paper died and the people are having a funeral for it. I'll be going to drive your Daddy home in little while, so I want you to mind your sister while I'm gone," replied Ma.

After the supper dishes were washed, Ma left to go get Daddy.

When they came home about an hour later, my father was ranting and raving about the no good Japs and Nazis and he smelled like Uncle Bill's sour mash tub.

I was later to learn that funerals of this type were a newspaper tradition.

By late the next morning my father had regained sufficient senses to explain our future plans.

We were going to be moving this coming week. Through some contacts my Aunt Eileen's husband had, Daddy had gotten a job at a car factory in Linden, N.J. This car factory was going to be making airplanes for the war. Aunt Eileen had also gotten us an apartment next to where she lived in Elizabeth, N.J.

*R. Allen Pender*

I found Elizabeth, N.J. on the map. It was south of New York, but not south enough to suit me. We would have to drive about four hundred miles to get there. By my calculations, we would have at least eight flat tires on the way.

Fortunately for us, the parts of our family that had moved already, sent us directions and said how much gas and oil we needed to get up there.

Now it was our turn to pack and load up. Daddy came home with a little open trailer hitched behind the Ford.

I was told to sort out my stuff, and I could only take those items I was using now. I had lots of old toys that I had out grown and books I already read. When I got down to the items I really wanted all I had was my flashlight, a bone-handled hunting knife, my pocket knife, a right handed catchers mitt, a baseball autographed by the 1936 N. Y. Giants, my crystal radio set and my slingshots with a bag of marbles.

All of the other stuff was given away, except my clothes.

We had a new Easy washing machine that my mother kept working overtime. She washed every bit of clothes we had. I helped her hang the wet clothes in the yard and take the dry clothes in. Ma took all the clothes and folded them neatly and placed them into boxes.

The same procedure was followed for dishes, glasses, pots, pans, and silverware.

Over the next few days a small mountain of boxes began to grow in our living room. Once something went into a box it couldn't be used, or even seen until we reached New Jersey. My mother had set aside certain things for us to wear or use that could be loaded at the last minute.

We had one of the first refrigerators made by General Electric. It was electric and could make a tray of ice cubes. The refrigerator was pretty small by today's standards, but we were the first family in our part of town that needn't get ice. The refrigerator was set out on the porch to defrost, after which my mother cleaned it inside and out. When she was all done, I helped my father load it onto the trailer.

It was cool outside, so we kept our food in a wooden box on the front porch.

During the next two days, I helped my father take furniture apart and load it on the trailer. The hardest thing to handle was that Easy washing machine. It was a round tub on wheels and had gear shift levels to make it wash or shift to the wringer. It was real cumbersome, but finally we woke up and took the darn wringer off.

My mother's favorite things were secure in the trailer. The refrigerator, the washing machine and her Sears Roebuck sewing machine were lashed to the forward end of the trailer. We took apart the kitchen and dining room tables; and then the beds.

My mother had taken all the clothes out of the dressers and put them in boxes. Now a problem arose. We didn't have enough room for all the boxes.

The situation confounded my mother and father.

"Why don't we just put the stuff in the boxes back into the dressers, and the other stuff into the refrigerator and washing machine," I chimed, as an eight year old experienced in the transportation of all kinds of stuff in my bib overalls.

"You know, that's a good idea, son," replied my father.

The only problem with this idea was that we had to practically unload the whole trailer to do it. But, in the end my father said, "By God, everything fits."

By that final Friday night the little house was empty. My mother had cleaned the inside and the keys would be left in the mailbox for Mr. Acker, our landlord.

The mattresses were the last things to be loaded and that would be done as soon as we woke up in the morning.

I had been away from home many times. But, that was to my grandmother's house only three miles away. A different thing was facing us in the morning. We were going overnight for along time to some place four hundred miles away. I was going on an adventure to a new place, but I was leaving a place where I knew every tree, every fence, every dog and every blade of grass.

I was consoled by the fact that I would see my family again and it would close the void that the war created over the past two months.

We were moving close to New York. And that is where the action was. If the Germans and Japs were going to land anywhere, it would be New York.

My young mind was busy envisioning all sorts of situations that would be occurring in a place and a future that at this point in time only existed in my imagination. The night took over and the movie screen in my head faded to black.

My folks were early risers. My father used to get to the newspaper at six a.m. each day, so they figured we would get on the road at five a.m.

My mother had made up a picnic basket filled with fried chicken, sandwiches, juice, cookies and fruit. My father had gotten four spare wheels with good tires for the Ford plus extra tins of gasoline. All we had to do now was to load the mattresses and cover everything with a canvas and we were ready to head north.

We had a route mapped out that would take us north to Richmond, Washington, Baltimore, Philadelphia, Camden, N.J., New Brunswick, and finally Rahway, New Jersey. My folks figured the trip would take fourteen hours and we would camp overnight at my Aunt Hazel's brother's house in Rahway, New Jersey.

# CHAPTER 6

# THE JOURNEY TO A STRANGE LAND

I woke up at the first crowing of Mr. Holder's rooster.

We were all camped out on the bare floors of our house.

My parents had already gotten up and my mother was making a fast breakfast for us to eat off paper plates.

One by one we went to the bathroom to wash our faces and brush our teeth. I helped my father roll and tie the bedding, which was then loaded onto the trailer. The canvas cover was pulled over everything and tied around the bed of the trailer.

My mother was making a final tour of inspection of the old house as my father brought the Ford to life.

The entire scene reminded me of the Circus people, who would arrive and leave in the dark of night, leaving only tire tracks as the legacy of their visit. In a few minutes all that would remain of our life in this place would be tire tracks in the soft soil.

The morning was clear and frosty. We knew it was going to get colder the farther north we went, and we prayed for dry roads. The radio had stopped giving weather reports, because the enemy could listen and use that information to their advantage. I wondered if the enemy listened to the Lone Ranger too. If they did, I'll bet they were bustin' to get a secret decoder ring.

After we were all settled in the car, Daddy put her in gear. And, like a mule straining at the plow, the Ford started forward with a lurch. As inertia took hold, the Ford moved out of the driveway into the darkness before us.

Our first destination was Petersburg, Virginia. There we would pick up the highway that went straight north. Direct to Washington, D.C.

As we rolled along the back roads of North Carolina, the Ford cheerfully pulled the load placed on its back. We would occasionally see a light come on in a house or a barn, as we moved through the early morning darkness.

I wondered whether the people saw us and knew where we were going.

The black darkness of night began to slowly change into the grey dawn of morning after we passed the Virginia line. Daddy was looking for a place to pull over, so the car and trailer could be checked. He didn't want anything to come loose.

"There's a fillin' station up a head, Ah can pull in there," said my father.

As we were pulling into the darkened filling station, a light came on inside. My father had pulled the Ford just inside the driveway, and we got out.

The front door of the filling station opened and a figure emerged. A husky man in bib overalls approached the car and asked, "Are y'all havin' trouble?"

"No", replied my father. We've been travelin' since 5 o'clock, and Ah just wanted to check everything."

"Where y'all headed?" The man asked.

"New Jersey", my father said. "Got a job in an airplane factory."

"Well, that is shoo more'n a pistol shot down the road, ain't it now?"

"Reckon so," replied Daddy. "We plan on takin' it easy, jest tryin' to get there in one piece."

"My missus is makin' coffee inside. We're closed now, but I'll he'p y'all check 'er over. Your wife an' yung'ins can go on in an' git warm, whil'st we check the Fo'wd."

"That's mighty kind," said my father.

"Well, Ah reckon were all in the same pot a' fish. My name is Virgil. See the sign, Virgil and Sons, Filling Station. 'Cept'in, my sons went on the bus to the Army, Monday last. Ah got me a job over Nawfauk, so I an' the missus are closin' this shop 'till the Lord knows when."

My father stayed outside with Mr. Virgil, as my mother, sleepy sister and I went inside.

"Y'all come in and sit. Ah jest made a fresh pot a coffee," said Mrs. Virgil.

"O, Ah certainly would enjoy that, thank you kindly", my mother replied.

"Virgil 'n' Ah were havin' awa mornin' devotion when Ah saw y'all come in awa station. Ah said, Virgil, go see if those people need he'p, bein' out so early, and with yung'ins."

"Thank you, but were fine. Mah husban' wanted to check and make sure aw'er packin' was still tight." replied my mother. And she then proceeded to tell Mrs. Virgil about our trip and why we were heading north.

Mrs. Virgil was a plump woman, younger than my grandmother, but older than my mother. And, the cat sure hadn't got her tongue, as she told my mother of their plans to survive the war.

"Virgil 'n me got married when he came back from the Big Wa' in France in 1919, an' we been hea evea since. Ain't that right Virgil,"she said turning towards the door where Mr. Virgil and my father were entering.

"Shoo nuf, Missey. Ah was with Alvin York, in the All-American Division."

My father was holding a box full of our preserved food.

"Virgil gave me some Alcohol for the radiator, and filled the tank with gas. And he won't take any money, but he'll trade for some peaches and beans. Is that right by you, Alice?"

"It's right by me, if it's right by Mr. Virgil."

"Y'all will need that gas'line more'n we needs the few pennies. Ah tole Jozeph, he best save that gas'line in the tins, causen pret' soon ain't gonna be none 'round. It's all gawn to the Wa'. But, those peaches will be a fine cake when awa boys come back, Rat so, Missey?"

"A-men, Praise the Lord."

"We all will be prayin' for your boys to come home an' eat that cake," replied my mother, as we were walking out the door towards the Ford.

"God bless y'all, and we'll pray for you goin' to that strange land. 'Member where y'all come from and who you are and that the Good Lord is watchin' over all."

"AMEN, Mrs. Virgil, Amen", we all said in unison as we took our seats in the Ford. With a final wave we pulled out of Virgil's driveway.

"Virgil said to go five miles to the next cross road, an' turn left. That 'll take us straight to Petersburg."

"Well, Ah believe Mr. Virgil knows all the roads 'round hea," replied Ma.

"Daddy. Who was Alvin York?"

"Alvin York was from Tennessee, an' he got the Congressional Medal of Honor for capturing a lot of Germans in the Great World War."

"Well, how come we gotta fight them again, did some body let them all loose?"

"That's what they call politics, son. We don't occupy people's countries and they promised not to make any more wars, but Ah don't think anyone was watchin' the hen house."

We had made the left turn where Mr. Virgil told us and now we were heading straight to Petersburg forty miles away.

I had gotten another road map at Mr. Virgil's and was plotting our course along the way.

"Daddy, how fast are we goin'?" I asked.

"Forty- five miles an hour."

"Ma, Kin Ah use you watch?"

"What for?"

"If Daddy tells me how fast were goin' an' Ah know the time, then Ah can figure where we'll be at lunch time."

"Let him use it Alice, it'll keep him busy."

Like a train conductor, I was announcing every little hamlet we passed through and providing mileage information to the next destination. My father was very appreciative of my efforts, but asked me to be a little quieter.

We passed through Petersburg and less than an hour later through Richmond. We stopped just past Richmond to go to the bathroom at a roadside restaurant. My father bought hot chocolate for me and coffee for him and my mother. Ma and I changed seats and I went up front.

We were now headed for Washington, D.C., one hundred miles away.

*THE SOJOURNERS*
*Life on the American Homefront During World War II*

As the rhythm of the road picked up again, Ma and my sister fell fast asleep in the back seat. I returned to my navigational chores.

My father asked me to keep watch for a filling station some where about fifteen miles south of Washington. I marked a circle on my map and began the countdown of all the little towns along the highway.

"Dad, Ah think we'll be in Washington around twelve o'clock. Do you think the President is home?"

"Why is that?"

"Well, maybe we could eat our lunch at his house."

"No, Ah think the President is too busy. Besides, we have to get to New Jersey and the President just might keep me too long in some kind of meeting, and Aunt Hazel will be holding supper for us."

Dad and I bantered back and forth on a myriad of subjects, such as why Virginia is called Virginia and Maryland is called Maryland. And, how come this and how come that. I think it eased the tension of his driving.

Finally we were approaching the circled area on my map. I had my eyes glued to the window for the tell tale sign of a filling station.

"There's a Richfield up ahead, Daddy."

Responding to my keen alert, my father slowed down and shifted the Ford to second gear. Even as careful as he was, the bump at the filling station driveway shook my mother and sister back to life.

"Where are we?" Ma asked.

"Jest south of Washington. Ah'm goin' to get some gas and check the awl and radiator. Maybe you need the women's room."

"Fine and Ah want to check the baby."

After we pulled up at the pump, my mother and sister got out and headed for the Women's Room. I got out my side and helped my father open the hood.

"Ah Kin only give you ten gallons," said the Richfield man." Were gettin' low and want to give everybody some before we run out."

"That's awright; we might make it on that. Ah got 'bout half tank."

"Where y'all goin'?"

"New Jersey"

"Well, Ah reckon Ah can fill'er up, y'all still have a ways to go. Local folks here got no place to go."

The engine oil and the radiator were fine, and we were blessed by a nice sunny day. Daddy paid and thanked the filling station man and we climbed back into the car. I jumped into the front seat before my mother had a chance to get to the door. But, she appeared quite satisfied to be in the back.

We crossed the Potomac River into Washington at ten minutes to noon.

I had been nibbling on fruit and cookies along the way, but I still was hungry for some fried chicken. My father was pretty hungry too. He was navigating through Washington, which had a lot of traffic. In the mean time I kept looking for a place where we could pull over and eat.

"Ah see a place! There's a park over there. See that trail goin' in there."

Following my advice, my father wheeled the Ford into the park. The car stopped and my mother handed my father the picnic basket from the back. Daddy carried the basket over to a nearby bench and we proceeded to set out a picnic lunch.

"This is really a nice place. Look! You can see the Washington Monument from here. Ah wonder why more people aren't here," my father quizzically remarked.

"Maybe it's not warm enough," replied my mother.

While we were eating, a brown Army car pulled up behind the Ford. Two soldiers emerged and started our way.

"Here come some people, Ma. Maybe they're gonna eat lunch."

"Excuse me folks", said the one soldier, who had a M.P. band around his arm. "Is that your car and trailer?"

"That's my car," answered my father. "Is anything wrong?"

"This is a restricted area."

"Oh, now! We thought it was a park and pulled in here to have lunch."

"Sir, you are almost in the back yard of the White House. Where are you people going?"

"New Jersey,"

The second soldier, who had been standing back, now came forward.

"It's O.K., Fred, these people from North Carolina are traveling to New Jersey and they just stopped for lunch. Go back and call in the situation. We'll escort them out to Rhode Island Avenue in fifteen minutes."

"Thank you, Ah certainly appreciate that. It is real confusing 'round here," said my father.

"No problem, we have tight security now. I'm sure you understand that."

"Ah shore do, we'll finish eatin' and skiddadle." replied Daddy.

The M.P. then turned and walked back to the Army car to join his companion.

We finished our lunch and carried everything back to the car. When Daddy fired up the Ford, the M.P. pulled up beside us and signaled for my father to follow him.

They led us around some turns and a few corners. Then they pulled to the side and waved to us to go straight ahead.

I could see the tenseness in my father's face as we moved up Rhode Island Avenue. There was a lot of traffic and there were trolley cars. The trolley tracks ran along the right side of the road. If we got to far to the right the car wheels would catch in the trolley tracks. If we stayed out far enough to miss them, some car would come behind us blowin' its horn.

"Let that bird blow his horn all he wants. Ah'm stayin' rat cheer", my father retorted.

Gradually, the traffic began to thin out and then the trolley tracks disappeared. We were out of Washington City.

I could see my father breathe a sigh of relief.

"That Washington is some mess. But now we got some open road."

"Ah was so embarrassed," stated my mother. "Here we are by the White House eatin' chicken and us with this dirty car and trailer. They must think we're from Tobacco Road or, something out of The Grapes of Wrath."

My father gave a little chuckle and said, "It worked out good. 'Cause those boys led us right to where we needed to go. Ah'd likely still be drivin' 'round Washington."

"Hey, Dad! Do you think the President saw us out his window?"

"Somebody sure did," snapped my mother.

"Well Dad, if he knew it was you, he probably would have made you come inside for a meeting."

"Meeting my foot," interjected my mother. "More'n likely jail."

"Oh now, it wasn't that bad, we only made a wrong turn. They don't put you in jail for wrong turns. Besides, we had a good spot for a picnic. How far is it to Baltimore, son?"

"Thirty miles, now."

"This highway goes smack through Baltimore. Gramps tol' me to take the highway from Baltimore to Wilmington. But the map shows that highway goin' through cities. This highway goes out back of Wilmington and Philadelphia and crosses into New Jersey at Trenton. After Washington, Ah'm not real happy about drivin' in cities," My father mused.

Baltimore had traffic. Not as bad as Washington. The highway snaked through the city streets and we all had to keep our eyes peeled for the highway signs. We didn't make any wrong turns and our eyes were agape at the brick row houses in the city. Naturally, I assumed everyone in Baltimore lived in this type of house. My concern was for the dogs in Baltimore. Where could they go to take care of their business?

The highway ejected us from the city streets of Baltimore into the Maryland county side. It would be close to a hundred miles to Philadelphia and my father wanted to check the car before we got near the city. At three o' clock in the afternoon and forty miles out of Baltimore, my father pulled the Ford into a filling station.

The old Ford sucked up a quart of oil. The man sold Daddy five gallons of gas and we all went to the bathroom.

*R. Allen Pender*

"That sign up yonder should interest you folks," Quiped the filling station man, pointing to a sign at the side of the road just beyond his property.

"How's that?" questioned my father.

"You're goin' into Pennsylvania. That's the Mason- Dixon Line."

We all looked with quiet contemplation. The Old South was behind us. And indeed as Mrs. Virgil had said, we were about to enter as immigrants into a strange new land.

# CHAPTER 7

# THE HIGH MARK OF THE CONFEDERACY

I think we did Jefferson Davis and Robert E. Lee proud as we moved out in the Ford, with Daddy and me waving towels and giving the rebel yell.

The filling station man was smiling and waving as we made our charge across the Mason-Dixon Line.

The Ford picked up the beat like one of J.E.B. Stuart's chargers and we attacked Pennsylvania.

"You two are crazed," hollered my mother above the din. "You're scarin' the life outta the baby."

The Ford kept moving, eating up the Pennsylvania road. But, my father and I reduced our merriment to light laughter.

"Ah got pret' near three quarters a tank a gas. That should get us to New Jersey," stated my father.

"Least wise this road don't have so much traffic." repied Ma.

"Let's pray Philadelphia isn't too bad," answered Daddy. "Sun-light is gonna be gettin' short an' Ah don't wanna be in some strange city in the dark."

The old Ford was doing its job, and a big sign welcomed us to Philadelphia at twenty minutes after four. This city wasn't bad, compared to Washington and Baltimore. There were a few turns and some traffic, but for the most part, the highway avoided the central part of the city. And we were able to cruise through at a moderate speed, which gave us all a chance to hit up on the picnic basket as we drove.

The sun was now sinking in the west, when a big sign announced, "BRIDGE TO NEW JERSEY AHEAD."

WHAT TRENTON MAKES THE WORLD TAKES, was boldly emblazoned on the side of the bridge. It sure looked like Trenton made a lot of stuff. There were tall stacks spewing forth the smoke of industry on both sides of the highway. Lighted factory buildings seemed almost human as they were animated by the energy of many hands inside producing the materials for war.

"Are those defense plants?"

"Yep, Ah reckon they are."

"Don't the people go home?"

"Shore they do. Some people work in the day, some at night. That way the factory can keep makin' things."

"Then some people gotta sleep durin' the day. How can they do that?"

"Ah guess if they're tired enough, they can."

"Ah sure wouldn't wanna do that."

I had a million questions to ask about night workers, like, do they eat breakfast before they go to bed and supper when they get up. If so, when do they eat dinner? But now as darkness was settling in, my father was concentrating on the road, concerned only with the last forty miles of this journey. And I filed my questions away for another time.

"Joe, sometime soon you best call Hazel! Let her know where we are."

"Ah will. She said to call after we pass the traffic circle in New Brunswick and cross over the bridge. Ah imagine that'll be in about a half hour."

None of us had ever seen a traffic circle. Four roads came into this thing that looked like a little round race track. All the vehicles wound up going one way around this circle, and then they would go off on whichever of the four roads they wanted. A problem could develop if you were on the inside and other cars were on the outside, then you couldn't get off onto the road you wanted. I'll bet some people rode around that circle for hours. We rode around the circle twice and only were able to get off by doing all kinds of waving at the cars around us.

My father said it was the "dam'est thing he ever saw," and my father never uses profanity.

Once we escaped the clutches of the cyclone inside that traffic circle, it was an easy two miles to the bridge that Aunt Hazel mentioned.

"Listen up now, Ah want every body to look out for a place that might have a telephone."

Not much more than a mile up the road, I spied what looked like a big filling station.

"Over there, Dad. Looks like a big fillin' station. They got trucks an' everything in there. Ah bet they got a telephone."

"We'll give 'er a try," replied Daddy, as he maneuvered the Ford toward the dirt driveway.

Slowly my father guided the Ford over the ruts created by thousands of cars and trucks to a spot near the office.

"Ah'll go in an' see if they have a telephone Ah can use. Y'All stay in the car," my father said, as he left the Ford, with the engine still running.

We could see him inside the office talking to a man who pointed towards something and Daddy then vanished in that direction.

In a few minutes my father reappeared, said something to the man in the office, who waved his hand in some sort of gesture and in the next moment my father, was out the door, heading back to the car.

"We only have eight miles to go. Straight up this highway." Daddy enthusiastically exclaimed. With renewed vigor, he took his seat behind the wheel.

As the Ford slowly moved out of the rutty station, he said, "They'll meet us in fifteen minutes at a yellow fill'in station at the bottom of the hill comin' into Rahway."

My father began a mileage countdown as we continued up the highway.

We were now surrounded by darkness and as we approached the six mile mark, all heads were scanning the road ahead for that yellow filing station.

"ENTERING RAHWAY", announced the small white sign on the side of the road. With it came a hill that made my father shift the Ford into second gear and up we went. As we crested the hill, there down on the right was the yellow filling station.

Daddy turned the lights on and off real quick a few times and the old Ford seemed to respond like a horse heading for the barn, as we started down towards the car now returning our light signal.

There probably is nothing in the world noisier, unintelligible, or more confusing than the caterwauling of four excited young southern females.

As the car was coming to a stop, my four cousins jumped on the running boards and were trying to get their heads in the windows before we could crank them down.

Within a minute the car sounded like the inside of a drum. Hands and faces were coming through the windows to touch and kiss anyone they could find. As they jumped up and down on the running boards, the Ford started rocking so much I thought it might get an upset stomach.

Finally the girls backed away as Aunt Hazel's brother, Tommy, came to the driver side window.

"Hello; Joseph and Alice. We've been praying all day for a safe trip."

"Ah can't tell you how good it is to finally get here, Tommy." Replied, Ma. "Ah thought we were goin' to the end of the world."

"Tommy, its sure good seein' you. Is your house close by?" Daddy asked.

"Real close, Joseph. Your Ma, Hazel and Ruth 'bout got supper fixed, so jest follow ma' car out that way 'n over'n that little bridge an' we'll be there in three shakes of a lambs tail."

We now had a small motorcade with a '29 Dodge in the lead.

We crossed the little bridge, made a right turn and drove up the street and under the railroad tracks. We followed Tommy as he made a left turn just past the railroad and went up the drive of big Victorian house.

A welcoming light on the porch had been turned on and Grandma, Aunt Ruth and Aunt Hazel scampered down to the car for another round of hugs and kisses. Never mind all the kisses, I just wanted to get my ground legs back and get in from the cold.

A long procession of females led us into the big house. The ladies got busy with their talk, just as they had done back home. The only difference was that the conversation was relocated over four hundred miles north. The words still sounded the same.

"Marjorie, show massa' Richard to the bathroom", barked my grandmother. "Have him wash for supper; 'n' make sure that rascal uses soap. Ah don't wanna see any soil on the towel, Ya Hea."

Things sure hadn't changed much. My grandmother was always having me cleaned. She had very high standards for cleanliness. And, I guess, I was her greatest challenge.

"Ah'll, take care a' him, Grammy," replied my cousin Margie, as she took my arm to lead me away. "Boy, you smell like chicken and gasoline and you got crumbs every where, even in your ears."

Once we reached the bathroom, Margie commanded, "Take off that shirt. An' what in tarnation do you have in your pockets?"

"Cookies Ah'm Savin'."

"Cookies! Now take those overalls off, 'cause we gotta shake you out. Richard A., you're a walkin' trash can."

Soon I was stripped to my underwear. My cousin lathered up a face cloth and began applying it to my face and arms with the precision of a modern day car wash. She shook out my clothes and dried me with a big towel.

"Get your clothes back on Chicken Boy, so Grammy can look you over before we eat."

"Well now, Richard A. looks all bright and shinein', like a new penny. Let me see your ears, most times you got 'nuff dirt in there to grow 'taters", Granma said as she took hold of my head to inspect my ears. "Ah declare! Narry a spect a' dirt in there."

"Good", I thought, now maybe we could eat supper.

The adults were all seated around the dining room table, while three of the youngest girls and me were put at the kitchen table.

"Momma", blurted my cousin Margie, "does the prayer in there count for our table too. Or, do we have to say our own?"

"No, y'all get in here an' we pray together," shouted back my Aunt Hazel.

"You pray Joey", commanded my grandmother.

"Yes, Momma," my father answered and he began the prayer.

"Lord Jesus, we thank you for delivering us to our family safely. And we thank you for the fine meal prepared for us. We ask that you protect our family members in the service and to end the war, so they can come home. AMEN."

And all the people said, "AMEN"

My Aunt Hazel made the richest dark brown gravy I have ever seen. Many times my cousins and I would just put it on bread for lunch. Tonight we're having it with boiled beef, mashed potatoes, and lima beans. Aunt Ruth was the cake baker and she had made a big chocolate cake. Of course you wouldn't get any, if you didn't finish your supper.

There was a lot of talk and laughter going on at the dining room table. My mother and father were recounting the details of our trip. And, at one point my cousin Betty poked her head in the kitchen and said, "Richard A., I hear you were almost in the White House. Were you goin' to have tea with Mrs. Roosevelt?"

"Ah don't drink tea, 'cept ice tea."

Obviously, my folks had told of our encounter with the M.P.s by the White House. And everyone got a good laugh.

It had been a long day. My sister, who slept most of the trip, was already down for the night.

After eating my chocolate cake, I went into the parlor to sit on the sofa and in short order fell asleep.

I was awakened by the crowing of a rooster. Slowly rousing, I felt like I was waking up from a dream. It was no dream. I was on a sofa in Rahway, New Jersey and it was a rooster other than Mr. Holder's, announcing the beginning of a new day.

Pretty soon the whole house came alive. With so many women and girls, the bath room was like the epicenter of an earthquake.

Daddy and Tommy were in the kitchen, sitting and having coffee while the chaos in the bathroom was going on.

Tommy, Aunt Hazel and the girls had already been to the place where we were moving. Our apartment had just been painted and they went over there to clean it up. They planned to head over there after breakfast and move our stuff in. We would all be back here for Sunday dinner and evening services at the First Baptist Church.

Good plan. One problem.

My father went to get something from the car and the old Ford looked sick. It had two flat tires on the drivers' side and was leaning over to one side like a fish about to turn belly up.

The old Sunday mornin' excuse had followed us to New Jersey.

We prayed not to have a flat tire through out the trip, and we were amazed by the fact we didn't. I guess God turned his attention in another direction after we reached Rahway. And "Pooooof" went the tires.

Luckily, we had one spare on the car and four on the trailer. So, by breakfast time, Daddy and Tommy had two replacement wheels on the car.

# CHAPTER 8

# A WALK THROUGH THE NEIGHBORHOOD

The voice of the waitress snapped me back from my momentary musing.
"Is everything all right; would you gentlemen like anything else?"
"I would like a cup of decaffinated coffee, How about you, Chick?"
"I'll have another O'Doules, please."
"R.A., I haven't had a real beer in about a year. A cop's life is the job and beer. It's no good. I had to stop the alcohol last year. I had an aneurysm in my aorta. They cut out the bad section and put in a piece of plastic. I lucked out, if that thing had blown, I would have been gone real quick. I still like the taste of beer and these things can't hurt me," he said, as the waitress brought another O'Doules.
"That's the same operation my Uncle had, but he didn't make it."
"I know, your cousin told me that at the funeral home. He also said, you were really shaken up by the death and you guys were real close."
"Well, we shared so many experiences and had common bonds and interests. It is almost like his death had taken some of my identity."
"Hey, R.A., do you want to walk off this lunch? We can take a short walk up around the old block."
"And look for ghosts?"
With a smile Chicky said, "There are probably a lot of them ready to start chasing us again."
"Let's go and see."
"No, no, R.A., don't grab that tab! Your money is no good today. Do you hear that Miss?" He said turning towards the waitress. "Don't take any money from this guy. He's my guest today. We'll be back in a little while. So, see if you can save this table."
"Thanks Chick. I'm goin' to hit the Men's Room. That O'Doules went through me quicker than water through a sieve."
With a chuckle in his voice, he replied, "Now you use the men's room, I remember when any tree or bush would do."
"T'aren't any left." I said, as I headed towards the Men's Room.
"That's because you killed them all." Chicky quickly came back.
The Tavern is on Lidgerwood Avenue. Directly across from the tavern is Garden Street, entering Lidgerwood Avenue at a right angle. At the common corner of Lidgerwood Avenue and Garden Street and running north at a forty-five degree angle, began our street, Rosehill Place.

When I came out of the Men's Room, Chicky was conversing with the bartender. Who said as I approached, "See you later fella's. Enjoy the afternoon."

Almost in unison, we gave a little wave and said, "Thank you." And, we walked out onto the sidewalk.

Waving his arm, Chicky said, "Every day we would walk down that street." Now pointing towards Rosehill Place. "We would cross over there and walk up along side this tavern, through somebody's garden in the back and there was the school yard fence. Further down was somebody's driveway and then the school gate. It always seemed to me that we climbed the fence more than we used the gate."

"Well", I said. "Fences and trees were made for boys to climb, natural challenges."

"R.A., are you ready to step back fifty-five years?"

"You know, if we were on planet fifty five-light years away and had a super powerful telescope, we could see ourselves as we were then."

"God, you haven't changed. I never knew a kid who had the wacky ideas, like you did. My mother said she never saw anybody with such a wild imagination as you."

"Chick, I take that as a compliment, thank you."

We crossed the street, moving in the direction of a three story, brick apartment building at the corner of Garden Street and Rosehill Place.

Stepping up on the sidewalk, Chicky stopped for a moment. "It has really changed. Hasn't it?"

"So have we." I replied.

In our time, the brick apartment building stood alone. A wooded area extended up Garden Street to the next cross street, New York Avenue. That area is now occupied by one family houses. The opposite side of Garden Street had been empty fields, except for a small area to the far end, where the State of New Jersey had a vehicle inspection station. That section is now an auto body shop and a junk yard. A large triangular piece of land separated Rosehill place from Lidgerwood Avenue. This property had been wooded along the Lidgerwood Avenue side and provided fields for horses to graze and a homemade baseball diamond where boys could play. Garden apartments now occupied the site.

New York Avenue, to our rear, had only two houses clustered together. Fields occupied the remainder of the street on both sides. Single family houses had now grown there to fill in the fields.

"Look, Chick!" I exclaimed, as we started to head up Rosehill Place. "All the trees are gone."

Norwegian Maples had once shaded the sidewalk along the entire length of Rosehill Place. The street had been defoliated.

*R. Allen Pender*

"It's nothing like the day you arrived, R.A. I remember that day clearly. I can still picture you and your family, with the car and trailer. If any body ever had straw sticking out of their ears, you people did. And here is this nine year old guy in bib overalls with a slingshot hanging out of his back pocket. We were hysterical. I went up and told my mother to come down and hear you people talk. It was really funny, like the movies."

"It was a real culture shock for us too."

As we continued to walk, my mind drifted back to that day. And with each step, I saw people and events come back to life in living color on the screen of my memory.

# CHAPTER 9

# WHO SHOT OUT THE STREET LIGHT?

After the flat tires on the Ford were changed, we had our Sunday breakfast. We weren't going to Church this Sunday morning, so I didn't have to wear Sunday clothes. Also, the girls had talked my Aunt Hazel into allowing them to ride with their Uncle Tommy, so they could help with the move. They also would miss Sunday school, which probably was their real reason for coming along.

Tommy sketched out the route we were taking on a piece of paper in case my father got lost following him. With all the preparations completed, we climbed into the cars for the final five miles of our journey.

It wouldn't be hard to follow Tommy. His car left a light cloud of blue smoke marking the trail.

We moved out into the same highway, by which we arrived last night. As we headed north, and entered Linden, there on the left was the airplane factory where my father would work. On the right side was an airfield, still under construction. Off to the right, I could see the smoking stacks of many factories. Pretty soon we were passing the Standard Oil Refinery, with its huge storage tanks and towers of steam spewing pipes.

As we entered Elizabeth, we were confronted by another one of those, unique to New Jersey, traffic circles. Fortune shone upon us, as there was very little traffic and my father was able to get off the circle at the right point, three-quarters of the way around the circle. We passed a couple of houses and watched Tommy make a right turn and go up this street past some fields. He took the left fork along the side of a big field and slowly stopped. My father pulled our rig up behind him.

Four box-like buildings were on the opposite side of the street.

A group of people were gathered in front of the second building. As we emerged from the car, my Aunt Eileen and her husband Ed appeared out of this group and crossed the road to greet my parents.

They then escorted my parents back over to the group and introduced my mother and father to the crowd. One lady, whose name I would later learn was Mrs. Mitchell, led my parents into the third building. She showed us our apartment, which was on the first floor in the front of the building.

Mrs. Mitchell's husband opened and blocked the large single outside front door and the two inner lobby doors. He directed my father to pull the car and trailer into the driveway between the two buildings. Once that was done, my father and I removed the canvas cover over the trailer.

The men, who were with the original little group, came over to the trailer and they were soon joined by others who came out of the buildings. One group began unloading the trailer while another group carried things into the apartment. My mother just stood like a traffic cop by the door, directing the cargo to its proper location. Mr. Mitchell came back with some tools and soon our kitchen and dining room tables were reassembled. My cousins were in the kitchen placing the unpacked dishes and pots and pans into the wall cabinet. Two men were helping my father reassemble the beds, while another group rolled out our parlor carpet.

Within the hour, all of our stuff was in the apartment. We still had some things in boxes, which my mother could put away at her leisure. But, for all intents and purposes, we were moved in.

My Aunt Eileen and another lady came in as things were being finished. They were each carrying pots of hot coffee and sacks of pastry, which they set up on our dining room table, which was now in the front parlor, for the lack of a dining room.

My father and I went outside to move the Ford and the trailer. And as we did, a familiar Chevrolet was pulling up to the curb.

"Gramps and Gramma are here!" I hollered and I ran to greet them.

My grandmother and grandfather were great huggers and kissers. And, in the next few moments I got more than my fill. I felt a little self conscious because a large contingent of kids had been standing by watching all the activity and I didn't want them to think I was a sissy.

Grandma and Gramps never came empty handed.

"Here son, help your grandma carry these sacks into the house." He said as he opened the trunk of the Chevy.

Dutifully, I obeyed. I picked up my load and led my grandparents to our new apartment.

Once inside, the hugging and kissing started all over again. I think my grandfather hugged and kissed ladies he didn't even know. But, that was Gramps.

He and Granma had brought sliced ham, potato salad, fresh baked bread and beer. Beer on Sunday! Even here, up north, they couldn't sell beer on Sunday.

Gramps was never one to let any grass grow under his feet. He was only up north a short time and he already had re-established his supply system. No wonder we had so many helpers.

While everybody was inside eating and drinking the beer, I walked outside to survey my new surroundings.

The same group of kids was still milling about in front of the building. Some of these kids looked my age; some a little older and some a little younger. Finally, one of the older boys said, "Hey kid, what is that thing hanging from your back pocket?"

"Thas ma slingshot."

They all giggled when they heard my voice.

Trying to mimic a southerner, the older boy said. "What do you all do with that there slingshot?"

"Ah shoot things."

"Like what, boy?"

"What eva Ah'm aimin' at."

"See that bulb on that street light, I'll bet you can't hit it. I don't think you could hit the broad side of a barn with a shovel."

Again the group went into a giggling frenzy and danced around mocking me by making believe their fingers were slingshots and they were shooting at each other. Some were ducking the shots and others were acting like they got hit.

While they were engaged in this merriment, I sized up the light bulb on the pole under a white metal reflector. The pole was about thirty feet from where I was standing. With one hand, I reached into my front overall pocket and drew up a glass marble. With my other hand I eased the slingshot from my back pocket. I quickly loaded, took aim and let the missile fly.

The mocking session came to an abrupt halt as the glass from the light bulb hit the street.

The attitudes now changed from one of challenge to one of respect.

The older boy, whose name was "Klinkey", was sort of the unofficial leader of the neighborhood boys. When the shock of the broken light bulb wore off, he said "Where did you get that slingshot?"

"Ah made it."

"Will you make one for me?"

"Nope. But Ah'll show y'all how."

"Good, we'll see you tomorrow after school. What's your name?"

"Richard A."

"Well we'll just call you R.A."

Their curiosity had been satisfied, and I had passed their rite of initiation.

I stood there feeling sort of like Gary Cooper, after he had dispatched some desperado, except I didn't have a smoking gun barrel to blow on.

My glow of victory was interrupted by my mother's voice, as she hollered out of the front bay window.

"RICHARD A., GET IN HERE. RIGHT NOW!"

Our parlor was still full of people as I walked in the door and my mother grabbed me by the scruff of the neck.

"Go get your Uncle Joe. He's out in the kitchen," she said to my cousin Betty. "And, you jest stand right here 'till your Daddy comes, you trouble maker."

"What's wrong Alice?" My father asked as he entered the room.

"Your son jest shot out the street light, Tha's what!"

"Why in tarnation would you do such a thing?"

Before I could answer, one of the new neighbor men chimed in. "Missus those bigger boys were teasing him. I saw the whole thing. It's a lot different around here, than where you came from. Your boy is going to have to be able to hold his own around here, or else he is in for a tough time. I wouldn't be too hard on him."

Gramps came up in the middle of the discourse. "Son, did you shoot out the street light?"

"Ah did." I sheepishly replied.

"And, how many shots did you take?"

"One."

"One! Well I dare say, that's good country shootin'."

Now wrapping his arm around me, he said, "Now you musn't damage anybody's property. That's wrong. But, I reckon you showed those boys where you come from."

Gramps had his own unique sense of justice. No matter what you did, right or wrong, if it was done with class and in a professional manner for a just cause, your actions were worthy of being defended.

"Daddy, don't you coddle that boy," exclaimed my mother. "He done wrong and should pay for it."

"Fine," said my father, as he took my slingshot and broke it through the crotch. "No more slingshots in this house."

"You stay inside and help us clean up. 'Cause we got to go back to Aunt Hazel's for dinner soon. An' Ah don't need any more trouble from you. Ya' Hea'?"

"Yes, Ma," I said looking over towards my four female cousins, who were snickering and making "shame, shame" signs with their fingers. I figured God didn't send a parrot this time to tell my mother. It was one of those four birds.

I still had two slingshots under the seat in the Ford. And I found a good hiding place. During my exploration, I noticed the exposed flooring under our front bay window. I would obey my father and not bring any slingshots into the house. I'd hide them outside up under the bay window.

# CHAPTER 10

# NEW KID IN THE CLASS

For the second day in a row, I woke up in a strange place. My body and brain had not yet been programmed for my new surroundings. I still woke up with the floor plan of my old home engraved upon my mind. And more than once I tried to leave my room and entered the closet instead.

I had tried to talk my mother into keeping me home from school for a few days. But, she was headstrong. Today she was going to take me over to the new school. I was ordered to dress in school clothes.

After breakfast, Daddy headed over to the airplane factory. It would be a big adjustment for him. But as he said, "a man gotta do what he gotta do." So, I guess I had to do what every one said do. And that meant school.

As the crow flies, the school was only one street over. There were shortcuts through people's yards to that street. But, Ma and I walked the long way around. It wasn't so bad, because the walk gave me a chance to check out the area and get my bearings.

The school was a big brick building with a large school yard, completely surrounded by a cyclone fence. As we walked to the main front entrance, I could see through the large windows. Kids were seated in the class rooms and I wondered where I would sit.

The school office was located at the head of the front stairs.

"Can I help you?" The plump red haired lady working in the office asked my mother.

"Yes, Ma'am," replied Ma. "I want to enroll my son. We jest moved hea' and Ah have his school records."

"Very good. Just fill in the information requested on this form and we'll get him a class."

My mother filled out the paperwork and gave it and the records to the lady.

"Oh, I see you moved to Rosehill place. I live two buildings down from you. You're from North Carolina. This isn't the boy who shot out the street light, is it?"

"The one and the same," replied Ma, as she glared at me.

My reputation preceded me. I was a dead duck. A marked man. This whole school must know about me. My every move will be watched. Any time trouble occurs, they'll round up the usual suspects plus the kid who shot out the street light.

R. Allen Pender

"I over heard some boys from my building talking about that last night. They were really impressed. You know, a boys thing. You can have a seat Missus Pendell, while I take these papers to the principal."

Within a short time the lady was back and said. "Mrs. Devaney, the principal is reviewing his records. And she'll see you shortly."

"That's fine." Ma answered.

We were sitting there for a few minutes, when a tall gray haired lady wearing glasses came in.

"Hello, Mrs. Pendell, I'm Mrs. Devaney, the Principal. Can you and your son come with me to my office?"

"How do you do, Mrs. Devaney. Certainly."

The Principal led us into her office and motioned for us to take a seat near her desk.

"I see Richard was in the fourth grade in North Carolina. However, he is almost a year younger than our average fourth grader. I also see that he never attended Kindergarten, which accounts for that year difference."

"That's right," said Ma. "We send our children to the first grade at five years old. We don't have Kindergarten."

"Well the kindergarten experience is very important. It provides the children with the opportunity to get along with each other and to become accustomed to the school experience. I am suggesting that we place Richard in the third grade. I am sure there are fine schools in North Carolina. However, it has been our experience that children coming from rural schools do not have the same level of maturity as our local children. Hence, they tend not to do as well as their peer group."

"I don't agree." My Mother snapped back. "My son can read, write and do mathematics as good as, if not better, than your average fourth grade student. Why don't you give him a test?"

"We don't usually do that. However, I am writing a note to our fourth grade teacher for their current study materials. And we can see how he handles it. The children will be breaking for recess shortly and I will ask Mrs. Yoder, our fourth grade teacher to bring those items down to my office. We should be ready in thirty minutes, so you can wait here or maybe you would like to go across the street to the Luncheonette where you can get a cup of coffee."

"I think I'll do that. A cup of coffee would be nice. We'll be back in thirty minutes."

I could tell Ma was in a bear fighting mood as we left the Principal's office. She didn't say a word until we were outside the school door.

"These arrogant Yankees, who do they think they are? Not mature enough. When we get back there, you do your best... Shoot out their street lights." she said looking at me with a sly smile.

"Ma, kin Ah have a hot chocolate."

"Sure nuff, you can."

We went into the little coffee shop and confectionary store across the street from the school. Ma ordered up for both of us from the lady behind the counter.

The lady could apparently see we were new to the community, and she and my mother began a conversation regarding their respective plights.

The lady told my mother about the impending rationing and how it would force her to close the store until the war was over. Ma told the lady about our current situation with the school. As they talked I watched the kids come out of the school into the yard for their recess break.

The kids were running around like corralled animals. Some girls were jumping rope; others were just standing around in small groups. The boys seemed to be separated into a different group and were much further back in the school yard. Several school teachers appeared to be monitoring the situation. These kids looked like normal run of the mill kids. And I couldn't see any reason to be fearful of this school. All I had to do was show this principal that I was qualified for the fourth grade. I wasn't going to worry about any test. I was going to let happen whatever was going to happen, after all I was only here for the wartime and not for a career.

A bell sounded and all the children were formed into lines. One by one, these lines of small humans were gobbled up by the brick building, until all that remained was the wind blowing across the school yard.

"Come on Richard, we better get back to the school before that lady thinks we can't tell time."

"Good luck." said the woman behind the counter.

"Thank you and I wish the same for you." Ma said as we walked out the door.

As I was walking up the school steps, I tried to imagine the feelings that General Lee had as he was walking up the steps of the McLean farmhouse at Appomattox to meet General Grant. He had the whole future of the South in his hands as he went to meet the enemy leaders. And now I was walking into the den of a Yankee school principal with the duty placed before me to uphold the integrity of my family, the South and the North Carolina school system. I must not allow these people to get the best of me. Suddenly, Mrs. Virgil's words of two days ago popped into my head." Don't forget who you are, or where you come from and that the Lord is watching over you." Any apprehension I had was gone and I was eager to meet the challenge.

The Principal and another lady were talking inside her office when we returned.

"Come in." She Beckoned." This is Mrs. Cower, our ungraded teacher. I have asked her to help me evaluate Richard. She specializes in children with special needs and we value her professional opinion in these cases. So, Mrs. Cower, you may proceed with the evaluation."

"Very well, Mrs. Devaney. Richard you can sit here at this table. And, if at any time you have a question, or don't understand my question, please speak out. Do you understand?"

"Yes, Ma'am."

"Richard, there are ten pieces of paper on the table. I would like you to write your name and age on each one at the upper left hand corner."

"Ma'am, do you want me to write or print?"

"Do whichever you please."

"Ah'll print five and write five." I said, as I began to fill out the papers as directed.

"I see you're left handed, Richard. Has anybody ever asked you to try writing with your right hand?"

"No."

"Can you do anything with your right hand?"

"Yes, Ah can."

"Would you give me some examples of what you can do with your right hand?"

"Well, I can catch a ball, pick fruit, swing and shift gears."

"Do you mean shift gears, like driving a car?"

"Yes ma'am."

With a perplexed look on her face, she turned towards my mother who gave an affirmative nod.

"Richard, can you show me on this globe of the world, where we are located?"

I placed my finger on the approximate position of the New York City area on the globe.

"Now I want you to write the answers to the following questions on your first piece of paper."

"One. What country do you live in?

Two. What State do you live in now?

Three. In what State did you formally live?

Four. What is the largest state in your country?"

I dashed off the answers as fast as Mrs. Cower asked the questions. And looking over my shoulder, she could see I had written the right answers.

"If you know the answers to this group of questions, write them below the answers you have already written. What is the capital of the United States? Who is the President of the United States? With what countries are we now at war?"

Again, I wrote the answers as fast as she asked the questions. And again she looked over my shoulder to check my answers.

"Now on the second piece of paper, I would like you to draw a tree in the middle of the paper."

"Mrs. Cower, what kind of tree do you want me draw?"

"What types of trees do you know?"

"Well, that tree rat there beside the winder is a red cedar, its evergreen. An' the big 'un further out is a maple an' the ones 'round the school yard are sycamores. Ah kin draw any kind you want."

"Can you draw an oak tree?"

"Shore nuff, summer or winter?"

"What is the difference, Richard?"

"Leaves. There aren't any in the winter"

"Summer. And can you draw an oak leaf separately?"

This lady didn't know that I had spent probably as much time in a tree as a squirrel. A tree was like a second home to me, so in the matter of a few seconds I was able to sketch a knarly old oak and a leaf.

"Now can you draw a boy by that tree?"

"Doin' what?"

"Well, just doing something boys do around trees."

Did this lady ever walk into this one? I sketched the side view of a boy with the front portion of his body obscured by the tree. Mrs. Cower picked up the paper and studied it. Finally she asked, "What is he doing."

"Peein."

I could tell she was embarrassed. She was struggling to retain her composure. Quickly, she picked up a book and asked me to read three pages out loud. It was pretty simple stuff and I had no trouble reading the short story. Finally, she wrote some arithmetic problems on one of my papers and asked me to complete them in ten minutes. I was done in less than five minutes.

"Thank you Richard. Mrs. Devaney and I will go over your evaluation. You and your mother can wait over in the office and we will be over to discuss your class assignment."

Ma and I walked out of the principal's office and before we got to the school office, she said, "You did real good, but why did you ever draw that picture? That woman must be wondering about what kind of family you come from. Some times you're good... an' then you ruin it by doin' bad."

My mother wasn't all that mad. She knew I had tricked that teacher and given them their comeuppance. I was laughing on the inside and I suspect my mother was too. I'll bet ole' General Lee and all my ancestors up in Heaven were laughing like fools.

We were waiting in the school office for only a short time, when Mrs. Devaney came in. She handed my papers to the office lady and then told my mother that I was being assigned to the fourth grade. She also said that I would be required to attend speech class twice a week to improve my verbal skills. I knew the real reason. They wanted me to speak their language. She also gave my mother a school schedule and informed her that the school lunch hour was from 11:30 to 12:30 and all children went home for lunch. With those things said, she informed the office lady that she would escort me to Mrs. Yoder's classroom. Ma gave me a peck on the cheek, straightened my tie and gave a little wave as I followed Mrs. Devaney into the corridor.

My classroom was on the second floor. Mrs. Devaney gave a tap on the door window and motioned for Mrs. Yoder to come out into the hallway. She was a nice looking lady, so much different than Mrs. Cower, the expert. She gave Mrs. Yoder a piece of paper that probably had all the vital background information about me. It probably said, "This is the boy who shot out the street light and pees on trees."

"I'll take care of him, Mrs. Devaney. Come on Richard, let me find a place for you," Mrs. Yoder said, as she opened the classroom door.

When I walked in all the kids were leaning out, or over their desks whispering to each other. My imagination told me they were saying, "That's the boy who shot out the street light."

"Boys and girls, this is Richard. He just moved here from North Carolina and we want to welcome him to our class."

A waving arm shot up in the back of the room.

"Yes, John," asked Mrs. Yoder.

I recognized the face, as one of those boys present at the street light incident.

"Richard lives near me and this desk by me is empty. Can he sit here?"

"For now, yes. However, I may have to change my seating chart later."

What she was really saying, was that if I screw up she was going to move me around. These Northerners had a funny habit of not saying what they were saying. They didn't talk straight on. They sort of come at your from around the corner. Another anomaly that I immediately noticed was the presence of three colored kids in the class, two boys and a girl. Back home the schools were segregated. Everything was segregated. I didn't understand what the up side of that situation was. I only knew that the downside meant that my school didn't have enough boys to make two teams for a baseball game and their school did. My butt is still sore from last summer, when I got caught playing in one of their after school games. Maybe things will be a little different around here. But, for now, I think I will just keep this situation secret.

# CHAPTER 11

# THE INTIMIDATOR

I wasn't settled in my desk for any length of time, when the lunch hour approached. Our hats and coats were hung in a little room at the rear of the classroom. They called it "the cloak room." Each row of students, by order, would file into the cloak room by the left door and exit from the right door with their hats and coats. Once dressed, the girls would lineup in single file in the corridor facing the stairway to the Girls Entrance. The boys would do likewise facing the Boys Entrance. I later found out the reasoning behind this arrangement. If you stood facing the front of the school, there was an entrance on each side of the school. The left side entrance was for girls and the right side entrance was for boys. Immediately down the stairs from each entrance were the boys and girls bathrooms. Girls on the left; boys on the right. No confusion, unless you didn't know whether you were a girl or a boy, or couldn't read.

The bell rang and the classes filed in order down the stairs and out the door.

"Come on. I'll show you the short cut." John said, as he grabbed my sleeve.

Just past the school fence, we turned left and walked up a driveway between two buildings. A path went between the garages at the rear of these buildings and through the middle of a garden, which extended all the way to the street and along the side of the building housing Cotton's Tavern. This route brought us to our corner and within three hundred feet of our building.

John Moccia lived in the same building as me. His family lived on the second floor in the rear. John was called Chicky, for whatever reason I never found out. He attached himself to me and became my guide in the intricacies of my new surroundings. Below Chicky, on the first floor, lived Robert. He was in the other fourth grade class. Robert's parents had just moved here from Pennsylvania. His father had been a Coal miner and he came here for defense work. Robert had an older brother in the eighth grade at the Junior High School. He was sort of a fastidious guy and never got involved in anything where he might get dirty. His name was Ivan and the older guys called him "Bloat." He had been aptly named. Robert was sort of like me, he didn't mind getting dirty. But, Bloat watched every thing he did and either hollered at Robert, or ran to tell his mother. I wished for Robert to get bigger than his brother and to slam him one in his fat mouth.

Out of the thirty-two families living in these four buildings, only Chicky, Robert and I were the same age. There were older boys like Klinky, Ducky, Waldo and Happy, Red, Wally and Breezy that went to Junior High School.

R. Allen Pender

Then there were guys like Butch, Alan, Sonny and Kluny that went to High School. Arthur and Tommy lived in the three story brick apartment building down on the corner and they were my age. However, we were still in the tail end of winter and our outdoor activities after school were limited due to supper and darkness. So for the present Chicky, Robert and I hung together.

Things were going along pretty good in school. Mrs. Yoder had me appointed to the school scenery committee. We were painting a mural on paper attached to the wall along the first floor corridor. All the kids on the committee were in the sixth grade, except me. They were going to have a Spring festival about Mexico and parents were going to be invited. In my area, I painted some tall cactus plants with a Mexican man and his burro peeking out from behind the cactus. Guess what they were doing?

Mr. Slavin was my speech teacher. He would come in twice a week for a forty minute session. There were about eight kids in the class, all from different grades and we would meet in the Auditorium. By the end of the first three weeks Mr. Slavin could say words like Dawg (dog), Awl (oil), Faar (fire), Waar (wire) and Y'all like a native. We were really making some progress. Six of the kids were colored, all from the South. The seventh was a boy whose family had come from Hungry and lived in New York, before moving to New Jersey. I was sort of bilingual. I could understand and speak the southern colored dialects and understood the various slang expressions. So, Mr. Slavin used me as sort of an interpreter.

These kids, including the Hungarian, would come to me in the school yard with little problems, mostly instructions they didn't understand, or words they couldn't pronounce. I always obliged. I was taught at home to obey the word of Jesus, to follow his example and to be a servant to others. As my Grandmother would say, "But for the grace of God, there go I."

With the help of Chicky and Robert, I assimilated into the main stream of the neighborhood and the school. It didn't come without paying a price and my association, even though minor, with the colored kids didn't help. Every school and every part of society has one of them. They can be labeled with various titles ... bullies, intimidators, self appointed rulers, or whatever. We had one. His name was John and he was in the sixth grade. John had to be in the forefront of everything that went on. He didn't like me. He would come by the mural as I was working and just stand there hurling insults. I was called "white trash", a "nigger lover," a sissy and a teacher's pet. The more I ignored him the more he came on. He continued to bait me at times where my reaction would get me in trouble. I told my father what John was doing and he said,

"You're gonna meet more like him. But, remember, every dog has his day, and yours will come."

I wasn't afraid of John. On the contrary, I wanted to go at him. When I didn't react to his provocations, he then developed a new strategy. He now directed his verbal attack at the kids I was associating with. Some of these kids were beginning to believe the venom John was spreading and now they began to politely distance themselves from me. Kids were now clucking at me behind my back and a few even openly called me a "chicken." I had the urge to lash out, but fortunately I was able to control myself.

As we approached the Spring of 1942, the country wasn't doing much better in the big war than I was doing in my little war. The Japanese had occupied most of the Philippines. The remaining American forces there were fighting gallantly on the Bataan Peninsula and Corregidor Island to resist overwhelming Japanese forces. German submarines were ravaging the ships in the Atlantic Ocean, while Hitler's Armies were inflicting heavy losses on the British in North Africa. It was a very bleak picture. Here on the home front men and boys were still leaving for military duty. They were replaced with a little red, white and blue banner. Families hung these banners in their front windows. Each banner had one or more white stars, to indicate the number of men who had gone to war. In time, many of those white stars would become silver... or gold.

When the weather was good, Robert, Chicky and I would go over to New York Avenue to play basketball. We had now teamed up with Arthur and Tommy, who lived in the brick apartment building on the corner. Both of these boys had come from Pennsylvania, and Arthur had a leather basketball. He was the kind of guy who would take his ball and go home, if he couldn't play. The High School boys had put up a backboard and a basket on a light pole and they would play after dark. New York Avenue had vacant land on both sides of the street, and little to no car traffic. So, before the bigger kids got home from Junior High School or High School we would play. As the afternoon wore on, the older boys would gradually appear and join in our game. As their numbers increased, we were eased off the court. However, many times they didn't have enough boys to make up two teams, so they would ask me or Tommy to play with them. I learned moves that they didn't teach in elementary school...and, how valuable that would become.

Mr. Harrison was the boys' Gym Teacher. He would come to our school twice a week. The boys from both fourth grade classes took gym together. To make things a little interesting, Mr. Harrison thought it would be a good idea to have a basketball game between the boys of each separate class. From that game, he would pick a team to play the fifth grade boys and from that game he would pick an all-star team to play the sixth grade. This sounded real good to me.

We had a nice game. My class won, but not by much; only one basket. Mr. Harrison picked George, Scotty and me from my class and Martin, Tommy, Robert and Charles from the other class. That Thursday we played the fifth graders. Again we won — this time by four points. Donald and Smitty from the fifth grade replaced Martin and Robert on the all-star team, which was now composed of five fourth graders and two fifth graders. Next Tuesday we would meet the sixth grade super stars. Our team had some pretty good athletes. George played a lot of basketball with some older boys in Linden, as he lived on the town line. Scotty and Charles were colored boys from South Carolina and they played regularly at a City play ground near their homes. Donald played for a Church team and Smitty had just moved here from another part of the city. And, of course Tommy and I played on New York Avenue.

That Thursday evening, after our victory over the fifth grade, Tommy and I walked over to New York Avenue. The bigger guys were already playing. We told them about our game coming up with the sixth grade and we wanted their permission for our team to hold a practice session on the court. The big guys listened to our pitch.

"Hey guys!" shouted Butch, who lived in the building next to mine. "Lefty and Red want to bring their team over here for practice tomorrow and Saturday. They got a game against some sixth grade wise guys. What d'ya say?" The game stopped momentarily and they went into a little huddle with Butch.

"O.K. kids. Bring your team over. We'll bring the balls and we'll have a real practice session."

Tommy, who Butch called Red, and I was really excited and amazed at the attitude of the big guys. We thought they would chase us away.

The next day at school we informed our team members of the practice sessions we arranged for Friday afternoon and Saturday morning. All the boys were agreeable, except Scotty and Charles. They had a longer distance to walk home and back, so we accepted that excuse. We all knew the real reason. The schools were integrated up here, but nothing else was. To come into our neighborhood to play meant crossing the White Line. It wasn't done.

The sixth graders were using every opportunity they had to mock and tease us. They were going to beat us bad and send us back to wherever we came from. We let all this baloney float right over our heads. After all, this was only a game and its outcome would have no bearing on the history of the western world. Or, would it?

We met by the brick apartment building, as scheduled, that Friday afternoon. And, we walked as a group to the basketball court. True to their word, Butch and the big guys came. There were five big guys in all. Butch was now playing for the Y. M. C. A. Men's AAU team. Two boys, each named John, played for Saint Mary's High School team. And the final two boys, named Dick and Ed, played for Thomas Jefferson High School.

After introductions, they formed us up for drills. They had us do dribbling and passing exercises. Then we started passing and layup practice. We were in the middle of blocking and passing exercises, when three colored boys on bicycles came down the street. It was Scotty and Charles. They were accompanied by a bigger boy.

"Hey, Eddie!" Butch hollered. "Does your little brother belong with this gang?"

"Yeah, he does."

"Then have him get his butt out here," Butch replied.

Scotty's brother, Eddie, was known to the other boys because he also played for Thomas Jefferson High School…and now three more joined in the practice.

These guys must have worked with us for almost two hours, before we realized that darkness would be coming pretty soon and it was time to quit for the day. Scotty's brother, Eddie approached Butch, who had taken on the Head Coach role for this session.

"Hey, Butch! These boys are going to play full court at the school. If they want, they can practice tomorrow at our court and learn what full court is like."

"Good idea, Eddie." Butch answered and then looking at us asked "Can you guys go to the South Broad Street playground tomorrow?"

Only Donald knew where the playground was located. But we agreed to go.

"What time, Eddie?" Butch asked.

"Say … ten o'clock."

We all nodded our heads in the affirmative, as Butch confirmed the time with Eddie. The bigger guys now started choosing up sides for a game, as we headed for home.

Except for family trips to Aunt Hazel's in Rahway, or to my Grandmother's house in Hillside, I hadn't ventured more than a half mile from home. My mother and I would walk to the A&P food store on the corner of South Street and Washington Avenue, which was about a half mile from home and that was the extent of my range. South Broad Street was two streets beyond Washington Avenue and the playground was way down near the intersection of Washington Avenue and Broad Street, the city center.

That Saturday morning our little band of aspiring basketball players met on the corner by the brick apartment building. Donald was an Elizabeth native and he would be our guide. Our journey would take us up Rosehill Place to South Street, where we would turn right and walk to Washington Avenue, one city block away. After crossing Washington Avenue, we walked two more blocks. Just past Saint Mary's School, we turned left on South Broad Street. We proceeded down the hill to the playground, which was on the upper bank of the river. We could have walked all the way down Washington Avenue to the playground. But, that lower portion of Washington Avenue and Pearl Street, along the river, was the colored neighborhood. And we would be crossing the color line. Our mentors were already there when we arrived. After putting us through some warm up drills, they broke us into two teams for a scrimmage game. We only had seven boys on the team. So Robert, who had joined us for the trip, was pressed into service. With four boys on each side, we began to play. Butch was coaching the offense and Eddie was coaching the defense. The game was like a stop action movie. They would give us instructions on the basic plays involved to move the ball towards the basket, or to guard the basket. If we didn't do it right, we had to start over. Once we got the knack of things, we were pretty receptive. As we played, Butch and Eddie were evaluating our different skills and moved us on the court to where each of us could play most effectively. When the session concluded, Butch got us into a huddle.

"You boys are doing Ok, now I have a little diagram where Eddie and I think each of you should play. Try to follow it and you should do alright. Keep the pressure on the other guys. Don't let them near the basket. Let lefty, who jumps like a kangaroo, and Scotty go in for rebounds. George and Donald, or Smitty have to try and keep open to take the shots. You other guys, work the ball into them. And don't take any wild shots. Ok, good luck."

We were full of enthusiasm as we retraced our steps back to our neighborhood. We were also hungry, as lunch time was approaching. A few of us were planning to mosey over to New York Avenue after lunch, but that depended upon the availability of Arthur and his ball.

*THE SOJOURNERS*
*Life on the American Homefront During World War II*

# CHAPTER 12

# SHOWDOWN ON THE BASKETBALL COURT

Basketball was not high on my mother's list of priorities. She had other plans for my Saturday afternoon. Ma was just finishing the clothes washing when I got home. The Easy washing machine had been stationed next to the wall hung porcelain kitchen sink and Ma was running the last pieces of clothing through the wringer.

"Start carryin' these baskets up to roof while Ah finish the wringin', ya hear!" Ma commanded. "As quick as Ah can hang these clothes, the quicker Ah can fix you lunch and we can go to the A&P."

So I grabbed the first basket and began my trip to the roof. The building had a flat tar roof, which was accessed by a staircase in the second floor hallway. At the head of the stairs was a copula with a door that opened onto a wooden deck built over the roof membrane. Clothes lines attached to vertical wooden supports were suspended back and forth across the deck. The families that lived in the rear apartments had clothes lines from their kitchen windows hooked to poles out by the garages in the rear. But, those families in the front of the building had to use the roof for drying their wash. It usually required three trips up and down to get all the wet wash up on the roof and this day was no exception. When my mother was hanging the wash, I would climb up on the copula where I had a good view of the entire neighborhood and the surrounding country. Naturally, Ma would make me get down as soon as she saw me perched on my little observation post. What she didn't know, was that before she got to the roof, I would climb through the sides of the roof deck and go to the very edge of the roof. Usually, I just spit a couple of times to see how long it would take for spit to hit the ground. The roof had great potential for a variety of covert activities and I did develop some long range plans to turn this roof into a slingshot nest. There were still some logistical problems to overcome, but I was working on that.

My mother was all business. She just wanted to get the clothes hung on the line and wasn't interested in my tour guide description of the panorama being displayed before us. She went about her work rapidly and as soon as she was finished, we collected the baskets and headed downstairs.

The next chore would be the trip to the A&P, but first came lunch. My mother always made me tomato soup and crackers for lunch. I really didn't like tomato soup that much. Apparently that was the only kind of soup that came in a can. My grandmother made good chicken, beef and pea soup. Whenever we went to visit her, she would give my mother a couple of jars of soup to take home. Now that beat anything in a can. We would be going there tomorrow and she just might have some soup for me to take home. But, for now I had to settle for canned tomato soup.

I had gotten a wooden wagon, which was kept in the basement. The main purpose of this wagon was to be a boy powered vehicle to provide trucking services to the family. Gasoline was in short supply, so cars were used only in an emergency and maybe for a short drive on Sunday. Aside from the little bus that traveled from Linden to Elizabeth, along Edgar Road, the shoe leather express was the main mode of travel. So a one boy powered wagon was a valuable piece of equipment. Some of our neighbors would call their food orders into the A&P or one of the three meat markets situated along Washington Avenue or Edgar Road. For a tip of 10 to 25 cents, me and my wagon would make the pick up and deliver the groceries to the customer. This little business generated about 50 cents a week. My mother never gave me a tip. Whenever I went to the store with her, I hoped she wouldn't buy too much. That way I would have some room in the wagon and could carry back some paying customer's groceries.

My mother was a frugal shopper. She bought only the bare necessities. We still had many jars of preserved food down in our basement storage bin. So, it wasn't necessary to buy any canned goods. My mother kept an inventory of everything down there in her head. The only snack food she purchased, was Ritz crackers. And, they could only be eaten with that tomato soup. Despite her frugality, Ma was a good cook and put out good healthy meals.

My Aunt Eileen was the exact opposite of my mother. She had a telephone, because her husband Ed was a supervisor at the Standard Oil Refinery. And, in the event of a fire or explosion, all the supervisors would be called to come in and help put the fire out. My Aunt used the phone to call her grocery and meat orders into a small butcher shop on Edgar Road. She bought everything in this little store. My mother would always chide her for spending so much money on food orders. My Aunt always bought the best meat cuts available and simply gave her husband the bill to pay. She didn't worry about anything.

Her exorbitant buying did have a positive trickle down effect on our family. Certain food items like meat, sugar, and butter were becoming scarce. Shop owners would save these items for their best customers. If you weren't a regular customer at one of these establishments, you were out of luck. My mother and Aunt developed a little buying group. Our meat needs were incorporated into her order and her grocery items became part of our A&P order. This system would become very important in the not so distant future.

The A&P, located on the corner of South Street and Washington Avenue, bore no resemblance to the current stores operated by that chain. If ten people were in that store at one time, the place was crowded. There wasn't any checkout. All business was conducted at the counter by a white haired man named Mr. King. Almost every one gave Mr. King a list of their needs, which he and his two assistants would scurry around the store to fill. They would snatch things off the shelves and pick things from the high shelves with a pole that had grabbers attached to its end. In short order the items were laid out on the counter. At that point, Mr. King would take the thick black pencil, which was tucked behind his ear, and mark and add the prices of the order on a paper sack. He was fast and accurate. The assistants would place the items in used corrugated boxes as they were added up on the paper sack. Ma would pay the man and I would load the boxes into the wagon. Some people phoned their orders into the A&P. These orders were set along the wall by the front door all marked in black pencil. All a pick-up person had to do was to holler their name and Mr. King would ring up the amount on his crank up cash register. I guess the A&P Corporation had people like Mr. King all over the country and they were forced to develop supermarkets when these people passed on. It's too bad, because these companies could have saved a lot of money by not having to buy big buildings with expensive check out equipment and employ modern day workers who aren't as efficient as Mr. King and his pencil.

Ma and I were finished with our chores by mid-afternoon. I was still keyed up about the upcoming basketball game and began to simulate game conditions in our apartment hall. I had a small rubber ball, which I would bounce down the hall and take a shot at a make believe basket on the kitchen door frame. Then, I would jump up, grab the rebound and start the whole process over again. Ma was making a cake in the kitchen and it didn't take too long for my jumping to get the best of her nerves.

"Do you have to do all that jumpin'?" She howled.

"I have to practice my jumpin' for the game, Ma."

"Well go do it somewhere else. That jumpin' is goin' to ruin this cake."

"Kin ah go to New York Avenue an' practice?"

"Go anywhere. Jest be back hea' by five o'clock."

With that said, I had my jacket on and was out the door. I ran across the back yard, around the garages and across the field behind the garages to the New York Avenue basketball court. When I got there some of the Junior High School boys were playing.

"Hey, guys! Here comes the little sharpshooter." Exclaimed, Ducky. "Boy, are you in trouble!"

"Trouble for what?" I asked.

"Klinky can't come out for a week on account of you." Happy replied.

"He shot Humphrey Bogart with one of your slingshots and got arrested," chimed in Wally. "And he told the Cops that it was your slingshot. They have it now at Police Headquarters."

"Who's Humphrey Bogart?" I questioned.

"He's in the movies, Hayseed. Klinky shot him on the movie screen in the Regent Theater. We all got thrown out and the Cops took Klinky to Police Headquarters ... and made his father come down and get him." answered Waldo.

"Wow! It weren't ma slingshot. I only helped him make it."

"Anyhow, those cops will be around watchin' you," stated Wally, as he took a shot at the basket.

Life was sure getting complicated in these parts. First, John in school, then the sixth grade basketball game and now I was on the Police wanted list as a manufacturer of illegal slingshots. I had to formulate some plans to keep myself out of trouble. At the moment the Police were my main concern.

I kept my slingshot making supplies down in the basement. So, I made a beeline for the basement. I took the inner tubes I had and stuffed them between the boards of someone else's storage bin. I hid the crotches on the inside of the coal bin and put the cord behind a board in Mr. Mitchell's workshop. I knew where everything was and I could easily retrieve my materials. If the Cops came looking, they would have a hard time finding the stuff.

Once the cache was secured, I went up to our apartment. I felt certain that any evidence linking me to the Humphrey Bogart shooting had been successfully concealed. This was the technique my Uncle Bill used to prevent the Revenuer's from destroying his liquor making equipment. As soon as he finished making a batch of liquor, the still and all the equipment was disassembled and spread to the four winds. Only Uncle Bill knew where all the pieces were.

"How come you're back so soon?" Ma asked.

"Jest were big guys over there."

Well then, go do some of your schoolwork. That's more important than basketball. Besides, were goin' to Gramma's tomorrow and you won't be able to do schoolwork there."

I picked up a book and went into the living room, turned on the radio and propped myself up in the bay window. From this vantage point I had a clear view of the street. Infrequently a car would pass by, going up or down the street. My main concern was a black '40 Ford with a 2 painted on its side. As the dusk of late afternoon began to shroud the neighborhood, I could not discern any movement resembling a Police dragnet. Suddenly, a group of people appeared from behind the rise of the hill in the field across the street and they were coming in my direction. It was my father and some neighbors, who just had gotten off the bus from the airplane factory.

"Hey, Boy!" My father exclaimed as he came in through the door. "What have you been up to all day?"

"Jest playin' basketball and food shoppin'."

"No problems, Ah guess."

*THE SOJOURNERS*
*Life on the American Homefront During World War II*

I wasn't about to tell my father that I might be the subject of an investigation into the shooting of Humphrey Bogart. So I said, "No problems today Daddy."

My father was looking forward to a peaceful Sunday off from work. The factories had made a rapid transition from peace time manufacturing to wartime production. My father was an inspector at the Eastern Aircraft plant. They made Grumman Hellcats and Wildcats for the Navy in this plant that used to make Pontiacs and Oldsmobiles. All factories were operating 24 hours per day, seven days a week. Workers, like my father had to work 8 hour shifts, six days a week. This would be my father's last Sunday off for sometime. He was scheduled to begin the 3 P.M. to 11 P.M. shift on Monday and he would be off on Wednesdays.

We had been alternating Sundays, by going to Aunt Hazel's in Rahway one week and to my Grandmother's in Hillside the following week. I didn't know how the change would affect us. But, the war had everyone fouled up. So, we had to make do with what we were dealt.

The old Ford was still faithfully serving us. It didn't get used during the week ... it only got started on Sunday, if there was enough gas. This Sunday we motored to my grandparent's house in Hillside, a five mile trip. My Aunt Eileen and Ed, her husband, were going with us. Ma had baked a cake and my Aunt made fruit salad. I got squeezed in the back by the window, while my mother and aunt sat in the back holding the cake, salad and my little sister. Daddy and Ed sat up front. I didn't like sitting with the ladies. They talked a lot and didn't say anything that was worth my overhearing. Dad and Ed talked about more interesting stuff, but I couldn't hear a thing from the back seat ... especially with two women yacking away.

Gramps and Gramma were renting a nice big house with a big yard. Big that is, compared to other houses around here. Not big compared to where we came from. The first thing you noticed upon pulling into the driveway was the banner in the window with four white stars. It always made me think of the ones not here for dinner. Cousins George and Hugh didn't have any living parents and for many years they made my grandparents home their address. It was good that they had a window for their stars.

Gramps and Gramma were lit up with big smiles and gave us all hugs as we entered the house. The overpowering aromas coming from the kitchen made us drool and forget that we had ever moved, and a war was on. Gramps was always a host and he would invite business associates, or someone he met somewhere to Sunday dinner. He loved a gathering and loved to have his family and friends around him to share his blessings.

This Sunday he had invited an elderly gentleman to dinner. The man, Mr. Seymour, was an engineer and he was working with my grandfather to develop better factory powerplant systems. Mr. Seymour was the consummate gentleman. His demeanor and dress were straight out of the Victorian Era. He was well schooled in the social graces, exhibiting all the proper courtesies during our introduction and the meal to follow. We later learned that Mr. Seymour had come from a wealthy family in Newark and that his father had been Mayor of the City around the turn of the century.

My Mother and Aunt had joined my grandmother and two Great Grandmothers in setting the table and placing the cooked food at the table. Meanwhile the men had settled in the parlor to discuss the events of the day. I had gone into the sun parlor, which my grandfather used as an office. As I was removing a book from the book case, I noticed a large black Buick entering the driveway.

"Gramma, someone is coming!" I hollered.

"It must be Doctor McCauley. I'll get the door." She said.

Gramma opened the foyer door and ushered in a slender red haired lady and a tall slim man wearing a black suit and black fedora. The first thing I noticed was his cleric's collar. My grandfather introduced the McCauleys' to everyone present. Doctor McCauley was the Reverend Doctor McCauley Pastor of a big Presbyterian Church in Newark. Although they didn't know each other, there was immediate name recognition between Mr. Seymour and the Reverend Doctor. Both men were members of established Newark families and both had graduated from Princeton University. My grandfather certainly knew how to pick his dinner guests. And, I got the feeling we were going to have some whooper of a prayer before the meal.

Gramma had outdone herself as the sumptuous meal was laid before us. Baked fresh ham stuffed with apple-cornbread dressing and roasted potatoes was complimented by greens and beans, sauerkraut, applesauce, glazed yams and creamed onions. Hot cornbread, butter milk biscuits, my Aunt's fruit salad and Gramma's gravy completed this meal fit for a King.

I think the appearance of the food had a definite affect on Doctor McCauley, as his prayer was to the point and very brief. He and Mrs. McCauley dug into that food with gusto. They couldn't get over the fact that this type of meal was a Sunday tradition for us and that my grand- parents apologized for our regular contingent of Sunday guests, who couldn't be present because of the War. My grandparents were called "Mom and Pop" by all of those people who graced our table. They had received letters from the many now in service, who were anxious for the day when they could again sit down to one of Gramma's roast pork dinners. If anything could inspire our troops to victory; Gramma's stuffed fresh ham was the thing.

The conversation around the table was light and interesting as we got to know the guests and them us. The good Doctor and his wife were interested in learning about our reactions to our new surroundings. And we in turn had questions concerning the customs and lifestyles of this area. Everyone had a good laugh when my mother told of our experience with Mrs. Devaney and Mrs. Cower at the school. At that point my Aunt Eileen cut in.

"Alice, did you hear what happened yesterday to the boy who lives in the building next to you?"

"No. What boy?"

"The one they call Klinky. He got arrested."

"What for?" asked Daddy.

"Mr. Ekker, his son is Wally. Mr. Ekker is an auxiliary policeman and he told Mrs. Mitchell, who told me, that Klinky was arrested at the movie theater for shooting Humphrey Bogart on the screen with a sling shot. And the police think there's a ring leader in the neighborhood that is a bad influence on these boys."

"Oh, That's silly, Eileen. Richard shot out the street light when we weren't here but two hours and he didn't get arrested."

Suddenly, I could feel all the eyes at the table shift in my direction.

"Shot out the street light, you say," interjected Mr. Seymour.

"One shot from the sling shot at thirty feet, Dave," Gramps proudly replied.

Wearing a sly smile on his face and winking at me as he answered, Mr. Seymour said, "One shot from thirty feet. That is good shooting."

"Well," said Gramma, coming to my defense. "Those bigger boys were teasing him and he had to standup for himself. I don't approve of damaging property, but I think he showed them a trick or two."

"The slingshot is a mighty powerful weapon, capable of changing the course of history." Interjected Reverend McCauley. "Remember young David and how he slew Goliath. God directed the shooter and the shot. No doubt young Richard is proficient with that weapon, but without some help he could have easily missed. We are living in desperate times these days and that may often require unusual actions to resolve a bad situation. Indeed these are the times that try men's souls."

"AMEN" Exclaimed Great Gramma Morisey. "We should pray for that boy who shot Mr. Bogart. May the Holy Spirit inspire him to do better things with his life, all to the Glory of God."

And all God's people at the table said, "AMEN."

I was really surprised by Reverend McCauly's dissertation concerning my street light episode. Initially, I thought he was going to call upon God to roast me with fire and brimstone. Instead, he displayed a tolerant, if not justifiable attitude regarding my actions. He even implied that God is involved in everything we do.

Sunday dinner in our family was conducted in a ritual like manner. When the main meal was finished, the men retired to the parlor and the ladies cleared the dining room. Immediately, the ladies went to work washing the dishes and silverware. When the scullery work in the kitchen was completed, the dining room table was reset for coffee and desert. For the men it was sort of an intermission; a time when they could discuss men things. During this period of digestion, I approached The Reverend Doctor McCauley.

"Doctor McCauley. Does God go to basketball games?"

"God is everywhere. And I'm sure He's at the basketball games. Why do you ask?"

I proceeded to tell the Doctor about our game on Tuesday and my problems with John, from the sixth grade. I related how our team was practicing hard and we could use all the help we could get to beat that sixth grade team. We needed God on our side.

"God is always on your side, Richard. But He won't help you win a game for your own glory. God wants you to play fairly, by the rules. Win or lose, it is the example you set by your playing that gives glory to God. We may lose the game, but if we play fairly by the rules, we win with God. Do you understand?"

"Yes Sir."

I knew the Reverend Doctor was right. But, I sure wanted to beat that sixth grade team. I was being humiliated by that John and a win for us would shut him up for good. As I lay on the parlor floor with the Sunday newspaper, I read the stories about our country's humiliating defeats at the hands of the Japs and Germans around the world. My problems were small potatoes compared to Mr. Roosevelt's. God sure had a lot of work to do and I really shouldn't be bothering Him about a little basketball game. So, I figured I would pray to God and ask Him to come to the game. If He was busy and couldn't make it, I'd understand. The worst thing that could happen would be for us to lose the game and that wouldn't have any impact on the world situation. If wise guy John were to attack me outside the safety of the school grounds, then I could employ the strategy Gramps and Mr. Seymour said our Military leaders were going to use. They were going to draw the enemy to the battlegrounds of their choice. I didn't know how well John played basketball, but right now that looked like a good battleground.

It seemed like an eternity as I waited for Tuesday afternoon. Finally the time had come. As a team, our game plan had been set. Scotty and I would go under the basket for rebounds and then get the ball back to Donald or Smitty. George would play back so we could get the ball to him if it rebounded off their basket. We practiced it this way, now all we had to do was to keep our heads and play as we were instructed.

The teams were given a few minutes to warm up by their baskets. Then Mr. Harrison called both teams to the center of the court. He explained the rules. Basically we would play seven minute quarters and he would be the referee. He also would make the substitutions for both sides, thus insuring everyone an equal opportunity to play.

The game started with a jump from center and the ball went to the sixth grade team. They immediately made a shot at the basket as Scotty and I scampered toward the net for the rebound. The shot missed and the ball was on my side of the basket. As I jumped, someone tried to jump over me from behind. Using a maneuver from New York Avenue, I was able to grab the ball with swinging out stretched elbows and with a rotation of my hips, the player behind me hollered and fell on the floor. I got the ball to Smitty, who got the ball to George down court. George was wide open and made the basket easy with no defenders around. My swinging elbows had caught John in the stomach and he got up from the floor yelling that he had been fouled. Mr. Harrison ignored his pleas. The sixth grade had the ball again and passed to John, who charged in for a shot at the basket. I was guarding him from the basket side and he tried to fend me off with a stiff arm, as he moved in for the shot. By standing still and ducking slightly, his out stretched arm glanced off the top of my shoulder. Immediately, I rose up and catching him under the armpit, John went sprawling to the floor. This time Mr. Harrison blew his whistle and called a foul on John for charging. I now had two free throws at the basket. I made the first free throw. The second bounced off the rim and was caught by Donald, who was able to score from under the basket.

As the play went on, the sixth graders were getting more erratic. John had them whipped into a frenzy, and they made one mistake after another. When the first half of the game was completed, we were leading 17 to 2. We didn't really have to score any more points. Our plan for the second half was to slow the game and prevent them from scoring. John had different plans, but Mr. Harrison was catching all the fouling and infractions perpetrated by the sixth graders. By the third quarter, John had fouled out and was sent to the bench for the remainder of the game. With him gone, the sixth graders began playing a better game. Unfortunately for them, it was too little, too late and we won 23 to 10.

John ended up with some bruises, which would be sore reminders of this game for some time. John was shown to be fallible and his attempts to control by fear and intimidation were no longer effective. We never became friends, as story lines of this type usually conclude. However, John kept a safe distance from me, which I surmise was more from embarrassment, rather than fear. I have to praise my teammates for their conduct. Naturally we were happy we won, but then we all walked away without any animosity or braggadocio behavior towards our opponents. The game was over and now it was just history.

When I walked into the house my mother was starting to prepare supper.

"How did you do?" She asked

"We won," I matter of factly answered.

*R. Allen Pender*

"That's nice. We'll be ready to eat supper by 5:30, so don't you stray too far."

"O.K, if' n I go to the basketball court on New York Avenue?"

"You jest be back hea' by 5:30. I don't want to be outside holler'n fer you."

I was just busting at the seams to get over to the basketball court to tell the guys what happened. I felt about ten feet tall and was anxious to bask in my fifteen minutes of fame. After changing my clothes, I took my short cut to the basketball court. My ideas about a glorious celebration quickly faded. This day the basketball court was empty.

## CHAPTER 13

## SPRINGTIME IN THE NEIGHBORHOOD

My father was sleeping when I went to school the next morning. I left a note for him on the kitchen table. It said "ARF, ARF. BOW, WOW, 23 to 10." My mother looked at me kind of funny when she read the note. But my father would understand.

We had turned the corner into Spring. Spring and summer were my favorite times of the year. I loved the heat and the light and all the warm weather sports and activity. My spirits were up after our victory over the sixth grade and now we boys were getting involved in all kinds of activities. We all got enlisted in the Papertroopers, the Airplane spotters and the Cub Scouts.

The Papertroopers were just like the name implied. We were given patches to wear on our jackets and we went around collecting newspapers, cardboard, bacon grease and old aluminum pots and pans. People now had to clean and flatten their tin cans and we picked them up also. On certain days of the month, we had to bring our loads over to the school yard where everything was loaded onto trucks. Each person was given credit for they brought in. As certain levels of collection were attained, the individuals were rewarded with a campaign button.

We were given cards with silhouette pictures of known enemy aircraft for the Plane Spotter program. We had to study the cards and we were given tests at the bi-weekly meetings. It was our job to scan the skies for these alien aircraft and report them to the Civil Defense Air Raid Warden in our neighborhood, who was Wally's father. This was a great activity and provided us with a reason to be up on the roof. We regularly had blackouts. All lights were to be put out at the sounding of the Air-Raid siren. Wally's father would then patrol the area wearing his white helmet and his armband. We would race up to the roof and signal kids on other roofs with our flashlights, as we watched the searchlights flicker back and forth across the sky searching for the enemy aircraft that never came.

The Cub scouts met once a week down in the basement of the three story brick apartment building. Arthur's and Tommy's mothers were the Den Mothers. The dues were 10 cents a week. We did little crafty things like making tin cans into flower pots, or bird houses. It was alright in bad weather. But, I had envisioned activities in which we would be preparing for survival trips into the uncharted N. J. wilderness. I thought we would be making slingshots, bows and arrows, snares, fishing tackle and survival housing. What would we do if the

Germans and Japs invaded the City? The only thing this outfit would be capable of doing would be to stand on some street corner, wearing our blue caps and yellow scarves and try to sell our bird houses to the invading troops.

We also had to memorize The Laws of The Pack and the Scouts Oath. The First Law was, "The Cub follows AKELA." I never found out exactly who AKELA was. I think it might have been Mr. Palmer, the Scout Master. But, more than likely it was a code name used to confuse the enemy. If we were ever picked up by the Gestapo, all we were required to say was our Name, Rank and Merit Badges, like Pendell, R. A., Bobcat. If we got tortured, the only other information we had was that our leader was AKELA. Their was no way the Gestapo would ever suspect Mr. Palmer was the leader of our Resistance unit, especially if they saw him tripping over chairs at the Cub Pack meetings.

The advent of Spring awoke the primal man living in my soul. I loved the outdoors and I looked forward to the balmy days ahead. My thoughts were centered on important things like; baseball, fishing, camping and climbing trees. Back home the great outdoors started at our back porch. Things were a lot different here, so I collected maps of my new area and began to plan forays into the surrounding country side.

The weather around here was as gloomy as the world situation. On April 9, 1942 Battan fell to the Japanese. American forces now only held the island fortress of Corregidor. Many Americans escaped the Japanese and fled into the jungles to join Philippine natives engaged in guerilla warfare against the enemy. General MacArthur relocated to Australia as the Japanese continued their march of conquest across the Pacific Rim. The Japanese appeared unstoppable as they devoured country after country from China down into to the South Pacific. But, on April 18, 1942, Air Force Colonel Doolittle led a force of 16 B-25 bombers from the pitching deck of Admiral Halsey's aircraft carrier, Hornet and bombed Tokyo. The Sleeping Giant was wide awake and all Japan knew it.

The attack on Tokyo was celebrated all across this country and while it didn't bring Japan to her knees, it raised the morale and resolve of this Nation. We knew that Japan was vulnerable. The City of Elizabeth, New Jersey was swollen with pride because her native son, Admiral Halsey, brought those airplanes to within striking distance of Japan. It was hard to believe that a man, who grew up a mile away from where I now lived, was taking the war to the Japanese. We could identify ourselves with him as a person from our ranks, one of the many we would ultimately recognize and support as our personal representatives on battlefields through out the world. The early Spring gloom was slowly being erased by blooming buds and the glorious sunlight of new Spring mornings.

Before we had moved into the neighborhood, the bigger guys had built a wooden backstop in the field across street. And now as the dreary winter yielded to the Spring sun, the baseball gods began their annual rites. Armed with shovels and rakes, hammers and nails, the bigger guys repaired the backstop and manicured the playing field. The playing surface had been ravaged by Ole' Man Winter and the horses from the livery stables on Edgar Road. Finally, the holes were filled and the ruts were smoothed and it was game time. This field did not posses the symmetrical characteristics of a regulation baseball diamond. Its bounds were dictated by the topography of the site and various ground rules were in effect to make up for the lack of regulation standards. As an example; a ball hit to right field and out into Rosehill Place was only a single. A ball would have to be hit into right-center field past the second telephone pole on Rosehill Place to be an automatic two base hit. A homerun in left field would have to clear the trees along Lidgerwood Avenue and any ball that went off or under the trees was a two base hit. As the field had to be shared with horses at various times, any ball that went into center field near a horse was a one base hit. A fly ball that went over all the horses and past the street sign was a home run. If there weren't any horses around, the ball was in play at all times.

The bigger guys were not as liberal with this baseball field as they had been with the basketball court. We would go over there and catch, or bat the ball around until they showed up. But, once they were ready to play, we were banished. There was an empty piece of property on the corner of Garden Street and Lidgerwood Avenue, right across from the brick apartment building. So, we decided to stake our claim to it. With scrap wood, we built a small backstop on the end of the property near the entrance to Cotton's Bar. As the word went out about our new ballpark, boys from school came over and in short order we were able to start playing. This was real sandlot baseball. We had old balls wrapped with friction tape. We had bats of all sizes. Most of the bats had been split and now they were screwed and taped together. What we lacked in equipment and facilities, we made up in enthusiasm. As long as the sun shone, we played. We didn't have any adult supervisors or coaches. We learned to play on our own and it all seemed to come in a natural way.

Baseball was my passion and like all passions, it got me in trouble and brought me to a cross road that Spring. I had started to skip the Cub Scout meetings to play baseball. I also spent the 10 cents dues money for soft drinks before the games. My mother was informed that I was 40 cents in arrears in my Cub Scout dues and was going to be severed from the organization. Suffice it to say, that Ma interrogated me thoroughly, especially with regard to the 40 cents. I was summoned, along with a parent, to a hearing before the Cub Scout Pack Leaders. Mr. Palmer, alias AKELA, called the court into session and asked me to present myself to the court.

"Is it true that you purposely missed the meetings of your den?" asked Mr. Palmer.

"Yes." I replied.

"It has been reported to me, that you have neglected your responsibility to your Den and this Pack to play baseball. Is that true?"

"Yes."

"Do you wish to be reinstated in this Pack, or do you prefer to play baseball?"

Without hesitation, I made my choice. "Baseball."

With the utterance of that word, I was drummed out of the Cub Scouts. Never again could I wear the blue cap and the yellow scarf. I was a boy without a Den.

My Mother and I left the meeting and she didn't say a word. She knew I was a maverick. I came from a family of mavericks, so it would have been useless to force me to conform. You can't change the spots on a leopard, even a young one.

In May of 1942 rationing was started. Every family had to register at the Rationing Board. The Local Board used our school to meet and register the people. Each family was given a ration coupon book with a value in points based upon the size of the family. Now, in addition to money, a person had to have the proper ration coupons to purchase the rationed items. Stores now had to price the various items with the dollar and point value as set by the Office of Price Administration. These prices were set in Washington and they were changed every week as the supply and demand changed. Everything was in short supply. Even with rationing coupons and money, there wasn't any guarantee that an individual could buy meat, sugar, butter, canned goods, gasoline, tires, cigarettes, shoes or liquor. Stores generally sold these items to their regular customers first and then if anything was left, they would sell to a stranger.

American ingenuity went to work making substitutes for those things we previously imported. Synthetic rubber was developed to replace the natural rubber we used to get from the Japanese held East Indies. Synthetic sweeteners replaced the sugar from Tropics and a substance call oleo margarine replaced butter. My father and other men began rolling their own cigarettes using Bull Durham tobacco and cigarette papers. Cars were parked to save gasoline, oil and tires. And, every day brought a new challenge to find ways to overcome the shortages.

Our neighborhood consisted mostly of displaced country people, so the Sring days awoke the growing season inherent in our genes. I don't recall how it started, but one evening some of the men began turning over the soil on the far side of the baseball field. In succeeding days they were joined by others until the whole neighborhood was involved in tilling the soil around the baseball field and in the field behind the garages. Every boy in the neighborhood got involved in breaking up the clods of earth, while the men came behind us to rake the land into a soft bed for the plants that would soon call this place home.

Mr. Mitchell had been growing tomato plants down in the basement. He had the little buggers growing in old soft drink cases, which had been set on planks straddling saw horses. And, he watched over those plants like a mother hen.

"Can't set them out 'till Decoration Day. That's the day for setting tomatoes, any sooner; they'll die."

Most men in the neighborhood were now working as shift workers at the various defense plants. So, it wasn't unusual to see a few men working in the gardens during the daytime. One day a couple of horse drawn wagons arrived; loaded with manure. They had come from the livery stable on Edgar Road. They dropped their loads near the gardens and turned back to get more. Pretty soon we had manure piles all around the gardens. Charlie, who lived on the second floor of my building, finally came with a wheelbarrow. We boys went to his aid with shovels and rakes to spread the manure over the prepared soil. When we got finished, we all stunk to high heaven and Charlie's wife scolded him for having all that horse manure delivered.

"Why did you get some much Horse manure, Charlie?" screeched his wife Angie.

"Well they didn't have any cow manure. Besides, it was free."

Over the next few days the odor of manure gradually dissipated. And I must say it did make the soil feel soft and rich. As the gradually warming days of May began to slip by, little green shoots began to break through the soil. Each evening people would go into their respective parts of the garden to pull weeds and separate plants. Little signs had been placed along the rows to indicate the vegetable that would germinate and grow in that location. Buckets of water were carried in and as the final act of the evening; the young plants were given a drink before bed time.

This Spring really amazed me. It seemed like some type of metamorphosis had occurred in the neighborhood. During the winter the people were fleeting images in heavy clothing, or voices behind windows and closed doors. Now they had emerged from their dens shorn of their winter coats to become an inclusive society. All most every one here was a newcomer, but there was a feeling of solidarity. Each evening would find people either gathered under the trees that lined the street, or off tending the gardens. Many were onlookers as the older boys played baseball across the street. Except for an air raid, there was little distraction. Six day work weeks, little money and rationing coupons didn't make for a materialistic entertainment oriented society. There was no pretension. Everyone was in the same boat. We all were hanging on for survival. And having come through the depression, these people were experts at surviving.

The ladies of the neighborhood would get together regularly to swap recipes and to pool ration coupons. Those, like my Aunt Eileen, who had a good connection to a butcher, would find out what meats were available and then purchase an amount equal to all the ration stamps in the pool. Somebody else would do likewise for sugar, or some other commodity. Shared meals were a common thing. Small groups of women would make one item, like stuffed cabbages, or tomato sauce, or meat loafs, or cakes and pies. These items would then be parceled out to the different families. Nobody had a lot, yet no one was left wanting.

"Waste not, want not", was the motto of the day. No food was wasted. Even the bones were boiled for meat stock. The traditional foods that had been our staple were now supplemented by dishes we never thought of. Stuffed cabbages, Kielbasa and pierogies were introduced by the Pennsylvanians. Fish chowder came from the New Englanders. The New Yorkers introduced us to spaghetti, meatballs and ravioli. We southerners taught the fine art of Brunswick stew and chicken and rice. The ladies of the neighborhood became quite inventive as they juggled their menu and added their personal variations to these different foods.

But, the greatest survivor of them all was out roaming the country side. Because his business was necessary to the war effort, my grandfather could get the maximum amount of gasoline. As he traveled from factory to factory around the state, he became acquainted with farmers, slaughter houses and other producers of food. He made all kinds of deals with farmers to raise hogs and steers for him. All in all, I guess he had deals with ten different farmers for all kinds of things. Then he made deals to swap one farm product for some other. It wouldn't be unusual for my grandfather to arrive with two potato sacks of ox tails, or a couple of buckets of beef kidneys I could just imagine what was going to occur when the field crops started to come in.

The land along Garden Street next to the three story brick apartment building was heavily wooded with wild cherry trees. On the Rosehill Place side of the apartment building there was a big yard with a thick stand of Sumac trees and brush boarding a fenced in yard of a block garage, where a man named Mr. Gavin kept a model A-B Mack chain drive truck with a canvas roof.

This piece of land along Garden Street was the ideal place for a secret guerilla camp. Arthur's father was the Superintendent of the brick apartment building, so the big side yard was off limits to all except those specifically invited in to play with Arthur.

As the Spring foliage began to thicken along the fence by Mr. Gavin's garage, Chicky, Robert and I began to plan and execute our secret shortcut to the woodlot on Garden Street. In order to avoid detection by Arthur and his parents we cut a narrow path in the brush along Mr. Gavin's fence. We did our work usually around four o'clock in the afternoon. Arthur would go into his apartment at that time to listen to the daily serials on his radio. Tom Mix, Jack Armstrong and Terry and the Pirates kept his attention as we trimmed the brush along the fence. After our work was completed, we could sneak quietly down the path without any body in the yard realizing we were there. As an added protection Chicky took some vanishing cream from his mother which he claimed would make us invisible. It was probably meant to vanish something else, because after smearing this stuff on our faces, we could still see each other.

"Your mother got gypped. This stuff don't work," complained Robert.

"Well, I saw it work in the movies," answered Chicky.

"Movies are make believe. They use trick cameras and stuff. Who did you see using it? The Three Stooges," retorted Robert.

"No! Abbott and Costello."

"Come on guys." I said, while wiping the cream from my face. "Let's just sneak down through the path real quiet like."

With out rustling a leaf, our patrol slinked through the bushes and finally emerged into some tall grass in the rear of the woodlot.

"Wow!" Exclaimed Chicky. "This is like Tarzan's jungle."

"I'll bet nobody was ever here before us," Robert answered.

"Probably Indians were here before us. A long time ago," I interjected.

The three of us scouted our new found land and made plans for our fortifications. We then returned through the bushes to our point of origin, solemnly swearing not to tell a soul about the new land we had discovered.

# CHAPTER 14

# DECORATION DAY

The days of Spring gradually got warmer and longer, until we reached the apex of the season on May 30. Although unofficial, Decoration Day was declared by all to be the beginning of summer. Its arrival signaled the beginning of the last two weeks of school and the day to set out tomato plants.

Mr. Mitchell had already begun to set the flats of tomato plants on the ground by the basement door when we began arriving with our wagons. One by one the wagons were loaded and we each started the overland trip to the garden in the field behind the garages. Mr. Mitchell was Chicky's uncle and his gruff manner instilled fear in our hearts.

"Don't you rascals hurt one of those plants. If you do, I'll have your hides," he admonished.

"Yes sir, Uncle Jim. Yes sir," replied Chicky.

As we arrived with our loads, men and bigger boys unloaded the flats and passed them to others, who planted and staked the plants in the soft warm soil. After a few trips with each wagon the work was completed and over 400 tomato plants were in their new home. Finally, the perimeter of the garden was marked off by pieces of white cloth tied to a string line that surrounded the entire complex. Now it was up to God to supply the sun and soft rain needed for a bountiful harvest.

Like all the other cars in the neighborhood, the old Ford was in hibernation. But, today it would awaken. After we had finished the tomato planting, my father poured two 5 gallon tins of gas into the tank of the car and then after belching a few clouds of blue smoke the old Ford fired up and cheerfully purred like a kitten. Something special was going on today.

I had planned for a day of exploration and work at the secret headquarters. But my mother's voice halted any plans I had made.

"Richard! You get in here and clean up. We have to go real soon."

"Where are we going, Ma?"

"We have to go to Rahway. No more questions just get a move on."

I liked going to Rahway. There was a river near my Aunt Hazel's house. My father and I had explored the river all the way up to Clark Township, which was a couple of miles from my Aunt Hazel's. Daddy promised that we would come back to fish the river when the warm weather came. There were a lot of woods along the river. It looked like a real neat place. Maybe we were going fishing today!! That would be better than hanging around the house with a bunch of bossy girls.

It was about a fifteen minute drive to Rahway. And, when we pulled into the driveway was I ever surprised. There to greet us was my Uncle Bill and my cousin Billy, all decked out in their Navy uniforms. They had finished their training and were on their way to new assignments. Uncle Bill was being sent to a ship in Philadelphia and my cousin Billy was going to a Marine base in California. No wonder Daddy and Ma were in such a hurry to get here. Nobody was at a loss for words as the adults bantered about the new experiences the war had brought. This day was reminiscent of past Sunday visits back home. We ate and talked as usual but, we knew the time of separation was again at hand.

My father idolized his older brother and prayed continually for his return from the war. On the ride home that evening, he remarked, "God has been good. He has given me the chance to see my brother one more time. If we didn't move, I would have missed this chance. I would say it's a miracle that our family is still intact so far from home. Praise the Lord."

At my age I didn't understand how God worked. I thought miracles came in a big puff of smoke like "Schazzam." ...And then before you would appear a big Genie ready to do your bidding. I didn't see anything miraculous in a war that would make people leave their homes, upset lives and make people work night shifts. Even this Decoration Day was different from any I had known before.

Today we didn't have a parade. Last year and every year that I can ever remember, we had a parade. The parade always started at 10 A.M. from the High School field and proceeded down Broad Street to the Monument by the River. The High School Band led the way followed by open cars carrying the Mayor, The County Commissioner and any other politicians who were hanging around. The American Legion Veterans of World War I marched in uniform alongside a wooden train body mounted on a truck chassis. The train body was called the 40 and 8, meaning the French Train cars in World War I carried 40 men and 8 mules. The VFW "Cooties" followed in the line of march. Led by their Color Guard carrying the Flag and an Honor Guard with silver rifles, the VFW members in their red caps threw hard candies into the crowd. The Spanish-American War Veterans came next, usually sitting in a flat wagon pulled by horses. Any Civil War Veterans remaining were driven in open cars. The ladies came next. The Daughters of the American Revolution and The Daughters of the Confederacy, mostly chubby ladies, marched in ranks behind each other. Last, but not least was the local Horse Calvary mounted in full dress upon their chestnut steeds. Everyone watching the parade clapped as each group passed by. But, the greatest ovation of the day went to the two street sweepers. Armed with a broom and a shovel, they brought up the rear ...behind the horses. Some individual, chosen for the day, set a wreath at the Soldier and Sailor Monument. Everyone stood at attention as the Honor Guard fired their salutes into the air.

This wasn't a day that was part of a getaway weekend to celebrate the opening of summer vacation spots. Rather, it was a solemn day when families gathered to fellowship and remember those who passed before us. We didn't have cookouts in the fashion of the 90's. We cooked in the kitchen and ate at the tables set-up in my Grandparents yard. After being led in prayer, the food came in profusion. Inevitably, someone would rise, holding a glass high in the toast position and looking toward my Grandfather say, "To the Flag."

Gramps would then stand up; holding his glass high, he would recite the poem he learned as a boy. This was the same poem he recited to the stunned gathering in his parlor, after we heard the news of the Japanese attack on Pearl Harbor.

At the conclusion of the poem, Gramps would always say, "The 4th of July is a day of great celebration and a day to party in the greatest country in the world. But, today is a day to remember the price we paid for that party... and the people who made it possible."

I missed that gathering this year. I missed the stories told about my ancestors and relatives. These people were always remembered with great love and joy as each story memorialized their madcap misadventures. But, this year there would be no stories; we as a nation and a family were busy paying for future July 4th celebrations.

The evidence of our payments was quite discernable. You had to look long and hard to find a house that didn't have a banner in the window. No family was living a normal life. Rationing and defense jobs made people form new habits and assume new identities. Even kids were not immune from the impact of the war. There was no candy, no ice cream, no cookies, and heaven forbid that you wore out the soles of your shoes. We became experts at cutting cardboard to fit the inside of a shoe with a hole in the sole. Friction tape was used to secure a floppy sole to the upper shoe. The newspapers and radio broadcasted the daily disasters occurring around the world. The nights were equally bleak as any unnecessary light was turned off and the top half of automobile headlights were painted black to avoid detection from the air.

We were digging in for the duration, however long that would be. Everything took a back seat to the war effort. Even everyday conversation centered on the war. At school, our daily scripture readings and prayers were directed to the war effort. It seemed like every facet of our lives was dedicated to the eradication of the Axis powers.

Early in May the Japanese thrust towards Australia was stopped in the Coral Sea. It wasn't what would be called a clear cut victory, since each side had heavy losses. However, the larger Japanese Naval forces retreated to prevent higher losses. On June 4, the superior Japanese fleet attacked Midway Island, the furthest and last American possession in the Pacific. By being able to decipher the Japanese code, Gramp's World War I friend, Admiral Nimitz deployed his smaller fleet around Midway Island. As the overconfident Japanese began their assault on Midway they were met by American carrier and land based aircraft. The ensuing battle wrecked havoc on the Japanese fleet and provided American forces with a decisive victory. One battle is not a war. But, this initial victory renewed the confidence and resolve of the country in our quest for victory.

My friends and I were busy constructing our fortress on the Garden Street lot. We dug two man fox holes and built brush covered roofs over the holes. There were two tall trees on the lot and we built a lookout platform high up in the branches. We ran the antenna wire for my crystal radio between the two trees and set the radio up in the fox hole. Everyone took turns putting on the earphones to listen for emergency messages. The radio only picked up one station, WOR. But, that was good enough for us. We had tin cans attached to strings running across strategic points on the site. The person calling in would pull on the string. A little Christmas bell was attached to each can. If somebody was on the opposite end of the string, he would jerk back; then the two would talk to each other. We drew pictures of Japs and Nazis and tacked them to the trunks of trees in the wooded area. Each day we would have a war with these pictures. Armed with our slingshots, we would move through the high grass and pick off the enemy. We had a good time, but we were also highly prepared.

As the last day of school approached, our secret camp was completed. Now we could devote all our efforts to those things boys are designed to do.

## CHAPTER 15

## THE SUMMER OF '42

The first official business of summer was to get a pair of "Keds." My mother and I walked to the Woolworth Store on Broad Street, Elizabeth to buy me a pair of "Keds." They were a canvas shoe with a molded rubber sole and came only in blue. I liked the high top sneakers with the white dot on the side, like the big guys wore. But, my mother was tough when it came to breaking tradition. Just like those knickers, it would take some kind of revolution to get a pair of sneakers.

"Ma, do you know that Jap soldiers wear "Keds." People might think I'm a Jap if I wear Keds."

"Where did you hear such nonsense?"

"I saw them in the movies. They wear Keds and knickers."

"Well, you don't look Japanese. You don't wear glasses and you have blonde hair and blue eyes. Nobody will mistake you for a Jap."

"Yeah, but Japs are good at disguises."

"Never mind all this silly stuff, you're getting Keds and were going to see if your school shoes can be fixed. For the life of me, I can't understand how one boy can tear up things so bad."

Even appealing to Ma's patriotism didn't work this time. So I ended up with blue Keds.

I wore the Keds home and gave them several tests along the way. I ran, then stopped short and turned around quick. Then I walked along the edges of the slate curbs and made a quick climb up on the statue of the Minute Man, by the Court House. I wanted to walk across the concrete railing where Broad Street crosses the river, but Ma jerked me back to the sidewalk.

"What in tarnation are you tryin' to do? Get killed!"

"I just want to make sure these Keds work, Ma," I yelped.

"The Keds are alright, it's you I'm not so sure of. Now mind yourself and let's get on home."

Young boys are not unlike members of the animal kingdom. They collect in little packs. Somehow these little packs meet up with other little packs and ultimately form a complete herd of baseball cap adorned critters. These Kangaroo like herds roam over the countryside in a circuitous manner stopping at various places along their route to engage in some type of spontaneous activity.

They have ears well attuned to the dinner bell, or a mother's screech, which is usually ignored until it reaches the pitch of an air raid siren.

Our little pack would start to assemble near the front steps of our building around 8 A.M. I could hear Chicky bounding down the stairs from the second floor as I was eating breakfast. If I didn't finish within five minutes, he would be back to knock on my door. When I heard the large front door of the building slam, I had my cue to go. Chicky, Robert and I would quickly scoot around the building and head for the garden behind the garages. The continuous slamming of the front door usually aroused Mr. Mitchell and we wanted to be out of sight when he came looking for the noise makers.

It was our chore to pull weeds in the big garden. We didn't mind doing it because it gave us the opportunity to monitor the vegetable growth and to estimate a time for some pre-harvest sampling. We had already become potato roasting experts. Over at our camp we would build a fire and then bury potatoes in the hot coals. When done, they were hot and black with soot. But, we ate every thing, charred skin and all. Right now we were keeping close watch on the corn, which we planned on roasting Indian style.

We went through the garden throwing the picked weeds into baskets, which we later deposited on Charlie's manure pile near the rear wall of the garages. As we worked, other little packs began to converge on the scene. Tommy and Smitty usually arrived with baseball gloves. This was our signal to finish weed picking and go home for our gloves.

"Goin' to play ball, Ma." I said to the crescendo of slamming doors, as Chicky and Robert and I raced into our apartments to get our gloves and then make a hasty exit before Mr. Mitchell had time to respond to the noise. With the speed of a cyclone we were out the front door and gone. Depending on the size of the pack that reached the Garden Street field first, we would start playing one-o-cat, or two-a-cat. As we started playing other little packs began to converge on the field. Donald, Gordon, Dickie and Tony would suddenly emerge from behind Cotton's Gin Mill. Billy, Walter and Ritchie would come from the New York Avenue direction and Nicky, Frankie and George would come up Lidgerwood Avenue. As each group arrived the structure of the game would change until we had enough boys to make up something resembling two teams. Ground rules were adjusted to make up for any deficiencies in player numbers. If each team had only two outfielders, right handed hitters were "out" if they hit the ball to right field and similarly left hand hitters were "out" if they hit the ball to left field.

Invariably, just as soon as all the legalities of the game were established, Arthur would come charging out of the brick apartment building. We always let Arthur play because he had a bat and sometimes a good ball. But, the big question was which side had to take him. Arthur wasn't a very good player and if things didn't go his way, he was apt to take his ball and go home.

R. Allen Pender

Tommy wanted to be a catcher, so I would trade my right handed catcher's mitt to him for the use of his right handed fielder's glove, which I had to wear in reverse on my right hand. We played without benefit of an umpire; more or less on an honor system. However, every once in a while an argument would break out that we couldn't settle. Jim Cotton was usually sweeping out his Bar and front sidewalk during our game times and since it was his slack time, he would watch us. Jim was from Ireland and I doubt he ever played baseball, but we enlisted him as an arbitrator.

"I saw da whole ting, He was out." He would say in his Galic brouge.

Or, we would holler, "Hey, Mr. Cotton. Wasn't that ball foul?"

"Ah yes, for sure, the ball is a foul one."

How could you argue with a guy that spoke with a kind of poetic lilt, besides he knew most of our father's and we would be in deep trouble if we didn't respect him as an elder.

We played the game until our stomachs growled, somebody's mother hollered, or the ball was lost. Being the only left handed hitter in the bunch, I was usually responsible for losing balls. If I pulled the ball good to right field, it went across Garden Street and into the woods. It then became incumbent upon me to produce a ball for our next game.

Usually, when he saw me later in day, Mr. Cotton would whistle and wave me to his saloon doorway.

"You sure made a fine hit lad. Aye found something you could use tomorrow."

Bringing his hand up from deep in his pocket, he would produce a baseball. They weren't new, but they weren't wrapped in tape either.

"Wow! Thanks Mr. Cotton. Where did you get it?"

"Oh now, the little people find them and bring them to me."

"What little people?"

"Leprechauns, Lad, Leprechauns. They trade for a bit of beer."

I didn't know anything about leprechauns, but I sure hoped they continued to find baseballs that they could trade for beer.

"R.A." said Chicky, as we walked home after the game. "Let's go to the camp after lunch and plan some stuff."

"What kind of stuff?" Robert asked.

"I saw some neat things in Captain Marvel Comics we could do."

"Captain Marvel!!" Exclaimed Tommy. "What do you want to do, fly around wearing a cape? It don't work. See that scar on my head. I already tried it."

"No! This is better. Let's meet at Tarzan's Jungle after lunch and I'll show you."

Since we had no urgent commitments that afternoon, we all agreed to listen to Chicky's plan and hoped it wasn't anything like his vanishing cream idea.

Our camp in "Tarzan's Jungle" was now well concealed by the maximum vegetation of the season. Our bunkers and tree stands were well shaded and obscured by the tree canopy and the thick ground cover. With an application of burnt cork to our faces and some small leafy branches stuck into our clothing at various locations, we were able to blend into our surroundings like chameleons.

Other than being concealed from each other, we didn't know how effective our guerilla training would be on the enemy. We needed to raise our training to a higher level. A mock enemy would be the ideal thing. But, where would we find anybody who would want to be a Jap or a German? We could declare war on the Cub Scouts, but they didn't meet in the summer. Since no attempts had been made to invade our jungle outpost, we planned to extend our training in commando fashion into the surrounding neighborhood.

One by one we navigated through the "jungle", taking care not to make any noise. Arthur usually ate his lunch in his tent next to the brick apartment building. Sneaking past Arthur was good training, but he really wasn't that formidable as an enemy, or an enemy sentry. However, it was always fun to sneak by Arthur and pretend he was a German guard.

Robert, Tommy and I were positioned in our respective bunkers when Chicky appeared out of the underbrush. Chicky had a brown paper sack under his arm and he motioned for us to follow him into the briefing area under the clump of wild cherry trees.

"Here, look at this," he said producing a handful of hollow tubes and a sack of dried peas.

Chicky began stuffing the dried peas inside his cheeks and then with the rapid fire action of a machine gun he began blowing the peas out through the hollow tube.

"We'll never hurt any Japs with those peas." Tommy interjected at the conclusion of the fire power display.

"Peas are only for practice, we can use poison darts for real war. The pigmies use poison darts. They sit up in the trees and shoot poison darts at their enemies." Chicky stated, as he continued to advocate his method of warfare.

"We can sit up in the trees all day in this jungle and not have anybody to shoot at. Not even Arthur comes back in here", snorted Robert.

Not to be dissuaded, Chicky continued his sales pitch. "If we can perch up in the Maple trees along Rosehill Place we can take target practice on anyone who comes along, like the people who walk up the street from the Wilson-Jones Plant on Elmora Avenue."

True, those peas wouldn't hurt anybody, especially if they were aimed for the backside. Since the main objective of this training was to infiltrate and harass the enemy, this tree top training sounded pretty good and we all agreed to give it a try.

The Norway Maples were a pretty easy tree to climb. The branches flowed upward, with well placed crotches enabling one to make a rapid ascent. Each of us picked out our own shooting platform in our respective trees. For a rapid deployment out of the tree, we tied off ropes to a branch above us, so we could drop the rope to the ground and slide down the rope for a fast exit. Over time this rope technique would become refined to a remarkable degree.

The day shift at the Wilson-Jones plant ended at 4 P.M. It was time to test our ambush. Perched among the leafy branches 20 feet above the sidewalk we waited for our unsuspecting victims to enter the trap. Shortly our victims would come into view as they made their way across our Garden Street baseball field.

Suddenly, from the opposite direction, came the closest thing we had to a real enemy. Mr. Mitchell and Arthur's father were coming down the street. They stopped at the spot where we peeled back the wire fence along the apartment building yard at the connection to Mr. Gavin's fence. They stood there talking while we observed the Wilson-Jones workers coming across the other field towards us. This could turn out to be a calamity if both groups passed beneath us at the same time. Mr. Mitchell and Arthur's father then turned and went back up the street, where they met Mr. Walley, the Air Raid warden. We could see that group in conversation as the task force from Wilson-Jones came into range. We waited until the last person had passed before commencing fire, or shooting. We aimed for the behinds of the targets and the people acted like they were being attacked by some sort of insects, as they waved their hands and arms to ward off the peas hitting them from behind.

We were elated with our tactical superiority as we watched our targets of opportunity move up the street and past Mr. Walley, Mr. Mitchell and Arthur's father. We then realized that we could not descend from the trees until the coast was clear and nobody could see us entering or leaving the trees.

Now Arthur's father left the group up the street and headed down in our direction. As he came under the trees, we each took one shot at his back.

Wiping his neck and looking around, but not up, he said," Those people are right, there appears to be some biting flies around here."

We were glued to the tree trunks as Arthur's father stopped for a moment under the trees. But then he continued on. We waited until he rounded the corner by Harry's Store before calling to each other. We planned an escape route into the clump of trees across the street in the big field after we bailed out of our trees. But, a clean escape depended on not being seen.

"Coast is clear." We echoed up and down the tree line. "Go!"

Blessed with the agility of alley cats, we were out of those trees and on the ground in a flash. As we made our way into the security of the high grass, we began to revel in our success.

"Imagine, if they were Japs, we would have got them all." Chicky proudly pronounced.

"You mean, if we had real ammunition." Robert quickly completed Chicky's statement.

Tommy was giggling, "Nobody saw us, and I shot Arthur's father and he didn't know it."

"Let's slip along the Lidgerwood Avenue side of the hill and come across the field by the path coming up from the bus stop. That way nobody will ever know that we were down in those trees."

"Good idea, R.A."

Our little band of commandos moved through the grass and brush along the side of the road until we came to the stand of Osage orange trees. These four tall spiney trees reached up from the cliff edge of the road about 75 feet into the air. We took note of the strategic features offered by these trees and filed that data away for future use.

We continued to move through the brush along the edge of the road until we came to a large immature stand of wild cherry trees. At that point, we cut inside the canopy formed by the cherry trees and began to move uphill into a large patch of wild rhubarb. We now had a clear view of the front of our buildings. Mr. Mitchell and Mr. Walley were still talking in front of my building. This was a bad omen. Remember, it was Mr. Walley who got the information about the Humphrey Bogart shooting. And that slingshot ringleader is still at large.

We slowly emerged into the open field pretending to focus on the plants growing in the big "Victory" garden. As we wended our way across the field, periodically we would stoop to inspect the growing plants and cast sideway glances at Mr. Mitchell and Mr. Walley to see if we were the center of their attention. We gradually moved diagonally down the field and crossed the street at the site of our ambush. It was now just about time for Jack Armstrong and Terry and The Pirates to come on the radio, so each of us headed for our homes, agreeing to meet after supper under the ambush trees.

Life wasn't all baseball and warfare. Gramps would stop by as he and Mr. Seymour were going out on business and invite me to accompany them. We went to many interesting places, but usually there was some work required of me on the trips. Mid summer meant the beginning of the field crop harvest and Gramps had his picking schedule all set to coincide with his business travels.

I learned a great deal about the geography of New Jersey and what crops grew where. Gramps would usually drop me off at a farm near one of his business calls and I would pick whatever vegetables were coming on until he returned. After making his arrangements with the farmer, we would pack the old Chevrolet with the baskets of produce and continue on our way.

We usually stopped for a good lunch. Gramps and Mr. Seymour knew all the places and their specialties. Under normal circumstances a hot dog or a hamburger would satisfy my desires, however Gramp would order a house specialty for he and I. Gramp said we had to cultivate our tastes and learn to enjoy these different foods. Some of those foods tasted terrible then, and still taste terrible now. I think my grandfather put on a life long charade as a connoisseur of fine foods. He may have eaten at some of the finest restaurants in the country, but the best meals in the world came out of my Grandmother's kitchen. Mr. Seymour and my Grandfather were never at a loss for conversation. They had stories about every conceivable subject. Mr. Seymour even had a camp up in the mountains. I saw mountains from a distance when we came up through Pennsylvania, but I was never in any mountains.

"Bill," said Mr. Seymour. "We should find out what kind of tenderfoot this boy is. Do you think he could survive in the woods up at the Camp?"

"I don't know Dave. He came from the cotton and peanut patches; I think he might get scared in those big woods."

Gramp and Mr. Seymour were setting me up. They were planning a trip to Mr. Seymour's camp and Gramp wouldn't take me if he thought I would be afraid in a strange place.

# CHAPTER 16

# MR. SEYMOUR'S CAMP

Looking northwest from the roof of our apartment building, mountains were visible at the horizon. They didn't look like large mountains, but maybe that's where Mr. Seymour's camp was located. In any event, I would find out by late Friday afternoon.

Gramp was picking me up on Friday and we would be going to Mr. Seymour's camp, where we would stay until Sunday. My mother packed some clothes, a towel, a toothbrush and some soap in a brown paper sack. When she was done, I secreted my slingshot and my knife in between the towels. I wasn't going to any strange place unarmed. Also, I had a map on which I planned to mark the route. I would show my grandfather and Mr. Seymour that I wasn't some tenderfoot from the peanut patch, but was really a commando, a part of the underground, America's last line of defense in the event of an enemy invasion.

Robert and Chicky came along as I was sitting on the front steps waiting for Gramps to arrive.

"You gonna be away all weekend, R.A.?"

"Reckon so," I replied.

"What kind of place are you going to?" asked Robert.

"Mr. Seymour has a camp up in the mountains. I don't know if it has a tent or what."

"Well, we're going to sit in the trees today and take shots at people going up and back from the corner." Chicky quipped.

"You best not get caught, 'cause their still lookin' fer the slingshot ringleader."

"They couldn't make us talk; besides you hid everything and nobody knows where."

"And I'm not showin' where 'till after the war is over. Right now you don't know who may be a spy and I got my suspicions."

Gramp's Chevrolet now appeared coming down the street. Ma and my Aunt Eileen were talking out in front of her building when he pulled up.

"Hi, Daddy." They sang out in unison.

"Richard is all ready. Now you tell me if he doesn't behave for you."

"He'll be fine, dear. We have a lot to do this weekend. He'll be too busy to get into trouble."

I didn't appreciate that "too busy" part of Gramp's statement. I wondered what he had planned for me. Gramp always had a motive for anything he did.

He didn't do anything without some sort of prearranging. I'm sure that there is some reason behind his plan to take me to Mr. Seymour's camp.

It was a little past noon and I had already eaten my lunch, when Gramp arrived. So, I was anxious to get started for the camp. But, Gramps always had his own agenda, so I expected some sort of delay before the trip started. However, it appeared today would be different as he abruptly greeted his daughters and signaled for me to enter the car.

"We'll be back Sunday," he said.

Before my mother or Aunt could answer, we were pulling out from the curb and heading down the street.

"How far is it to the camp, Gramp?"

"Well, we first have to pick up Dave and some other people and then stop for some things, so we should be there for supper."

As I had come to know my Grandfather's behavior translated into language and considering the present time of day, that meant we would be actually traveling forty percent of the time and stopped in conversation with somebody sixty percent of the time. Hence, the camp was approximately sixty miles away.

We were now headed for Gramp's house in Hillside. When we arrived, my Grandmother was pouring homemade soup into jars for us to take to the camp. Naturally, she had me sit down for a bowl full as Gramp went off to pack his traveling bag. When he returned, we kissed Gramma goodbye and headed for our next stop, which was a butcher shop in Newark. We went in by the back door and the butcher alerted my Grandfather to a pile of packages set near the door. Gramps in turn instructed me to carry the packages out to the car. I performed my chore as Gramps and the butcher were engaged in a conversation of some sort regarding the jar of clear liquid Gramps had brought in to the butcher.

I sat in the car waiting until Gramp finished his business. He emerged from the butcher shop with a big smile on his face and said, "Now to pick up the rest of the gang... That Karl really liked that drink and he gave us some fine sausages and frankfurters."

If that stuff in the jar was anywhere near as potent as Uncle Bill's sour mash, that butcher was in for some weekend.

Mr. Seymour lived in a big brownstone building with another man named Dr. Wherry. The building was in a fashionable area of Newark, overlooking a park. The Doctor had offices in the building as well as his residence. I helped carry their "grips" to the car and get them seated in the rear. These two men didn't look like they were headed for a camp as they wore shirts and ties and waistcoats on this summer day.

After Mr. Seymour and Dr. Wherry were situated in the back seat, Gramp piloted a course through Newark to the town of East Orange. East Orange was next to Newark and there wasn't any noticeable difference between it and Newark. I would learn that in addition to East Orange there was a Town called Orange, another called South Orange and another called West Orange. Why they picked the color orange, or a fruit to name a group of towns, I never found out. Why not East Apple, or East Purple? Who knows? Anyway, a man named Casebolt lived in East Orange and we stopped to pick him up.

Mr. Casebolt was a lawyer and he was dressed in a fashion similar to the other men. After he was seated and Gramp got the Chevy rolling again, the men began passing around a paper sack containing a jar of what I would learn was homemade apple whiskey. It must have been good because the jar was in constant circulation until it was emptied.

"Bill has more in the trunk, don't you Bill?" asserted Mr. Seymour.

"I have plenty Dave, all better than bottled in bond."

"Good friends, good food and good whiskey, all the necessary ingredients for a good weekend," stated Mr. Casebolt. "We do have food, don't we Bill?" questioned Mr. Casebolt.

"Eddie, do we have food aplenty! And I have to stop at the Greek's for a fine ham." Gramp answered.

I had no idea what a Greek was, but since they had hams, they couldn't be too bad.

As we traveled up South Orange Avenue, the city began to thin out until forests and fields replaced the buildings of the city. The topography got increasingly hilly, until we got to a place called Kenvil, where the Greeks were located and our ears popped. The altitude caused our ears to pop, not the Greeks.

Two short men named Chris and Jimmy were the Greeks. They had a combination store and luncheonette fronting on Route 46 in Kenvil. I don't know how they got the ham that they cooked for my grandfather, or the manner of payment, but those jars appeared from the trunk again. I was pushed off to eat ice cream in the luncheonette while the men gathered around the trunk of the car.

Finally we got going again. The mountains got steep as we rode Route 206 into Sussex County. I kept marking our route on my map and noted the various landmarks along the way. Considering the rate at which those jars from the trunk were being emptied, my map marking might ultimately be my source of survival.

We turned off Route 206 at a red barn in Andover Township and followed a dirt road up over the hill to a place along the Paulinskill River called Stillwater.

In the village of Stillwater was an old Inn called the Stillwater Inn. We pulled into the parking lot and the gang quickly made for the Bar room. I was allowed to have a soda and then I was dispatched by the bar tender to the river where a man helped me fill up buckets with minnows, which would be used for bait. Fortunately these buckets had covers, so I carried them up to the car where my Grandfather was getting some more jars from the trunk. The buckets of minnows were placed in the trunk along with all the other items.

Stillwater was an interesting place, so I stayed outside. Cows were grazing in the pasture beside the Inn and across the road a grist mill was making flour. It sure was a lot different than the industrial area where we now lived. Nazi's and Japs would probably never come here. Besides watching cows and fishing there wasn't much else to do here.

In due time the group emerged from the Inn and loaded back into the car.

We headed out of the village and up a hill and around some turns and down and up some more hills and turns until there smacking me right in the face and looming straight ahead was the leading edge of the Appalachian Mountains.

We turned off on to another dirt road between two fields of corn and then, about a mile later, we turned into a narrow dirt lane that terminated in a barnyard.

Gramp stopped the car in front of a spotless white farmhouse and got out. He walked over to the house and began talking with a man, who had been sitting on the porch, but now rose with an extended hand of greeting. As if on cue, our passengers alighted from the vehicle as Gramp and the gentleman started walking to the car. Gramp called me and told me to go with the white-haired lady, who had just emerged from the kitchen.

"Hello, Jimmy" our passengers began exclaiming one by one as they reached out and shook hands with Jimmy and then began to form a semi circle near the rear of the car as Gramp opened the trunk.

Meanwhile, the white haired lady led me into an antiseptic white kitchen.

"Here are your sheets and pillow cases," she said pointing at four packages wrapped in brown paper.

Dutifully, I picked the packages up and carried them back to the already opened car trunk.

As everyone began to assemble back into the car, Gramp gave Jimmy some change for the sheets and mentioned something about seeing him around milking time.

Leaving the barnyard we proceeded to follow two tire tracks through a gate in the pasture. The tire tracks ran along a hay field and a cornfield then began a bumpy twisting ride up and down hill through the woods. Finally the trail ended at a green cabin and I could see a body of water, partially obscured by trees, beyond the cabin.

Gramp instructed me to start unloading the trunk and bring the items down to the little wood deck by the cabin door.

As I started to remove things from the trunk, the four men marched down to the cabin and as they unlocked the door and before they entered the building, they formed up like a barbershop quartet and began to sing:

"Catchin' fish. Catchin' fish at the Kittatinny Club. Oh! I wish I could catch fish at the Kittatinny Club."

This ritual ended with a big "hurrah" and they all fell inside the door.

I can't remember how many trips I made back and forth to the car... But, it was quite a few before I had everything on the deck by the door.

Finally, without any ritual, I entered the hallowed halls of the "camp."

The building was shaped like "U." A wide Dutch door opened into the main room from the rear. The right wall of the main room was a huge stone wall and fireplace. The stuffed head of a Bull Moose hung above the fireplace to oversee all the activities and to guard the liquor bottles marshaled on the sideboard. A Kitchen was located behind the stone wall and two barracks like bedrooms extended rearward from the main room and kitchen. There was a considerable drop in elevation from the rear to the front of the house as the land sloped down to the lake in front. A large Adirondack type front porch was constructed across the front of the building and was appropriately furnished with Adirondack rocking chairs.

A small bathroom had recently been built onto the building off the front porch on the south side. An outhouse was still functioning about 50 feet beyond the kitchen on the north side of the building.

The building did not have any finished interior walls. The backside of the exterior sheathing served as the interior wall surfaces. The spaces between the wall studs were filled with photos, animal skins, hands of playing cards and fishing lures. This was not a place intended for ladies.

In the dormitories, single steel frame beds were lined up next to each other Army style. Wooden doors at the end of each dormitory opened to expose the sleeping area to the outside. A sliding screen door behind the wooden door was the only barrier between Mother Nature and my bed.

I was instructed to deliver the sheets and pillow cases to our passengers, who had assigned beds in the dormitories. After I performed this chore, Mr. Casebolt assigned me to the last bed near the sliding screen door. I was then instructed in the art of bed making, World War I style by Mr. Casebolt, a former officer. The men then changed into their "camp clothes." Mr. Seymour changed into a white Lee overall suit and settled himself into one of the Adirondack chairs on the porch. The other men changed into Khaki shirts and trousers and then adorned their heads with floppy fishing hats.

Gramp took charge of all the food out in the kitchen and I carried the buckets of live bait down to the dock where Mr. Casebolt and Dr. Wherry were bailing the rain water out of one of the six wooden rowboats tied to the dock.

"Here, young fella, we'll put those shiners into this live well." said Mr. Casebolt, pointing towards a box made of screening material setting in the shallow water near the dock.

The box had a door on its topside, and when I opened the door, I could see that a couple of large rocks inside the box kept the unit anchored to the lake bed. I poured the minnows and the water from the pails into the box as Mr. Casebolt instructed me from the nearby boat.

Mr. Casebolt and Dr. Wherry continued to get the boat ready and had all their fishing tackle lain out on the dock.

"Bill said he'll have supper ready in about an hour Doc, so we can fish up this side of the lake and then do the other side after supper. How does that sound?"

That's fine with me, as long as we got some sippin' whisky in the boat, Eddie."

"Son, do you think you can bail out the rest of these boats so they can dry out before the sun goes down?" Doc asked of me.

"I guess I can." I replied, as I climbed into the first boat and grabbed a small pail that was lying in the flooded boat. I started to scoop up water and pitch it over the side, as Dr. Wherry and Mr. Casebolt eased the other boat away from the dock.

There must have been a lot of rain, or these boats leaked badly. They were full of water. I kept at it steadily until one by one the swamped boats took on a new posture at the dock. Mr. Seymour had been watching me from the porch and he gave a cheer when I climbed out of the last boat.

"They should be nice and dry in an hour." He said as I walked up the gravel path to the porch. "Maybe you can take me and your Grandfather for a boat ride later. Do you know how to row?"

"Sure." I said, knowing full well I had never rowed this type of boat. But, I just watched Mr. Casebolt row away and it didn't look that hard.

"What I need to do first, is to make some fishing tackle. Do you think that there may be some line and hooks around, Mr. Seymour?"

"Try looking in the cabinets below the windows in this corner of the room." said Mr. Seymour pointing to the wall behind his rocking chair.

Low cabinets were built out from the southwest wall of the big room. There were about five cabinets in all and they contained everything from nails to a big can of poker chips. I did find about twenty feet of cord, not real fishing line, but it would do. There was a rack for fishing poles in the corner of the room. A couple of rods and reels were set there. I didn't want to touch them because they obviously belonged to someone. But, there were two loose hooks stuck into the rack. All I needed now was a cane pole, or something that I could make into a fishing pole.

There was a vast forest outside, millions of trees. All I needed was a nice slim branch to make my pole. I found a hatchet in one of the storage cabinets. Between it and my knife, I was sure that I could fashion myself a fishing pole.

"Gramp," I said, walking into the kitchen where my grandfather was organizing the week-end food. "I want to go out in the woods and find a branch to make a fishing pole."

"Alright, but don't go too far, because we'll be eating soon."

I went out the kitchen door and past the outhouse. Immediately I was into dense woods. Huge Chestnut Oaks, Red Maples and Beech trees created a canopy of leaves that allowed only slivers of twinkling light to splash down into the inner forest. The under story was a thick shrub of mixed Blue Berry and Mountain Laurel. The ground beneath my feet was very rocky and was covered by a thick layer of composting leaves that exuded an earthy mushroom like scent. As my eyes adjusted to the dim light of the forest, I could pick out some young saplings trying to poke their way up from the forest floor.

I had a wide variety to choose from as I inspected each little tree for the characteristics I perceived was needed to make a fishing pole. Finally, I chose a Maple sapling about eight feet tall and cut it off at ground level. With my knife, I cut off the short branches and the leaves. Then, I skinned the paper like bark from the shank and admired what I thought would be a fine fishing pole, worthy of any young Indian who ever roamed these parts.

Coming out of the woods, I noticed a soft spot near the wood pile. I was able to kick off the turf and uncover some big earth worms. Clutching the pole in one hand and the worms in the other, I ran over towards the kitchen door. Fortunately, the men who came to the camp weren't well versed in domestic matters and they had left a collection of tin cans among other garbage outside the kitchen door. Quickly I made one of the cans into a worm container and proceeded up to where Mr. Seymour was seated on the porch.

"It looks like you have just about everything you need to go fishing," said Mr. Seymour as he saw me approach with my hands full.

"All I have to do is put the line and hook on this pole and I'm ready to go fishin'. I got some worms, but I'm goin' to go get some more."

"What are you going to do with a fish, if you catch one?"

"I'm going to cook him over a fire and eat him."

"Do you know how to do that?"

"Sure. Back home we did it all the time."

"Suppose a bear or a fox comes along and wants your fish. What would you do then?"

"Well, I would just have to pull out my gun and shoot that bear or fox."

"Where, all of a sudden, did you get this gun?"

"Same place you got the bear and fox, Mr. Seymour."

We both laughed. Mr. Seymour had one of those sly senses of humors. He liked a joke and he liked to joke and see the funny side of things, so you had to be alert, because you never knew when he was putting one over on you.

"Gramp, are we ready to eat?" I said, while running from the porch to the kitchen.

"Why? Are you hungry?"

"Some. But I want to go fishin' before it gets late."

"I got some of your grandmother's baked macaroni and soup warmed up. And, I'll cut some of Chris's ham for you. You can eat now. The men can eat when they come in. How is that?"

"Good, Gramp," I said grabbing a plate and some silverware.

Gramp set out my food on the table in the big room, beneath the head of the Bull Moose, which hung above the fireplace.

With both the front and rear doors opened, the breeze filtered across the room and I also had a good view of the woods in back and the lake in front. With his work done in the kitchen, Gramps took up residence on a cot out on the porch, near where Mr. Seymour was rocking. The sun had moved over towards the West and it looked like a few more hours of daylight remained.

Gramp and Mr. Seymour were engaged in a conversation concerning the flag which flew from a mast mounted on the corner of the porch. From what I could over hear... it appeared that a boy's camp was located about a half mile north of us on the lake and each day at sundown they shot off a cannon to signal the lowering of the flag. Gramps was concerned that maybe we should have the same respect for the flag as the campers. Mr. Seymour felt that if Gramp wanted to show more respect, he should hang the flag out when the Y- Camp had reveille in the morning and he could start making coffee at the same time. I think that ended all conversation about the flag.

"Gramp, I'm heading out to go fishing," I hollered as I ran out the front door and started for the steps down to the walkway.

"Stay close to shore on this side of the lake," warned Gramps. "I'll ring the bell when I want you in."

"O.K." I replied, heading for the boats.

I got my new fishing tackle and bait into a boat near the outside edge of dock. Fortunately, the water was turning to glass. I didn't know the reason for this phenomena which occurred late every afternoon, but I was sure glad it happened when I was about to make my maiden voyage. I had impaled a worm around the hook attached to the end of my line before the boat was released from the dock. Slowly the boat I slid away from the dock and I angled her on a course up the north side of the lake. With just a few strokes of the oars, the boat easily glided along its course.

I was about twenty five feet off the shore and drifting two hundred feet northeast of the dock when I made my first cast. I really threw the worm and line out and it plopped into the water beside a half submerged tree. Before the boat moved another ten feet, the line took off like a shot. I was just able to grab the pole before it was pulled into the water. As I held the pole up, the line was zig zaging through the water. This had to be some fish and he was moving towards deeper water. As I hung, on the boat started to head back towards the dock, but much further off shore.

"What have you got there?" A voice hollered.

"I don't know, but he's pullin' the boat."

"Reel him in, Reel him in."

"I can't, I don't have a reel," I replied to Mr. Casebolt and Doctor Wherry in the approaching boat

As their boat tied up to mine, Mr. Casebolt asked, "What kind of fish is it?"

"I don't know, I got one look at it and it looked like a torpedo."

Mr. Casebolt was now in my boat and he was helping me hand haul the fish up to the boat.

"Throw me a net, Doc," he urged.

Doctor Wherry complied and Mr. Casebolt held the net in the water as the head of the fish came toward it. "My God Doc, the boy has a pickerel that's as big as a log."

A few seconds later the pickerel was in the boat. I had never seen a pickerel. The sucker looked like a barracuda and he was slashing back and forth in the net.

"We have to get him unhooked and into the live well." Mr. Casebolt commanded.

"Where is that? I asked."

"Right where you're sitting."

Sure enough, the seat of the boat opened up and exposed a wooden tank built into the boat which allowed water to come in and keep the fish alive.

Mr. Casebolt unhooked the fish and placed him in the live well. I was sure happy about that.

"I'll row the boy's boat in, Doc. Then we can eat and come back out."

"I'll follow you." Doc replied.

"Did you catch anything, Mr. Casebolt?"

"Not even a weed," he answered dejectedly. "We'll do better after supper. Where did you get that fishing tackle?"

"I just made it."

"I'll have to talk to your grandfather about that. If you're going to fish here you can't use this homemade crick fishin' stuff like they do down south."

"Yes, Sir." I said. But, in my mind I thought, 'You're a big New Jersey lawyer with real good equipment and you got skunked. I got me a pickerel as big as a log on a piece of twine and a maple branch.'

I saw Gramp and Mr. Seymour coming down to the dock as Mr. Casebolt rowed the boat in. We weren't that far out in the lake, so Mr. Seymour and Gramp saw the battle with the fish from the porch.

"Hand me a line," said Gramp as we pulled up to the dock.

I threw him the rope tied to the ring on the transom of the boat, which he pulled and tied to a ring on the dock.

"Let's measure and weigh that monster," suggested Mr. Casebolt, as he opened the livewell beneath his seat.

The pickerel didn't have enough room to swim in the live well, but he would snap and jump. Mr. Casebolt reached in and grabbed the fish behind the gills and lifted him out of the well. Doctor Wherry came over with a tape measure and he laid it up against the fish as Mr. Casebolt kept it immobilized.

"Forty two and one quarter inches!" exclaimed Dr. Wherry.

"This fish must weigh seven pounds, if he weighs an ounce."

"Do you think he's that heavy, Eddie?" asked Mr. Seymour.

"Do you think a bear or fox might come along and want this fish, Mr. Seymour?" I chimed out recalling our earlier joke.

"That fish would do in a fox for sure and he could give a bear a hard time. I'm certain of that." Mr. Seymour said with that coy smile of his.

"Let's have some roasted pickerel tonight. This fish is too big to be hanging out in this lake eating up the bass. I'll do the honors, but young Richard is going to learn to clean him. O.K. Richard?"

"That's alright with me, Mr. Casebolt."

Quickly, Mr. Casebolt flipped the fish over and smacked the top of its head against the corner of the livewell. The big fish went limp and was no longer a thrashing biting threat.

"Let's bring this guy up to the sink outside the kitchen and clean him up. Here, He's all yours Richard."

I was now standing on the dock, as Mr. Casebolt handed me the huge fish. I grabbed the fish in the gills, emulating Mr. Casebolt. I performed the feat like it was the most natural thing for me to do and something that I had experienced many many times. This fish was big and I walked rapidly, leading a small parade up the gravel walk towards the outdoor sink by the kitchen door. I couldn't get there fast enough and I was praying that this fish didn't come back to life before we reached that sink.

My father had taught me how to clean fish a long time ago. I was used to Bream and mud catfish, not monsters like this. Everyone, except Gramp, who knew what I could do, was impressed by my handling of the chore. They expected to have some fun with me. Maybe they thought I would be squeamish or get sick performing this nasty detail But, I placed that fish in the sink and took my bone handled knife from the sheath attached to my belt and unzipped that fish from his rectum to his jaw. I reached in and removed the fish's inners; then with the back side of my knife, I scrubbed the outside of his body free of scales. In a few minutes the fish was rinsed clean and ready to be cooked.

"We can build a nice fire tonight and roast that fish in the fireplace. I'll fix him all up like we used to do those big Pike up in Canada. This fish will melt in our mouths." Mr. Casebolt kept on talking as he carried the fish into the kitchen and tried to place it on top of the ice cube tray in the little electric refrigerator. The fish was too big. So, Mr. Seymour, the engineer, came to the rescue. He put the fish in a big tub and then filled the tub with ice cubes and cold water. He then placed a piece of cardboard over the tub and packed newspapers on the top, underneath and around the tub.

"We can make some more ice cubes, but I think that fish will keep quite a while the way it is." Counseled, Mr. Seymour.

"That's good Dave." Gramp interjected. "Richard and I have to go back to Jimmy's farm for milk. The food is all out on the table. The boys can eat and we'll clean up when we get back."

"O.K. Bill, but watch out for Indians in those woods."

"What Indians is Mr. Seymour talking about, Gramp?"

"Oh! Just those Indians from the camp up the lake, they go on the warpath every once and a while."

I wasn't that worried about Indians, but Mr. Seymour said bears and wild cats roamed around here. I had my knife and slingshot on me. I felt pretty safe. Besides we would be riding in the car, or would we?

The sun was going down as Gramp and I started walking up the road. He didn't even flinch as we walked past the car. I kept waiting for him to turn and walk towards the car. But he never did.

"It's getting dark Gramp, did you bring a flashlight?"

"No, we won't need one. I know this road well."

It was about a mile walk to Jimmy's barnyard. Except for the little sky we could see above the road, night was rapidly closing in on the shaded forest. At last the sky started to lighten up as we broke out of the trees and the road passed the cornfield near the barnyard.

I was very happy to see the cow barn come into view on the left. Jimmy and his sons were busy finishing their milking chores. I hung back as Gramp went over to talk to Jimmy.

I was standing near the gate in front of the cow barn when Gramp and Jimmy started walking in my direction.

"Is this the big fella who is going to help you haul the milk back, Bill?"

"This is my grandson, Richard. He just caught a forty two inch pickerel."

"You don't say. I better count all my cows to make sure he didn't use one of 'em for bait to catch a fish that size. Your milk is here in the cooler. I'll get it out." Jimmy said as he walked into the little white block building.

Jimmy set a big milk can outside the door of the cooler. "Here she is; all yours."

Gramps and Jimmy conversed a little more as I stared at this big can of milk.

"Grab a handle son and let's start back."

"What are you going to do with all this milk, Gramps?"

"Oh, we need milk for Kittatinny cocktails and Dave is going to make wheat cakes in the morning."

"What is a Kittatinny cocktail?"

"When we get back I'll make some. The boys have them before they go to bed and then when they wake up in the morning. It's a tradition here."

Some tradition I thought. I wondered if carrying a heavy milk can through the woods in the dark was part of the tradition too. During his lifetime, I can remember my grandfather doing some strange things. But, this was one of the strangest.

By now the woods were submerged in black darkness. It was so dark that I couldn't even see my grandfather on the other side of the milk can. Every once and a while Gramp would want to stop and rest. I would urge him on in the hope that soon we would see some light from the camp.

A bear or a werewolf could be standing right in front of me and I would never know it. It could have been a bear or a werewolf carrying this milk can with me. They might have already eaten my grandfather and I didn't know it.

I knew we were going up a hill, a long hill. Finally, we were at the crest and I could see a faint light in the distance below us.

"Hey, Gramp, we're almost there. We just have to go down this hill."

"Yep, that must be the camp. We don't have too far to go."

What a relief, I don't know what I would have done if some bear or werewolf had answered me instead of Gramp. Fortunately we were heading down hill and the light from the cabin was getting progressively brighter.

At last we stumbled up on the back porch. Gramp and I carried the can into the kitchen and everyone was enlisted to find receptacles to store all this milk. Gramp did what he could to reorganize the refrigerator so all these containers of milk could be accommodated.

Doctor Wherry and Mr. Casebolt had returned from their evening fishing just before we arrived with the milk. Fortunately they didn't catch any fish, which would have further strained the capacity of the refrigerator.

"Bill, I'll make some cocktails out of some of this milk before it spoils," volunteered Mr. Casebolt.

Now I was going to find out what a Kittatinny cocktail was.

Mr. Casebolt took this steel container and filled it with milk. Next he broke two eggs and dropped them into the container. One of those jars of clear whiskey suddenly appeared and a good part of that went into the container. A little sugar was added then a lid was installed on the container. Mr. Casebolt shook the container above his head for a few minutes. He poured some of the mixture into a glass and then sprinkled a little cinnamon on the creamy head.

As fast as these containers of cocktails were made they were guzzled down. Mr. Seymour used some of the milk to make a gigantic pot of wheat cake batter. It took a little while, but most of the surplus milk was consumed. I often think how much easier it would have been to bring back less milk.

The men had a fire going in the big fireplace. There were a lot of hot oak embers beneath the burning logs. Mr. Casebolt raked these out to one side. He had gotten the big fish out of the tub and placed a rod up through the fish, which had been wiped with butter and salt and pepper. Each end of the rod was rested on short log sections over the hot embers. Immediately, the big fish began to sizzle and within ten minutes it was done.

Mr. Casebolt took the fish off the fire and laid it on a big piece of cardboard. He removed the rod and then squeezed some lemon on the fish. Everyone gathered around the table with a fork in their hand and began to pick away at the giant fish. I ate my share; after all it was my fish. All of the men said it was the best they ever tasted. But I think their taste buds may have been numbed by Kittatinny cocktails. To me, it tasted like roasted fish.

Gramp and Mr. Seymour went back to the kitchen. The big tub, where the fish was kept, was really used to make hot water for dishwashing. It sat on a two burner stove next to the cooking stove on the backside of the fireplace in the kitchen. Both of these burners were fueled by propane tanks mounted outside the kitchen window, behind the sink.

Because the fish had been in the big tub, Gramp and Mr. Seymour were only now starting to make hot water to clean all the supper dishes and pots filling the sink. I was pressed into service to get all the garbage and food waste off the table and out of the kitchen.

I packed the garbage into paper sacks and then took them outside to a rusty fifty five gallon drum. The garbage was placed in the drum and Gramp said they would burn it in the morning. The drum had a lid to keep the animals out in the meantime. There were quite a few sacks of garbage and I'll bet some animals of the night were watching me put that stuff in the drum.

Gramp, Mr. Seymour and Doctor Wherry were in the kitchen washing and drying the dishes while I removed the garbage and cleaned the floor. When these chores were done, the men adjourned to the big room for more talk, drinks and a game of cards.

There was a big bright light that shone down on the gravel walk and the dock. All sorts of flying insects were attracted to the light and they flew around its beam in a dizzying fashion. Every so often an insect would fly into the hot bulb. You would hear, "plink" and then see the bug going down towards the earth in a tailspin.

The new bathroom was built in an odd place. It was like an appendage constructed onto the outside wall of southern dormitory. There wasn't any entrance to the bathroom from the inside of the house. The only door was facing the stairs which went down off the porch. Conceivably, if the bathroom door was open, a person could sit on the toilet and be seen from the dock and beyond.

I wanted to wash up and get ready for bed, but there wasn't any tub or shower in the bathroom. I got my towel and soap from the sack by my bunk and then went into the big room to confront my grandfather with my dilemma.

"Gramp, where can I take a bath? I don't see any bathtubs around here."

"We don't need a bathtub. We got the lake," he replied. "Get into the water by the dock and take a bath."

Holding my soap and towel, I walked out onto the porch. The beam of light with its million insects beckoned me down to the dock. Beyond the light, the woods were black and dark and so was the lake water in front of me.

When I reached the dock, I turned and could see the lighted cabin immersed in an atmosphere filled with flying insects. As I stripped off my clothes and was contemplating an entry point into the lake, I could see dark winged creatures flying low over head on sorties through the sea of insects.

"What kind of birds would be out at night?" I said aloud to myself.

I quickly realized, they weren't birds, they were bats.

Without any wasted motion, I eased my self off the dock and into the lake between two boats. I did a fast lather and rinse job on myself and quickly bounded back onto the dock. I gathered up my clothes and made a beeline for the bathroom. In this little lighted sanctuary, I could dry and dress without fear of attack by some denizens of the night or the deep, who might be lurking down by that dock waiting to capture me with my pants down.

As I walked from the bathroom across the porch to the big room, I didn't recognize any trees or shrubs. Instead, my imagination conjured up bizarre creatures and apparitions of the night observing my activities from their nocturnal sanctuary. The night light and mountain breezes provided the breath of life which animated the trees and shrubs of the forest, creating an army of hideous and grotesque creatures before my eyes.

The big room was filled with a mixture of wood smoke and cigar smoke. The men were so engrossed in their card game that they were oblivious to the metamorphosis taking place outside as the peaceful daytime woodland was changed into an enchanted hostile forest.

I was now protected within the walls and surrounded by the oasis of light the building provided.

A long big day had ended and I was anxious for the comfort and security my bunk would provide. The cooling breezes were filling the room from the open windows and the screen doors at both ends of the dormitory. As I hunkered down in the blankets, with my face inside the screen; I was safe and just six inches separated me from the hostile forest outside.

## CHAPTER 17

## MISTY SMELL OF MOONSHINE

Little fingers of light were dancing across my face and they gently woke me into the new day. Orange day lilies were bowing easily in the morning breeze and their fronds were rubbing the screen six inches from my nose. I didn't even know they were there. I could hear various birds trumpeting their morning breakfast call and the breeze rustled the leaves of the small white oak and the rhododendron just beyond the screen. The creatures of the night had vanished as light penetrated the forest.

As I walked out to the bathroom, I could hear a strange bellowing and splashing noise coming from the direction of the dock. At first I thought it might be an animal or a sea monster feeding in the lake. But, then its head came up out of the water and I could see it was Gramp.

"Good morning son," he hollered. "Tell Dave that I'll be up in a few minutes to start breakfast."

With that, I headed for the kitchen.

A good sized fire was going in the big fireplace to temper the morning chill. Mr. Seymour was in the kitchen and he had coffee brewing and was making adjustments to his big pot of wheat cake batter.

"Mr. Seymour, Gramp said he would be up in a few minutes to start breakfast."

"Good, Bill is going to make bacon and eggs and I have the batter and the griddle ready for hot cakes." Mr. Seymour replied in his raspy voice.

"You know," he said. "It would be nice to have some fresh blueberries in those hot cakes."

"I saw blue berries along the shore of the lake, right down that little path from the kitchen. Near where I caught that pickerel."

"Oh, there are a lot of blueberry bushes over there. Here let's you and I walk out there and get some. Eddie and Doc aren't awake yet, so we have time."

I grabbed a pitcher and the old gentleman and I headed off on the path just beyond the garbage can.

Mr. Seymour stood out on the path as I squeezed into the bushes that overhung the shore of the lake. The blueberries were out in profusion and I kept picking as we moved along the narrow path. The pitcher was about half full when we reached a small opening where a rotted wooden rowboat was lying up near a huge rhododendron bush. A rusty chain and lock secured the boat to a nearby tree.

"Who belongs to this boat, Mr. Seymour?"

"Some men were supposed to buy this lot around the time of the Great World War. They put this boat here, but they never came back. Don't know whatever happened."

Of course, Mr. Seymour was talking about World War I, 1917 to 1919, which was 23 years ago.

"This is a neat spot. That rhododendron bush is big enough to be used as a house." I remarked.

We had collected a sizable amount of blueberries and decided to head back to the kitchen when I was surprised by a sharp explosion.

"That's the cannon at the Y camp, waking them up. Pretty soon they'll blow their bugle and raise their flag." Mr. Seymour responded with authority.

"Look here, Richard." Mr. Seymour called as we moved down the path. "See this plant," he said pointing to a small very pale purple stalk with an upturned pod on the end. "This is called an Indian pipe and it means that an Indian emptied the tobacco from his pipe on this spot."

"How long ago?" I answered with skeptical inference and thought of the nighttime forest. Maybe that Indian was out here last night?

"Hard to tell," Mr. Seymour replied. "This has always been Indian Country, so some spirits may still roam these parts." He said with that sly smile of his.

We were within sight of the kitchen door, so I knew I was safe from Indians. The only thing that would draw Indians to the cabin was the smell of bacon frying. If that didn't attract any Indians, then there were none around.

Gramp was cooking slab bacon when we walked into the kitchen. Mr. Seymour cleaned the berries and then poured them into his wheatcake batter. He had a black iron griddle setup on the two burner stove where hot water was usually made.

After he had finished cooking the bacon, Gramp began frying eggs in the one inch of rendered bacon fat remaining in the skillet. Gramp always told everybody about his cooking skills. And, a person has to be a good cook in order to fry eggs in this fashion. If the cook isn't fast enough, the egg white will shrivel up in the hot grease and all that will remain is a well done fried yoke. Gramp cooked plenty of eggs in case he had some defects.

Again, after breakfast we had the kitchen police detail. It wasn't bad because everybody pitched in.

With the kitchen cleaned up, the men sought after their own interests. Mr. Seymour settled into a rocker to read, and Doctor Wherry and Mr. Casebolt were intent on catching some fish. Gramp had paperwork to do for his company and I wanted to explore my environs.

I had my bone handled knife on my belt and my slingshot in my back pocket. I filled my pockets with marbles and so armed, I felt invincible.

My plan was simple. I would move into the woods away from the cabin in a pattern of increasing concentric circles about 100 feet apart. That way I would have a good fix on the cabin's location in the event I had to make it back fast. I also made a map on which I could note landmarks.

The greatest landmark was the mountain range across the lake. The Kittatinny Ridge of the Appalachian Mountains ran northeast to southwest without interruption. Mr. Seymour's camp was to the left of a notch in the ridge. A Fire tower is located on a mountain top southwest of the lake. I also noticed last night that the sun set just to the right of that tower. With all of this information noted on my map, I set out to explore the area.

I doubt that anyone ever thoroughly mapped this area in detail. The data would be useful if we ever had to retreat into this area and establish fortifications.

With all the big tall trees in this area, Robin Hood and his Merry Men would be right at home. The Germans and the Japs would never have a chance against the Merry Men in this forest.

As I moved along my recon route, I noticed low walls of piled up stones. Who made them and why? They were great cover for riflemen and I duly noted their locations. I would have to ask Gramp or Mr. Seymour how these piles evolved.

Although I was able to identify many trees, there were some that were new to me. I picked some leaves for identification purposes and noted the locations on my map. I wanted to be prepared In the event Robin Hood might show up some day.

Over the course of the next several hours, I wound my circuitous route through the woods on either side of the cabin. My goal was to explore all the land between the lake and the top of hill behind the cabin.

There were four cabins next to our cabin on the southeast lakefront. A two tire track driveway branched to the left off the lane into our parking area and it ran behind the four cabins and ended. The woods beyond that last cabin were thick with large trees, however the land immediately behind those cabins and going up hill away from the lake, was thick with mountain laurel and smaller trees. Groves of grey birch trees grew in off that side of the lane and a small grassy meadow topped the hill on that side.

I had my slingshot loaded and at the ready as I skirted the edge of the mountain laurel and moved up hill just beyond the last cabin. The shrubs were thick and higher than my head, making visibility impossible. I may have been 150 feet up from the driveway behind the cabins, when I heard a snorting noise coming from inside the laurels. I momentarily froze and then the snort came again. This time fear got me and I ran back towards the driveway. I heard some commotion behind me and turned to see three deer run out of the laurels and start to go diagonally uphill behind me. When I stopped, they did too. Their ears were up and they twisted their necks to get a good look at me. We all stood still for a moment looking at each other and then as I moved my foot to continue on, their white tails came up and they bounded away.

I was still shaking from the encounter as I ran down the driveway toward the camp. When I reached the lane I had a choice. I could go left to the cabin or right and continue up the hill. I decided to go up the hill. The deer had gone up hill also, but they were then about 500 feet from where I am now.

I was anxious to review the topography over which Gramp and I walked with the milk can last night. And, I needed the time to calm down. I didn't want the men to know that I jumped some deer and they scared the wits out of me.

The road going up the hill was pretty steep. At one point it switched to the right, then back to the left and followed a stone row to the top of the hill. There was an open area on the right side where the road made the right/left switch. The burnt up and rusted skeleton of an old car was crumpled into the stone row in the far corner of that area. I wondered what the story was behind its demise. Maybe Mr. Seymour knew. From what I could determine by the body style, the car was a late 1920's or early 1930's model. I'm sure the driver was up to no good when he had this wreck. I wondered why the carcass of the car was never removed.

Grey birch trees inhabited the right side of the road going up the hill and big oaks inhabited the left side. This was a strange situation, since all this land was the same age, why shouldn't the trees be the same? Another question for Mr. Seymour. When I came to the top of the hill, I carefully walked into the little meadow on the right, where I half expected to see those three deer again. The meadow wasn't that big, more like a one acre field of tall grass with a few cedar trees and a few blue berry bushes. The field was ringed by birch trees.

With my slingshot at the ready, I slowly picked my way around the field constantly aware of my exit route should that be necessary. Other than song birds hanging out in the surrounding trees, there were no surprises. I eased my way back out into the road and crossed to the other side.

The road from the end of the camp parking area to the top of the hill ran right along the course and next to a stone row on the left side. Just past the top of the hill, the road veered to the right and then switched back to the left as it went sharply down hill. The stone row continued up over the hill and down the opposite side into some hemlock trees at the base of the hill, where a swampy valley between the rises of the hills is located.

At the top of the hill, just off the road on the left side there was a narrow opening in the stone row. Gingerly, I stepped through the opening into a small moss covered clearing. I noticed a narrow trail heading off at a slight angle to the left. I hadn't gone very far along the trail when I came upon a few piles of old horse manure. Then in a soft spot, between stones, I saw horses hoof prints. Another mystery to be solved. Who was riding horses through the woods? And who belonged to these woods? The path didn't go too far before it merged with a narrow clearing running northeast, almost parallel, but 1000 feet to the rear of the lake shore. Telephone poles were placed along its length as far as I could see.

I retraced my steps back up the path towards my point of entry. Rather than taking the path to the road, I decided to walk parallel to the stone row and see what the swampy valley looked like. I hadn't gone 25 feet off the path when a bird, about the size of a chicken, jumped out of a bush right in front of me. The bird had a white feather breast, which was puffed out and its tail feathers were spread fan style, like a turkey. The bird was jumping up and down and back and forth. Its wings were doing a slow beat in time with the cackling call it was making as it performed this dance. Naturally, it scared me and I didn't know if it was going to attack or fly away.

I kept my slingshot aimed right at that bird's chest and I slowly moved away to the right. After I had moved a short distance, the bird disappeared back into the bushes. It was gone without a trace. I would have to ask Mr. Seymour about that bird. Now I was moving much more carefully and looking in all directions at one time. The way these animals popped up and appeared out of nowhere was downright scary.

I was now walking along the stone row towards the point where the hill broke off sharply towards the valley. This was also the point where the road started to turn to the right. Again I heard a snorting noise. This time the noise was off to my left. I Froze. The snort came again, now it was in front of me. Next, the slender neck and head of deer appeared from behind a tree. A front leg attached to that deer appeared and began to stomp the ground in between snorts. I had enough. The animals in these woods were out to scare me. I never heard of a deer attacking a person, but I wasn't taking chances. I had a marble loaded into the pocket of the slingshot and with one swift movement I pulled the bands back and let the missile fly in the deer's direction. As fast as I was, the deer was faster. It had turned at my movement and bounded down the side of the hill. My marble just bounced harmlessly off a tree behind the deer.

As I got up on the stone row to cross to the road, seven deer ran out from the hemlock trees at the bottom of the hill. With out stopping they ran across the road and vanished into the forest.

Taking a cue from the deer, I started off at a jog for the cabin. Every so often, I would turn and look over my shoulder to see if any animals were in pursuit. I didn't like the attitude of that chicken like bird, or those deer. I'll bet they told other animals about me.

"There's that kid with the slingshot, the one who caught and ate the big fish. Watch out for him, he's trouble."

The word was probably being circulated throughout the forest as I ran down the road towards the cabin. After passing the little meadow at the top of the hill,

I started accelerating down hill. I passed the bend in the road and the burned up car. Finally, as the road straightened out, the back door of the cabin came into view. The path in front of me was clear and one last look over my shoulder did not reveal any pursuers. The biggest problem I faced now was momentum. I had built up a lot of it on this downhill sprint and if I couldn't slow down fast enough, I would crash right into the back of the cabin.

Fortunately, Gramp's car was parked just off my line with the back door of the cabin. I veered my involuntary moving legs towards the rounded back fender of the Chevrolet and with extended arms, made contact with the car's rear quarter. I didn't have the velocity or mass sufficient to damage either me or the vehicle. I only left two palm prints on the dusty car as I caromed off the vehicle and continued downhill at a much slower rate of speed.

The big main room of the cabin was empty when I burst through the screen door. A pile of smoky embers in the fireplace was all that remained of the morning fire. Even the kitchen was empty, as I wandered through it to get a drink of water at the sink.

"Richard, is that you?" came the questioning sound of my Grandfather's voice from the porch.

"Yeah, Gramp," I replied, walking out of the door onto the porch.

Gramp was seated at a small round table in a corner of the porch by the flag. He was simultaneously playing solitaire and talking with Mr. Seymour, who was seated in a big green rocking chair reading a book as he conversed.

"Son, I want you to come with me. I have to go see Jimmy and then I have to go over to the "Mountaineer's Cabin" near Blairstown."

"O.K., Gramp." I answered, knowing my grandfather had some sort of chore scheduled to occupy my attention.

"I'll fix a nice ham sandwich for you to take for lunch and then we can go."

"All right," I replied, moving to follow my grandfather, who had gotten up from his card table and was heading towards the door to the big room.

Gramp went into the kitchen and slid the platter with the remnants of the Greek's ham from the refrigerator. He lined up two pieces of bread and began to fill them with pieces of meat carved from the ham bone.

"Now that's a fine looking sandwich," he said in a manner designed to convince me of the quality meal I was about to partake. "I'll bring this bone home to your grandmother. She can make a nice bean or pea soup from what is left."

I wondered if my grandmother knew how lucky she was to have a man like my grandfather, who would bring her soup bones from all over creation, especially bones from a Greek ham.

I munched on the sandwich as we walked towards the car. Once inside the car I felt secure enough to put the sandwich down for a minute. I didn't see any animals stalking me and I knew that once inside the car I was safe because these animals couldn't open the doors.

As Gramp drove up the road in first gear, I kept my eyes peeled for activity on either side of the road. These animals were slick, I didn't see nary a one of them, but I knew they were watching us.

The Chevrolet made the top of the hill and Gramp shifted to second as we started down hill and around the switchback. The road leveled off after we passed the hemlock trees and drove between the corn fields on either side of the road.

After we swung into the barnyard, Gramp got out of the car to look for Jimmy. Obviously Jimmy wasn't nearby. Gramp talked some with the lady from the house and then came back to the car.

"Jimmy won't be back 'till around three o'clock. So, I'll catch him later. We'll go over to the mountaineer first."

Gramp drove down the farm lane to the township road, which is called Old Schoolhouse Road. He made a right and we drove along that road, which did some zigging and zagging, up hill and down hill, as its course ran parallel to the mountain ridge visible on our right. We crossed a little bridge where a stream came out of a swamp and then formed up into a little pond on the opposite side of the road. White ducks were swimming in the pond and walking all over the road. The ducks must have been trained to avoid cars, because they moved to each side of the road and gave us room to pass.

Not to far from the duck pond, Gramp directed the Chevy off the road onto a rutty little drive that looked like it was heading straight to the mountain ridge. We pulled into a little yard where some chickens were scurrying about and couple of white geese came honking at the car. A small white cabin was set off among some trees that backed up to the mountain. A billy goat was peering at me from behind a screen fence enclosure out in front of the cabin.

In short order a tall slender man in blue bib overalls emerged from the cabin. This must be the "mountaineer."

"Howdy, Ale," said Gramp, as he walked toward the "mountaineer", who shooed the barking geese away.

"You can't hear yourself talk for the noise those critters make. Follow me. I have your stuff in the well. Who is that armed guard there with the slingshot?"

"That's my grandson Richard. He's helping me this weekend. Up to the start of the war, his uncle made some of the finest sour mash in the Tidewater."

"Well he'll be all right, so long as he only runs this stuff and don't drink it. Makin' and drinkin' don't mix. I learned that back in Brooklyn."

"Brooklyn," I thought." What kind of 'Mountaineer' comes from Brooklyn?"

I didn't say anything as I followed the two men up alongside the cabin. Behind the cabin were some rundown chicken coops that were now being used for some other purpose. A Spring house, a building a little lower than an outhouse, was built over a small brook that came out of the side of the mountain.

"Watch yer step." Said Ale, as he opened the Spring house door. By the way, Ales real name was Al. My Grandfather's dialect played tricks with a lot of words. This mountain man from Brooklyn must have scratched his head many times in wonder as my Grandfather and his associates called him … "ALE." I even heard Mr. Seymour say Ale instead of Al. And, Mr. Seymour was an educated man from Princeton. Gramps had that kind of effect on people.

The inside of the Springhouse was dark and damp with a musty smell, accompanied by the sound of running water.

"Let me get the light," said Ale, reaching inside the door and pulling on a long cord.

A single bulb came on to reveal the dank interior. The little brook coming into the building cascaded over a lip into a round stone walled pit. The water level was only a few inches below the rim of the pit and it was hard to tell how deep the pit was.

Ale began hauling up on ropes, which were attached to the walls of the Springhouse. From the depths of the pit, a milk case surfaced near the rim of the pit. Ale tied off the rope and lifted the case clear of the water.

"There's one. You fellows can empty it out and I'll pull up another."

The case was full of large bottles, capped and filled with liquid. Gramp and I started to carry the bottles back to the car as Ale pulled more cases up and out of the pit. Gramp had empty cases and empty bottles in the trunk of the car. We filled the empty cases with the fresh bottles and carried the empty bottles back to the Spring house. These trips continued until we had eight cases stowed in the trunk.

"Now don't forget," Ale warned my grandfather. "This is double run stuff; it has to be cut with fifty percent water. Don't let anyone drink it straight or it will take the top of their head off."

Gramp and Ale went off out of my hearing to conclude their business deal. I went and sat in the car while they talked. The goat and the geese kept me under close observation. Each time I moved, they moved. Gramp finally came out from behind the cabin and got into the car.

"Let's go son, we got some real work to do."

Gramp turned the car around and we reversed the course that brought us to the "Mountaineer's" cabin.

It was only a few miles back to the lane into Jimmy's farm. Just as we turned off School House Road into that lane, there was Jimmy talking to a lady in front of the bungalow at the beginning of the lane.

*R. Allen Pender*

When he saw us, Jimmy signaled my grandfather to pull over in front of his truck, which was parked in the road.

After Gramp moved the car in front of the truck, Jimmy walked over to the driver side window.

"Hey, Bill, I'm glad I caught you. I had to go into Newton for a few things and then make a drop off here at my mother's house. I'm going to this next house down the lane. My son is working inside; I'll show you what we're doing. Follow me."

An apple orchard on the right side of the lane separated Jimmy's mother's house from an old two story white farm house that set on the edge of the rise where the road dipped down and then rose up again into Jimmy's barnyard.

Jimmy had pulled out ahead of us and drove further down the lane. He parked on the road and waited for Gramp to stop behind the truck.

"We're fixing this old house up for the hunting season. The boys can come and pay us to stay here and then hunt the property. Come on in."

The old house was void of any furniture or floor covering. All the walls, the ceiling and the woodwork were painted white. Jimmy hollered for his son Ben, who was working up on the second floor. And, while he waited for Ben to join us, we had a quick tour of the empty rooms on the first floor.

"We're going to put wood stoves here, upstairs and in the kitchen." Jimmy said, pointing to the various locations. "The hunters will have heat and we have some oil lamps for light. Tell your boys what we have, if they feel like hunting this winter. When do you close up the camp down at the lake?"

"We'll lock up for the winter after our October meeting, which will be around Columbus Day. How much land do you have here, Jimmy?"

"I own from in behind those two houses up at the corner of Fairview Lake Road all the way down to where School House Road makes that bend heading to Blairstown. I used to own down to the lake, but the "Y" and I made a deal to swap the lakefront down near the Blair property for that hillside behind Goddard's three cabins on the lake. Birch trees and laurel are growing in there now, but you can still see the furrows where we used to plant corn. All told we have three hundred and sixty acres."

Ben had now come down from the second floor and Jimmy directed him out to the truck, where whatever materials he needed were located.

"Did you get everything you needed over at Al's place, Bill?"

"Ale took care of me fine," replied Gramp. "We have everything in the trunk."

"O.K., let's head up to the milk cooler. I have your can of branch water ready."

Jimmy gave his son Ben some instructions regarding the materials he had just brought and then he got into his truck and drove to the barnyard.

Gramp and I pulled up as Jimmy was walking towards the milk cooler.

"Can we set this can by your rear seat, Bill? It has about five gallons of well water in her."

I was wondering why Gramp would come out to the farm for five gallons of well water. Back at the camp we had a big lake and a well; there was a lot of water back there. I didn't say anything. I just watched as Gramp and Jimmy wrestled the big milk can into the back seat.

"I may come down after supper to see how you boys are doing and maybe have a taste of this batch."

"Very good, Jim. We'll be looking for you."

Turning to me, Gramp said, "Now son, you hold onto that handle on the can. We don't want any of this water to spill."

I leaned backwards over the front seat of the car to hold onto the milk can handles as Gramp wheeled the car across every rut and rock in the road back to the cabin.

Miraculously, we reached the cabin without spilling a drop. Gramp pulled the car down close to the kitchen door.

"We'll put everything up on the porch," Gramp said as he climbed out of the car and opened the trunk.

We repeated the same procedure that we did over at Al's, only in reverse. And, after what seemed like an eternity of endless trips, all the bottles had been safely placed on the porch. The only chore that remained was to carry up that milk can full of water.

Gramp and I wrestled the milk can out from the back of the car. The can was heavy, and the inertia of the sloshing water inside the can made it really rough to handle. The movement of the water inside made the can appear to have a will of its own. Move forward and the mass of water splashed up the back wall of the can. Stop and the water would splash forward. If we moved too fast the water would splash back and forth with almost enough force to knock some one down.

We had to go around the car and then about twenty feet to the porch steps.

"Hey, Gramp! If you back up the car we won't have to walk so far with this can. We can just walk straight across to the porch."

"That's the easy way. You always want to do things the easy way. Besides, we have to load the car again, so why move it."

"Well, you could always move the car back. It's easier to move the car than this can."

"This is good exercise for us. You need some good exercise."

No matter how I put it, Gramp wasn't about to move that car. It was my idea, not his. So, we had to do things his way. It took us a while, but we finally got the can up on the porch.

The other big milk can, the one we had milk in last night, had to be cleaned on the inside. Gramp told me to take it down to the lake and fill it up with water and then empty it and to do this until the water ran clear of any milk.

I lugged this can down to the dock. And, as I went, I put my mind to thinking of an easier way to clean the son of a gun. EUREKA! I had it. Instead of putting lake water into the can, I would put the can into the lake.

When I got to the end of the dock, I removed my shirt and my shoes and socks. I put my sling shot, marbles and knife into a can that was setting on a big rock at the lake shore. There was a smell like a baby throwing up when I removed the cap from the can. WOW! Without the cap, I eased the can down, top first into the lake. Water began to rush into the can and before long I couldn't hold onto it anymore and like a sinking ship it continued to fill and head for the bottom.

As the can sank, it discharged a smokey whispy plume that rapidly dissipated into the waters of the lake. Once the can came to rest on the bottom, I followed in after it.

The water off the end of the dock was less than three feet deep, so I just eased myself in by stepping on some rocks by the dock abutment and gradually made my way into belly high water. The submerged can was easy to move under the water. I found that I could make it act like a submarine by elevating the bottom of the can. With that action and several submersions, the can appeared to be free of the milk residue. Getting the can out of the water was the easy part.

I could bring the can to the surface by inverting it under water. Once it breeched the surface, I inserted the cap and the can floated. Like a ship, I pushed the floating can around the dock into the low water along the lake shore. Being free of water, the can wasn't heavy and I could drag it up on the shore. I removed the cap and shook out any residual water, then set the open can in the sun to dry. It didn't smell like a sick baby anymore.

I also had to dry myself off. The sun was doing a good job on the exposed parts of my body. But, my Levi's felt like they weighed twenty pounds. I had brought a pair of shorts with me, not knowing whether I was going swimming or not. So, I slipped on my shoes and grabbed my socks and shirt and headed up to my bunk. Once in the bunk room, I changed into the shorts and took my Levi's over by the kitchen to hang in the sun.

"Is the can clean, son?" Gramp said as I walked by him and Mr. Seymour on my way to hang out my Levi's.

"It's down drying on the dock, Gramp. I'll bring it up after I hang my pants out to dry."

Mr. Seymour and Gramp had put a lot of the bottles up on a table on the kitchen side of the porch. Mr. Seymour was dropping a glass bulb into each of the bottles while Gramp was taking samples from the bottles with an eye dropper.

He would put some drops in a little white dish and then add some other chemicals to the dish and watch for a color change, which he compared with a glass slide.

I went back down to the dock to get the can while all this testing was going on. The milk can looked clean and dry to me, so I carried it back up to the porch.

"Here she is, Gramp. All clean."

He took a towel and reached inside the can and wiped it around. "It's fine Dave, which bottles are ready?"

"All of these bottles over here have been checked," Mr. Seymour said pointing to a group of bottles set on the left side of table.

Gramp counted and poured those bottles into the can which was just cleaned.

Handing me three empty bottles, Gramp instructed me, "Rinse these out at the kitchen sink and bring them back here."

I did as told. Gramp then instructed me to fill and dump ten bottles of water from the milk can with the water into the can where he was pouring the alcohol. When that was done, I stood at the ready until he called for more water. This procedure went on until the can was more than half full.

Mr. Seymour would periodically take a sample in a glass and put his hydrometer into the sample. He then made a few calculations and told Gramp how many more bottles to add to the mixture. This process went on until we had emptied all the bottles we had gotten from "Ale, the Mountaineer."

Mr. Seymour had another ingredient in a tube. They looked like berries, he said it was Juniper and he poured it into the can. Gramp took what looked like a little boat oar and began to stir the mixture.

"Here son," Gramp said, handing me the paddle. "You keep stirring while we get the jars ready."

As I began to stir, Gramp vanished in the direction of the kitchen and Mr. Seymour resumed his reading in the big green rocker.

"I'll be over in a while to test the batch," Mr. Seymour announced, as he lit one of his small thin "Between the Acts" cigars.

I sat on a small box like square stool as I stirred the mixture. Every so often I would get a whiff of the aromatic pungency developing inside the can. I didn't know what kind of fumes this stuff was producing, but in my opinion it was getting stronger every minute. I think the aroma finally drifted over to Mr. Seymour's rocker, because he got up and headed in my direction.

With a soup ladle, he withdrew a sample from the can and poured it into a glass. Again he measured the specific gravity of the solution with his hydrometer and then he did a smell and taste test.

"It's done," he said. "Tell your Grandfather, we can start filling the jars."

Once I walked into the cabin, Gramp wasn't hard to find. His ability to sleep and snore was legendary. I just walked in the direction of what sounded like two lions fighting and there he was, stretched out on a bunk fast asleep.

"Hey, Gramp!!!" I hollered. "Mr. Seymour says that the booze is ready."

Gramp was immediately awake; almost like a switch was turned from asleep to awake without hesitation.

"Son, start taking some of those jars by the kitchen sink out to Dave and I'll be right along," he said rising from the bed.

Following his dictate, I carried jars out to the table on the porch. Mr. Seymour began lining up the jars as I continued to place them on the table.

Gramp arrived with a funnel. He held the funnel while Mr. Seymour ladled and poured the liquid. Gramp showed me how to assemble the cap and gasket with which I sealed the full jars. Once we got organized, this primitive assembly line began to crank out jar after jar of high quality bathtub Gin. After gramps was assured that I had the caps on tight enough, the jars were put into the original corrugated Mason Jar cases and stacked next to the porch railing.

Gramp and Mr. Seymour gave me a break by cleaning up and securing the Gin processing equipment.

I was anxious to get out on the lake, where the fish awaited me. I also wanted to explore the lower end of the lake, where some people had a bus and some other small cabins.

"You did a good days work, son." Gramp said as he released me from my duties. "I'll ring the bell when supper is ready. You be careful in that boat. Your Mother and Grandmother will never forgive me if you drown or get hurt. You come right in when I ring the bell."

"I'll stay in close to shore, Gramp." I replied in a reassuring and confident manner as I bounded down the stairs toward the dock.

## CHAPTER 18

## OF URBAN INDIANS AND A RACCOON TALE

I eased my boat away from the dock and headed towards the southern end of the lake. The afternoon sun was still high and hot as it moved to the West. A slight breeze blew across the lake creating ripples that picked up the Sun's reflected rays and broadcast them like sparkling diamonds across the waters surface.

Fairview Lake is about one mile long and a quarter mile wide. Mr. Seymour's camp was located near the middle of the Eastern shore. The property on which Mr. Seymour's camp was located extended up the lake in a northeast direction about one thousand feet to a boundary with the "Y" Camp. There were four houses right next to each other on the south side of Mr. Seymour's Kittatinny Cabin. After those houses there wasn't anything until the very end of the lake.

You would think that there would be a lot of people out enjoying the water on a hot summer afternoon and there was some swimming activity going on at the "Y" camp, also some people were out at the Boy Scout Camp across the lake, but except for Mr. Casebolt's boat, way across at the other end of the lake and my boat, nobody was out on the water.

The breeze was coming down the lake and it was gently pushing my boat along. I only had to maneuver the oars to maintain my course, keeping my boat in a controlled drift close to the shore. The water was about four feet deep as I drifted about fifty feet off shore. I could look down in the shade along the side of the boat and see the rocky lake bottom. It was fun and I could see where the drop offs to deeper water took place. As the boat neared the end of the lake, the lake bottom was clear and sandy. At the end of the lake, the shell of a house was set back from the shore line. It was decorated with Indian symbols and had a circular fire pit out in front of the building. Nobody was around and I made the gradual turn at the end of the lake to follow the shore line around and up along the opposite shore. Another shack like building was set back a few hundred feet from the shore. And nobody was there either. As I continued on I saw a bus with some towels and things hanging out on line tied between trees. This side of the lake got very rocky, with some huge rocks only a few inches below the water surface. I actually got hung up slightly on a few of these rocks as I navigated for deeper water. Water lilies grew in profusion in this lower western quadrant of the lake. Hemlock trees shaded the greater portion of this area and they appeared to conceal a cluster of cabins beneath their canopy. As I continued northward, a large Grey boathouse and big wooden dock were followed by a big open field going up to the base of the mountain. I later learned this was Camp Altaha, a Boy Scout Camp.

Mr. Casebolt and Doctor Wherry were fishing up in a little cove that I was approaching. I didn't want to bother them so I set my course for the camp dock on the opposite side of the lake. Before heading out into the deep water, I decided to bait up and toss my line in the water. It was steady rowing across the deep water as I was bucking the wind, which wanted to push me back in the direction I had just come.

Although the lake is only a quarter mile wide, it seemed like a lot of miles as I rowed toward the center. By now I was pretty proficient with the oars. I also was learning how to gage the wind and the drift. Also, now I could pick a point behind me and row on a line that would bring me to my desired destination. In short, I was becoming a real hot shot with the boat.

I really had those oars churning water as I crossed the middle of the lake. At one point my fishing pole jumped like it was going to fly out of the boat.

"Must have caught some weeds," I murmured as I grabbed the pole and hooked it between my legs.

Gramp was down on the dock as I made my approach. I brought the boat in a little past the north side of the dock and as I drifted south, I cranked on the oars and brought the boat into its berth with enough power to enable me to get into the bow and secure the boat to the dock.

I no sooner had the boat tied up, when my abandoned fishing pole started to move again.

"Your line is caught on something!" Gramp hollered.

I grabbed the pole and began pulling my line in, when suddenly this yellow fish with black stripes came up splashing with my line.

"You got a perch! A big perch!" shouted Gramp. "Put him in the live well."

I got hold of Mr. Perch, unhooked him and put him in the live well.

"I must have hooked him out near the middle of the lake. Something almost pulled the pole out of the boat. Maybe, I can cook him over the fire tonight?"

"He caught another fish, Dave!!" Gramp proudly called up to Mr. Seymour.

"Another pickerel? "Mr. Seymour responded.

"No. A big perch." I answered.

Gramp helped me secure the boat and my equipment, after which I dispatched the perch and carried him up to the sink outside the kitchen.

A little sign was posted on the bulletin board by the bar sideboard to inform people not to leave dead fish or fish parts around because they attracted turtles and raccoons. Well, that is exactly what I wanted to do.

When I was picking blueberries, I saw a spot along the lake shore that was littered with freshwater mussel shells. Mr. Seymour told me a raccoon was more than likely the critter that made that mess and I wanted to draw him out to see what he looked like. I might be able to use some of this perch for raccoon bait.

As I dressed the perch for cooking, I put the head and the inner parts of the fish into a tin can. I planned to use those parts later for raccoon bait.

"Richard, you sure can catch fish. At the rate you're going there aren't going to be any fish left in this lake in a few years." Mr. Seymour quipped as I came up on the porch with my latest prize ready for open fire roasting.

"Tonight, I'm going to catch a raccoon, Mr. Seymour."

"How do you plan to do that?" he asked.

"I got some raccoon bait an' tonight I'll show y'all how to catch a raccoon."

"Well, I guess if anybody can do that, you sure can. I'll be anxiously waiting to see that feat," said Mr. Seymour as he returned to reading and smoking his little cigar.

I went into the kitchen and wrapped my fish in waxed paper. I was able to create some room in the refrigerator for the fish, which was nowhere near the size of that pickerel of yesterday. I cleaned up all the mess I had made, except for cleaning me. By now my slender sweaty body had been exposed to clouds of wood smoke, cigar smoke, Gin and fish. Today, I would take my bath in that lake before the night creatures came out.

There was plenty of late afternoon sunlight available after I changed into my bathing suit and made my way down to the dock. Gramp was seated in a wooden lawn chair next to the dock as I approached.

"I'm going to take a bath, Gramp," I said as I walked by.

"That's good son, you'll be all cleaned for supper. When you finish we can go up and put the supper on the table. Everybody should be hungry. Today was a very busy day."

That was an understatement as far as I was concerned. I had a busy day, I don't know about anyone else. But, the thoughts of the loading and unloading of bottles and the stirring and pouring of liquor quickly faded as I eased myself into the placid lake water. As I lathered up, the clean fresh smell of soap supplanted my other odors. I submerged myself and then began to swim around the dock area like a river otter.

The men who came to this camp were obviously more interested in fishing and other activities, than they were in bathing and swimming. The lake bottom around the dock was very rocky and walking was quite difficult. Getting into the water from the dock required the precise placement of feet on some strategically located slippery rocks. Other than Gramp, I didn't see any other man swimming in the lake. This was probably an area of low priority, since not too many kids and fewer women came here.

I didn't know if I would have the opportunity to come here again. But if I did, I would bring goggles, so I could dive under the water and move these rocks to make a better swimming area.

"Come on, son," called Gramp as he prepared to walk up to the cabin.

"Let's go get supper ready."

At his beckon, I climbed up on the dock. I grabbed my towel and soap and followed my grandfather up the gravel path to the cabin.

I have to give my Mother some credit. She was smart enough to pack sufficient changes of clothes in my paper sack. After the wash and swim, clean dry clothes felt real good.

Gramp was preparing our supper. He had hot dogs and beans, slices of ham, Jewish Rye bread and lettuce and tomatoes. There were also some steaks that Mr. Casebolt was going to cook in the fireplace. He and Dr. Wherry liked to stay out on the lake until the sun started to go down. They didn't like to lose any fishing time.

Mr. Seymour ate a big bowl full of lettuce, tomatoes and cucumbers. Gramp and I ate lettuce and tomatoes with our franks and beans and slices of ham. I had plenty to eat and I had my fish for later.

The salad was kept on the table. Gramp put the beans and franks in the kitchen oven where they could be kept warm for Mr. Casebolt and Dr. Wherry, who were due in soon because the sun was beginning to dip down behind the ridge in the west.

As that blazing sun cast its fiery fingers into the western sky in what looked like an attempt to hold onto this day, I could hear the steady clunk of oars from a wooden boat. Mr. Casebolt and Dr. Wherry were coming in for supper.

"Throw me the line," I called to Dr. Wherry, who was seated in the rear of the boat.

"Thank you, young fella," he said passing the rope into my outstretched hand as Mr. Casebolt backed the boat into the dock.

"We got two nice pickerel, Doc and I did," said Mr. Casebolt. "We'll put them in the live well and maybe take them home with us tomorrow."

Not to be slighted, I announced, "I got me a big perch that I'm going to cook tonight over the fire."

"Well now", Dr. Wherry proclaimed, "We better watch out or this young fella is going to catch all the fish in this lake."

"At least we won't starve, Doc. He cooks what he catches."

With a slight smile and in a satirical tone, Doc Wherry sent a friendly jibe the competitive Mr. Casebolt's way. "He's out fishing you two to one and if he learns to cook better than you, we just won't have to go through East Orange any more on our trips up here."

As he climbed out of the boat and followed his friend onto the dock, Mr. Casebolt patted me on the head and gave a small oration obviously for Doc's benefit, but directed at no one in particular. "Well, I know he can't out drink me... Not yet anyway. You gotta watch these cane pole crick fisherman, especially ones with a knife and a slingshot hanging from their back pockets. They're just cut ups, who can only shoot the bull. Ha! Ha!"

I guess his comeback to Doc at my expense made Mr. Casebolt happy. That was alright for now. I had other concerns and needed to devote my energies towards the execution of my plans for tonight.

When I first got here, all the men were teasing me about being afraid of the Indians at the other end of the lake. At dusk, war canoes full of feathered dressed Indians started racing down the lake. They were hooping and hollering just like Indians in the movies. There must have been about twenty of these war canoes spread across the lake and racing to God only knows where.

"Richard, Here come the Indians!" shouted Mr. Seymour. "You better hide before they catch you." And he continued to rock in his chair.

I heard Doctor Wherry and Mr. Casebolt holler, "The Indians are coming!"

But, when I looked, they were still sitting at the table eating and drinking.

To be sure, not a one of them had enough hair to warrant a scalping. But, why would the Indians be only interested in catching me and not Gramps, or Mr. Seymour? These men didn't know I had been studying and practicing commando tactics for over a year now. True, my efforts were to be directed at Japs and Germans. I didn't have any gripe with Indians. I even thought that they had joined us. But, just in case these were some sort of renegades, I would take a tactical position.

I eased my way around the outhouse and down the little path towards the blue berry bushes on the lake front. I really wasn't very far from the kitchen door over which was mounted a yellow light bulb to serve as my homing beacon. I waded into the blue berry bushes right up to the point where the lake water lapped at the shore. In the dimming light I could see the war canoes returning up the lake towards their origin.

Suddenly, to my left I heard voices.

"Camper! Yeah you with the red hair. What's your name?"

"Harold, Harold Birnbaum. Why?"

"Birnbaum, what is your buddy's name? Yeah. The guy in front of you?"

"I'll ask him, I don't know. He came on a different bus."

"I didn't come on a bus." Piped in the third voice, "My parents brought me."

The first voice was obviously that of an irritated teenage camp counselor.

"What is your name idiot?" Barked the counselor.

"My name is Herschel Mandel and I live in Maplewood." The third voice sheepishly responded.

"Can't you guys paddle right; you're pushing us into the shore."

With that statement said, I could hear the branches scraping on the metal canoe, which was on a collision course with the bushes on my left.

"PUSH OFF!" Bellowed the counselor. "OFF, NOT IN, YOU DUMMIES."

In my best deep voice, I broke my silence. "PUSH OFF DUMMIES"

"WHO SAID THAT!" the counselor exclaimed.

"ME, GHOST OF THE WOODS, KEAWAMMY." I came back with my deep voice.

"Something's in there. GET OUTTA HERE, QUICK, QUICK."

The canoe was almost abreast of me now. Another foot closer and I would be able to reach out and touch somebody. Would that ever scare the wits out of them?? Wow! The bushes and the dark woods behind provided me with real good cover. Those campers went into a frenzy. They were nothing but a bunch of arms with wild flying paddles, splashing like crazy in an attempt to quickly get away from these bushes.

Finally in their fury, they succeeded in getting out into deeper water and I could pick up the sounds of their talk.

"Was something in the bushes?"

"It said it was a Ghost."

"Never mind what it is, just paddle back to camp."

Gradually their voices merged into one garbled sound as they faded into the distance.

INDIANS. Some Indians. Herschel and Harold from Maplewood. Maybe they were going to raid us for our Jewish rye bread. Indians, "oye ve."

These Indians had side tracked me from my main mission, which was to set a trap for a raccoon. As I emerged from the bushes and started to head for the porch, I could see the half headlights of a vehicle coming down the road towards the cabin.

The vehicle was a pickup truck and it pulled smartly into the clearing behind the cabin. Jimmy Carlin, from the farm got out and proceeded towards the back door. Based on the conversation earlier today, I knew he was coming to sample the batch of gin we made this afternoon. I didn't want to get in the middle of that drinkin' stuff, so I continued on with my plans to trap a raccoon.

Gramp had burned up all the garbage this afternoon in the rusted out drum out beyond the wood pile. I checked and all the steel trash cans were empty. The only garbage we would have would come from this evening's meal. I had the idea to trap a raccoon inside a garbage can and edible smelly garbage was to be my bait.

While I was planning my moves out side with the garbage cans, Gramp came out on the porch to get a few jars of that gin.

"Hey, Gramp," I hollered. "Is the fire going yet?"

"It sure is. Eddie is getting ready to cook some steaks in the fire place."

"Good. I'll come in and cook my fish."

"That will be fine." Gramp said as he went back inside with the freshly mixed gin.

I went into the kitchen and got my fish from the refrigerator. The level of noise from the big room began to increase, and I presumed that the gin Gramps brought in had started to talk. I rubbed my fish with salt and pepper and stuck a skewer up through its body.

Mr. Casebolt was squatting in front of the fireplace holding a folding type of grill that held steaks. Every so often he would let the grill dip down and the flames would shoot up and sear the meat.

"I like it burnt on the outside and rare and hot on the inside. That's the way to eat beef." Mr. Casebolt said, as I slid in next to him and held my fish in close to the hot coals.

"I should have brought some 'taters to bury in those hot coals. They would go good with those steaks and this fish." I announced.

"Do you cook over a fire often?" the older man asked.

"All the time." I responded. "My friends and I even cook eggs and corn in a fire. We cook everything."

"Wow! You're like a regular frontiersman. An outdoors man, able to live off the land. Isn't that so?"

Before I could answer, Mr. Seymour came to my rescue from Mr. Casebolt's teasing. "He's also a dead shot with that slingshot, Eddie ... and a mixer and bottler of fine gin."

"Well, leastwise I'm closer to being a real Indian than those make believe Indians from the "Y." They make noise like an Indian, but they can't even paddle a canoe. And, whoever heard of Indians with names like Harold and Herschel?"

"Who are Harold and Herschel? "Asked Doctor Wherry, as he leaned in to inspect the steak Mr. Casebolt was cooking.

"Harold Birnbaum and Herschel Mandel, two Indians in one of those War canoes that got stuck in the blue berry bushes near where I caught the big fish."

"Did you help them out, Son?" asked Gramp.

"Sort of," I answered. "I was hiding in the blueberry bushes and made like I was a Ghost... Boy, did they ever get out of there fast. I don't believe any Indians 'round here are going to give me any trouble."

Whether it was the gin or the story of my Indian encounter, all the men had a good laugh. They didn't know it, but my next joke would be on them.

Gramps got platters from the kitchen for the steaks and fish, which were placed on the table. Everybody took turns picking on the meat and fish.

"Jimmy, you should have been here last night. We had this big pickerel, that my grandson caught and Eddie cooked it in the fireplace. It was delicious."

"This perch is real good. I like perch, but my pond is too small. If I put perch in there they would eat up all the blue gills and young bass. So, Sonny Boy, if you catch perch and can't use them; bring them over to me. They sure won't go to waste ... and, you tell your 'Pop' to let you come fish in my pond the next time you come up."

"You have a fish pond, Mr. Carlin?"

"I got two. Since 1937. The Government paid to put them in. Stocked and everything. Fish are getting the right size now for some good fishing."

"That sounds good, thank you." I said and began to clean up the steak and fish remnants from the table. "I'll take care of this stuff, Gramp."

"Very good, son. Very good."

My Grandfather and the other men probably thought that I was being a nice obedient boy, but in fact I wanted some good tasty garbage.

Those steak bones and fish bones were going to make some good raccoon bait.

I cleaned the platters and the utensils and put them away. Then I picked through the food waste and got some nice meaty bones and a little bit of fish flesh. Along with my can containing the fish head and innards, I felt that I had enough raccoon bait.

The men were busy with their gin and talking and probably happy that I was out of the way. Although Gramp didn't do it, I know some of these men liked to talk about women and use foul language. This wasn't done in our family and I was happy not to hear such stuff. Anyway, the challenge of catching a raccoon was much better than talking about women.

I slipped out the kitchen door and began the next phase of this operation.

My idea was to get the raccoon to climb into a garbage can without turning the can over. That was the trick. As I gazed around I saw some materials I could use to accomplish this feat, as Mr. Seymour called it. First, there were a few masonry blocks lying under the porch and then there were a lot of split fire wood logs on the wood pile. As I mulled over the resources available to me, a design began to form in my mind.

Both metal garbage cans were empty. So, I would take one can and use the split firewood to build a stacked wood wall around the garbage can to keep it upright. I would use the masonry blocks to build a set of steps up to the rim of the can. This way a raccoon could easily walk up and jump down into the can to get the bait.

My plan sounded good and simple and I started to implement it without haste. It really didn't take me very long to assemble this first part of the trap.

Now came the hard part - How to keep the raccoon in the can after he takes the bait. AH! HA!

The second garbage can. I tied the steak bones and package of fish parts to some fishing line and placed them down in the trap. I put a good sized rock down in the trap and pinched the fishing line under it. Next, I fed the line up over the porch railing and tied it through the handles of the second garbage can. Now if a raccoon got into the lower can and pulled the bait, the line would come out from below the rock and the upper garbage can would fall part way into the lower can trapping the raccoon. The trap was complete and set in a very short time. Now everything was up to Mr. Raccoon.

I went back inside and shut off all the outside lights.

I wandered over to the bathroom and washed my face and hands. Then I came back to the kitchen, got a Pepsi and found myself a seat atop the storage cabinets in the big room.

The liquor and the stories were flying fast and furious. If as many fish were caught or animals shot as told in these stories, then the planet should be devoid of any wild life. I sat quietly and listened. Concurrently, I scanned through a pile of hunting and fishing magazines. No doubt many of the stories told here tonight had been published in these magazines at one time or another and were now being told as first person experiences. All this stuff was somewhat entertaining, but I had my ears open for the sound of falling garbage cans.

A flashlight was kept on the liquor sideboard for use by anyone who needed light to go to the bathroom at night. Some intuitive spirit moved me to go and pick up that flashlight. At that time Mr. Casebolt was telling a story about an encounter with a bear in these woods, during the construction of this cabin.

"We decided to call it a night and go to sleep. There was only a part of the roof over the dormitory off the kitchen, so that's where we slept. Fools that we were, we left all the food on a table in what's now the kitchen. We had lumber and materials all over the place. Four of us just got comfortable in our bunks when…"

CRASH! BANG! YEEEOWWW! SNAAAARRRLLL!

Mr. Casebolt was stopped in mid sentence by the commotion occurring outside.

"What in God's name is going on out there?" he exclaimed.

I was out the front door in a flash and had the light trained on the garbage cans below me, which were rocking back and forth. The trap had worked better than expected and there was one mad animal inside that can.

"PUT THE KITCHEN LIGHT ON!" I hollered.

Somebody obliged. And the next thing I knew, Jimmy and Mr. Casebolt were standing down by the moving garbage cans. All the other men were standing up by the kitchen door.

That raccoon was banging around inside that can and snarling to beat the band. Pieces of wood were falling away as the raccoon got his momentum going inside the can.

"Sounds like a 'coon is in that can," Jimmy observed.

"How did it get in there?" Mr. Casebolt asked.

"Looks like somebody made a trap." Jimmy replied

"WHAT DO WE DO NOW?" Mr. Casebolt excitedly asked.

From up on the porch, I said in a very innocent manner "Mr. Casebolt, while you skin that one, I'll set a trap to catch another."

That punch line brought down the house and the men went wild with laughter. I have to admit, that the line was not an original creation of mine, but was an old Burlesque joke that has been adapted to fit various skits over the years. What really made it funny and I didn't know this until later, was that it was a version of this punch line that Mr. Casebolt was going to use in his bear story. I just beat him to the punch line, so to speak.

Jimmy finally moved more of the wood away from the cans, so the whole mess fell over. The top can came out of the bottom can and it was followed by a nasty snarling boar raccoon. He took a good long look at each of us, sort of like committing our identities to memory and then ambled off into the dark.

## CHAPTER 19

## GRAMPA'S ROCK AND THE
## START OF A NEW TRADITION

After the fun was over, I straightened things up in the garbage can area. And as a token of appreciation, I placed the raccoon bait near a tree where I last saw the boar. We had fun at his expense, so I felt he deserved a prize.

Inside, the party seemed to have picked up where it had left off. I had a busy day with plenty of excitement and now my bunk was beckoning me to return for another night.

I don't know if it was the cool evening breeze or sheer exhaustion, but I think I was asleep before my head hit the pillow.

Even out here in the woods, Sunday was the Lord's Day as far as Gramp and a few other men were concerned. I don't recall my grandfather being a pious Bible thumping individual, but he respected Sunday and so did I when I was in his company, like today.

Gramp was already up and doing his morning exercises out on the porch, when I awoke. I wandered out to see him, but I was more interested in breakfast than exercises.

Without skipping a beat in his exercise routine, Gramp said. "Come on, son, we'll go down to the lake for our morning bath and then we can get dressed for Church."

"What about breakfast, Gramp?"

"Dave is going to make some hot cakes and sausages; they'll be ready when we come up."

"OK." I said as I turned to go back into the bunk room for my bathing trunks and towel.

By the time I returned, Gramp was already in the lake cavorting like a seal.

I gingerly eased myself into the water, lathering up my body as I went. Finally, I was totally immersed in the chilly water and anxious to get out. Quickly, I climbed back on the dock and retrieved my towel.

"Would you hand me my towel there, Son?" Gramp asked as he started to come up out of the water. "And get my robe over there on that chair."

I dutifully obliged, especially when I noticed Gramp was butt naked.

"Oh, is that water delightful. Just the thing to wake up your body and get it refreshed for the start of the day."

Gramp was always saying things like that. I don't know if he was trying to convince me or himself about the benefits of these supposed health enhancing practices. It would be a few hours before the sun's warming rays would touch our side of the lake. So right now, I was downright cold and wanted to get every last drop of water off my shivering body. If Gramp didn't feel the cold like I did, he had to be more than human, or just plain faking it. And he sure didn't have fur like a polar bear.

After Gramp got into his robe, I headed lickedy split to the bunk room. I wanted to get dry and put warm clothes on before I became a blue Popsicle. As I reached the turn at the porch stairs, I could see that Gramps wasn't far behind.

It didn't take long for me to dress and comb my hair and present myself in the kitchen to get some breakfast.

"Well, is young Dan'l Boone ready for another exciting day?" Mr. Seymour sang out, when I entered the kitchen.

"Not today, it's Sunday and we can't play or get dirty on Sunday."

"Oh, why is that?"

"Somewheres God told my mother that I had to wear my Church clothes all day Sunday and I couldn't get dirty."

"Oh, yes. I almost forgot," Mr. Seymour relied. "They had that same rule when I was a boy."

"God was around back then too."

"Certainly, and even when my father was a boy, they had that rule. Boys break a lot of rules, so God made a lot of rules for boys to obey. That way there were so many rules, a boy couldn't break all of them."

"I guess that's about right. It sure seems like there are a lot of rules."

Gramp now arrived in the kitchen and surveyed the scene. He grabbed a plate and began to fill it with a few of the hot cakes and sausages that Mr. Seymour had already prepared.

"I'm only going to take a taste, Dave. My grandson and I have to get to Church, or his grandmother will have both our heads."

Following my grandfather's lead, I loaded up a plate with hot cakes and sausages. I'll be darned if I was going to be hauled off to Church on an empty stomach.

Gramp was dressed in his business clothes, white shirt, tie, vest and jacket. I, on the other hand, wore jeans, a polo shirt and Keds. At least me and my clothes were clean, even if I wasn't dressed to normal Sunday standards.

"Where are we going to Church, Gramp?" I asked as we walked out toward the car.

"I think today we'll go to Swartswood, there is supposed to be a new Church there. Usually, when Charlie is with me we go to Blairstown. But, Charlie isn't here today, so we can try Swartswood. I can buy the papers there too."

I didn't know Charlie, I didn't know Blairstown and I didn't know Swartswood. I just didn't want to go to some strange Church that would be after more than the ten cents that I had planned to give.

Swartswood wasn't very far from the camp. Maybe, five miles. I marked the route and the landmarks on my map as Gramp drove. There was a White Methodist Church on the corner as we came into Swartswood.

"Is that the Church, Gramp?" I asked, as he maneuvered along the road looking for a parking space.

"No, I think we're going into that building, where those people are going." he said, as he found a place to park and brought the Chevy to a stop in front of a white building with green trim. There was a sign on the building that said "LOUIE'S HOTEL." We got out of the car and crossed the road to another white building with green trim. This building had a sign that read "LOUIE'S LAKE HOUSE."

A lot of people were walking down towards "Louie's Lake House" from another complex of white and green buildings called "LOUIE'S PINES."

We followed along as they went down the stairs into the barroom of the "Lake House." The place was crowded, standing room only.

"I heard that they had a lot of services here on Sunday and that they are very fast." Gramp related as we pushed into the crowded barroom.

In short order a Preacher came out and started speaking in some language that I didn't understand. I focused on Gramp, who was acting like he knew what the man was saying. Some of these other people responded at times to the preacher in the same language. I didn't have any notion of what was going on, until some men came around with baskets. That I knew... And just as Gramp had said, the service was fast and ended after the baskets were passed.

We had stayed back, at the rear of the room and were able to exit before the bulk of the crowd made for the doorway. Ahead of the crowd, we walked down the road to a place called "STRUBLE'S" where they sold the Sunday newspapers. Gramp purchased the various editions he wanted and then we walked back to the car.

"Hey, Gramp! What language was that preacher speaking?" I asked as we crossed the road in front of the crowd forming near the front of the barroom.

"I think Italian. I think most of the people who come here are from Brooklyn. This is their vacation resort."

That comment sort of answered my next question as these people, by their dress and physical appearance did not fit the stereotypical description of a Sussex County dairy farmer.

"Even if we didn't understand everything, we still went to Church and it was a nice fast service. That should satisfy your Grandmother."

I knew Gramp would come up with a way of justifying our attendance at an Italian Church Service. What he told my Mother and Grandmother would be something else again. But, as far as I was concerned, my Grandfather took me to Church.

We reversed our course and headed back to the camp.

Mr. Casebolt and Doctor Wherry were up when we returned. They and Mr. Seymour were busy cleaning and straightening up the cabin. Their "grips" were all packed and set by the rear door. I could visualize the next assignment arranged for me.

"Son, we have to load up all the bottles on the porch, then everybody's luggage."

Here I go again, doing the Mason Jar shuffle. The cases were heavy, so I had to take some jars out, carry the case up to the car and then carry the loose jars up to refill the case. I took care of this chore while the men cleaned the cabin. Once the cases were taken care of, I carried the men's bags up to the car. My own stuff was back in my paper sack and stuck inside the trunk of the car.

I thought everything was loaded in the car. But, the men kept walking back and forth through the rooms of the "camp." They checked this, that and some other thing until they were satisfied that everything was either in the car or secured in the building. At first, I thought maybe they were going to have some little ceremony ... like when we arrived. But, no. They finally came up to the car and squeezed into their seats.

It was only early afternoon and I wondered why we had to go so early in the day. This was wartime and blackout conditions prevailed after dark. The top half of a car's headlight was painted black and road lighting wasn't that good anyway. So most traveling was done during daylight hours. But, more importantly, I think Gramp wanted to get home for Sunday dinner.

As the old Chevy groaned going up the hill, I could pay one last mental visit to those places in the forest now permanently etched in my mind. In my imagination I could see the creatures of the forest bidding me adieu' from their camouflaged positions.

The car wound its way through the forest and into Jimmy's barnyard.

I had to get out and leave the sheets and pillow cases with the lady at the house. Except for a few chickens, the barnyard was quiet. Nobody was around. As we drove towards the township road, we could see all the cows lying under the apple trees.

The return trip home was much more subdued than the trip up here. I guess everybody was tired out from resting. Every once and a while someone had something to say. But, for the most part it was very quiet.

We were one of the few cars on the road as we traveled down Route 206. This was the summer of '42, gasoline rationing was in effect. Many people had their cars set up on blocks for the duration. Gasoline, tires and car parts were hard to come by. If you couple that with shift work and people continually leaving for the military, we weren't a very mobile society.

I had my map out and I marked the landmarks along the way as we went down Route 206 to Route 46 and then a short way on Route 10. A few miles south of the Ledgewood traffic circle we turned off onto the Morris and Sussex Turnpike. That road went up through a place called Mount Freedom. Gramp told me that this was a famous Jewish resort. He said Jewish people came from all over to go here; I'll take his word for it. As we drove through I saw a place called Saltz's Hotel and another place with cabins. There were some people out walking along the roads, but I didn't see any Ferris Wheels or Rollercoasters. Most of the people I saw looked older, so I don't know what kind of resort this could be.

The road brought us right into Morristown and past the house George Washington used for his Headquarters during the Revolutionary War. The road was now called Morris Ave, and it went all the way to Eliizabeth. Gramp had to go over some back streets to drop the passengers off in East Orange and Newark, but finally we arrived in Hillside.

All of the immediate family was at Gramma and Gramp's house when we arrived. My mother and father and baby sister Joyce, Aunt Eileen, Ed and baby Patricia were there along with my Grandmother, Aunt Rosemary and the two great grand mothers.

I was right; Gramma was ready to set out the Sunday dinner.

We had no sooner stepped out of the car, when my great grandmother Deering peered out of the kitchen window and hollered, "We knew you scallywags would make it to dinner. Is that boy clean? Have him get in here so's his mother can look him over."

I don't know what it is with grandmothers and such. They always want to look at boy's ears and heads. What do they expect to find?

"Here boy, let me look in your ears," my great grandmother said when I walked into the kitchen.

Wouldn't it have been something if some kind of animal had jumped out of my ear, like in a cartoon?

"Go get washed up, you smell like a smoked fish. What do you people do at that camp that makes you smell like burnt wood?"

"I took a bath in the lake, Gramma and I had to dry off by the fire."

My mother had brought clean clothes for me with her, so I headed off to the shower in the basement. In a short time the smell of the camp was gone and Gramp, who took a bath upstairs and I were permitted to join the family at dinner.

Gramp told everyone about my escapades over the weekend and I told them about the fish, the deer and the grouse. I didn't say anything about making gin or going to the Italian Church. Neither did Gramp and it was left that way.

Great Grandma was right. My clothes did stink to high heaven from the wood smoke. I didn't notice it so much when I was at the camp, but the next day at home, I could really smell them.

On Monday morning it was business as usual and I met Robert and Chicky under the trees out front. I regaled them with my stories of the weekend and showed them my map.

"If the Japs and Germans come, we can hide out in those hills like guerillas and they will never find us. But, first we have to get some bikes; otherwise it's a long walk up to those mountains.

It wasn't long before I was back to my day to day routine with Robert and Chicky and the rest of the boys.

The summer wore on and the vegetables started coming out of the gardens in profusion. We were eating fresh picked vegetables every night. Some of the women, my mother and Aunt included, began to can the produce. Some women knew how to make spaghetti sauce and others made pickles and garden salads put up in jars. The shelves in our basement larder began to fill again.

The same process was going on at my Grandmother's house. We would go over there on Saturdays or Sundays and my mother and grandmother would always have something to preserve. I had my same jobs, husking corn or shelling peas. Life never changes.

The summer was moving into to August, when my mother informed me that the whole family was going to the camp for two weeks.

This was going to be some trick since there was only one car, Gramp's. Secondly, the camp had to be vacated at three o'clock on Friday in case some men showed up to fish and we couldn't come in until 10 A.M. Monday. There were some wrinkles in the whole deal, but Gramp usually came up with some sort of a solution.

Fortunately, Eileen couldn't go until the second week. So that freed up a seat in the car. My father was off from work on Wednesday and he didn't have to be back until midnight on Friday. He was going to take the train from Newark to Blairstown and Gramp would meet him at the train station. Things began to fall in place as the count down to departure began.

My mother and grandmother planned the menu and established who would bring what foods. When the weekend came to a close, my mother had all our food and clothes packed in boxes.

Gramp and Gramma arrived on Monday morning. We had a rough job of packing the car. There were so many boxes of food and clothes that there was very little room left to sit. My sister was small, so she could sit on my mother's lap. At least some room was saved that way. Finally, after what seemed like an eternity of moving things around and repacking boxes, we were able to leave.

This time we didn't have to circle through Newark and East Orange to pick up people. Good thing. There wouldn't have been much room in the car.

The route from Elizabeth, by way of Morris Avenue, through Union, Springfield, Summit, Chatham and Madison to Morristown was direct and provided me the opportunity to renew my acquaintance with the landmarks along our route. There were a couple of turns in Morristown were we could go wrong, but I had them highlighted on my map.

Gramma had an egg carton full of home made candy. She made Rice Crispy balls flavored with cocoa and stuck together with melted marshmallows. She kept feeding them to me; probably because I wouldn't shut up as I called out every landmark and turn on the trip.

We stopped again at Chris and Jimmy, the Greeks, place in Kenvil. Again, they had a ham ready for Gramp, who introduced everybody to Chris and Jimmy. I already knew Chris and Jimmy from my earlier trip, so I was one up on everybody, but Gramp. I'm sure some of those little jars exchanged hands, although I didn't see that happen. But then, why would Gramp put the ham in the trunk of the car?

Soon we were out on the road again, heading for the Ledgewood Circle with Netcong and Route 206 to the north. We passed Lake Muskconectcong right in the center of Netcong and then a few miles further, Cranberry lake fronted right on the highway.

We were getting closer, when we passed through Andover. The next landmark would be the red barn at the corner of Route 206 and Sprindale Road. This was a gravel road that ran straight up and over the hill to Fredon. Gramp always took the left at the base of the hill, onto Fredonia Road, which made a serpentine climb up the hill and then a rapid decent down to route 94.

"Hey, Gramp" I asked, when we passed the single room Fredon School at the bottom of the hill. "How come you don't drive up this hill, when we go home? Wouldn't it be shorter than going into Newton, like we did on the last trip?"

"That's a tough hill. Someday, when we don't have a load, we can try it."

Gramp continued on across Route 94 in the direction of Stillwater. The road forked, with the left leg winding its way into Stillwater village. Someday I will go down that right leg to Middleville. On the map it looked like a shorter route. Both roads eventually connected with Fairview Lake Road, 3 miles from the camp.

We didn't stop at the Stillwater Inn, but continued on right through the village and up Fairview Lake Road.

Gramma and my mother were starting to get a little antsy as Gramp wheeled the car up and down and around the bends on Fairview Lake Road.

"Where in Gawd's name is this place, Bill? If we get there in one piece it'll be a miracle."

"Don't worry Gramma, were almost there. About two more miles to go... Do we have to stop at Jimmy's farm for sheets, Gramp?"

"Oh, yeah, I 'bout forgot. Good thing you reminded me, son."

"You get sheets from a farm!" My mother exclaimed.

"The lady that lives at Jimmy's farm does the laundry for the camp, Ma. You'll see."

We were now turning down the dirt lane towards Jimmy's barnyard.

"I smell cows, lots of cows!" Exclaimed my mother

"Oh, Jimmy has a lot of fine cows, dear. Richard and I will come back here for the afternoon milking. We'll help Jimmy and then bring fresh milk back to the camp."

Gramp's words went through me like a knife. Not only was I going to milk cows, but we were going to do a repeat of the milk can carry through the woods feat. I was already tired as I thought of that ordeal.

"Watch out for those chickens, Bill." Cautioned Gramma, as my grandfather wheeled the Chevy up the hill toward the right hand turn in the barnyard and then came to a stop.

"I'll get the sheets," I said, jumping out of the car into the middle of a bunch of scattering chickens.

The white haired lady came out of the house as I started to walk toward her. Gramp was following close on my heels and said, "Good day, is Jimmy about? Also, give my grandson sheets and cases for six beds."

"Jim's hayin' up in that back field. Don't expect him back 'till milkin' time. The boy can come with me for the linens."

I followed the lady into the white kitchen and she piled me up with brown paper packages containing the sheets and pillow cases. Gramp was waiting outside when I emerged and paid the lady as I carried the load to the car.

"I sure hope these sheets don't smell like cows," said Ma, as I plunked the packages down on the rear seat.

"We'll see Jimmy later, when we come back for milk," Gramp volunteered while getting back in the driver's seat.

The chickens scattered again when Gramp started up the Chevy and drove onto the two tire tracks that went around the back of the barn, between the two corn fields and into the woods.

We passed the stand of hemlock trees and began the twisting uphill climb to the birch stand at the top of the hill.

"What do you do if someone is coming the other way?" questioned my mother.

"I never had that problem, but somebody would have to pull over or back up," Gramp answered.

Fortune would smile on this day and no other vehicle would come at us from the other direction.

"HEY DEER, HEY GROUSE!!" I hollered out the car window, when we came to the top of the hill. "I'M BACK!"

"I'm sure you made their day," my mother returned. "All the animals are probably heading for the next county."

"I don't think that boar raccoon is gonna be too happy either," Gramp interjected.

"We're there," I yelped when we passed the remnants of the burned up car at the last bend in the road. "The camp is straight ahead."

Gramp brought the car to a stop in the cleared area behind the cabin.

Turning to me he said, "I'll go open everything up. You help your mother and grandmother unload the car and bring everything down by the door."

I knew the routine well. My mother and grandmother weren't going to be carrying boxes and bags downhill to the cabin door; I was raised with a certain degree of chivalry and knew better.

The ladies and my sister followed along behind Gramp. I don't know what their immediate reaction was upon entering the building. However, when I arrived with the first load of things from the car, my mother hollered out from the other side of the screen door: "Don't bring anything inside until this place is cleaned."

I obeyed my mother and stacked everything out on the landing by the back door. I had the food on one side and the clothes and things on the other side. When I was finished, I walked into the cabin.

My mother and grandmother were busy cleaning the kitchen.

"Start putting the boxes of food on this table and no place else," my Mother commanded as she and my grandmother cleaned and arranged different areas to their satisfaction.

For the next hour or so I brought in and placed different items at locations they designated. Everything was now in the building, but the cleaning continued on for the remainder of the afternoon. Ma and Gramma were continually grumbling about the quality of the housekeeping and they washed and rewashed every dish, pot and pan, knife and fork.

In the meantime, Gramp busied himself with some things out of their sight, until he felt it was time for him and me to go back to Jimmy's farm for the afternoon milking.

"Rose, Richard and I are going back to the farm. We'll be back with milk and corn."

Without waiting for her answer, he motioned me towards the car. I walked out and get into the passenger seat.

"We should be on time for the milking," Gramp said as he started the car and moved out towards the farm.

Sure enough, when we got there the cows were just moving into their milking stalls.

"Hey, Bill, you're right on time!" shouted Jimmy from the barn door.

"I'll give the boy a bucket and some towels and he can wash these cows down once they're in the stalls."

I had done this many times before, so I went over to Jimmy and he supplied me with the equipment needed.

"Here Son, Ben and Abe are hookin' 'em up in the stalls, they'll tell you where to start cleanin'."

"Start up there on this side." said Abe as I walked into the barn.

I grabbed a small stool and began to clean the udders. I went down the line from cow to cow until I had worked my way around the barn. Ben, Abe, Jimmy and Freddie were right behind me with their stainless buckets milking faster than the milking machine Gramp showed me at Walker-Gordon Farms in Plainsboro.

They had a good system working and it didn't take all that long to milk some 30 cows.

Gramp was waiting by the car for me. He already had a milk can and five big burlap sacks stuffed into the car.

"What's in the sacks, Gramp?"

"Corn. Nice sweet corn."

I could only guess what we were going to do with so much corn. I couldn't wait to see my mother's face when we came in with this load.

It was almost suppertime when we returned and Ma and Gramma were still trying to warm to the idea of staying the week in this cabin. They had cleaned just about every area of the cabin. The only things they didn't touch were the moose head hanging above the fireplace and the various stuffed animals hanging on the walls and rafters.

The table in the big room was all set for supper. Ma and Gramma whipped up a nice meal of potato salad, baked lima beans, lettuce, tomatoes and the ham from Chris and Jimmy's. I didn't care what we had to eat. I just wanted some food and a few hours of light to swim and maybe fish some.

"You wait for me to go down to that dock with you." Cautioned my mother. I don't want eyes taken off the baby while we're here, so you watch her while I clean up in the kitchen."

"I'll cleanup," volunteered Gramma. "You go down to the lake with the children. Y'all can have a nice swim 'n we'll be down in a little bit."

That was music to my ears and I ran into the dormitory and got my swimsuit. I was changed and down on the dock waiting as my mother and sister slowly made their way down to the lake.

I had forgotten that my mother had never been here, so I was obligated to give her a brief orientation before I could finally go into the water.

"I didn't know you could swim here." Said Ma, who enjoyed the water and was a very good swimmer. "I thought this place was just for fishing."

"It is Ma, but there isn't any other place to take a bath, so we have to wash in the lake."

"From what I've seen of this place, I don't think these men care about cleaning anything, including themselves."

Ma was right. The men who started this camp weren't all that concerned with women and kids. The lake was beautiful, the water clean and the dock is ideal for sun bathing. But, there wasn't any place where a person could enter the lake without climbing on or over rocks and then, if successful, walk onto a slippery rocky lake bottom full of sharp stones.

We made do. Where the dock met the shoreline, we cleaned some of the stones off the lake bottom and sprinkled some gravel from the walk into that area. The water was about 2 or 3 inches deep at that point and was an ideal place for my sister to play. Bigger folks could climb down to a couple of rocks off the end of the dock and do a surface dive into the water.

Gramp and Gramma came down to the dock in their bathing suits before Ma and I had entered the water. Gramp then gave a demonstration on how to enter the water. He stepped down on a couple of rocks then dove into the water. He swam out to a point where he could be seen feeling for the bottom.

"Here it is!" He shouted as his body began to rise until he stood chest high in the water. "I found this rock. Swim over here, Dear." he said to my mother. "So you will know where the rock is."

My mother obliged and soon she was standing shoulders above the water.

"Come on Richard!" she called. "Let's see if you can swim out to Grampa's Rock."

And as "Grampa's Rock" it would become known to a generation of cousins yet to come. This rock eventually would become one of those benchmarks in life by which personal achievements are measured. The individuals in this new generation of youngsters would proudly proclaim the time and date when they each reached that ultimate plateau in the summer of their lives... "That was the day I swam out to Grampa's Rock."

"Gramma was standing off the end of the dock washing up. She was able to get in the water, but getting out was something else. Climbing over rocks was not one of my grandmother's favorite things. But, Gramma was smarter than the whole bunch of us. She had a pair of these slip on canvas shoes that she wore right into the water. She could walk right over to low end, where my sister played, and step up on the shore.

Like my mother had said, "I thought this place was just for fishing."

I had wanted to do some fishing since we got here. But, I was kept busy with chores and meals and other things to the point where the sun was now getting ready to drop behind the mountain at the western end of the lake. The best time of the fishing day was almost over and I had yet to wet a line.

Schools of bait fish were breaking the surface of the now glass smooth lake. These smaller fish were feeding on insects somehow caught at the water's surface. Periodically, a large splash or swirl would occur as the next higher member of the food chain would seek his dinner from among the smaller members of the community. I wanted to be out there, but here I was, confined to the dock with some ladies and a toddler.

"Let's go for a short boat ride." My mother suggested after she had dried off from her swim. "I would like to see what some of these cottages on the lake look like." Turning to me she said, "I'll row and you sit in back and hold your sister."

"Foiled again," I thought. Mothers aren't supposed to row boats. Besides, I came to this place before my mother. I know these boats.

Ma surprised me. For a lady, she could row quite well. She must have rowed a boat sometime in her early life, because I had never seen her row a boat until today.

She rowed nice and easy past the four bungalows to the south of the camp. Once she was satisfied and saw what interested her, we switched places and I assumed control of the oars.

I took sort of a circuitous course back to the dock and along the way, I pointed out various landmarks around the lake.

As we pulled into the dock, the cannon sounded at the "Y" camp.

"They do that in the morning when the flag goes up and then in the evenin' when the flag comes down. Next thing will be a bugle call."

The Bugler began to play almost on cue, as we began to emerge from the boat, now secured to the dock. Looking up, we could see Gramp taking in the flag from its mount on the corner of the porch. He and Gramma picked up all the things on the dock and brought them up to the cabin. The lights were on inside the cabin, which was good, since darkness came quickly once the sun ducked behind the mountain.

I could see that Gramp had been busy while we were having our swim and boat ride. He had transformed the kitchen into some type of processing plant. Huge pots filled with water were setup on the gas range and the big tub was set up on the two burner hot water heater. Cases of Mason jars were stacked in the kitchen with more in reserve out on the porch. The sacks of corn were lined up along the porch rail near the kitchen. I didn't know what we were going to do, but I did know that it had something to do with corn.

Other than the corn, which we had brought in earlier, I suspect that these other items must have been brought and stored here at some earlier date.

I played dumb to the whole setup. I figured that they would let me in on the plot soon enough... especially where my participation was required.

Today wasn't the best day in terms of my outdoor life and from the looks of that kitchen; it was going to go downhill from here.

Gramp, Gramma and my mother had been sitting out on the porch in the Adirondack rockers, while I investigated things close by the house and down by the dock. As darkness stated to overtake the woods, they moved inside for protection against the bugs of the night. The lights inside the cabin attracted a dizzying array of insects, which pounded their bodies against the screened windows like suicide pilots; I was always amazed by the volume and diversity of bugs that those lights attracted. I wonder why Gramp hadn't thought of some way to capitalize on this phenomenon. I'm sure there is some market for dead insects.

As soon as the folks went inside, I put all my fishing stuff in the boat I had selected for myself. I planned to shove off at the crack of dawn. If I got up and out before everyone was up and fed, I could have some good uninterrupted fishing time. To make this plan work, I had to get to bed early, which wasn't too difficult since there was little to do here. We had a radio that produced mostly static, old magazines and newspapers to read and that was about it.

My mother and grandparents were seated at the big table in the main room when I came in. There was no other furniture in the room. An alternate seating place was on the stowage cabinets along the base of the south wall of the main room. I tried to sit there and read some magazines and newspapers, but it was too dark. The only light in the room was suspended over the big table. It looked like something that was taken from a pool hall. That light probably came with the chairs that were placed around the table. They were those dark banjo backed chair frames with cane seats, typical barroom furnishings of the 1930's.

I imagined that someone made a deal with some bar that was either closing up or being renovated and the camp became the beneficiary of all this wonderful stuff.

Gramp was regaling my mother with a story about something or other, while she and Gramma sat at the table paring and slicing vegetables for the pot of soup, or other dishes we would eat in the coming days.

No mention was made of the preparations out in the kitchen and I didn't even ask.

"I'm going to bed now, Ma," I said, as I made the rounds of the room to say good night to everyone.

*R. Allen Pender*

"You had a busy day, Son. Get a good night's sleep." My grandmother said as she gave me a pat on the cheek and a kiss on the forehead.

My game plan was to get to bed early, but I was really tired. A day with my grandfather can have that effect on a body.

# CHAPTER 20

# PEACHES, PEARS, PRESERVES AND BEARS

We slept in the south dormitory. The beds were cast iron frame single World War I style garrison cots and mattresses. The bunks were lined up along the wall of the dormitory. Ma had made up the beds and she had the head of each bed back at the wall. I changed my bed around so my head would be where everyone else's foot would be. This way my head would line up with screen door at the end of the dormitory. I wanted to sleep with my head facing east, so the breaking dawn would hit me in the eyes.

My plan worked well. I awoke as the first glimmer of light started to push away the darkness of the night. The cabin was quiet, except for the snoring of my grandfather and the constant ticking of the Regulator clock hung near the back door in the big room.

There was a chill in the air as I dressed and then quietly made my way into the kitchen. It was 5:30 A.M. when I went by the noisy Regulator clock.

I opened a fresh box of corn flakes, poured some in a bowl, doused them with milk and gobbled the concoction down. I also buttered a couple of slices of bread, which I stuffed in my jacket pocket to use either as bait or a snack, whichever came first.

I wasn't quite prepared for the sight that greeted me as I walked down to my boat. I couldn't see the lake. The entire body of water was shrouded by a grey mist. I couldn't see the mountain ridge across lake. The mist was rising up from the water like a scene from a horror movie.

I could see southward along the shoreline. Visibility was about 50 feet off the shore, so if I kept my boat at that distance I would be able to navigate until the mist lifted.

I unhooked the boat from the dock and eased it out into the calm water. My planned course would be on a sight line just off the docks of the four cottages south of our dock. The land projected out slightly beyond the fourth cottage and then cut back in to form a shallow cove that extended down to the end of the lake. I set the boat on a course that would take me to the upper edge of the cove. Depending on visibility, I could correct my course once I reached that point.

I had a big can full of nice juicy nightwalkers… and I selected one to bait up my hook as I slowly glided by the first dock south of our camp. My father had picked up a used bamboo fly rod for me. I still didn't have a reel, so I had to jury rig the line when casting or retrieving. And this morning, I just threw the baited hook and bobber off the back of the boat.

Everything was quiet, except for the slight slap of water against the side of the boat. The sky above the trees to the east was slowly changing to lighter shades of grey as daylight crept in on us. This was exactly like a scene I had read about in one of the outdoor magazines. The person in that story was fishing just like me. He stopped to light his pipe and at that moment a huge bass took his bait and the man didn't know whether to grab his pole or his pipe. He lost the pipe, but caught the fish. I didn't have a pipe, but I did have some bread to munch on and that's what I did.

The boat was now approaching the point where the shore projected out before cutting back into the cove. I had to adjust my course to keep my bait out of the weeds and rocks close to shore. As I set the rod down and began to row in the direction of deeper water ... the line went taught and pulled the rod tip across the back of the boat. Quickly, I released the oars and grabbed the rod.

I could feel the darting movement of a fish on the other end of the line. Holding my rod tip up with my left hand, I began to pull in line with my right hand. The fish darted around some, but it didn't make any moves like that giant pickerel did. A couple of minutes later I had a good sized perch in the boat.

I had neglected to watch where the boat was going during the brief battle with the fish. As I sat back in my seat and began to unhook the fish, I heard a large splash behind me. Turning around, I saw that the bow of the boat was heading into some bushes near the shore. I quickly dropped the fish and grabbed the oars. As I rowed out slightly into deeper water I could see some movement in the woods behind the bushes. I retrieved the fish from the floor of the boat and when I stood up to put the fish in the live well, a mother bear and two cubs appeared at a small clearing in the foliage. About 100 feet of water separated us. The bears sat and watched me and me them. However, as soon as I moved the oars, they turned and moved off into the woods.

I must have scared them as they were feeding on the blueberries that grew around the lake. I wonder if they saw me catch that fish and wanted it for breakfast. I just sat there in the boat amazed at what I had seen and I shook like a leaf for the next few minutes.

The mist was now rising off the lake and the sound of birds began to fill the air. Some crows made their appearance in a few tree tops along the lake shore. As I made the turn at the end of the lake to head up along the west shore, the suns rays began to come across the tops of trees on our side of the lake.

I baited my line again and heaved it out beyond the back of the boat.

Suddenly, from across the lake, I saw smoke rising from the camp. Gramp was probably up and had started a fire in the fireplace. The sun would warm things up in about an hour, but right now it was cool.

I had one perch and would land another as I crossed the middle of the lake on my way to the dock. I wasn't sure that I should tell my mother about the episode with the bears. She might restrict me to the cabin, or otherwise curb my independence. I would just have to play this one by ear.

"How long have you been up?" Boomed my mother from the corner of the porch.

She was about to go into the bathroom, when she saw me bringing my boat into its berth.

"I caught two nice perch, Ma. They'll be good for lunch," I said in an attempt to evade her question and yet make a statement that I didn't have to defend.

Ma went into the bathroom without answering me, so I figured that she was satisfied with my answer. I placed the two perch in the floating live well and then made my way up to the main room.

Gramp had made a fire in the fireplace and now he was seated at the big table all dressed in his business clothes, sipping a cup of coffee. Gramma was out in the kitchen preparing his breakfast, when I walked into the main room.

"What's that I hear; you got two perch?"

"Yeah, Gramp. Two nice perch. I think I could have got more if I stayed out longer. But, I didn't want my mother to worry, since it's her first time here."

"It's good you're back. I have to leave soon to do some work, so you stay close to help your grandmother."

If one were to look at his situation logically; the question should occur, "why does my grandmother need help on what is supposed to be a vacation?"

Those sacks of corn, the Mason jars and the pots in the kitchen provided all the clues necessary. We had brought "canning time" with us. This was no vacation, it was a portable food factory and we were the workers.

In a short time my mother came in from the bathroom and then Gramma came out of the kitchen with a big platter of fried eggs, bacon and toast. We all set about making that food disappear. And when we were done, Gramp got up, bid his goodbyes and walked out towards his car. In a few minutes the Chevy was out of sight and here I was, left with two women and a toddler. There was no car and no phone, just woods.

"Richard, when you're finished eating, would you start husking the corn on the porch. Gramma and I will get things ready in the kitchen after we cleanup breakfast."

I was familiar with this process and knew my place in it. "OK, Ma," I replied and I got up from the table to get about my chore.

I transferred the husking operation to the base of the wooden kitchen steps, where it was a short walk to the drum where Gramp burned the garbage. I put the clean ears of corn into a big pot near the kitchen door and I allowed the spent husks to accumulate at the base of the stairs. Periodically, I would grab an armful of husks and carry them over to the garbage burner.

Every so often, Ma would open the kitchen screen door, grab a few ears of corn and duck back inside. This went on for some time. I kept husking and one by one the large sacks emptied. The garbage drum was stuffed full of husks and they were drying fast in the mid morning sun. Maybe, we could burn them this afternoon. If not, garbage was going to start backing up to attract the raccoons and maybe those bears.

When I walked into the kitchen, it was some sight. Huge pots were steaming on the stove. Ma and Gramma were filling jars with corn mixtures that they had cooking in other pots. There were piles of corn cobs all over the place. They were putting jars in and taking jars out of these boiling caldrons.

My next chore was to get the corn cobs out of the kitchen. There wasn't any room in the garbage burner, so I chucked the cobs out into the woods.

We all stopped for a quick ham sandwich lunch between batches of boiling jars.

The final products were starting to accumulate at different spots. There was whole kernel corn in one place, creamed corn in another place, corn with peppers in a third place, and so on. By mid afternoon the final batches were done. As the jars cooled, Ma put a little tag on each one and I placed the jars back into the original Mason jar cases. By 3 P.M, the kitchen was cleaned, the jars were packed and the labeled cases stacked.

Ma and Gramma finally got out of the kitchen. They were sitting out on the porch catching a breeze and enjoying a cool drink, when I heard the sound of a vehicle coming through the road in the woods.

A couple of minutes later the Chevy wheeled into its parking place. Gramp had returned.

"Oh son, come with me. I need me a hand for a second," He said as he opened the screen door.

"Sure" I replied, rising from my seat at the table.

I followed Gramp outside to the opened car trunk.

"Here, let's carry these boxes in and set them on the porch."

Looking into the trunk, I saw more cases of Mason Jars.

Where in the world did all of these Mason jars come from? Gramp must have cornered the market for Mason jars. But, being a dutiful grandson I helped empty the trunk and carry the cases of jars to the porch. I had to laugh a little, because we used up all the corn and didn't have anything to put in these jars.

WRONG. After the jars were carried to the porch, Gramp said.

"I have a few things in the back and front seats that have to come in."

AND HOW. There were bushel baskets and paper sacks full of assorted vegetables. It looked like the factory was going to run another day.

Not only another day; but every day. The next morning Gramp left with the cases of finished product and returned in the afternoon with more Mason jars and fresh produce. My mother and grandmother worked like beavers in that kitchen. When the day's production was done, it was time to prepare supper. The only relaxation they got was in the evening. I wasn't much better off, but I was able to squeeze some fishing in before dark.

Fortunately, Gramp didn't leave Wednesday morning. My father was en route to Blairstown via the Delaware Lackawanna and Western Railroad. He was supposed to arrive at the Blairstown Station around 10 A.M. If nobody was there to meet him, he was lost. He didn't know where we were... and he sure wouldn't know where he was. There are a lot of woods around here and to try and find us would like trying to find a needle in a haystack.

It was decided that Wednesday would be a slack day. Gramp wasn't going to business and we were pretty much caught up with the "canning." We still had a few cases of empty Mason Jars, but very little raw produce.

Gramma and my mother were going to prepare a nice dinner for my father. Everybody was going to rest a little today. I wanted to do some exploring in the woods and thought my father could come with me. We could also get in some fishing, which Daddy loved. It really looked like today and tomorrow had some good possibilities.

As long as we didn't have to "can" today, I didn't have to get up at a super early hour to get a little fishing time. Also, since Gramp didn't have to go out on business today, this morning was much more relaxed.

After breakfast, I got the boats all ship shape while Ma and Gramma got the cabin straightened out. We were all getting ourselves physically and mentally prepared for a vacation day.

At the appointed time Gramp and I left for the Blairstown train station.

We took Old Schoolhouse Road into Hardwick along the base of the mountain. We went past the lane, where we had turned in to go to the "Mountaineer's cabin. The dirt road, which was covered with oil and gravel, wound up and down hill along fields and woods for about eight miles. We left a steady stream of dust in our wake until we finally came to a narrow paved road that went down hill and emptied onto the main street of Blairstown.

The business center of Blairstown was a short street that looped off of and then back onto Route 94. There was a little A&P store in a white building with a covered wooden sidewalk. In my opinion this street could have been used for the set of a cowboy movie. It had that 19th century look and I wouldn't have been surprised if I saw someone like Tom Mix or Gene Autry coming down Main Street.

The train station wasn't too far from the center of town. We pulled into an empty parking area. There wasn't anybody waiting for the train. Obviously, we didn't miss my father's train, or else he would have been here waiting.

My grandfather knew about everything. He told me how this railroad went up to Scranton and how the engineers built a cut across route 206 in Andover that saved 21 miles of track. He had all these little tidbits of information and don't ever question his statements, because he would show up sooner or later with some kind of documentation to prove his point.

One time some man made the mistake of questioning a statement Gramp made about San Francisco. Pity that man. Gramp called for a blank piece of paper and on it he drew a map of the city of San Francisco. Someone later checked his drawing against a published map of that city and found Gramp's map accurate to the smallest detail.

Gramp continued to spin one railroad story after another as we sat waiting. He talked like he knew some of these historical railroad magnets personally. Maybe he did and maybe he didn't. I just listened and didn't question. Last year I did question one story about an uncle of his, who discovered the Comstock Lode. He made me read a book called "The Silver Kings." It was about his father's uncle, a man named Jim Fair and his partner Mackey, who were a couple of real scalawags and they did in fact discover the Comstock Lode and then caused all kinds of mayhem out in Virginia City, Nevada.

Now, I just listened and if I heard something questionable I did my own research.

The shrill loud long blasts of a locomotive quickly brought an end to the story telling. The train was coming and it wasn't very long before the huge locomotive seemed to materialize out of the heavy foliage surrounding the track. Slowly it bore down on us as the Engineer sought to bring the train to a stop in the proper place.

My father was the only person to get off the train, which was a good thing, because we didn't want to miss him in the crowd.

"Hey, Dad!" I hollered to make sure he saw us, despite us being the only people at the train station. And, then I ran over to greet him and help with his bag.

"Are you ready for some good fishing, Dad? I already caught two nice perch."

"Well it sure sounds like everybody is having a good time. I sure am anxious to see this place."

"Oh, we are having a grand time, Joe. It's a wonderful place and we have the best of food."

Gramp kind of neglected to say that most of food had been put in Mason jars. I was happy to see my father and to have a little companionship today and tomorrow. My Dad had liked to hunt and fish and I thought we could explore the woods together, especially since I saw those bears. So I didn't plan to say anything about the canning. I'd leave that up to my mother.

*THE SOJOURNERS*
*Life on the American Homefront During World War II*

After we got into the car, Gramp headed out of the railroad parking lot and made a turn in a direction different than that from which we had come. Of course my father didn't know where we going, but Gramp saw the puzzled look on my face.

"I have to see a man up the road here. We'll go back by way of Stillwater. It's a nice ride, Joe. You'll like it."

My father didn't have any choice. But, my grandfather's behavior was nothing new to him. He had seen it all. I wanted to get back and go fishing, but both of us were trapped.

Gramp turned off onto a dirt lane about two miles away from the train station. Again we ended up in some person's barnyard. Gramp got out of the car and went over to greet a man seated by the side of a faded red shed. They stood and talked for a while and then Gramp signaled us to come out and join him.

As Dad and I walked over towards the shed, Gramp and the man went inside. We followed. Once inside the man pointed to a group of baskets and said,

"There's your stuff."

Gramp then delegated baskets for each of us to carry out to the car. I showed my father the routine and we got everything loaded. I'm sure some prearranging went into this stop. Gramp did very few things on the spur of the moment.

My father was somewhat bewildered by Gramp's need for baskets of peaches, peppers, cucumbers, cabbage and carrots. But, I wasn't.

Daddy should have known how lucky we were today. Gramp only made one stop. I've been with him on days when he made more stops than a local bus.

My mother and grandmother gave my father a big "Hello" when he arrived. They were in high spirits considering today was a vacation day and he was probably the cause. My sister clung to my father like a magnet. So yours truly was left to unload the car.

Ma and Gramma were not too pleased to see the baskets of produce being set on the porch. It meant tomorrow was going to be a production day.

My father didn't have to be back at work until 11 P.M. tomorrow night. The train coming from Scranton to Newark would pass through Blairstown at 6:45 P.M. Daddy was planning on catching that train and things should work out; if Gramp was back in time for supper.

Before we set about getting ready for lunch and doing some swimming, Gramp had us load up the car with all the finished cases of canned food.

"I have to go on business down near the city tomorrow," blurted Gramp. "I'll drop this food off at the house so we have some room in the car for Friday."

On seeing the size of stacks and then looking in the boxes, my father questioned," How much of this stuff is there? And, where did it all come from?"

"We can talk about that later," My mother replied. "For now let's just load this stuff and then have a nice lunch."

Dad was quite used to Gramp's antics and knew he was at the bottom of everything, so he just quietly helped to load up the Chevy.

The baskets of fruits and vegetables that just came in were sitting out on the porch near the kitchen door. The peaches had attracted a swarm of fruit flies of such proportion that my mother made me move the baskets out beyond the wood pile.

Lunch was finally served and our vacation day could begin in earnest after having suffered a few false starts.

Gramp was the first one finished with his lunch, dressed in his bathing suit and down at the dock. We all followed suit, however not until all the lunch stuff was put away and everything else cleaned up.

I had my swimming time and that was fun, but I wanted to be out fishing. My father had to devote time to my sister, who played in the shallow water. After several hints and much cajoling my mother finally relented and permitted me to go by myself in a boat.

"You stay where I can see you," she said

That was some statement, because you could stand on the end of the dock and see just about every part of the lake.

This time I nosed the boat towards the north end of the lake. I was full of nervous energy and anticipated a battle with a big fish, like that pickerel I had caught in this same area.

Slowly I rowed up along the shore. I went past the little clearing with the rotted boat, then by the big fallen tree and the little cove with the big rock bar. I passed the end of our property and came to the Rusty Knife Cabin, where some "Y" Camp counselors had all their laundry hung out across the porch. The landmarks around the lake were now becoming more familiar to me and their locations were becoming imprinted in my mind.

The residents of the Y Camp must have been off doing something. Their log bunk houses were vacant, although I could see things inside through the open sides. I wondered if Herschel and Harold, the two Indians from Maplewood were still here.

The Y Camp had two sections Camp Minisink and Camp Kittatinny. The entire camp was at the north end of the lake with one section along part of the shore on our side of the lake and the other section along the opposite shore. Inland from the north end of the lake was a large log dining hall where both camps ate their meals. From what I could observe, the younger kids were housed on our side of the lake.

They had athletic fields and tennis courts over near Fairview Lake Road. That road went past the camp and then wound its way up and over the mountain. I wasn't on that road yet, but some day I would go up on that mountain.

Everything was quiet on the lake as I slowly moved around its perimeter. A light breeze was blowing me south along the west shore of the lake. I only had to row slightly to maintain my course. Every once and a while I would check my bait. Nothing was biting. Maybe the fish were on vacation too.

My folks were the only people out swimming on this whole lake. Maybe my mother was right that this lake was only for fishing. I saw "Y" kids swimming, but not anybody else. As a matter of fact, I haven't really seen anybody around the few cabins that dotted the lake. I did hear some mumbled voices coming from the area near one of these cabins, but I didn't see anybody.

The folks were still out on the dock as I proceeded up the east shore.

As I came closer, my father swam out to meet me.

"Did you catch any fish?" he asked, grabbing onto the transom of the boat.

"Not a bite," I replied. "I don't think these fish start bitin' till 6 o'clock. Anyhow that's what Mr. Casebolt said."

"You and I will go out after supper, 'n maybe we can get a big one."

With that he let go of the transom and sprinted towards the dock. I continued on my course and brought the boat into its berth.

Apparently, my mother had told my father about the canning operations that had been going on over the past few days. He was only staying until late tomorrow afternoon and didn't want to spend his time off and a train ride to go some place to can vegetables. We were supposed to vacate the camp by 3 P.M., Friday. Right now it wasn't all to clear where we were going and how Gramp was going to get my Aunt Eileen and Cousin Patricia up here on Monday. In any event, tomorrow, Thursday, would be the only day left to can the produce we just brought in.

I'm sure Gramp was thinking of some scheme to get the canning done and to cover all his bases. It wasn't like him to retreat from a preconceived plan. His brain must have been going overtime.

My father never disagreed with Gramp. My mother did. She was one of the few people who could get the best of him, without his getting mad. My father was just never interested in the same things as Gramp. My father also denied having technical expertises in any of the areas where Gramp was involved. Gramp left him alone and treated him like a distant in-law. This was fine by my father. Gramp didn't bother him like he did others in the family, who more readily did his bidding only to eventually realize that they were inextricably caught in his snare and had a tough time getting out.

Today was one of those times that my father displayed his amicable non threatening demeanor that drove Gramp nuts. Each time Gramp suggested something which would lead back towards the canning issue, my father would circumvent the issue by introducing a variety of other subjects where Gramp had no interest or expertise. Unable to provoke an argument, or even develop a discussion, Gramp retired to take a nap.

Gramma went through life with mixed allegiances. She was devoted to her husband, which was no easy chore, considering his idiosyncrasies. She was also devoted to her children and grandchildren. She was the oil that was constantly being poured out to soothe the waters that Gramp stirred up when he tried to rock everybody's boat.

I can recall several times when Gramp, in an effort to get his way, would proclaim, "I'm the head of this family and we do what I say."

He may have gotten results with that type of remark when his children were young, or financially dependant upon him. But, that was no longer the case; yet he continued to think he could wield power over his children and their families. Gramp even claimed the families of his sons and daughters-in-law as part of his regal domain.

I remember one time when my father's older brother Bill, who is now serving in the Navy, was present during one of Gramp's tirades. Gramp had made one of his famous, "I'm the head of the family speeches."

My Uncle Bill said, "My brother was unfortunate enough to marry into your family, not me. And we're not joining."

Except, maybe to use him as a standard, against which to measure the quality of sourmash liquor, Gramp never had very many kind words for my Uncle Bill after his refusal to be included in Gramp's Royal Court.

My grandmother had a gift. Despite her husband, everybody loved her. She had a way of making and enforcing the peace. Gramma was not loud or boisterous, but soft and quiet, almost condescending. She had the ability to make my grandfather see what the real priorities of the moment were. Naturally, he claimed the ultimate decision as his own, but we knew where it really originated.

My mother and Gramma had a little conversation after Gramp went in to take a nap. The conversation was brief and then I saw Gramma do a slight wave of her hand, palm outward across her body below the shoulder. That was her signal that she knew what the situation was and she had it under control.

We had a great afternoon. First, I led my parents and sister down the trail along the lake. Ma had brought a little pail along to pick blueberries. I showed her all the spots where Mr. Seymour and I had been. She picked a lot of berries and after we came back near the cabin, it was my sister's time for a nap. Ma wanted to rest a little too, so they stayed at the cabin while Daddy and I walked up the road towards the top of the hill.

I showed my father all the places where I had encountered animals on my previous trip. We walked into the spot where the grouse had jumped out at me. Mr. Seymour told me that a grouse puffs up to look fierce and tries to distract a predator from its nest. I'm sure that any baby grouse that were here then are gone now. No grouse popped out at us this time. There were plenty of fresh deer tracks going up and down into the little swampy valley beyond the crest of the hill. We didn't see any deer, but their evidence was all around. We encountered lots of droppings and a few fresh beds. We saw a scrape, where a buck tore up the ground and a few saplings where he rubbed his antlers. Yes indeed this was very active deer country.

I told my father about the bears I saw at the other end of the lake.

"I'm sure they roam all over this area. What with that "Y" Camp down there, these cabins and the farm, they probably can find a lot to eat. I'll bet that those bears have been around the cabin looking for food. When we go out in the boat later, you show me where you saw the bears and we'll look for tracks."

I was beginning to feel like Daniel Boone as my father and I roamed through this world inhabited only by creatures of the forest. I tried to visualize this area as it may have looked 100 years ago. Was it a primeval forest where bears, wolves, mountain lions, foxes and bobcats roamed along with deer, elk and wild turkeys? Did Indians hunt and camp here? There was so much I wanted to know. And as the years went by I did learn a great many things.

First- Fairview Lake was called Sucker Pond back in 1896.

The land we were now on was once part of a tract of over 800 acres granted to a person named Thomas Lightfoot and surveyed by the King's surveyors in 1744.

Mr. Lightfoot's heirs subdivided the property in half, right down the middle, from the Kittatinny Ridge or Pacqulon, its Indian name, to what is now Old Schoolhouse Road. A family named Losey became the owners of the northern part of the tract and a family named Stahley became owners of the southern half.

The Stahley's were farmers and most of their land was cleared for farming. An old lime kiln that once belonged to them is still visible just off the lane going to the West side of the lake. Most of Jim Carlin's farm including his farmhouse was part of the original Stahley farm.

The Losey farm was on the road to Flatbrookville, now called Fairview Lake Road. The place where Mr. Seymour's camp is located had belonged to the Losey's and was used as their wood lot.

A great many trees had been cut off these lands to provide timber for building and firewood to heat homes and to fuel the furnace at Wintermute's foundry on Old Foundry Road. An ice house once stood on the shore of the lake right where the dock is now. The Stahley's and Losey's both had ice houses. They cut ice off the lake in winter and stored it in these ice houses from where they distributed it to local creameries in the warm weather. The roads in and around the lake were made by the Losey's and Stahley's so they could harvest their wood and ice. The rock walls throughout the area are the result of this road building and field clearing activity.

A man named, Sanford Robinson of Philadelphia, came along in 1896 and purchased lake front property where the three cabins, just south of our camp, sit today. Mr. Robinson and others were going to stock the pond with fish and made an agreement with the Stahley's and Losey's permitting them access to their property.

Mr. Seymour and his friends came along in 1901 and purchased a couple of lakefront lots from John Kitchens and John Johnson, relatives of the Losey family. After the present cabin was built in 1909, the group, now called the Kittatinny Club, purchased the balance of the 15 acre woodlot.

So, I guess 100 years ago this was a pretty industrious place. All the woods were devoid of trees and the wildlife were hunted for food, or had moved into other areas. Now in 1942, the forest around here is maybe about 40 years old in places. Jimmy was farming the area just behind the three cabins until not too long ago. Birch trees and mountain laurel have grown up in that field in a very short time. They are the first plants to take hold and someday they may be succeeded by oaks and beeches.

There is a great deal of history surrounding this area. And as my father and I walked and talked, I wanted to find out more and more.

Our walk had brought us right back to the cabin. My sister was just waking from her nap. Gramma was in the kitchen preparing supper, which would be ready in about an hour and a half.

"Why don't we take a boat ride until supper is ready," my mother suggested.

"Let's do that Alice. I'm anxious to see the lake."

My father rowed, my mother and sister sat on the rear seat and I navigated from up in the bow. We went down past the three little bungalows with the grass lawns. The name "Goddart" was emblazoned on a shingle hanging from a post in the lawn between two of the houses. No one seemed to be around and my mother wanted to peek into these houses to see how they were furnished. My father wasn't too keen on that idea. He felt that someone might see us and we could be treated like "peeping toms" or charged with breaking and entering. Cool headiness prevailed and we rowed on past the cabins.

We beached the boat at the very end of the lake and went ashore. My mother was interested in the shell of a house that stood about 50 feet back from the shore line. Other than a fireplace, the building had no improvements. It looked like people camped here. The lake bottom here was nice and sandy. Apparently someone had cleaned out the rocks to make a nice swimming area.

My father and I walked over to the approximate spot where I had seen the bears. We could see where they had stripped the bark off some dead trees looking for insects. We walked back a little further towards a white shed type building with red trim. Near that building we saw some bear droppings.

"They've been around here. Not today, but fairly recently," said Daddy.

This little building sat in just off the lane, which came from Jimmy's farm to the cluster of small cabins in that southwest corner of the lake. I learned later that this cabin belonged to Blair Academy, who owned a 500 acre tract of land west of the lake.

We finished our explorations and returned to the boat. We continued our tour up past the cabin colony and then began a trip across open water towards supper.

Gramma was still working her magic on the propane fired stove when we returned.

"Do you need help Mother?"

"No, Alice. You can set the table. Then we can bring everything in."

I must say each meal up here was like a Sunday dinner. There was no fast quick stuff. Everything was either beef, pork or lamb roasts with all the trimmings. Gramma even had her constant pot of homemade soup cooking at all times.

We had a good supper, but I was more interested in the clock. I was anxious for us to be finished by 6 o'clock so Daddy and I could be out on the lake for the peak fishing hours.

"All right, all right. We'll clean up here. You two can go out in the boat," my mother said as she read my ants in the pants attitude at the table.

I was down to the dock in a flash. My father followed a few minutes later.

"Which way should we go? I'll row you fish," he said getting into the boat.

"Let's go up this side towards the camp. Then we can cross over to the other side and come down by those rocks across the lake," I replied like I was some guide leading an expedition.

I had caught two perch and a crappie by the time we got to the Rusty knife cabin. Midway across the lake between the camps, I landed a nice largemouth bass. He probably weighed 2 pounds. Then as we came down past the last counselor's cabin, just before the big weeping willow along the shore, I got a hit that almost tore the rod from my hands.

It became a real tug of war as the fish kept going under the boat. I had to keep changing positions to deal with him. The fish finally came up along side the boat and Daddy netted him. It was a nice pickerel. Not like the monster I caught with Mr. Casebolts help. But, a nice fish never the less.

"We better get in and take care of these fish, son." Daddy advised as we saw the sun was sinking behind the mountain.

"I guess we better. There is a lot more fish out here to save for another day."

"Dad, after we show everybody the bass and pickerel, maybe I should let them go. I have three more perch in the live well. Maybe tomorrow, I can give them and this crappie to Jim Carlin. What do you think?"

"I think that will be fine. We have plenty to eat here and we don't want to see these fish go bad."

"Good."

Gramp and my mother came down to the dock to see the fish I had caught. Everybody thought it was a good idea to release the bass and the pickerel. Those two fish were giving me some nasty looks when I opened the livewell in the boat. After much groping and grabbing, I was able to get hold of each fish and return it to the water. I already had three perch in the big floating livewell to which I added two more perch and a crappie.

The sun had now sunk down below the mountain and we all headed up to the cabin to start a fire. Daddy had brought some marshmallows, Campfire Marshmallows, which we planned to toast in the fireplace.

Gramp had fire going in no time at all and we sat close to the smokey opening impaling our marshmallows on the end of thin twigs. The whole idea was to see if you could toast the marshmallow to a light brown color without setting it on fire. One mistake, a little too close to the flame and WHOOSH, the marshmallow would ignite and turn into a black carbonaceous mass. Other times, the marshmallow would get too hot and melt off the stick and fall into the fire.

Gramma sat at the table talking and cutting vegetables for tomorrow's meals, while Gramp read. I didn't hear any more talk about canning. I guess everyone was letting a sleeping dog lay for now.

In a short time the fire died down and us along with it. It was a busy day and bed was a welcome refuge.

I awoke before everyone, except Gramp. He was down at the lake again doing his polar bear thing. Of course he was going out on business this morning and had to be fresh and clean. I still don't know how he could tolerate that cold lake water in the early morning. But, he did.

I was sitting at the table eating some cereal when he came up from his bath.

"Have to get going early, so I can get back early. We have to get your father to the train after supper. I can't wait until this war is over so people can drive again."

Gramp went into the north dormitory, where Gramma was sleeping. A few minutes later he came out in his business clothes with Gramma tagging along behind in her robe.

Instinctively, she headed for the kitchen and began preparing his breakfast.

Maybe it was the smell of bacon cooking, or coffee brewing that woke up my parents because they suddenly emerged from the south dormitory. My sister was still asleep.

"Son," said Gramma. "Would you take this garbage out of the kitchen for me?"

"Sure, Gramma," I replied as I got up to go into the kitchen.

"Also show your father how to burn the garbage in the big drum," Gramp instructed as I went by. "You have to do it when there isn't any wind, or else the embers may fly around and set the woods on fire."

I carried the paper sacks of trash out to the "fire can", as I called it. After depositing the sacks in the can, I noticed something irregular over where I had put the baskets of produce. I could see some of the baskets turned over and moved to different locations.

On closer examination, I could see that the baskets were raided. Most of the peaches were gone or had big bites out of them. Chewed up peppers and cabbage were strewn all over.

"Gramp! Gramp!" I hollered as I ran into the house. "Some animals have raided the peaches and vegetables."

All the adults quickly returned with me to the site of the carnage.

"Looks like bears." My father quipped, as he studied the trail of debris that went up past the car towards the top of the hill. "They are probably sleeping off their meal in that laurel near the top of the hill."

"Those weren't the best peaches, Bill. I hope those bears don't get a stomachache. God knows those animals probably needed a good meal and He spared us from canning bad peaches."

Gramp had nothing to say at her response. But, we all knew the canning was over for this week.

## CHAPTER 21

## GRAMPA'S LAKE – EPILOG

That Thursday was a good day. Gramp took off with his load of preserved food. My mother and Gramma relaxed. They sat out on the porch, or down by the dock enjoying the summer day. Daddy and I followed the bear tracks up to the top of the hill and into the little meadow. They were gone for now, but we knew they weren't far away.

We had an early lunch, after which Daddy and I took the perch, live and in a bucket to Jim Carlin. He showed us his fishponds and then after having a nice conversation with my father, he drove us back to the camp in his truck.

Gramp got back in mid afternoon, so my father and I had time to fish and swim before supper and the ride to Blairstown for the 6:45 train.

Ma and Gramma spent Friday morning cleaning the cabin. This place was probably never cleaned as much in its 33 year history as it was this week.

Then, by 5:30 Friday afternoon, we were back in Elizabeth, N.J., the land of War plants and oil refineries.

Monday morning we were all set to go again. My mother spent practically the whole weekend washing clothes. Eileen's husband Ed, had a problem similar to my father's, as far as time off went and they both were making arrangements to take the train to Blairstown on their day off. This looked like it was going to be a replay of the past week, only the car would have more passengers. My aunt Eileen has a daughter, Patricia, who is the same age as my sister Joyce. Fortunately these girls were small and they didn't take up too much room.

Ma, Aunt Eileen and Gramma didn't can any vegetables this week. Instead, they preserved fruits and made jam and jelly. I believe that it may have been the result of his need to compete in a tough 19th century society, during his early years, that Gramp cultivated his ego. In speaking of himself, Gramp had once said, "I am the smartest man I know..." And this week he got a little smarter. Thanks to some bears, who ruined 5 baskets of fruits and vegetables, he now kept his fruit in Jim Carlin's milk cooling shed and brought the baskets down to the camp when my grandmother needed them.

Gramp, in his own mind might have been the smartest person he knew, but it was only as long as he listened to Gramma.

Before long the week was over and I was back in my neighborhood. School came pretty quick, but the summer memories lingered long after.

Gramp, Mr. Seymour and I would go up to the camp every fall in October. I would rake the leaves from around the building and Gramp would burn them in the fireplace. We would pull the boats out of the water and close the camp for the winter. In the Spring we reversed the process.

Mr. Seymour came with us every time until he died in 1950.

As the years went on and the war ended, our whole family and friends would spend those two weeks at the "Lake" each summer. Gramp would have weekend parties for the men in May and October. Of course they all helped in closing the place for the winter and opening it for the summer.

All of my cousins spent some part of their youth swimming in the lake and participating in the interaction of the family. Since they all came along at different times, each will have different memories of those summers.

These very early years established a family tradition that was somewhat exclusive to the life and times of my grandparents, "Two weeks at Grampa's lake." The place and the situations brought us all together as a family unified under my grandparents. Many times we were unified in our opposition to Gramp and his ideas, like spending two weeks preserving food, or drinking gallons of unpasteurized raw milk. One time we were unified in grief, when the state police came in to inform us of the death of my Uncle Jack's four-year-old daughter, Kathleen.

But most times we were unified in zaniness, like the time Jack had a few beers too many down in Stillwater and mistook the gate into Jim Carlin's hay field for the lane to the camp. My father and I were with him when he drove through two haystacks before realizing he wasn't on the road.

When my cousin Ned got older, he started coming with me and Gramp. One time Gramp bought a potato sack full of beef liver. Ned and I ate beef liver for about four days. We also had to lay all the beef liver out on the kitchen floor and cut it up and package it into parcels for delivery to his daughters and anybody else, who he thought liked liver.

Gramp fancied himself as a great chef. On one trip, he bought a basket of tomatoes with the idea to make his own homemade tomato sauce and serve it to us over linguini and sausages.

He put the tomatoes, whole tomatoes, into a big pot of water and set them to boil on the stove. After the tomatoes had boiled for some time, he mashed them up with a potato masher. Now the pot was full of tomato parts including skins and seeds. He probably threw in a few spices, but they wouldn't have mattered, because he added hot Italian sausage to the mix.

He thought this meal was great when he served it to us. But, it was hardly edible. The sauce was merely spicy hot water with flecks of tomato parts over linguini. The linguini would have been better with nothing on it.

The sausage was really hot beyond anything we were used to. So the next morning Gramp made us pancakes from Bisquick. Just Bisquick and milk, no other ingredients and accompanied by hot Italian sausages. He said the maple syrup made them taste "divine."

Over the course of years, Ned and I had many gastronomical disasters at the hands of our grandfather. It is amazing that we survived.

Gramp made lamb stew one time. We ate it for 3 days. It was a very fatty lamb and then again, maybe it wasn't a lamb at all. Gramp thought something was lacking in the stew, so he added rice. A Lot of Rice. So what we ate over the next three days was more like Lamb Glue than Lamb stew.

Alec McFee, a man of Scotch origin, was a friend of my grandfather's and he started to make trips up to the camp with us. Maybe it was some Scotch tradition or spirit of the Highlands, or whatever that prompted Mr. McFee to make a big gigantic pot of oatmeal every time he came. Ned and I ate so much oatmeal that I thought we were going to turn to stone and sink in the lake.

The War ended and in 1948 Gramp bought a Pontiac Station Wagon with a wood body. This wagon was just what he needed to cart the family produce, Mason jars and everything else up to the lake. A short time later, when I was in High School, I started driving to the camp in my 1937 Chevrolet.

Gramp had retired from the wartime boiler chemical business and now in his mid sixties, he decided to make a career change.

The Newark Star Ledger was a local area newspaper that was interested in growing statewide. Gramp convinced the circulation manager that within two years he could triple their circulation in the northwestern part of the state. The Ledger gave him the job and Gramp enlisted our aid. Every Saturday afternoon I would drive up to the camp with Ned or his cousin Butch, or somebody else and we would meet Gramp. We would have a little time to fish before having supper, then go straight to bed. We would get up around 4 A.M. and drive to a diner somewhere. It could be Augusta, Sparta, Byram, Newton, Oxford, Chester or God knows where and we would meet some other men and boys. All of us had a pancake breakfast, nothing else, just pancakes. At a predetermined time a truck from the Star Ledger would arrive and dump off bundles of Sunday newspapers. These newspapers were loaded into the various cars and we spread out in the predawn, running through rural neighborhoods, waking up every dog in the county, delivering free samples of the Sunday Star Ledger. In the following week, Gramp would return to the area and sell subscriptions to the Star Ledger. We were paid $5 for our efforts each Sunday morning.

"Can you take some more boys with you next week and do Lake Mohawk all by yourself? We'll give you an extra $10." He asked me one Sunday.

"I'm sorry I can't, Gramp. I'm leaving for the Army tomorrow morning."

My grandfather stood still and for the first time I can ever recall, he had nothing to say.

I had left my grandfather's antics to my cousins. They would have to endure his eccentricities for the next several years. I am sure each one has a favorite story of Gramp and GRAMPA' S LAKE.

My Uncle Billy would start laughing and couldn't stop at the mere thought of an event that took place in 1962.

In 1961, Uncle Billy needed someone to assume control of the financial portion of his auto parts business. This was right up Gramp's alley, since he knew the auto parts business and was an accountant. Despite the fact that he was in his mid seventies, he took the job.

Gramp and Gramma moved to an apartment building on Grove Street, Montclair. Gramp had the best of all worlds. He could walk to Uncle Billy's shop on Glen Ridge Ave. and go home for lunch, if he wanted to. He enjoyed what he was doing and at the same time he was collecting his pension and Social Security. He had no restrictions.

One Friday afternoon in October, 1962, Uncle Billy gave me a call at my automotive shop in Rahway, NJ.

"Richard. Your grandfather just called me from up in Stillwater. He wants you to come up to my place and pick up the key to his apartment. He says your grandmother left the food for the weekend on the dumbwaiter. They're up at the camp, with guests and have nothing to eat."

Without making any comments, I said, "OK, I'll be there in about an hour." I made the appropriate arrangements with my employee and my wife and went to Montclair.

Along the way I kept thinking, "The smartest man in the world leaves food on a dumbwaiter and then blames my grandmother. Gramma didn't carry packages and load cars. He did."

The camp wasn't up near the Arctic Circle or some place beyond civilization. There are supermarkets in Andover and Newton. Any number of restaurants can be found within a fifteen minute drive of the camp. Yet, the smartest man in the world can only think to call his grandson, sixty miles away to solve his dilemma.

Uncle Billy came with me and we delivered the groceries to the camp. Gramma and Gramp along with their guests, Mr. and Mrs. Hayes were happy to see us. Gramma fixed us something to eat and then we had to head back.

"Oh boys," said Gramp. "Could you take these sacks back with you?"

"What are they?" I asked.

"Oh, this is the garbage from home; we brought it instead of the groceries."

Gramp lived well into his mid 90's and he continued to be a boss right up to his last day. He didn't like his lunch, so he fired the cook in the nursing home where he lived and then died.

The Mountains and the lake are still there, so is the old camp. Jim Carlin sold his farm around the time the War ended. Gramp wanted to buy the farm, but nobody had any money at that time. It was purchased and cut into various parcels. Jim had envisioned a Country resort on the property extending down to the lake. He was far ahead of his time.

The land and its features will remain until God reclaims the earth. But, the people of my parents and grandparents generation have left us just as the sun goes behind the mountain at the end of the day. Their spirit and memory are kept alive by those of us who remember them in the sunlight of their days.

The world and the things in it continue to change. So our time or times like ours will never come again... And maybe that's how it should be.

## CHAPTER 22

## BATTLES ON THE HOMEFRONT

How quickly the summer ended. Before we could blink an eye, we were back in school preparing for another bleak winter season. It had been a very busy summer and I would often find myself gazing out the window and visualizing the sights and sounds and even the smells of those glorious summer days.

It was the first Spring and Summer here for most of us. Everyone in the neighborhood got to know everyone else. All the boys of the neighborhood were now galvanized into a common little society. Despite the differences in ages, we all worked together in the "victory gardens" and played baseball on the various homemade fields scattered around the area.

With the advent of Fall, came the football season. Our baseball parks now changed into little football stadiums. Except for Arthur, none of us had any football equipment. We played tackle football without any protective equipment. There were plenty of bumps and bruises. But, there never were any broken bones, or other long-term injuries.

When the long shadows of "Indian Summer" set in and the days were warm and the evenings cool, little campfires came to life in the open fields after darkness descended upon the neighborhood. We placed potatoes under the coals of the fire to roast. We also gleaned the gardens throughout the community for last remnants of the harvest season. We usually ended up with a lot of small green tomatoes that never made it to the ripening stage. While our potatoes roasted under the coals, we cooked our green tomatoes on sticks, marshmallow style, over the fire.

Our movements around the fire created grotesque shadows that danced about on the dark ground. Embers shot into the air from the disturbances within the fire, creating a scene reminiscent of primitive ritual and mystery.

It was after all the time of the year when many species started their period of dormancy. The summer foliage was withering and the birds were leaving for warmer climates. The sap would be going down in the trees and little boys would start releasing the pent-up energies generated by the heat and freedom of summer in preparation for a winter of conformity.

The campfires and the wild running games of the night prepared us for the coming end of our season and the final release of our free spirits in one glorious holiday, HALLOWEEN.

The 5 and 10 cent stores downtown, like Woolworth's and Green's had a few factory made costumes. But, most of the costumes we had were homemade and they were supplemented by masks and false faces purchased elsewhere.

The week before the holiday we started our preparations. We carved Jack-O-Lanterns out of anything from a pumpkin to an apple. In school we made black cats with articulating legs and witches on broomsticks. Hand drawn jack-o-lanterns were pasted up in just about every window of the school.

We even learned some Halloween songs to sing in celebration of this autumnal ritual. Songs of witches, black cats and hob goblins, along with the darkening nights worked our imaginations overtime.

The activities around our evening campfires started to get a little more frenzied night by night as we closed in on the "witching holiday." The only damper to our spirits was the sound of the air-raid siren.

"Get those fires out now!" Mr. Wally, the Air-Raid Warden would holler as he charged through the field to observe his area of responsibility.

The cheerful fires now changed quickly into acrid smelly plumes of smoke that wafted through the neighborhood.

"Who urinated on those fires?" Mr. Wally cried. "Do you want to poison everybody with the stench?"

Some voice would always reply, "We put the fire out quick, didn't we?"

Mr. Wally was hampered by the darkness and couldn't identify any of the culprits, who vanished into the cover of trees and bushes. Many of us found our way up to the roof and watched the searchlights scan the skies. Reinforced with our aircraft identification cards, we anxiously waited for Jap Zeros and Mitsubishies, or maybe planes of the German Lufwaffe to come in for the attack. The Standard Oil Refinery in Bayway was a prime target; they would want to hit that. So was the Eastern Aircraft factory, where the fighter planes were made. Some person said Staten Island was a big target. I don't know why, we never went there and I didn't know anyone who did.

We knew that if a real attack came, it would be on Halloween Night. The civil Defense people knew that they would precipitate a war with the kids if they had an Air-Raid Drill on Halloween Night. I'm sure President Roosevelt told them not to have any drills that night. Japs and Germans were enemies enough, never mind starting a war with the kids of this country.

"Ma, what are you going to get to give out for Halloween?"

"I don't know yet, I'll have to see what's available," she would reply to my continuous questioning.

Of course she knew. The women in this neighborhood had an intelligence system as good as anything the Government had. They knew what everyone was giving out for Halloween… And they were sworn to secrecy.

On October 31, we had school as usual in the morning. But, when we went home for lunch, we could return to school in our costumes. The afternoon was party time.

All the kids in the school marched around the schoolyard in their costumes. The teachers selected different kids for prizes, like "The Most Original" or "The Funniest", things like that. I can't remember who won any prizes; I was only interested in the cup cakes and Kool-Aid. Again, the mothers got together and made sure that there were just enough cup cakes and not many extras.

When school ended we went home to wait for "Trick or Treat" time, which was after supper. Little babies could go around with their mothers in the daylight, but school kids, like us had to wait for darkness.

As I remember, it was a bright clear Halloween night. All of the houses and apartments were lit up as gangs of kids roamed the streets. Robert, Chicky and I systematically covered all the buildings in our area. We made mental notes on who was giving out what and passed that information on to other kids we met in our travels.

The adults got into the spirit of the holiday too and they seemed to enjoy it as much as the kids did. The whole day was a deviation from the daily reminder, that we were a nation at war. I often wondered if the Japs and Germans had fun holidays like Halloween. Dressing up and going around collecting things to eat is a lot more fun than a war.

People gave out homemade cookies and cakes, wrapped in tissue paper. There was very little in the way of store-bought candy. The rationing and the lack of confections had already closed the local candy stores and soda fountains. The 5 and 10 cent stores had some candy corn and a few other imitation candies, but nothing else of interest.

"Hey guys, if you go to Mrs. Kluin's house, she'll make you duck for apples, they have money in them! She said there's even a quarter in one," reported a member of a passing group of vagabonds.

"Wow! Let's go try for that quarter," yelped Chicky and we went off on the run to Kluin's house, which was right behind the backstop on the big baseball field.

Sure enough, Mrs. Kluin had a big tub on her kitchen floor full of floating apples. We had to peel back our masks and with our hands behind our backs, we had to select a specific apple then plunge our head into this tub and snare the apple in our teeth. We each were able to get an apple, but mine was the only one with money... a penny. I think that quarter story was made up. Nobody had a quarter to waste.

It was a fun night. Our sacks were full of stuff like apples, cookies, roasted chestnuts, popcorn balls, a few pennies and little cakes wrapped up in orange napkins.

Despite the number of kids in all age groups running through the neighborhood, there wasn't any trouble. There never was. It was like we lived under a code where we looked out for each other, adults as well as children. This was never more evident than on Saturday mornings.

There were four movie theaters in uptown area of Elizabeth. The Regent and the New were on Broad Street, The Ritz was on East Jersey Street and the Liberty was on Elizabeth Avenue. Usually, the bigger guys got together and made the decision regarding which movie would be seen and all the boys in the neighborhood would collect in one huge gang and walk to the movie theater. The group would consist of all ages, third to eighth graders and sometimes a few older guys.

Most of us had a quarter in our pockets. It cost 14 cents to get into the Regent, or the Ritz and 9 cents at the New Theater. The Liberty was 10 or 11 cents, which depended on whether they were having a vaudeville show or a double feature. The vaudeville shows usually consisted of a Dog Act or a Magician.

We weren't usually that interested in Dogs or Magicians. Our tastes gravitated more to the weekly serial segments, like Superman, Tom Mix, or Zorro. The serial playing was the decisive element in our selection process. Theater owners were smart enough not to put some love story or musical on the same bill as a good serial. The kids would desert in favor of an action movie at a competing house and never forgive the management for the faux pas.

The movie industry was keeping up with the War and producing films about the exploits of Americans on all the battlefronts of the world. We were introduced to such heroes as Dana Andrews, Van Johnson, Humphrey Bogart Edward G. Robinson, Ward Bond and John Wayne. Gary Cooper, Randolph Scott and Spencer Tracey also provided the inspiration that would lead us to victory. William Bendix was the guy from Brooklyn in every movie from Guadalcanal Diary to Action in the North Atlantic. Lloyd Nolan and James Cagney and John Garfield gave the enemy trouble at every turn. And, who can forget Tyrone Power as he took his submarine on a Crash Dive in an undersea battle with the enemy?

Each week we fought the War vicariously along with these stars of the silver screen. The movies made us feel good about who we were and fortified our resolve to keep our country free from the foreign oppressors... I guess that's what they were intended to do.

Those Saturday forays to the local movie houses taught us more than Patriotism, we also learned a lot about economics. Most of us had a quarter to go to the movies. If we went to the Regent or Ritz, the price of admission was 14 cents that left 11 cents remaining. A box of Mason Dots or Juicy Fruit from the vending machine cost 5 cents. That left 6 cents remaining, which we would pool to buy Texas Wieners at a little place on Elizabeth Avenue that had a service window at the sidewalk. The foot long Wieners cost 15 cents. That meant each of us could have 4 inches of the Hot Dog for 5 cents. If we went to the New or Liberty theaters, with lower admission costs, we would have enough money to buy a 5-cent soft drink to split and wash the wiener down.

Considering the different ages of all the boys involved in these Saturday outings, I cannot recall a single instance where one of the older boys took advantage of a younger boy. It didn't happen. Not even an extra half-inch bite on a hot dog. Sure everybody was rough and tumble, but the older boys looked out for the younger ones. There was certain cohesiveness in that neighborhood that began with the adults and filtered down through the children and there was always accountability. If you did wrong, you were going to pay for it. Like the time, when the boys were at the movies and "Klinky" was caught after he shot Humphrey Bogart with the slingshot.

The local Police knew everyone in the neighborhood. Other than giving the Air-Raid Warden a hard time, or shooting peas from the trees, there wasn't any crime in the neighborhood. Except for one day, when an episode of national prominence occurred, centered on a toddler, whose family lived in my Aunt's building. The little boy was branded with the letter "A" on his leg.

Police swooped into the neighborhood and rounded up the usual suspects, which were all of us boys. The story made headlines in all the regional newspapers, including the New York Daily News. True Detective Magazine ran an account of this bizarre crime, where some boys took this youngster into the fields and branded him. The Police hovered about, they visited our homes and we even were transported to Police Headquarters for interrogation.

Of course, we all denied having any part in such an act, nor did we see any suspicious strangers in the neighborhood. The Police were having a hard time trying to come up with the item that branded the boy with a large perfect capital letter "A." This investigation went on for a few weeks.

I remember being home on the day Mrs. Mitchell came to see my mother. She had a cake of soap in her hand.

"What does this look like, Alice?" she said holding the cake of soap for my mother to see.

"Why, it's an 'A', just like the one on little Joseph. Where did you find it?"

"I'll show you," she said as she walked over to the steam radiator in our living room. "We had a leaking steam valve on our radiator and after Jim fixed it, I went to clean up his mess. When I wiped the valve down, I saw this 'A' on the back side of the valve."

Using the opposite side of the same cake of soap, Mrs. Mitchell reached behind our radiator valve and pressed the soap against the valve body. A perfect letter "A" had been impressed in the soap. EUREKA!! The crime was almost solved.

Almost solved, because if the letter "A" was on the radiator valve, how did it brand Joseph? Was the plot even more sinister than was earlier believed? Did Joseph's parents brand him as punishment for something, or did his siblings do it? Maybe some sadists broke into their apartment and did the deed. Remember, U.F.O.'s or space aliens hadn't been invented yet, so they couldn't be blamed.

The Police now centered their investigation on the radiator and in due course the case was cracked.

It wasn't a crime and it wasn't a hoax, because Joseph was really branded. It was an accident. Joseph did it himself.

The toddler liked to stand on the stem handle of the radiator valve, which was near the window. From this perch he could watch and interact with the kids playing out side. He apparently slipped from his perch and momentarily wedged his leg between the radiator valve and the wall.

The hot valve burned his skin in that instant. It was no doubt painful for the brief moment when it occurred, but the contact wasn't prolonged and the child was probably distracted from residual soreness by other activities. Only after his mother discovered the burn mark did the story take on the exaggerated proportions that were reported in the press.

Our neighborhood had ended its brief fling with fame and we were able to return to our normal lifestyles of pea-shooters, slingshots and campfires in the fields.

In the latter part of 1942 the American War machine was rapidly developing. But, we still had a long row to hoe. The Axis powers were still dominating the world fronts as we approached the first anniversary of the War. American industrial facilities had made the transition into the production of war materials, often producing products far different from their peacetime pursuits. Women and high school students were entering the work force to replace male workers, who were constantly being called to military service. Individuals had to change their lifestyles by moving to different locales, or by taking new jobs and acquiring different skills for wartime occupations. Personal desires and ambitions had to be put on hold for the duration. However, as a nation we were gaining offensive momentum. In August, U.S. Marines landed on Guadalcanal in the South Pacific. This would be the scene of fierce fighting for the next six months, as we took the War to the Japanese.

On November 8, my Uncle Bill participated with the Naval landing forces as American and British Armies invaded North Africa, beginning the Allied initiative against Hitler.

Here on the American home front, mobilization and production efforts to supply the war materials needed on the world fronts was operating full blast, 24 hours per day. Shortages were rampant and rationing was an accepted, although not a preferred way of life and a source of constant civilian discontent. Our displeasure was directed at the Axis powers, which were responsible for our situation. Cartoons depicting the demise of the Axis leaders were placed on every billboard, telephone pole, and factory bathroom door. People wrote their names on shells and bombs and planes. Every person wanted to special delivery their own personal knockout punch to Hitler and Tojo.

Christmas 1942 was a prime example of the War's impact on our way of life. The profusion of cakes, candies and sweets that we enjoyed in past years, was now a memory. The foods we enjoyed were in short supply. And, forget new toys or decorations. Christmas products, which had been made of metal and glass in prior years, were now being made of wood, paper and cardboard. But, we made do. Old toys were reconditioned and passed on to someone else. My mother made doll's clothes for my sister's dolls, then repainted and refurbished her dollhouse. These gifts looked as good as any store bought items. And, the barter system was in full swing, as people tried to meet the desires of their families by swapping anything from books to baby buggies.

The commercial part of Christmas was severely restricted by the world at War. Blackout conditions prevented lighted displays, stores lacked products, shift work schedules and gasoline shortages prevented anything but local travel. Every family had someone in the service or involved in the war effort somewhere, so there were long lines at the Post Office as Christmas packages full of a little bit of home were sent to those relatives spread around the world.

We were all impacted by a common situation and united in a common effort. Our fondest desires were for peace at home and abroad, the return of our servicemen and women and the return of our pre-war lifestyles. This year the anniversary of the birth of the Prince of Peace took on a new tone. It was not a holiday of parties and merry making, but rather a celebration of hope and prayer. This year was very somber, compared to Christmas seasons of the past.

We were gathered at my grandparents' house on Christmas day for our dinner. The crowd was smaller than past years, but what we lacked in quantity, Gramma made up with quality. Despite shortages and rationing, Gramma could still drive that kitchen stove and produce mouth-watering aromas. I don't recall what we had for dinner that day, but I'm sure the entree did not come through standard channels of procurement. I'm sure the person, who supplied the meat for us to enjoy, was gaining similar enjoyment from Gramp's homemade apple whisky that was provided as a necessary inducement and part of the payment for our meal.

We had finished dinner and the men were sitting in the parlor, waiting for dessert to be served, when a yellow taxicab pulled up outside.

R. Allen Pender

Three men dressed in dark clothes wearing wool hats got out of the taxi and started removing big bags from the trunk of the taxicab. After they had finished; the taxi drove off and the three men, two tall and one extremely short, started up the front walk.

As soon as I got a frontal view of the men, I said, "Hey Gramp! George and Hugh are coming up the front walk."

"WA'll I'll be," snapped Gramp as he looked out the window while heading for the front door.

George and Hugh were my mother's cousins. They were merchant seamen and for the past few years they had been sailing the North Atlantic in those convoys bringing war materials to England and Russia.

Gramp had the front door open before the sailors reached the front steps.

"Hey Pop," hollered Hugh. "Are we on time for dinner?"

"I could smell roast pork as we sailed into New York Bay. And knew right where it came from," exclaimed George.

"Come in, come in. Get out of the cold," Gramp clamored. The group, made their way into the parlor, dropped their baggage and began a series of homecoming greetings as the family members began to fill the room.

Gramma quickly set three places at the dining room table and brought back the main course. The rest of the family sat down for coffee and dessert, as the sailors took places for the dinner Gramma placed before them.

Hugh had introduced the little man accompanying them. His name was Mr. Selman. He was a Russian Jew and they stowed him away aboard their ship, while they were in the port of Murmansk, Russia.

I can only guess what prompted them to do this. They had been sailing in convoys to England and Russia since 1939 and each time they returned, they told us stories about the conditions in Europe. Here, we only knew what the newspapers printed. However, they told us about Hitler and his treatment of Jews and other minorities. These were things beyond comprehension. And, they were eventually determined to be true.

We are a God fearing Christian family, defenders of the faith for untold generations. As descendants of early American settlers, we believed our God and our nation were the sacred authorities in our lives. However, we have a rebellious side to us also. Inbred in us is that same independent spirit that started a nation, rebelled against a King, and later, split the Union.

I'm sure George and Hugh saw their actions as a way to spit in Hitler's face and now they were enlisting our aid to complete the deed. Of course they came with complete confidence in our ability to do so.

Mr. Selman knew little English. He had relatives in Canada and Hugh and George thought my grandfather could use his resources and connections to get

Mr. Selman across the border to his new home. Gramp was willing to help, but it was a project that could take some time considering wartime constraints.

Mr. Selman steadily ate as the continuous bantering around the table centered on his plight. Periodically, he would raise his head from his plate and smile in the affirmative as a reaction to some word he understood. By using a series of words and gestures, Hugh and George would reassure Mr. Selman, that his situation was being addressed. As these exchanges took place, the little Russian man would smile and lightly applauded his benefactors.

Again, all the men adjourned to the parlor, as the ladies cleared the dining room. At my grandfather's direction, I went into the sun parlor and plugged in the Christmas tree. My Grandparents always placed the Christmas tree next to a front window, where it could be seen by people passing by. This year, because of blackout conditions, the tree was placed away from the windows next to the entry to the sun parlor.

Mr. Selman got all excited as the tree came to life. I didn't know if he had ever seen a Christmas tree before this. But, being Jewish and coming from Russia, this could have been something new to him. He came over to where I was standing and began to examine the tree very closely.

He began to touch the various ornaments and presents beneath the tree. Then he straightened up real quick, and with a big smile on his face he said something in Russian and raised his finger to exclaim the point. He then thrust his hand into his pocket and pulled out some paper money. He took the paper money and twisted it up on one end and flared it out on the other end. I began to get the idea as Mr. Selman leaned over and tried to attach the money to a branch on the tree.

Suddenly, the tree began to move and Mr. Selman with it. Within a split second Mr. Selman and the lighted tree were prone on the floor. The poor man didn't know what had happened and was in a state of shock when Gramp and I picked him up off the floor. I picked up the tree, which wasn't really damaged from the episode. However, Mr. Selman was ranting and raving in Russian and was offering my grandfather money in what appeared to be an apologetic offering. He apparently thought he had damaged a religious icon and was willing to pay for his redemption.

Gramp assured him that everything was all right and then he fixed Mr. Selman a drink of home made liquor and we made a few jokes and laughed at the incident to let him know that he didn't break any laws or hurt our feelings. I got some string from my Grandmother's junk drawer in the kitchen and then I found and tied Mr. Selman's paper money onto the Christmas tree. I could see that made him happy. His debut in America was pretty auspicious, and his gift was placed on our tree.

Gramp had a Jewish friend named Maxie and he had placed a call to him while the men were eating. Maxie was well connected into the Jewish community in Newark and he obviously made a few phone calls after receiving Gramp's call, because soon Maxie and another man arrived at the house. The man with Maxie could speak Russian. Mr. Selman lit up brighter than our Christmas tree when that man spoke to him in Russian. His reaction was one of pure wonder; like a little child seeing his first 4th of July fireworks display or Birthday cake. Mr. Selman was beaming from ear to ear as he talked with that man.

When he first arrived at my grandparent's house, Mr. Selman was cautiously reserved, sticking to George and Hugh like glue. I couldn't blame him. He came from a place where nobody could be trusted. Why should he trust us? Why did he trust two American seamen, who weren't Jewish and didn't speak Russian? Why was he willing to risk his life stowed away on a freighter crossing U-Boat infested waters? Like the Jews of the Exodus, I'm sure Mr. Selman had a lot of second thoughts about this whole episode. But now all his apprehension was gone and his faith and courage were rewarded, as he was delivered to the modern day Promised Land on the birthday of our Jewish born, King of Kings.

Gramp's call had triggered a reaction in the Jewish community and they were prepared to handle situations like this. They would provide Mr. Selman with a place to stay and they would arrange and oversee his travel to Canada.

Maxie and the Jewish man sat and talked with the men of my family for some time. It was an education for me as I heard the stories concerning world situations from the people involved. I saw the people involved. One even fell into our Christmas tree. This evening's events made the war real to me.

I saw a man liberated and made free. Mr. Selman had attached a face and a personality to the victims of war. They weren't just pictures in Life magazine or the Newsreels. They were real people; people who could come into our house and eat at our table and yes, even knock over our Christmas tree.

Finally, it came time for Maxie and his friend to leave with Mr. Selman.

"Bill, we're sorry to take up so much of your time on your Christmas holiday."

"Maxie, that's what this day is for, to share the hope and joy we have in Jesus, The Prince of Peace."

"Well, your family certainly gave a wonderful gift to a Jewish man and his people this Christmas... Shalom!"

"Merry Christmas, Maxie, Merry Christmas. We're glad we could help."

One year ago, we were provoked by the savage attack of the Japanese Imperial Navy and now a victory medal in the form of a Russian Ruble hangs from the Christmas tree. We won a very small battle in a great war. One man was freed from the oppressor. Millions more like him had to be freed before this war would end. But, today was exciting. That the gift of freedom could be bestowed on a refugee of war on Christmas is miraculous. What a way to celebrate.

Over the next few months Mr. Selman became a periodic visitor. He was a furrier by trade in Russia. But, here we were in need of defense workers and since Mr. Selman was an illegal alien, he had no papers to get a job. So, he was established in a little business of renovating and restyling fur coats, while he awaited transportation to Canada.

Before the Depression started, my grandfather bought my grandmother and his daughters fur coats. Somehow, Gramp made arrangements with Mr. Selman to restyle these coats and in due course he came to our home to measure my mother and get her coat.

My mother had a full-length leopard skin coat. She hadn't worn it in years, because it was too long and didn't conform to the styles of the late '3Os and early '4Os. Mr. Selman took the coat after convincing my mother that he knew the latest styles and would fashion the coat to her specifications.

Near the end of winter Mr. Selman returned with the finished product. He had cut the coat and shaped it to her liking and even had enough material left to make a pill box type of matching hat. My mother was thrilled with her "new" coat and wore it everywhere from late Winter to Spring.

Ma was active in the P.T.A. at school and helped in the art class. We didn't have a full time Art Teacher and my mother was trained in that field. Ma loved to wear her coat and hat to school for the various meetings and days of teaching... And I think she wanted to show off a little.

It didn't go unnoticed.

Our usual route home from school took us out the school gate and around the back of the vacant store building and up through the yard behind Cotton's Gin Mill. The colored kids, who lived down on Washington Avenue usually walked straight up Edgar Road to Washington Avenue. Generally, there was never any trouble. But, on this particular day, something went array.

Apparently, someone in our group had made a comment to someone in their group, or visa versa, as the two groups converged before going their separate ways. While the respective parties were exchanging insults, I heard someone say.

"Yeah, And there is that Pendell boy, his mother is a Nazi."

"Who said that?" I shouted, quickly turning to face the crowd.

"I did," said a boy named Walter Samuel, from the ungraded class. "Your Mama wears a leopard coat like Rommel. She must be a Nazi and you one too."

This was something I couldn't take. My family members were serving this country at all points on the globe and this guy calls my mother a Nazi.

"You better take that back, else were going to have some serious fightin' to do."

"I take nothin' back," he scowled. "You make me."

That response ignited my fire and we went at it. The kids formed a big circle around Walter and I, who were now locked in combat.

I don't know how long we fought, but it had to be broken off because everyone had to go home.

The fight was resumed the next day after school and lasted a total of three days after school.

When we met on the field of honor for the fourth day of the conflict, Walter said, "I can't fight today, my mama wants me home early. Besides, I think you fight too good to be a Nazi."

Walter never directly took back his statement about my mother. But, that was all right. We knew who won the fight and we both departed the field with our honor intact.

We used to avoid the Washington Avenue neighborhood when we went to the movies. Someone would always have a comment for our group when we marched through their neighborhood.

The next time we went to the movies, we paraded right down Washington Avenue. This time someone standing along the way said, "There goes that Pendell boy, the one Walter Samuel couldn't beat."

## CHAPTER 23

## THE OUTSKIRTS

Cities always interested me. Why are they located where they are? Who came there first and why? We know cities didn't just one day pop up where nothing had previously existed. There had to be some rhyme or reason behind their development. Elizabeth was a funny kind of a city. It had its central business area, with a tall courthouse and a tall office building called, The Hersch Tower, located on Broad Street. There was the Port area fronting on the Arthur Kill. The Port had its own shopping area along First Street and it was connected to the center of the city by Elizabeth Avenue on the south side and East Jersey Street in center. East Grand Street made the northern connection. A little more than a mile and a half separated First Street in the Port from Broad Street.

The central city was surrounded by a U shaped road that began at the Arthur Kill, on the south side of the city. At this point it was called Bayway Avenue. This road made the connection to the Goethals Bridge, connecting New Jersey to Staten Island, New York. Bayway Avenue's leg of the U was interrupted by its intersection with U. S. Route 1 at that notorious New Jersey invention, the traffic circle. West of the Bayway Circle, the road became South Elmora Avenue. After South Elmora Avenue crossed the road to Rahway, aptly called Rahway Avenue, the name of the street became just plain Elmora Avenue.

Between Jersey Avenue, which went to the town of Roselle and Westfield Avenue, which went to the town of Westfield, Elmora Avenue had it's own shopping district, including a movie theater. On the other side of Westfield Avenue, the road's name changed again. From this point until it's terminus at the Elizabeth Dumps on the other side of U.S.1, near Newark Airport, it is called North Avenue.

The curved part of the U shaped road entered the Townships of Union and Hillside before its final leg down to the Elizabeth meadows and the dumps. The bulk of the city was confined within this looping road. The city developed from the center of the loop outward, with rural and semi-rural undeveloped pockets still exiting inside and outside the bounds of the road.

Within the loop there is a myriad of neighborhoods, each with their own character and basic ethnic background. More often than not, the areas are identified with an ethnic Catholic Church, which reflects the makeup of the community.

The north side of the Port section, near the Singer Sewing Machine Factory, is mostly Polish located in Saint Adalbert's Parish. The central port area had been and still is predominantly Irish in Saint Patrick's Parish. Their neighbors to the south live in an area called Frog Hollow on the north bank of the Elizabeth River. A lot of people in Frog Hollow are of Polish or Slavic ancestry. A good portion of this neighborhood is consigned to the Elizabethtown Gas Company for their Gas plant and storage tank.

From the south bank of the Elizabeth River to the Linden meadows and west to U.S. 1 was the Bayway section. There are a lot of people of Polish or Slavish ancestry. Their church is Saint Hedwigs. Situated northwest of Frog Hollow and bounded by Elizabeth Avenue in the east, Spencer Street on the south. The Elizabeth River on the west and South Street on the north is Peter's town, or the "Burg." This is an Italian neighborhood centered on Saint Anthony's Church.

Between Elizabeth Avenue and East Grand street, just east of Route 1, is Saint Michael's Parish. At one time this area was a solid German community. Even though other people have gradually moved into the area, some vestiges of German culture still exist. There are still some German merchants in the area to go along with the Alexian Brothers Hospital and Saint Marks Lutheran Church. The Kerihead Irish community was established east of Route 1 between the railroad tracks separating East Grand Street from Magnolia Avenue. Sacred Heart Church on Route 1 is the focal point of this community, which extends north to North Ave.

The North Elizabeth section extends to the Newark border on the north and the Hillside border in the west. A large portion of the community, west of Route 1 off North Avenue is largely Irish in its makeup. The Blessed Sacrament Church at North and Adams Avenues and Saint Catherine's Church on North Broad Street divided the faithful between them.

The Westminster neighborhood off Salem Avenue near the Hillside border is composed of large upper income homes. The Pingry School, a prep-school for boys is located in that area, as is the Elizabeth Town and Country Club.

West of North Ave and north of Westfield Avenue is the Townley section. Union Township forms the northern boundary of this upper income single family home section. This is Saint Genevive's Parish, an area of established families, with no ethnic identification.

The Elmora section is on the south side of Westfield Avenue. A large Jewish community resides in this area. Not that it is exclusively a Jewish section, but a greater number of Jewish people live here than appeared to live in other areas of the city.

Our neighborhood is in Saint Mary's Parish in South Elizabeth. We are squeezed in between Bayway on the South, Elmora on the north and the city of Linden on the west. It appears that some Irish families originally moved to this area from Elizabethport. They farmed this area, which they called "Quality Hill." This neighborhood is on the outskirts of the city.

Many of the streets in the area have yet to be paved. We even have a small cemetery, St. Mary's Cemetery, where Washington Avenue ends and Edgar Road begins.

Ours is a relatively new neighborhood when compared to the established sections of the city. There are multi family buildings housing the people coming into the area from other regions of the country. Many of these buildings were built during and after the World War I era, just a scant twenty plus years ago.

Our school is Woodrow Wilson, School 19, the latest school built in the city. George Washington, School 1, is in the original port settlement of the city. So, as a rule of thumb, the school numbers reflected the growth of the various sections of the city. Also, our neighborhood still had a lot of vacant land.

Three short blocks after crossing South Elmora Avenue, Lidgerwood Avenue becomes Linden Avenue, Linden. The Lidgerwood Hoist Company is on one side of the street and the Morey La Rue Laundry is on the other side of the street. After those companies, it is a wilderness of bull rushes and cattails along a dirt road for almost two miles to Wood Avenue, Linden. There are two cemeteries between Linden Avenue and Route 1, in Linden, near Wood Avenue.

U.S. Route 1 forms the border for the east side of this swamp area and the Pennsylvania Railroad forms the western boundary. On the opposite side of Route 1, cows graze in pastures along the northbound side of the single lane highway right up to the ever-expanding property of the Standard Oil Bayway Refinery.

Lambert's Dairy Farm is on the other side of the Railroad tracks and Juzefyk's Livery stable is just north of our school on Edgar Road, next to Saint Mary's Cemetery. The horses that live there graze in the cemetery, in Mr. Ives field on Edgar Road and in the big field in front of our house. Every so often the horses would run behind our house to the fields along New York Avenue. What ever would set them off, I don't know, but all of a sudden they would take off across the street and run right up our driveway.

Cattle grazed and corn grows where North Avenue touches the Union and Hillside town limits. As it goes into Hillside, North Avenue crosses Ursino Lake, which belongs to the Elizabethtown Water Company. Once it was the reservoir and the prime source of water for the city. It may have become obsolete as the city grew, but it sill is there and is a haven for wildlife.

Elizabeth is a compact city, as far as cities go. There are four Junior High Schools that feed one High School for Boys, one High School for girls and one Vocational High School. So there is a pretty good chance of eventually knowing almost every boy in the city in your age group.

I guess, if I had to pick a city to live in during this period, Elizabeth would be a pretty good choice. We have the best of all worlds despite the circumstances and the fact that the choice wasn't ours.

Boys love swamps, woods, other people's fruit trees, roofs, places to swim, places to fish, places to play ball and other people's gardens. We had it all and then some. The only problem we have is transportation.

Bicycles are in long in demand and short in supply. Even if your parents had the money, a bicycle could not be had. Robert, Chicky and I resurrected a couple of pre-war bicycles. These bicycles might have even been pre-World War I models. One bicycle has balloon tires, a manufacturing style that came on the market in the 1930's. The other bike is a girl's model with skinny tubeless tires.

We constantly have flat tires. The balloon tire isn't as bad as that tubeless tire. At least the balloon tire has a tube, which can be patched. Right now there are more patches showing on that tube than there is tube showing. The rubber is dry rotting and becoming porous. The tubeless tires are in much worse shape. For one thing they're older. The only way they can be patched is with a metal plug, which has to be feed fed through the leaking spot into the inside of the tire. A piece screws from the outside into this metal plug creating a seal. I think we spend more time fixing these bicycles than riding them. Each time, as we work on the bicycles, we make outlandish plans for trips to exotic places on these two-wheeled stallions. Unfortunately, the repairs are usually short lived and after a day two we're back fixing the machines again.

The "shoe leather express" is the most reliable of all the modes of transportation. It isn't always the most pleasant, especially on rainy or snowy days. In combination with the number 44 bus, we can make safaris out to Linden Pool and to Jackson's Pond out behind Winfield Park. The Old Mill beside the Rahway River in Cranford is another favorite attraction and the prime camping and swimming area is a hike away at the Reservoir in Clark. The 44-bus fare is 5 cents each way. So for 10 cents apiece and a good pair of shoes, we can escape the fringe of the city and roam the hinterlands of Union County.

For urban travel, primarily for errands, the scooter is a pretty efficient mode of travel. It is constructed of a wooden milk crate attached to a 2 by 4. One half of a roller skate is attached to the front of the 2 by 4 and the other half attached to the rear of the 2 by 4. The scooter is well adapted for down hill travel on paved roads. The range of the scooter is limited. The A and P at South Street and Washington Avenue is the outer limit of its range, because the return trip is mostly up hill.

We nailed orange crates onto the scooter over the rear set of wheels. This enables us to pick up groceries or perform other errands as needed and paid for by people in the neighborhood. We work for tips. Every so often, someone will have an order too large for one scooter. In that case two and sometimes three scooters are dispatched to complete the errand. Afterward the tip is split three ways. Scooters are a pretty good mode of cheap transportation, but the metal skate wheels make them as noisy as a locomotive. We can never sneak up on an enemy while using a scooter. We need a tactical vehicle that can coast down hill and ride up hill with a minimum of effort; a vehicle that can carry a small load, be quiet and is easy to store. A bicycle fits the description, but none are available, so we have to come up with something else.

On those long dark winter days, when we are confined due to foul weather, we hang out in the basement of the building. Mr. Mitchell has big workbench set up down there. We use it as a place to make model airplanes.

The model kits cost 10 cents and include plans, balsa wood pieces and tissue paper to cover the model plane. Using a razor blade and glue, called Dope, we cut and glue the various pieces outlined on the plan. Slowly the skeleton of an airplane takes shape. Finally, all the parts are assembled and the tissue paper skin covers the frame. A power plant, consisting of a rubber band and a propeller is installed. The rubber band is attached to the fuselage near the tail and is stretched slightly as it passes through the fuselage and is then attached to the propeller shaft, which is nothing more than a piece of wire hooked onto the propeller. The finished product is now ready for a test flight.

The planes flew. Not far, but they flew. It took longer to wind up the rubber band than it did for the band to unwind when it was released.

We thought that by releasing the planes from the garage roof they would fly further. They did. Even though the rubber band driven propeller stopped, the planes had a longer glide path.

"Hey, these planes probably could fly across the garages, if we flew them off the roof," Robert commented, pointing to the top of our building.

Chicky and I scanned the projected flight path and simultaneously nodded our approval.

"We can make little paper men and put them in the airplanes and give them a ride," Chicky excitedly commented.

"Hey, yeah, this is a good idea. Let's do it," I responded.

We gathered up our planes and headed for the roof. Chicky stopped by his apartment to get some paper and a scissor to make little men.

When we got out on the roof, it was a lot colder and the breeze was a lot stronger, compared to the garage roof. We slipped through the wood frame railing surrounding the clothes drying platform and walked across the roof deck to the short parapet wall that encircled the building. Now, at about 25 feet from the ground, we could see our goal, the garden behind the garages.

"If we wait for the wind to come from behind us, it will help the planes go further," Robert interjected, as he surveyed the situation.

Commenting on his profound statement, I said, "Let's put a paper flag up by the clothes lines, then we can tell which way the wind is blowing."

Chicky, who was busy making little men to fly the planes, got up and stuck apiece of paper into a split in one of the uprights supporting the laundry lines.

"That should do it," he said, returning to his little men. "I have these guys ready to fly," he said, holding up a pair of paper figures, "Let's put them in the planes."

"We should give them names," Robert replied. "So we know who is flying our planes."

"O.K." I replied. "What is your man's name, Robert?"

"I'm going to call my man Tom Bill."

"Tom Bill!" exclaimed Chicky. "That's two first names. How can a person have two first names?"

"Well, Tom and Bill were two neighbors of ours in Pennsylvania. They worked in the mines. They were neat guys. I want to name my man after both of them."

That sounded reasonable enough for me. I didn't care what his name is, as long as he can fly the plane.

"What is your guy's name gonna be, R.A.?" asked Chicky.

"I'm gonna call my guy Joe Biddy."

Both Robert and Chicky came back in unison with the same question. "Who is Joe Biddy?"

"Joe Biddy is nobody, it's an expression. Down south young guys, who don't know what their doin', are called young peckerwoods. When they get older and still don't know what their doin', Church goin' people call them Joe Biddys. Up here people call those kind of people "dumb S.O.B.'s. I figure anyone goin' in these little planes has got to be a dumb Joe Biddy."

Joe Biddy and Tom Bill were placed in their respective aircraft. The propellers were turned to wind up the rubber bands. Holding the propellers, Robert and I held the planes steady on the roof parapet.

"Let us know when the wind is right," we hollered to Chicky, who was monitoring our impromptu windsock.

"Let them go!!" he suddenly yelled and dashed over to the launch site.

Robert and I released the propellers and the two little aircraft grabbed hold of the air and started off on their mission. They flew out straight until the rubber bands unwound and the props stopped. The planes then started on a downward glide towards the garages.

The slight tailwind carried the planes to the front edge of the garage, where they hit and fell to the ground.

We raced down the stairs from the roof to the backyard and then out to crash site.

There was some damage to each of the planes, but it wasn't severe enough to cancel the program. We retrieved our aircraft and brought them down to Mr. Mitchell's workbench for repairs. We would repeat this scenario many times as we made subsequent flights in our effort to have the planes clear the garage roof.

Finally, we came up with a combination of propeller and rubber band that gave these planes enough power to clear the garage roof.

As we continued our aircraft research with these little models, we began to think on a larger scale. What would prevent us from making a model that one of us could actually fly?

"I got a book for Christmas last year. It has instructions on how to fly an airplane," I said to my fellow aviators. It was true; my Uncle Ed had given me a book called, "Flying and How to Do It," by a man named Assen Jordanoff.

This is a good book. It has every thing anyone needs to know, if they want to fly an airplane. Back before the War, Ed and his friends had an airplane. It was a World War I surplus airplane. The plane had two wings and two open cockpits. I'm sure they used this book to learn how to fly.

I remember sitting in that airplane out at the little airfield where it was parked. That plane could fly for about ten miles before it had to land and have the radiator refilled with water. Most times, Ed and his friends would just takeoff, fly around in a circle and land. We could probably build an airplane like that one, especially with this book, that can teach us everything.

Each day after school, I brought the book down to the basement. Each of us would take turns reading and looking at the cartoon type illustrations.

"If we build this plane, who is going to fly it?" Chicky asked.

"I can," I replied. "I have a leather aviator's cap that my Uncle wore under his racing helmet."

"You can fly first," said Robert. "Because it's your cap, but maybe we can see if the cap fits us and we can choose who goes second."

"O.K., but we need stuff to make the airplane first."

"I heard the bigger guys say that they got wood for their forts and things from the trash over at the Wilson-Jones company," Robert contributed.

"Let's get a wagon and go over there and see what they got," chimed Chicky.

We didn't know what we needed, so we trooped over to Wilson-Jones to see what was available.

They had a big trash pile outside their receiving dock. In the trash was a lot of cardboard, waxy paper and wood from packing cases.

"Hey mister!" Chicky hollered to the man working inside the open dock door. "Can we have some of this wood laying out here?"

"Go ahead take what you want, but, don't make a mess," he answered.

We got busy and dug into the pile. Before long we had a big pile of packing case wood loaded on top of our little wagon. It took one guy pulling and the other two keeping the load stabilized on the wagon to get the wood moved. We struggled when we had to move over rough ground, but for the most part, the trip wasn't too bad.

Over the next few days, we pulled and straightened the nails from the packing crates. The pieces of wood were separated by size, although we didn't know what sizes we were going to use.

The plans from one of the model planes would be used to make our air frame. Of course we would have to adapt those plans to the materials we had available.

A great deal of time was expended on securing the raw materials necessary to manufacture this airplane.

"Look what I found," said Chicky hauling in a wire bound orange crate. "This might make a neat cockpit."

After taking turns sitting in the orange crate, we agreed that with a few modifications the crate would make a good cockpit.

Robert found a big baby carriage that someone had thrown away. The fabric part of the carriage was shot, but it had a real strong under carriage supporting the four wheels. It would defiantly support our plane.

Gradually, over the winter, the airframe began to take shape. From time to time, we would return to Wilson-Jones for more wood and we continually scrounged the neighborhood for any other useable materials.

We made the fuselage and wings in different sections, so we could get the pieces out of the cellar door.

The model airplane plans called for the wing to be above the fuselage. We had many discussions concerning the wing location. Would the fuselage hang below the wing, like a small observation plane, or would the fuselage sit on the wings, like the new fighter planes. It was clear that our plane would not have the horsepower like the current fighter models. We didn't even have an engine yet... Even if we did find an engine, we couldn't get gasoline. First, because it was rationed and second, we didn't have any money to buy it, even if it was available.

Our flying book helped us make the decision. A wing above the fuselage might have an effect like a kite and we would need less horsepower. That was good, because we didn't have any horsepower any way.

Very few people were driving cars, or even had cars, since rationing began. The row of garages behind the buildings was made to accommodate the cars of the tenants. The decline of the automobile population gave rise to some vacant garages. We picked out one and moved our frame sections in for final assembly.

According to our flying book, older aircraft were covered with a painted fabric skin. We didn't have any fabric and maybe we could use some of Mr. Mitchell's old house paint, if he was in a good mood. But, this was wartime. We would have to do like the rest of the country and develop a substitute skin covering.

Chicky was right on top of the situation and made this suggestion. "What about all that brown shinny paper over at Wilson-Jones? It's a lot thicker than the paper we use for the model planes. It might make a good skin. What do you think, R.A.?"

"It's worth a try. It sort of beats anything we have, which is nothing. And we probably can make it stronger with paint."

"Let's take the wagon and this old baby carriage over there and load up," Came Robert's response.

The trip to the factory scrap pile was fruitful. Not only did we come back with a load of brown paper, but we also found some strapping material that could come in handy.

Since the garages had no heat or light, we could only spend a little time each day after school and on Saturdays, assembling the airplane.

Towards the end of January, the thaw came and with it, the promise of Spring. The fields and garden areas were soft and gushy. Only clumps of brown grass tied the earth together. Water would squish out underneath our feet as we moved from clump to clump. It was approaching the best time of the year for our first test flight. The winds of February and March would soon begin to dry out the soft wet ground. And it is our intention to have a soft landing.

The brown paper was working out real good. It was surprisingly tough and we could cut and fit it to the various sections of the plane. We found some roofing nails that had big heads; they were used to attach the paper the frame. The moving parts, like the rudder and the elevator on the tail section were a little more difficult to deal with and for now anyway, we decided to do without ailerons. We might put them on later, if we get to powered flight, but for now we were having enough trouble with the elevator and the rudder.

I removed my slingshot making materials from their hiding place. We cut pieces of inner tube and used them to make strap hinges for the rudder and the elevator. Old clothesline we had found was used for control cables. There wasn't enough room to run the control cables inside the fuselage, so we ran them along the outside of the fuselage to the rudder and elevator.

We did find enough money to buy some large hook eyes to guide the lines along the side of the aircraft. Surprisingly, the rudder and elevator worked. Not perfect, but they worked well enough for our planned test glide.

The final assembly onto the wheels and under carriage will take place on the garage roof, the day of the flight. Meanwhile, we felt that we needed to build some type of power assist to launch the bird from the roof.

This last detail had us stumped for quite some time. We thought about building a wooden incline for the plane to roll down. We didn't feel that the plane would get enough launch speed that way.

"Too bad they don't make real big rubber bands, and then we could have a wind up propeller," complained Chicky.

"That's it," I shouted. "We can make a big rubber band and have it work like a slingshot."

"How are we gonna do that?"

"Here, I'll show you," I said, picking up a section of inner tube from the slingshot supplies. "We cut across the tube and we'll get bands. Then we slip one band through another and then back through itself and we keep doing this for as long a band as we want."

"Oh! That's the way they made belts in the Cub Scouts," Chicky said, now understanding the theory.

"I guess were gonna need a lot of inner tubes," Robert interjected. "There's a junk yard in Linden over the other side of Dark Lane Bridge. Maybe we can get some more tubes there."

"We can look in all these garages, too. There might be some around here," Chicky suggested.

"On Saturday morning we can go over to that junk yard, but, let's look around the neighborhood first," I chimed.

That day we looked in some of the unlocked garages and did find five inner tubes.

Out of the 32 apartments in the four buildings, there were only 7 cars in operation. We let our need be known to all the neighbors, especially the ones with cars. For whatever rhyme or reason, all the car owners had saved their used inner tubes. By the end of the week and before we went to the junkyard, we had 19 tubes.

Arriving at the junkyard on Saturday morning, with our wagon in tow, we addressed the man working there, "Mister, do you have any inner tubes that you don't need."

"Where are you guys from, the Boy Scouts, or something?"

"Yes, sir," said Robert. "We're collecting things for the Scouts to make Christmas presents for the men in Service."

"Christmas! It's been over for a couple of months."

"Next Christmas," said Robert. "It takes a lot of time to make and get these presents around the world."

"I guess it will," the man answered. "O.K., go over in that side of the yard." The man said pointing to a location near the railroad tracks. "Anything you find over there, you can have."

"Thank you, Sir," we answered in unison and we scampered off in the direction he indicated.

"How did you think up such a crazy story?" I questioned Robert, when we reach our scavenging location.

"I didn't. The man did. I just played along with him."

Chicky couldn't keep from laughing. As a matter of fact, he was almost hysterical.

"Cut it out Chicky!" we commanded. "Hearin' you, that man is gonna know he's been fooled and he'll sic his dogs on us."

Suddenly Chicky ceased his hysterics. "What dogs? I don't see any dogs."

"Dummy, all junk yards have dogs. Where have you been?" charged Robert.

"Alright guys. I'm sorry. Let's look for inner tubes."

Once we got about our business, we discovered that the junkyard was a veritable gold mine of interesting stuff. Chicky spent more time picking up and examining useless stuff, than he did looking for inner tubes.

"Chicky, don't bother us with that stuff. If you find an engine we can use, O.K. but, otherwise look for inner tubes," I retorted.

We concluded our expedition with a full load of inner tubes. We even found some truck inner tubes. It was a successful week. We had enough inner tubes to make probably the largest rubber band in the world.

The better part of the next two weeks was spent cutting and weaving this huge rubber band.

Things were really coming together. The days were now clicking off towards Easter and fair weather. We got more excited with each passing day, while we waited for the right weather conditions for the flight.

As a nation we were making advances against the Axis powers, as the Spring of 1943 approached. American and Allied forces were pushing Rommel and his Italian partners across North Africa. The Japanese advance had been stopped in the Pacific. Admiral Nimitz's fleet in the Pacific was gradually growing as new fighting vessels and aircraft carriers were being churned out of our ship yards. They were set to be manned by the steady stream of citizen soldiers and sailors now being prepared in the training camps around the country.

From his base in Australia, General MacArthur has formed a team with the Australians that would start his drive back to the Philippines. Combined Army, Navy and Marine operations began the assault on Japanese held islands in the Pacific, while increased Naval and submarine presence in the Atlantic reduced the previously effective Nazi wolf packs.

In a little more than a year and a half the energies of this country have begun to bear fruit. The morale and resolve of the people in the factories and the fields of this country could never have been at a higher level. We knew what it would take to win the War and crush the oppressors. We also knew that it wasn't easy and that even if victory wasn't around the corner, it was within sight.

Despite a situation that prevented us from having those accouterments consistent with youth, like; candy, cookies, ice cream and bicycles, we were also caught up in that spirit that made us Americans feel invincible. If Jimmy Doolittle could take off and bomb Japan from the pitching deck of an aircraft carrier and Americans could produce materials that our men were using in the four corners of the world to defeat the enemy, then it shouldn't be any problem for us to launch our airplane from the garage roof.

The gradually warming days and longer hours of sunlight provided us the opportunity to speed our work in preparation for the launch. The warming weather also triggered the gardening instincts in some of the older neighbors. Charlie and some of the older boys turned over the soil in the garden behind the garage. They also raked it out and spread lime on the surface. Continued thawing and early Spring rains will work the lime deep into the soil. Charlie also rebuilt the manure piles along side the garden. This past fall, after the harvest, he threw all the spent vegetable plants and vines on the manure piles and turned them under. The winter had done its work on this compost pile and it was now ready to fertilize this year's crops.

The rubber band we had made from the used inner tubes was almost 20 feet long. We planned to tie one end to a clothesline pole on the front side of the garages and the other end to a telegraph pole on the backside of the garages. These two poles were not lined up with each other, but that was all right since the angle created by the offset poles would direct the plane across the flat garage roof towards the path that ran across the garden at 9 degrees to the garages. To the left of this path was the soft soil of the garden and to the right were two of Charlie's manure piles. The path would make an ideal landing strip for our flight.

"Are we going to test the catapult?" Chicky asked, after the band was tied to the poles.

"Of course," replied Robert. "We don't know which way this thing is goin' to shoot off the plane."

"We need something to substitute for the airplane, so we can test the launcher," I contributed.

"Let's practice with the baby buggy part that is gonna be used for the airplane wheels," came a suggestion from Robert.

"Good idea," I said. "It'll be almost like usin' the plane itself."

It became a pretty tedious chore that we chose. Each time the baby buggy under carriage was shot off the roof, one of us had to climb down the pole, retrieve the piece, tie a rope on it, climb back up the pole and all three of us would then haul the wheeled section back onto the roof for another attempt.

Our efforts did not go without reward. We did develop consistency in our catapult. We knew the exact spot on the band to load the carriage and the right amount of pull on the band to exert the necessary force for a trajectory to the garden path. If it worked with the carriage, it should work for the plane. We painted white spots on the band and on the roof mark our loading a pulling points.

We were ready for the real thing. Manned flight off the roof.

We had a half-day of school on the Thursday before Easter and would be out of school the entire next week. We planned to make the first flight on Saturday morning. This was good, because we had all day Friday to get the plane sections ready. The fuselage was all assembled. We had to install the wings and under carriage and that work would be done up on the roof, Saturday, before the flight.

Chicky had a million and one questions concerning the airplane. "How high do you think it can go? Do you think it will fly all the way to New York Avenue? Do you guys think that each of us can have a plane of our own?"

"Sure, Chicky," Robert replied. "We'll probably have our own Air Force."

"We'll have to get more flying caps, because R.A. is the only one who has a flying cap."

"Well Chicky, I think if we can make an airplane, I think we might be able to make flying caps too," I responded.

It was a good thing that the plane was in sections, because if it were one piece, we wouldn't get it up on the roof.

The assembly was moving along very smoothly that Saturday morning. The fuselage and the under carriage were located on the paint marks. The band had been stretched to its proper place and was tied to a bracket that we had put into the roof deck.

We just started to install the wings, when two wagons, each pulled by a single horse, came up the garden path from New York Avenue.

"That's just what we need now, more horse manure," Robert intoned.

We continued on with our project and attached the wings as the manure was off loaded onto Charlie's pile.

"As soon as those horses leave we'll fly the plane," I said as I climbed into the cockpit and pulled my goggles down over my aviator's cap.

The two wagons had deposited their loads on Charlie's compost pile and then turned back and started to exit in the direction they had come. As we were watching the horses and their wagons depart, a loud booming voice shattered the morning calm.

"WHAT ARE YOU KIDS DOIN' ON THAT ROOF! GET DOWN FROM THERE, RIGHT NOW!"

It was Mr. Mitchell at his booming best. Next he was joined by Charlie, who had come to inspect his manure.

"You boys better come down before you get hurt," he calmly said.

"We'll be down as soon as we launch our airplane," Robert advised.

"You Kids can't fly an airplane off the roof of a garage. Who is in that thing?" Charlie asked.

"R.A.," answered Chicky. "He's the only one who has a cap."

While Charlie was trying to talk us off the roof, Mr. Mitchell was alerting parents. Soon Robert's mother and Chicky's mother were at their kitchen windows.

"Get off that roof right now," they commanded their respective sons.

The noise and commotion brought other people to their windows and into the back yard.

We were running out of time. If we didn't get off the roof soon, we were going to be in trouble for disobeying, our parents and the other adults.

"O.K., guys. Launch the plane and get off the roof," I said.

"We're coming down," said Robert as he and Chicky released the bracket holding the rubber band.

I felt the immediate sensation of movement as the rubber band shot me and the plane forward. We were catapulted out over the edge of the roof. I held back on the stick anticipating a response to the feeling of lift under the wings. Instead the little machine lost its forward momentum and nosed down. It glided like a stone into the big fresh manure pile. My flight lasted maybe all of 5 seconds. Except for the stinky landing, it was glorious.

"Are you trying to kill yourself?" said Charlie and Sonny as they came to extricate me from the wreck.

"No," I said. "I just want to fly."

"You just did, you crazy fool," said Sonny. "About all of 50 feet."

"How did it feel R.A.?" said Chicky running up to join the crowd of rescuers. "It looked great. If that manure pile hadn't been there the plane would have gone further."

"It was too quick of a flight, Chicky. We need an engine. We need power."

"Young fella," said Charlie. "What you and this airplane need is a bath."

From that day forward, Charlie and some of the other adults would call me "Stinky." But, they did so with a smile.

From time to time, I would go back and relive that flight. I would measure the distance of the total flight from its starting point on the roof to landing place in the manure pile. It was close to 100 feet. If the adults didn't make such a fuss, we could have tried it again.

## CHAPTER 24

## WHAT EVER HAPPENED TO LEROY RAVIOLI?

It didn't seem possible that another school year was going to end very soon. We had been preparing for summer since Easter and this year we had grand plans. Last year had been a time of orientation, but this year we had our act together and we were ready for a busy summer. Also, as fifth graders, we would become the big shots of the school in September as sixth graders.

George came up to me in May and informed me of a boy's baseball league that was being formed by the County and was going to hold tryouts in Warinanco Park. This was great news to me because my Uncle Bill sent me a left-handed first baseman's mitt, all the way from Algiers in North Africa. Now I didn't have to play handicapped with a right-handed glove.

"You have to bring your birth certificate to prove your eleven years old," relayed George.

"I'm only ten, but maybe my mother can give me a note sayin' I should be eleven, but we came from North Carolina were everybody is a year younger."

George had sort of a baffled look on his face as he tried to understand my answer. "Well ... that may work. The Tryouts are at 6 o'clock in the park. My father will walk with us to the park, if we meet by my corner."

I informed my mother of my plans when I got home from school.

My mother was very cooperative. "I don't have a copy of your birth certificate handy, I had given my copy to the school. But, I can write you a note to whoever is running this baseball league."

That sounded good to me.

Ma fixed me an early supper and after eating, I headed off to meet George.

Warinanco Park is located in Roselle at the border of Elizabeth and Linden, about one and a half miles as the crow flies and a 45-minute walk from my house. Even last year as nine year olds, we would roam off as far as Clark Township without adult supervision. We made many forays afield during those youthful years and never had a calamitous incident. Rivers, ponds, fruit trees, woods, railroads, junkyards, abandoned buildings and even cemeteries were attractions for us devotees and followers of the Huckleberry Finn life style. God must have been very busy watching over us and keeping us out of harm's way and it is a testament to His Grace, rather than our ability, that we survived into adulthood.

George and his father saw me coming as they exited Spotford Avenue at the corner of Lidgerwood Avenue. I had just crossed South Elmora Avenue and was moving at a jog to join them two short blocks away.

George's father was a tall husky gray haired man, who held a cigar in his mouth even when he talked. "So, this is the lefty who hits the ball up on the school roof. Are you all set to show these guys from the county what you got?"

"I sure want to play ball this summer. If I were still at home, I would have played in the boy's league last year. But, 'causen of the War, we had to move."

"Well maybe this year you boys will have a chance," replied George's father.

We made small talk as we wended our way up Lidgerwood Avenue to Park Avenue, Linden. We went across Dark Lane Bridge, which carried traffic across the main line of the Pennsylvania Railroad. Park Avenue ended at St. George Avenue and the park entrance was on the opposite side of the street. Warinanco Park was very large, especially for two little boys and we had to walk halfway across the park to get to the place where the tryouts were being held.

"Eleven and twelve year olds stay here by the bleachers. Thirteen and fourteen year olds go across the road to field one and all boys over fifteen go across the road to field eight." These orders were being barked by a man in real baseball pants wearing spikes. George and I followed his orders and went to the bleachers.

As we sat in the bleachers another man came by and passed out sheets of paper. On these papers were mimeographed instructions and places for us to fill in information. They also gave out little yellow pencils for us to write with and to return with the paper.

After all the administrative work was concluded, the man in the baseball pants stood in front of the bleachers and told us to be quiet. Somebody mentioned that this man was an umpire. We all knew umpires didn't take any nonsense and that they didn't like kids. We also knew that umpires were never kids themselves. This was the first time in my life that I ever saw a real umpire, so I had to believe everything that was said about these mysterious people. I don't know where umpires lived, but the only place they were ever seen was at a baseball field. I didn't know if umpires were related to vampires, but I wasn't going to get one mad.

Pretty soon some other men came along. "All outfielders come with me," said the red headed man walking with the bat towards the right field foul pole.

"Infielders form up near first base," shouted a slim dark haired man.

"I want all pitchers and catchers to line up behind the backstop," hollered the umpire.

I decided to go with the infielders. That umpire was kind of scary.

"You must be a first baseman," said the slim man. "You're left-handed and you have a first baseman's mitt. First base is the only place a lefthander can play in the infield. Can I have your paper? And you will be our first baseman for now." Looking at my paper, he said, "Do they call you Lefty or Richie?"

"My real name is Richard, but my baseball name is Lefty."

In due time the slim man had players lined up at the infield positions. He then walked over to home plate, where he had gotten the catchers from the umpire and lined them up by the plate.

"All right boys. I'm going to hit ground balls to each position. I want you to field the ball and throw it to Lefty at first. Lefty, after you get the throw, get the ball back to the catcher. I will call the next group of fielders in each line up when I'm ready. Does everybody understand? O.K. boys, here we go."

There were only four boys at first base and I was the only one with a first baseman's mitt. So I figured that my chances for making this league were pretty good.

Some of the infielders made some pretty bad throws, but I got anything within reason. I fielded the ground balls hit to me and made good throws to "home." So, I figured I did pretty good.

While we were working in the infield, George was with the group in the outfield and they were doing pretty much the same as us.

After everybody had several chances, the slim man brought us infielders over to the bleachers.

"Boys, as I call your name I want you to grab a bat and go up to the plate. Each batter will get three pitches to hit. After you take your swings report to Mr. Woods in the outfield and he will send an outfielder in to hit."

My name was called fourth and guess who was pitching? The umpire.

When I got up he laid three nice pitches in to me and I ripped them out to right field. So far so good.

After I reported to the outfield, I got a couple of chances at balls hit out there and was hoping that the coaches saw me make the catches.

After the batting was completed, the Umpire wanted all of the pitchers out by the mound and all the catchers back by the plate.

Quickly, I ran out to join the pitchers as the infielders were just hanging around.

Under the watchful eye of the umpire, the pitchers were winding up and throwing about ten pitches apiece to a catcher behind the bat of the red headed man, who just stood at the plate and didn't swing at any balls.

"Next," shouted the umpire and I took my turn to make my pitches.

"Wait a minute, where is your paper?"

"The infield man has it," I replied

"Are you an infielder?" the Umpire asked.

"I play anywhere, even pitch and catch," I sharply retorted.

"How can you pitch with a first baseman's mitt?"

"Give me the ball and I'll show you."

The umpire obliged me and I made ten good pitches.

After I had finished, we were gathered again by the bleachers. The red haired man now took control.

"Boys, we will be grading your tryout and the boys selected will be notified by mail next week. Good luck to all of you."

On the walk towards home George and I relived every moment of the tryout. We were really wound up and would have a hard time resting until we knew our baseball fate.

"I saw everything and you boys were terrific, I don't see how you two guys can miss," George's father said in an encouraging manner between puffs of cigar smoke. And we knew he was right.

My mother had the envelope with my name on it propped up against the lamp in the parlor. I had been pestering her every day as I awaited notice from the league. Finally, on Thursday, it arrived.

"YOU HAVE BEEN ASSIGNED TO THE RED SOX TEAM OF THE UNION COUNTY MINOR MIDGET LEAGUE. REPORT TO THE STADIUM OFFICE AT WARINANCO PARK BETWEEN 9 A.M. AND 12 NOON ON SATURDAY FOR YOUR CAP, T-SHIRT AND GAME SCHEDULE. BRING PROOF OF BIRTHDATE WITH YOU AND HAVE YOUR PARENT SIGN THE PERMISSION PORTION OF THIS NOTICE."

WOW! I made it.

The next day at school I saw George and he made it too. George was assigned to the Yankees, but we would stay friends and we arranged to meet the next morning and go for our shirts and caps.

On Saturday morning, George and I met again, this time we made a solo trip to the Park... as we would ultimately do twice each week during the summer.

The stadium was past the ball fields and tennis courts near the outside of the park in Roselle. It wasn't too hard to find because the kids in all age groups were going there to get their uniforms. So, we just followed the crowd.

The stadium was all concrete, sort of like the Roman Coliseum, except it didn't entirely surround the football field and running track in front of it.

George and I went inside under the concrete seats. The red haired man, Mr. Woods and a tall slender man, Mr. Kron, were seated at a table with all the papers in front of them. Open boxes containing hats and T-shirts, were labeled with the team names and lined up along the wall.

We got into the line of kids waiting to present their paperwork to the men at the table. As Mr. Kron checked each kid off on his teams' roster, Mr. Woods gave them the appropriate hat, shirt and schedule. The system worked very well until it came to me. I didn't have a birth certificate and I was under age.

"Red, how we handle this problem?" asked Mr. Kron.

Mr. Woods and Mr. Kron began examining my paperwork and discussing my qualifications to play.

"Most of the time we have older kids trying to play in the younger leagues, now we have an underage player who wants to play with older kids. This is a switch," exclaimed Mr. Woods.

"Let's get his tryout sheets," stated Mr. Kron as he got up and went to a group of boxes filled with papers. He groped around in the papers for a while and finally came up with a handful of paper sheets.

"Here it is, Richard A. Pendell, Birth date, none. See note from mother. Well, at least he didn't lie, Jim. And, he's been given good marks by the tryout team. What do you think?"

"His mother signed the permission slip and he is in the fifth grade. I say, let him play."

"Done," said Mr. Kron as Mr. Woods reached into my team's box for my cap and shirt.

"Thank you," I said as George and I made a hasty exit before they could change their minds.

There were only four teams in our league; The Yankees, Giants, Dodgers and Red Sox.

Our league did not resemble any of the latter day youth baseball organizations, such as the Little League, in any fashion. No Adults were involved at the game level. We played on regulation sized fields according to official baseball rules. The kids ran the games themselves. A teenager, apparently employed by the Park Commission, would show up at game time with the bases, catchers' equipment, 2 balls and 3 bats. Both teams would use the same catcher's equipment and the same bats. The teenager had a scorebook and he would stand out behind the pitcher and be both scorekeeper and umpire. It was also his job to see that everybody on each team got in the game.

Our games usually started around nine o'clock in the morning and over the course of the summer we would play each team around six times. By summers end we would know the names of almost every kid in the league. My team, the Red Sox was made up of boys from the port section of Elizabeth. I didn't know any of them, but they all went to Catholic Schools, like St. Patricks and St. Adalbert's in Elizabethport. They had names like, Murawski, Majorowski, Sullivan, and Gillen to name a few. George's team, the Yankees, was composed of boys from the City of Linden. George lived at the city line, so I imagine that was the reasoning behind his placement on the Yankees. The Giants were composed of kids from Roselle and the Dodgers had kids from Roselle Park and a few from other towns, like Westfield and Rahway.

During the course of that summer we were given the opportunity to play baseball. And that is what we did. Play kids baseball. There wasn't any pressure on us and no team was crowned champions at the end of the season.

After the season began, some alterations were made regarding the length of the base lines and the pitching distance. Most of these adjustments were made by the players themselves and the league officials went along with it.

Some of these twelve year olds could pitch pretty fast from the shortened pitching distance and it was hard on us younger guys, who had to either bunt or walk to get on base.

The best part of the whole deal was, getting your name in the paper. All of the box scores were printed in the Elizabeth Daily Journal. So, twice a week our baseball exploits were circulated throughout the County. It took me most of the season to register something in the Hit column of the box score. But, just seeing that in the paper made my season.

I was just beginning to hit my stride when the season came to an end. Next season I would be one of the experienced guys in this league. This years twelve years old would be thirteen next season and would have to move on to a higher league.

Next season couldn't come soon enough for me and my mother. I was continually improvising a baseball park inside the house and was driving her crazy with bouncing balls and taking batting practice with curtain rods and any tiny object that could simulate a baseball, like mothballs and wadded up paper balls.

On days when the weather was good, I would pitch a rubber ball against a target on the garage wall. In order to have some batting practice, I would move in close to the wall. While holding a bat in one hand, I would pitch the ball against the wall and then attempt to hit the rebounding ball. Eventually, to increase the degree of difficulty, I used a very small sponge ball and a thin piece of broomstick for a bat. Over the winter months, I would practice this activity when there was a lull in other activities.

As winter wore into Spring, I kept my eyes peeled on the sport page of the Elizabeth Daily Journal. Finally, one day there it was... YOUTH LEAGUE TRYOUTS.

The time and date were marked on the calendar and I began crossing off the days. The neighborhood boys and I began playing at school or on our field in early Spring, so we were in pretty good shape when tryout time arrived. I was the only one from my neighborhood who played last year. Most of the guys thought I was crazy then. But, after seeing my new cap and getting my name in the newspaper, they became believers and everyone wanted to tryout this year.

When the day for the tryouts came, we all went in one group. I was sort of the guide, because I had been through this before. When we got to the field, it was mobbed. I never saw so many kids. Mr. Kron, Mr. Woods, The Umpire and a few other men where there and they were huddled in a conference.

"All boys who played in the 11 and 12 year old league last year go over to the right field foul pole," bellowed the umpire.

The boys who were trying out for the older leagues had already gone to different fields, so this mob was just for the four team league. WOW!

We veteran players gathered at the foul pole with Mr. Woods. He had us fill out the same kind of papers as last year, but when they were given back to him, he marked the name of our last years team on the paper.

Looking at the group of us, he said, "I remember most of you boys and because we have so many here tonight, you boys who played last year will not have to tryout. We will place you on a team, so look for a card in the mail next week."

With that we were free to go. Hot Dog!

I hung around as my guys tried out and I renewed acquaintances with some of the other veteran ball players. We didn't see how all these kids would fit on four teams. But, hey, we were all set, because we're returning from last year.

Sure enough, about a week later a card came informing me that I was assigned to the Red Sox again. Robert, from my building made the Pirates. Tommy made the Cardinals and Donald from the sixth grade was on the Red Sox.

The league had really grown. This year there were ten teams. And they were going to have playoffs and a Champion at the end of the year.

I arrived at my first game ready to pickup where I had left off last season. The only familiar face I saw was Donald from my school, everyone else was a stranger and none had played on this team last year.

"Where do you play?" Asked a boy named Ricadulli.

"Pitch, first and the outfield. I played on this team last year."

"Well this year my father is the manager and he says Don pitches and Leroy Ravioli plays first. You can probably play some in the outfield. Our team is altogether from our neighborhood."

I had to go to Mr. Ricidulli and inform him of the league rule that requires every boy to play a minimum of two innings. I must say he obeyed that rule explicitly and I never played more than two innings. Everybody, except me and Donald, was from the Peterstown section of Elizabeth. That was an Italian neighborhood in downtown Elizabeth.

Donald was a big boy at that age and he did pitch well. He threw a straight fastball and had good control of it. The Red Sox were doing quite well and were undefeated as we approached the end of the first half of the season.

I was getting little playing time and was quite disgusted with my situation on the Red Sox. Robert, my neighbor was playing for the Pirates and they hadn't won a game.

"We don't have anyone who can pitch," complained Robert. "We had a good pitcher named Gray, but he moved."

"Hey, Robert. How about if I pitch for your team?"

"You can't, you're on the Red Sox."

"But, if you put Gray's name down on the scorebook, nobody will ever know."

"Let's find out tomorrow, R.A."

The Pirates had a teenager assigned by the league for a manager and after explaining the situation to him, he was agreeable to giving our plan a try.

The Pirates were playing the Cubs on this particular day and they were from the same area of town as the Red Sox players. Also, they were the major challenge to the Red Sox Championship hopes.

It was a good game and the Pirates came out on top for the first time that season. The Pirates also sprung to life in the next two games as we beat the White Sox and the Braves. Could we be spoilers in this league, as our next opponents were the undefeated Red Sox?

I knew the jig would be up the instant I was seen, but I decided to go for it any way.

That big-mouthed Ricidulli kid was the first to see me on the Pirate's side of the field.

"Hey, you're supposed to be on our team," he hollered.

"I quit and joined this team," I answered.

I then heard Ricidulli say to his father and some of the players, "He's the lefty, the guy who beat the Cubs, that's him."

Next a contingent of Red Sox along with Mr. Ricadulli came to me and said, "You've been assigned to our team, you can't play for anyone else."

"That's what you think," I replied. "You didn't let me play, so I jumped teams."

While we were arguing, Mr. Kron and Mr. Woods were walking along with the scorekeeper in tow.

"Just what is going on here?" asked Mr. Kron.

Mr. Ricidulli went on to explain how I was assigned to his team and shouldn't be allowed to play for anyone else. Also, that I had played for the Pirates under an assumed name and had won three games.

"Is all this true Lefty?" asked Mr. Woods. "Your real name isn't Gray, it's Pendell, right?"

"Yes, sir."

'Why would you want to play for the Pirates? The Red Sox could be the League Champions."

"Well Sir, the Red Sox don't let me play. They put Leroy Ravioli in my position and won't give me a chance to pitch. The Pirates need a pitcher and I'm A Pitcher. And, I just want to play ball."

"George," asked Mr. Woods of Mr. Kron. "What do you think?"

"This is what it is all about, kids playing baseball. Jim, give that lefty the ball and let's sit down and watch a game."

The Red Sox did ultimately win the Championship, but not on this day. With a second half wining streak, including two victories over the league Champion Red Sox, the Pirates were becoming contenders. A poor showing in the first half of the season could not be overcome in the race for the Championship. But we proved we were winners and I started to gain a local reputation among my peers for winning ball games.

Over the next several years my friends and I continued to progress through the various levels of youth league play, including the Junior High School team. Finally, out of our group, just George and I made the High School team. With the help of my team mates, many of whom who started with me, on other teams back in the youth leagues, I was able to accomplish an outstanding record in American Legion Baseball and High School Baseball. After being selected to the All- County and All- State Scholastic baseball teams for three years, I was named the leading High School Pitcher in the State in my Senior Year, based on an undefeated season and sixteen consecutive victories.

These things may never have come to fruition, had it not been for those people on the Red Sox, who chose to play Leroy Ravioli over me. I forced Mr. Kron and Mr. Woods into making a decision that obviously altered my youth.

Who knows? I might have gotten discouraged, like a lot of kids probably did. So I owe Mr. Kron and Mr. Woods a debt of gratitude. But, if it wasn't for Leroy Ravioli, none of this would have happened. I often think about Leroy and wonder what became of him.

# CHAPTER 25

# JERKING THE BELLS AT SAINT MARY'S

We lived in St. Mary's Parish. It was a geographical area. Somewhere off in the vast reaches of space a Catholic prelate in some office cut up all the real estate on the earth and assigned the pieces and the people who lived in those pieces to a specific Church Parish. Our piece happened to be in St. Mary's Parish.

One day a priest and some parishioners from St. Mary's came into our neighborhood. They went from door to door taking a survey to determine how many people, and of what ages lived where. When they could get an ear like my mother's, they would explain the necessity of providing a religious education to their children, of which I was one. Their activity sort of reminded me of the Missionaries who went to foreign lands to convert the heathens.

We weren't heathens; we just didn't have cars or gas to get to those churches we would normally attend. Also, shift work had cut into what had been normal church attendance. St. Mary's had all the answers. It was within walking distance and we kids could go to religion class on Mondays after school. They even had a special service on Sunday morning when kids could go to Church without their parents.

My mother fell hook, line and sinker for their pitch. My mother thought I was a heathen.

My father sided with my mother on the issue, although his reasons were not as altruistic. My father wanted to get a job in the Standard Oil Co.'s refinery. Even though my father had my Aunt Eileen's husband Ed, as an inside contact, a man named Tom Glackin, who lived around the corner on Stewart Place, was the hiring boss. And, Mr. Glackin was a bigwig in St. Mary's Church.

It was said, that if a person were to get a job in the Bayway Refinery, he had to be Catholic and Irish. It was also said, that years earlier Irish immigrants would arrive in this country with notes directing them to *Tom Glackin's Kerosene Factory*. I wonder if Mr. Rockefeller knew about that name.

My father thought my presence in St. Mary's would aid the family fortunes. Now all he had to do was to become Irish.

Our family name is British in origin, so it wasn't too difficult for my father to manufacture some Irish ancestors who came to this country when Tom Glackin was only a gleam in his Great- great- great Grandfather's eye. Yes, this St. Mary's thing might work out real well. Well, that is for everyone but me.

Mr. Mitchell worked at the Bayway Refinery. Last Christmas he gave out tickets to all us kids so we could attend a Christmas show put on by the Standard Oil Company. The show was held at Battin High School, which is the Girls High School in Elizabeth. It was a real nice show. They had a dog act, some singers, a choral group and some acrobats. They gave each kid a small box of hard Christmas Candy. That was fantastic. We hadn't seen candy for some time. That Mr. Rockefeller, who owned Standard Oil, must have had some connections to be able to get all this candy during the War. I was hoping that my father would get a job in the Standard Oil Co. Maybe they would give him a job where they kept the Christmas candy.

Almost every kid in my class had been signed up for the religion class at St. Mary's. That is all, except the colored kids and Irwin, who is Jewish, what ever that is. It's a strange thing too, because Irwin and the colored kids lived closer to St. Mary's than we did. I guess their parents didn't want to get jobs in the Standard Oil Refinery.

One Monday afternoon we arrived as a mob at St. Mary's School. A stern looking Catholic Nun herded us into groups according to our age. Again, I was left standing alone as all my friends were assembled into classes.

"Don't you belong to this group?" said the stern Nun pointing towards my group of friends.

"Yes Ma'am," I replied.

"Then why aren't you with them?"

"You didn't call my age out."

"Are you, or are you not in the same class with these people?"

"Yes Ma'am, but I'm a year younger. So, maybe I ought to come back here next year."

"That's right Sister," chimed my friend Thomas. "He comes from some place down South where everybody is a year younger than other people."

I could see the Nun was baffled by the discourse taking place, so she just pointed her finger at me and then at the group. I followed her direction and fell in behind Thomas.

We found out very soon that Nuns do not have a sense of humor. Leastwise, this group of Nuns sure didn't.

After seating us in the classroom, the Nun began passing out these thin blue books. Once all the books had been passed out, the Nun took a position at the blackboard.

"Boys and girls, my name is Sister Michael Francis," she said as she wrote her name on the blackboard. "And I want you to write my name on the top of the inside cover in your Catechism. Are there any questions? Yes, young man," she said responding to George's raised arm.

"Is Sister or Michael your first name, or is your last name Francis or Michael Francis?" George asked.

I thought it was a good question, but obviously the Nun didn't.

"My name is Sister Michael Francis period," she said pointing to what she had written on the blackboard. "I am married to the Church!"

I was ready to raise my hand to ask the next logical question, but I could see from the redness of the Nuns face, which was shrouded by something resembling a white picture frame, that another question of that order could be disastrous.

This was a new experience for most of us, so we did have a lot of questions. I wasn't acquainted with the structure of the Catholic Church and how it related to my world.

Single women were called Miss. Married women and widows were called Mrs. Married women took the last name of their husbands. George's question was not out of order. He simply wanted to know if she was a Miss or a Mrs.

Since nobody would answer our questions, we had private discussions in which would speculate on many of the answers to questions like;

"Are Nuns Bald?"

"Do Nuns wear underwear?"

"Do Nuns have mothers and fathers?"

"How many Nuns are married to each Priest?"

"Who does the cooking?"

"Why are they called Nuns?"

Instead of answering questions, they only wanted us to memorize the answers to questions in the blue book. No explanation. No background. Just memorize the answer and forget the reasoning.

Being a Catholic did have some benefits. First off, we didn't have to be in Church as long as when we were Baptists. Then there were Comic strips and crumb buns.

St. Mary's Church was really a very crowded place. The services weren't that long, but they had had a lot of them. A large group of people was always gathering out on the sidewalk for the next service. Suddenly, Mr. Glackin and his helpers would throw open the Church doors and a mob would descend out of the Church onto the already over crowded sidewalk. If you got caught up in the movements of the wrong mob, you could just as well be pushed back into Church for the next service. It could go the other way too. The mob moving down the street towards the A&P could move a body in their direction so fast that the person thought he had already been to Church.

Amid all this turmoil, a Jewish man, named Mr. Levin had a couple of planks set across some saw horses right at the curb in front of the Church. He sold the Sunday newspapers. There was the Newark News, the New York Daily News, The New York Mirror, The Herald Tribune and the New York Times.

My mother always gave me 10 cents to get the New York Daily News. But, often the crowd was so bad that I couldn't get to the part of the plank where that paper was located, so lots of times I ended up with The New York Mirror. I liked the comic strips in the Sunday papers. The Herald Tribune had the best comics, so sometimes I'd let myself get pushed to that part of the stand.

I had 15 cents each Sunday to buy crumb buns at Bartone's Bakery, which was located 50 feet south of the Church property. This little bakery was so crowded that you had to be 7 feet tall to be seen and have a set of lungs like a tiger to be heard. I liked to go into that bakery and watch lady tie the cake boxes. She had a spool of string hanging down from the ceiling and she could take the cake box, give that string a few twists and then snap the string and that cake box was tied neat as could be. I had a difficult time getting waited on in that bakery. I usually had to wait until the crowd left before I could be heard.

I had to develop a system to deal with this situation. And, strange as it may seem, my mother gave me the idea.

When my parents took me to the movies, we just went without any concern given to the starting time of the show. We would often arrive in the middle of the movie. After the movie ended, it would start all over again. We would sit there through the next show until my mother said, "Let's go. This is where we came in."

Since all the Catholic services were alike, I decided to be late for one service, then sit there through the next service and finally leave at that point where I had come in for the previous service. I made sure to sit in the back, so people saw me coming in, but few saw me leave. I got the whole service and had the newsstand and bakery all to myself.

Two of my friends from school, Thomas and George, were pretty much in the same boat as I was. We realized that if we pooled our collection money, which would have come to about 30 cents, we could enjoy a nice Sunday morning repast.

It took a few weeks, but finally we came up with a scheme. We would just avoid Church altogether. We weren't going to miss much. The Pastor gave a speech every week about how much money he wanted to raise by the War's end, so he could eventually renovate the Church. They sang a few songs and said a few prayers in a garbled tone that I really didn't understand.

We felt that we were getting enough religion as it was. Those Catechism classes taught us nothing. A bunch of parrots was all that was needed to memorize the answers to questions in the blue book. We got a better religious education in the Public School, where we read a scripture passage each morning and recited the Lord's Prayer before our Pledge of Allegiance to the Flag. I often wondered if the Catholic School kids did the same thing. I know they recited a prayer about God's Mother that really confounded me. To me, it sounded like she was swimming with some monks around the Queen Mary. I know that the Queen Mary was being used as a troop ship in the War, so maybe the prayer was for the benefit of our soldiers and sailors at sea. I knew Jesus had a mother named Mary, but God, The Father, who lives in Heaven didn't have a mother as far as I knew. But, then again, there are a lot of things I will never know or be able to explain.

In order to be seen, we would attend the School children's service.

Facing the Church, the boys would gather on the right side and the girls would gather on the left side. We would walk through the gathered girls making sure to say hello to any girls in our Catechism class.

"Good Morning, Sister," we would say to the Nun who stood by the Church steps in front of the gathering of boys. Then we would drift into the crowd of boys, gradually working our way to the back of the pack.

"Boys take your hats off and follow me!" commanded the nun at the head of the steps. With those words the assembled multitude began a single file march into the Church. Near the right side front door, where the boys were entering, was a spiked iron fence with a small gate that was always left open. A path went from the gate up along the side of the Church and then exited onto a street behind the Church.

Fortunately for us, the inside perimeter of the fence had a thick wall of Cedar trees. Once inside that gate and behind those cedar trees, we would be screened from the view of anyone in front of the Church.

We hung back as the line moved forward; we then assumed a typical commando posture and slipped through the gate. We crouched among the cedars until the boys ahead of us had entered the Church. Making sure to keep our bodies below the lower edge of the stained glass windows, we stealthfuly moved along the Church wall towards the back gate.

"We did it," said Thomas. And for the first time in our lives we saw the backside of the Church.

"Which way do we go?" George asked.

"The priests live in that house on the other side of the Church. We don't want them to see us, so we better go this way," I said pointing to the right.

"What's down here?" Thomas questioned as we walked down the narrow street behind the Church.

"I donno," I replied. "I don't live around here." Thomas, George and I lived over near the Linden line, on the fringe of the parish, so this neighborhood behind the Church was new to us.

The sign at the next corner indicated that we had just come down Race Street and were now at the intersection of Race and Pearl Streets.

"I know where we are! That's the beginning of the colored neighborhood, where Joseph in my class lives. And down there is Washington Avenue where

Charles and Catherine from my class live. Do you guys want to go down there and see the live chickens in the chicken store next to the Chink's Laundry?"

"I don't think so," Thomas responded.

"Richard, where does the street go if we go over by the train tracks?"

"Well, George that other street goes along the tracks to the old closed down Railroad station at South Street. We can then circle around South Street back to the bakery before Church lets out."

Since the idea of live chickens didn't appeal to anyone, we turned left towards the railroad tracks.

We probably had a good half hour of freedom before we could be the first people in the bakery, or at the newspaper stand. So we walked up Burnett Street to South Street, past Tripoli's Italian food store. At the next corner the A&P appeared and around the corner, on Washington Avenue, was the bakery.

As we hid in the A&P doorway and looked down Washington Avenue, Mr. Levin was the only person in sight as the crowd for the next service had not yet begun to form.

"Let's get into the bakery and then to the newspaper stand real quick," urged Thomas.

"We gotta go slow and easy," said George. "Or else people will think we're up to no good."

"That's right Thomas. If anybody says anything, we can always say that the Nun let us out of Church early to buy her crumb buns. How does that sound?"

"Alright I guess, but do we know for sure that Nuns eat crumb buns?"

I could understand Thomas's apprehension, after all this type of mission was new to him and George.

"How come you're not in the Choich wit all the kitz?" said Mr. Levin as I walked up to the newspaper stand.

"I went real early this morning with my father. He's working the 7 to 3 shift today. I came back to get the Daily News and some crumb buns for my mother."

"Daily News, 10 cents," Mr. Levin said as he handed me the thick newspaper.

George and Thomas were standing in the A&P doorway giggling when I returned.

"What did Mr. Levin say to you? Did he know you didn't go to Church?" Thomas managed to ask between giggles.

He said, "Daily News, 10 cents." That's what he said. Now let's go to the bakery."

"What can I do for you men?" said the dark haired lady in the white uniform behind the counter.

I was the first to bark my order since I was a little more experienced in this type of operation. "I'll have 15 cents worth of crumb buns and could you tell me how much a jelly donut costs?"

"Five cents for a jelly donut," she said as she reached for the trays of buns.

"I'll have one of those too."

"You must be flush today. Did you come into some money?" the lady said with a slight laugh.

I had that dime that was supposed to go into the collection basket. This way I would still have a nickel left.

"I made a little extra money this week."

"Oh, and are you going to treat your friends?" she said looking at George and Thomas.

"They have their own money," I replied.

"Oh, you all hit it big this week. Right?"

She handed me my order and then Thomas and George placed their orders. People were just getting out of Church when we walked outside and headed south on Washington Avenue toward our neighborhood.

We pulled it off and had a jelly donut to boot. Now all we had to do was to figure some way out of that Catechism Class.

One good thing about the War was the fact that a lot of things could be blamed on the wartime situation and nobody would question them. All we had to do was to make these Nuns forget who we are and that would be that. It would be just like we were moving away. They didn't know our families, so we could easily move to some imaginary place.

"The Government isn't going to allow folks to just up and move," interjected George.

This was true. People couldn't just quit their job and move to some other job in some other place. Everyone was essentially in government service and there was a procedure involved whereby a person had to apply to a Government Agency for permission to transfer from one Defense job to another. We had to keep all these things in mind as we planned our deception on the Nuns.

"Loose lips, sink Ships," was a motto posted to warn people not to discuss Defense related business. Spies could be anywhere and by discussing things like production figures, product changes, material movements and troop locations; we could unwittingly be supplying the enemy with information. We had to employ this same type of tactic to our Nun operation, code named, "Black Birds."

Our deception could be revealed if some of the other kids in our class informed on us. Particularly girls. They had big mouths and thought it was their duty to broadcast any and all information to the world. We had to begin a propaganda program to indoctrinate our peers with false and misleading information that would prepare the Nuns for our departure.

Getting our father's fictional jobs was one way we could explain our relocation to another parish. We also had to think up some kind of story to explain our appearance at home on Catechism days, particularly when the weather was bad. Most of our mothers were house wives and didn't have jobs outside the home, so we had to come up with a plan that would keep us out of sight during that hour when we were supposed to be getting religion.

There is an old inactive school on Grier Avenue behind St. Mary's Cemetery. This school was probably the school that served the neighborhood before our current school was built. A lot of kids, mostly kids who went to St. Mary's school, went there to play basketball and softball. It was a good spot, just far enough to keep us out of sight from our homes and the Nuns at St. Mary's School.

For foul weather, we had our fortified camp with its semi-subterranean bunkers. No mothers or Nuns would ever look for us there.

The plans were starting to fall into place. We had gotten our Sunday evasion tactic down pretty good after three third weeks of execution. On the fourth Sunday we performed the same maneuver, except I felt something was different. When I reached the back gate, I turned to see some more boys following us.

"What are you doing Everett?" I said to the first boy.

"We've been watching you guys for three weeks and we want to try it."

"There's too many," said George. "You guys will ruin it for us."

"Yeah," Thomas agreed. "You guys can try it after we stop coming to Church."

"Where are you going?" Everett asked.

"We have to go to a different Church, because our fathers are getting new jobs," I answered.

Andy popped out from behind Everett and asked, "Are you going to change schools too?"

"No, just Churches and Catechism class. They have their own Church at the company where our fathers are goin' to work. You know, just like the Chaplains they have in the Army."

"Oh, yeah," said Everett, with a sort of befuddled look on his face.

Given the wartime conditions and all the changes we had to accept, the fable told to Everett could be within the realm of possibility. I wonder if this story would work on the Nuns. In any event we had planted the seed with Everett.

This day we took the new members of our band to see the live chicken market.

"Is this what you guys do every Sunday... Come here to see smelly chickens?" Everett complained as he grabbed his nose.

"No, sometimes," Thomas said, "They have ducks and turkeys."

"Come on," implored George. "Let's go around back by the river where they throw the chicken's inners for the river rats."

By the minute, Everett was getting to enjoy this escapade less and less. "It's almost time for me to go home. I can go down South Broad Street to my house."

With that he and his two companions, Andy and Tony blew out of the chicken market and headed for South Broad Street.

We laughed like fools as we watched them move down the street and we began our circuitous route back to the bakery.

The smell of those chickens did linger in our noses for a little while. Hopefully, the smell would go away before we got to the bakery.

"Do they really have Churches in factories, Richard?" Thomas asked.

"Don't be silly," said George. "He was making that up."

"Well, it sounded like it could be true. They have a nurse at my father's factory. Why not a Priest?"

"Well, I told that to Everett 'cause tellin' him somethin' is like tellin' the whole world."

We made it to the bakery ahead of the crowd and had our usual round of jelly donuts.

## CHAPTER 26

## REVENGE ON THE DENTIST

We put a lot of effort into evading Church and Catechism classes. It was like a juggling act, we were trying to keep a lot of balls in the air at one time. On one hand we were trying to deceive the Nuns. On the other, we had to keep our parents in the dark concerning our activities. Our worst enemies were the kids who went to our school; the girls in particular. They were always threatening to tell somebody if we didn't do their bidding. Most times they just wanted help with schoolwork; Art projects for the most part. This was one of the inconveniences we had to suffer. Sometimes I think we could have expended a lot less energy if we complied with the rules of society. But, that wouldn't be any fun. It didn't offer a challenge.

We weren't doing anything different than the rest of society. The wartime economy and the accompanying restrictions made innovators out of everyone.

We weren't a society of "black marketeers" or lawbreakers. However, homemade wine, whiskey and cigarettes were every day commodities; by products of the "victory gardens." Nothing was being withheld from the war effort. Quite the contrary. Besides boosting morale, these innovative products relieved demands on the local merchants whose activities were regulated by the OPA.

We kids were only following the rebellious example of the adult society. The American spirit was alive and well on the home front. Our neighbors were busy producing the necessary materials for our forces to use in the global advance against the enemy; those people responsible for our shortages and incontinences.

By the time school opened in September 1943, American troops had chased the Germans and Italians across North Africa, Sicily and were now on the Italian mainland fighting towards Rome. In the Pacific, General MacArthur was hopping across New Guinea en route to the Philippines. Admiral Nimtz and his Pacific Fleet had become a formidable Navy, a mobile air force and an infantry afloat as they moved from island to island securing a route to Japan.

We followed the action of our Armed Forces through the Saturday newsreels at the movies. Each week we emerged from the theatre with an enhanced sense of pride and invincibility. We were Americans, we could do anything, or at least we thought we could. Our Uncles and cousins, older brothers, and parents are the people taking the War to the enemy, both on the foreign and home fronts.

Our job, as kids, was to stand on the sidelines, watch and stay out of trouble; which was easier said than done.

Our gang was trained to perfection in combat techniques. We were all good shots with slingshots or peashooters. We could repel out of trees on ropes just like the Phillipino soldiers in "Back to Bataan." We were experts at camouflage and concealment, blending in with our surroundings like chameleons so we could pepper fat ladies and cats with our pea shooters. We could live off the land, having been able to infiltrate and raid every garden and fruit tree for miles around. We were an army at its peak of training and looking for a battle.

The opportunity finally arrived during the winter early in 1944.

Despite my protests, my mother had signed a card saying I could be treated by the School Dentist. I didn't have any tooth problems, but somebody in their infinite wisdom felt that each week so many children had to be treated by the School Dentist. So, problems or not, periodically my name would be picked to go to the Dentist.

I had been there five or six times already. Each time the Dentist, Dr. O'Doyle, propped my mouth open; chose a tooth and began to drill down to my toes. Dr. O'Doyle clamped his teeth down on the cigar he continually kept in his mouth and laid the pressure on the drill 'till the thing started to smoke. No matter how much I complained, my mother felt that we were saving money by my going to the School Dentist. This guy was a sadist and my mother was thrilled that I got free dental care, even if I didn't have anything wrong.

Everett, from my class and me were picked to go to the Dentist one day in February. It had snowed a few days before and the ground was still covered with snow. Both of us were not too thrilled at the idea and we had to accompany a group of six more kids from the lower grades.

I was entrusted with an envelope containing the records for all of the students. This gave me an idea and I needed a confederate to assist me in my plans.

As we walked towards the Dentist office located in the Bayway section, I began to formulate my plan.

"Hey, Everett!"

"What R.A." he replied as we walked at the head of the small entourage.

"Do you really want to go to the Dentist today?"

"No. What's on your mind?"

"I can slip our records out of this envelope and then after we get there, I'll give the Nurse the records and we can skip out of the Dentist office."

Everett had experience with my evasion tactics at Church and now we were taking that experience to another level. He was quick to nod in the affirmative.

The Dentist had a bossy, nasty nurse. Maybe it was his wife. She was somewhat like the lady who ran the orphanage in the "Our Gang" movies. She didn't like kids.

There is an empty field across the street from the Dentist office. In the field is a Billboard facing the Dentist office. Our escape route would take us right behind the billboard, where we could wait until the coast was clear.

Everett was to wait for my signal and then we would bolt from the Dental office and head for the billboard.

Our little group entered the waiting room and the younger kids took seats on the chairs in the waiting area. A few minutes later, the Nurse came out of the Dentists room.

"Who has the records?" she said with a scowl.

Without saying a word, I handed her the envelope and she turned and went into the Dentist's room.

As soon as the door shut behind her, Everett and I bolted out the door into the outside air.

We made tracks straight for the billboard. We had just made cover when the Dentist and the Nurse came out the door to look for us.

"What should we do if they come over here, R.A.?"

"If they start coming this way, we can bombard them with snowballs. We can't let them catch us alive. I'll move to the other end of the billboard where I can whip snowballs left handed and they can't see me."

"R.A., do you think we're in trouble?"

"I imagine. So if we throw snowballs at them, how much more trouble can we get?"

The Dentist and Nurse went out into the street, then the Dentist looked in our direction. He pointed to our tracks in the field and they started to come our way.

Everett and I quickly made some snowballs when the Dentist started in our direction. As soon as he walked into the edge of the field and saw our tracks leading to the billboard, I signaled to Everett.

"Fire!" And with that we sent a barrage of snowballs in the Dentist's direction.

The Nurse ran back towards their office while the dentist tried to dodge the snowballs. One of my throws found its mark and slammed into the Dentist's shoulder. Quickly he retreated to his office and went inside the building.

Using the billboard as a screen between the Dental office and us, Everett and I retired from the field of battle.

We had won this skirmish on the field, but we under estimated the enemy's strength and communication capabilities.

After roaming around for a while, Everett and I headed to our respective homes for lunch.

"Is that you, Richard?" my mother hollered from the kitchen when she heard the door open and close.

"It's me, Ma," I answered in return while walking towards the kitchen.

When we were finally face to face, my mother very coolly asked, "So how was school this morning?"

"O.K."

"Weren't you supposed to go to the Dentist this morning?"

"How did she know that?" I thought. We were never told before hand when we were scheduled to go to the Dentist.

"Yes."

"Well ... what kind of work did he do?"

"None," I said as I took a seat at the table.

"Why not?" She asked in her cool tone.

"I left before it was my turn."

Slowly turning up the heat, Ma said, "I know. Mrs. Ferrarra from the School office was already here and told me what you did. Mrs. Devaney wants to see you and me in her office after lunch."

Ma didn't say as much as I thought she would. However, as she poured my soup I started to get a stinging feeling in the seat of my pants.

My mother said very little during the time I ate my lunch and then walked with me back to the school.

We went up the center stairs to the office. Ma and I had climbed these same stairs only a couple of years back. Then, we were united in our efforts to conquer the school system. Today I was returning as a prisoner of war. Turned in by my own mother.

Mrs. Devaney peered over the top of her glasses at me, when Ma and I entered her office. The light coming through the window behind her framed her in such a fashion that she looked like a Gestapo officer.

She rose and slowly moved around the desk towards me and as she came, she began a litany about the benefits of a school dentist and my obligation to obey orders for the safety of the other students. Her tirade lasted for about five minutes and then she asked me, "Why did you do such a thing?"

"I didn't want to go to the Dentist. He's a horse doctor."

"You could have told someone that you didn't want to go. You denied some other child the benefit of seeing the Dentist."

"If I told someone that I didn't want to go, I'd be made to go anyways. That dentist works on teeth that don't need fixin'. I don't feel like suffering pain just to keep that Dentist busy."

"That's enough young man. I know you never went to Kindergarten and that's where we are sending you until you show us that you have grown up."

My mother didn't say a word during the whole proceeding.

Mrs. Devaney had her plan all worked out. Mr. Flatley, the custodian showed up at her door with my books and work. Mr. Flatley knew me, because I once had to spend some time in his boiler room for shooting staples at the hall lights.

"Take him to the Kindergarten, Mr. Flatley."

"Yes 'uum," Mr. Flatley replied and he escorted me out the door.

"What is it this time, boy?" Mr. Flatley asked as we moved down the corridor towards the Kindergarten.

"I threw a snowball at the Dentist. And, now they're sending me to the Penitentiary."

"Did you hit 'em, Lad?" Mr. Flatley asked.

"I got him on the shoulder."

"Do you think it was worth it?"

Without hesitation I said, "Yeah!." ...And I quickened my steps towards my chamber of confinement.

"This is Richard, boys and girls. He's been bad and he's been sent here so you can teach him some manners," Mrs. Hale, the kindergarten teacher announced as I made my entrance into the realm of five year olds.

The little Kindergarten kids didn't faze me one bit. I was more concerned with what my father would do when he came home.

When three o'clock came and I was released from my first tour in the Kindergarten, all the boys in my class were waiting to hear my story. Everett had told them most of what happened. But, they wanted to hear it from me. Everett had turned states evidence on me and didn't receive the punishment that I had. The Powers to Be singled me out as the ringleader and I had to take the brunt of the punishment. But, I had the satisfaction of scoring a direct hit on the Dentist making today a victory day for the kids.

I could just see tomorrow's newspaper headlines: U.S.FORCES LAND AT ANZIO and LOCAL BOYS ESCAPE DENTIST.

Although he didn't approve of my methods, my father understood my reasons and reserved his decision pending further investigation. I was however restricted to my building until that investigation was completed.

I was never vindicated or pardoned and had to spend one full week in the Kindergarten. But, the incident did get the attention of the Board of Education and controls were placed on the Dentist, who happened to be the Mayor's brother-in-law. These controls limited his discretion in selecting treatment and thus prevented any unwarranted drilling and pulling.

Score one victory for the kids and the American way of life.

My school life wasn't all trouble. Whenever there was some program that had redeeming civic or social values, I was always put on the list. I guess they figured I needed as much exposure to decent things as possible.

I was uneducated when it came to ethnicity and religion. After all, I came from a place where everybody had pretty much the same origins and religious beliefs. Here it was a different story. This place was a melting pot.

Not only where there people here from other States. There were people from foreign countries too.

The house next right next to the big field was sold to a foreign family. They had a boy my age and two younger girls. Right away we had trouble with that family. Whenever a baseball was fouled or thrown past the homemade backstop along their property line, the father would run out and grab our ball. He would then start ranting at us in some foreign language after which he would disappear with or ball. In a few minutes he would return and wildly throw our ball back accompanied by some more foreign expletives.

As of yet the son hadn't come out to join us, so we couldn't ask him about his family.

Breezy was from New York and he had seen foreigners before. "The lady looks like a Spanish woman," he said with conviction.

Somebody else asked, "Do you think they came from Spain or Mexico? Mexicans are Spanish people."

"Probably Mexico," he replied. "My brother told me that there are a lot of U-Boats out in the ocean; so they couldn't have come that way."

We all agreed that the family was Mexican. We now had to come up with a name for the boy. The Cisco Kid was Mexican and he had a sidekick named Chico. So that was it. We would call this boy, who we had never spoken to, "Chico."

Someone did speak to him one day and told him that he could join us on the ball field, if his father stopped taking the ball.

Chico, whose real name was Albert, became a regular with our gang even though he went to St. Mary's School. His family had come from a place called Holy Rosary in "The Burg." For a foreigner, he spoke pretty good English. Sometime later we found out that his family had come from Holy Rosary Parish in the Peterstown section of Elizabeth, which was called "The Burg." They weren't Mexicans. They were Italian. You could have fooled us, but the name "Chico" stuck.

Robert came running up to where we were gathered one day and announced, "A Pollock just moved in over on Edgar Road."

"A real Pollock?" somebody asked.

"A real live Pollock!" Robert exclaimed. "He has a Pollock's hat and coat and everything."

None of us had ever seen a Pollock before, including Breezy from New York and Chico, the Italian. So our little band marshaled its members and headed over to where Robert had seen the Pollock.

Sure enough, there was a man hoeing his garden, who looked for all the world like a Pollock. He wore a gray Dutch Boy type paint cap on his head and a gray jacket with buttons clear down the front.

"I'll talk to him," Robert said. "I learned a couple of words from the Hunkies up in the coal mines."

"Are Hunkies the same as Pollocks?" someone asked.

"Practically the same," Robert replied. "That's how I could recognize this man when I saw him."

As we approached, Robert waved his arm in greeting. "Hey, Pollock, Yak she mash."

"Yak tis she mash," the man replied with a big broad smile on his face.

"Dobsher," said Robert.

The man stood there talking Polish at a mile a minute, while Robert tried to remember another Polish word. Finally he said, "John Quey."

At that point we all waved at each other and the Pollock kept doffing his Cap.

We were quite impressed with Robert's command of Polish. Andy in my class is a Hunkie from Pennsylvania. I'll have to get Robert to teach me some words so I can impress Andy.

Someone in the School System must have realized that the effects of the War were creating a very diverse student body. The influx of Defense workers from any and all backgrounds and regions had fostered this change and now, for the sake of harmony, the schools took a lead in educating the students about these differences.

Previously, I had thought a Jew was somebody who didn't work for a manufacturer of War materials. They were people like Mr. Levin, who sold newspapers, and Mr. O, who came through the neighborhood selling blankets and sheets and household supplies. He would collect quarters from people and when a certain amount had been collected, he would bring the merchandise that had been ordered. He operated some sort of credit program. Harry Dombrowsky operated the corner grocery. It was a little food store, like a convenience store. Harry's was an immigrant from Russia, like Mr. Selman. His son Seymour was in the Air Force. The family of Irwin in my class came from Germany. Irwin's father wore a black coat and he wheeled a little cart around the city stopping to sharpen knives and repairing umbrellas. Then there was the "Rag Man." He had a horse and wagon. There was a cow bell on the wagon that he rang to announce his coming. He would ring the bell and holler, "RAGS, RAGS." He bought rags, paper and any other kind of junk. Another man with a horse and wagon would come by selling fruit and vegetables. He was the Vegetable Peddler.

As I learned about the War and Mr. Hitler in particular, my distain for him and his Nazis continued to grow. We found out how they persecuted people and chased them from their homes. The Jews were his enemies. People, who sharpened knives, were furriers, who ran corner stores and sold dry goods, along with the Rag Man and the Vegetable Man; these people were his enemies? Well, now he had some real enemies to worry about.

American Armies were moving up the boot of Italy, Russians were moving west from Leningrade and on June 6, 1944 the greatest Armada the world has ever seen would be deploying American, British and other Allied troops on the beaches of France. Mr. Hitler was going to find out what happens when you pick on little people.

Each of our days in school started with a Scripture reading from the Bible, the recitation of the Lord's Prayer and the Pledge of Allegiance to our flag. Our school assemblies had the same ceremonies and we sang songs praising God and Jesus at our Thanksgiving, Christmas and Easter programs. I don't recall anyone complaining.

A program of field trips was initiated to the various places of worship around the city. Fortunately for me Saint Mary's wasn't selected on the tour. It's a good thing because my cover could have been blown if some Nun recognized me. Instead of Saint Mary's we were going to Saint Patrick's Catholic Church, down in Elizabethport.

It was a pretty good program. Each week we went to a different church. The Pastors we visited gave us a talk about their particular denomination and we could ask questions. The locations and architecture of the various Churches reflected the lifestyles of the various ethnic communities as they came and settled in this city.

Some of the Churches were real interesting.

Going into The First Presbyterian Church of Elizabeth was like visiting a movie set. The Church was built way before the Revolutionary War and right down to the paint on the walls, it was perfectly restored. Thomas Jefferson or George Washington, or any other Colonist would feel right at home in its setting. A separate building off to the side of Church had at one time been an Academy that was attended by Alexander Hamilton and Aaron Burr. In later years, after the Revolution, these two schoolmates would be involved in a duel that cost Alexander Hamilton his life. Aaron Burr was a vice President of the United States in the first term of Thomas Jefferson's Presidency and he went and got himself in all kinds of trouble. This former patriot was destroyed politically and subsequently received the scorn of the American Government. The Academy fared much better than its two illustrious graduates. It prospered and grew. It was moved to Princeton, N.J. and ultimately evolved into Princeton University.

The Church property is located next to the Union County Courthouse. Between the Church and the courthouse is a graveyard where many of the early settlers of the town are buried. It would be hard to escape going to Church here, like we did at Saint Mary's. We would have had to make our escape around the tombstones and I don't think I would have been too comfortable with that.

The Jewish Synagogue on East Jersey Street and Route 1 was pretty neat. Only adults went to their services, which I liked. Their services were on Saturday, which I didn't like. Of course, I had no choice in selecting my religious preference and that Saturday business would not fly with me, even though they didn't have Nuns.

People from the Elizabeth Daily Journal newspaper took pictures during our visit to the Synagogue. My father practically hit the ceiling a few days later when a picture with me appeared in the paper. A small group of us, wearing those little black Jewish caps, were standing with the Rabbi, who was showing us the scroll.

"I'll never get that job at Standard Oil if Mr. Glackin sees your picture at the Jewish Synagogue. He'll think were Jewish," my father ranted.

"All Mr. Glackin has to do is read the story and he'll see it was something to do with school," I replied.

I could see by the look on my father's face that this situation did not have a simple solution.

"Mr. Glackin can't read," Daddy blurted.

"Well, I could go and steal his newspaper. If he can't read, why does he get a newspaper?"

"For pictures like this, that's why."

I was not in a good position. The picture might make people think I'm Jewish, especially since I've been AWOL from St. Mary's. I could only think of the consequences if my parents found out.

I decided to make the supreme sacrifice. I would return to St. Mary's.

The summer and the end of the school year were approaching. I would only have to go to St. Mary's maybe one or two times. I could tell the Nun that we had moved back into the Parish.

The timing was good. Allied troops had landed in France and they were moving towards Germany. The war would probably be over before school began in September and everybody could return to their normal lives. We could go back to where we came from and forget all about Mr. Glackin, the Standard Oil and the Nuns.

R. Allen Pender

## CHAPTER 27

## BREAKOUT AT THE SLAUGHTER HOUSE

The summer of 1944 held a lot of promise. Allied Forces had broken out of the Normandy beachheads and were starting to make a run for Berlin.

In the Pacific our forces, under General MacArthur, had fought across New Guinea: while Admiral Nimtz wagged a combined sea and land campaign against Imperial Japan. Troops of the U.S. Marines and U.S. Army were landing and taking Japanese held islands in the South Pacific in a steady march towards the mainland of Japan.

On the Home Front we began to relax a little, as the threat of any Japanese or German invasion of the American homeland was no longer a viable consideration. Rationing still existed and the need to supply war materials was at an all time high, as we needed to support the large and continually expanding war machine now sweeping the globe. But, despite the inconveniences, morale was high and after seeing the positive impact of their labor on the battlegrounds of the world, our people were proud and full of confidence as they carried out the tasks assigned in their unified commitment to victory.

We knew that the war would end soon. I hoped by September, so I didn't have to go to those religion classes at St. Mary's and my father could forget about getting a job at the Standard Oil Co.

This summer our activities wouldn't be all that different than that of the past few summers. There was still baseball - a lot of baseball. And, of course victory gardens were still the center of attraction for the neighborhood. Also, being a little older now meant having a little more freedom to explore more area beyond the neighborhood.

My Grandfather bought me a membership in the YMCA for my birthday. It cost him $6. It was O.K., but I had to go to downtown Elizabeth and be there between 8 and 9:30 A.M. on Saturdays. We had a Gym Class and then some swimming instructions. I didn't like the idea of going alone. Sure, there were other kids there, but none from my neighborhood.

Before school had closed for the summer, our teacher asked each person to stand up and tell the class about their summer plans.

Most of the girls were going to read books and help their mothers cook and sew. What a dull summer, I thought.

"And, Richard, what are you going to do this summer?" Missus Riley asked.

"Well, to start with. I go to the YMCA every Saturday for swimming. Then I will be going with my Grandmother and Grandfather up to the mountains to spend two weeks caning vegetables. Then I will be working in our neighborhood garden and of course in my spare time I'll be playing baseball, fishing in the Rahway River and swimming at Linden Pool." I didn't say anything about helping my grandfather make "Bath-Tub Gin." I'll save that information for another day.

"That sounds like a very ambitious summer program. Did you leave any room in your schedule for reading or studies of any kind?"

"No, Ma'am. I am going to be too busy for reading, except for the newspaper."

I could see the direction Mrs. Riley was headed. She was recruiting for a summer library reading program. Most of the girls were interested, but the boys were going to do some of the same things I planned to do. About six or seven boys said they were going to the YMCA too.

"HEY, RICHARD!" Thomas hollered as soon as we got out of the school building. "How much does that YMCA cost?"

"It costs $6.00 for the year. But, you can pay 25 cents a week."

"Wow. I'm gonna tell my father. Can I go with you Saturday?"

"Sure. All you have to bring is a towel. We don't wear bathing suits."

As one boy heard about the YMCA, he would tell another and so it went until we had quite a good-sized gang heading to the YMCA that next Saturday at 7:30 in the morning.

We had a raucous little crowd, bound to wake up anyone we could on our way to Madison Avenue, Elizabeth. As we went by the house of some schoolmate, we would stand out in front of their house calling their name until we got chased. We were an obnoxious little bunch.

The routine started all over again when we came home from the "Y." On most Saturdays we would eat lunch at home then meet again for another trip to Elizabeth to see the movies.

Linden Pool is another destination, mostly during the week. The Pool is located in Wheeler Park on Route 1 between Wood Avenue and Stiles street. The Park is about a 2 mile trip from our street. For 5 cents each way, we could travel by bus. Or, we could walk. It cost 11 cents to get into the Pool, so if we walked, additional money would be available to spend at the refreshment stand.

We usually brought a lunch of Spam sandwiches and took the bus. That way we spent less time walking in the heat and more time in the pool.

Our parents didn't want us to walk to the Pool. Because, it would be necessary for us to walk either along a desolate section of Route 1, opposite the Standard Oil Refinery, or down Linden Avenue, which runs parallel to Route 1 on the east and the railroad on the west. Linden Avenue started at Park Avenue and was a dirt road with swamps on both sides of the road along its mile and a half length to Wood Avenue, the main street in Linden. Midway down the road was a Railroad siding next to, which was a slaughterhouse.

Further down the road on the left side is a large cemetery. "Breezy" told us that they buried Gypsies there. It was a pretty spooky place.

Every once and a while we would venture down to the slaughterhouse.

Sometimes the corrals outside the slaughterhouse contained steers and at other times horses.

We liked to play RODEO with whatever animals were penned there. Taking turns - one by one - each boy would climb up on the corral fence and light onto the back of whatever poor animal passed by. Naturally, this activity stirred up the animals to the extent that someone working inside the slaughterhouse would come out to investigate the commotion.

"GET OUT OF HERE YOU KIDS," hollered the man, who wore black rubber boots and a bloody white coat. As he wildly cut at the air with the big knife in his hand, we made a rapid exit from the area. We didn't stop running, or look back until we reached Park Avenue.

We wanted to get "even" with that man. And we came up with a plan to open the corral gates and let the animals run loose. It would have to be at night. Since it was very spooky down there at night, we confided our plan with some of the bigger guys.

A few days later, Chicky's cousin Ducky approached us at our baseball field. "I was told to tell you guys that you should go down by Dark Lane Bridge at 8 o'clock tonight."

"What's gonna happen there?" Someone asked.

"Never mind, just go up on the bridge."

After supper we gathered at our Garden Street baseball field. We all brought our gloves and bats and taped up balls to the meeting site. An evening baseball game was good cover and our parents wouldn't be looking for us until dark, around 8:30 or 9 P.M.

Dark Lane Bridge carried Park Avenue over the Pennsylvania Railroad Main Line. There was a sidewalk and a fenced in railing on both sides of the roadway. It was a great place to stand and spit on the trains passing below. The smoke from the belching steam locomotives passing beneath the span would curl up around the sides of the bridge creating a moment of complete darkness. Maybe that's where the name Dark Lane came from. I don't really know, because it was a pretty dark place without any smoke. Rumor or legend has it, that someone hung themself below the bridge, which added more mystery of the place.

To confound anyone watching our activities, we decided to head up Elmora Avenue and then proceed south on Rahway Avenue towards Warinanco Park. We then went east on Park Avenue towards Dark Lane Bridge.

It was ten minutes to eight when we passed the clock in the store window on Park Avenue. At our present rate of speed we would cross Elizabeth Avenue and start to ascend the bridge in five more minutes.

Bell's Auto Junkyard was on the bridge side of Elizabeth Avenue and it backed up to the railroad.

"Look over the junkyard!" Tommy yelled. "There's a red flashing light comin' towards us."

We were half way up the bridge and could now see a series of red flashing lights.

The first vehicle, a '39 Pontiac Linden Police car, came up Elizabeth Avenue and squealed around the corner on Park Avenue then shot up over the bridge. Another police car and a fire engine followed the lead car.

"Something is happenin'," yelled Chicky. "Let's get to the top of the bridge."

There was a multitude of red flashing lights coming from the direction of the slaughterhouse... And we could see more red flashing lights coming down Route 1 towards Park Avenue.

Two Elizabeth Police cars came from Lidgerwood Avenue and pulled up and across Linden Avenue forming a roadblock.

Four Elizabeth policemen got out of the cars and appeared to be looking down Linden Avenue. We could see the flashing lights, but the tall bull rushes and cattails obstructed our view of the road.

Suddenly, we heard some unintelligible hollering and saw the policemen dive into their cars. They had no sooner got into the protection of the cars when three horses, at a full gallop, raced by the cars and headed down Lidgerwood Avenue.

"STAY UP THERE, YOU KIDS!" one of the Policemen hollered when we started down the sidewalk towards Linden Avenue. We just wanted a better look. But, the Policeman looked mad and kept waving at us to stay back.

Flashing red lights began to appear in every direction within view. Another Elizabeth Police car turned off Lidgerwood Avenue and pulled across Park Avenue halfway up the bridge.

One of the Policemen got out of the car and ran over to where we were standing.

"What are you kids doing here?" he bellowed.

"We're on our way home from the Park," Robert answered.

The Policeman looked us over as we stood their clutching a collection of antiquated baseball equipment. "Where do you ball players live?"

"Rosehill Place, Garden Street, Lidgerwood Avenue, New York Avenue," we blurted in unison.

"I want to get your names and addresses," he said, pulling a pad from his pocket.

Two more horses suddenly shot out from Linden Avenue along side the Police cars, which formed the roadblock. A Police car further down Park Avenue, nearer Route 1, took up the chase and followed the two horses down Lidgerwood Avenue.

"What's going on?" Robert asked.

"Some wise guys let the horses out of the pens at the slaughter house. What do you guys know about that?"

"Nothing," we said, shaking our heads like a bunch of puppets on strings.

"Well, I'm going to take your names and a detective will probably come around to see you tomorrow."

The Policeman proceeded to take our names and addresses and told us to stay where we were until they could release a police car to follow us home, because right now they didn't know where all the horses went.

After taking all the information, the Policeman walked back to his car. A few minutes later, that car turned back and slowly went down the bridge; pulling up next to the two cars forming the roadblock.

We could see that the cops in the cars were talking with each other, but we couldn't hear what was being said.

"They're pointing up here," Chicky excitedly yelped. "They know we know something."

"Shut up!" Robert scowled. "If you act like that; they will think we know something."

"Pipe down," said Chico. "Just act like nothin' happened."

This type of dialog went on for several minutes. Most of us didn't say anything; we were too busy trying to take in all the activity.

"I wonder where all the horses went? There must have been a hundred in that corral," I mused.

"Be quiet," Tommy urged. "The police are coming back here."

The Elizabeth Police car backed part way up the bridge. The Cop that took our names, leaned out of the window and said, "O.K. boys, walk behind this car. We're gonna escort you guys to Elmora Avenue."

Like a ragtag mob of prisoners, we followed the Police car on its slow cruise towards South Elmora Avenue, a half mile away. Small groups of people had gathered at the corners of Spotford and Kenneth Avenue to see what the Police activity was all about.

"What happened boys?" somebody hollered from one of the groups.

"Some horses got loose from the slaughter house," Robert answered.

"Oh," came the reply. "We thought maybe there was some sabotage along the railroad."

"Nope, just horses," Chico returned.

"Wow! This is like we're in a parade. We could be famous," Chicky chirped.

"Famous for what, seein' some horses run down the road?" Tommy shot back.

"Well, we were there where it happened."

"No we weren't," Robert said trying to keep Chicky quiet. "We were a half-mile away from where it happened, and we only saw five horses running."

The police car stopped by the Sun Brite Laundry on the corner of South Elmora and Lidgerwood Avenues. Our friendly officer got out and signaled for us to cross the street. "Get straight home you guys. I don't want to see you out anymore tonight."

When we got to the opposite corner, the Police car turned around and went back towards the scene of caper.

We laughed hysterically for the next few minutes as we walked up the street. No doubt we were suspects, especially after our previous experiences at the slaughterhouse. But, we really didn't do it and we really don't know who did.

Our neighbors were all seated out under the trees and on the front steps when we came innocently walking up the street.

"What happened down there boys?" Mr. Mitchell asked from his seat under a tree, where he sat puffing his pipe.

"Someone let the horses loose at the slaughter house," I answered.

"Were you boys down there?" Robert's father asked.

"No." answered Robert. "We went down Lidgerwood Avenue to see what was happening."

"I better not hear that you were down to that slaughter house!" My mother snapped.

"I wasn't there, Ma. Somebody else let the horses loose."

"You should have seen it Mom," Chicky said addressing his mother. "We saw cops chasin' horses down Lidgerwood Avenue."

"Where were you boys to see all this stuff?" Chicky's mother asked.

"Up on Dark Lane Bridge." Chicky proudly asserted.

Robert and I looked at each other. That Chicky was so excited and he couldn't keep his mouth shut. If he wasn't careful the whole story would come out and we would be in hot water.

The adults more or less bought our story of being at Dark Lane Bridge because of our interest in the police activities taking place. But, they were also unanimous in scolding us for not being where we were supposed to be at that hour of night. Of course we didn't do anything, nor did we really know who did. But, we were at the scene.

R. Allen Pender

The next day, around mid-morning, two detectives arrived in the neighborhood. They had the names and addresses of all the suspects, us included.

"How come you guys are always around when something happens?" said the stocky detective with dark hair.

He was referring to the shooting of Humphrey Bogart at the theatre downtown, the branding of little Joseph and the various complaints filed by Mr. Ecker, the Air Raid Warden. We were notorious bunch and of course we were high on the prospective suspect list for this recent caper.

"You guys were chased from the slaughter house recently. The Forman down there gave us a description that fits you guys," said the taller detective with light colored hair. "We know you guys have been hanging around there, riding the animals and just causing trouble all the time."

"Yeah, but we can't go down there at night. Ask our mothers," Chicky responded.

"That's right," I added. "It's too spooky at night."

"How many horses got away?" Robert asked.

"Three," Replied the stocky detective. "But, we'll ask the questions."

"Now boys, what do you know about this thing? Who did it?"

Shaking our heads, Robert, Chicky and I responded in the negative, "We don't know."

Chicky suddenly raised his hand, "I think I know."

"WHO?" The two detectives said in unison as they glared at Chicky.

We also glared at Chicky. Was he crazy? Was he going to tell about our being tipped off by his cousin? He had us scared.

"Somebody who wanted a horse," he said.

The detectives were getting mad at the answers they were getting from us. "We have your names and addresses. If we find out you guys haven't told us the truth. We'll be back."

We watched as the detectives moved down the street. We were also careful not to make any suspicious moves that might give away the fact that we had some knowledge of the caper.

"Be quiet and act normal," Robert snarled at Chicky, who was having a difficult time containing himself. "Wait until they're gone."

We all followed Robert's advice and slowly walked over to the big field.

"Where do you think the three horses went?" Chicky asked as we walked into the field. "Maybe we should go down by that cemetery and maybe we can find them. They're probably giving a reward for whoever finds the horses."

"Forget it," Chico shot back. "Let's stay away from that place until the heat is off."

"HEY!" I yelled. "Here come the O'Donell brothers delivering the Elizabeth Journal. Let's see if there's a story about the slaughter house."

The O'Donell brothers ran from building to building dropping the newspapers at their customer's doors. We knew who was working and wasn't home so we could borrow a paper, read it and put it back without anybody being the wiser.

Jack and his wife Clair, who lived on the first floor across the hall from my apartment, worked at the Aircraft Factory and they wouldn't be home right away. So we read their paper.

The Headlines of the Day amplified the progress of the War and focused on the advance of General Patton's Third Army, as it fought through France on its way to Berlin. Despite the importance and preponderance of War news; there screaming out at the bottom of the front page was a small story headline - HORSES FREED FROM ABATTOIR.

We would have missed the story if the headline didn't mention horses, because none of us knew what an Abattoir was. Now we knew.

The story went on to report that three horses were still at large and Police were investigating what appears to have been the work of a group of vandals.

"Wow, front page," exclaimed Tommy.

"Yeah, we're real news makers," chimed Chico. "Those Cops will never leave us alone now."

"I think we ought to forget about those horses and that slaughter house," Robert advised.

"Well, at least we made the newspaper. I'm gonna cut that story out of the paper, when people put it down at the collection bin in the cellar."

"What are you gonna do, Chicky... Paste it on your bedroom door?" Tommy laughingly replied.

"Hey, at least there's a story about us in the paper. R.A. is the only one who had a story about him in the paper 'till now. That was the time he went to the Jewish Temple."

"That story wasn't about me anymore'n the story about the horses is about us. We were just near there that's all."

We returned the newspaper and made our way back into the big field to survey the crops growing in the big garden.

# CHAPTER 28

# THE COUNTER SPIES

Our summer routine didn't differ much from the past year. The only difference is being our sizes. We all seemed to be starting to grow like weeds and that was accompanied by voracious appetites and increased levels of strength and energy. No ripe fruit trees or vegetable gardens were safe from our feeding frenzies.

We were all now at that crazy stage of life, a limbo between childhood and young manhood... too big to be small and too small to be big.

We had outgrown our small baseball fields and had to move on to the regulation size fields at Warinanco Park, or use the big guys' homemade diamond in the big field across the street. This wasn't much of a problem since the bigger guys were either going into defense jobs or the Military. In three short summers, those fellows who were entering high school when I moved here were now entering the Service.

Tommy had wanted to be a catcher, so when Alan down the street went into the Navy, he gave Tommy his catching equipment.

Gradually we began to inherit all the things of our predecessors. The meeting place on the concrete steps down by Harry's store, the big wooden backstop in the big field, the big field itself with its campsites and TARZAN'S rope swing in the Osage orange trees and the basketball court on the New York Avenue light pole were now ours.

With the increased strength came an increase in responsibilities. We had to begin filling the gap left by the bigger guys. There were kids now a few years behind us who had to be educated in the ways of the neighborhood. We had to let some of these younger boys tag along on our trips to the movies and Linden Pool. Gradually they would inherit our camp in Tarzan's Jungle and our weeding duties in the big gardens.

We were on to bigger and better things, like spreading horse manure and picking vegetables. In September we were moving on to Junior High School and a whole new life at a different school. This was our last summer as kids. Next year we would be young teenagers.

Breezy was already in Junior High School and he regaled us with stories about how tough it was. We would be going to Theodore Roosevelt Junior High School, located on Bayway Avenue in the Bayway section of the city. It was quite a walk from our neighborhood and we had to cross Route 1 to get there. If we lived on the other side of the railroad, two streets away, we would have had to go to Alexander Hamilton Junior high School, which was probably the same walking distance.

I was anxious to go to Junior High School and I didn't care one way or the other, which one. This was my opportunity to leave my checkered Elementary School past. I had two strikes against me when I entered Elementary School. Remember, I was the kid who shot out the street light and made a fool of the Principal and Mrs. Cower, who didn't want me to enter the Fourth Grade. Then I was caught taking target practice on the hallway light globes with a staple gun. Hitting the dentist with snowballs was probably the high point of my Elementary School Career and probably set a record for conduct that wouldn't be broken for some time.

As the end of the summer approached, it didn't appear that the War would be over before school began. That meant that we would probably be living here through another school year.

My father had resolved himself to the fact that he wouldn't get a job in the Standard Oil Company. However, because of his Union Membership and Newspaper affiliations, my father got a part-time job, at the Elizabeth Daily Journal. He worked on his days off, which were weekdays. This made him happy and anxious for the War to end, so he could return to his profession in the newspaper business.

The Japanese and Germans were no longer capable of mounting an invasion on the American homeland. They had to concentrate all their efforts in slowing down the Allied march toward Berlin and Tokyo. We began to relax our efforts in training to quell a potential invasion. It wasn't that we were abandoning the war effort, on the contrary. We were at the forefront in protecting the Country from subversive elements. Using our cover as Paper troopers, collecting old newspapers, we sought to uncover Fifth Columnists – saboteurs and spies working for the Axis Powers.

The Chinese Guy, who ran the Hand Laundry on Washington Avenue, was the only Oriental in the community. When we went by his store, we could see that the packages of laundry were plainly visible and the writing on the packages was Chinese.

"How do we know that the writing on those packages is Chinese and not secret Japanese messages?" Robert asked.

"Maybe, we should hang around there and see who goes in," Chicky suggested. "He could be passing messages to German spies."

"How will we recognize a German spy?" I asked.

"That's easy," Tommy responded. "They wear fedora hats pulled down to shade their eyes and have the collars of their coats turned up. Most of them have shifty eyes and smoke long cigarettes."

"Well, I guess anybody that is wearing a Fedora hat and an overcoat in this summer heat, has got to be guilty of something," I answered.

We decided to concentrate our paper collection efforts on Saturday to the vicinity of the Chinese Laundry.

We stationed Chicky with the wooden wagon right in front of the Chinese Hand Laundry. The rest of us scattered out in the surrounding area to knock on doors and look in alleyways for old newspapers. Two lookouts were stationed a few hundred feet north and south of Chicky. Chicky would signal them in the event that any of the passers-by would enter the Chinese Laundry. The lookouts would try to ascertain the identity of anyone entering the Chinese Laundry. Meanwhile, the rest of us would frequently return to the wagon with every little bit of paper we could find.

"Did anybody go into the laundry yet?" Chicky was asked.

"No. The Chinaman is in there all alone. He can see me out of his window and every once and a while he waves at me."

Things were pretty dull for a while, until finally someone came down the street and went into the Chinese laundry. It was Breezy. What was he doing just walking into the Chinese Laundry? Breezy couldn't be a spy. His brother was at sea on an oil tanker. But, then his family had moved here from New York. His parents never got involved in the main stream of the neighborhood. Maybe they were spies of some sort. Breezy probably didn't know his parents were spies. He was probably just a courier for his parents.

Tommy nonchalantly stopped Breezy as the later walked back up the street carrying the brown packages he picked up at the Chinese laundry.

"Hey, Breez, where are you going?"

"I'm goin' home. What are you guys doin' around here?"

"We're collecting newspapers for the Paper troopers," Tommy replied, without compromising our cover. "Do you go to the Chinese laundry a lot?"

"Yeah, my father has to have a clean white shirt every day and my mother can't do them because of her job. The Chinaman is pretty good. I come here every week."

"I have to go down an' check with Chicky to see how much paper we got. I'll see you later," Tommy said, ending the subtle interrogation and he headed off toward Chicky to file his report.

As Tommy and Chicky were talking, a gray, dusty 1938 Dodge sedan pulled up at the curb by the laundry. A man got out of the car and went into the laundry.

After the man went into the laundry, Tommy and Chicky began the wave signal.

"Something must be goin' on," I said to Robert. "Let's get back to the wagon and see what's up."

We could see the dirty Dodge parked at the curb… and it did have a familiar look. Chicky could hardly contain himself when we joined the group.

"It's Sharfenburger, the German. He's in the Chinaman's place. He gotta be a spy."

Mr. Sharfenburger lived on New York Avenue, right behind our row of garages and next to our big garden. He had a high wooden fence surrounding his property and he was very secretive. He never came out to see what was going on in the big garden right next to his fence. We only saw him go in and out in the dirty Dodge.

We busied ourselves around the wooden wagon as Mr. Sharfenburger came out of the Chinese laundry and left in his dirty Dodge.

"That's it," Chicky exclaimed. "We gotta set up surveillance around his house. I'll bet he has a secret radio transmitter in his attic. No wonder he's always chasing everybody away from his fruit trees."

With our quarry identified, we packed up our paper collecting equipment and headed for the next place to conduct our mission.

Mr. Sharfenburger's house was in an ideal place for our under cover activities. We could look directly into his rear yard from the garage roof. We dug a foxhole on the New York Avenue side of the big garden. From that point we could observe the front of the house without detection.

Arthur had a cardboard periscope that he got from some parade years back. That thing was neat. A guy could hunker down in the foxhole, out of sight, and see everything going on above ground with the periscope.

We went to Bell's junkyard and found some copper wire that we attached to my Crystal radio antenna. We now had a long antenna wire that we could stretch across the clothes poles near the garages. We had a super antenna that would pick up Sharfenburger's transmissions to any German submarines lying off the coast.

Day after day we manned our posts. One or two guys would sit on the garage roof, secreted among the branches of one of the Sumac trees growing behind the garages, spying on the activities going on in Sharfenberger's yard. One or two other guys would man the foxhole to observe the front of the house. The antenna wire for the crystal radio was draped into one of the vacant garages. I took the crystal radio set into the house when we were not out on our observation posts.

I don't know what kind of action we would take if something subversive did happen on our watch. We had a set of hand signals, which were to be used by the guys in the foxhole and those on the roof. Periodically, we would test the signals just to make sure we remembered them. The group observing the subversives would signal the other group, who would then rush from their position to join the signaling group. Needless to say, we had many false alarms.

R. Allen Pender

The crystal radio set picked up WOR real good, but we never heard any other signals, like a spy would use.

Our observations did generate some positive information. During our surveillance we could watch the progressive growth and ripening of the fruit on Sharfenberger's trees.

A big Cherry tree was just inside his fence near the rear of the garages. A Pear tree was located deeper in the yard along the fence that separated his property from that of Mr. Allen on the south. Mr. Allen had a high green wooden fence along his south property line, near our Tarzan's Jungle Camp. Deer had been entering his yard to feed in his garden, so he raised the fence up high and left a gap down low between the fence and the ground. He had Raspberries growing all along his back line, next to the back of the garages, to Mr. Sharfenburger's fence.

Our intelligence gathering indicated that it was time to raid the raspberries. The cherries would be next and the pears last, closer to the Fall.

The first phase of the mission would involve enlarging the gap below Mr. Allen's fence, so we could crawl into the raspberries. This was easy since we could operate under the cover provided by the brush near our secret campsite in Tarzan's Jungle. The second phase of the operation would consist of an airborne assault from the garage roof into Mr. Sharfenburger's cherry tree. From the first phase of the plan we would learn the best way to attack the pear tree from Mr. Allen's yard.

Mr. Allen had an old father-in-law, who was home all day and he worked in the garden. We could watch his activities from the garage roof. The man generally finished his gardening at about 4 P.M. We think he went in the house to drink homemade wine. Then we made our move.

We made a burrow under the fence, just big enough for us to crawl through. A couple of rocks were put into the burrow to conceal our activity. When the time for the raid came, we could quickly remove the rocks and crawl into the garden.

Mr. Allen had to walk from the bus stop on Edgar Road to his house on New York Avenue. His routine was the same every day and he got home around 6 o'clock. Shortly after getting home, he would take his big white dog for a walk in the fields on the other side of New York Avenue. That was the time for the raid…In and out real quick; while that dog was away.

Two Chow dogs lived cross the street from Mr. Allen in the last house before the New York Avenue fields. As soon as Mr. Allen left his house with his dog, those two chow dogs would start barking like crazy. They would stop after he passed their house and then they would start up again as he passed their house on his return. Our plan had to be carried out in the time between the dog barks.

The evening of the planned raid had arrived and we watched Mr. Allen coming from the bus stop through Sinnott's barnyard.

"Let's get in position guys," Tommy excitedly barked. "Mr. Allen is comin'."

"You go first, R.A.," Robert suggested.

"All right, but you guys watch. I can hear the dogs, but I won't be able to see anybody coming out of the house."

"Watch me," Chicky responded. "I'll climb up in that big Sumac tree near the fence. I'll wave if someone's comin'."

The rocks were removed from the burrow as Chicky scaled the Sumac tree. I got in position at the base of the fence and waited for the dogs to bark.

There was no mistaking the bark of those Chow dogs. They could probably be heard a couple of miles away.

In a flash, I was under the fence and into the raspberries. The old gentleman, who worked the garden, had done a good job. The raspberry bushes were laid out in nice straight rows and our burrow came out right in the middle of two rows.

I was able to crawl along on my side and sample the berries dangling from the heavy-laden branches of fruit. I was careful not to pick too many berries from one spot as I crawled down the row stuffing the ripe berries into a paper sack. I could see Chicky up in the tree when I turned from side to side to pick berries from alternating sides of the row. So far, so good…I was midway across the yard when the dogs started barking again. Quickly, I turned and crawled on my belly to the burrow and hastily exited the yard.

I was greeted like a hero by my comrades, who quickly placed the stones back in the burrow. As the early evening light receded from among the wild cherry trees in Tarzan's Jungle, we sat in their flickering shadows and stuffed ourselves with sweet pilfered raspberries.

We were all pretty smug at the success of this operation.

"Sharfenburger's cherry tree is goin' to be a lot harder," Robert stated. "There's no cover if he sees us an' we have to get back on the garage roof real quick."

"Yeah gettin' over his big wood fence isn't too easy. Then getting' out of that tree fast, is a problem," Chicky volunteered.

"We have to think of a good system. And I have an idea."

"What have you got R.A.? I hope it's not the rubber bands from the airplane," Robert sarcastically announced.

"Almost," I said. "Ropes."

"ROPES!! Are you crazy, R.A.? Is this gonna be something like the way we used to slide out of the trees?" Chicky asked.

"I got an idea. Let's get some rope and try it."

We had some good ropes that we had used for repelling out of the trees and off the fire escapes. This wasn't cotton clothesline. It was "Horse Rope." I don't know where it came from, or how it got the name Horse Rope. It was another one of those items that boys older than us had used and it was passed to us as they out grew its need. We kept these ropes and an assorted collection of items down in the cellar of our building in a little niche near the tenants' storage bins.

"Let's take these ropes up on the garage roof over by the big garden."

"I hope you know what you're doin' R.A.," Chicky mused.

"Don't worry about it Chicky," Robert said grabbing up a pile of rope. "We'll let him go first."

There was a wooden pole with steel rungs at the end of the row of flat roof garages where the path went into the big garden. Quickly two of us were up the pole and onto the garage roof. The ropes were passed up and then the rest of the gang climbed up the pole and joined us on the roof.

Several more poles were set in the field along the backside of the garages. These poles supported a power cable about an inch and one half in diameter, encased in a lead sheath. The cable was very flexible and I had even seen bigger guys hanging on it then dropping the eight or so feet into the soft soil of the field.

Sharfenburger's fence came up to about one foot from the back wall of the garages. The cable ran across the back of his yard and Mr. Allen's yard to a pole behind Mr. Gavan's Block Garage.

We could just reach the cable from the garage roof and we threw a rope over it and tied a slipknot in the rope so that it dropped to within two feet of the ground.

"O.K. guys watch this," I said grabbing the rope and swinging out into space. The cable flexed under my weight and I released my hands and landed upright on the soft turf.

One by one, the rest of the boys made the same trip and then climbed back up the pole to do it again. Each of us got to learn our own landing style and how much the flexing cable would impact our landing.

Sharfenburger's fence was made of wood planks nailed to horizontal 4 x 4's that were supported by vertical 4 x 4's every eight or so feet. In order to get out of the tree fast, a boy would have to swing out of the tree and land on the horizontal 4 x 4, which was about 4 feet off the ground. From that point it was an easy swing over the fence and a drop into the small space between the fence and the rear wall of the garages. A few feet away there was an opening, which separated two rows of garages… an ideal getaway route.

The cherry tree was only a few feet inside the fence. Some of its outer branches actually swept the edge of the garage roof.

On the first mission, one boy was to be sent into the cherry tree to test the system. The others would support him from the garage roof. If the first person were successful, then the rest of the boys would go on succeeding missions. Only one boy would be in the cherry tree at a time.

On the afternoon of the first mission we secured a rope to the cable at a spot in line with some branch openings. It looked like an ideal spot to make the leap onto one of the main branches of the tree.

The mission was set to go after supper. Chicky would man the foxhole outpost to watch Sharfenburger's house. If he saw anything that would endanger the mission, he would use a flashlight to signal the rest of us up on the roof. Three quick flashes meant there was a problem. Two long flashes meant the coast was clear.

"You go first, R.A. This is your idea."

"Alright, give me the sack for the cherries."

Tommy handed me the bag we had made that was to be attached to the belt. I unhooked my belt and then passed the belt through the slits we had made in the sack. "I'm all set," I said as I adjusted the sack to a good picking position.

Sharfenburger's yard was quiet and there didn't seem to be any activity around his house. We all watched as Chicky came down New York Avenue, past Sharfenburger's house and entered the foxhole.

I was ready at the rope when two long flashes of light came from Chick's foxhole.

"Go." Robert quietly said.

In a second, I was down on the fence rail and then made the step across to the main branch of the tree. I squeezed the rope under my arm into my armpit as I quickly placed cherries into the bag. After about three minutes, I felt that I had enough cherries and I swung out to the fence.

The plan worked perfectly. I was over the fence and hit the ground running.

I ran down to the other end of the garage and climbed the pole back to the roof.

"How come you got out so quick? Everything is quiet. You could have stayed longer," Robert exclaimed, while I unloaded the cherry bag into a bucket.

"It was too quiet. Almost scary. Do you want to try it now?"

"Yeah, I'll go," he said, as I handed him the cherry sack.

Robert followed the same route I had used and was quickly in the tree. Nerves had probably gotten the better part of him too. Because, a few minutes later he was out of the tree and over the fence.

"WOW!" he said as he rejoined us up on the roof. "I could see Sharfenburger everywhere when I was in that tree."

We decided to call it a night at that point. We concluded that the mission was a success and we had out foxed the Germans. In this case, one German... Sharfenburger.

Chico ran down and got Chicky out of the foxhole. We moved our operations over by the backstop in the big field where we gouged ourselves with cherries.

We were pretty satisfied with the success of our commando raids.

The next afternoon we all gathered on the concrete pad in front of Harry Dombrowsky's store to relive our exploits of the night before. It's amazing how six minutes of daring can develop into a story that takes longer to tell than do, particularly if a lot of animation is involved. We also had to plan tonight's mission.

Another foray into Sharfenburger's tree would be exciting, but we were a little tired of cherries right at the moment.

While we were trying to make up our mind and decide what would be satisfying to our pallets... Mr. Allen emerged from Sinnott's barnyard next to Jim's Ice House.

"I think we're in trouble guys, Mr. Allen looks like he's headin' right for us," Chicky nervously disclosed.

"Maybe he's going to Harry's store," Robert answered. "Just ignore him like nothin' ever happened."

"Hi, fellas," Mr. Allen said with a smile. "Would you boys be interested in making 50 cents each?"

I'm sure all of us thought the same thing at the same time. Fifty cents was a lot of money. It was equal to two Saturdays of movies and a couple of hot dogs.

Tommy's father knew Mr. Allen well, so we let Tommy speak for us.

"Sure Mr. Allen. What would you like us to do?"

"My father-in-law needs some help picking the fruits and vegetables in my yard and my neighbor, Mr. Sharfenburger, had to go to Pennsylvania. His mother is very sick and he asked me to find someone to pick the cherries on his tree before the birds eat them all up. I'll pay each of you 50 cents and you can take home some fresh produce too."

I don't know the reason, but somehow the fruits and vegetables we got paid to pick didn't taste the same as those we acquired on our secret missions.

# CHAPTER 29

# JUNIOR HIGH SCHOOL

Junior High School was a lot different than our old Elementary School. We were mixed in with a new group of kids and we had different teachers for each subject. We also had shop classes. The seventh grade split the year between wood shop and print shop. The eighth grade had Metal Shop and Mechanical Drawing. Ninth graders could choose any shop class they wanted.

We had gym class that had a locker room where we changed our clothes and wore gym shorts and a T-Shirt. We also had to wear an athletic supporter, which was an embarrassing thing to ask your mother to buy, since they didn't know anything about those things.

The girls were starting to change too. They started to change shape and to take on proportions similar to that of grown women. I think it was because they had to get special gym suits too. Girls and boys no longer had Gym together. They had it at the same time, but the girls had their own Gym, behind the Auditorium curtains.

There were more after school activities here than we had in Elementary School.

Beginning in September, each grade had a football kicking team, punting, place kicking and drop kicking and we had matches between the other Junior High School teams. After Thanksgiving we had class swimming teams and we participated in meets at the Elizabeth YMCA. The swimming meets were nothing fancy, just freestyle heats and relays where each boy swam the length of the pool once. After Christmas, we had basketball. Each class team played a corresponding class from one of the other three Junior High Schools and the team with the best record was crowned City Champion for that grade. We came close, but we weren't Champions. In the Spring we had a track meet at the Stadium in Warinanco Park. All the Junior High schools were there at the same time and we competed by grades. We did the running broad jump, the shot put throw and the quarter mile relay race. We came in third out of four schools, which wasn't too bad since we were the smallest Junior High School in the city.

March, April and May was the time for baseball. Our Gym teacher, Mr. Ciambelli loved baseball and we would practice every afternoon at a place called "Simmon's Field", which was actually next to the Standard Oil Refinery in Linden. We had a lot of good players and enough boys involved to have two teams for a game every day. This year we weren't the Junior High School League Champions, but we won more than half of our games.

*R. Allen Pender*

Sports weren't the only extra-curricular activity. We had clubs like; the Art Club, the Visual-Aids Club, and an Orchestra. Then there was Social Dancing. That was attended mostly by girls. Some of the ninth grade boys went, but for most of us, the sports programs were more compatible with our life style.

Dancing, or anything having to do with dancing or girls, could get a guy into a lot of trouble. We prohibited girls from all our activities. They just weren't physically or mentally compatible with our type of interests. They were becoming young ladies, while we were still in our aboriginal stage.

We were interested in sports and roasting potatoes in smoky campfires. We liked to hang around the river and play in the swamps. We liked fishing and swimming in the reservoir. We liked to hitch rides on the horse and wagons that worked in the Standard Oil and returned to Juzefyk's Livery stables each night. We liked to clean the horse stalls on Saturdays and then be treated to a bareback ride on the huge draft horses. Of course we were magnetically attracted to anything resembling a garden, a fruit tree, or something edible.

Girls on the other hand were getting interested in clothes and make-up. Hairstyles were becoming another priority. Add the dancing to these differences and the huge gulf between boys and girls is quite visual.

These differences started on a collision course one evening in October.

There was a lot to celebrate that October. Allied Forces in Europe were moving steadily towards the German homeland. American forces had landed in the Philippines and were starting to liberate the various Philippine Islands as they sought to regain and avenge the early war losses at Bataan and Corregidor.

We had a great harvest season. The gardens yielded bumper crops to which we were able to add that which we were able to collect from Mr. Allen's and Mr. Sharfenberger's yard. All the canning was done and the food was stored in each individual family's storage bin in the basement.

We had warm days, but the evenings were getting darker and cooler as we approached the witching time of Halloween.

One evening we were out in the growing shadows of the season. We had picked a few of the remaining late season tomatoes that had been clinging to the vine and were now roaming around seeking targets of opportunity on which to unload our gushy missiles.

We had taken some target practice on a few inanimate telephone poles when Robert alerted us to a moving target coming up Lidgerwood Avenue from the direction of Elmora Avenue.

"A girl is coming up the street. Let's scare her."

It was Arlene. She and her family lived up over Cotton's Gin Mill. Arlene was in the ninth grade and she had blossomed into proportions that were the envy of a lot of the girls.

From our positions in the Garden Street field we watched as Arlene started to come into range on her walk up the sidewalk towards her home.

Chicky hurled the first tomato, which splashed into the street some twenty feet from Arlene's position. Arlene squealed and yelled when she realized she was under attack. Immediately she started running towards her home.

Tommy and Robert then unleashed their salvos which hit the sidewalk behind Arlene. I was last and threw my soft red missile up ahead of the fast charging Arlene.

As the soft tomato fell to earth, it collided with Arlene's head.

SPLAT!!!

"You got her R.A!" Chicky yelled, as the girl reached the safety of her front door.

"What a shot," shouted Tommy. "That was one in a million."

We knew Arlene wasn't injured and we had no intention of hurting her. She was a girl and girls were meant to be scared, or so we thought.

After Arlene entered her door, we excitedly ran from the scene to look for another outlet for our mischievous inclinations. We still had some tomatoes remaining and they were looking for a suitable target.

Quickly we distanced ourselves from the site of the Arlene attack and made our way to the abandoned train station on Dehart Place. We were intent on using our remaining tomatoes to attack an unsuspecting passenger train on the Pennsylvania Mainline. However, the only train that came along had no passenger cars and what seemed like a thousand boxcars. We were denied the thrill of a human reaction to our mischief as we peppered the slow moving boxcars with the remnants of our ammunition.

As darkness began to settle-in we decided to call it a day and we all headed for our homes on Rosehill Place.

"What were you up to tonight?" my father asked just as soon as I came through the door.

"Just hangin' around with the guys."

"Oh, yeah? You weren't out throwing tomatoes by some chance ... were you?"

"Well ... we threw some at a train full o' boxcars."

"Somebody said you threw some at Arlene down the corner."

"Oh, we just meant to scare her."

"You hit her in the head. DIDN'T YOU?" my father said with a sudden rise in the tone of his voice. "That girl was just coming home from getting her hair done for her first school dance tomorrow night. AND YOU MESSED IT ALL UP!"

I knew I was in real trouble when my mother joined in the attack. "That girl's head is full of tomato seeds. Mrs. Faughnan just went to all the trouble of fixing that girls hair for the dance and now it's ruined."

"HER MOTHER AND FATHER WANT TO SEE YOU RIGHT NOW. COME ON," my father bellowed as he got out of his chair and grabbed a jacket.

I didn't know what kind of punishment was in store for me, but what ever it was, I was sure it wasn't going to be pleasant.

I walked ahead of my father, neither of us saying a word, on the trip down to Arlene's house.

A group of men were standing out in front of Cotton's Gin Mill, which I thought was rather unusual.

"Here he is, Fred," someone in the group said as we approached the building.

Fred, Arlene's father emerged from the barroom. He had some brown objects swinging from the hands he held at his side.

When we drew closer, I could see what they were... BOXING GLOVES.

Grabbing a pair of the soft leather gloves from the steely eyed Fred, my father said to me, "Here, put these on."

Quickly Two of the men in the crowd jumped out to help me lace up the gloves. Two more did the same for Arlene's father, Fred.

"Here, move over under the street light," Mr. Cotton suggested.

Once we had moved under the streetlight, the crowd formed a circle around me and Fred.

"I'll be the Referee," said Mr. Thomas, stepping into the circle.

"He's all yours, Fred," My father said, as Mr. Thomas signaled us to the center of the circle.

"No hitting below the belt and I'll stop the fight when I think it's gone far enough. Now go back to the edge of the circle and come out fighting."

Fred had me by about four inches and sixty pounds, but most of it was a beer belly. I was fairly tall for my age and was pretty quick on my feet, so I just danced around parrying Fred's jabs. Every once in a while he would hit me on the upper arm. He didn't hurt me because I could roll with his punches. I never punched back even though I had a few openings. It took me a while to understand the meaning of this fight. It had been "cooked up" by the men of the neighborhood and gave Fred the opportunity to be a hero in his daughter's eyes; it was his way of avenging the hurt done to her and concurrently punishing the culprit. Me.

I don't know how many minutes we fought, but it wasn't too long before Fred signaled Mr. Thomas that he was finished.

No one was declared the winner. A wrong had been avenged in an honorable and just manner, and a lesson was learned. The matter was closed.

It could have been a lot worse for me. I think I was lucky for having a boxing match to resolve the problem. My mother promised that if I didn't learn my lesson and give the girls some respect she would send me to dancing school.

The waning daylight of November and December put a crimp in our night-time activities. We were pretty much limited to school activities ... and homework. The teachers probably thought we didn't have any life beyond school and they piled on the homework.

Homework did have a plus side. I had so much of it that I wouldn't be able to attend St. Mary's Catechism classes and still get my homework done for the next day. My mother bought into this scam, but she was smarter than I thought and she added some homework of her own to my busy schedule.

We opened each day at school with a reading from the Bible. Sometimes it was a Psalm and sometimes it was a passage from one of the other books of the Bible. But, in any event, I had to make a notation as to what passage was being read every day. That evening I had to pick up our Bible at home and write the passage of the day for my mother. After I read it to her, she asked questions. Even though she didn't read the passage, she knew what it meant. I think going to St. Mary's might be easier than my mother's homestyle brand of religious training.

A lot of our schoolwork, except math and science, concerned the world situation. History was being written every minute of the day. Geography was alive. Each of us could point to different parts of the world where we had relatives serving in the conflict. All of these things related to our every day life.

We saw the Grumman Hellcats being ferried out of the Eastern Aircraft plant in Linden to points where they would be made available to our carrier pilots. There was a steady flow of tanks and trucks moving along the mainline of the Pennsylvania Railroad, destined for some port of embarkation.

Despite the fact that our forces were rapidly pushing the enemy back to their homelands, we were still experiencing Black outs, rationing, air raid drills and shortages. These things were now a standard part of our daily lives and although we didn't like it, we accepted it.

Synthetic items were developed to replace those products impacted by the War. Margarine came in a kit that included a white manufactured fatty substance that got mixed with another yellow compound to produce an imitation butter. Because of the shortage of shoe leather, we had to tape up a lot of floppy shoe soles, until they came out with NEOLITE replacement heels and soles.

One manufacturer came out with patches for pants. The patches came in standard plain colors. After the color was selected, the patch was placed over the tear, on the inside of the pants and heated with an iron to make a neat repair. There wasn't much available in new clothes. Most of us wore hand-me-downs

R. Allen Pender

from either relatives or neighbors and as time wore on, some of our pants had almost as many patches as original cloth.

My mother was very skilled with her Kenmore sewing machine. She made clothes for my sister and cousins and altered clothes for anyone in the neighborhood.

Plastics were starting to replace glass and metal products. Christmas ornaments, which were once manufactured of glass in Europe, were now being manufactured by American companies, using plastic. Synthetic rubber replaced natural rubber that we formerly imported from Southeast Asia. There wasn't enough synthetic rubber to make tires for domestic cars. It was all going to the war effort. A large piece of rubberized fabric called a "boot" was installed inside a worn out tire to give a few more miles. It was something like the pants patch, only bigger.

Ladies stockings, once made from silk imported from Japan, were history. Ladies first used a leg makeup to color their legs in an attempt to imitate the appearance of silk stockings. American genius developed a new synthetic fabric called NYLON. A variety of products that ranged from rope and parachutes to ladies stockings are made from this miracle fabric.

In an effort to provide our troops with advantages in the battlefields, American industry developed new products and entire new fields of technology. New words are being added to our language on a regular basis. Radar, Sonar, Flying Fortress, Superfortress, Liberty Ship and Jet Aircraft are just a few of the additions to the American lexicon. Another American character placed his imprimatur on walls or any other standing structure around the world big enough to print "KILROY WAS HERE."

The Federal Government even built a little town on a tract of land along the Rahway River where Linden, Cranford and Clark Township came together. They called the place Winfield Park and it housed people who built the Liberty Ships at the Kearny Ship Yards.

We were fiercely proud of the accomplishments of our troops on the battlegrounds of the world. We were equally proud of the important work on the home front that was contributing to the Allied success. That pride was due to be raised another notch at Christmastime in December, 1944.

When the first man set foot upon this North American continent he not only started the development of the most unique nation in the history of mankind; his arrival also signaled the beginning of the American Psyche. It's an attitude. That attitude dumped the King's tea in Boston harbor, then those people wrote him a letter that more or less told him to put his crown where the sun don't shine. Our history is replete with manifestations of this attitude. During the American Revolution, when asked to strike the colors of his burning ship, The Bonhomme Richard, Commander John Paul Jones replied, "I have not yet begun to fight."

That phrase and others born in the heat of battle, like "Damn the torpedoes, full speed ahead" and "Praise the Lord and Pass the Ammunition" were widely publicized examples of the American attitudes during the stress of battle.

In mid December, 1944, the line of the American Armies advancing on Nazi Germany was struck by a fifty mile wide wedge of German armor and infantry. American soldiers fought fiercely to repel this attack in the worst weather conditions the European continent had seen in recent history. Hitler had assembled all his reserve infantry and tanks to make this final desperate assault in hopes of capturing allied gasoline and supplies sufficient to crush the Allied advance. This fight over a seventy mile front was called the BATTLE OF THE BULGE. Out numbered and scattered in miserable weather, so overcast they could not get any air support: Small pockets of Americans valiantly held against the German onslaught. The 101st Airborne Division was surrounded in the small town of Bastogne. A contingent of German soldiers approached under a flag of truce to demand the surrender of the surrounded Division.

As the Nation prayed for a break in the weather, which would permit the use of superior American Air power to crush the German thrust, The 101$^{st}$ Division Commander, General Anthony McAuliffe responded to the German demand with one word, "NUTS!"

Clearing skies backed up this bit of American stubbornness and on December 23, The Air Force began to make a junk pile of Hitler's tanks.

It wasn't any cakewalk into Germany. Hitler's forces were never again able to mount an assault as massive as they did at the "BULGE." But, that didn't stop them from fiercely resisting the Allied advance into Germany.

In January, my Uncle Bill was sent home to the Naval Shipyard in Philadelphia.

Uncle Bill served on an LST. He was in the European-African-and Middle Eastern Theater. Beginning with the Invasion of North Africa, he was involved in just about every beach head in those theaters of operations, including, Sicily, Anzio and finally Omaha Beach.

He was promoted to the rank of Chief Petty Officer and had earned enough "Points" to return home for discharge.

Uncle Bill was a great baseball fan and he loved the N.Y. Giants. One of the first things he did after being discharged was to order tickets for the Giant's season opener in the Polo Grounds in New York.

# CHAPTER 30

# THE END AND THE BEGINNING

For us, Uncle Bill's homecoming was a harbinger of Spring and a hopeful indication of good things to come...the War's conclusion.

In February, General Douglas MacArthur's Army completed the liberation of the Philippines and re-took Manila. U.S. Marines were steadily moving up the Japanese home islands; securing those key locations for air bases to be used in the final assault on Japan. On February 19, U.S. Marines made a landing on Iwo Jima, six hundred sixty five miles from Tokyo.

In March, while forces in the Pacific were engaged in the bitter fight for Iwo Jima and sea battles raged closer and closer to the Japanese mainland, Allied Forces entered Germany.

The closing perimeter around Germany began to reveal atrocities that boggled the mind. We had heard of Hitler's desire for a Master Race and his miss-treatment of Jews and others not suitable for his grand plan. But, I don't think American troops were prepared for the sights they encountered when they liberated the NAZI concentration camps. Millions of people were enslaved, tortured and killed because Hitler saw them as enemies of his demented Third Reich.

The extreme of man's inhumanity to his fellow man is described in many ways, but there are not enough suitable words to describe such treatment and such sights. It was a "Holocaust."

This could have been the fate of Irwin's mother and father, or Mr. Selman; men, women and children, whose only crime was their existence during the reign of lunatics.

To say the American public and military was enraged at the disclosure of these atrocities is put it mildly. The German military had to pay the price for this genocide and no quarter would be given.

By April 1, 1945, seven Allied Armies had crossed the Rhine River and were overrunning Germany on the march toward Berlin. Meanwhile, the Allied Air Forces were relentlessly pounding the German cities and industrial centers into ruin.

Russian Armies were moving towards Berlin from the east. On April 1, in the Pacific, American Army and Marine units landed on the Japanese Island of Okinawa. Even as they were losing the organizational ability to prosecute the war, the enemy troops, both in Europe and in the Pacific were not yielding an inch of ground without stiff resistance.

It looked like this April was going to be a momentous month in the history of the world and this war.

Indeed it was.

On the morning of April 11, I was given money and told that when school finished for the day, I was to take the bus to my Grandmother's house in Hillside. My mother had been taken to the hospital. A new baby was due and I was to stay with my Grandmother until the event had taken place and my mother was released from the hospital.

I could have taken the 44 bus from Edgar Road to Broad Street for 5 cents. But, I elected to walk and keep the nickel. At the corner of Broad Street and Caldwell Place I got the number 50 bus which traveled up Broad Street to North Broad Street in Hillside. I could get off the bus at the corner of Coe Avenue and North Broad Street. It was then a one block walk to my Grandmother's house on Salem Avenue.

I reached Gramma's house just as my father was leaving to visit his mother, who was very sick, and had been admitted to Saint Elizabeth's Hospital in Elizabeth. Then he was going to see my mother, who was in Elizabeth General Hospital.

"You have a new sister. I brought your clothes and things so you can stay here with your grandmother until your mother comes home. I'll see you tomorrow." With that he was gone in a blur of blue smoke that came from the tailpipe of my grandfather's car, which he borrowed for the event.

The next morning Gramma packed my lunch and I reversed the process and commuted back to school in Elizabeth. I walked to school from the end of the 50 bus line and saved another nickel.

That afternoon, April 12, 1945, I took the #50 bus again to my grandmother's house.

The bus had just crossed North Avenue and came to a stop in front of the Benedictine Academy, a private girl's school. Some girls got on the bus and they were crying.

Someone asked one of the girls what was wrong and I heard them exclaim, "President Roosevelt has died."

"Impossible," I thought. "President Roosevelt was always our President; he can't just up and die right in a critical part of the War."

"Gramma!" I said as I burst through the kitchen door. "Some girl on the bus said President Roosevelt died!"

"Well, I wouldn't know," she answered. "I've been here in the kitchen pretty much all day. What with your mother havin' a new baby, we'll be havin' folks a' comin' to eat. I'll put the radio on and maybe we kin hear."

I followed my grandmother into the parlor and sat down in front of the big radio with the light up dial. The very same radio that I listened to a few years back, when the Japanese bombed Pearl Harbor.

Sure enough all the news was about the death of President Roosevelt at a place called Warm Springs, Georgia. The Vice-President, a man named Harry Truman was sworn in to be President. Nobody seemed to know anything about Harry Truman. It was almost like President Roosevelt was the president forever and now a man that people called "Harry Who" was in charge of our destiny.

I was all caught up in the news about President Roosevelt, when I noticed that my father was in the kitchen talking to Gramma.

"Come with me now, son," he commanded as he stood beneath the dining room archway. "We have to go meet Uncle Bill."

"Uncle Bill?" I thought we might be going to see my mother and the baby. How did Uncle Bill fit into that picture?

My father was unusually quiet as we drove down Salem Avenue and then turned right onto North Avenue.

Uncle Bill was now working for the Gas Company and we saw him at the corner of North and Morris Avenues, standing next to the '35 Ford coupe car that belonged to the Gas Company.

My father pulled up behind the black coupe, got out and went over to where Uncle Bill was standing. I was told to stay in the car.

The two men stood there talking with a posture that indicated to me that something wasn't right.

My father was dabbing his eyes with a handkerchief when he returned to the car.

"The baby gave your mother a lot of trouble, so she isn't feeling well. Don't tell her about this meeting with Uncle Bill. Your grandmother died and I don't want to upset your mother."

I answered in the affirmative even though I didn't really comprehend the situation.

President Roosevelt died today. My grandmother died today. My mother was in the hospital with a baby. What else could happen?

The next day I made the round trip bus ride to school again. My life was fairly normal, except I couldn't go home. Although it had only been two days, I did miss my after school activities, particularly baseball.

After I entered the classroom that morning, my teacher Mrs. Hughes approached me. "Richard, could I see you outside in the hall?"

I couldn't imagine what she wanted. I had clean clothes and took a bath every day. Some kids had problems in that area, but I didn't.

"Richard, where are you living? We have heard that you may have moved because what has happened in your family. If you feel that you need to take off until your father gets over the bereavement period it is alright with the school."

"I'm just staying with my grandmother in Hillside until my mother and the baby come home. But, I wouldn't mind takin' a couple of days off."

"BABY, WHAT BABY?" Mrs. Hughes exclaimed.

"My mother had a baby girl the other day in Elizabeth General Hospital."

"Didn't somebody in your family die in Saint Elizabeth's Hospital?"

"Oh, yeah. That was my grandmother."

"Are you sure? Is your mother Alice Pendell and your father Joseph? Those were the names in the obituary."

"My father is Joseph, Jr. and my grandmother's name is Alice the same as my mother. I thank you for your concerns, but I think someone didn't read the newspaper right."

The situation was a lot more confusing for my father.

Engle's funeral Parlor in Elizabeth was in charge of my grandmother's arrangements. Someone there had prepared the notice for the newspaper and they got some of the family relationships confused, particularly in light of the fact that my mother wasn't present when the arrangements were made.

We didn't have a telephone at our house, so people couldn't verify what had happened. With both my sister and I staying at my grandmother's, most folks thought it was my mother who died.

Floral pieces came from places where my grandfather did business and from professional organizations believing it was his daughter who had died. Cards and flowers came from friends of my Aunt Eileen's thinking the deceased was her sister. My father's co-workers at the airplane factory sent all kinds of stuff. A floral piece even came from the "Boys at Cotton's Gin Mill."

My mother had a few rough days after the baby's birth. She had no idea that her mother-in-law had died. When she was finally released from the hospital she became quite busy informing people that she hadn't died.

By the end of the month it had been firmly established that my mother was alive.

Hitler wasn't that lucky. On April 30, at 3:30 P.M., as Russian shells were exploding above his underground bunker, Adolf Hitler fired a bullet into his head. Without dignity or honor, the madman who sought to build a super race, was dead among the rubble his lunacy created.

Months earlier Mussolini was treated to an undignified death at the hands of Italian partisans and Italy was totally defeated.

The Allied High Command accepted Germany's unconditional surrender on May 7, 1945.

Church bells rang, factory whistles blew and from the smallest towns to the largest cities, people filled the streets to dance and celebrate Victory in Europe.

Europe was in shambles. Its cities were in ruin. People were without homes, jobs or anything that closely resembled a normal life. We are a liberating nation, not a conquering nation and to us and our liberating armies would fall the task of helping these nations rebuild. But, first we had to direct our attention to the last obstacle to peace – Japan.

The battle to secure Okinawa was brutal and it was an illustration of the fanatic nature of the Japanese soldiers and citizens. This island, which was secured on June 21, was the final door to open in preparation for the invasion of the main islands of Japan… and the Japanese defenders knew it.

Their attitudes toward life, death, honor and national loyalty are totally different than ours and even those of the average German soldier. Despite the attitudes of their leaders and the political pressures involved, the average German soldier was raised according to Judeo- Christian values the same as us. The Japanese on the other hand had a far different set of beliefs that did not value human life as we do.

President Truman had to weigh the situation and make a decision regarding the invasion of Japan.

The Air Force was softening up the Japanese Islands as troops were being marshaled from around the world to create an invasion force. The President's military advisors felt that the Japanese would fight to the last person, women and children included, to repel an Allied invasion. Because of the nationalistic attitude of the Japanese people, our military leaders calculated that the landing forces would suffer an extremely high number of casualties.

This was not acceptable to President Truman, particularly in light of an alternative.

While he was at the Potsdam conference meeting with Allied leaders, President Truman received a message informing him of the successful explosion of a uranium bomb in the New Mexico desert on July 16, 1945.

President Roosevelt had been alerted to this possibility by Albert Einstein. He initiated a program that employed scientists, under a cloak of secrecy since 1939 to perfect this bomb. Although the average person knew little of what was going on, scientists here and in Germany were racing to successfully complete similar work. The destruction wrought on Germany and her resources slowed their progress, while the U.S. forged ahead.

The uranium bomb is 20,000 times as powerful as TNT and has the capacity for mass destruction.

Despite the mass bombing of her cities and warnings of greater devastation, the Japanese ignored all offers of surrender. After being informed that estimated

Allied invasion casualties would be one million or more, President Truman made his decision, drop the uranium bomb on Japan.

Early in the morning of August 6, 1945 a B-29, named The Enola Gay, took off from Tinian Island bound for Japan with a uranium bomb. At 8:15 A.M. that bomb was dropped over Hiroshima setting off a reaction that devastated the city and raised warfare to a new level. A second bomb was dropped on Nagasaki on August 9. Japan was beaten and although the formal ceremonies would not take place until September 2, the war was over.

Those two Atomic bombs, to date the only nuclear weapons ever used, set off a political reaction that will last beyond all of our lifetimes.

# CHAPTER 31

# RETURN OF THE AUTOMOBILES

It was over. All of the fear associated with war was over.

Of course everything didn't return to normal over night. There were a lot of loose ends that had to be tied together.

We were operating on a war-time economy. As their government contracts began to expire, industries had to convert back to their peace time pursuits. This meant layoffs and occupation changes again. New industries such as plastics, electronics, and food processing had been developed for war time needs. These new industries readily converted to produce products for the consumer market and absorbed people displaced by the defense plants.

The War had inspired many technical developments and the methods used to produce these items. For each major industrial group there were untold numbers of smaller sub-contractors engaged to supply the needs of these industries.

Young men were still being drafted to provide manpower for the world wide peace keeping force needed to insure the peace. They had to fill the ranks of those men and women, who had served for the duration and were now returning home to resume their lives.

The G.I. Bill of Rights was instituted to help the veteran return to society. This program provided financial assistance for education, home buying, or starting a business.

The de-mobilization after the War was almost as impressive as the mobilization for the War. The resilience and ingenuity of the individual American was without peer. We were a different country and far different people, almost unrecognizable, when compared to the sleepy nation that existed in 1939. There was no turning back from the new challenges and unlimited opportunities being presented each day.

After a depression and a War, people could see their potential and visualize the American Dream. It was within their grasp.

No, we weren't going back to the turnip patches, or the coal mines.

My father was luckier than most. Right after the War ended he was able to get back into the newspaper profession at the local paper, The Elizabeth Daily Journal.

The Eastern Aircraft plant where he worked was going to be converted back into an automobile factory, producing Buicks, Oldsmobiles and Pontiacs. Some people were staying on, but others were looking for post war opportunities.

*THE SOJOURNERS*
*Life on the American Homefront During World War II*

Americans were on the move again. Rationing slowly evaporated and as consumer products started returning to the store shelves, it wasn't long before ration coupons were a distant memory.

1946 was the first production year for post-war automobiles. Of course the automakers didn't have time to design and re-tool for exciting new models, so the '46 cars were made from the same parts as the '41 cars, except for some changes in the trim.

The demand for new cars was high, but the supply was limited. People had to put their name on a waiting list. The car dealers weren't dumb. They knew they could sell every new car that came in and didn't have to make any deals, or accept old clunkers for a trade-in. And, that was exactly what the buying public had… old clunkers. All of the older cars were pre-war and a lot were pre-depression. Most of these things were held together by chewing gum and bailing wire. Tires and auto replacement parts were not available during the war. Most of these cars were in such bad condition that junkyards wanted to be paid to take them in for scrap. Before the War, Japan was a big customer for American scrap metal. Right now, they themselves were a pile of scrap. So, until some new markets opened up, there was a surplus of junk cars.

Again my friends and I were called upon to perform our service to the country. We were needed to help reduce this scourge of junk cars.

"Hey, kids. You want a car? Come with me and just take it."

That was a frequent offer that came our way from anxious people, who were just informed that their new car came in. If they didn't come and get it right away, the car would go to the next person on the list.

It was our civic duty to assist these people and we didn't refuse anyone.

Fortunately, most of the garages in the back of our buildings were empty. Many of our neighbor's cars started to disappear when gasoline rationing was instituted during the early days of the War. Of the 32 families living in these four buildings, only Mr. Mitchell, Mr. Hartigan, Mr. Harrison, Mr. Berry and Mr. Carley had cars.

Mr. Mitchell used his '29 Dodge only on one weekend a month and that was during the summer, when he and Mr. Kluin went fishing in Raritan Bay. Mr. Hartigan had a 1930 Ford. You knew he was coming from a mile away. The engine made the typical Model A chirpping sound, only this car was louder than normal. Mr. Harrison had a '36 Dodge that was always kept in the garage. He moved the car out of the garage, usually on nice days, so he could smack golf balls into an old rug he had hung on the back wall of the garage. He had his own small driving range right inside his garage. Mr. Berry had a '38 Hudson Terraplane. He commuted every day to work in Mountainside. He managed a Standard Oil gasoline station for the family of a man, who was killed in the War.

Mr. Carley was an Elizabeth firefighter. He had the only car around that wasn't black. He had a baby blue '38 Plymouth that he took out only on Sunday.

The cars we collected never had any gas in their tanks. It required a lot of boy power to push these jalopies, usually from several blocks away, to our storage area in the vacant garages. It would have been a lot easier to drive these clunkers in, but we didn't have enough money to buy gasoline ... and even if we did, not one of us had a driver's license, or was near the age required to get one.

We needed fuel and motor oil to feed our growing stable of derelict beauties, which now included two Model A Fords and a '29 Dodge 4-door sedan.

Pepsi-Cola was 6 cents for a 12 once bottle. By comparison, gasoline at 14 cents per gallon and a jar of bulk oil at 20 cents a quart was a lot cheaper. The oil in these engines was black as tar and almost as thick. We could get Re-refined oil at either the Refine oil station on Rahway Avenue or Sears-Roebuck for 79 cents per gallon.

We needed about 4 gallons of oil and about 10 gallons of gasoline to get these beauties running. That was about 4 dollars and 56 cents more than we had, or one heck of a lot of Pepsi's.

"My father drains the gas out of the hoses at the station where he works," Robert volunteered. "He gets enough gas that way so he don't have to buy any."

All of our minds went into gear when we heard that statement.

"We can try that at Marshall's Esso over on Edgar Road. Maybe tonight!" Chicky emphatically suggested.

"OK," We all nodded in agreement.

"Marshall's Esso Station" was set on the point where Lidgerwood Avenue and Edgar Road came together and formed Washington Avenue as the road continued on into Elizabeth. The station must have been built when this area was a cross road between Elizabeth and Linden.

The station was a little white square building with a red tile roof. Mr. Marshall had to work on a lift outside if he wanted to grease a car, or fix a tire. There were two gasoline pumps... one ESSO REGULAR and the other ESSO EXTRA. The station wasn't open at night. Mr. Marshall generally went home around 6 o'clock, which was usually our suppertime.

We all met by the wooden backstop in the big field after supper. Earlier that afternoon we had stashed a one gallon tin can in the bushes by the backstop.

"I saw Mr. Marshall go," Chicky reported as he emerged from the wooded area on the Lidgerwood Avenue side of field.

"Robert, because your father works in a gas station, you work the gas nozzle and I'll hold the can," I said.

"Good, let's get in and out real fast before someone sees us," Chico counseled.

Our War time training, perfected to evade capture when we shot peas at fat ladies or raided gardens, came in handy for this mission. With the stealth of commandos we migrated through the woods and crossed Lidgerwood Avenue into Marshall's Station. No one was around.

Except for a nightlight in the little building, the place was dark. Some light was coming from the open door of the Oasis Tavern on the other side of Edgar Road, but the men in there were too busy to care about us.

The pumps were locked, but the hoses were free. Robert slipped the hose out of the side of the pump and placed the nozzle into the waiting can. He squeezed the handle and I heard the sound of a quick splash of liquid.

Chico followed Robert's lead and already had the hose from the second pump down near ground level. I quickly placed the open can under the nozzle. Chico squeezed the lever on the nozzle and another splash of fuel found its way into the can.

We had collected almost two cups full of gasoline. I don't know how Robert's father got enough gas this way to run his car all week. He must have had another trick or two, because we would have to drain the hoses of a hundred pumps to get a decent amount of gasoline.

"There's another station over on Elmora Avenue. Let's try it," Robert suggested.

"Good idea," Chicky answered, as if he were making the decision for all of us.

"Let's go," Chico countered.

We had to go across the big field, then diagonally across the little field at Garden Street. We came out at New York Avenue and Elmora Avenue. The station was located up one block near the corner of Erico Avenue.

This station had four pumps. We quickly went to work and drained the four hoses.

"If we do this every night for a week, we might get enough gas to start one of the cars," Chicky informed us in an academic tone.

"Yeah, we'll be able to start one, but it sure won't run for long," I answered. "We might fill this can if we do this ten more times."

"WOW," Robert replied. "We better find some money to buy gas."

"We need to make some big money fast," Chico interjected.

"Soda Bottles," said Chicky. "We can find soda bottles and return them for the deposits."

"How about collecting and selling newspapers to the rag man," I contributed.

"We can still haul groceries from the A and P for tips."

It took us quite a while to earn and save the money needed to fuel up the cars. In the meantime we cleaned and pampered the buggies so they appeared roadworthy when their hour of power appeared.

"What are you guys doin' with these cars?" Warren asked one day after seeing us push the cars in and out of the garages.

"We're gonna fix 'em and sell 'em," I answered.

"I may know somebody who might want to buy one," he said. "How much are you askin'?"

"Ten bucks each," said Robert.

"That's a lot for one of these clunkers," Warren replied.

"Yeah, but we have a dollars worth of gas in each one and they got fresh oil."

The next day Warren showed up with Wally.

"Can you start these things up?" Wally asked.

"Well, we can crank them or push them. Do you know how to crank a Ford?"

I asked Wally.

"I know how. Let me see 'er."

We pushed the two Fords out of the garage so Warren and Wally could get busy hand cranking the Fords.

First some gasoline was squirted into the carburetors, the spark was retarded, the hand brakes were applied with the gearshift in neutral and then Wally and Warren engaged the cranks at the front of the cars.

The first few turns of the crank produced little results.

"R.A., you squirt some gas into the carburetor while I crank," Wally commanded.

I did as he directed and the Ford made a couple of puffs and that was all.

"Do it again, she's about ready to go," he clamored.

After a few more squirts the engine sputtered, but kept on going. It was going so slow that you could almost hear each one of the four cylinders firing.

"Somebody, advance the spark!" Wally hollered.

Chico reached inside by the steering wheel and as he moved the spark control lever, the engine began to pick up its tempo. The engine continued to run and as it did, it slowly enveloped us in a cloud of blue smoke.

"She hasn't run in a long time," explained Robert. "She'll clear up pretty soon."

I don't know where Robert got all his information, but I think it really was wishful thinking instead of real knowledge.

Amazingly, the smoke cloud began to disappear. The engine still generated smoke out of the tailpipe, but it wasn't as heavy as it had been. Maybe Robert knew what he was talking about.

"WHAT ARE YOU BOYS DOING?" shouted the shrill excited voice of a woman. "YOU ARE GONNA RUIN ALL THE LAUNDRY HANGING ON THESE LINES WITH ALL THAT SMOKE."

Remember little Joe, who branded himself on the radiator? It was his mother hollering out of her ground floor kitchen window. There was some laundry hanging on the lines that extended from the rear windows of the apartments to poles planted against the garages. But, not that much.

"THE SMOKE IS ALL GONE," Warren, who was never at a loss for words, hollered back.

"IF MY KIDS GET SICK FROM THAT SMOKE, I'LL CALL THE COPS AND TELL THEM WHO CAUSED IT," she said as she slammed down her kitchen window.

"Us and the Cops have been down that road, with her already," Wally vented sarcastically. "Maybe we'll get our pictures in the newspaper, or in True Detective Magazine. You kids will get a lot of free advertising for these cars."

Wally and Warren went into a little huddle.

"Look, we'll take both cars, but we won't pay ten dollars each."

"We'll have to talk it over," Replied Robert. And, we went into a huddle.

"Two cars for fifteen dollars and we won't charge for the oil and gas," Chico announced when our huddle broke.

"Deal." said Warren as he reached into his pocket for the money. "Do you guys have titles for these cars?"

"Sure," answered Robert as he retrieved the documents given us by the previous owners, from the door pockets of the cars. "Here they are, all signed and everything."

Warren handed the money to Robert.

"You get behind the wheel of that car," said Wally. "I'll push you over to our garages. Put it in gear and try to start it while I'm pushing."

Their garages were across the common back yard around 250 feet away.

Warren popped the clutch as Wally pushed and in a cloud of smoke the second Ford came to life.

We had made a real deal. We had fifteen dollars and one car left. All of our attention could be focused on the remaining Dodge.

We took the battery from the Dodge over to Mr. Marshall's for a quick charge and we also bought 5 gallons of gas.

"What are you boys going to do with this gas and the battery?" Mr. Marshall asked.

Pointing at Chico, Robert replied, "We're helping his father get an old car started."

Chico was somewhat surprised at the statement, but he played along.

"That's good, because I don't want to sell something that could get you hurt," Mr. Marshall said as he took the wagon that held the battery over to the charger.

"I'll give you the gas now. The battery will be ready in an hour."

We paid Mr. Marshall and put the cans of gasoline into the wagon for the trip back to the garage.

"You know?" Chicky said. "It would be neat if we could take the Dodge out for a ride."

"We don't have license plates," Robert replied.

"We could make some," Chico said. "We could go get some old license plates off a junk car at Bell's Junk Yard and paint them this year's color."

"If we ever got caught, we would be in big trouble," I said.

"Sure, we could get caught and get a ticket and we might lose our drivers license," Robert casually answered.

"None of us has a Drivers license!" I exclaimed.

"Then we don't have anything to lose," Chico came back.

"Right," Chicky chimed in. "How could they do anything to us?"

Something didn't seem right, but as a group we decided to paint up some license plates.

This year's colors were white numbers on a black plate. This was easy. Mr. Mitchell had loads of white paint down in his basement workshop. All we had to do was to get a set of plates from the junkyard. We had an hour to spare while the battery was charging to look for some plates.

After we returned to the garage with the gas, we went looking in all the other garages for old license plates. In one garage we were surprised to find a set of plates nailed to the wall. These plates had orange numbers on a black background. What a find. All we had to do was to paint the numbers white.

While Chicky went off to Mr. Mitchell's workshop in the cellar to get some white paint, we went to get the battery from Marshall's ESSO.

Chicky was already in the garage repainting the numbers on the license plates when we arrived.

Robert and I were selected to reinstall the battery because his father worked in a gas station and my uncle used to make and drive racecars. I guess everyone felt that genetics had given us the qualifications to carry out these chores.

It really did take the two of us to lower the battery into its place under the front seat of the car. Amazingly we got the battery back in its original position.

"Let's try it R.A.," Robert anxiously intoned as we reinstalled the front seat cushion.

"O.K.," I responded. "Make sure it's out of gear."

Robert was on the driver's side, so he hopped in behind the steering wheel.

"I'll pull the choke and you crank it," I told Robert as he settled into the drivers seat.

The engine made a couple of turns and fired up.

I pushed the choke in slowly, as I remember my father doing and the engine smoothed out and ran a lot quieter than the Fords.

"Let's see if I can move it up a few feet," Robert announced for our approval.

We all had watched our fathers and others drive cars, so we knew the basics and had done dry runs on cars that weren't running. All of us had practiced using the clutch and shifting gears, but this now was a real live running car.

"Do you know where first gear is?" I asked.

"Right here," said Robert, as he held his foot down on the clutch and moved the gearshift to the various positions.

"Let's try it," I said.

With that command Robert throttled up the engine and eased up on the clutch. He didn't have the combination of engine speed and clutch release quite right because the car hopped forward instead of taking off smoothly.

He made several short trips, about 20 feet, going forward and then in reverse and he got a little better each time.

"Do you want to try it?" Robert asked me, as he backed up close to the garage and brought the car to a stop.

"Sure," I agreed.

He put the gearshift in neutral and applied the hand brake. We switched seats and I assumed control of the vehicle.

Chico and Chicky got into the back of the car as I prepared to take off. "I'm next," they both hollered as they took their seats.

On the first attempt, I wasn't much better than Robert. The car bucked and lurched forward. Quickly I depressed the clutch pedal and gave the engine a little gas and slowly released the clutch again. Gradually it took and the car moved forward.

We all took turns doing the same thing…driving back and forth. It took a while, but each of us finally got accustomed to the clutch.

We were fortunate that we had a sizable common yard behind the apartment buildings. Our forays with the car got longer and longer until we were circling the yard in first gear.

"We got to see if we can get the car out on the road. There are never any cars out on New York Avenue. And, I have the license plates all finished," Chicky said after one session of driving around the back yard.

"Somebody will see us if we drive out the driveway. We would never make it to New York Avenue," I said.

"Let's see if the path through the back garden is big enough for a car to drive through to New York Avenue," Robert suggested.

"Sure," said Chico. "The horse and wagons come in from New York Avenue to bring the manure for the garden.

The dirt path through the garden had been baked hard by the hot summer sun. It was almost a straight shot from the end of the row of garages, down the path to

New York Avenue. The manure man had even put a couple of pieces of wood down by the curb, so he could drive his wagon up on the path.

The old Dodge was ready. It had freshly painted license plates, almost a half a tank of gas and was all cleaned up for its return to the road.

Somehow the word of our venture got out among our other friends. At the appointed hour, on a Saturday at noon, we had about a dozen kids hanging around to watch us drive out to New York Avenue.

Because my uncle was a racecar driver, I was selected to drive the Dodge out of the garage, across the yard and down the path to New York Avenue.

I drove in first gear all the way and eased the car down and across the curb onto New York Avenue.

Robert was next. He wanted to drive down the street make a K-turn and come up on the other side of the street. We were progressively going further and further along New York Avenue, until we were eventually making our K-turns at the intersection with Garden Street and the intersection with Grove Street.

Robert, Chico and I were taking turns at the wheel and everyone else had either packed into the car, or was standing on the running boards as we made the trips up and down the street.

We were really having a good time and didn't pay too much attention to anything but the road, until Robert started to make a K-turn at Garden Street.

There, appearing out of nowhere was a black and white Ford with two police officers inside.

We knew we couldn't out run them, so Robert stopped the car at the curb and climbed into the back seat.

"License and Registration," demanded the one policeman, who approached the driver's side. "WHO'S THE DRIVER!" he demanded, looking at the vacant driver's seat.

"We don't have one," I said from my position in the front passenger seat.

"ALL RIGHT, EVERBODY OUT AND LINE UP BY THE CURB," he commanded.

"DO ANY OF YOU HAVE A DRIVER'S LICENSE?"

We all shook our heads in the negative.

"WHERE IS THE REGISTRATION FOR THIS CAR?"

Again, we all shook our heads.

"This car has painted license plates, George," the second cop reported.

"FICTITIOUS LICENSE PLATES."

The first cop, George, had his ticket book out and he was pacing back and forth in front of us.

"LET'S SEE, NO REGISTRATION, NO DRIVER, NO DRIVER'S LICENSE, PHONEY LICENSE PLATES, OVERLOADED VEHICLE. NO INSPECTION STICKER. I COULD GO ON HERE FOREVER. THIS IS JUST

TOO MANY TICKETS TO WRITE AND WHO AM I GONNA' GIVE 'EM TO?"

He folded up his ticket book and placed it in his back pocket. Removing his revolver from its holster, in his booming voice, he said, "I'M NOT GONNA WRITE ANY TICKETS. I'M JUST GOIN' TO SHOOT YOU GUYS."

Putting the revolver back into the holster, he said, "BULLETS COST 6 CENTS. I CAN'T WASTE THAT KIND OF MONEY ON YOU GUYS... YOU, PENDELL, I KNOW YOUR FATHER. CAN YOU DRIVE THIS CAR?"

"Yes sir," I answered.

"GOOD. WE'RE GOIN' TO FOLLOW YOU UP THE STREET AND YOUR GOIN' TO DRIVE THAT CAR INTO THE FIELD AND BACK WHERE IT CAME FROM... AND I DON'T EVER WANT TO SEE YOU GUYS OUT DRVING UNTIL YOU GOT A LICENSE. NOW GET GOIN'."

I got behind the steering wheel and slowly drove the car up the street. I turned into the field and returned up the path to the garage. I was shaking like a leaf by the time I shut off the engine.

"See," said Chico approaching the car, "I told you we had nothing to lose."

# CHAPTER 32

# CHRISTMAS SURPRISE

Our romance with the automobile wasn't over. As a matter of fact, it had really just begun. Our desire for mobility, fueled by our increasing age, had been stifled by the Wartime constraints. Our episode with the old Dodge demonstrated our desire for some degree of emancipation. Our parents knew that. A lot of things were not available to us because of the depression and then the War. We knew it wasn't anyone's fault. It was the way life had to be during those times. We were just trying to make the best of a bad situation.

We sold the old Dodge to a high school boy for 15 dollars. Besides having a lot of fun and getting in a lot of trouble, we cleared almost 5 dollars apiece on the entire venture. I had wanted a bicycle for some time. None were available because of the War. Even if one was available, there wasn't any room in the family budget for such an expense. Because of the car episode, we all were restricted to an area close to home until Spring. We knew cars were out of the picture... at least for the next four years. So, we spent our spare time looking at bicycle ads in magazines. We also planned fantasy trips on these new bicycles we didn't have.

"Why should we get you a bicycle for Christmas?" My mother would say admonishing my almost daily request. "You can't go anywhere 'till Spring."

"I could use the bike to go to the store for you and other people." I would say in an attempt to appeal to her sense of economic benefit.

"If I have a bike, I won't be looking for a car to drive." I said, trying to induce guilt. "Or, maybe I can go down to the slaughterhouse and get a horse." I said to make the situation seem ridicules. But, as my mother knew, it was not something that was beyond my attempt to try.

By Christmastime 1946, new bicycles were beginning to make their appearance in Sears-Roebuck and a few other stores. My friends and I made it a point to visit every possible place in the Elizabeth area that sold bicycles.

We probably were big pests to the storekeepers, who guarded the bicycles and watched our every move as we inspected each of the display models down to the tiniest detail.

Each of us had our own tastes; although we would be satisfied with any new bicycle. Chicky liked the purple Elgin that Sears Roebuck had sitting on display. Robert liked the red Schwinn in Solomon's Sport Shop and I liked the maroon Columbia in the window of Acme Firestone on North Broad Street.

"Hey, Dad, do you know where the Acme-Firestone store is on North Broad Street?"

I said approaching my father, who had just settled into his soft chair to read and relax before supper.

"No, I don't. What happened there?"

"It's right up the street from the Journal. Nothing happened there. They sell Columbia bicycles.

I could meet you, when you finish work on Saturday and show you the model they have in the store."

"How much does it cost?" He asked as he turned the pages of the newspaper.

"I think its $29. But, it might be less if you put it together by yourself."

"I'll talk to your mother about it and we'll see."

That was always the standard answer. "We'll see." At least that was a better answer than a straight out no. It was more like a definite "maybe."

I gave it a rest for a few days; although I did leave some subtle hints in strategic locations. The inside cover of a comic book was taped to the wall over my bed. A smiling boy on a Columbia bicycle waved from the advertisement to greet my mother each time she entered my room. I commandeered any type of publication that displayed a picture of a bicycle. This stuff was placed on every shelf, radiator and cabinet. I hoped my parents would be subliminally convinced to buy me a bicycle, or at least realize that the avalanche of paper wouldn't stop until I had a bicycle.

Chicky and Robert were conducting similar campaigns. Our parents were no doubt in communication with each other and had joined forces in applying some heat to our efforts.

"How are you goin' to ride a bicycle in a jail cell?" Chicky's mother exclaimed one day when we were discussing the bicycle campaign in her presence. "The country's not at war anymore, so they can spend their time now chasin' you hooligans. You characters are public enemy number one."

I could see public enemy number one, but what is a "hooligan?"

Fortunately, there was a new threat that diverted the government's attention away from us…COMMUNISTS.

In his speech at Fulton, Missouri, Sir Winston Churchill warned the world of the threat that lay behind a "Communist Iron Curtain." The Soviet Union, with the aid of our World War II ally, the Red Army, was advancing its influence into war torn Eastern Europe. The United States was supplying aid to Greece and Turkey under the Truman Doctrine. The European Recovery Plan, known as the Marshall Plan was helping to restore prosperity and growth to Western Europe. Both of these plans were designed to prevent the communist influence from expanding into the areas of our allies, or countries we had liberated from the Nazis.

*R. Allen Pender*

Beginning with their takeover of Russia in 1917, the communists began to expand their influence into Eastern Europe and the Balkan states. What eventually evolved was a collection of communist states known as the Soviet Union. The communist ideology took advantage of depressed world economic conditions to enlist followers all over the world; even here in the U.S.A. World War II temporarily curtailed communist activities while we all united to defeat the common foes - Germany and Japan.

With the War over, communists began emerging again. They didn't believe in God.

They believed that the State should control people's lives. Everybody and everything should belong to the State. No one person should owned anything. Everybody was entitled to share in the labor and possessions of everyone else and the State controlled who got what. The Communist Party was to run the government and everyone was to be subservient to the Communist Party. This definitely wasn't the American way. We just finished fighting a war to keep dictators off our soil, so we weren't about to buy into this Communist propaganda.

But, these communists were real sneaky. They wanted to take us over politically and they were infiltrating just about every part of American life and they had allegiances to Russia. Most of their big spies were looking for military secrets, like the atomic bomb. But, the average spy was looking for any kind of information that would help advance the cause of the Communist Party. Some of these operatives had established themselves in various trade unions and labor movements where they could influence workers. Some commies were writers; others were in broadcasting and the entertainment industry. My father told me a lot of communists were school teachers and college professors. The underlings, people who sympathized with the communist movement and did some of the bidding of higher ranking "Comrades were called "Pinkos" or "Fellow Travelers."

Nazis and Japs were easy to recognize. But, these communists looked and talked like anybody else, except they asked lots of questions. We really had to be on our toes to deal with this threat. We wouldn't give anybody any information.

"Say boys," said the man rolling down the passenger side window of the dirty black sedan as he pulled up to the curb on Garden Street, near where we were standing. "Could you give me directions to New York Avenue?"

That was a pretty suspicious question. This man was wearing a fedora hat, a shirt and tie, and a dark over coat. New York Avenue was mostly fields. There were a few houses on one end, so why would someone want to go there…unless some communists were going to meet on the dark street and exchange secrets.

"We think it's down Lidgerwood Avenue about a mile on the left." Robert replied. Sending the Commie off on a wild goose chase.

"Quick, let's go back to New York Avenue and see what these Reds are up to." Chico said when the car moved away.

Our gang ran down Garden Street to the corner of New York Avenue. The brush and wild cherry trees growing along the vacant side of Garden Street gave us plenty of cover to watch the activity on New York Avenue.

We had been in our lookout posts for about ten minutes when we saw the same car slowly coming up New York Avenue, from the direction of South Elmora Avenue. The car slowed and came to a stop in front of one of the two 4 family houses on that part of the street. The man got out of the car and mounted the front steps. A light behind one of the two doors came on and the door was opened for the man to step inside.

"Pass the word" Tommmy whispered. "We'll wait ten minutes to see what happens."

"What do you think is goin' on?" Chicky asked.

"More an' likely a cell meeting." Robert returned.

"What's a cell meeting?" I asked

"A bunch of communists meet somewhere to pass along instructions and carry out plans." Chico answered.

"Who gives them instructions?" Chicky questioned.

"Russians from Russia." Tommy snapped back.

It wasn't too long before the front door opened and the man escorted a woman down the front stairs to his car.

"It looks like Wanko's sister." Chico whispered.

"What do you think they're up to?" Robert asked.

"The cell meeting is probably someplace else." I offered.

When the car drove by us I could see where Wanko's sister had moved close to the driver and he had his arm around her.

"These communists may be sneaky." I said. "But, unless there's no heat in that car, they sure are acting real friendly towards each other."

"We'll have to watch Wanko's sister." Tommy retorted. "She doesn't look like she's up to any good- especially with that new hairdo."

"I heard she got a job at the Standard Oil." Chico added.

"That's it," Robert echoed. "She's probably givin' away Standard Oil secrets or something to that guy in the car."

"We'll have to put her under surveillance." Chico intoned as we broke off our under cover operation and started back up Garden Street towards the street corner.

"I'll watch her." said Tommy. "She goes by my building on her way to work; n'she comes back again around 5 o'clock. I've noticed she's starting to wiggle some. Maybe it's from the high heeled shoes."

259

"Yeah, that girl has changed." Interjected Chicky. "A couple of years ago she went sleigh riding and roasted potatoes with the guys. Now she's snuggling up to some communist in a car."

Securing the country from communists was important. But, the Christmas campaign for a bicycle was a priority. The closer we got to Christmas, the more secretive my parents became. I couldn't get any kind of answer, much less a positive one, as to where my request for a bicycle stood. The other guys were pretty much in the same boat. Nobody knew anything.

Our parents knew we were old enough to know that some elf named Santa Claus didn't slip into our house and stack presents around the Christmas Tree. But, I had younger sisters who thought he did, so I had to play along with the myth.

A few days before Christmas, I went with my father to buy a Christmas tree. Daddy believed that the closer to Christmas, the cheaper the trees got. He always said they were fresher and wouldn't drop their needles real quick. I couldn't understand his logic since all the trees arrived together at the lot a few weeks back and somehow the trees we always got weren't endowed with a surplus of greenery.

"We got lots of decorations to fill up those bare spots." He said. "Besides, this tree is a lot easier to carry home."

My father and I carried the tree back from the lot over on Edgar Road. We put the tree down in the basement. Tradition had it that Christmas trees were put up on Christmas Eve and never earlier. I don't know who made that rule, but we weren't going to break it.

"Tomorrow." meaning Christmas Eve, he instructed - "I'll probably be a little late coming home from work. So, I want you to set the tree in the stand and get the decorations out of the bin in the cellar. Your mother will tell you how she wants the tree decorated and I'll finish it when I get home."

The instructions were simple enough. We didn't have to go to school on Christmas Eve. We were on vacation and didn't have to go back to school 'till after New Year's Day. I had all day to set up the Christmas Tree.

"You wait until I'm done cleaning before you bring that tree in here." Ma chastened. "An' shake that tree hard so any loose needles fall off. I don't want to keep running this vacuum cleaner n'gettin' it stuffed full of needles."

I went down to the basement and dragged the decorations out of our storage bin. In a short time I was joined by Chicky and Robert, who were on a detail similar to mine.

"Let's look around down here to see if our parents are hiding any gifts down here."

Chicky suggested. "I can't find any thing in the usual hiding places in my apartment."

"I found some things for my sisters hidden up stairs. But, I didn't see anything for me." I replied.

"I can't find any gifts for me either." said Robert. "Do you think we're still in a lot of trouble?"

"Could be we're not gettin' anything." I responded.

The three of us began a systematic search of the basement area and nothing turned up.

"The only thing down in this basement that we might get ... is some coal from the coal bin." I remarked.

"I guess our sins have caught up with us." Chicky announced in a very dejected tone that bordered on crying.

"Well. It's too late for us to do anything now. So I guess we better get about puttin' up our Christmas Trees." Robert advised.

Little by little, I started to carry the decorations upstairs. My mother started separating things out in the order they would go on the tree.

Around 2 o'clock in the afternoon, she said "You can bring the tree in now."

My mother had the living room arranged so that the Christmas Tree could be set in the front bay window. During the War years we had to put the tree in some other corner of the living room, where it couldn't be seen from the outside. Now every family was placing their tree in a window for the whole world to see.

I got the tree erected. Then my mother took over. She directed my every move when it came to installing the lights. I must have put those lights on four times before she was satisfied.

"I'm goin' to fix supper. After we eat; I'll put the ornaments on. Leave the tinsel for your father to put on this evenin'. He's the only one who can put that on right."

"Good." I thought to myself. "I'm done."

It was now late afternoon and daylight was rapidly waning. Now would be a good time to plug in the tree lights and see how the tree looked from the outside. Surprisingly, the lights came on as soon as I put the plug into the outlet. My mother and father had purchased these tree lights before I was born. They were the type of light where one burned out or broken bulb would prevent the entire string from lighting. Every Christmas, for as long as I can remember, my father would spend most of Christmas Eve trying to get the lights working. Tonight he wouldn't have to do that. It should make him happy.

I went outside to admire my handiwork. The tree lit up the bay window with a mix of colors that softly twinkled through the bending boughs of the cedar trees, which grew in front of the window.

As I stood outside in the cold December wind, I heard a squeaking and sometimes creaking noise coming down the street towards me. I stepped out into the street to see what noisy thing was coming in my direction.

A small light was switching back and forth and I could discern in the fading light a person coming on a bicycle. When he rode under the street light by Stewart Place, I could see it was my father.

He came to a screeching halt near where I was standing out in the street. He was riding the maroon Columbia!

"I helped the man at the Firestone Store put the bike together. I think we probably didn't oil or adjust everything right. You take this bike n' put it in the cellar before your sisters see it. We can bring it up later; after they've gone to bed."

"Wow, The new Columbia!" I said, as my father dismounted and headed for the house.

I was walking on air as I wheeled the new bike to the rear basement entrance. I noticed the front tire was rubbing on the fork and the rear wheel was also out of line. The seat and handle bars weren't tightened completely and the chain needed adjustment. They forgot to put oil into the coaster brake. The headlight worked fine. The bike had all new parts. It just had to be reassembled. It is a miracle that my father didn't have an accident riding this bike home. Yeah, it needed some work, but I had a new bike.

Christmas Eve is probably the longest day of the year. At least it seemed like it. I couldn't wait to get to work on the bike. But, I had to keep cool and not be anxious, until my sisters went to bed.

I was itching to get my hands on the new bike parked in the basement. Despite the fact that my mother had supper ready before 6 o'clock and my father got busy hanging the tinsel on the tree, the evening went slow. The girls had to be ready for bed by 7:30 so my parents could go to the Candlelight Service at 8 o'clock. I had to stay home with the girls while the Service was underway. Hopefully they would go to sleep.

"The quicker you get to sleep, the earlier you can get up to see your presents." I cajoled my younger sister, Joyce. The baby sister, who wouldn't be 1 until April, was in her crib oblivious to all that was going on.

My parents would be back in about an hour and a half. If my sister was asleep at that time, I could help my parents set the presents out around the tree. I wanted to slip down into the basement to see the new bike. If my sister wasn't sleeping, she might hear me go out. I wasn't afraid of her seeing anything, but she might tell my parents that I went out and I'd be in trouble again. I wanted to tell Robert and Chicky about the new bike, but right now there was no way to do that without leaving the apartment. It was just as well because they were involved in their family's traditions at the moment.

It was a long hour and a half. The clock seemed to be standing still. I tried to find someway of occupying myself, but all I could think of was the new bike in the basement and the adjustments that it needed. I could be doing that work right now. Officially, by the rules of Christmas, the bike wasn't mine yet. It had to have a tag and be placed in the vicinity of the Christmas tree. I don't know how far away from the Christmas tree something could be placed and still be called a Christmas present. I guess it depended on how big your living room was, or who made the rule.

Finally, after what seemed like an eternity, my mother and father returned. Ma went into check on my sisters.

"They're asleep. Let's get the big presents from Jack and Claire's. Richard can help you put them together. I'll get the smaller things."

Jack and Clair lived in Apartment 2, across the common main hall. They had a son the same age as my baby sister. He didn't have any idea what was going on, so his mother and father let my parents keep the big gifts over in their place.

I helped my father carry back boxes containing a doll house, doll carriage and a tricycle; all of which had to be put together. While we were gone, my mother brought out the other gifts from their secret hiding places. She would never let us see where she was keeping everything. I saw some packages under her bed, but couldn't find anything else.

The doll carriage and the tricycle weren't too bad to put together. I did both of them while my father started with the doll house. I could see he was getting frustrated with the directions and the loads of little parts that came with this doll house.

"I'll put the doll house together, if you get the bike up from the cellar." I suggested.

Glad to be relieved of the chore, which had the prospect of keeping him occupied late into the night; my father quickly accepted my offer.

Assembling the doll house wasn't as bad as my father made it seem. I laid all the parts out and identified the various pieces according to the instructions. It took some time, but it wasn't that hard.

The house was beginning to take on the look of a pre-war Christmas. Metal products had returned. The doll carriage had a steel suspension system and rubber tires. The tricycle was the same. The wooden and cardboard products of the past four years were now history. There was no more conclusive example of our nation's return to peaceful industry than the moment the door opened and my father wheeled in the maroon Columbia bicycle.

I was stimulated to finish the doll house so I could get busy with the bike. I had all the tools and rags lying by to adjust and clean the bike.

My mother took over once the doll house was assembled. She had made little curtains and bought little pieces of furniture, which she carefully placed in the house. As I watched her work, I wondered how long it would take for my sister to mess up my mother's interior decorating job.

Ma brought out fruit cake and cookies for all of us to munch on as the evening wound down. Fruit cake wasn't one of my favorite foods. I was too sweet. My mother said we had to have fruit cake at Christmas. Not any fruit cake. A&P fruit cake was the only acceptable brand. Somehow I don't think any of the rituals we followed were established at the birth of Jesus in Bethlehem; over nineteen hundred years ago. Maybe I'm wrong, but I don't think Mary and Joseph invited the Shepherds in for fruit cake.

It was getting pretty late and I was almost finished reassembling the bike. I had taken the wheels off the bicycle and carried them down to the cellar, where I kept oil and grease. I packed the wheel bearings with grease and oiled the coaster brake. The bike had been wiped clean and I was finishing the final adjustment of the seat and handlebars when Ma made a final inspection of the tree and the presents surrounding it.

"I think we're all finished and it's time for bed." She said scanning her handiwork

"I'll be a little longer, Ma. I want to get everything adjusted so I can ride the bike in the morning."

"You mean after Church in the morning." She shot back.

I had forgotten about that one little thing. The reason we have this day and the reason I got the bike.

It was really difficult to fall asleep. I could still smell the freshness of the new rubber tires and feel the fit of the seat and the handle bars. I was ready to ride and conquer the road.

I was awakened by the commotion being created by my sister, Joyce. The sun had barely started to creep above the eastern horizon...and she had the whole house awake. The baby sister, who was 10 months old, didn't know what was going on, but that didn't stop her from adding her screechy music to the festive atmosphere initiated by her older sister. She wanted to be part of the action.

Getting up that early did have its positive side.

The first Church service on Christmas morning was at 7 a.m.

There was only one thought on my mind; the inaugural ride on that maroon Columbia.

The quicker I got to Church, the quicker I got home to put the rubber on the road.

I got dressed, ate some cereal and was out the door like a flash. If I missed that early service, I would be stuck for another hour... And, I couldn't afford that. It felt like I ran about 2 feet off the ground all the way to the Church. The place was really crowded and I was able to squeeze in along the back wall.

"How come you're not at the school children's service?" The gruff looking usher said to me as he tried to find seats for the late comers. "I'm seeing people here that I haven't seen since Easter." He whispered sarcastically.

It was Tommy's father. He was like one of the bosses of the Church.

"I came early because I want to get home and try out my new Bike." I quietly replied.

"Alright for today, but don't let me catch you at any service other than the school kid's service." He replied in a tone which indicated that he thought he was ordained with some sort of divine authority.

I nodded my head in agreement and he continued on with his duties.

During the course of the service, I slowly inched my way across the back wall towards the entrance door. I planned to bolt out the door at the conclusion of the service. I didn't want to get caught up in the throng that would jam in the doorways as the faithful tried to exit the building in a race to beat each other to either the newspaper stand or the bakery.

The final benediction was to be my signal to get ready to make a hasty exit. My weight was against the inner door as I anticipated the Pastor's final "Amen." When it came, I moved like a flash. The door swung open almost hitting Tommy's father, who had already opened the outer doors and was starting to reach for the handle on the outside of the inner door. If he had been one step closer that door would have got him in the face.

I was by him in a blur. There were so many people around and he was recoiling from the surprise that I doubt he ever knew who opened the door.

I was down the front steps in two jumps and hit the sidewalk running.

The Nativity scene had been setup in the Church yard next to the sidewalk. Everyone entering or leaving Church was expected to stop and reverently admire the Crèche and the figure representing the Infant Jesus, which had been placed in the manger after the Christmas Eve service.

"I'll be back later with my bike. Thank You Jesus." I blurted as I ran past the symbol of this Holy occasion. My only thoughts were centered on the maroon Columbia sitting in our living room just waiting to be ridden.

## CHAPTER 33

## KNAVES OF THE OPEN ROAD

That Christmas morning was sunny and cold. There was very little wind. I created the only wind which bathed my face on the run home from Church.

"You're red as a beet!" My mother exclaimed as I burst through the apartment door disturbing their peaceful morning.

"I ran all the way home. I want to take the bike out."

"Are you sure you went to Church? Don't lie to me." She questioned with that jaundiced look in her eye that underlined her words. "I know you. Remember!"

"Honest, Ma. Ask Tommy's father. He saw me there." Tommy's father not only saw me there, I almost mashed his face with the Church door. But, I didn't tell her that part.

"Alright, But, you be careful with that bike. It cost a lot of money. And don't go too far away."

"I'm only goin' to ride it 'round the block; I won't be far."

I navigated the bike out of the living room and into the common hall of the building.

As I was negotiating through the interior lobby doors, I heard Robert's voice.

"R.A.! I'll be out in a minute. Wait for me."

"O.K., I'll be right out front."

"Wait for me too!" Chicky hollered down from his upstairs apartment.

"We will!" I answered.

By the time I got the bicycle out the front door and down the front steps, Robert emerged from the driveway on a red Schwinn.

Chicky wasn't far behind and he rendezvoused with us on the sidewalk by the driveway.

"The purple Elgin! The purple Elgin! I got the purple Elgin." He exclaimed with a smile that went from ear to ear. "I didn't think I was goin' to get anythin'. My father kept the bike hidden in my Uncle Jim's garage. I was really surprised this morning. My mother and father sure fooled me."

Christmas dreams had come true for all of us.

Of one thing we can always be certain. A natural law of the universe; in the same class as the law of gravity, or the first law of thermodynamics... That when two or more boys are gathered together with bicycles... there is going to be a race.

"Let's see who can get down to the corner first." Chicky suggested.

"O.K." Robert and I concurred in unison.

The streets were still void of any regular traffic. Automobiles had yet to return in any significant numbers to regain control of the streets. Consequently, we had plenty of open road for our balloon tired mounts to conquer.

We wheeled our bikes out into the center of the street.

"On the count of three we mount up and go." Chicky announced.

"You count!" Robert answered.

Each of us had a foot on one of the pedals as Chicky began his count.

With the shout of "THREE" we were off.

From the light pole by our driveway to the mail box down the corner by Harry's store was about 100 yards. Robert jumped off fast and led to the corner. I was about a half of length behind him and Chicky brought up the rear. This race really didn't prove anything. The bikes were new and we were new to the bikes. After a few adjustments, a longer race might prove something.

After we had reached the mailbox and turned the corner we saw Arthur and Tommy coming out of their building. Each one had a brand new bike.

"Rollmasters" Said Arthur. "The best bikes made."

"Do you want to prove it?" Robert shot back. "We'll race you down Garden Street around the corner on New York Avenue to Grove Street."

Tommy just rolled his eyes when Arthur agreed to the proposition. I guess he felt that his far superior bicycle would make up for any shortcomings he might have as a rider. But, we all knew differently.

To make things fair we all agreed to a rolling start. We knew Arthur couldn't get on his bike until the rest of us were half way down the street. We all felt this would be a fairer test of boy and machine... and Arthur wouldn't have any excuses if (when) he got beat.

The five bicycles, with their riders mounted, slowly rolled up to the starting line. The tree just before the front door to Tommy and Arthur's building was designated as the starting point.

"Go!!" Shouted Robert as the five racers, lined up abreast, approached the imaginary starting line.

The pack took off like a swarm of bees. Robert had the lead again as we dove into the corner at Garden Street and New York Avenue. I pulled even with Robert as we passed Scharfenberger's house. Tommy and Chicky were right on our tails. It was hard to tell, but, I think I had Robert by half a wheel when we reached Grove Street. He didn't dispute it. After all we had come in ahead of the highly touted Rollmasters and that was our goal.

Arthur was nowhere to be seen. There were only four of us at the finish. Arthur wasn't even still riding on New York Avenue.

"Where did Arthur go?" Tommy excitedly questioned.

Turning around and seeing no Arthur, we all shrugged our shoulders.

"Let's go back and find him." Tommy urged. "I could get in trouble if his mother tells my mother that we ran off and left him."

Not wanting to see one of our group in trouble over Arthur, we reversed course and headed back towards Garden Street.

When we turned the corner onto Garden Street, we could see the lone figure of Arthur halfway up the street. He was walking beside his bicycle. Approaching him we could see that front wheel of his bike was wobbling.

"What happened to you?" Tommy asked as the group formed a little circle around Arthur and his damaged bike.

"My bike wouldn't turn the corner and it went across New York Avenue and hit the curb. I can't race anymore. I have to go home and see if my father can fix the bike."

"He probably can." We assured Arthur before we left him with his problem and headed back to the corner.

Given Arthur's track record; we all felt that there was probably nothing wrong with the bike. He probably just couldn't handle the corner at any kind of speed.

Coming up to the corner, we could see more bicycles coming towards us. Breezy and Chico were coming down Rosehill Place on new mounts. Smitty was coming out of his Lidgerwood Avenue driveway on a small blue bike. Donald and Gordon came wheeling out from behind Cotton's Gin Mill on a pair of Schwinns. One was green and one was red. Two more bikes were coming from the direction of South Elmora Avenue. It looked like George and Nicky. Dennis, John and Billy suddenly appeared from around the corner on New York Avenue.

Some of the younger kids; boys, like Billy, Jackie and a girl named Betty were also out making maiden voyages on their new wheels. Pretty soon their were enough bicycles converging on the corner of Rosehill Place and Garden Street that it resembled a summer hatch of grasshoppers.

These bicycles represented a certain level of emancipation. The War years had really restricted our movements. Most of us were now in the early teen years and looking to spread our wings a bit. The bicycle provided that opportunity and we would have to be satisfied with this mode of transportation for the next four years…until we could get a license to drive a car.

Three months of winter remained. The restrictions imposed on us would be lifted in the Spring, which according to my calendar is March 21, at the latest, or possibly earlier, depending upon what the groundhog determined when he was roused from his den on February, 2.

The combination of weather and early winter darkness confined our activities to the immediate neighborhood. I was doing some errands on the bike and that activity demonstrated a need for a few accessories.

"Ma, I could carry more on the bike if I had a basket and a luggage rack"

"How much do they cost?"

"I can get a big basket and a luggage rack at Sears & Roebuck for around six dollars."

"That's almost as much as the whole bike cost. How much is the basket by itself?"

"About Three dollars and fifty cents."

"How much money do you have?"

"I have almost two dollars. But, if you loan me the rest, I can pay you back with the deliveries I can make for you."

"Let me talk to your father about it."

My mother was not one to be fooled when it came to money. One of my Uncles said she could squeeze a penny so hard that Abe Lincoln would jump right out of his coat. Whatever it was, I knew I was in for some bargaining.

I had presented my case to my mother, who would confer with my father. Of course I wouldn't be privy to their discussions, nor would I be allowed to address then jointly and present my arguments on the matter. This was not some type of democracy. It was a family and they were the rulers and all decisions were final.

My reasons for wanting the accessories for the bike were not that pure. Sure, I wanted the basket and carrier so I could haul more groceries. But in the bigger picture, I needed those accessories to carry my outdoor equipment on our planned fishing expeditions into the wilds of the Clark Township Reservoir and the Rahway River.

Of course my mother knew nothing of the travel plans we boys had been making. It was going to be a wild and exciting Spring and summer. We would become bicycle riding Knights of the Open Road.

"Your father and I," my mother announced, "Have decided on the bicycle basket thing. Since you have two dollars: we will loan you a dollar and a half towards the basket. You can pay us back by doing twelve grocery orders for me. If you're good, we may get you the luggage carrier for your birthday."

My mother sure knew when she had me in a corner. Her terms were tough. I got a 25 cent tip from everybody else for picking up their groceries. My mother demanded a 50 per cent discount. I should have been happy that she didn't ask for a cut on each of my other deliveries. She was tough to do business with. But, I got the basket.

Robert, Chicky and I continued with our war-time jobs. We collected newspapers, pots and pans. The Papertroopers had long been disbanded. Now we sold our scrap on the open market.

The Rag Man, I never knew his name, we always called him Rag Man, came around once a month. He had a horse and wagon. He would ring a cow bell and holler, "RAGS, RAGS."

R. Allen Pender

He always seemed to know when we were in the area. He usually came on a Saturday morning. The Rag Man would drive his horse and wagon right up to the empty garage where we kept our stuff. He bought everything; newspapers, rags, metal of all kinds, wire and just about any other kind of junk. I don't know what he did with this junk, but he seemed to enjoy buying it from us. We were happy. Some months we got almost three dollars, which we split three ways.

Chicky was a soda bottle expert. He looked through all kinds of garbage to find deposit bottles. The small Coca Cola type bottles had a 2 cent deposit paid on them and the bigger quart size bottles were worth five cents.

Chico worked a deal with Harry's Store on the corner. On Saturdays, Chico would take a box with an assortment of candy and soda from Harry's Store on consignment. He would then parade these wares up and down the line of cars waiting to go through the Motor Vehicle Inspection Station on Lidgerwood Avenue. He added a few cents to the price he would have to pay Harry for the stuff he sold.

Chico would go up and down the Inspection line peddling his wares and Chicky would follow behind watching to see who bought soda. Most of the drivers in line threw the empty bottles into the field along the side of Garden Street. Chicky would watch for the discarded bottles and in some instances he would ask the driver if he could return the bottle for him. Every once and a while a driver gave him a tip for doing that, unaware that he was getting the 2 cents back on the bottle.

On a nice Saturday, with a big Inspection Line, they could almost make a dollar apiece.

Robert and I could make about 50 cents apiece on a Saturday. We each had a few steady clients for whom we would pick up and deliver their Saturday grocery orders. The new bikes cut down the trip time to and from the A&P. Walking with a wagon took twice as long. But, it could carry twice as much. I saved enough money to buy the luggage carrier onto which I mounted a wooden box. The large basket and the wooden box gave me a cargo area of almost the same size as the wagon.

Each day our lifestyle would change a little more. The shortages of the War years were rapidly becoming memories. This was good for my business. The Saturday runs to the A&P were now supplemented by short quick runs to places like John's Meat Market, The Washington Meat Market, and Tripoli's Italian Market. Most of these stores were expanding their inventory and people were buying those extras that weren't available to them during the War.

The products were becoming better too. Somebody came up with this stuff called oleo margarine during the War. It was a butter substitute. Originally this white fat back like stuff came in a package with another ingredient that looked like a yellow egg. These two ingredients were mixed together to form, depending on one's eye sight and the degree of lighting in the room, a product which resembled butter.

Real butter was coming back. So the food companies went to work and began to produce a product which looked like and cost less than butter. The American consumer was now becoming a discriminating buyer.

Instant coffee was another Wartime innovation meeting with success in the marketplace. Each day a new group of products, derived from wartime technology would surface on the scene. Tires of synthetic rubber, refrigerators, washing machines and a totally new product, the clothes dryer, drew people to stores like a magnet.

A few people had moved out of the neighborhood at the conclusion of the War. They were quickly replaced by local boys returning from the War. The boys brought wives with them and then in short order...BABIES. Lots of babies. People you would never think would have a baby were having them.

Chicky's mother, Chico's mother, Smitty's sister, my Aunt Eileen, Breezy's sister, the wives of all the Thomas brothers and even Wally's mother. Wally was ready to graduate High School. He bought the old Dodge and his father was an Air Raid Warden. Something strange was going on with all these babies arriving. It was like some sort of epidemic.

It may have been strange, but it was good for business. These babies needed a lot of things from the drug store and other special stores. I started to make quick runs to Paskow's Drug Store on Washington Avenue and Kolker's Baby store on Elizabeth Avenue.

Returning from one of these runs, I passed what had been a vacant store on the corner of Grove Street and Washington Avenue. A new delicatessen business had opened there and it had a big paper sign in the window. I didn't know what a delicatessen was, so I figured that I would hurry home and ask my mother.

"Ma, there's a new store opening on the corner of Washington Avenue and Grove Street. It's called a Deli'cat'sen and the man who owns it is named Cole Slaw. What's a ELI'CAT"SEN?"

"A WHAT?"

"There's a big paper sign in the store window that says...OPEN, DELI CAT' SEN COLE SLAW."

"A delicatessen is a store where they sell lunch meat and salads and pickles and such. They don't have those kinds of stores where we came from. And, Cole Slaw is a salad; not a persons name."

I thought I was learned in the ways of the community. Not knowing what Cole slaw and a delicatessen were really showed my ignorance. My mother made all kinds of salads and pickles so she never had to go to a delicatessen. I guess there were a lot of people around here who couldn't do those things and that is why someone invented a delicatessen.

My mother couldn't argue too much with my expanded range on the bicycle making deliveries. It was more like a job and I was providing a vital community service. She also allowed me to go to the Bayway Community Center, which was next to our Junior High School, twice a week to play basketball. All the boys in the neighborhood went and we were usually accompanied by an adult. There was little chance to get in trouble, especially in the winter. My behavior since Christmas was worthy of a Good Conduct Medal.

School, deliveries, basketball and cold dark afternoons limited our free time. Gradually the days began to lengthen and then on February 2, the Ground Hog predicted an early Spring. Our restrictions would soon be lifted and we could take to the road once again.

## CHAPTER 34

## THE ISLAND IN THE SUN

That Ground Hog was right. I don't think any Spring was ever as early and as glorious as this one. The days were sunny and the temperatures mild. Baby carriages were parked all over the place by our buildings. The new mothers had set their new charges out in the mild air to snooze and grow in the peaceful afternoons.

Our restrictions were lifted. We had our bikes and sunny days ahead. Yes Sir, all was well with the world, or would be if it weren't for those Russians. They were doing a lot of saber rattling and walking in and out of the United Nations. The newspaper people called all this posturing "The Cold War."

We had more important things to do now. We had no time to worry about Russians.

I was on the Junior High School baseball team. We practiced every day at a place called Simmons Field in Linden. The field was about 3 blocks behind the school next to the Standard Oil Refinery. Our league games against the other 3 Junior High Schools were played in Warinanco Park, part of which is in Roselle. On game days, I could ride my bike to the park since my house was on the way from school to the game. All the other guys on the team lived in Bayway and they rode their bikes from their homes to the park.

With the exception of the opening day of Trout Season in April, baseball was the only game in town.

Opening day of Trout season was usually more ritual than pleasure. Early April could have some raw wet days and they were usually reserved for the opening day of Trout season.

We caught the 44 bus going to Winfield at 6 A.M. We boarded the bus wearing our hip boots, knapsacks and fishing vests loaded with all kinds of hooks, lures and containers of worms. We carried our rods, which were always ready to poke at someone on the bus.

"Have your nickels ready, boys!" The driver hollered as somebody held up the line trying to find their money hidden among all the stuff they were carrying.

Once boarded, most of us stood up for the trip. It was a little hard to sit down and then get back up again with all paraphernalia we were wearing.

Winfield Circle was the end of the line for the 44 bus. The Rahway River flowed under the wooden bridge on Raritan Road, just west of the circle. From this point we followed the river down to our favorite spot on Jackson's Pond above the first dam in Winfield.

People were already picking out their spots along the river in anticipation of the 7 A.M. opening. Some people were gathered around camp fires to ward off the morning chill.

We spread out along a stretch of the river, where we would first try our luck. The rods, reels and worms were ready with time to spare before the Ranger blew his whistle.

"Remember the Sucker I caught here last year?" Chicky chirped. "You guys made me throw it back. If I catch it again, I'm goin' to cook it and eat it. Did you ever cat a Sucker, R. A.?"

"No. But I ate plenty of Catfish."

"Catfish! Does it taste like Tuna Fish?" Robert asked.

"It tastes like a cat." Tommy answered. "That's what they give you in a Chinese Restaurant."

This kind of banter went on for the next few minutes. Finally 7 o'clock arrived and all the lines went into the water.

The stream was high, fast and muddy colored. I don't know how a fish could see our bait.

"Robert got one!" Tommy yelled.

Sure enough, Robert climbed up on the bank and hauled in a 7inch Brook Trout.

"I got something big!" Chico yelled. "Somebody help me with this."

We could see his rod bending to a point where it looked like it would break. Tommy quickly ran to his aid.

"This thing gotta be a monster." Chicky squealed, when we all ran over to join the battle.

The monster finally yielded and slowly came towards the shore. The fierce battle was coming to the end and the monster reared its head out of the murky water.

"It's the branch from a tree." Robert howled as he waded into the water to grab the monster by its butt end.

"It put up some fight though." Chico responded. "I hope I can get this line untangled. The darn thing took my worm."

"What are you using for bait?" Robert asked after seeing Chicky cast his line far out into the river.

"It's a lure my Uncle Jim uses when he goes ocean fishing."

"That thing is bigger than the fish around here. It's probably scarin' them away. You can't catch anything with that."

"Maybe. But, it does cast good." Chicky answered in an attempt to justify his position.

By noon time we all were pretty wet. But, we did catch some fish.

Robert had the Trout and a Blue Gill. Chicky and I each had a Blue Gill. Tommy had a Trout and Chico got a small Catfish.

Chicky wanted to eat the fish despite the fact that each of us brought lunch.

"You know how to clean fish, R.A.; you do that and we'll make a fire." Robert said to me as he gathered up the catch.

I cleaned the little rascals and prepared them for roasting over the fire.

We sat around the fire eating our lunches hoping to dry off some. The fish were mounted like popsicles on a stick. The sticks were stuck into the ground just beyond the flames of the fire. When the fish were done we passed them around for everybody to have a bite.

The flesh was sticky, sweet and smokey. But, we enjoyed it. We were one with nature.

Shortly after lunch we all decided that it was time to go. Satisfied with our first foray of the season into the field, we headed back to the bus stop.

"You smell like a bon fire." My mother complained when I entered the door. "Get those smelly clothes off and take a bath. Did you fall into that river?"

I often wondered what would have happened if my mother was Daniel Boone's mother. The country would probably still be settled this side of the Appalachian Mountains because Daniel had to go home every day for a bath.

Spring gradually warmed into summer and another school year had ended. Hopefully an endless exciting summer of new experiences lay ahead. The bicycles provided us with the mobility to accomplish those things that we only dreamed about a few years ago.

Each of us was on a team in the County League in the Park. When we weren't playing baseball we took trips to Linden Pool or the Clark Reservoir. In the swamps down on Linden Avenue we picked cattails and caught frogs and snakes. We saw Herons and Egrets and other exotic birds in a setting that subliminally tricked our imaginations into thinking that we were in the Florida Everglades.

We were planning on going up to Mr. Seymour's Camp later in the summer. I could hardly wait to tie into the big fish up there. This looked like it was going to be the best summer ever.

Early in July, Gramp came by and asked my mother if I could go with him to Long Island.

During the War my Uncle Jack married a girl from Long Island. He had been living out there since being discharged and now he bought a bowling alley. Gramp was going out to help him and he wanted me to come along. I knew my grandfather. If he was going to help Jack; then I was going to help Gramp. I wondered who would do the most helping.

I had never been to Long Island. It was another place to see and broaden my horizon.

R. Allen Pender

The trip took us across Staten Island where we got the Staten Island Ferry to New York.

Gramp knew his way around. We had to cross a bridge into Brooklyn and then get on a road that went by Coney Island. This was all new to me. In my wildest imagination I could not conceive of so many people in so many buildings. It was unbelievable.

"This is the center of the world. Everything happens here" Gramp said.

Since I never saw anything like New York, I had to agree with him.

After we passed Coney Island we drove and drove some more. It looked like the road had no end. We saw farms and open spaces. Gramp told me that they raised a lot of ducks out here. I didn't see any. But then, why would anyone want to come out here, except to raise ducks.

After what seemed like an eternity, Gramp said, "We're here Sayville, Long Island.

The Montauk highway is the main street in Sayville. The town straddles each side of the road. There are a few side streets off the 2 lane highway and Jack's bowling alley is on one of those streets. His building couldn't have been more than 100 feet from the highway.

"Hey, Pop...and Richard. Glad you could come over!" Jack exclaimed when we entered the front door.

Jack was standing behind the circular bar situated on the right side of the ground floor. A curtained divider running from front to rear separated the bar area from the 4 bowling alleys, which occupied the remainder of the ground floor.

One man was sitting at the bar drinking a beer. If it weren't for him and Jack the place would be empty.

"Put your stuff down and I'll show you around."

There is a kitchen and rest rooms to the rear of the bar. A steel stairway next to the right wall led to the second floor where there are 8 more bowling alleys. Two men were working up on the second floor. They were refinishing the surface of the bowling alleys so the facility could comply with the standards of the American Bowling Congress. Jack introduced us to the men and then we went back down stairs.

"This place was once a movie theater. Back during the War it was changed into a bowling alley. A lot of people in the area worked for Republic Aviation making airplanes, so this was one of the places they could relax. Most of those people are gone now. The town and this area is more of a vacation place now."

Gramp immediately went behind the bar for something cool to drink.

"Do you want a Coka Cola or Ginger Ale, son." He yelled out while reaching into the bar cooler.

"Have a Coke, Richard. After you finish, Pop can mind the bar and I'll show you around the town."

"That sounds good. I heard you were by the ocean."

"The bay is straight down this street and on the other side of the bay is Fire Island and the ocean."

It's a nice little town. It took us all of about 15 minutes to drive around it. We went down the street from bowling alley. The street dead ended at the Great South Bay. Jack turned left and went a short distance to what looked like a creek loaded with boats.

"That is where the ferry leaves for Fire Island across the bay." Jack said, pointing at a parking lot with a sign that said "FERRY."

We slowly drove on a narrow road along the creek and looked at all the small boats moored along its length. An open air type of seafood restaurant, sitting on pilings, is located next to the bridge where the Montauk Highway crosses the Creek.

Jack turned left and went a short distance back to the street where the bowling alley is located. The rest of Main Street consists of a couple of small stores and a little diner.

"Did you ever bowl or set pins?" Jack asked.

"No. This is the first time I was ever in a bowling alley."

"We've been getting some summer vacationers in here to bowl. Right now we're just using the downstairs alleys, because they are working on the alleys up stairs. I'll show you how to set pins. It's easy. Most of the pin boys around here are working the summer leagues in Islip."

I knew there was some reason I was here. Setting pins didn't sound too bad. Besides, Jack was trying to get this place started…and he's family.

At the back end of the alley is a pit. The pins get knocked into this pit and the back wall stops the ball. There is a foot pedal at the end of the alley. Stepping on this pedal raises metal spikes up from beneath the alleys surface and the pins are set on these spikes. When the pedal is released the pins are set in their proper positions.

"You just return the ball and clear the pins away after the first ball. You reset the pins after the second ball or a strike. Sit up on this board between the two alleys so you can set the pins on two alleys."

Jack and I practiced for a couple of minutes. "I think I got it."

"People probably won't come in 'till it cools some after supper. You and Pop go over to the diner and eat and then we'll see what happens tonight."

I wanted to eat ham, but Gramp said we had to eat this diner's meatloaf. Gramp said this little diner had the best meatloaf chef this side of Chicago. I'm sure my Grandfather ate a lot of meatloaf in his time, but if this chef is so good, why is he out here at the end of the world. I was too hungry to argue.

"You don't want to fill up too much. It'll be harder to set pins if your stomach is too full. After the alley closes we'll come back here for wheat cakes."

"I guess this diner makes the best wheat cakes this side of Chicago."

"He makes beautiful wheat cakes. They're so big it's hard to eat more than one."

I would have to see these wheat cakes. Gramps idea of quality was a lot different than that of the real world. I am sure the chef made big wheat cakes. They are probably used around here for boat anchors

The meatloaf was edible. It came with canned green beans and lumpy potatoes. The bread and butter were good. I ate everything in the little basket.

Jack went home for supper when Gramp and I returned.

Gramp got behind the bar. He put on an apron and straightened up a little. He said he was going to try a glass of beer from the tap to make sure it was the right temperature. I'm sure Gramp wanted everything to be perfect while he was in charge of the bowling alley. In the mean time I tried to bowl. I had a difficult time finding a ball to fit my hand. When I found one that fit pretty good, I rolled it down the alley like I saw people do at the Bayway Community Center. After each roll, I walked down the alley, returned the ball and reset the pins. This activity kept me occupied until Jack came back.

Three or four people came in and sat at the bar. I was sitting at the scoring table at one of the alleys reading, when Jack called me.

"Hey, Richard! We got some people here who want to bowl. Set up alleys 1 and 2."

Jack switched the lights on in the alleys and then he proceeded to fix the people up with shoes and scoring sheets. I walked back to the pits and made my self comfortable on the board between the alleys. The pins were set and I was ready to try setting pins.

Two men and two women seated themselves on the bench serving alleys 1 and 2.

"Hey, boy!" One of the men cried out. "We want to take a couple of practice balls."

I didn't know what the custom was in this game. So I hollered back. "Go ahead!"

I wasn't prepared for the explosion which occurred on either side of me when these two balls whizzed in and scattered those pins all over the place. When the pins stopped flying around, I jumped into one pit, returned the ball, reset the pins and then I did the same thing in the next alley. Before I had a chance to sit down these two balls were coming back at me again. This time I knew what was going to happen and I was resolved to the fact that I had been sentenced here to pay for any bad thing I did, or would ever do for the rest of my life.

The ladies were up next. They were much slower than the men and provided me some relief. They each rolled two practice balls and then the game began.

I didn't know how to score this game. All I did was to keep track of the balls. Reset the pins after a strike or after the second ball. That's what Jack told me and that's what I did.

I got into a rhythm after a while and I was able to swing from alley to alley fairly smoothly. Also, it didn't take too long for the sweat to begin to pour out of me. I had my shirt off and my T-shirt wrapped around my forehead to keep the perspiration out of my eyes.

Gramp was in his glory. Every so often he brought a tray full of beers over to the people who were bowling. He had his white apron on and he paraded over carrying the tray like some waiter in a movie. It would have been funny, except I was sweating to death. Finally there was a little break. I think the ladies had to go to the bathroom. Jack had seen my distress and he came over with a cold soda and a towel.

"You're doin' great."

"When do you think they'll be done?" I asked

"Pretty soon, I'm sure."

The ladies came back and the pins started flying again. After what seemed like an eternity, I heard one man say, "last game."

Gramp brought them another round of beer and the action started up again. By this time I was kind of punchy. I was just hoping the game would end. Finally it did. I made a beeline to the men's room to rinse the sweat off my head and upper body.

When I returned to the bar the men were settling up their bill with Jack. Each man came over and gave me a dollar.

Turning to me, Jack said. "You get 15 cents for each game. Each person bowled 6 games. That's a total of 24 games at 15 cents. Here is $ 3.60."

Three dollars and 60 cents plus a 2 dollar tip. Wow! That's more money than I made home in a month.

Jack had a stall shower set up out back of the kitchen. I had brought a lot of T-shirts and underwear with me. I also had several changes of clothing. My mother knew that I would have to change clothes more in the heat and in case anything happened to me, she didn't want me taken to any hospital or doctor in dirty underwear. Right now, I just wanted to be out of my sweaty clothes.

The water from the shower felt real good as it rinsed the salty sweat from my head and face. In a few minutes I was out and dry, feeling human again.

The last patrons left the barroom around 10:30. Jack cleaned the last few glasses in the sink and then cleared his cash register.

"You go home Jack. Richard and I can lock up." Gramp commanded." We're goin' t' go for some wheat cakes then we'll come back here and go t' bed."

Jack checked the door in the back and I checked the exit door on the second floor. Everything was locked, so the three of us headed out the front door.

"I can drive you to the diner, Pop." Jack said as he locked the front door and gave Gramp the key.

"No, no, no. It's a nice night. We can walk. We can use the fresh air."

Jack got into his car and drove off towards his home. Gramp and I started walking up the street towards the Montauk highway.

Gramp was always lecturing me about something. He meant well. I guess it was his way of passing along the lessons he learned from his life experiences.

Tonight his discourse started out on the value of work and business.

"If you take care of business, you'll always have enough business to take care of." He began as our walk progressed up the street.

The events of the day apparently triggered the subject matter for this evening. I didn't know if it had something to do with my pin setting, or Jack's management of the bowling alley. But, the thrust of his lecture dealt with discipline and how we should pay attention to details. He really got into his subject using people he knew or heard of as examples of good and bad practices.

Gramp didn't even stop for a breath as we rounded the corner and started walking along the Montauk Highway. He was busy regaling me with stories about personalities which ran the spectrum from Thomas Edison the inventor to Jack Johnson, the boxer and John McGraw, the manager of the old N.Y. Giants, when I noticed that the highway was getting darker the further we went. It was then that I realized that we had walked across that little bridge spanning the creek by the outdoor seafood restaurant. The diner we went to earlier wasn't in this direction.

I kept trying to break into the conversation, but Gramp was on a roll. The more he talked the faster he walked.

"Gramp!" I hollered, stopping in my tracks.

He walked a few more feet before he realized that I wasn't by his side.

"What's wrong?" He asked, turning back to see me standing on the side of the road.

"Gramp, that sign just up ahead says BLUE POINT 1 MILE. Is that where the diner is?"

"Oh! We must have made a wrong turn. You should have let me know that we were going the wrong way."

Never one to admit to a mistake or cry over a bad situation, Gramp just turned around and said. "Come on; let's go back. This is nice walk. Just the thing to give us an appetite for wheat cakes."

We must have been the last two customers in the Sayville diner. The counterman didn't seem real enthused when he had to make up more buckwheat batter. He even started to put out the lights while we were eating the wheat cakes.

Gramp kept trying to engage the man in conversation. However, the counterman ignored him and continued with his cleanup chores, which I took as a signal that this guy had a long day and wanted to go home. So did I.

We had to walk only a block back to the bowling alley. Gramp and I were going to sleep on Army cots up on the second floor bowling alleys.

There is a big exhaust fan and a lot of windows up on the second floor. It was warm, but not hot. The breeze from the fan felt good and I had no trouble sleeping. Gramp could sleep on a picket fence. I think he was asleep before he had completely lain down.

The sound of birds and the soft morning light gently woke me. Gramp was already up and had gone downstairs. He was either in the men's room or the kitchen because I could hear water running. I had that good shower last night, so all I had to do was wash my face, brush my teeth and comb my hair.

Gramp had coffee brewing in the kitchen while he was in the men's room washing up. I went into the lady's room and cleaned up.

"Do you want ham and eggs for breakfast?" Gramp hollered as he rooted through the big commercial refrigerator in the kitchen.

"OK", I said walking into the kitchen. New York Law said that every bar like Jack's had to serve food. Jack had ham, swiss cheese, liverwurst, eggs, milk and soup in the refrigerator. Around the bar he had little tables with red and white checkered table cloths. I guess he had the basic ingredients for a restaurant and satisfied the law.

Gramp and I had breakfast. We put away the cots and I started sweeping the floor.

Soon after Gramp unlocked the front door, the men who were refinishing the bowling alleys arrived. After exchanging some pleasantries they went upstairs to be about their business.

Jack arrived a little while later and he showed me how to clean the men's and lady's rooms and install new paper towels and toilet paper. After that he gave me a big soft mop which is used to wipe down the bowling alleys.

Gramp was behind the bar checking all the bottles getting ready for a day of bartending.

It didn't take us long to have the place all cleaned up ready for the afternoon and evening crowd.

Jack and I went over to the Drug store on the main street for ice cream sodas. He told me about all the good things to do around the town. He knew I liked to fish and he was going to ask a friend of his if I could borrow a pole for the week. I could go fishing right down at the end of the street or over by the Ferry Dock. Or, if I felt adventurous, I could take the ferry to Fire Island and fish in the ocean.

"The afternoons are slow around the alley. Nobody comes in to bowl early. It's like last night. People come in after supper. You can have the whole afternoon to do what you want."

"If I can borrow the pole, maybe I'll go fishin' tomorrow. I can probably do some crabbin' right over by that bridge."

"My friend Carl will probably in later this afternoon we can ask him and he'll tell you the best places to go."

Things were looking up. I was really excited about fishing and being out and about by myself. Everything around here is within walking distance. They even sold bait down by the ferry. I am gonna catch me some fish.

At noon time, Jack made some ham and Swiss cheese sandwiches. The men, Art and Jim, who were working upstairs, came down to join us at one of the tables with the checkered table cloths. Jack got beers for everyone but me. I got a cold Coke.

"What do we have here Jack, a greenhorn?" Remarked Jimmy, the man wearing glasses. "Drinking Coke is for sissies. He should have a nice tall Rheingold with that sandwich."

"He's too young Jimmy. Besides, my sister would kill me if she found out he was drinking beer."

"He sure looks big enough. What are you going to do with your time out here, Lad?"

"I set some pins last night and maybe will tonight too. Then maybe I can get some fishing in during the daytime."

"I got to see if I can borrow a rod for him. He's a fresh water guy and all his stuff is home." Jack interjected.

"No problem." Jimmy answered. "I have a nice Bay rod out in the car he can use."

"Are you sure you won't need it?" I asked.

"I probably won't go fishin' 'till my son-in-law comes out here from the city, around the end of the month. We'll go out to my car as soon as I finish this sandwich."

"You'll need a rig with some hooks and sinkers. You can get them at the sport shop over here by the highway or at the bait shop down by the "Fairy Dock." Jimmy instructed as he took the rod out of the trunk of his car. "Tell the guy in the store that you are going for snapper blues. That's what is bittin' now."

"Gee, thanks." I said. "I'll go to the sport shop after lunch and then I can get this ready for tomorrow."

Jimmy and I walked back inside and I placed the rod out in the kitchen to keep it safe.

"Where are you going fishin'?" Asked Art, the bigger of the two men.

***THE SOJOURNERS***
*Life on the American Homefront During World War II*

"I'll probably go down here by the end of the street, or maybe over by the creek, first. Then, I'll see. Maybe somebody will tell me another place. I'd like to go by the ocean sometime.

"That's good." Art replied. "You can take the "Fairy" boat over to the island."

"He should really enjoy that." Jimmy said and laughed. Art and Jack laughed along with him.

I didn't know what the joke was, but it probably was something funny between them.

I had plenty of money in my pocket. My mother had given me ten dollars and last night I made five dollars and sixty cents. So, after lunch I went over to the Sport Shop.

The man there was nice. He knew what kind of rig I needed. They didn't cost much so I got two. He also sold bait. He said squid was the best bait at this time of year. So I bought a squid in a cellophane package.

He had a lot of nice stuff in the store. He had genuine LEE RIDERS, the best blue jeans available. He also sold Daisy Air Rifles. They were outlawed in New Jersey. But over here they were legal. The regular Daisy repeater cost $3.50. I vowed that if I have another good night in the bowling alley, I will come back and buy that rifle.

Later that afternoon, Gramp and I walked over to the outdoor seafood restaurant.

Attesting to the freshness of their fare, the restaurant has a big sign on top of the shanty like building. "THE FISH YOU EAT TODAY, SLEPT LAST NIGHT IN GREAT SOUTH BAY." I don't think you could get anything fresher than that.

Inside is a bare bones dinning room. Screening covered the open windows and the wooden picnic type tables didn't have table cloths. The menu was written on a chalk board hanging on the wall.

"We'll have fish and chips." Gramp said to the middle aged lady who took our order.

There were two other people in the restaurant. I guess we were just ahead of the dinner crowd, because It didn't take very long for her to return with our order.

"You know." Gramp said as the lady set down our plates. "I had fish and chips in London, where they serve it in a newspaper."

"Is that right?" The lady replied. "We can't do that here or the Board of Health will close us up."

Well, so much for trying to impress that waitress I thought and I dove into the fried fish and potatoes waiting to hear Gramps reply, which never came.

While Jack was out for supper, a group of boys and girls came in. There were six of them and they looked college age. They wanted to bowl, so Gramp and I took them over to the shoe rack to fix them up with shoes. Once they were set, I went and turned the lights on in Alleys 1 and 2. Gramp was dressed up in his bartender apron and he brought them over a tray of beers.

They appeared to form two teams and they started their game right away. The boys didn't roll the balls as hard as the men last night. The group seemed to be having a good time. Gramp kept them in fresh beers and I guess they bowled for almost two hours.

The night was still young when they finished. I was sweated up pretty good, so I went out into the kitchen to rinse off in the big sink. When I came out, Jack gave me some money.

"They bowled 18 games and left a 2 dollar tip. Four dollars and seventy cents."

Wow! My little treasury was getting fatter. I had a coke and sat down at a table to rest awhile.

I don't think fifteen minutes had passed, when another group of adults came in the door.

"Richard!" Jack hollered. "Set up alleys 1 and 2."

I went back into the pit and put the lights on again. This group of 3 men and 3 ladies arranged themselves into some kind of teams and they started bowling. About an hour latter I noticed that they must have switched sides. They continued on for another hour, then they switched around again. They were drinking beer and having a good ole time. This group, both the men and ladies were good bowlers. They finally stopped at 10:30 P.M.

I was so tired and sweaty that I could hardly walk down the alley and out to the kitchen.

I stuck my head under the kitchen faucet to cool and rinse myself. I was anxious to get into the shower, but I walked back to the bar first.

"Some job, Richard. They had 36 games and left you a 5 dollar tip." Jack proudly announced.

"That's a 15 dollar night!" I exclaimed and I quickly thought of the Daisy Air Rifle. It's mine, or will be tomorrow.

Jack stayed open as long as he had customers. After the bowlers left, 5 or 6 people were sitting at the bar. I guess that's the nature of the business.

I took a shower and changed clothes.

"Gramp. Do you want to go over to the diner?" I asked

"No. I'll stay here with Jack. You go over, son. The door will be open when you come back."

This time there were a couple of people in the diner. I went in and sat at the counter.

"Do you want wheat cakes again? The counterman gruffly asked.

"No. I'll have scrambled eggs and ice tea."

"Rye or white toast."

"Rye."

Setting a big glass of ice tea in front of me, the counterman asked," How come a young feller like you is out so late?"

"I was settin' pins over in my uncle's bowling alley."

"Are you Jack's nephew?"

"Yeah. I came over here with my grandfather to help Jack awhile."

"That's good. Jack is a nice guy. Listen, you want some bacon with those eggs?"

"OK."

That ice tea and the food made me feel whole again.

"Can I have a check?" I asked the counterman.

"Don't worry about it kid. I'll catch you tomorrow. Tell Jack, Gus says hello."

"Thanks, Gus." I said walking out the door.

Gus was a nice guy, even if he made lumpy potatoes.

Gramp and Jack were cleaning glasses as the last patrons were going out the door.

"We'll have to refill the coolers with bottled beer first thing in the morning."

"Richard, if I leave you a note with what I need, can you get the cased beer out from that little room beside the kitchen and fill up the cooler?"

"Sure he can Jack." Gramp replied before I had a chance to understand and respond to the question.

"Leave the note right on the register and I'll take care of it as soon as I wake up."

"Good boy."

I went upstairs and dragged the cots out while Gramp and Jack were finishing downstairs.

The windows were open, the fan was on and I was ready to rest my aching body.

Gramp was up before me again the next morning.

He was busy in the kitchen when I came down stairs.

"I'm going to make ham and cheese omelets. How does that sound?"

I never had a ham and cheese omelet, but I figured I would give Gramp the benefit of the doubt. "That should be alright, Gramp. I'll start getting the beer out while you cook." I took Jack's note and identified the cases he wanted out at the bar. The room was actually a walk-in cooler. I had no trouble loading the cases on a hand truck and wheeling them out to the bar.

I didn't want to fool around this morning. I wanted to get the beer put away and then sweep the floors and alleys. The rest rooms had to be cleaned too. And then, I had a date at the sport shop.

Jimmy and Art came in, said hello and went right upstairs. Jack wasn't far behind them.

I had already put the beer in the cooler and put the empty cases outside. I had finished the rest rooms and was now in the process of sweeping the floor.

"You got busy early today, Richard."

"Yeah. I want to get everything done so I can go over to the sport shop this morning and then maybe go fishin' after lunch."

"Didn't you get everything you wanted yesterday?" Jack asked.

"I need a couple more things and then I should have everything."

"The sport shop should be open by 10 o'clock. You will probably be done by then."

I was done my chores for the morning and I hotfooted it over to the sport shop.

"Did you catch any fish yet, young fella?" The man behind the counter said when I entered the store.

"I'm goin' to go fishin' after lunch. I want to get a couple of things first."

"Well, what do you need?"

"I want a pair of those Lee Rider britches."

"OK. Do you know what size you wear?"

I didn't know my size, so the man measured my waist and then reached up on the shelf and pulled out a pair of denim britches.

"All you gotta do is roll up the pants legs to the length you want and you're set. Is there anything else?"

"Yeah. I'd like the Daisy Air rifle and some tubes of BB's."

It was done. The man pulled out a cardboard box from another shelf and there it was all oiled and blued... The Daisy Repeating Air Rifle. I gave the man two five dollar bills and he gave me back some change. Everything cost about six dollars, but I wasn't counting.

With my new purchases in hand, I headed back to the bowling alley.

Jim and Artie were sitting at the bar having a beer and talking with Gramp, who was behind the bar.

"Here he comes, the super pin boy. We've been hearing about how hard you were working. Where have you been, laddie, shopping?" Jim asked.

"Yeah. I went over to the sport shop and bought a pair of Lee Riders." I replied pulling the denims out of the bag. "And this." I said, laying the cardboard box on the bar.

"An Air Rifle. What are you gonna do with that?" Artie asked.

"I'll do target shootin' and such. I always wanted one of these, but they don't sell them over in New Jersey."

"He's a good shot, Artie. He can hit anything he wants with a slingshot." Gramp proudly announced.

"Well, I'll tell you what you gotta do with those dungarees." Jim chimed in. "You put them on and then wear them in the water. After they're all wet, you let them dry on you and they'll take the shape of your body."

"Yes, sir." Artie agreed. "That's what they do in the Navy."

I wasn't going to argue with them, because I didn't know what went on in the Navy. I just said, "Maybe I'll do that if I go over to the beach at the ocean."

"That's the thing to do. I guarantee ya." Jim answered.

Jack said I could make myself a little shooting range down in the cellar. There wasn't a full basement under the building; just a dugout area where the furnace is located. Everything else is dirt, like a crawl space.

I got some tin cans and set them up on the dirt and zeroed in the Air Rifle. I was probably down there about 45 minutes just shooting up those tin cans. After I was satisfied with the gun's performance, I called it a day. It was lunch time and time for fishing.

Jack was going to make sandwiches again, but since I had a lot of money, I wanted to go over to the diner for a hamburger.

"I'll have a California Hamburger and a Chocolate milk shake." I said to the red headed waitress wearing a pink uniform with a little white cap. She was behind the counter. Gus was working at the grill and he had his back to me.

"How do you want that done, Honey?" She said, shifting her body onto one hip.

"Regular, cooked hamburger." I answered, somewhat taken aback by her posturing.

She tore my order from her pad, stuck her pencil back into her hair and sashayed down to where Gus was working the grill. She hung my order on a clip above his head and then continued down to the milk shake mixer, which is next to the display case containing pies, cakes and other desserts.

Gus had his spatula going at the grill. He had eggs and fried potatoes cooking on one side of the grill. Without breaking stride, he opened the refrigerator next to the grill, took out a hamburger patty and slapped it on the grill. He quickly grabbed a plate from the rack beside him and in one swift move of the spatula; he slid eggs, bacon and fried potatoes onto the plate. Turning around, he passed the plate to a waiting customer sitting at the counter

"Hey, Jack's pin boy." he said when he saw me sitting at the counter. "Is the California for you?"

"Yeah. I'm eattin' my lunch out today, 'cause I'm going fishin' this afternoon."

Turning back to the grill, he continued talking to me. "Goin fishin'. That's good. You work 'till late at night; you need some time off for fun. Hey! If you catch some fish you bring 'em over here. Gus knows what to do with fresh fish."

"Ok. If I catch anything, I'll bring it here."

The redhead was back with my milk shake just as Gus was assembling the hamburger.

He passed the plate to her and she set it down in front of me. "Is there anything else you want, Honey?" She said with a quirky smile.

"No. I'm fine fer now."

I ate my hamburger and polished off the milk shake. When I was finished, I signaled the waitress for my check. I had heard that waitresses call men "Honey" and parade around so they can get bigger tips.

I left her a tip and I could see her watching to make sure I did, as she walked up to the cash register to collect my money.

"Maybe we'll see you later big boy. Bring us back some fish."

"I'm gonna try." I said as I headed for the door.

I knew she was just trying to have some fun with me. But, she did get me a little unnerved. I've been used to dealing with teen age girls and this was a women. I'll bet she was about 22 or 23.

I made my way back to the bowling alley. I had to get my pole and the squid, which was in Jack's refrigerator. I hope Gramp didn't eat it for lunch.

When I returned to the bowling alley, Gramp, Jack, Jim and Artie were sitting at a table eating and drinking beer.

"Do you want a sandwich, son?" Gramp asked as I approached the table.

"No thanks. I just had a big California hamburger and a milkshake at the diner. I'm goin' to get my stuff and go down the road to fish for a while."

"Oh, so you were over at the diner. How is Marlene?" Artie asked.

"Who is Marlene?"

"You didn't meet Marlene! She's that cute redheaded waitress." Artie shot back.

"She waited on me, but I didn't know her name."

"Did you leave her a good tip?" Jim asked.

"I left her a tip, I don't know if it was a good as she was workin' for."

All the men started laughing; I guess Marlene had some sort of a reputation around here.

I knew the men were having some good natured fun with me. And, I didn't mind.

Luckily, Gramp hadn't eaten my squid. I put the bait and the rest of my tackle in a little bucket. I put my bathing suit on under my jeans and then slipped my hunting knife onto my belt. I was set to go. The men were still sitting at the table when I walked out of the kitchen.

"I'll be goin' down the end of the street and then maybe over to the ferry dock. I should be back before 5 o'clock."

Gramp knew I could handle myself around water and boats. And I was used to going to different places; I wasn't a little boy anymore, so he wasn't too concerned for my welfare. "Have a good time and come back when you're hungry." He said and I was out the door.

There is a cable running through some short pipes at the end of the street. I guess it's a barricade to prevent someone from driving into the bay. On the other side of the barricade is a little beach area. It isn't sandy. The beach is made of ground up clam and oyster shells. Gramps told me that they have so many clam and oyster shells out here, that they grind the shells up and pave roads with them.

It's a good thing I wore my sneakers. I was going to take my pants off and wade barefoot out into the bay. But, those sharp shells were spread out into the bay too.

I took my pants off and cut up some squid for bait. I had to wade out quite some distance before the water was over my knees. Then I made my first cast into salt water. I made several casts, each time I let the bait sit awhile before reeling in. Maybe I was wrong, but I was employing fresh water tactics to salt water fishing.

After one cast, I started to reel in and felt a slight tug on the line. It didn't feel like a fish biting. I had some drag on the rig as I reeled in, but I couldn't feel movement as I would with a fish. Soon I got the rig close enough for me to see a big crab clinging to the squid. The little bucket with my bait was suspended from my belt, which was draped across my neck and shoulder. Bending down, I herded the crab into the bucket. Once he was out of the water, the crab let go of the squid. Over the course of the next hour, I caught five more crabs in the same manner.

I waded back to shore. I wasn't catching any fish here. Maybe I had to be in deeper water.

Picking up my pants, I decided to walk over to the ferry dock. The water had to be deeper over there.

A group of people were lined up along the pier. They didn't have fishing rods, but they did have some kind of a rig at the end of a line.

"What do people use for bait over here?" I asked the man sitting in the bait shack.

"They're crabbin'. Some have a chunk of fish in a crab trap. Others use a line tied to a piece of fish. With that you need a cloth net, cause that crab is gonna let go once he comes out of the water."

"Do you sell crab traps?" I asked the man.

"These are them." He said pointing to what looked like triangular baskets made of window screen.

"How much is one with a piece of fish?"

"I'll give you one with a piece of fish for 2 dollars. I usually get 3 dollars from the city people, but you don't sound like one of them."

"I already caught five crabs on squid." I said pointing to the bucket.

"Those are nice crabs. But, you don't want to waste squid on crabs."

"I got the squid because I might go over to the ocean and fish in the surf."

"When are you going over there?"

"Maybe tomorrow. I have to come here and get the ferry."

"Here let me have your squid. I'll put it in my refrigerator and you can get it when you come for the ferry. That way it won't go bad out in this heat."

"That's good. Thank you." I said placing the 2 dollars and the squid on the window counter.

"Here, don't go over where those people are crabbin'. Go around back of my shack. More crabs there."

I grabbed up my belongings which now included a new crab trap.

"Thanks a lot. I'll see you in a little bit." I said heading off to the back of the shack.

The bait shack was on the creek side of the wharf, just a head of the mouth of the creek.

I situated myself behind the shack and then lowered the baited trap into the water. I let the line go slack and waited a couple of minutes then hauled the trap up for inspection. Sure enough, I had a nice big crab in the trap. He was transferred to the bucket and I lowered the trap again. Every few minutes I would catch another crab. Within the hour, the bucket was almost full to the top with crabs. I either had to stop crabbing or get another bucket. I decided to stop and head back to the bowling alley.

"What are you gonna do with all those rascals?" The baitman asked when he saw my catch.

"I'm gonna see if my uncle wants to cook them at the bowling alley, or I might take them over to Gus at the diner."

"Oh, you're with Jack. I stop in there for some beer every so often. Got some in the ice box right now."

"I'll tell him I met you. I'm goin' back there now. I'll have to clean up and get ready to set pins tonight."

"Better you than me in this temperature, Boy. I'll see you tomorrow when you come for the ferry."

I bid the man goodbye and started the trek back to the bowling alley.

Between fishing rod, bucket, crab trap and crabs, I must have resembled a Gypsy peddler walking down the road.

Gramp was tending the bar when I walked in the building.

"Hey, Gramp. do you think Jack would want some crabs?" I said, displaying the bucket full of the critters.

"Jack went home for his break. He'll be back so we can go to supper. We can ask him them. Boy, you sure got a lot of them." Gramp commented when he looked in the bucket.

"I could'a caught more if I had a bigger bucket. But, it would be harder to carry it back here."

I put some water and ice on the crabs to keep them alive. I didn't want them to dry out in the summer heat. Jack was impressed with the catch when he came back. But, he didn't know how to prepare crabs.

"I can take them over to Gus. Gramp and I'll be goin' over there to eat pretty soon. Gus said for me to bring anything I catch over to him."

"Yeah. Good Idea." Jack answered. "Gus makes good crab cakes."

We all agreed that Gus's Diner would be the final repository for the crabs.

I got all cleaned up and put on my new Lee Riders. It was close to 5 o'clock when Gramp and I went to the diner. There were a few people in the diner. Not as many as lunchtime. I didn't see Marlene. A woman, I would later learn was Gus's wife was helping at the counter. Gus was relaxing and talking to some people when we came in.

"What do you have in the bucket, Pin boy?"

"Crabs." I said. "Hope you can use them."

Gus looked into the bucket. "Wow! You do have some crabs. Nice big ones too. Oh, we can use them. I'll make crab cakes and a crab meat spaghetti sauce. They won't go to waste." He then carried the bucket into the little rear kitchen and we could hear him emptying the crabs into something.

Gramp and I sat down at the counter and looked over the menu posted up on the wall.

"Jack says you make good crab cakes. That spaghetti sauce sounds good too." I said when Gus came back with the bucket.

"I make the crab cakes. My wife makes the spaghetti sauce." He answered, pointing at the woman down at the other end of the counter.

I selected a hot roast beef sandwich platter.

"You should try the beef goulash." Gramp commented.

"No. I think I'll stick to the roast beef." I answered. Beef goulash sounded like something made from old shoes. It didn't sound very appetizing.

Gramp liked to brag that he ate all kinds of exotic stuff. I like to stay with the tried and true things.

"How is he? A good boy, Pop?" Gus asked when he returned with our food.

Gramp liked to brag about his family. Everyone was a champion of some kind. Uncle Billy had been a champion auto race driver; Jack had won amateur bicycle races when he was a boy. And now me. What was I?

"He's a great baseball player, Gus. He pitched a no-hit, no-run game for his high school team."

"Junior High School Team, Gramp." I tried to say. But Gramp kept going and I couldn't get a word in sideways.

"In a few years he'll probably be playing for the New York Giants. He's a great fisherman too. A few years back he caught a record breaking pickerel"

New York Giants and record fish. Gramp really knew how to embarrass me. It's a long way from playing with 14 and 15 year olds to the New Your Giants. About the only thing I could do in the Polo Grounds, is buy a hot dog. Yes I caught a big pickerel. But It was not a record of any kind, unless you say, it was the biggest pickerel caught by anyone in our family. That might be some kind of family record.

Gus knew what was happening. He could see my face lit up like a red traffic light.

"I know he's a good boy, Pop. I'll have Gus's special crab cakes for him tomorrow."

"I'll have them for supper tomorrow night. I want to go fishing in the ocean tomorrow afternoon."

"I'll save you some. Gus 'll take care of you."

This evening was a replay of the past two nights. I went into the pits about 7 o'clock and set pins until past 10 o'clock. I made a little over 7 dollars. But, I came out tired and soaking wet with sweat.

"You can go over to Fire Island early tomorrow, if you want. I'll sweep up and restock the beer in the morning." Jack volunteered. "You won't have to come back until later in the afternoon."

"That sounds good. I can bring some lunch with me, or do they sell stuff over there?"

"If you want to buy something cold to drink, there's a big hotel over there called DUFFY'S. You can go into the barroom and buy a coke or ginger ale. That's about all you can buy."

"I'll have Gus make me a sandwich tomorrow, when I'm on my way."

"I'm goin' to stop at Gus's for breakfast tomorrow. If you want I can get you a sandwich." Jack suggested.

"What time are you goin' to be there?" I asked

"About 8:30." Jack answered. "Do you want to meet me?"

"Yeah. That'll be good. I can get a real good diner breakfast and Gus can make me a sandwich."

After having a nice shower and putting on clean underwear, I set up the cots on the second floor and was asleep before Gramp came to bed.

Jack was already at the diner when I arrived. He was sipping a cup of coffee and talking to some of the men seated at the counter. The diner was busy. But, he kept the stool next to him reserved for me.

"Hey, Reechard." He yelled his usual greeting to me. It is something like a French pronunciation of my name and Jack has always called me that since I was a little.boy. "Gus is making me ham and eggs. What do you want?"

"I'll have that too. I feel like havin' a good big breakfast this morning"

"How is my honey this morning? Do you need a menu Sweetie?" Marlene said, as she slinked up in front of me with her order pad at the ready.

I decided not to be shaken by her antics and remained cool. I didn't want her to think her wiggling was having any effect on me. "No. I'll have scrambled eggs and ham with toast, orange juice and milk." I coolly replied.

"Don't we have a good appetite this morning." She quipped, while she scratched the order down on the pad. "You must've had some busy night last night."

"I did." I dryly answered. She could take that anyway she wanted. But, it really meant that I set a lot of pins.

"She's quite a looker." Jack said as Marlene wiggled her way down towards the other end of the counter.

Jack laughed when I said, "She doin' it all fer bigger tips."

"You got her figured out. Don't you?" He said.

"I reckon. I been told what waitresses do."

Marlene was back shortly with our breakfast. Giving me a little wink and a smile, she said, "If you boys need anything else just give me a call."

"I wonder how many times a day she puts on that act for the guys who come into the diner." I said as she walked down to her next customer.

"Yeah, she's a tease alright." Jack said with a chuckle. "Just like those Coochie Coochie dancers that used to come with the carnival back home."

"I knew Jack and some of his friends used to sneak in under the tent to see those dancers…and we both had a good laugh.

As we ate our breakfast, Jack and I talked some about the days before the War. It was a far different life then than now. Some things I had already forgotten. But, people like Jack and Gramp and my other relatives were not quick to let go of the past. They never let me forget our history, our traditions and our faith.

Gramp loved being a bartender. He already had his apron on and was arranging things behind the bar when Jack and I walked in the door.

Since Jim and Artie were working on the alleys upstairs, we really only had to cleanup down stairs. I volunteered to do the rest rooms and Jack went over to cleanup around alleys 1 and 2. With two of us working, the chores were done very quickly.

I began assembling everything I needed for my trip to the ocean. I had all my tackle in the bucket, which was with the rod and reel out in the kitchen. I had on my new Lee Riders, which got pretty sweated up last night. It didn't matter because they would be washed in the ocean, like Artie suggested. I went upstairs to where I kept my clothes. My hunting knife was up there and I needed my baseball hat.

Jim and Artie were doing their work on the alleys when I went upstairs, got my stuff and began to put my knife on my belt.

"Where are you goin' with that Bowie Knife?" Artie clamored.

As I was threading the belt back through my pants, I walked over to where he and Jim were working. "I'm goin' over to the ocean fishin'."

"You're goin' t' take a ride on the fairy boat, eh." Jim commented.

"Jack and I got everything done downstairs, so I'm goin' to go fishing. I got a bunch of crabs yesterday. I gave 'em to Gus over at the diner. I'm goin' over there now and have him make me a sandwich for lunch."

"I'll bet you're just goin' back to see Marlene." Artie remarked.

"Since I don't know where I'm goin, she said she might come with me." I lied.

"Half the guys in this town have been tryin' to get her to go somewhere. I think she may be funnin' you, son." Jim commented.

"We'll see." I answered and went down the stairs.

The crowd at the diner had thinned out when I got over there. Marlene was sitting down at the end of the counter smoking a cigarette and drinking coffee.

Gus saw me coming in the door with all my fishing stuff.

"Where are you goin' Huckleberry Finn?"

"I'm gonna go fishin' over at the ocean. I need a sandwich to take for my lunch."

"You know what? I just made tuna fish salad. Hows about I make you a nice sandwich on Italian bread with lettuce and tomata? Sound good?"

"That will be fine."

"Marlene, get him a banana an' a apple. Pie too. You look like a guy who eats blueberry pie." Before I had a chance to answer, Gus called Marlene. "Blue berry pie."

"This is gonna be some lunch, Gus."

"A big boy like you gotta eat good."

I saw Marlene cut the pie and wrap it up. She brought it up to the register where Gus was putting the sandwich in a paper sack. "Here you are blueberry pie for my blue eyed baby."

I know she was trying to get me to blush. That would have made her day. Instead I remained calm and cool. I knew she was a teaser and I let it go at that.

"He needs a good lunch. He's goin' fishin' over on the island."

"Oh, you're goin' on the fairy boat." She answered. "You better watch out for all the fairies. They like sweet young things like you."

"Fairies. I'm not afraid of any fairies, or ghosts or hob gobblins."

She and Gus started laughing. I didn't know what the joke was. I thought it might be the manner and dialect of my speech. I put my lunch bag into the bucket, paid Gus and started for the door. "Have a good time, Sweetie. Don't let those fairies get you." Marlene said with a little wave as I pushed the door open.

"I don't know what all this nonsense was about fairies. It was probably some local myth; like down on the Outer Banks, where the ghosts of Blackbeard and other pirates are said to be roamin' about. It's all for the benefit of tourists and people like me with straw stickin' out of their ears." I thought aloud to myself on the way to the ferry dock.

I walked out along the Montauk Highway, past the street where the bowling alley is and up to the shell covered road along the creek next to the outdoor seafood restaurant. I ambled along looking at all the boats docked along the creek. People were on some of them, but most appeared vacant. The creek bent a little bit and I could see the bait shack up ahead.

"How's my young friend doin' today? Looks like you're ready for some serious fishing." The baitman called from his beach chair in the door of the shack.

"Yes sir, I'm headin' over to the ocean. I'll be needin' my squid."

"Sure thing young man. What did you do with all those crabs?"

"Gus at the diner is gonna make crab cakes and spaghetti sauce. I'm gonna have crab cakes for supper tonight."

"You are, eh. You'll have to beat me over there." The bait man chuckled.

He went and retrieved my squid from the refrigerator. He also told me that the ferry would be coming in very soon.

"There prob'ly won't be many people gettin' off this time a day. So you jest get over there and jump on as soon as she ties up."

That baitman sure knew what he was talking about. I had no sooner gotten over to the ferry's berth, when a stream of cars started coming into the parking lot. There were a few small groups of people already there. I eased over close to the waters edge and waited.

A few minutes later the crowd that was in the parking lot began cheering. I looked out towards the Bay and saw a boat approaching. It didn't look real big and it wasn't shaped like the ferry from Staten Island to New York

The people in a couple of the groups began singing, "The ferry is coming, the ferry is coming, hi ho the merry-o the ferry is coming."

R. Allen Pender

As the singing started to get a little faster, the people joined hands and began dancing around in a circle.

It looked a little weird to me. But, then what did I know? I'm a stranger around here.

This might be some sort of custom. Maybe that is why some of the people were looking at me kind of strangely. Maybe I was supposed to dance too.

The boat slowed down as it approached the wharf. It wasn't a real big boat. It wasn't something that you could drive a car onto. I always thought ferry boats carried cars. But, then I was only on a ferry one other time and that one carried cars too. I stood watching as the boat was slowly eased into its berth. The baitman was right; there were only a few people on the ferry. Just before the boat came to a full stop, a mate jumped off and grabbed a line to secure the boat to the dock. There was a little two step stairway for the passengers to board. All the people had lined up by the stairway waiting for the mate to assist in boarding. Quickly, I climbed over the gunnel; the same way the mate got off.

I sat down on the bench seat in a corner right up against the wall to the pilot's cabin and the gunnel. The portion of the boat behind the cabin was just an open deck. Wood planking formed the bench type seats that ringed the outside perimeter of the deck. A roof covered the deck, but the sides were open to the weather. An inner ring of bench seats encircled the roof supports in the center of the deck.

I sat in my corner entranced by the procession of passengers. The first person to come aboard was an elderly lady, who everyone seemed to know. She wore a lot of make-up and had a fox stole around her neck. She was accompanied by two of the strangest looking dogs I ever saw. The dogs were little things and they didn't look like they had heads or tails. They looked like two little cushions of fur and long hair.

The parade continued with a man, who looked something like Ronald Colman, but he wasn't Ronald Colman. He wore brown and white shoes, a tweed sports jacket and a hat like Robin Hood's, with a big feather. He had a tan silk scarf around his neck.

All of the people getting on this boat were all dressed up like Astor's pet goat. As I watched, I could see these people throw a glance at me. It was quite obvious that I didn't fit the dress code.

Some of the men getting on wore bright colored silk trousers and jackets, patent leather shoes and scarves around their necks. By contrast, I must have resembled a pumpkin in a pea patch. The people weren't too quick to take seats near me. Maybe I smelled or the bait smelled.

Just about everybody was carrying packages of some sort. There were the obvious suitcases and then there were packages that looked like they were filled with groceries.

Slowly the boat filled with all these people, who were kissing each other and calling everyone "Dahling." It was quite a show for this country boy.

As the launch sped across the water, I tried to avoid the stares of the passengers by looking around the Bay at sights new to me. I was probably just as strange looking to them as they were to me.

It seemed like a long ride, because I didn't have someone to talk to. But, in reality the ride was only about 20 minutes in duration.

The sounds of the engines suddenly changed and the boat began to slow for its approach to the dock.

There was a large crowd on the dock and they were waving at people on the boat, who were waving back and calling to members of the crowd.

I was the last person off the boat and I walked smack into this incredible sight on the dock. Those on the dock were obviously happy to see their friends from the boat. Men were kissing and hugging men and women were kissing and hugging women. The dock was littered with kid's toy wagons pulled by those who had come to meet the boat. People were loading their baggage and sacks into the little wagons.

I skirted around the activity as best and fast as I possibly could. A wood plank walk went straight up from the dock, past some cottages to the sand dunes. I walked up and over the dunes and there it was, the Atlantic Ocean.

Looking up to my right was a large weather beaten building. It was Duffy's Hotel, right where Jack said it would be.

I walked right down to where the surf was lapping the beach. I took my shoes off and laid them and the bucket in the dry sand. With a piece of squid cut for bait and threaded onto the rig, I waddled into the ocean.

The waves were breaking out in front of me and the surf was washing my thighs. It didn't take very long for me to be thoroughly saturated. The noise was unreal as the rollers crashed in front of me and heaved my line back. I would just reel in and cast out again. I got into a rhythm of casting and then getting rinsed by the wave. It was a lot of fun. I didn't feel any strikes on my bait. But, I thought it a good idea to reel in and check it.

I took a few steps backward towards the drier sand as I reeled in the rig. Just as I turned to swing the baited rig; I was scared out of my wits.

Six guys wearing little tiny leopard skin bathing suits came leaping up over the sand dunes. As I watched in astonishment, they went into some kind of ballet dancing routine. My watching didn't seem to bother them. In fact, I think it may have encouraged them, as it appeared that all their gesticulations where being directed towards me. I was getting somewhat unnerved by the performance and thought it might be a good time to take a break. I picked up my shoes and the bucket and started up towards Duffy's Hotel to get a drink.

R. Allen Pender

I put my shoes on when I reached the steps up to the Hotel's porch. I also strapped my hunting knife back on my belt. I left the rod and bucket by the door and walked into the bar room.

It is a huge room with a big bar along one side. There weren't any customers seated at the bar.

"Can I get a Coke?" I asked the bartender, who looked like he was going to die from boredom.

He reached under the bar without saying a word and came up with a frosty bottle of Coke.

"Do you want it opened?" He said as I fished up a soggy dollar bill from my pocket. I was smart enough to understand that his statement meant my Coke was to be taken out. Four men were dancing as two couples on the other side of the room by the jukebox. I saw them turn and stare at me for a second. "I think it is time for me to get out of here." I said to myself grabbing my Coke and making a hasty exit.

Before I knew it, I was down the wooden walkway and at the ferry dock. The ferry wasn't there and I didn't know how long I had to wait. The dock was empty, so I made myself comfortable next to a little shed just off to the side of the dock.

Gus had made me a nice sandwich. I ate that along with the fruit and pie, all of which were washed down by the cold Coke.

After finishing my lunch, I practiced casting out in the bay. I still had squid on the hook just in case some hungry fish came along. I kept myself occupied in this manner until I saw the small outline of a boat approaching.

"Hallelujah" I thought to myself. "I'm getting off this devils island."

It wasn't long before the ritual I saw earlier, began to repeat itself. People in bathing suits pulling little wagons began arriving at the dock. As the boat started to come closer, the people began hollering and waving. As soon as the vessel tied up, the hugging and kissing started all over again as the passengers disembarked.

I started making my way to the ferry when it appeared that the last of the people were getting off.

Again, I climbed over the gunnel and took a seat by the cabin.

Gradually the crowd on the dock disbursed and I was the only passenger on the boat.

The mate released the lines from the dock and swung over the side near where I was sitting.

"You came over here not too long ago." He said.

"I did. But, I don't think this is my kinda' place."

"The fairies got to ya', did they?"

"No. But some strange acting people dancin' over the sand dunes and lookin' funny at me did."

"Those are the fairies! The whole place is full of 'em. "They come here from New York City. Mostly show people. Men with men and women with women. We're happy they stay over here on this island."

"Is that what fairies are? I thought the fairies were like ghosts, but these people are weirder than ghosts."

The mate laughed and shook his head, knowing that I had just received some sort of initiation on the road to adulthood.

I don't think anyone was ever happier to see the mainland than me.

Artie and Jim were sitting at the bar when I walked into the Bowling Alley. Gramp was playing bartender and Jack was out in the kitchen with a salesman.

"How come you're back so soon?" Artie asked.

"There are weird people over there, real weird." And, then I proceeded to tell them about the guys dancing over the sand dunes and Duffy's Hotel. I related how the people acted and dressed on the boat and on the dock.

"Well they're Bohemians. They act like that." Gramp said.

"I didn't hear anyone talkin' Bohemian or any other kind a foreign language."

"No." Gramp replied. "Bohemians are artists, actors and dancers. They live a different lifestyle."

"They sure do! They're weird." I replied.

Everyone was having a good laugh at my expense.

"I have to get these damp pants off and take a shower." I said, starting to go upstairs for dry clothes.

"Did you go into the ocean with your pants on?" Jim asked.

"Yeah, I did. I got to let them finish dryin.'"

I got some clean clothes from my bag upstairs and then went down to the shower in back of the kitchen. When I undressed, I noticed that my underwear and legs were kind of blue.

It felt real good to get the salt off my body. But, even after washing, I noticed that I was still blue from the waist down.

"How did the guys in the Navy get the blue dye off their legs?" I announced to the gathering at the bar.

"It had to be War (wore) off." Said Artie, trying to make a pun. "Again, everybody had a good laugh at my expense. Admittedly, I had to laugh too.

I gave up all thoughts of going back over to the ocean. I liked to roam around the waterfront down by the Bay. There were a lot of interesting things to see. There are commercial fishing docks where the boats unload their catches of fish, clams and lobsters. And, then there are all sorts of private pleasure boats moored in the various marinas. It was a nice place. Nobody was jumping out at me from behind sand dunes.

R. Allen Pender

When I wasn't roaming around or setting pins, I went down in the furnace room and shot targets with my Daisy Air rifle.

I really got to be a good shot. My favorite trick shot was to shoot out the flame on a candle, without hitting the candle. I practiced this shot for several hours on end and must have fired several thousand BBs into the crawl space below the building.

I told Jim and Artie what I was doing and they didn't believe me.

"Come on down to the furnace room and I'll show you." I said eager to demonstrate my prowess. They agreed and followed me down to the little shooting gallery. I lit the candle sitting in the dirt of the crawl space and then moved back against the opposite wall.

I loaded the gun and took a steady aim. A squeeze of the trigger and ...Poof, the candle went out. Jim went over to inspect the candle.

"Yep! He shot that flame out without touching the candle."

Both he and Artie were impressed and they told my grandfather so. I felt good and it sort of made up for the jokes the pulled on me.

A few days later a smell started to emanate from the bathroom. It got progressively worse over the next couple of days.

"Smells like something is dead under the building, Jack." Jim said.

"I better call an exterminator and have him look" Jack answered.

An exterminator came over and went down into the crawl space. He returned about a half hour later." I think I found the problem, come on outside."

He had a dead rat lying on a piece of cardboard. "It looks like somebody shot this rat with BBs and it went under the building to die."

"That kid is really a good shot." Artie laughingly replied, "He can hit things he ain't even shootin' at." Everybody laughed, except the rat.

## CHAPTER 35

## THE MECHANIC

"How did your underwear get blue?" My mother asked as she separated my clothes for washing.

I told her what Jim and Artie told me and how I waded into the ocean to break in the denims like they did in the Navy.

"I think they just knew a "Huckleberry" when they saw one. What other crazy things did you do?"

I told my mother about most of my activities. But I didn't tell her about Marlene, the fairies or the rat. Most of my story centered on how hard I worked and about the money I made.

"I'm glad you were of some use over there instead of thinkin' you were on some kind of vacation."

The BB gun didn't go over too well. My mother could not see its necessity. She also couldn't understand how someone would sell a gun to a boy.

"They're legal over on Long Island" I said. "Everyone over there has one. That's how they kept the German Submarine crews from landing during the War."

"Who told you such nonsense, the same people who told you to wade into the ocean in your new britches?"

"No it was someone different. That was the last BB gun in the store, 'cause everyone is buying them to shoot at Russians, who want to land on Long Island."

"Such stories." She said. "I don't know how you could believe all that nonsense. But, if I hear you do any damage with that gun, I'm goin' to take it away."

I interpreted my mother's words to mean that I could keep the gun as long as she didn't learn of any damage I did with it. The solution was simple, don't let her learn anything.

The time spent over in Long Island at the bowling alley provided me with a nice little treasury for the remainder of the summer. My needs weren't great. I had the money to buy a bait bucket and live bait for my fishing trips to Mr. Seymour's camp. Most of the outings with my friends took place at the reservoir in Clark, where we fished with worms.

The reservoir is the property of the Middlesex Water Company. It is a long skinny lake a little over a mile long and about 300 feet wide. Featherbed Lane crosses the reservoir at its western end and Raritan Road also crosses the western quarter of the lake east of Featherbed Lane. Woods completely surround the reservoir, except at its southeastern end where the dam and pump station are located. The woods are surrounded by Madison Hill Road, which connects to Raritan Road on the south side. It circles around to join Westfield Avenue coming up around the woods and a few little streets on the north side.

Altogether, the reservoir is surrounded by over 3 miles of roads.

The water in the lake is clear and clean. The fishing is also very good. Many a day we made nice catches of Bass, Pickerel, Catfish and Yellow Perch. Every so often we would meet up with another gang of kids who had discovered this pristine place like we did. There was never any trouble between the various groups. Quite the contrary. We often exchanged bait and respected the other group's fishing or swimming space. Over the course of the past few summers, this reservoir had become one of our favorite places.

There was one draw back…it is private property. It belonges to the Middlesex Water Company. We acted like it was our private property, but it wasn't. The New Jersey State Police patrolled the area and periodically they would show up to chase us. If the police showed up on the Westfield Avenue side, we would swim across the reservoir to the Madison Hill Road side. To catch us the police would have to drive a 3 mile circle around the reservoir. When we saw them coming we would swim back to the opposite side again. The police either got tired, or figured we weren't worth the trouble, so the game usually ended after the second trip.

As the crow flies, the reservoir is about 4 1/2 miles from our homes on Rosehill Place. We made the trip on bicycles a few times, but the trip was 6 1/2 miles one way. The bicycles were kind of cumbersome, especially if we made overland trips through the woods, or were chased by the police. The bus on the other hand cost 5 cents and delivered us to Winfield Park. From there we walked through the woods, across Jackson's Dam to Valley Road, then back into the woods to the reservoir. It is about a 2 mile walk from the bus stop. We went this way many times, following a trail laid down by who knows how many generations of boys with worms and fishing poles.

This summer though, some changes were beginning to take place

We could hear the sound of hammers banging while we walked from Winfield Park through the woods to Valley Road.

"What do think that is?" Robert questioned.

"Sounds like someone building a house." Chico replied.

Chico was right. Except it wasn't one house, it was a sub-division of several houses over near the horse riding stables off Valley Road. The post war housing boom had started in Clark Township. In a few hours we would learn how the new construction would impact our lives.

As was our practice, we would pick out our favorite spots and start fishing. Slowly the sun would begin to take effect on our bodies. The warming would encourage us to begin shedding clothes. Pretty soon we were all sitting around in our underwear. At this point, the time had come for us to enter the water. Just as soon as one person went in, everybody went in.

Today was no different from any other summer day. We caught a few fish for lunch and they were hooked to a stringer dangling in the cool water. In the meantime we were cavorting in the water like a school of porpoises.

We were having such a good time in the water that we were totally oblivious to anything going on around us.

"COPS, COPS!" Someone yelled.

Sure enough. One Cop was standing on the opposite shore and another was walking towards us along the shoreline on our side. Without any hesitation we were out of the water, grabbing our clothes then disappearing into the woods.

Abruptly, the woods ended and we were standing in someone's backyard where a lady was hanging up clothes.

Startled, we all stared at each other without saying a word. Then as fast as we arrived, we departed down her driveway across Madison hill Road to the woods beyond.

There we were standing in the woods in dripping wet underwear and laughing like fools.

"Did you see that lady's face?" Chico asked. One by one, we would try to imitate the look on the frightened woman's face and then we all laughed hysterically.

We didn't know it at the time, but we had just run headlong into the beginning of "suburbia", a word which had yet to be coined. Civilization was encroaching on us and our days of skinny dippin' were rapidly coming to an end.

We got dressed and hung out in the woods for a little while. We thought that the police had cordoned off the area and set up a drag net for us. Our fish and fishing tackle were still secreted in the brush over by the reservoir. We eased up to the edge of the woods along Madison Hill Road to survey the situation.

We sure didn't want to cross the road anywhere near that lady's house. We expected to see several police cars patrolling up and down the road. But, we didn't see any as we hung to the woods and walked along looking for a good place to cross back into the woods by the reservoir.

With stealth gained from our World War II training in Tarzan's Jungle, especially that part where we had become efficient at covert operations designed to invaded private gardens and fruit trees, we calculated our crossing back into the woods by the reservoir.

"The cops saw us with our clothes off." Robert announced. "They probably won't recognize us with our clothes on, even if we walk down the road."

"We have to get our stuff over by the Rezy." Chicky intoned. "We still have to get back in the woods without them seein' us."

"Once we're around the bend from the lady's house, we can cross back into the woods without anyone seein' us." I related.

"I'll stand out by the road." Chico volunteered. "When everything is clear, we all can charge across the road."

The plan worked to perfection. When the foliage along the road obscured the lady's house from our position, Chico emerged from the woods and began walking along the side of the road. He then turned and walked across to the opposite side, from where he signaled us to charge across the road.

Pumped up by adrenalin and hearts racing, we charged across the open no-mans land of Madison Hill Road.

Quickly, we sought the cover of the trees and brush in the woods. We didn't see even one solitary car on Madison Hill Road, never mind a fleet of Police cars.

"They're probably hidin' out by our stuff, so they can grab us when we come back." Chicky hypothesized.

"Alright then," I suggested. "We can sneak up on them and we can lay low until they leave."

Everyone agreed that was the best tactic and in the fashion of experienced Indian warriors, we began to carefully steal through the woods.

Stepping slowly and carefully to avoid breaking twigs or branches, we gradually advanced to our swimming area. After what seemed like an eternity, we arrived at our spot. Much to our surprise nothing had been disturbed.

"Everything might be *booby trapped*" Chicky warned. And, he immediately began to check for signs affirming his suspicions.

Nothing was booby trapped. There wasn't any troop of State Police hiding in the trees or lurking in the shadows of the forest ready to grab us.

"I wonder where they are?" Chicky questioned.

"They prob'ly went to lunch." Robert answered, as each of us picked up our gear and retrieved the fish.

"Let's go over by Jackson's Dam and make a fire to cook these fish." Chico suggested.

We all agreed... and the band of outdoorsmen picked up the trail to return to an area near the bus stop, where we would camp and roast our fish.

We gathered up twigs and nice looking firewood on our march along the trail to Jackson's Dam.

When we arrived, we scouted out a nice little place to build a fire. Each of us had brought a potato to bury and roast under the coals of the fire. This was going to be a great meal — roasted fish and soot covered baked potatoes. Each of us had a peanut butter and jelly sandwich and the whole mess would be washed down with grape Kool-Aid.

The potatoes were buried in the first coals of the fire and the fish were mounted on sticks implanted in the ground not too close to the flames.

I am sure we looked like a veteran group of pioneer mountain men as we sat amidst the swirling smoke of the cooking fire and munched on our peanut butter and jelly sandwiches. None of us had much to say. We all were engrossed by the moment and watching to see that the fish didn't burn.

"I think we should eat first and then go swimming." Chico said, trying to wipe the charcoal from the potato skin off his mouth. "Maybe then we wouldn't be so dirty and smell so bad."

He did have a point. Daniel Boone and those boys didn't have to take a bus, or get chased by State Troopers. They could go swimming anytime, any place they wanted. They really had the cat by the tail.

We were trying to have the best of all things in our little world. But, we could see the world around us changing and us changing also.

In a few short years we had grown from pre-war Depression babies into young teenagers getting ready to witness the coming of the second half of the twentieth century.

Things were a lot better now than during the War, but there are still plenty of problems.

We are now in the Atomic Age. Are we going to blow each other off the face of the earth, or learn how to harness atomic power for peaceful pursuits? People called us kids juvenile…the rest of the world is really juvenile when it comes to knowing and handling this atomic energy.

It seemed that our life and the changes to it were racing along like a runaway train.

Before we returned to school in September, Chicky and his family moved away. They went to a place called Clifton, which was somewhere past Newark. Robert's Aunt and Uncle from the coal region of Pennsylvania moved into Chicky's apartment. His uncle, like many others from Pennsylvania had come here to work in the G.M. plant in Linden. That factory, where airplanes were made during the War, now produced Buicks, Oldsmobiles and Pontiacs.

In 1948, the British Colony of Palestine was given its independence and became the Nation of Israel. It was a great thing…a homeland for the Jewish people, who suffered so greatly at the hands of the Nazis. Those people who came there knew the cruelties of war and almost immediately they were thrust back into war against the Arab nations, which opposed the formation of this new country.

The Soviet Union, now occupying East Germany, flexed its muscles by throwing a blockade around the western sectors of Berlin in an attempt to starve that portion of the devastated city under Allied control. The Russians probably only had a chance to drink a few vodka toasts over their success, before President

Truman initiated the Berlin Airlift which would fly in supplies to the beleaguered city around the clock at 3 minute intervals. By the time the Airlift ended the Russians had hangovers and 277,000 flights had brought in 2 million tons of goods.

The Chinese Communists resumed their fighting with the Chinese Nationalists led by Chiang Kai-shek. Each group was struggling to control China before World War II. They had stopped fighting with each other to deal with the common enemy, Japan.

The same situation applied in Indo-China. Ho Chi Minh and his Comunist army were fighting to remove the colonial power, France. Indo-China had provided the French with riches during their period of colonial rule. Like China, the fighting started before the Japanese conquests and subsided during WWII. The fighting had now resumed, but at a much more aggressive level.

India, now emerging from under generations of British Colonial rule, is engaged in a bloody religious civil war.

On any given day, there is conflict of major proportions somewhere in the world. We woke up daily to wonder where and how large the next conflict would be.

Our Junior High School years had passed with little notice. The most significant thing about Junior High School was girls. We were made to dance with girls at something they called Social Dancing. It happened about once a month for about an hour. Most of us guys had two left feet.

Although girls were beginning to have a little more appeal; at our age what was a boy going to do with a girl. Take her for a date on your bicycle? How about a bus ride to the movies? It also cost money to do these things... and that we didn't have to spare.

High School offered great promise. High School kids could get jobs and eventually cars.

There are three Public High Schools in Elizabeth. I am going to Thomas Jefferson, an all boy's school. Battin High school is for girls and Thomas Edison Vocational and Technical School is Co-ed.

As exciting as High School was, it was also scary. Over the past few years, I noticed that a few of the guys in my neighborhood, who graduated High School, went to college; the rest went to the military. A few had even been drafted in their senior year of High School.

I had three years before I came to that fork in the road and that was scary. For now I was going to enjoy High School. I planned to get a job, save some money for a car and maybe even date a girl on some special occasion.

I got off to a great start in Jefferson High. My homeroom teacher and American History teacher is a nice Southern lady from Virginia. Her name is Miss Stuart. J.E.B. Stuart, the famous Confederate Calvary General was her grandfather. Obviously she recognized my family name and made some inquiries about my pedigree.

Unfortunately for me, she explained that because of my breeding and family background, she would hold me to a higher academic and behavior standard than the other unfortunate students who came from less established families.

Jefferson High School received all the boys from the City public schools. There were stories of how tough life was in this school of over 800 boys. Most of those stories were just that, stories.

This school was very orderly and had a high level of discipline. Sure, there were a few wise guys, but they were culled out and dealt with.

If a person wanted an education, it was available at Jefferson. The school had an excellent academic rating and had graduated a host of people who became leaders in their fields.

Breezy was on the football team and Tommy was on the cross country running team. I had played freshman football, but this year I decided to try cross country. I felt that it would help me keep in shape for the baseball season.

I worked out with the team and ran in all the races. I was always able to finish the 2 1/2 mile course, but I was never fast enough to place in a position that gained points. The good runners were thin and small. By contrast, I was tall and weighed almost 160 pounds. I liked basketball and I did well in Junior High as a freshman, but I wanted to get a job so I could have some money when the baseball season rolled around and I couldn't work. Basket ball would have to wait.

I answered a want ad for a job in Murray's Houseware and Hardware store on Elmora Avenue.

Murray was looking for a boy with a bicycle, who would work around the store and make deliveries. No body else applied, so I got the job. The wages of 35 cents an hour for 22 hours a week would net me about 6 dollars a week. Some of my school mates worked in the Food Fair; just up the street from Murray's store. Some of those people made 50 cents an hour.

Maybe I should have gone to the Food Fair for a job, but I only planned to stay at Murray's until the beginning of baseball season. I didn't tell Murray that.

Murray's store is little and the work wasn't hard. Most of the time Murray would leave for a while when I came in. I guess he was taking a break from his wife, who was left in charge. His wife is a red haired lady, who was always going to the hairdresser. She had the biggest lips I ever saw. I really never got that close to her to find out if her lips were big, or she missed her mouth with her lipstick. Maybe the hairdresser painted her mouth.

Every day Murray would ask me if I brought my bicycle. Each time I would say yes. But, in the entire time I worked there, I never made a delivery.

R. Allen Pender

I don't think I was cut out to be a store person. For me it was too dull. Just to make the time to go by, I had to make work, or make it look like I was working.

The store was open until 9 P.M. on Thursday. I would usually have my supper hour with a couple of my Classmates, who worked in the Food Fair. We would go to the White Castle on the corner of Elmora and Westfield Avenues. With the coupon that was printed in the paper every week, you could buy 5 White Castle hamburgers for 20 cents. I cut out a lot of coupons, but the offer was limited to one coupon per person.

Murray thought I might be stealing from him, because he would see one of my friends knock on the store window and then I would lean out and hand them something.

Grabbing me by the shoulder, he said in a very demanding tone, "Answer me. What are you giving to those friends of yours? Or, do I have to do an inventory of this store to find out what is missing?"

"Here." I answered, pulling a wad of White Castle coupons from my pocket. I extended my hand out toward him with the evidence and said, "5 hamburgers for 20 cents. Want one?"

"No. They're not kosher."

"Neither am I. And, if you inventory this store the only thing you will find missing, is me. I'll be back tomorrow for my pay."

"No it's all a mistake. Come to work tomorrow. Tomorrow is pay day. If you want me to pay you today, I will."

"OK. Pay me now."

I had no sooner answered when his wife, with a big smile on her face, like the Cheshire Cat, approached us and handed me the little brown pay envelope. She didn't say a word. Because she could surely see by my composure, that I felt insulted and had lost all respect for their authority.

Without another word I took the envelope and walked out the door.

I went over to the White Castle and told my friends what had happened.

"Are you going back?" My longtime schoolmate Walter asked.

"No. I'm goin' to retire for a while and eat hamburgers. Let me borrow your jacket for a minute."

Walter looked a little confused, but he obliged me.

I left my jacket in the booth and carried his out through the door opposite the one I came in.

Next, wearing Walter's jacket, I came in the other door, presented a coupon and ordered 5 hamburgers.

EUREKA, it worked. I had used 2 coupons. I shared the 5 hamburgers with everybody at the booth and then we all got up and did the penguin walk out of the White Castle.

*THE SOJOURNERS*
*Life on the American Homefront During World War II*

Baseball practice would start in March, so I would have had to leave Murray's in less than a month anyway. But as one door is shut, another one opens.

On Saturdays Robert worked for his father at the gas station in Westfield. He and Donald, along with a few others had started hanging out at the Town House Luncheonette located in the bank building on the corner of South Elmora Avenue and Edgar Road. The Donahue's, who are our neighbors, have just bought the business and they installed a pin ball machine.

Robert and Donald are pinball fanatics. Every day after school they can be found near that pinball machine. The whole idea of pinball is to beat the machine and rack up free games. I started to go there now that I have retired from Murray's.

In the meantime, a group of men are building a used car lot on the opposite corner of South Elmora Avenue and Edgar Road. The car lot is called Bayway Motors and it has a huge neon sign that say's BAYWAY MOTORS. On the sign are animated neon monkeys that keep jumping over the Bayway Motors letters on the sign.

One afternoon the boss of the car lot saw Robert playing the pinball machine and asked him if he wanted a job after school and on Saturdays. Robert explained his situation with his father, but he could work during the week. The man was agreeable if Robert could find someone to work on Saturday. At that particular moment I walked into the Luncheonette.

"R.A., do you want a job on Saturdays," Robert asked as I walked up to him and the man in the flashy sport jacket.

"Doin' What?"

"Working in the car dealership across the street." The dapper gray haired man answered. "I'm Dick LeGrande, the owner and we need some boys to keep the cars clean and running. I'll pay you five dollars for working Saturday. What is your name?"

"Richard Pendell. They call me R.A." For short.

I could almost make in one day what it took me a week to earn at Murray's. Plus this job wouldn't interfere with baseball. Talk about God being good. Working on cars and getting paid for it, unbelievable.

"It sounds good to me. When would you want me to start?"

"Come in Saturday morning and see Donald in the garage. He'll take care of everything. Robert and Richard. Sounds like a good combination. See you later boys."

Robert and I were probably selling ourselves short. We had a lot of automobile experience and Mr. LeGrande was going to benefit for our work on the junk cars.

We had to damp wipe the cars down every day. Then we started them up and checked the oil and water. We physically inspected the outside of the cars for damage or flat tires. If a car wouldn't start we would find out if it had a dead battery or some other cause and report it to Donald.

When somebody bought a car, we would pull it out of the line and drive it over to the garage and get it ready for delivery. Donald showed me how to use the battery charger and the wet wash procedure. Another man would come by about once a week to compound and buff the paint on cars that had just arrived on the lot. Donald spent most of his time in the garage waxing the cars.

This was almost like play to me and I was getting 5 dollars for it. It wasn't long before I was changing tires and installing batteries. This job had one negative aspect …I wanted drive one of these babies out on the road and I had a year to go before I could take the driving test.

Donald wasn't a real mechanic. He knew a lot about cars, but was all thumbs when it came to fixing them. I wound up doing some light mechanical work, like replacing spark plugs and installing points and condensers. I changed headlights and other bulbs. This type of work made the job interesting, especially when it came to finding the trouble with a car.

My work hours were good. I could come home from school, get my homework done and have the evenings free to hang out at the Town House. The High School basketball team played Friday nights in the Elizabeth Armory. We would go to the game and afterwards flock up to the Regent Sweet Shop, next to the Regent Theatre on Broad Street. A lot of girls went to the basketball games and then up to the sweet shop. Most of these girls only recognized you if you pulled up in a car. Any kind of car.

I used to daydream and wish that Mr. LeGrande would come up to me and say, "Richard, I want to reward you for the remarkable work you have been doing. Take any car on the lot to the basketball game on Friday night and here is an extra five dollars to buy all the girls ice cream sodas."

Of course that never happened and I would have to wait until my senior year in High School before I could drive a car up to the sweet shop after a basketball game.

Of course, I had to get a car first.

The baseball season came and I made the varsity team. There were only two sophomores on the team Ron and me. Ronnie and I were reserves on the local American Legion Team last summer.

We had played against each other through our years in the Youth leagues and Junior High School. Ronnie had gone to Lafayette Junior high School. It felt like I made the major leagues when the coach, Abner West, issued me a uniform and a varsity jacket.

"Hey, Lefty." Ronnie always called me Lefty. "We can walk up and down Broad Street on Thursday night in our varsity jackets." He said with an enthusiastic smile.

The stores stay open Thursday nights until 9, in Elizabeth. Just about every High School kid in the city was either walking or driving up and down Broad Street. I don't think the stores made a dime off all these kids. The kids spent their money in either The Regent Sweet Shop, or Pamel's Sweet shop up the other side of East Jersey Street.

Ronnie was going to milk this varsity jacket stuff for all it was worth. He wanted every girl in Elizabeth to swoon before him in his varsity jacket. I agreed to meet him Thursday evening, just to see what effect he had on the throng. I couldn't see what good it would do to meet girls if you didn't have a car to put them in.

We walked up and down Broad Street many a Thursday night. Ronnie greeted every girl he saw.

But, we might as well have been fishing without any bait for all the good we did. Each Thursday night ended up the same, we bought ourselves a 30 cent sundae in the Regent Sweet shop.

Despite our differences, Ronnie and I became good friends through High School. He is the only child in a family long established in the city. His father even bought a one of those new 10 inch Television sets. Whereas, I am a WWII migrant into the city and live on the outskirts of town and we need a new refrigerator. He is outgoing and involved in all kinds of school activities. I do my work and I'm reserved. We just came from families with different lifestyles. This was no more evident than one Easter vacation morning when Ronnie and his father stopped to pick me up for baseball practice.

"He's out in the kitchen eattin' his breakfast." My mother said, answering the door.

Ronnie walked out into the kitchen to get me moving.

"Are you eating fish for breakfast?" He exclaimed, walking into the room.

"No. These are fried grits. Want some?"

"It sure looks like fish to me. I knew you people were a little different, but fish for breakfast."

I took a lot of good nature ribbing because of my rural background; most of it instigated by Ronnie. He started to get all the guys on the team calling me Huck Finn. I obliged them by sticking a trout fly and spinner on my baseball cap.

As a whole, the team had a mediocre season. I'm a left handed pitcher, and I had a 2 and 4 won-lost record. If a few bad breaks didn't occur, I could have been 5 and1 or, 4 and 2. But that is the way the game is. Almost don't count, except in horseshoes. However, I did set a County record by appearing in more games than any other pitcher. Most of it in relief. But my season was good enough for me to be named as an Honorable Mention player on both the All County and the Newark News All State Team.

Now the laughs were on Ronnie. I made him carry my bag onto the field for the summer American Legion Games. He would fuss and fume and threaten me with the same treatment when he made All County next year.

Our Legion team played 2 evenings a week and Sunday morning. We won the County championship and advanced to within one level of qualifying for the State Championship series.

We had a good season and maybe with a little more luck we can get into the State Championship series next year.

Robert and I continued our work schedule at the car lot through the summer, except when Robert had to go with his family on a car trip to California. I filled in for him for two weeks. There weren't any problems, because just about everybody had a summer job. All of our interests lay in the same direction, except for Tommy. He was interested in girls; the rest of us were interested in cars.

My father finally got a car, a '39 Nash 6. I don't know where my father got it from, but it was a real clunker. The engine had twin ignition, which meant that each of the 6 cylinders had 2 spark plugs. The engine was pretty tired and the spark plugs fouled out just about every 2 weeks. If the car was driven harder, the plugs failed a lot faster. It was my job to keep the spark plugs clean.

I kept a box in the car's trunk with clean spark plugs and dirty spark plugs. When the engine started to misfire, I had to locate the bad plug and replace it with one of the clean plugs. The engine had so many spark plugs that I lost track of where I had replaced plugs. The dirty plugs were always oil fouled. I had a wire brush and a little file to clean out the black carbon.

One weekend my father and I went up to Mr. Seymour's camp to help my grandfather. All the spark plugs in the car were cleaned and Daddy bought an extra 2 gallon can of motor oil.

That Saturday morning, my father drove the car very easy and I guided him along the route. When we got to Andover, he turned off the highway and headed up over the hill to Fredon. From this side of the hill it is a gradual climb, but the other side, by Route 94, is steep. Gramp drove over the hill this way to get to Stillwater, but coming back; he took Route 94 into Newton and then picked up route 206, circling around the hill.

"Which way do we go now?" My father asked when we came out of Stillwater and approached the intersection of Route 94. It was Sunday afternoon and we were on the return trip home.

"You can go left into Newton, or take the shortcut over the hill straight ahead."

"It's a shortcut, Huh? OK. We'll try it." He said slipping the car into first gear to cross the road.

Dad started climbing the hill in first gear. About a quarter of the way up, he shifted into second.

The car went a little bit then began to make a grinding noise. It then shuddered and stopped. The car then began to roll backwards down the hill. Daddy stopped it and shifted back into first gear.

"I think we stripped second gear." He said very calmly and started to climb the hill again in first gear.

It felt like it was taking us 3 days to get to the top of that hill. Once we got there, my father put the car in high gear and more or less coasted down the other side.

"You know" He said when we came to the junction of Route 206. "That is a pretty good shortcut."

Dad drove the rest of the way home using first and third gears.

Of course the little detail of removing the transmission and getting it fixed fell upon me.

We didn't have any facilities for fixing a car. My father didn't even rent a garage. He parked the car at the curb in front of the building and I went to work on it right there. It was tight when I had to crawl under the car. However, I was able to remove the floor boards in the front and do most of the work from the driver's seat.

I got the transmission out and put it in the trunk of the car. I could only work on it during daylight, because we didn't have any electricity out at the curb.

Charlie from upstairs told me what parts I needed. He did a lot of work on cars. I called my Uncle Billy at his auto parts store and told him what Charlie said I needed. Gramp stopped in at Uncle Billy's store all the time. So he brought the parts to us.

Charlie worked on trucks down at the Standard Oil Refinery. He told me how to take apart the transmission and get it clean inside. It was full of black gear oil and metal chips from the stripped gears. I emptied as much as I could into a cut off can and then wiped the inside with rags. It sure was a mess. I had to siphon some gas from the car's tank and slosh it around inside the transmission case to get all the black residue out.

With Charlie standing over me directing my every move, the transmission was disassembled and reassembled with new parts. I got some gear oil from Mr. Marshall's and filled up the unit.

The transmission was heavy and awkward to handle going back in. My father helped me get it into the clutch and up to the back of the engine. I finished bolting everything back together.

The car was ready for a test run.

*R. Allen Pender*

    Earlier, my father had given me the keys. I needed them so I could get in and out of the trunk and lock up the car. I had an extra set made over at Carey's Hardware Store: just in case I had to start up the car to work on the transmission at some other point in time, I wouldn't have to bother my father. Or, maybe some emergency would arrive and I would have to move the car.

# CHAPTER 36

# THE GREAT RACE

The saying goes," That the idle mind is the Devil's work shop."
Our minds are anything but idle…and we are under some devilish influence; CARS.

Richie's brother, Walter got a car near the end of the summer. Walter was going to be a senior in High School and the rest of us juniors.

We chipped in for gas and rode all over. We went to some neat places like Keansburg and then swimming at Duck's Nest in the Parlin sand pits. We even went to Asbury Park one night for a hamburger. We made regular trips to 5 Points in Union for hot dogs. We were really living it up.

Tommy was the next one due to get a license. Robert and I couldn't get a license until March. Bragging a little, I showed the guys the keys I had to my father's car. That gave Tommy an idea. His father liked to have a few beers after supper, and then he fell asleep. Tommy would get his car keys and then we would go get a copy made.

Bruno's Truck Stop over on Route 1 near Grier Avenue had a key machine. Walter would drive us over there to get the keys made.

The plan worked perfectly. Tommy's father fell asleep on time and we got the keys made.

Robert and I planned to give Tommy driving lessons the next night after his father fell asleep.

The car is a big black '36 Packard. Tommy's father always parked it by wooded area of Garden Street.

For the first couple of nights we taught Tommy how to use the clutch and gear shift. He started the car and moved it back and forth, maybe 20 feet at a time.

By the third night we had him driving to the end of Garden Street, stopping and then driving in reverse back to the parking spot.

The time had now come for him to go solo. He had to drive to the corner of Garden Street, turn right and drive to Grove Street and make a U-turn at the intersection with Grove Street. Coming back, he had to make a K turn on Garden Street and backup into the parking space.

Tommy was as nervous as a cat in a burlap sack. He was trying to drive the car and look in all directions at the same time. His head looked like it could turn all the way around like an owl.

"Suppose my father or somebody is watching?" He nervously hypothesized.

R. Allen Pender

"If you don't watch where you're goin', you're going to hit a pole and your father will hear you wreck." Robert cautioned.

The street was empty of cars and Tommy made his trip successfully, although quite slow.

Slowly, over the next couple of weeks, Tommy's skill and confidence increased.

Robert in the meantime figured out how to beat the pinball machine.

He had watched the man come and collect the money from the machine. By hitting a little lever inside the machine the man gave him a couple of free games. Robert made a mental note of where this lever is located.

"We need a little drill." He said to me.

After I figured out what he wanted to do and understood the project, I said, "There is a thing like a screw driver with a little chuck on the end for a fine drill. When the handle is pumped up and down the drill turns."

"Where do you think they sell them, R.A.?"

"I saw them in Sears and Roebuck."

"Let's go downtown Thursday night and get one." Robert responded with a gleam in his eye.

Getting the drill was easy. Boring a hole in the side of the pinball machine is something else. Chico picked up some putty and a steel wire. We all gathered around the pinball machine. Donald played and as he did, Robert drilled into the side of the pinball machine. He slid the drill over to me after he got through. Chico gave him the piece of wire and Robert slid it through the hole. He wiggled the wire some then he hit the lever. While Vince, the owner of the luncheonette was down at front end of the store; Robert quickly racked up 16 free games. A little putty was smeared over the hole and we all had a free night of pinball.

We lived a charmed life. It didn't seem like anything could go wrong. The more things we did, the more confident and brazen we became.

Gloria is a woman about 25 or more years old. She lived with her brother and his wife in my Aunt Eileen's building. She worked part-time at the Town House. She smoked cigarettes and drove a 1932 Chevrolet.

Because I worked in the car lot and people saw me working on my father's car, I was gaining a reputation as an automotive expert.

"Would you look at my car, R.A." She said one day when I walked into the Town House.

It's bucking and hard to start. I'm afraid of getting stuck somewhere."

"Ok." I said, ordering up a Cherry Coke.

"OH! GREAT. It's out back." She enthusiastically replied, tossing the keys across the counter.

"My tools are up by my house. I'll go get some after I finish my drink."

"Drive the car over there." She said "That way you can see how it runs."

*THE SOJOURNERS*
*Life on the American Homefront During World War II*

Wow! I thought. She thinks I'm old enough to drive. What an opportunity. Every time I get into a situation like this, I have to remind myself to be calm. I have to think of the old Bull and the young Bull story.

The young Bull and the old bull were out walking and they spied a herd of heifers down in a pasture at the bottom of the hill. "Let's run down and get us a heifer," the young Bull said. "No, the old Bull said." Be patient. We'll walk down and get them all."

"Ok." I said, pretending to be professional. "When I finish this drink, I'll look at it."

"Take your time, have another Coke. I'll be here until 8 tonight. Let me know if you see anything it needs."

"Alright. I'll probably work on it up by my house and I'll be back later." I couldn't believe my good fortune. This is like leaving the hen house door open for the fox.

I finished the second Cherry Coke and spinning around on the stool, I gave Gloria a wave and said, "I'll see you later, Gloria."

"Oh. Thanks a lot. I'm so grateful you can look at it."

The '32 Chevrolet 2 door sedan is a boxy little car. Her car is tan colored and she keeps it very clean. The body didn't have any dents or crumpled fenders like you would expect to see on a car this age. The car was hard starting, but finally I got it going. The engine ran rough as a cob. The motor oil was as black as tar and the air filter didn't look like it was ever cleaned. Black smoke was coming out of the exhaust and the engine picked up about 200 RPM when I lifted the air filter off. There in the yard I made some adjustments so I could drive this thing home.

Just like an old pro, I climbed into the driver's seat and drove the old Chevy out of the yard. I drove that car up South Elmora Avenue to Lidgerwood Avenue like I had been driving it all my life. I pulled the car into the back yard by the vacant garage where we kept our newspapers and stuff for the Rag Man.

There was still enough re-refined oil left from our days with the old clunker cars to change Gloria's oil. It was a lot easier crawling under her car than my father's Nash.

I cleaned and reset the gaps on her spark plugs and the reset the ignition point gap. She really could use new spark plugs and spark plug wires. The points were pitted and could stand replacement. I cleaned the oil bath air filter and checked the rest of the car over. The gas tank was full and the lights all worked. This car hadn't been maintained for some time. Gloria probably only put gas in it and forgot about everything else.

I got the car to start with one push on the starter. The engine was now running nice and smooth, but I hadn't given the car a road test.

It was almost supper time when I finished. As I was heading into the house to wash up and eat, Robert was coming up the street after his afternoon job at the car lot.

"I got something to show ya. Look out in front of the junk garage."

Robert walked down the driveway with me. When we came into the backyard," He asked. "Is that Gloria's car?"

"Yeah. She wanted me to fix it some. I'm goin' to bring it back over to the Town House after supper."

"Wait for me." He snapped. "I'll meet you at the car as soon as I eat."

Both of us went into our separate apartments. I went into the bathroom and washed up.

"Is supper ready yet, Ma?" I hollered.

"Why? Where do you have to go that is so important?"

"Nothing special. I'm just goin' to meet the guys for a game at the school yard."

"I have stuff ready, if you want to eat now."

I didn't care what my mother had cooked. I wanted to just eat and go.

"How come you're in such a hurry?"

"Well, you know with everybody workin' after school, we don't get much time together while it's still light out."

"That's true. But don't stay out too late."

Quickly, I finished my meal, bade my mother goodbye and was out the door.

Robert was sitting in the car waiting when I arrived.

"What took you so long? We have to get out of here quick before people start comin' home and see us."

I jumped into the driver's seat and started the car and drove out of the alley way between the buildings. The street was clear. Most of the women were probably in cooking supper and the men hadn't gotten home from work yet. Tommy's father got home earlier than most of the other men and he usually stopped in Cotton's for a few beers. We didn't know who might see us when we went by Cotton's, so I elected to turn onto Garden Street and go to Elmora Avenue from New York Avenue.

Tommy was standing on the front steps of his building when we went by. Robert hollered from the car and told him we were going to the Town House. Tommy waved back and ran into his building.

Robert was really excited, but it was an uneventful trip. The car ran pretty good, but with some traffic on South Elmora Avenue we really couldn't let it out.

"How come you're back so soon?" Gloria asked when Robert and I walked in and sat down at the counter.

I told her what work I had done and what I thought needed to be done. But for now the car ran pretty good, only I didn't give it a good test run. She was elated and set up Cherry Cokes for me, Robert and Tommy, who was now coming through the door.

"Will you be able to do that work" She said referring to the run down, I just gave her.

"I just have to get the parts and I can do the work on any day, but Saturday. 'Cause I work in the car lot that day."

Gloria and I made the arrangements for the next week. I would get the parts and work on the car a couple of afternoons.

"My brother said I might need tires pretty soon. Would you look at them too?"

"Sure"

"And, if you want to take the car for a good test ride now, I'll be here until 8."

I could see Robert and Tommy's ears perk up like those of a deer.

"Come on guys. We'll take it out on the highway. The traffic has died down." I announced.

The three of us piled into the car; with me at the wheel.

"She thinks you have a license. She thinks you have a license. I can't believe this."

Tommy squealed and wiggled like a baby with a wet diaper.

"Be calm. Be calm." Robert chastened him. "R.A. has the situation under control."

I started the car and drove out of the luncheonette driveway and headed for the Bayway Circle. I only went a quarter of the way around the circle onto Route 1 South.

We had only gone a short way when we came to a red light at Myrtle Street. Also waiting at the light was a 1931 A Model Ford Woody Wagon. The back of the woody was filled with chicken crates.

Tommy was trying to lean out of the window and get the attention of the driver in the chicken truck. "Want To Race! Want to Race!" he kept hollering.

The light changed and the chicken truck took off. We followed behind driving on the inside lane of the highway. When we reached the light on Park Avenue, just a short distance down the road, the chicken truck was waiting.

"I'll race you to Wood Avenue, the driver hollered to me through the open window."

When the light turned green, I stood on the gas and wound that car up through the gears.

I was running alongside the chicken truck in high gear and the pedal on the floor. All of a sudden that chicken truck just shot off in front of me like a rocket and all we could see were feathers flying from the back of the truck. The chicken truck was pulled off to the side of the road at the Wood Avenue traffic light. I pulled off next to him.

I'll bet that fooled you." He said with a laugh.

"What in the world have you got in that thing?" I exclaimed

He lifted the cowl panel and there it sat. A bored and stroked Mercury with twin carburetors." He smiled and laughed.

"I'll bet you do more'n haul chickens." I said after seeing that engine.

He looked at me with a big grin. "Some times I got to make fast runs from South Jersey to Newark at night. Ya know these chickens can get mighty thirsty." He bellowed, laughing again.

"If you boys are interested in racing, There's gonna be some races right here at Linden Airport the Sunday from next. They're gonna have sport cars and souped up cars and plain stock cars like you got. Just put some wide tires on that thing and you can run with the street cars. There's a sign up the road all about it."

"That sounds neat, R.A., let's go read the sign." Robert implored.

Our friend in the souped up chicken truck took off and so did we; to read the sign at Linden Airport.

It was true. A road racing course was going to be set up at Linden Airport, next Sunday. It cost 5 dollars to enter a car and they had all kinds of classes.

"How are we goin' to get Gloria's car on a Sunday?" Tommy asked.

"I'm goin' t' work on the car next week, so I'll tell her I have to finish it on Sunday." To me it sounded like a plausible story. I hoped Gloria would buy it. Besides we didn't have to pay the entry fee until the car was given the OK to race.

With enough excitement under our belts for one night, we drove up the highway towards the Town House.

"Hi, Gloria." I said, as the bunch of us trooped into the Town House. "The car doesn't run too bad and it does need tires. With new ignition parts and tires it should be in pretty good shape."

"Can you get tires?" She asked.

"I'll go up to the vulcanizing place at South Street and Rahway Avenue and see what kind of tires he has to fit your car."

"Oh, that will be good." She said as she continued to work and line up Cherry Cokes along the counter. "Let me know how much money you are going to need, because I won't be around after next Thursday. I'll be going with my brother and sister-in-law up to Pennsylvania next week end."

I could almost hear the eye balls at the counter snapping back and forth when she finished her remark.

"That can work out good, just in case I have to finish something on the car over the week-end."

"Don't spend your whole week end working on the car. You boys need some time off for fun."

"We'll manage to squeeze in some fun time." Robert confidently answered...and everyone at the counter nodded in agreement.

"What is the biggest tire I can put on a '32 Chevy?" was the question I posed to the man at the vulcanizing shop.

"Why do you want to change the tire size?" The man replied.

"Well, we want to race the car at Linden Airport this coming Sunday."

"Maybe I can match up some other wheels with bigger tires, if you bring the car over here."

Can you do that?"

"Sure. How about tomorrow?" I answered.

"You may have to leave it here for a day. I got a lot of other things to do and I'll have to fit it in when I got time."

"That's alright. Maybe I can tune it up and do a few other things while the car is here."

"When you bring it, just park there along side that wood garage." He said pointing to an old wood structure in the rear of the tire shop.

"OK. Thank you, Mr. Sieberling." I didn't know if that was the man's name or not. The side of his shop building is painted yellow and Sieberling Tire and Vulcanizing is spelled out in large black letters across the side of the building. The man didn't correct me, so maybe that is his name.

The next morning, Donald at the car lot did us a favor. I gave him a list of parts that I needed for Gloria's car and he called the order in to Jimmy's Auto Parts. I got the discount that dealers get, so I saved some money and Jimmy's delivered the parts.

Gloria had given me some money; more than enough to pay for the parts. I would have to find out how much the tires were going to cost before Gloria took off for the weekend. Tomorrow was Tuesday already. If Mr. Sieberling could come up with something for the tires by Wednesday, we would be in good shape before the weekend came

Tuesday morning I loaded the parts and my tools into Gloria's car. She had parked under the trees by Mr. Gavin's garage, just up from the yard of the brick apartment building on the corner.

I had to make it around the corner on Garden Street to New York Avenue and then down to South Street without any of the neighbors noticing that I was driving. Once I cleared the corner by the apartment building where Tommy lived, I was in good shape. New York Avenue was mostly vacant, except for a few houses down where New York Avenue intersected De Hart Place and the Railroad. That didn't bother me, because nobody down there knew me.

Tommy came out as I was putting the things in the car.

"I'll stand on the corner and wave to you when the coast is clear, then you pick me up after you drive by the building."

"OK. I'll watch you." I replied in agreement.

Tommy took a station where he could see inside Harry's store and then cover the entrance to his building and the sidewalk up Rosehill Place.

I fired up the old Chevy as Tommy positioned himself. First he looked into Harry's store and then he ran out by the road and waved frantically to me.

Not wanting to be noticed, I eased the Chevy out of its space and into the street. Despite Tommy's frantic waving, I drove the car carefully around the corner and stopped by the woods on Garden Street.

"You were driving so slow somebody could have come along and seen you." Tommy admonished as he opened the door and climbed into the passenger seat.

"You have to do things normal, like you're supposed to be doing them. Otherwise people will get suspicious and then you'll get caught." I answered, slipping the car in gear and moving forward towards New York Avenue.

Tommy was nervous. "I can't imagine we're doin' this in broad daylight." He said as his head twisted every which way looking for someone who might tell on us.

"We're not robbing a bank. We're just drivin' a car down the street. Nobody's gonna bother us unless we speed or get in an accident." I said in an effort to keep his spinning head from drawing attention to our mission.

We made it to the vulcanizing shop without any problems and I parked the car where I was told.

"Let's go see Mr. Sieberling. Be calm and let me do the talkin'. I don't want him spooked."

Tommy agreed with my instruction and decided to stay by the car.

"Are you just going to use the bigger tires for the race and then for everyday?" Mr. Sierberling asked when I walked into the back of the shop.

"Well, right now the car needs tires and we can only afford one set. So, we have to get something that we can use for the race and for regular driving"

"I have an idea." he said. "I have a set of Buick tires and wheels that should bolt right on that car. I'll loan them to you for the race. That way I can recap the tires on your car and we can swap them back on Monday."

"That's a good idea." I replied.

"Take that floor jack and knock off your wheels while I roll these other tires out."

"OK." I eagerly replied, grabbing the big floor jack. I then headed back to where Tommy was standing by the car. I explained the plan to him and then the both of us got busy loosening the lug nuts.

The jack was placed under the straight front axle and the car was lifted high enough to remove the wheels. The Chevy's wheels had no sooner hit the ground when Mr. Sieberling arrived with two Buick wheels. Quickly, Tommy and I mounted the wheels on the car and let down the jack so we could move to the rear of the car.

The jack was placed under the differential, the rear end of the car. Mr. Sieberling came with two more wheels and Tommy and I made the exchange.

"How much is all this going to cost?" I asked

"When you come back Monday we'll put the four recapped tires on the car for $24 dollars."

"That's real good. I'll see you Monday."

The car handled differently with the wide tires, but I could feel it getting more power to the road. I retraced the route we had taken earlier, but instead of going up Garden Street, I drove out to Elmora Avenue and down to the Town House.

How can we get more speed out of this car? I wasn't just satisfied with the bigger tires. I wanted to think of other ways to get more power. I was going to put new points and condenser and spark plug wires into the engine. That would help a little bit, but not as much as another carburetor or some internal engine work. We didn't have that kind of time or money and we had to give Gloria a regular car when she got back, not some souped up machine.

Tommy and I were pondering this problem over a couple of Cherry Cokes at the counter in the Town House when Donald from the car lot walked in for his coffee break.

"Hey, Donald! Can you answer a question?"

"What is it? I'll try."

"If we wanted to make that old Chevy go faster. What could we do that don't cost a lot of money?"

"That's a tough one. Maybe you can run a straight pipe instead of a muffler. That's what these guys do that race up on Route 22. They put a cutout in the pipe so that they can open and close the exhaust. If the cops catch you with those things open you're in for trouble. Beside that, I don't really know how to soup up a car."

"Thanks anyway, Donald."

"Maybe we can take the muffler out of Gloria's car." Tommy mused.

"Let's take a look at it." I replied, downing the remainder of the Coke.

"Naaa! I don't think that 'll work." I hollered out to Tommy, while I lay on my back under the car. "The muffler is almost in the middle of the car. We could set the car on fire if we took it out."

After crawling out from under the Chevy, Tommy and I sat on the running board to ponder the problem.

"When my uncle raced regular racing cars, they didn't have mufflers. The exhaust came out on the side in front of the rear tires." I related

"Maybe we could do something like that?" Tommy said, questioning the possibility.

"They make a flexible exhaust pipe. I saw Donald use some at the car lot so an old clunker could pass inspection. Let's ask him where he got it."

Donald was outside the garage washing up a green Hudson when Tommy and I approached.

"Hey, Donald. Remember when you used some flexible exhaust pipe to fix an old car?"

Where do you get that stuff? That's what we need for the old Chevy."

"I have some here." He answered. "But, there are different sizes. The parts store sells adapters to go from one size to the other, but you have to take the exhaust apart to find out what you need."

"Would you help us; if we take it apart?"

"Sure get it apart. Then call me and I'll see what size pipe and clamps are needed."

We had four days to complete the work on the car before the race. I didn't want to fool around with the exhaust until Gloria left for the weekend. I decided to follow the original plan and tune up the car. She could see me working on it and I didn't want things to look strange… and Gloria did stop to see how I was progressing when she reported for her evening shift at the Town House.

"Are those the new tires? They look kind of funny."

I explained to her that these were loaner tires and her tires were going to be recapped and ready Monday. "And they will cost 24 dollars for all 4 tires."

"I thought they would cost a lot more. I have to get inside now. When you come in later, I'll give you some more money for the tires."

She turned and went inside and it looked like she was satisfied with the story.

The tune up was almost done by supper time. I had a few things left to do, but they could wait until tomorrow. I locked the car and could see across the street, just as Robert was leaving the car lot to go home.

"Donald has some of that flexible exhaust leftover." Robert reported, as I joined him on the walk towards our building.

"The whole exhaust system under the car is rusted bad." I commented. "Maybe Gloria will go for a new muffler. If she does, then we could cut the pipe in front of the muffler and hook up the flex pipe. I'll have to talk to her later."

On the short walk home, Robert and I continued to talk and speculate about our success in the upcoming race. We really didn't know what to expect. I had seen my Uncle Billy race midgets and sprint cars on circular tracks. They were wild. Our race is going to be a road race on paved airport runways. It couldn't be anywhere near as bad as the dirt tracks where my uncle and other professionals raced. Besides, they are wild guys and they race for money. We're going to be in an amateur race for maybe a trophy. How bad could that be?

Gloria was behind the counter at the Town House, when we returned after supper. I informed her of the rusted condition of the exhaust system. She knew about it. A mechanic in a service station had told her the same thing. I said that I would replace the muffler and pipe if she would pay for the new parts. She wanted to pay me for doing the work. But, in good conscience, I couldn't charge her, because I was really ripping the exhaust system apart for the race. Of course I didn't tell her that.

The next day I finished tuning the engine and then I started removing the exhaust system.

Talk about rust. The muffler and tailpipe were nothing but big rust flakes. It was impossible to loosen the clamps holding everything together. All the parts had just rusted into one piece.

I borrowed a hack saw from Donald at the car lot and cut everything apart. By the time I was finished with all the sawing, I had pieces of rust in my hair, my ears, all over my face and down my shirt. But, the ancient exhaust system was out from under the car. Gloria had given me enough money to cover the cost of the parts and tires by the time she, her brother and his wife left on Thursday.

The car was almost ready for the track. The exhaust had to be hooked up, but everything else was ready. We even put 10 gallons of Hi-Test gas in the tank. Somebody told Robert that if we used Hi-Test we could advance the ignition timing a little bit and the car would go faster. It was worth a try.

Saturday morning, I drove the car across the street to the car lot. Without the muffler the car already sounded like a race car. I had to go easy; otherwise I would wake up the whole neighborhood.

Robert, Chico and Tommy met me at the car lot for this final phase of preparation.

We were able to slide the flexible steel pipe that Donald gave us, over the front exhaust pipe from the engine almost up to the manifold. We clamped the pipe to the chassis and then under the running board on the drivers side. Tommy and Chico took out the headlights while Robert and I worked on the exhaust. Donald was the overall supervisor making sure nobody broke anything.

It didn't take long to do the work. We made a final check of the car including the oil, water, battery, fan belt, brakes and tire pressure. We couldn't do much more. The car was as ready as we could get it. We put my tools, some extra oil and water and a jack on the rear floor of the car and locked the buggy up until Sunday.

We all tried to ignore tomorrow's race for the remainder of the day. But, each of our adrenaline levels was rising to a point of uncontrolled anxiety. I was hoping that the excitement wouldn't keep me from sleeping. After all, I was driving tomorrow because my uncle was a race car driver and I had an old racing helmet and goggles. Robert would be the head serviceman in the pits, because his father had a service station. Tommy and Chico would help Robert, if needed.

We spent the afternoon and early evening playing what we called fast pitch stickball in the school yard. Each team had a pitcher and a fielder. We used a rubber ball that was pitched to a box marked out on the school wall. When we could find somebody to be an umpire, he would stand behind the pitcher and call balls and strikes. The batter used a broom stick. If a ball was hit and it was fielded cleanly, it was an out. Over the school fence was a home run and a ball hitting the fence on a fly was a double. A ground ball past the pitcher and fielder was a single. We could play this game for hours and tonight it was just the thing to tire us out and ease the tension.

The stick ball game, then a few pinball games and a couple of Cherry Cokes were enough to erase the pre-race jitters. We stayed until Vince started closing the Town House around 9 o'clock and then we made our way home, agreeing to meet at the car lot at 7 o'clock Sunday morning.

So we didn't have to lie totally, we all told our parents that we were going to see the races down at Linden Airport. Because of our interests in cars and the fact that the races had been advertised in the newspaper, it would seem like the logical type of event to attract our attention. Consequently, no suspicions were aroused when we got up early and left home without having breakfast.

We had to get the car out of the car lot yard before Vince came to open the Town House.

That car was going to make a lot of noise with the open exhaust and we didn't need to attract anyone's attention

We saw the Sunday newspapers and the bags of fresh baked goods sitting in the Town House doorway. Vince hadn't arrived yet.

Quickly we piled into the car and I fired the engine up. My foot was on the gas pedal like I was walking on an egg and I eased the car out of the driveway and up to the traffic light on the corner, which lucky for us, was green.

In a micro second we were out into the Bayway Circle. Traffic on the highway was very sparse, just as would be expected on a Sunday morning. The engine made a lot of noise when I gave it the gas. So I would gas it some to get up speed, then back off the gas and let the car coast until the speed began to drop. I repeated this activity along the highway until we came to the little diner just past Stiles Street and almost across from the airport.

I coasted into the diner's parking area, which was pretty crowded. With the race across the road, it was boom times for this little diner, which normally catered to the people working at the General Motors plant.

Tommy and I grabbed two stools down near the far end of the counter.

"We're gettin' our stuff ta' go. Your buddies can sit here." Said the man sitting next to Tommy, as he and his companion rose from the stools.

"Thanks." Tommy replied waving to Robert and Chico and pointing to the seats.

After we all were seated, the cook behind the counter turned to us and said, "We have a breakfast special this morning for all people going to the races. Scrambled eggs, bacon, or pork roll, home fries, toast and coffee, or in your case milk for 45 cents. What'll it be gents?"

"We'll all have the breakfast special, with coffee." Chico announced. We had planned on having breakfast here, so everyone nodded in agreement. Tommy wanted pork roll, but the rest of us had bacon.

I think they had everything cooked ahead of time, because before we could say anything else, the heaping breakfasts were set before us. We ate like we had never seen food before. I was anxious to get into the airport, so I wasted no time finishing the breakfast. People were standing behind us ready to take our vacant seats. When I got up to walk down to the cash register, some guy quickly took my seat. Robert and Tommy followed behind me, but Chico wanted another cup of coffee.

"Make it to go!" Robert hollered down to him. "Come on, we have work to do to get ready for the race."

"Are you all racin'?" The grillman at the register asked.

"He's drivin'." Tommy replied, pointing at me "We're all mechanics, here to help out."

"A lot of fancy fast lookin' cars have gone in there. It ought to be some tough racin'. I hope you boys know what you're in for."

"His uncle was a champion midget car racer before the war. He even has his own helmet and goggles." Robert retorted.

The grillman sort of rolled his eyes and shrugged his shoulders at the brief resume' he just heard outlining some rather whimsical qualifications.

There were more cars in the parking area now than when we had arrived. I was careful not to blow anyone away with the open exhaust. I eased the Chevy out of the diner driveway into the highway and over to the airport entrance.

It looked like a carnival. Colorful tents were all over the place...and there were cars everywhere.

There were two lines entering the airport. The line on the left rode under a sign saying SPECTATORS AND PARKING. The line on the right said COMPETITORS. That was us.

"Are you fellas racin' this car?" The man at the gate asked when our turn in line came to his station.

"Yes sir, we are." I answered.

"OK. I want to ask a few questions. Fill out the drivers name and sign the bottom of the card. That's a release in case you get hurt or wreck the car, the airport isn't responsible. And are you over 18?"

"Sure." I said taking the card, filling it out and signing my name.

The man then stuck the card behind the windshield wiper and told me to; "Drive down to that fella in the red shirt. He'll inspect the car and if it passes you pay him 5 dollars and he'll tell you where to go."

The man in the red shirt lifted the card from the windshield and began to write and talk at the same time. "'32 Chevy two door, Pre war, street class. Stock, no modifications, novice driver." He said looking into the engine compartment. He walked around the car and shook the front tires. "Everything looks OK. Five dollars, boys."

After I paid the 5 dollars he wrote something on the side and back windows with a yellow crayon. "Go down this path all the way to the end. You'll go past all the cars in the different classes. Give this card to the man in the red shirt and he'll show you where your class is pitting."

Talk about cars. There were all kinds of cars. We slowly rolled past cars that looked like they belonged in the movies. There were European looking sports cars. Fancy roadsters like the Cord and Auburn were lined up next to Alfa Romeos and Jaguars. Indianapolis type championship roadsters occupied an entire section next to regular open wheel sprint cars.

Colorful tents were set up in the areas where the fancy cars were parked. I even saw what looked like a guy in a tuxedo making drinks in one of the tents.

The cars got shabbier and shabbier the farther down the line we went. The regular souped up jalopies that started to revive short track racing a few years ago were out in profusion. The street racers, like the guys from up on Route 22 were all there. Post War and late model factory stock cars were pitting next to pick-up trucks. Finally, at the very end of the line was something that looked like a junk yard. That was our group.

The man in the red shirt and sunglasses approached as I arrived in the area. He looked at the yellow writing on the windows and the asked for the card.

"I'm the Pit Steward. Park over there next to that Ford marked number 11. You'll be number 12." With that said, another man in a white sport shirt, standing behind him, quickly wrote big 12s on both doors with white shoe polish.

"Who's the driver?"

"I am." I said raising my hand which had been resting on the open window.

"We are going to have a driver's meetin' for this group in about 20 minutes. Don't miss it or you will not race. I'll explain the rules after which you will get five practice laps around the track. This group will have a 10 lap race starting at 11:30. Save your questions for the driver's meeting."

This guy isn't fooling around I thought as I assumed my position next to number 11, a 1935 Ford sedan. The other guys had already gotten out of the car before I parked it and now they took the tools, oil and the jack from the back floor. They put our stuff out on the ground behind the car, in the same fashion as our neighbors, or rivals.

I didn't want to stray to far from the car for fear of missing that driver's meeting. But, looking up, I saw Chico and Tommy walking back up the path we had just come down. Robert and I got busy and took the spare tire off its mount on the back of the car. The other crews were taping over the headlights and tail lights. We had already removed the headlights, so we just taped over the tail lights. The water and oil were OK. We were ready to race.

Robert and I sat down on the running board of the car. I had my helmet and goggles at my side ready for the driver's meeting and the practice laps, when Chico and Tommy returned.

"You should see some of these cars." Chico blurted. "They gotta be worth a lot of money."

"Paul Whiteman, The band leader is up there. He has a real expensive sports car. He even has this tent with a waiter." Tommy excitedly spit out.

"Good." Robert replied. "After our race we'll go up there and have a drink with 'em."

The man in the white shirt appeared out in front of the cars and began announcing through a megaphone, "DRIVER'S MEETING OVER HERE."

While we were walking up to where he was standing, the man in the red shirt appeared. The man in the white shirt handed out pieces of paper on which was printed the map of the race course and the rules we must follow.

The Steward in the red shirt explained how the race was controlled by flags that we were to obey. Green meant RACE, while yellow means slow down and red means stop. If a black flag is waved at you, get off the track. A white flag means there is one lap to go and a checkered flag means that the race is over. He emphasized a lot of other things, mostly safety. Since we were amateurs, he didn't want to see any rough riding or somebody taking unnecessary chances. If we did any of those things, or didn't look like we knew what we were doing, he would black flag the car.

Fortunately for us there are only 12 cars in our class. Gloria's Chevy is number 12. The odd numbered cars were to go out first for their practice laps. We even numbered cars were to stand by on the pit road awaiting our turn. The course over the airport runways and taxiways is almost 2 miles long. It has left turns and right turns and a couple of long straightaways. Some of the turns are marked off by orange barrels and hay bales. We were told to do the first couple of laps under the yellow flag at no more than 50 miles an hour on the straightaways. If everything was OK, we would be given a green flag to go as fast as we wanted.

I was the last in line for my group. I had my helmet on with the goggles above the visor.

*R. Allen Pender*

Like the dirt track drivers of old, I had a cowboy bandana tied around my neck that I could pull up to cover my nose if things got dusty. I didn't have Kid driving gloves like my uncle used to wear. I had a pair of paint covered work gloves, which Mr. Mitchell left down in the cellar.

The Steward in the red shirt came down along the line of cars telling us to restart our engines and get ready for the practice session.

"Where did you get that helmet?' the Steward asked after I started the car.

"It's a copy of one my uncle used to wear when he raced before the War. My grandfather got it for me. I had a complete racing outfit when I was a little kid."

"Is that right? Where did your uncle race?"

"He ran the Triple A circuit."

"What is his name? I knew a lot of triple A guys."

"Bill Morisey."

"Sure. I heard of him. What is he doing now?"

"Him and his brother-in-law opened an auto parts business in Belleville, N.J."

"That's nice to know. You take care out there and don't try to drive like Wild Bill."

I wondered how he knew my uncle's nickname. I wasn't about to ask because now we were being flagged for our turn on the track.

We ran single file for the warm up laps. The car rode through the turns nice after 50 miles per hour on the straightaway. Then came the green flag. The Studebaker in front of me just didn't have it and I passed him on the first straightaway. A '37 Pontiac was ahead of him and pretty quick down the straight, but the car looked like it was going to roll over in the turns and the driver had to slow so much to keep the car under control, that I was able to get by him and drive away before he could get his speed up again. Two Model B Fords now separated me from the front running '36 Ford. One of the Bs started to smoke and got black flagged. I eased off some for the next couple of laps to concentrate on my speed and gear shifting in the turns. That '36 Ford could beat me on a straight road, so my only tactic would be to run through the turns faster.

The practice period ended, and the next group of cars from another class was lined up ready to enter the track. I drove back to my pit spot.

"How did it run, R.A.? It sounded pretty good from here." Robert said.

"I don't think it got enough power for the V-8 Fords down the straightaway, but I think the Chevy got a little more gear in the turns. Those Buick tires sure make a difference.

For the next hour and a half or so, different groups were going out to practice. I think they wanted to get us amateur groups done early and then the pros and the fancy sports cars would be the main events in the afternoon.

*THE SOJOURNERS*
*Life on the American Homefront During World War II*

The car had been checked over and we were resting on the grass, when the man in the white sport shirt and megaphone marched up in front of the parked cars.

"LINE YOUR CARS UP BY NUMBER ON THE PIT ROAD."

They were going to start the cars in the order of their arrival this morning. I was last.

Well actually I was starting 11th since the one Model B Ford had engine problems.

The cars were lined up in five rows of two cars each, with me all alone in the sixth row.

After we were lined up we made one lap around the track and the green flag was thrown.

The Studebaker was left in the dust by one of the Model Bs. I shot past the Studebaker on the first straight and closed in on the Model B. The Pontiac missed the first turn after the second straightaway, went through the hay bales and continued on down an unused runway. He was off the course, so no yellow flag was thrown.

My system of braking and downshifting before I entered the corner was working well.

I got by the Model B by powering out of a turn while he was braking. I was passing a car almost every lap, but I couldn't gain on those two V-8 Fords. I could see them wallow in the turns, but then they were like greased lightning on the straights.

A '37 Buick, a '36 Hudson Terraplane and two Fords were a head of me. The Buick had plenty of power on the straightaway, but it and the Hudson both lost time in the turns. I gained slowly on all of them, but there wasn't enough race left for me to win, unless everybody broke down.

I finally over took the Buick and then on the last lap I caught the Hudson coming off the last turn. I was happy to see that checkered flag. We were directed to make one more lap under yellow, the file back into the pit area.

I could see my friends jumping up and down when I made the turn onto pit road. Then I saw something else. Standing next to the Steward in the red shirt was a familiar figure in green work clothes...my Uncle Billy.

O boy! Was I caught, or was I caught.

Uncle Billy wasted no time. He ran over and jumped on the running board of my; rather Gloria's car.

"What do you think you're doing? Park that car and I'm going to whip your backside all around this race track. What if your mother finds out what you have done? Don't you know racin' is dangerous? You know nothing a bout racin'. You're just a young fool." He hung onto the side of the car and berated me until I had the thing parked.

Uncle Billy stood about 5 foot 8. I was very athletic and I stood almost 6 foot tall and 170 pounds going into my junior year of high school. The racing helmet made me look almost 2 inches taller. He stepped back from the car when I got out.

"Alright, I'm caught. Now what was that first thing you were goin' to do to me?"

Uncle Billy looked up at me and then shook his head and began to lightly laugh. "Let's go get a soda and talk about this."

The man in the red shirt was standing near us. "Bobby, this is my nephew Richard." Uncle Billy said introducing me to the Steward. "Bobby and I raced together for a long time. So you have to watch out, because you're in my kind of place right now. A lot of these people know me and now they know you."

"Hey, Bill! Really! How old were you when you told the promoter you were 18?"

"Come on Bobby… Let's not make it any easier on this guy."

"Well, the apples don't fall far from the trees. Do they?" He said giving me a pat on the back.

I told my Uncle the whole story; about Gloria's car. About racing the chicken truck. About the tires and exhaust system.

"This story is as bizarre as the time your Uncle Jack worked for the dry cleaner and he loaned the clean suits out to his friends on the weekend. He got caught when some guy came looking for his suit on Saturday and Jack had loaned it to some friend who was going on a talent show."

Uncle Billy started laughing. "Good God! It runs in the family. For now, this is between you and me. We had to race during the Depression to make a living. You have other options. A lot of the guys I raced with are either dead or crippled. You don't want to worry my sister like I worried your grandmother. Today you were lucky. You didn't wreck that lady's car and get hurt. Hey, you drove a great race. Be satisfied with that."

We finished our drinks and walked back to the pit area. Uncle Billy knew a lot of the racers in the sprint car and champion roadster group, where he stopped to talk and introduce me to car owners and drivers. After that we stopped to look at the modified stock cars. These are the jalopies now racing on the local tracks. Uncle Billy knew just about everybody in this group. Most of the guys, like Roscoe Hough and Johnny Rodgers, were former midget car racers and now they had taken to this relatively new form of professional racing which was being banded together into a new sanctioning body called NASCAR.

My uncle told me stories of how some promoters would run off with the proceeds of the race before the main event was finished, so they didn't have to pay the drivers. There also wasn't any uniformity of rules from track to track. NASCAR was designed to correct those problems and protect the interests of drivers and car owners from unscrupulous track owners and racing promoters. The tracks had to obey NASCAR rules before a race would be sanctioned.

Rules also applied to car owners and drivers. These new restrictions created more competition within the ranks of the competitors. Who could cheat without being caught? Who could come up with the latest "trick" to gain the edge on the competition. It would be interesting to see if this idea catches on.

By the time we got back to my pit, I started to get the idea behind Uncle Billy's tour. There is a big network here. Everybody sees everything. Step out of line and it becomes common knowledge. I was a marked man now. Unless I changed my name, my nationality, or color, I would never race anywhere if these people knew that I didn't have my Uncle's blessing.

I had come in third in the race. But, when I got to the pit, Robert gave me the bad news.

"We've been disqualified. The Steward said we broke the rules with an underage driver."

"Do you know what you have to do now?" Uncle Billy asked.

"Yeah, we gotta get out of here and fix this car back to what it was… and grow older."

# CHAPTER 37

# THE '37 CHEVY

After we loaded everything back into the car, Robert and Chico said that they wanted to stay a little longer and see some racing. Tommy elected to return with me to help clean the car and install the new exhaust system.

People were turning to look at us while I slowly drove along the pit road towards the airport exit. I know what they're thinking and saying, I thought trying to avoid the stares. "There goes the underage kid who was disqualified."

"Hey, R.A!" Tommy yelped. "Some people are waving at us."

"Wave back." I said and turning quickly I saw two red shirted Stewards waving at us.

"They're probably happy that we're leavin'."

I started to sweat when I saw two Police cars outside the gate. The man at the gate raised his hand to hold us up, then to my relief the Police stopped the traffic on the highway and waved us on.

"I still don't understand how you got caught." Tommy said in a questioning manner.

"The Helmet." I replied. "That steward recognized the helmet. It's my Uncle's trademark with that black stripe going down the middle. They had raced together before the War. Like a dummy, I mentioned my Uncle's name. That and one quick phone call did it."

"It was a good race though." Tommy consolingly replied.

"I'm blackballed now. If I ever try to drive again without my uncle's permission, I'll be chased from every race track on the east coast. These guys have a big grapevine and they're loyal to each other."

"Is he gonna Tell your mother?"

"No. We're gonna keep it between us."

Depending on the amount of business, Vince usually closed the Town House early on Sunday afternoons. It wasn't yet 1 o'clock and we had to get in near the garage at the car lot without being seen; especially by someone who would tell Gloria what we were up to.

"Do you want to stop at the White Castle?" I asked Tommy when we crossed Park Avenue.

"Good idea. I am hungry."

Up at the next corner, we crossed the highway and I wheeled number 12 into the parking lot of the small White Castle. This was a good place to kill some time and fill our bellies.

"We gotta get into the car lot so Vince doesn't see us." I told Tommy. "Maybe I should drive down to Grier Avenue and come up Garden Street to Edgar Road, then turn quick on Elmora Avenue into the car lot."

"Why don't you just let me out of the car by the corner? I'll just walk over to the Town House and wave to you if the coast is clear and you can drive right into the car lot. A lot of people could see you and hear you the other way."

"That is a lot simpler." I said. "That's what we'll do."

We ate up our sack of White Castles and continued on our way. I pulled over to the curb by Gus's ESSO station at Edgar Road and the Bayway Circle. Tommy got out. He ran around the corner to the Town House and the next thing he was running back to the car.

"It's closed." He said climbing back into the car.

Those were magic words and I quickly drove around the corner into the car lot.

The new muffler and tailpipe were secreted along the side of the garage and Donald had left a hose out so we could wash the car.

By 4:30 the car was cleaned, the exhaust installed and the headlights replaced. The new recaps would be ready tomorrow. Everything would be back to normal and nobody would be the wiser.

Tommy and I took the car back over to the tire place and parked it along side the garage.

We had to walk home, but we didn't have to keep looking over our shoulder to see who was watching us.

"God, those race tracks are dirty places." My mother complained when I walked in the door. "You're as dirty as your uncle used to be and you have been only watching the races. What were you doing; crawling in and out of the cars? I don't want this to become a habit. Remember, I know what race tracks and race track people are like. I also know you were eating those White Castle hamburgers, you reek of onions."

I didn't need much encouragement to shed my clothes and climb into the bath tub.

Much to her delight, the car was ready for Gloria early Monday afternoon. She took it on a little test drive to Roselle. When she came back to the Town House, she was brimming over with excitement.

"That car never ran so good. It runs like a race car and sounds so good."

Robert almost fell off his stool and I started laughing. Gloria looked at us like we were a couple of nuts. She didn't understand how profound her statement was.

"Could you tell me why there is a lot of yellow writing on the side and back window?"

"Oh." I said trying to come up with a quick answer. "I think the tire man might have done that to make sure the right tires went back on the car. We'll clean it off for you."

"No, no. You guys have done enough. I can take care of that."

Up to that point the "Race" had been the high point of the summer. It was relived time and time again in our evening bull sessions.

It took me a little while to understand that what we did could have become a disastrous situation. Racing Gloria's car was not the prudent thing to do. But, of course, I had to learn this lesson the hard way.

My father had an ulcer in his stomach. One morning at work he got terribly sick. The ulcer had perforated and he had to be taken into surgery at Alexian Brothers Hospital.

The hospital is down on East Jersey Street, Elizabeth. My grandfather took Chicky and me there one time. That is the hospital where they make beer in the boiler room. I hope my father's doctors and nurses didn't hang out in the boiler room.

My father didn't take the old Nash to work. He only used the car on the weekend. He was working at the Elizabeth Journal since the end of the War and it was much easier to get there by bus than to find a parking spot for the car in the Broad Street, Elizabeth area.

The route of the 44 bus, which we could get on Edgar Road, went down East Jersey Street and past the hospital on its way to Elizabeth port. I thought it was a terrible shame that my mother had to take the bus to the Hospital when I could drive her there in the car. I thought that there might be some kind of law that would let people without a license drive in an emergency, or at least there should be a law like that.

"Wouldn't it be nice if I could drive you down to the hospital, Ma?"

"Oh, yes it would be, but you don't have anything to drive."

"The old Nash is just sitting down the street lookin' for someplace to go."

"That old Nash is goin' to have to wait for your father to get better. Haven't you caused enough problems with cars already? I'll take the bus."

"I just thought it could be an emergency situation, like the War. If we were being invaded, or there was an air raid, nobody would ask to see a driver's license."

"The War is over. We never were invaded… and there isn't any air raid. I'll take the bus."

The visiting hours at the hospital were over at 9 o'clock. I went there in the afternoon and my mother went in the evening. My sisters stayed with my Aunt until my mother came home. It was a nice arrangement, especially for me.

I had that set of keys to my father's car that I carried around in my pocket just in the event of some sort of emergency. I could hear those keys talking to me, "Let's start the car. Let's go somewhere." These keys were getting downright nasty and suddenly I found myself walking down towards the Nash.

"The battery could go dead if the car isn't started for a long time." I thought, trying to justify the situation in my mind. This is maintenance. It is the proper thing to do. Nobody will get mad at me for taking care of the car. I had convinced myself that I was doing the right thing and before long I was seated in the driver's seat of the Nash.

"What are you doing?" Tommy asked peering in the car window.

"Just keepin' the battery charged up while my father is in the hospital. Come on in."

We sat there for a time with the engine running. We were talking and listening to the radio, when Robert came along.

"Are you guys goin' somewhere?"

"No. I'm just runnin' the car to keep the battery up."

Robert climbed into the back seat and the three of us continued to hold a conversation on a variety of subjects as the evening light started to wane.

Eventually the subject came back to cars.

"R.A., do you think this car could beat Gloria's car?" Robert asked

"This car is a six cylinder with twin ignition. It's a lot heavier than Gloria's car. But, it got more power."

Robert, Tommy and I debated the subject until we wore it out.

"Look, I'll show you how much power this thing got." I said putting the car in gear and releasing the hand brake.

"Better hold on Tom, Barney Oldfield is at it again. Hey, where's your helmet R.A.?"

The two of them were laughing and giggling when I pulled out of the parking space and turned down Garden Street. I intended to make a sprint down the vacant part of New York Avenue and then make a 180 degree turn at Grove Street and head back to Garden Street.

"COPS! COPS! Tommy yelled pointing to a pair of headlights down near DeHart Place.

All I could think of was that cop George. With anybody else we might have a chance. But, that George knows us too well. I was just about halfway down the street with the car still in second gear. I got off the gas and on the brake and pulled over to the side of the road. I would make a nice polite K turn to avoid suspicion if the car was a Police car.

The other car was still down by DeHart Place. If it was a Police car, I could be turned around and back on Garden Street before he cruised up the street. I swung the car out into the middle of the road; then quickly backed up to start the leg of the K turn…when;

"CAARASH", the car shuddered and I heard the sound of breaking glass.

"You hit a fire hydrant!" Robert yelled.

"What fire hydrant?" I exclaimed, putting the car back into first gear. I was anxious to get out of there, especially if that other car or someone heard the noise.

"A big empty street. What is a fire hydrant doing there?" I cried.

I didn't know if the other car was a Police car, or if it heard or saw me hit the fire hydrant. I wasn't looking back to see if it was coming after me. I just leadfooted that Nash back to Rosehill Place.

I had to make another K Turn to put the car back in its parking space. I switched the headlights off just in case the other car was following me. At this point I was real nervous. I didn't know the condition of the fire hydrant and what the left rear fender of the car looked like. In my haste to park the car in the dark, I climbed the curb and hit a tree with the right front fender. Again I heard that familiar sound of glass breaking.

Finally, I got the car parked without any more damage. The right front fender was crumpled and the headlight was smashed. The bark was skinned off the tree. The left rear fender looked like a prune and the tail light was beyond recognition. Red paint from the fire hydrant was all over the fender and rear bumper.

"We better go back through the yard to New York Avenue and see what the fire hydrant is like." I said once the car was shut down and parked.

I expected to see a geyser, like Old Faithful, shooting water 20 feet in the air when we went around the garages into the back field. But, everything was quiet. We cleaned up the remnants of the tail light lens and left the scene.

"How are you going to explain this, R.A.?" Robert asked.

"I got a week before my father comes home from the hospital. And, he won't be able to drive for a while. I'll have to think hard on this one. I can probably bang the fenders out. But, where the devil can I get a headlight and a tail light for a Nash?"

I really had my tail caught in the screen door. I needed Divine intervention to get out of this mess.

Returning to the scene of the last crash, I cleaned up as much of the broken headlight as I could in the dark. I hoped that the wrinkled fender and broken headlight wouldn't attract any attention before I had an opportunity to rectify the situation.

The damage didn't look that bad in the dark, but the next morning it looked beyond hope.

I spent the major part of the day running around looking for a headlight and a tail light for the Nash. I was beginning to believe that this was the only Nash in existence. Suffice it to say that I had come up empty handed.

*THE SOJOURNERS*
*Life on the American Homefront During World War II*

I had been over in Bell's junkyard in Linden looking for the parts and was riding my bicycle home on Lidgerwood Avenue when I saw this man kicking and beating on an old Chevy. When I got closer, I saw that it was Klinky's father.

"Can I help with anything?" I said coming to a stop at the site of this mayhem.

"Not unless you have 50 dollars. I'll sell this car to the first person that comes along with 50 dollars."

"Sold!" I said. "I have the money home."

"The Chevy dealer was going to give me 50 dollars on a trade-in for my new car, but this thing just stopped dead right here. I'll walk home and meet you by your house. I have the Bill of Sale at home anyway."

Mounting back on the bicycle, I said, "I'll see you in a few minutes."

I think I rode that bicycle faster than I did Gloria's car in the race. I wanted to get home and get the money before Klinky's father could change his mind. I had been saving my money for such a purpose. I didn't think it would come this soon, but I had saved close to 100 dollars.

I was in and out of the house in a flash with 50 dollars in hand. Klinky's father was just coming up the street and I met him down by Harry's store.

"Here's the 50 dollars Mr.Klinkman."

"Alright, Richard. Wait a few minutes while I go up in the house for the Bill of Sale."

"I'll be out by our porch. I have to get some tools to see if I can get the car running."

"Well, I think its going take an expert to get that car running." He sarcastically answered.

Klinky's father signed the Bill of Sale and handed it and the keys over to me.

"I'll have my father change it over when he comes out of the hospital."

"Good luck. I hope you can get it off the street down there."

I wasted no time getting back to where MY car was parked. I lifted the engine compartment panels. When I turned on the key, the gas tank gage registered half full.

I took the distributor cap off and snapped opened the points with a screwdriver. I got a spark out of the coil wire. Klinky's father had left some tools, tire chains, rope, motor oil, grease and a siphon hose in the storage area behind the rear seat. I had learned a few tricks in the car lot. I siphoned a little gasoline from the tank into a cola bottle I found lying in the vacant lot near the car.

After pouring a little gas down the carburetor, I tried to start the car. It fired up, ran for a few seconds and quit.

"It's not getting any gas." I said aloud.

I tried again and it did the same thing.

There is a glass filter bowl with a stone filter element in the gas line ahead of the carburetor. It looked kind of rusty. I loosened the clamp holding the bowl and took it off. Rusty gas and water came out of the bowl. The stone filter was supposed to be cream colored. This one was rust red. I wiped the glass bowl clean and put it back in place without the filter element. When I cranked the engine over the bowl filled up and then the engine fired. The '37 Chevy had come back to life.

This was a little '37 Chevrolet 2 door sedan. It didn't have any trunk and the spare tire was mounted on the back of the car. I used the rope that was behind the rear seat to tie my bike to the spare tire and rear bumper. With everything secured I started for home. It was a calm uneventful trip; after all I was almost legal. I had a signed Bill of Sale. I drove up Lidgerwood Avenue, across South Elmora Avenue and then up to Rosehill Place. I parked at the curb, next to the big field, across the street from the banged up Nash.

It was pretty ironic. I was looking for parts to fix the Nash and ended up with a whole car that is probably better than the Nash.

"Ma! Do I have a surprise for you and Daddy?" I loudly announced boisterously entering the apartment.

"You have. What kind of surprise?"

"I bought a car for you."

"You did what?"

"I bought a car." I repeated and then I proceeded to tell her the whole story about Mr. Klinkman and the car. I left out the part where I drove the car home.

My mother didn't know exactly what to say. She didn't like the Nash because something was always breaking at the wrong time. I extolled the virtues of the Chevy and of course my mother knew Mr. Klinkman and how well he treated the car…except for changing the gas filter. "Your father and I were going to buy a Chevy like that, but we bought the Ford instead."

"I'll go with you to the hospital tonight and tell him about the car and see what he wants to do about getting a new Title and the car registered."

"That will be good. He's gonna' need a reliable car if he still wants to sell real estate out in Clark Township on the week ends."

I invited her out to see the car. But, she said that she didn't have time now. "I know what that car is like. I see it every day going in and out of the driveway."

I was just as pleased. I didn't want her, or anybody else getting close to that Nash.

I was really proud of myself. I spent the rest of the afternoon going over that car with a fine toothed comb. Behind the rear seat I found a genuine Chevrolet repair manual for this model. The car had a heater, but was absent the optional radio. One by one my friends arrived on the scene and I repeated the story of how I came to acquire this car. I showed them everything from the engine to the storage space behind the rear seat. All of the guys were impressed with the car, but most of their questions were directed toward my situation with the Nash.

When my mother and I arrived at the Hospital that evening, I told my father the story of the deal with Mr. Klinkman... and of course I said nothing about the Nash.

"That was a good deal" Daddy said as he scanned the Bill of Sale. "The Bill of Sale for the Nash is in my top dresser drawer. Bring it over tomorrow and I'll sign it, then you can call a junk yard to take the Nash. Make sure you take the license plates off the Nash. Go to Palermo's on Wood Avenue, Linden and get the applications to change the license plates from the Nash to the Chevy and then bring everything over here for me to sign."

My father felt that he was going to have a tough time getting the Nash through the State inspection. There were just too many things wrong with it. "He should see it now", I thought to myself. This little Chevy could be the answer to prayers, his and mine.

"A man, who works at the Journal, wants to buy a new car next Spring. He will sell me his Plymouth for the trade-in value: If I want it. This Chevy could hold us over 'till the Spring and then you can drive it."

My father either read my mind or knew of my ulterior motive. I was as happy as a flea in a dog pound.

The next morning I took the 44 bus to Linden. Palermo's Real Estate and Insurance was also the Motor Vehicle Agency. The building is located next to the railroad on Wood Avenue. My father worked for Palermo Real Estate on the weekends. The company was selling building lots that had been cut out of farms in Clark Township. The ladies in the Motor Vehicle knew my father and they took care of me immediately. They knew the situation with my father and they gave me all the forms necessary to put the Chevy on the road.

After getting the papers, I reversed my tracks and took the 44 bus back to Elizabeth and down to Alexian Brothers Hospital.

My father was sitting up in bed when I arrived. He still had some hoses, or tubes hooked up to his body and he sure didn't look too good. I had filled out all the information required on the forms while sitting on the bus. All my father had to do was to sign the forms. We made some small talk and I assured him that I had enough money to pay for the new Title, which is 1 dollar and 50 cents.

When my visit was concluded, I made the bus trip again back to Edgar Road. All the papers were temporarily put inside the big cabinet in the living room. The next order of business was to contact a junk yard to haul away the Nash.

I rode over to Bell's junkyard on Elizabeth Avenue, Linden on my bike.

"Does the car run?" The man asked.

"It runs, but it's banged up a little bit."

"Is this the car you were looking for parts for yesterday?"

"Yeah. I met a man on the way home and bought his Chevy. Now my father wants to junk the Nash."

"Do you have a signed Bill of Sale?"

"Yes I do." I said removing the document from my pocket and handing it to the man.

"Ok." He said handing the paper back to me. "If you want to drive it in, I'll give you 15 dollars. If I tow it, I'll give you 5 dollars."

The 15 dollars sounded real good to me. But, the 5 dollars was a lot safer. The way my luck was running with the Nash, I didn't want to tempt fate.

"When can you come and tow it?"

After I gave him directions, he said. "That's not far. I'll come in an hour. You be there?"

"I'll be there waitin'." With this part of the business concluded, I hopped back on the bike and made a rush for home. I had already removed the license plates from the car. But, I also wanted to get the radio. I was going to take the battery out, but that battery wasn't much good anyway.

I did get the radio out with about 10 minutes to spare when, true to his word, Mr. Bell's helper arrived with a tow truck.

"Are you the one who ran into the tree?" The driver said, surveying the damage around the car

"Yeah, I got nervous and jumped the curb."

"You don't have a license, Do you?"

"No. How did you know?"

"I did something similar one time. Isn't it funny how much better people drive when they have a license in their pocket?"

I couldn't argue with that question. Then I went on to tell the driver how well I drove in the race at the airport and then how I got caught.

"You'll do fine when you're legal. But, if I were you, I wouldn't try drivin' on the streets 'till you get your permit."

He was hooking up the Nash to the tow truck as we talked. When he had finished and was ready to go, he asked for the Bill of Sale and then pulled 5 dollars from his pocket.

"Take it easy sport. Don't hit anymore trees." he cautioned.

Putting the 5 dollars in my pocket, I gave the tow truck driver a wave and watched the evidence of my crime being dragged down the street.

"How in the world did you pull that off?" Tommy asked when he saw the tow truck leaving with the Nash.

"The Man Upstairs must have been watching this whole deal. And, I'll bet He was involved somehow. I'm just wonderin' what He's gonna want me to do to pay Him back."

"Does it work like that, R.A.?"

## THE SOJOURNERS
### Life on the American Homefront During World War II

"I don't know. But, somehow I think I'll find out one day."

The next morning, accompanied by Robert and Tommy, I went back to Palermo's with all the papers. I had some money left over from the purchase of the car, so we stopped in at Associated Auto Parts on Wood Avenue. I bought spark plugs, ignition points, spark plug wires and a new fuel filter. By the time my father got out of the hospital, the car had been all tuned up and the oil changed.

I even cleaned out the carburetor, and I must say that the little Chevy purred like a kitten.

Just to keep a good feel for the clutch, I moved the car backward and forward in the parking space and it seemed to satisfy me for now

I picked up an antenna from the Pep Boys on Elizabeth Avenue and installed the radio from the Nash. It didn't really fit, but I was able to jury rig it under the dash board.

The Chevy was a reliable car and actually became like a member of the family... something like having a dog or some other pet. During his convalescence, which was during the last half of the summer and into early fall, my father used the Chevy almost every day to ride out to Clark Township to sell real estate. When he got home in the evening, I would pamper the car so it was clean and serviced for the next day. I had a vested interest in the car. Come March I would be driving it.

That September I started my junior year in high School. I continued to work in the car lot on Saturdays. Sometimes when they were busy, I would work after school with Robert. Tommy and a couple of other fellows from high School had a job with a tree surgeon. When they needed extra help, I would go with them. Most of the time we cleared building lots for new homes in Linden, Kenilworth and Clark Township. We didn't use any power tools. Everything was done by hand. Tommy and the other guys worked after school and weekends. Sometimes I worked after school, but most of the time I worked on Sundays.

I had a busy schedule with these part-time jobs and homework from school. However, we still spent our evening time at the Town House and at the Elizabeth YMCA.

Fortunately, or unfortunately, depending on how one views the situation; we had very little interaction with our female counterparts. The city had a Boy's High School and a Girl's High School. Unless a boy had maintained contact with some of the girls he knew in Junior High School, the chances of getting acquainted or socially involved with girls in our age group was slim. The girls probably didn't realize how lucky they were.

I'm sure the girls would not be interested in our lifestyle which included jobs, sports, pinball, White Castle Hamburgers, fishing, carousing and cars. On the flip side girls cost money and our funds were pretty much dedicated to our lifestyle, most of all to cars.

All of us would be driving in the Spring. I planned to play High School Baseball in the Spring, so I needed to work all fall and winter to sock away all the funds I would need in the Spring to support my car. My priorities were in order and I was moving ahead with the plans for the next year of my life.

One evening in September, my father came home and made an announcement that appeared for the moment to derail my plans.

"I bought a house in Clark." He proudly announced.

The way in which he made the announcement made it seem like we would be moving next week. However, that wasn't to be the case.

The house my father bought from a man named Louie was not fully built. Mr. Louie began building the house before the War. The basement and the exterior block walls had been erected before the shortage in building supplies curtailed all activity for the duration.

After the War, Mr. Louie went back to work on the house and finally got it enclosed. Now he had run low on money and needed to sell the house in its unfinished state.

Through Palermo's Real Estate, Daddy became involved with several builders for whom he was selling lots and new homes. By shaving his commission on future sales these builders agreed to send people over during slack times to finish the major parts of the house. Dollar wise it was a good arrangement, but it would be some time before we could move in.

The house is located on a dirt road with fields in the front and woods in the rear. The Rahway River and Jackson's Pond are on the other side of the woods. The swath of land between our rear yard and the river is currently being cleared for a roadbed. A section of the soon to be built Garden State Parkway will be passing about 300 feet beyond our back yard. Some houses are being built in Clark Township, but for the most part it is still farmland. There really is no center of town unless you count the White Diamond Hamburger stand and the Clark Rest Bar on the corner of Raritan Road and Central Avenue as the town center. There are some stores and businesses on Westfield Avenue coming up from Rahway, but not enough to be considered a shopping district. High School students in the Township are bused to the Regional High School in Springfield. That is probably where I will attend in my senior year.

"We probably will be able to move in by the beginning of next summer." My father intoned the following evening after we made our first trip to the house.

Summer would be the best time to move in, since the structure didn't have any heat. It didn't have much in the way of plumbing, or electrical service either. It did have a roof, doors and windows. My father figured that we could do a lot of the interior work during the winter after he got some kind of heat put in.

My mother immediately put a new austerity plan into effect to save the money which would be needed to buy the materials to make a home out of this house. Squeezing pennies and stretching dollars was her forte'. A Depression and a War made her well qualified to manage the financial end of this project.

## CHAPTER 38

## THE NEW HOUSE

As the crow flies, the house in Clark Township is only 4 miles from our current home in Elizabeth, but in terms of development, it is light years away. The Township is surrounded by the undeveloped parts of other developing suburban towns. Westfield and Cranford, both to the north are well established commuter communities with all the amenities associated with a suburban hometown; however their outer fringes bordering Clark are still developing. Roselle to the northeast has always been considered a neighborhood of western Elizabeth. Linden has historically been an industrial community. Winfield Park, alongside the Rahway River was an undeveloped wooded area before it was spun off from Linden, during the War to create a community for shipyard workers. The remainder of northern Linden is still wooded or farmed. Clark was formerly a part of Rahway, a sleepy railroad town. The northern parts of Rahway and Woodbridge to the west are still actively farmed as is Scotch Plains to the Northwest.

I liked going out to work on the house. I usually went on Sunday, unless I had work with the tree surgeon. But, now as cold weather was approaching, that work started to ease up until the Spring. When we reached the house, my father would explain all the chores to me. Shortly thereafter he was usually picked up by one of his real estate associates to spend the day selling lots at one of the farms they were carving up and I was left alone to complete my duties. I didn't mind at all, because he also left the Chevy.

Clark didn't have a police force like Elizabeth. They had two police officers and one part-time auxiliary officer. A white building up on Westfield Avenue, that was smaller than a 2 car garage served as the headquarters building. Every so often the State Police would cruise through the town, but I really think the only reason they came here was to get hamburgers at the White Diamond.

I went about my chores diligently and fast. The quicker I got done, the quicker I could start cruising around town in the Chevy. I'm sure my father had his suspicions about my activity. He knew a lot of people in this town and this was no place where you could get lost in a crowd. Besides, I left evidence.

"I could swear," he'd say. "That when I parked the car here it had a half tank of gas. Now it only has a quarter. How do you explain that?"

"Oh," I'd say. "I siphoned some out t' clean the paint brushes."

"My friend Frank saw a car just like ours driving away from the White Diamond. It's funny. As much time as I spend in this town, I have yet to see another car like ours, with those fake white wall tires and a raccoon tail on the antenna."

"They're popular now. Everybody is buying them. Real whitewall tires aren't available for all cars yet. Besides, they'd be too expensive for older cars."

"Well, I thought maybe you knew that fella, since he goes to the White Diamond and this house smells like a White Diamond hamburger."

"I had them a long time ago… and I think the hamburger smell sticks to the wet paint. It'll probably go away when we air out the house in the Spring."

"I'm sure a lot of things will change in the Spring." He said with that quirky raised eyebrow look of his.

He knew what I was doing. Like me, he was probably praying for Spring, when I would be driving legal. Right now he wasn't too excited. There wasn't enough traffic out here for me to get in trouble. I could possibly hurt myself, but the chance of hurting someone else was very slim.

As a freshman and a sophomore, I had played football and ran cross country in the fall. Now as a Junior I was only going to play baseball in the Spring. Between school work, part-time jobs and working out at the house, there was little time in my schedule for any extra curricular activities. I was even getting a couple more days a week work in the car lot. My only spare time was at night, which had to be dedicated to homework or, hanging out at the Townhouse Luncheonette. In competition for my time, homework usually lost out.

My focus was on the coming Spring and obtaining a driver's license. Work and saving money to fund my future automobile exploits were the preoccupations that won me over and lured me away from school work.

By Thanksgiving time heat had been installed in the house.

My mother would show up every couple of Sundays to see how things were going. She drove me nuts.

I painted the kitchen and the cabinets three times before she settled on the color. The same went for the bedrooms. My color perception and hers were quite different. We bought white paint; to which coloring was added from little tubes. Everything was hand mixed - by my hands. She would match the color in the paint can to a piece of fabric, or something else containing the color she wanted.

"That's exactly the color I want. Don't change anything. Do you hear?"

"I won't change anything. I'll paint everything with this paint." And I did exactly that.

Unfortunately for me, when the paint dried on the wall it was a different shade from the color in the can.

"It's different. What did you change?" She would blurt.

"I didn't change anything. Here's the same can of paint. Look at the color. Now watch while I paint some of the wall again. Come back after the paint dries and see what color it is."

"I know you're doing something, because you don't like my colors."

"Ma, I don't care what the colors are. After we move in I'll only be sleeping here at night and the lights will be out so I won't know what color anything is."

"Where are you gonna be that you will only be here to sleep?"

"I'll have my car and I'll be workin'."

"I wish you would care as much about this house as you do that car. Mark my words, that car will be your undoin'."

It took quite a while, but the house did get painted on the inside. The next fiasco erupted over the door knobs.

My father was buying materials for the house from a surplus place in Linden. He was getting real good a deal on stuff, but most of it was used materials. One day I had to help him unload a couple of crates of door knobs from the car. The knobs were made of glass and came in a variety of colors. Some of the knobs were dark purple, others were amber, some were green and some were red. He even got the brass shafts that went through the passage sets that were set into the mortises cut in the doors. My assignment was to install all the knobs throughout the house while my father went off to the real estate office with his friend Frank. At first appearances, it looked like this was going to be an easy chore. I just had to screw the set screw in the knob down onto the shaft then pass the shaft through the door and install the knob on the other side in the same fashion as the first knob. I would get this job done real quick and then I could drive over to the White Diamond for a hamburger.

Wrong again. The shafts were worn in the area where the set screw made contact. I turned the shaft to find a spot that wasn't worn. No such Luck. These shafts had been worn on each flat side. The set screws were worn too. To do this job right I needed new screws for the knobs and new shafts. The house didn't have a telephone, so I couldn't contact my father. I assumed that he had left everything up to my ingenuity.

I needed something that would fit into the set screw hole and could be tightened down on to the shaft locking the knob in place. The next hour was like being on a scavenger hunt as I looked through the house for something that would work in this situation. I found some scraps of copper wire that were smaller than the screw hole in the knob. This might work if I could jam the piece of wire down the hole and then tighten the screw.

Luckily, we had the tools I needed; an ice pick and a pair of cutting pliers.

I snipped little pieces of wire and drove them down the screw hole with the ice pick. It seemed to work. The knob became tight on the shaft. The job took a lot longer than it should have, but all the knobs were nice and tight.

Nice and tight that is until my mother made her next visit.

"Where did these God awful door knobs come from?" She bellowed as she opened and closed one of the bedroom doors. Her force in opening the door had caused the wire to move and the next thing the knob was spinning around in her hand. One door after another succumbed to her attack until there wasn't a door knob in the house that worked.

All my labor had gone for naught. But, my father was really the person in trouble for buying these gaudy door knobs.

"Look at the money that's been wasted on these things. Get some screws and shafts and have Richard put the knobs back on." She commanded my father. "I'll make up some thing to cover these knobs."

She did. My mother got busy and knitted little hat like things to slip over the door knobs. It would have been frivolous and against her economic nature to buy new door knobs. As far as I know we had the only house in the world where the door knobs had hats

The hats on the door knobs were a good idea and they complimented the rope tied around the refrigerator to keep the door closed. I'm sure that there aren't too many people who have a refrigerator like this one.

Last year around Christmas time, my mother's pride and joy, the old early 1930's General Electric refrigerator just up and quit.

The weather was cold enough for us to keep our perishable food in box mounted on the outside window sill. The emergency lasted a little more than week because my parents were preoccupied with Christmas preparations and they needed an opportunity to shop for a new refrigerator. As long as the cold weather held out, Christmas had a greater priority than a refrigerator. Right after the New Year they bought a brand new Norge refrigerator from Jay and Dee Appliances down on Washington Avenue.

Jay (John) and Dee (Dominic) are a couple of guys from the South Street neighborhood and they opened an appliance store next to St. Mary's Church. Consumer goods, like refrigerators, washing machines and now gas or electric clothes dryers, which replaced backyard clothes lines, were coming back on the market and the demand was high. The designs were also different. Wringer type washing machines like my mother's Easy were passe'; although you couldn't tell that to my mother. The designs were new and different. Washing machines are now automatic and they spin dry. All a person has to do to operate one is to open the top lid or the front door, which has a round window in it and load your clothes and soap. A turn of a dial and the machine takes care of the rest. For some reason the new refrigerators are sort of domed shaped. I guess that is so you can't store stuff on top of them. The new refrigerators have a freezer compartment in the upper part of the unit. New things called frozen foods have started to come on the market. I don't know which came first the freezer compartment or frozen food. I suspect frozen food was a War-time invention that has now found a peace-time use.

Before the War washers and refrigerators were made of steel. Now everything was made of stamped sheet metal and plastic. In an effort to get things out on the market, quality control wasn't all it could be. The Norge refrigerator was one such victim of Post War material fatigue.

I don't recall who did it, but we only had the refrigerator for a short time, when somebody pulled too hard on the door handle and the thing snapped off. The handle was made of pot metal, a die cast white metal, that couldn't be brazed or welded like steel. A replacement part wasn't immediately available; so my mother, with my help, tied a piece of cotton clothes line around the new refrigerator to keep the door closed tight. We taped the rope to the back of the refrigerator, so it wouldn't move. We could open the door by pushing up on the rope to release its hold on the door and then reverse the process by pulling the rope down over the closed door to keep it sealed. In its present condition, the Norge is a lot better than having to open the window and fish around in a wooden box perched on the outside window sill. The refrigerator had a light that came on when the door was opened. Whereas at night, we had to use a flashlight to find things in the window box.

We were steadily progressing towards the day when the refrigerator with the rope would join the covered door knobs. On moving day another family oddity, an heirloom of sorts, would add its character to the new house - Grampa's Cabinet.

Sometime back in the '20's my Grandfather came into possession of 5 large hand carved, Mahogany colored cabinets, each one about twice the size of a normal refrigerator. The cabinets had bi-fold doors in the front. The doors were Gothic in style with carvings of Medieval Knights standing guard at the opening. Depending upon which family member you talk to, there are several different renditions of the story on how he acquired these cabinets. The truth therefore lies somewhere in the middle.

We know Gramp's had some business arrangements with Senator Homer Capehart of Indiana, who was also involved in the infant Radio business. Gramp was also associated with a man named J.J. Holcomb, President of a company called Holcombe and Hoke of Indianapolis, Indiana. At that time, during the "Roaring Twenties", a factory in Indianapolis manufactured Gramp's Ever-Ready battery for electric vehicles, submarines and for radios; which required Direct Current.

Somebody, I don't know who, said these cabinets were made to house the first combination Wurlitzer music machine (Record Player) and a Capehart Radio. Apparently the cabinets and the music machines were made for display at a trade show in Chicago. How Gramp got involved, I don't know. But, legend has it that somebody owed him money at this show and he took the cabinets in lieu of cash. It does seem like the kind of thing Gramp would do. He probably thought he got a bargain.

It is sure amazing how things worked out. Gramp had five children and he also had five cabinets. I think he saw the cabinets as some sort of legacy. He would always tell everybody how valuable these cabinets were going to be in the future and that he was going to give them to his children. He did... as wedding presents to his daughters. His sons, Bill and Jack and their wives wanted no part of these "White Elephants." But the spouses of the daughters were stuck.

Much to everybody's consternation, Gramp would periodically arrive to inspect the cabinets to make sure that they were taken care of and that they were located in a place of high visibility suitable for the class they brought to a residence.

Gramp also had a collection of paintings by the watercolorist, Fred Cozzens. Mr.Cozzens specialized in painting sailing ships. He was commissioned to do paintings of all sorts of ships and some of his well known works are in the hands of collectors. The paintings Gramp has are nice, but they aren't the famous or valuable works of this man. Again, Gramp felt that these paintings would be worth a tidy sum in years to come. To date he hadn't given away any paintings, but he did designate who would get what painting after his death. I'm sure everyone wished he had done the same thing with the cabinets.

Life wasn't all school and work. From December on, The High School basketball team played on Friday nights in the Elizabeth Armory. We all went to the games and then later to the Regent Sweet Shoppe. A lot of girls from Battin High School went to those games. But, it didn't do us any good - no car.

After Christmas, some of us on the baseball team would meet a few evenings a week at the Elizabeth Y.M.C.A. March was two months away, but we wanted to be in shape before the good weather came, so we could devote all our energy to baseball skills. March was also the month in which I would be eligible to take the driving test. I was all for any activities that would make the days pass quickly until that landmark hour.

Slowly things started to come together. The house was almost ready and we planned to move the day after school let out for the summer. In February, my father bought a '46 Plymouth from a man he worked with. The old Chevy had a month vacation before I got behind the wheel full time. And I made good use of the time. I went to the Pep Boys on Elizabeth Avenue and bought some red seat covers for the car. I also got a sealed beam conversion kit and new floor mats. I put on a steering wheel cover and one of those steering knobs. I was really giving this car a treat.

Bayway Motors, where I worked on Saturday, was giving out latex monkeys as a promotional item. The monkey was like one you would see with an organ grinder. It was molded with a little red jacket and a little red cap. It had a long tail and a silly smile on its face. This was just the accoutrement that was needed to finish the interior decoration of my car. Donald, my boss, said I could have as many as I wanted, but I only needed two. The little monkey would squeek when it was squeezed. I hung a monkey on each of the sun visors. They looked neat.

The paint on the exterior of the Chevy was touched up and the car was spotless when that all important day arrived.

Tommy went with me to the Motor Vehicle Test Area, by the Elizabeth Armory. He had just gotten his license in February, but didn't have a car yet. I was being accompanied by a licensed driver and that's what counted.

"How long have you been drivin'?" The State Trooper asked when I gave him the form from the written test.

"Probably 5 or six years." I replied.

"He even drove race cars." Tommy volunteered.

"I worked with my uncle and drove a lot of stuff, but, never on the roads."

The trooper had sun glasses on so I couldn't see the expression on his face. Except I know he wasn't smiling. He attached my test sheet to clipboard and gave the car the once over as he walked around to the passenger side.

"Get in!" He said opening the passenger door.

"Where to?" I asked, climbing behind the wheel.

He outlined a course he wanted me to drive and then sat back to watch me.

I performed flawlessly. I made all the proper hand signals and kept to the legal speed limit. I made K turns and parallel parked like I had been doing it all my life.

"I guess you have been driving for sometime." The trooper said handing me my test sheet. "Now you can do it legal."

The great milestone had been reached. The rite of passage completed. There were no drums sounding or brass bands playing, only the clicking valve noise of a six -cylinder Chevrolet reverberated in my head.

# CHAPTER 39

# PLAY BALL

Baseball. Nothing else mattered.

I went to school to play baseball. I really only had four classes a day. I had locker duty for one period and study hall for one period and we were excused from seventh period Gym to go to baseball practice. I got my homework done during the study hall and locker duty periods. I got it done. Not that it was the best quality— but passing.

At 2:15 each day, a group of boys crowded into my old Chevy and we headed for our High School home field in Warinanco Park. Elizabeth didn't have an athletic complex for its sports programs. Some of the other High Schools located in the smaller towns in the county had home fields with locker rooms and everything. Elizabeth had Williams Field next to Edison Vocational High School. It was used for football, but not much else.

Our Baseball team, track team, soccer team and tennis team all called Warinanco Park, which is located in the Town of Roselle, our home field. As it is, Warinanco Park is probably the most familiar athletic site in our baseball playing lives. Most of us had spent many a summer playing in the County Youth leagues, which take place in this park. The American Legion baseball team, on which a lot of us play, call this park its home field.

This is an open field. The closed fields of all the other High Schools are fenced in and have a big cage behind home plate. I personally think that it takes a somewhat higher level of discipline to play on this field. Errant throws, wild pitches, or passed balls are not going to be stopped by some big cage. Here the ball can roll 50 feet to a back stop, or something hit into the outfield can roll forever, until stopped. Most of us had played in this environment for a long time, so we did have the home field advantage when other teams came to play.

Last season we had a mediocre team. But, this year we were looking forward to a successful season, because most of us played on the local American Legion team that won he county and state sectional championships last summer.

The American Legion team is composed of players from all the Elizabeth area high schools, public, private and parochial. Whereas most of the other Legion teams in the county and maybe in the state are really local high school teams wearing a different uniform.

Our Legion coach is a man named "Buzzy Fox." The Buzzer, as we call him behind his back, has spent almost all of his life, with the exception of a period with the Marines in the battle of Okinawa during the War, as a baseball, basketball player, or coach at just about every level of the game that you can imagine.

By contrast, our high school coach, Abner West, didn't have the playing experience the Buzzer had. But, he was a student of the game and had an academic approach in his coaching style. Using his connections to college coaches and professional players, Mr,. West sought and brought back the answers to help each of us, individually, improve our technical skills.

Our growth as players, the result of the combined tutelage of these men, was beginning to be manifest in our performance on the field. We had devastated Roselle and Roselle Park in a couple of pre-season scrimmage games. This looked like our year and we felt confident going into our season opener against Columbia High School.

The Gods of baseball did not favor us in this first game. It was more like a soccer game than a baseball game. Whatever could go wrong went wrong. We had more earned runs than Columbia, but they had more runs period - all unearned. I was the starting pitcher, so I got credit for the loss. So much for a perfect season.

The second game against Hillside wasn't any better. I wasn't credited with the loss, but again the ball was kicked around like a soccer game. Games three and four were much the same way and I was credited with the 5 to 1 loss against Irvington, a team against whom I had pitched a perfect 1 to 0 no-hit game in last season's American Legion Tournament...

We had lost four games in a row and our next game was against Union, a perennial power and one of our arch rivals. I had been the winning pitcher in the Union County American Legion championship game against Union last summer, so I'm sure they were out for revenge. We were really depressed and needed something to spark us into turning this season around. A win over Union would go a long way to revive our lagging spirits.

The game was almost a replay of the first four games of the season. I wasn't hit hard, but errors came at the most inopportune times. The lead see-sawed back and forth; until we were tied 5 to 5 in the fifth inning. Union had a runner on second base with two outs in the bottom of the fifth. I wanted to get the third out in this inning so bad I could taste it. I got two strikes on the batter at the plate. He popped the next pitch foul right over near the Union on deck circle. As our catcher, Jack Hudson, ran over to get under the ball, the player in the on deck circle stuck out a bat and tripped him. Jack fell, but he was still under the ball. I ran over to make the catch and someone threw dirt in my face. I missed the ball, but landed a left to the jaw of the guy who threw the dirt.

The Union bench erupted and came charging at me.

I didn't know, who was who and I punched at the first person in a maroon hat who tried to grab me. Later I learned that I had punched one of the Union coaches in the nose. My Jefferson team mates, those in the field and on the bench, had come to my rescue and a wild donnybrook ensued.

After the umpires and whoever else helped to restored order and, calm the riot; both teams were sent to their respective benches. Our Coach, Abner West was the only person left sitting on our bench during the melee. The umpires then decided to throw two people from each team out of the game and resume play. Whittey Possenreide and Ralph Oriscello, a kid from our JV team, who was just standing behind the bench watching, were ejected. The real culprits were still in the game and I threw a third strike past the batter.

"That is the first time this season you guys have acted like a team." The Coach remarked when we came off the field.

We didn't beat Union. The game ended in a 5 to 5 tie. For us it was like a win. At least it wasn't a loss.

I was the pitcher in our first win a few days later. I pitched a no-hit, no run game against Perth Amboy. Before the season came to an end, I ended up with seven straight wins in our team's total of 16 victories. It turned out to be a pretty good season.

A girl I knew from Junior High School asked me to take her to the Battin High Junior Prom. Well really, Don, a class mate of mine, was seeing a girl, who I also knew in Junior High School and the other girl was her friend. Don was really the intermediary who asked me. It would be like a double date and I had the car. Hey, why not.

Ronnie wanted me to go to the Jefferson Hugh Junior prom too. He knew a girl who had a friend. Of course I had a car. I was in demand. But, one Prom was enough. Especially when I found out what the costs were.

A store on the corner of Elizabeth Avenue and Bridge Street rented tuxedos. For $12.00 they supplied jacket, pants, shinny black shoes and a funny shirt like thing that had a bow tie attached to it. I had to spend $2.50 for a wrist corsage for the girl and then we were expected to take the girls someplace after the Prom for something to eat.

I had known this girl, Joanne, since the seventh grade. She is a nice girl, but I was never socially involved with her, or any other girl for that matter.

A week before the Prom, Don and I met with these two girls, over pizza at Spirito's Restaurant to discuss the plans for Prom night.

Spirito's is located in the Peterstown section of Elizabeth. It is unofficially the official Italian restaurant of Elizabeth. The restaurant is really the back room of a bar, or at least it started that way. Nothing fancy here. The walls are lined with booths and tables fill the center of the room. Somewhere back in time the owners developed patience for the high school patrons and the place has been crowded ever since. This is my first time at Spirito's. Without knowing it, Don,

Anne, Joanne and I are continuing the tradition by becoming another generation of first daters or Prom goers to frequent Spirito's.

The only thing Joanne and I had in common was the years we spent together in class at Roosevelt Junior High School. I don't think we ever said more than 10 words to each other over that three year period.

She is a good looking girl and I am pleased that she thought to ask me, or have Don ask me to her Prom. I don't know how these girls went through the selection process and whether I was the first or last selection. I was probably at the top of the list, only because I had a car.

"Joanne, I have a problem with going to the Prom." I said. And then after seeing the look of surprise and dejection on the faces of those at the table, I realized my words had conveyed the wrong message. "What I mean to say is ... my problem with the Prom is that I can't dance."

"IS THAT All?" she laughingly responded as the color returned to her face. "Don't worry about that. I'll have the whole Prom to teach you."

The rest of the evening was filled with light talk about the color of flowers and the logistics of getting to and from the Prom. This is a big deal. The event of a lifetime for these girls.

The Prom may be a big deal for the girls. But it is a bigger deal for my mother.

"Who is this girl? Do I know her mother? Where do they live? How long have you known her? When am I going to see her?" The questions came at me like a barrage.

"He gets a car and the next thing he's takin' some strange girl we don't even know to a prom." My mother would lament to anyone within earshot.

"Why don't you go with some girl whose mother I know?"

"Ma, I'm not marryin' this girl. I'm only going to her school prom. She invited me."

"Why don't you invite some girl whose mother I know to your school Prom?"

"I don't know any girls whose mother you know. And I'm only going to this one Prom."

I had almost reached the point of canceling this whole Prom deal. But, then I thought about the disappointment I would cause. I could handle my mother easier. Fortunately I had a picture of my Junior high School graduating class and I showed Joanne's picture to my mother.

Satisfied that Joanne was a Caucasian, my mother's parting remark was. "Well I still would like to meet her."

"Maybe you would like to get a gown and come to the Prom with us." I facetiously answered.

"Wouldn't it shock you if I said yes?" And then she left in a huff.

Going to a girl's house to pick her up and then having to meet her parents scared the wits out of me. I imagined all kinds of things. After all this mother and father had to trust the well being of their daughter to some galoot like me. I wouldn't even trust me.

Surprisingly, her parents were most cordial and put me at ease. She really was pretty in her crinoline gown and Hollywood hair-do. They took a few snapshots of us, mostly of her: I was just an accessory, like the wrist corsage. After the photo session, we departed to pick up the other couple. Don was already at Anne's house when we arrived and I was introduced to her parents. They also were very cordial and after a short conversation, we left for the High School Gym in the well scrubbed Chevy.

The girls had to introduce the boys to the receiving line of teachers as we entered the decorated Gym.

"This is my escort, Richard," was the way Joanne introduced me to her teachers and friends. I was comfortable with that and it was interesting to see how regal girls become when they let others know that they have their own squire.

True to her word, Joanne spent the evening trying to teach me to dance. Periodically we would break for cookies and punch and some small talk with some class mate. But, for the most part she kept me occupied. Some of the guys there were real good dancers and I felt a little bad for her in having to spend so much time with a person with two left feet.

When the Prom ended, we took the girls to a place called "Phil's" out on Route 22 in Scotch Plains. It was a non-alcoholic night club that catered to teenagers. They had a limited menu of hamburgers and such, along with ice cream and sodas. The place had dance floor and juke box music. It also wasn't expensive.

We ate something, danced to the juke box and made small talk around the table. We didn't discuss anything profound. Most of the talk concerned our summer plans and our excitement about our senior year in high school. It was an enjoyable informal time.

During the course of the evening I mentioned that my family was moving to Clark Township at the close of the school year.

"You won't be attending Jeff next year, then?" Don asked

"I don't know. The coach is trying to work something out between my parents and the Board of Education, because I might be ineligible to play at another high school. I'd like to stay where I'm at."

When the little party ended, everyone climbed wearily into the Chevy and we started back to Elizabeth. I dropped Don and Anne off at her house and then continued on to Joanne's house.

"I had a wonderful time." She said. "I know you're going to have a very busy summer playing baseball and working. I hope we can keep in touch."

"I will call you. I want to get a copy of the Prom pictures to show my mother."

"Oh, good. Call me anytime."

I escorted her to her door, and said good night. I made sure she was safely inside before I returned to the Chevy.

I had always thought girls were more sophisticated, or experienced in this dating thing. It always looked like everything just came natural to them and they were comfortable with it. But, then I thought that she was probably just as scared and nervous as me … and that this was her first date too.

I was picked for first team All-County honors in the Elizabeth Journal, Newark News and the Newark Star-Ledger. My team mate Ronnie got picked for the Elizabeth Journal first team and third team in the Newark News. I also was a third team selection on the All-State team. Ronnie had to carry my glove again for the American Legion season that started as soon as the High School season ended.

Our team started the Legion season where we had stopped the High School season. The team was unbeatable in county play. My friend Ronnie was always alerting me to the professional baseball scouts in attendance at each game.

"They're watchin'. They're interested in us. We do good this year and next year. We'll get signed. Big money. Come on Lefty. Throw strikes."

After winning our second county Championship in as many seasons, we were invited to play an exhibition series up in Massachusetts as a tune up prior to the New Jersey State Tournament. The games were to be played on Friday evening in Amesbury, Massachusetts and on Saturday afternoon in Haverhill. It was a nice deviation from our normal routine of games and practice. The host American Legion Post up there had even arranged a beach party for us at Salisbury Beach. The beach party interested us more than the games, since we had little deviation from baseball since March.

I was busy the week preceding the trip. This was the last week of school. Each day I came home and loaded whatever my mother had ready into the Chevy and drove out to the house in Clark. The big pieces of furniture would be brought out on Saturday. I wouldn't be home on Saturday, so it was my job to put the things in the places she had designated. She had everything planned right down to where the linens went in the closets. I was also going to work full time in the car lot this summer and I would start there Monday. Our baseball games were usually started at 6 o'clock, so work really wouldn't interfere with playing, except if we had to travel far or leave on a Friday, like this week. The bosses at the lot didn't mind and they even encouraged me.

# THE SOJOURNERS
## Life on the American Homefront During World War II

Gramp volunteered to loan me his Pontiac woody station wagon for the trip. I left the '37 Chevy for his use. Friday morning we were part of a six car caravan, led by Jim Devine's red Packard that left from the Argonne Post Clubhouse on West Grand Street. I carried all the teams equipment plus four players, not including me. Ronnie had commandeered the front passenger seat and acted like I was his chauffer. I didn't mind. We were off on a carefree, no pressure weekend. Life was good and we had the cat by the tail.

Amesbury, Massachusetts is north of Boston, almost in New Hampshire. It was a good thing we left early enough. It took almost eight hours to get up there, which barely gave us enough time to get dressed and go to the ball field. We brought food and drinks with us, but we stopped several times along the way to shake our legs and empty our bladders.

The local American Legion Post had sandwiches and fried chicken for us when we arrived. They also had canvas Army cots setup for us in the big meeting room. We barely had time to down some chicken and a few sandwiches before leaving for the field.

A pretty good crowd had gathered by the time we reached the ball park. Somebody had really touted our team as one full of all-stars. I hated such publicity. It was easier to look like a fool than an all-star and a baseball game is liable to go either way on any given day.

Buzzy planned to give the reserve players some playing time on this trip. It was a good opportunity for them and it gave the first team players some rest before the opening round of the State Tournament next week.

When the public address announcer gave the player introductions I thought he made a mistake and announced my name as the starting pitcher for Amesbury. He didn't. The opposing pitcher has the same exact name as me, the difference is, he is right handed and I'm left handed. Also this boy is French Canadian and doesn't speak a word of English.

It was a close game. But, the reserve players pretty much carried the game. I only pitched one inning and some of the other players were spotted into the game just to make things interesting. It was a fun game for us, not the usual pressure.

People came down out of the stands after the final out to talk to us and ask questions about our home town and the environment were we live and play. A very short Catholic Priest came up to me and introduced himself.

"My name is Father Bergeron. What is the name of your grandmother, your father's mother?"

After I told him my grandmother's maiden name and where she came from, He said;

"I am your cousin; many times removed of course. Your grandmother's grandmother was a Bergeron, the same as me. The family was split apart many years ago and you are from the part we call Acadian, La Louisian."

"I know my father had told me that at one point in his life he had been taught by French Catholic Nuns. I don't know where it was, but I'll sure tell him I met you. How about the boy on the other team who has the same name as me? Are we related?"

"No. That boy's family name has been changed from the French to be the same as yours.

Your family name comes from the English. This I know. That is how I know you, Reechard."

The little Priest then laid his hand on my forehead and prayed in French.

I could see my riders waiting impatiently for me to be through with the Priest so we could go to the beach party. After a few more words the Priest and I shook hands and bade our farewells.

"What was that all about?" Ronnie asked.

"Ron. You won't believe me if I tell you that that Priest and I are related and it goes back almost two hundred years."

"Aw! Get out!"

"Like I said. You won't believe me."

Ronnie was a little dumbfounded by my statements, but his mind quickly shifted to the beach party. "Come on! Lefty! Let's get to the Post, so we can get changed for the party."

The American Legion Post did have a small locker room with a shower down by their bowling alley in the basement. I'll bet Ronnie had scouted this out before we went to the ball field, because as soon as we got inside the Legion building he made a beeline for the basement with his towel and clean underwear. None of us knew where he was going. I followed him down into the basement and made the discovery for myself.

"Hurry up Lefty. Get your stuff and get down here before anyone else finds this place."

"I don't have to hurry, Ron. Remember, I'm drivin'. Everybody has to wait on me."

Eventually, much to Ronnie's consternation, we all got showered and dressed for the party. The entire group left in a procession, now led by one of the local Legion members. We couldn't have left early, even if we wanted to. I had no idea where we were going. I just followed the pack.

About 15 minutes later the caravan pulled into the yard of a house nestled among some sand dunes. After we emerged from the station wagon, Ronnie just stood in the yard with a look on his face, like he had just died and went to heaven.

A micro second later, I heard the music and the female voices. Now I understood the reason for Ronnie's semi-comatose condition.

"Come on Ron! Let's get in an' get some of those girls before they're all gone." I said to snap him out of the starry eyed trance.

Right now, I was more interested in the smell of burnt beef, wafting up in a smokey haze from the opposite side of the building.

Ronnie charged off in the direction of the music and I went off in the direction of the beef smoke.

He didn't know it, but it looked like all the girls were out back; around the Barbeque pit.

At this moment their interests were probably similar to mine - Food. And there was plenty of it set out on a table under a canopy along the back wall of the house.

All of the other guys must have gone into the house, because I was all alone when I entered the rear yard. Alone that is, except for all these girls, who surrounded the cook busily at work at the grill.

"Reechard!" The cook, my new found cousin the Priest, hollered. "Come eat."

He then turned and said something to the girls standing by his side and immediately two dark haired beauties came over and took me by the arm to a table nearby where we all sat down. Two more girls arrived with plates and silver ware. The girls all introduced themselves.

"We know who you are. Richard. The Father's Acadian cousin." Cooed the dark eyed girl, named Peggy. "Come on, let's eat" she said taking both my hand and my plate.

Together, the four girls and I filled our plates at the long table. By the time we returned to our table, Father Bergeron had arrived with a platter of hamburgers.

As we were getting reseated, the rest of the team came out the house and into the yard with Ronnie in the lead.

When he saw me seated with the four girls, the look of astonishment on his face was priceless. It was so spontaneous and perfectly timed. The look was something Hollywood would have paid money to see.

"How did you get all these girls?" He whispered to me after he had recovered.

"I didn't. The girls got me.'

"I still don't understand how that happened."

"My cousin." I answered, pointing to Father Bergeron over at the grill.

"Oh yeah! And, I suppose all these girls are your cousins too."

"Are you girls my cousins?" I asked the cute young things adorning my table.

The girls played their part to perfection and gathered in close, putting their arms around me. Then in sultry voices that drove Ronnie crazy, they said. "Oh, yes. He's our cousin and we won't let him get away."

Finally, I introduced Ronnie to the girls and that made him happy.

Apparently, Father Bergeron and the parents of these girls had come down from the French speaking Provinces of Canada. For what ever reason; they settled in this area. Two of the girls, Peggy and Emily were cousins. Not my cousins, for which I was grateful. They wouldn't let me out of their sight for a minute. Both catered to me and kept me company all while we were at the beach house.

"Would you like to go up to the Beach?" Peggy proposed. "We can walk."

"Sure. You just lead the way."

Without anyone noticing, the two girls and I slipped away from the party and began walking to the beach. I really didn't know what their expectations were. But, in my mind I could visualize the three of us cavorting in the surf on some isolated beach. My visions of this scene were shortly dashed as we approached the brightly lighted amusement area of the beach. The place was crowded with vacationers and it had an area that had carnival rides and games of chance.

As we proceeded along this midway we came to a booth where a man was trying to entice people to throw baseballs at dishes, cups and saucers mounted up on wooden racks at the price of three balls for 25 cents.

"Oh, come on Richard. You can do that" Begged Peggy.

I had a girl on each arm and both were tugging me towards the dish game. I fished in my pocket for a quarter and handed it over to the pitch man. He handed me three well worn baseballs.

In rapid succession I hurled the three balls and three dishes exploded. The pitch man gave me a coupon and said. "Care to try again?"

Emily squealed. "Do it again for me."

Not to be accused of partiality, I gave the coupon to Peggy and another quarter to the pitch man.

Again I threw the three balls and three more dishes exploded. The man gave me another coupon, which I gave to Emily.

"Here. Go again." Came the voice of a man standing behind me, where a small crowd started to gather. I turned to see an arm holding out a quarter, which I took and gave to the pitch man for three more balls.

Again. Three throws, three blown up dishes and another coupon, which I handed to my sponsor, the man with the quarter.

I later learned that these coupons were given out at all the stands and people collected them until they had enough to redeem the prize they wanted. That is why a crowd was forming behind me and people were pressing forth with their quarters.

Peggy and Emily were collecting the quarters and passing back the coupons as I kept disintegrating the crockery.

It wasn't long before the pitch man was trying to move around in a booth that was full, almost up to his knees, in broken dishes, cups and saucers. "I have to close up now folks. Come back tomorrow."

What he meant was... It was time for me to leave.

The girls and I saw the rest of the sights on the midway and then we returned to the party.

Except for our Business Manager, Jim Devine, Ronnie and a few people from the Amesbury Post, everyone had left the party and the rest of the team had returned to the Post.

"Where the devil have you been? We have been waiting for you forever. We have a game tomorrow, or don't you remember?" Jim harshly scolded me, lighting up his red Irish face.

"The girls and I were having a fun and I lost all track of time."

"I'll bet you did. You and Ronnie get back to the Post and go to bed. Tom here will see that the girls get home."

"Good night Richard. We'll see you tomorrow at the game in Haverhill." Peggy said blowing a kiss.

Jim Devine was faking his wrath. "Never mind this stuff." He sternly said to me with a quick wink of his eye that gave away his true tempermant.

Ronnie was going crazy. He had a million questions. "Where did you go with those girls? What did you do? How did you handle two girls?" He went on and on.

"Ron" I answered. "It was just a typical double header."

I thought he was going to beat the wooden doors of the station wagon to a pulp with his fists. "I had to stay here all night with the chaperones while you're out skinny dippin' or something with two girls. Not just one girl. Two girls. It isn't fair."

"I had nothing to do with it. They asked me. I was only being polite."

Ronnie could not be calmed no matter what I said and he even woke up the next morning with the same thoughts on his mind.

We were treated to breakfast at a local diner type restaurant. Our team's co-sponsor, Hersh Motors, the Ford dealer in Elizabeth picked up the tab. The only thing Ronnie had on his mind was girls. Our Coach had girls on his mind too. But, for a different reason. He wanted our attention on baseball, not girls. Right now I wasn't too high on his popularity list because of last night's escapade. It seemed like everybody was treating me like some mad rapist, when all I did was break a bunch of dishes.

"Are all the girls coming to the game in Haverhill?" Ronnie continually asked.

"I don't know. I only heard Peggy say that she would see me at the game in Haverhill."

"Can you find out for sure?"

"How? I don't know where they live. Besides, Buzzy doesn't want me riding all over creation with all the team equipment in my car. Maybe they'll come by the Post while were waiting to make the drive to Haverhill."

"I know. You're acting like you don't care, so you can have all of these girls to yourself. I'll bet you got something already cooked up you crafty lefthander. Crafty lefthander, that's what the newspapers call you. They should add the word, Slick."

We had to go back to the Post and put our cots and things away. While we were playing over in Haverhill, the Ladies Auxiliary was going to set the room up for a banquet supper honoring us and the Amesbury and Haverhill teams.

I was inside the building and Ronnie had gone to sit outside by the Post's cannon. The next thing I knew, he came charging back inside.

"Lefty, Lefty. I gotta talk to ya outside. Quick, come on outside. I have to show you something."

When we got out of earshot of Buzzy, he said. "They're here. The Girls are here. They want to talk to you. See if you can set up something for after the game."

"Like what? We're goin' to have banquet dinner here at five o'clock"

"Maybe after the dinner. See what you can do."

"Alright! Alright! Put your tongue back in your mouth and let me see what they want to do."

Emily was driving the '47 Ford. Of course I knew Peggy and had met two of the other girls in the car. She introduced me to two more girls, who I don't remember seeing at last night's party. We talked about our schedule for today, including the five o'clock banquet. They said they would see me at the game. In the meantime they would try to figure out something for this evening. Before they left, I introduced Ronnie to the girls, especially the two new girls. That made him happy.

Haverhill is about a 10 mile drive from where we are staying. Our game was scheduled for 2 o'clock. Buzzy wanted to get over to the field around noon, so we could have a good workout. He really wanted to keep us under control.

Today's game was almost a repeat of yesterday's game at Amesbury. The reserves did most of the playing. Ronnie played 4 innings at third base before yielding to a reserve player. I was put in for two innings. I think Buzzy wanted me to flounder before my newly created fan club. But, that didn't happen. I went through the Haverhill line up like I was breaking dishes.

"We can meet you guys over at the Post around 7:30. We know a good place to go swimming. How does that sound?" Peggy asked.

"That sounds real good. How many of us are going?"

"We can fit six girls in our car. You pick out four or five guys to bring in your car and then we'll see who rides with who."

Ronnie went out of his mind when I told him of the plans. He had a grin on his face like the Cheshire cat for the rest of the afternoon.

The banquet dinner was nice. Naturally, in addition to the food, we had some speeches where everybody patted everybody else on the back. The people did do a good job and they were very hospitable. We can't deny that. Personally, I wanted to thank whoever made arrangements for those girls to be at the party. I think that was sheer genius.

The dinner didn't last much beyond 7 o'clock. The guys on the other teams wanted to be off doing their normal Saturday night things. A few people, including the two colored boys on the team, hung around to play pool and darts. Some of our guys were going to take in a movie. But, before any of us had left for the evening, Buzzy made the announcement that there would be a bed check at 10.00 P.M. I don't know how he planned to punish any violators. He wanted everybody in so we all could have an early breakfast and then attend a Non-denominational Church service, which he said was sorely needed by some, before heading back to New Jersey.

Ronnie and I recruited our catcher, Eddie and Right fielder Jay to join the swimming party. True to their word the girls arrived at 7:30. I followed their Ford until it pulled off about a mile from the Post. Jay and Eddie went into the girl's car. Emily and Peggy climbed in beside me in the front of the woody wagon. And Yvonne sat in the back with Ronnie.

I followed the Ford on some back roads and over hill and dale until finally it pulled into a clearing off some road out in the country. The girls quickly stripped to their bathing suits, which they wore under their street clothes and raced across the road. They climbed over a pipe guard rail and jumped into the water below. We followed along right behind them.

If any body had developed any warm adventurous feelings that they wanted to share with any of these girls, the cold water of this creek quickly froze their libido, short circuiting those urges. We swam around for a short while. It didn't seem to bother the girls, but it was just too cold for us.

After the swim we ended up at a roadside Drive In where I saw and tasted fried onion rings for the first time in my life. We danced to some juke box music and made small talk until it was time for us to return to the Post.

There were a few hugs and squeezes and then as we watched the tail lights of the Ford vanished down the road, we knew the night was over and the precious moments were now just memories.

By tomorrow evening we would be back in our world, several hundred miles to the south, ready to return to reality...

*R. Allen Pender*

When we went for breakfast Sunday morning, everybody wanted to look at the local newspaper and see if our game had gotten any press. Instead, interest in us was replaced by an event that had occurred halfway around the world; around the time we were out with the girls... the Army of North Korea had invaded South Korea.

South Korea is supported militarily by the United States. This is a small place near China.

People are always fighting over there. It didn't seem like anything for us to worry about.

This little War would probably be over in a week. We put the news of the day aside and expressed our disappointment on not receiving any press coverage.

After the short prayer service at the post, the caravan started for home.

Ronnie kept reliving the week-end on the trip home. He sure made it sound like I had a wild time.

I didn't try to correct him, or argue the point. I let him think what he wanted to think.

The ride home was long and hot. We had to stop in Rhode Island for lunch and gas. I was taught in school that Rhode Island was the smallest State in the Union. I don't think they measured it the same way we were driving across it. I didn't think we were ever going to get out of Rhode Island, but we finally did. Connecticut was just as bad.

We all were pretty weary by the time we rolled across the George Washington Bridge into New Jersey.

Suddenly everyone in the car was revived. It must have been some sort of a homing instinct, or the smell of the fresh New Jersey industrial air that snapped them back from their malaise.

We were all in high spirits, laughing and joking about the week end. The world was our oyster and we were ready to take on all comers in the State Tournament, which would start for us this coming week in East Orange.

It was about 5 P.M., when the caravan pulled up to the Legion Post on West Grand Street in Elizabeth. Some people were waiting for their sons. After unloading my passengers and receiving our schedule for the coming week, I headed for my new home in Clark Township.

## CHAPTER 40

## HIGH JINX ON THE ROAD

My mother was happy that I got home with my grandfather's station wagon in one piece.

"I was worried all weekend, that you would wreck his car somewhere. That is a long trip for a driver like you without any experience."

"Did the Police call you, Ma?"

"No. Should they have?"

"Only if I was in wreck or in trouble. You don't have to worry unless they call you and then the time for worrying is over."

"You're incorrigible ... and, I still think you're too young to be runnin' all over the country."

I told my mother and father all about the trip. I told them about our new cousin, the Priest, and the French boy, who had the same name as me. I didn't tell them anything about the girls. My mother's imagination would put Ronnie's to shame. I didn't want to open a can full of worms and have a set to with her, like we did over the Prom.

My father did remember the name Bergeron and knew it was on my grandmother's side of the family. They had originally settled in Nova Scotia and some of them were later exiled to Louisiana. He didn't know how this was all tied together since it was so long ago. I'm sure the Priest knew. In hindsight, I probably should have talked to him a little longer to find out. Instead, I was more interested in partying.

The move to Clark on Saturday must have gone well, because the house looked like we had lived there forever.

On Monday morning, it was business as usual. I was back at the car lot and had a day off from baseball. Tomorrow evening and Wednesday we would have practice. A best of three game series in East Orange would start Thursday evening.

Over the course of the next few weeks we blew through the competition. East Orange, West New York and Philipsburg fell to us in rapid succession. None of the three game series had to go to the third game. Richie Jones a hard throwing right handed pitcher and I held the opposing teams to a total of four runs in our march to the State Championship series against Brooklawn of Camden County.

The local sports writers were having a field day with our exploits and to read their articles, one would get the impressions that were the greatest things to come along since sliced bread.

I believe the spark behind all the publicity is our Manager, Jim Devine. He used to work for the Elizabeth Journal and now is in the public relations business. I think I am right, because a lot of what I have heard him say out at the games has ended up in print. Not that publicity is bad; it has brought people out to the ball park. But, it also can be embarrassing. I'm just a plain kid. I don't want people looking at me as some sort of an athletic freak.

My father is really the one suffering the abuse. He works in the Composing Room of the Elizabeth Journal. Each time a story about our team is run, it is usually accompanied by individual pictures of me and Ritchie Jones. For fun, my father's co-workers have switched the names under each picture and plastered the proofs around the shop. I am left handed and Richie is right handed, but the major difference and the source of the joke is that Richie is colored. It amused the guys in the shop. After a while, my father learned to roll with it.

I was always worried that the opposing team would read our press and then shove it down our throats. After traveling down to South Jersey, that is about what happened. It was a low scoring close game and we lost. Richie relieved me in the fifth inning with us trailing by one run. The Coach wanted me to get some rest, so I could start the next day's game. Our team never made up the deficit and we lost our first game of the season.

After the shock wore off, Eddie, our catcher, Ronnie and I were taken out for a nice steak dinner by Eddie's father, who had come down to see the game. It was a great morale booster.

We stayed in Cundy's Motel in Westville, near the Delaware River. Between the noise of the frogs and some cutting up by our two young batboys, it is amazing that we got any sleep.

We battled back the next two days in a couple of hard fought contests. When the final out was recorded, we were the State Champions by five runs. Mentally and physically we were exhausted and we had a week to recover before heading for the Middle Atlantic finals in Bristol, Connecticut.

I skipped practice Tuesday and Wednesday to go up to the camp with my grandparents.

I fished and swam and enjoyed some of my grandmother's good cooking. I missed a big photo session on Wednesday. But, by Thursday I felt rejuvenated and ready to play again.

Friday afternoon we boarded a chartered bus for the trip to Bristol, Connecticut to meet the championship teams from New York, Connecticut, and Rhode Island. At least this time I didn't have to drive.

This is a single elimination tournament, meaning one loss and you are out. On Saturday at noon we were to play Manchester, Connecticut. The winner of this game would play the winner of the Schenectady, NY- Pawtucket, Rhode Island game under the lights at 8 P.M. for the championship.

## THE SOJOURNERS
### Life on the American Homefront During World War II

Late Friday afternoon our bus arrived at the Endee Inn in Bristol. All the teams in the tournament are staying at this hotel. Our entourage was billeted on the third floor, except for Ronnie and me. We each had separate rooms on the fourth floor. The hotel elevator only went to the third floor and a security guard, in the person of a large tough looking matron, who we nick named "Big Bertha", had been posted at the stairway. She knew who had to go up to the fourth floor and when they had to come down. Anything else, she had the authority to apprehend the culprits.

Buzz y was taking this precaution, because Ronnie and I were the two most likely individuals to sneak off and get into mischief. He probably was conditioned by my Massachusetts escapade.

After supper, we walked around town some, had ice cream and then went to our rooms, like good little boys.

We had a nice big breakfast the next morning, after which we headed out to the ball park to get familiar with the surroundings and have a work out before our noon time game.

Muzzy field is one of those old time minor league baseball parks. It isn't run down or anything. As a matter of fact it is in excEileent shape. The architectural style is old fashioned with a covered grandstand that wraps around the field from midway down the right field line to midway down the left field line. A six foot high solid fence surrounds the outfield. Evergreen trees grow on the opposite side of the outfield fence, shielding the field from the possibility of off site diversions. Each team had a covered dugout and ours was on the third base side of the field.

I always made it a part of my routine to pitch a round of batting practice at every pre-game session, even on days when I was going to be the starting pitcher. Today was no exception. In my mind this effort gave me the opportunity to see how I physically felt on a strange pitchers mound and the impact the situation had on my control and selection of pitches. Today's situation provided us with plenty of time to workout and then return to the hotel to shower; have a light lunch and dress for the game.

Today, for some reason I was well relaxed and not a bit apprehensive about my unknown opponents. The surroundings, the other team, the attitude of my own team, the pressure or the importance of this game, none of these things; nothing intimidated me today.

With the exception of a couple of games, this season has been one of low scoring games where the victories have been gained by a one run margin. This was not to be the case today. Our team drew blood in the first inning and continued the assault throughout the game. The next thing I knew it was the sixth inning and we were leading 9 to 1. I had given up one run on two hits back in the third inning and since that time no opposing batter had reached first base.

I couldn't do anything wrong. I either struck out the opposing batters or they harmlessly tapped ground balls to the infield. Therefore, I was kind of surprised when with two out, none on in the bottom of the sixth, Ronnie called time out and came running over for a conference at the mound.

"Hey, Lefty" He blurted. "See those two girls in the stands, two rows up from the dugout. They want to know if we want to meet them after the game."

"How do you know that?" I sharply answered, annoyed that my rhythm had been interrupted.

"They've been sending notes down to the bat boy."

"OK, we'll meet them. I don't know what we can do, because we have a game tonight and we don't have a car."

"I'll send a message back saying that we'll talk to them after the game." With that said, he bounced back to his position at third base.

Right now we had three innings to go and that was foremost on my mind. We scored two more runs and I kept the home team off the bases for the next three innings. The score was 11 to 1. We had won the right to play the final game tonight.

The girls were waiting at the gate and with Buzzy trying to quickly shepherd us onto the team bus, Ronnie was just barely able to tell them to meet us at the Inn in one hour.

"We have, at most, three or four free hours this afternoon and no car. What are you thinking, Ron?" I asked, as I sat down next to him on the bus.

"After we get dressed, we can meet them outside the Hotel. Maybe they got a car."

"I guess we'll just have to play it by ear and see what they're like."

This afternoon was no problem. It was at night that the security guard could give us trouble... and, only if we tried to come back into the hotel after the curfew. We needed a route to circumvent the guard, just in case we hit it off with these girls.

After I showered and dressed, I set out on a reconnaissance mission to explore the fourth floor. There had to be a way to breech the hotel's security...And I was determined to find it.

Satisfied that I had solved the problem, I marched back down the hall towards Ronnie's room. As I approached, he was just coming out of the door.

"Why the big smile on your face? What are you up to?"

"Come on." I said "let's go down to the second floor."

"Why the second floor?"

"I want to check something out. I think I know a way we can get around that lady."

Ronnie followed me and the two of us went down the stairs to the third floor. We took the elevator to the first floor. Exiting from the elevator we walked down the corridor to the stairs and then walked back up to the second floor.

"What are we doing?" He impatiently asked.

"You'll see in a minute." I said leading him down the second floor corridor.

At the end of the corridor I opened a window. "OK. There it is. Come on." I said, reversing course back towards the elevator. "Let's go meet the girls."

"There it is? There what is?" Ronnie asked in apparent confusion.

"I'll tell you when we get outside." I answered in a manner designed to protect the secrecy of this mission.

"Look around this side of the building." I said to Ronnie; once we were out on the sidewalk. "There it is. The fire escape."

"The fire escape! You want us to climb four floors up the side of this building?"

"No. Only two floors. We go out the window on the fourth floor and climb down to the window on the second floor. Coming back, we go out the second floor window and climb up to the fourth floor."

"It sounds kinda risky."

"It'll be dark. No one will see us."

"That's just it. It'll be dark and dangerous."

"Well, are these girls worth the risk? You gotta figure that out."

My experience so far with New England girls has led me to conclude that they are punctual. These two girls were not to be the exception. Irene and Cynthia were right on time; the only problem is that it is already 3 o'clock in the afternoon and we have to go to dinner with our team at 5 o'clock.

Maybe it's a cultural thing, but girls down home seem to be kept locked up and they aren't as forward, nor do they roam around free, like the girls up here. I have to admit that it is a pleasant difference. But, right now one that needs getting used to. The girls didn't have a car, so we walked. They showed us around the town of Bristol and we stopped for an ice cream soda.

Ronnie and Irene had started to become a pair. First he was holding her hand. Then in the ice cream parlor, he had his arm around her. By the time we had finished our walk and were approaching the hotel, Ronnie was a case of raging hormones.

"I hafta see her after tonight's game. Are you gonna help me?"

"The game isn't goin' ta' be over 'till around 10 o'clock. Are you willin' to climb down the fire escape, in the dark for just a short time with this girl?"

"Yeah! Yeah! And you gotta help me. Because you owe me one from Massachusetts."

"How do I owe you one from Massachusetts?"

"Because it's your fault we have curfews and bed checks and whatever else."

"Alright. I'll come with you. But, not because I have to see any girl. I just like climbing up and down buildings in the middle of the night."

In the night game, Richie pitched a one hit shutout against Pawtucket, winning 6 to 0. Next week we would travel to Pittsfield, Massachusetts to play in the Eastern U.S. Finals. A win there would propel us into the U.S. championship series in Miami, Florida.

Buzzy was so happy, he decided to relax the curfew until 11 o'clock. It was a good thing, because by the time we got back to the hotel, it was well after 10 o'clock.

Just to make it look good and to provide a little deception, Ronnie and I got some snacks down in the lobby before going up to our room. We told everyone, that we were tired and that we were going to have some snacks and go to bed.

Instead we got up to our rooms, showered and changed clothes in about 10 minutes.

"We've got to be very quiet." I cautioned him as I climbed out of the window onto the steel fire escape frame. Slowly and silently I climbed down to the third floor. I waited for Ronnie to catch up and then I proceeded down to the second floor.

Once there, I looked through the window to make sure the corridor was empty. I eased the window open and crawled inside. Ronnie followed behind me and we headed for the stair well. We quickly descended the stairs and went out the open side door. The first phase of the plan worked. We were outside the hotel and the girls were waiting across the street.

Irene and Cynthia had seen us go out the fourth floor window and come down the fire escape. Ronnie and Irene greeted each other like long lost lovers that had been separated for a long time by the ravages of war or something else. Cynthia's mind was on the same page as mine. She was hungry. She and I led the way to an all night diner that she knew about.

Ronnie and Irene stayed behind us and every once and a while along the way, they stopped for a quick smootch. Cynthia and I went into the diner and took a booth. Ronnie and Irene went into the vacant telephone booth along the side of the diner.

After I gave our food orders to the waitress, I asked Cynthia. "Is my friend safe with Irene? I don't want him to get in any trouble."

"Are you kidding? She's just a big tease. She'll lead him on and drive him crazy and then she'll drop him like a hot potato. Tomorrow she won't even remember his name. This is her hobby. I've seen her do it lots of times."

"I sure hope he realizes that. We won't be here after tomorrow morning, so I hope he doesn't think he got somethin' goin' here."

From where I was sitting, I could look straight at the front door of the diner. Cynthia must have wondered what was wrong with me when I almost fell into my coke.

"Big Bertha", the security guard walked into the diner.

Evidently, she was a regular here. Because, the waitress behind the counter greeted her by name. "How are you tonight, Sharon? How come you're in so early?"

From where we were seated Cynthia and I could over hear every word of their conversation.

"I was supposed to work until 12, but they let me go at 10. The Connecticut team went home this afternoon and the night game ended at 10. I guess they figure everybody is too tired to cause trouble."

"Who won the games?" the waitress asked.

"The New Jersey team. They say that they just tore everyone up. We were tipped off that they had some troublemakers. But, I think they just got tired out and went to bed."

Cynthia leaned over and whispered to me. "You didn't have to climb down the fire escape."

"Don't tell Ronnie. Make like you don't know anything. We're going to go back the same way."

She shriveled her shoulders and covered her mouth to conceal a laugh. "You are bad. But, I'm going to watch you guys climb back up the fire escape."

"OK. I'll wave to you when we reach the top."

Finally, Ronnie and Irene came into the diner. He passed right by "Big Bertha" and never knew she was there. Cynthia kept giving me coy smiles. She was excited about her part in the secret that we both shared. She was a good sport and didn't let the cat out of the bag.

Ronnie wasn't too interested in eating. He ordered cokes for him and Irene. I think he was just taking a break to wet his lips and he wanted to get back outside in the dark with Irene.

Cynthia and I remained seated, enjoying our food and making small talk, after Irene and Ronnie ran back outside to re-convene their meeting in the telephone booth.

I don't know where the time went, but something made me look up at the clock on the diner wall. It was almost 12:30.

"Are you girls allowed to stay out this late, unescorted?" I asked Cynthia. I was afraid that we might get in trouble for keeping them from going home.

"No there's no problem. Our parents know where we are right now."

"They do?"

"Irene's father is the Police Chief. We have the whole police force watching out for us."

Was I ever glad that Ronnie was with Irene and not me? I had a good laugh over the whole situation...and then I suggested to Cynthia that the hour was getting late and the party should break up. She agreed. We paid our bill and we went outside to pry Ronnie and Irene out of the phone booth.

He was reluctant to leave. "Ron, I'm tired. I want to go to bed. You can stay out if you want. But, you'll have to climb the fire escape by yourself."

That made him change his mind. "Alright, let's walk back slow."

I was chuckling to myself all the way back to the hotel. Every so often I would turn around to look for a police car. Instead, I would see Ronnie trying to grope Irene and that made me laugh all the more. Cynthia was laughing too. She knew what was making me laugh. The only one who didn't know what was going on was Ronnie.

We walked up on the dark side of the street across from the hotel. I was very polite and said good-night to the girls and wished them well. Ronnie was hanging back.

Finally, I had to say, "Ronnie, say good night Irene. We have to get up that fire escape."

With that, I left the group and headed across the street towards the side door of the hotel. Ronnie was only a few steps behind.

Once inside, we made our way up to the second floor.

"Come on, Ron." I whispered, after peeking out of the stair well door to make sure the corridor was empty.

Silently, we made our way down to the other end of the corridor and opened the window to the fire escape. After getting out on the steel landing, I shut the window and started the climb up to the fourth floor. Once there, I opened the window and had Ron go in ahead of me. I turned and looked down and across the street. I could see the girls taking in the whole scene. I waved to them and they waved back. Just as I was doing that, a police car turned the corner and slowly drove down to where the girls were standing.

Ronnie stuck his head back out of the window just in time to take in the scene below. "Oh, My God. The cops are gonna pick them up."

"Don't worry about it." I cautioned

"What do you mean with the 'Don't worry about it'? They could be in trouble." He excitedly replied.

"No, they're not. It's her father. He's the Police Chief. They're goin' ta' get a ride home."

"Who told you that?"

"Cynthia."

"You mean they've been watchin' us all the time! Why didn't you tell me?"

"I didn't know the number of that phone booth where you were hanging out... Come on, get inside. Before some one sees us."

"What else do you know that you're not telling me?"

"Not a thing, Ron. Not a thing."

The next morning after breakfast we loaded our things onto the bus for the trip home.

Before we left Buzzy and Jim Devine called for our attention. Standing up in the front of the bus, Buzzy was the first one to address the group. "We had two good games. Our hitting finally came through for us and our pitchers could relax a little, which I'm sure they appreciated. We will have practice Tuesday, Wednesday and Thursday, at the Park. Our normal time, 6 o'clock. Friday we will meet at the Post at 12 noon to take the bus to Pittsfield. Eat lunch, or bring stuff to eat, if you want to. It will probably be a long trip. We should be there before supper. Now Jimmy wants to say a few things."

"This was a great week-end guys. We are proud of the way you played and proud of the way you behaved. There were a lot of Legion Officers around this week-end and they had nothing but positive comments about your play and behavior. That is the reason the Tournament officials decided to lift the curfew and suspend the security chaperones. We want to thank everybody for not causing any embarrassment."

I knew who Jimmy meant with the comments about not causing embarrassment. He was looking straight at me.

Ronnie then poked me in the side. "Did you know about them suspending the security?"

"No. Do you think I would be climbing up and down the side of a building for the fun of it?"

Ronnie went back into his fantasy world with Irene. I relaxed and enjoyed the trip home.

The practice sessions this week were really press conferences, interviews and photo opportunities. Not my favorite things. I was glad when noon Friday arrived and we got on the bus.

We got into Pittsfield around supper time and the first thing we did was go to eat. After supper we checked in to the Hotel Berkshire. Ronnie and I were assigned to a corner room on the third floor. After getting settled, we met up with some of the other guys and walked around the business district of Pittsfield. As was our habit, we wound up at an ice cream parlor.

There would be only two games this week-end. Both on Saturday. In the afternoon, the New England Champion is to play the Chesapeake Champion …and then we are to play the winner Saturday night under the lights. Each team has been assigned a time for a morning practice session. After that the field is off limits, except for the games.

After a team meeting in the hallway, Ronnie and I returned to our room in order to prepare for bed.

I was laying on the bed reading about myself in the local paper, which gave the Tournament a big spread. Ronnie was in the bathroom getting ready to take a shower, when all of a sudden I heard all kinds of screaming and Ronnie ran out of the bathroom in his shorts.

"There are girls in the bathroom." He blurted.

"Why would there be girls in our bathroom?" I said, getting off the bed to investigate the situation.

Sure enough. There was a girl in our bathroom. It was also their bathroom. Our room and theirs shared a common bathroom, which meant that certain courtesies or precautions were required to deal with the situation. Simply, when using the bathroom, the opposite room door had to be locked from the bathroom side. Common courtesy also applied so one party wouldn't lock the other out of the bathroom. We agreed to knock on the door before attempting to enter the bath room and they would do the same.

These girls were really ladies. They were about 21 years old. We could tell, because they smoked. They were part of a crowd that came from Milford, Massachusetts to see tomorrow's games. We had no sooner gotten the bathroom situation under control, when Buzzy opened the door to make his bed check. I could see his point. We really shouldn't be partying tonight with an important game tomorrow.

At practice the next morning, I learned that I would be the starting pitcher tonight. I tried to forget about that for the rest of the day. We just hung around all day. There wasn't anything to do, but rest. Later on, in the afternoon, we learned that we would be playing the Massachusetts Champion. They had defeated the team from Washington, DC. Even though we all were staying in the same hotel, the people on the other teams were like phantoms. Because of the scheduling, none of us ever saw each other.

We went out for an early supper. After which we suited up and went to the ball park.

It was a little after 6 o'clock when we got to the stadium. The lights were already on, despite the fact that we still had plenty of sunlight. The game would start at 8 P.M., right around sundown. Last week was our first night game. All of our other games had been played in daylight. This was the first time I was going to pitch under the lights and I didn't know what to expect. The quality of the lights can make a big difference in the game.

I had pitched some batting practice here this morning and I was pretty comfortable with the surroundings. However, I wasn't prepared for what started to occur the closer we got to game time. People, droves of people carrying signs and banners started filing into the ball park. Then a high school marching band, in uniform came in and filled the area behind the screen in the home plate section. When it was time for the opening ceremonies, Wahconah Stadium was filled to over flowing. Spectators were even lined up inside the playing area, along the right and left field foul lines.

We didn't score in the top of the first inning. As I walked out to the pitchers mound to take my warm-up tosses for the home half of that inning, that high school band greeted me with a din so loud that I couldn't hear myself think.

Ronnie ran over from his third base position to talk to me. "Are you scared?"

"No I'm only scared of the batters. I hope that drum and bugle bothers them as much as it does me."

On each pitch the band would start up and the drum would boom and the crowd would holler if the umpire called a ball. The only way I could quiet this crowd down was to throw strikes and that's what I did for five innings.

We had scored one run in the third inning and I was protecting that lead going into the sixth inning of this nine inning game. So far I was averaging at least one strike out an inning and no balls had been hit to the outfield. I had been keeping the ball down. I threw an assortment of curve balls, sinkers and cut fast balls that tailed in and down. As a result, anything they hit was down on the ground. A few of these grounders had been beat out for infield hits, but so far nobody had gotten into scoring position. I wasn't going to try to overpower these guys. Working the ball in and out down around the knees was doing the job, so I wanted to keep it that way.

With one out in the bottom of the sixth, our shortstop bobbled one of those ground balls, putting a runner on first base. I walked the next batter after going to a 3 and 2 count. For the first time in the game they had a runner in scoring position and our one run lead was in jeopardy. I threw two balls to the next batter. Before I could step back up on the mound,. Buzzy called "time "and walked out onto the field. He raised his right arm to signal for Richie, who had been warming up on and off, almost the whole game.

I turned the ball over to him and walked off the field to the rousing applause and cheers of the crowd and the beat of the drum, which kept time with my steps. My attitude at this time was such that I didn't know if was jeering or cheering... and whether they appreciated my performance, or they were happy that I got pulled.

Richie inherited a 2 ball count on the batter at the plate. His first pitch was drilled out off the right field wall, scoring the two runners on base. A series of several more hits ran the score to 5 to 1 before their side was retired to end the inning.

There is a fundamental law that governs baseball; one team is going to win and one team is going to lose. I guess that other team didn't read about us in the newspaper, or maybe they did and it inspired them to shove it down ourrthroat. We got a few more runs and so did they. But, we didn't win the trip to Miami; we were three runs shy.

We were a somber group that boarded the bus for the trip back to the hotel.

Later at the hotel I was sought out by some members of the winning team, including the opposing pitcher.

"We knew we were going to win it once they took you out." My left handed opponent, Ralph Lumenti stated. "Our guys were frustrated. They couldn't get the bat on anything you threw. No matter what the box score says, you didn't lose that game."

It was a nice compliment. But, it didn't get me a ticket to Miami. They wanted me to come with them to a team party across the state line in New York. They were going to have beer, food and girls. I was tempted, because right now I was in the doldrums. But, knowing the mood of our team and our leaders, I thought it best to decline. This game would just about complete my tenure on this team. Ronnie and I along with a few others would be starting our senior year in high school very soon. Next season we would be moving on.

Everybody on our team was licking their wounds. They were trying to play the game over in their minds. Some even blamed the Coach for taking me out and putting in Richie. Did he know what was going to happen? He's a human being, not a fortune teller. He played the averages. It worked before. I've replaced Richie and he has replaced me. Two different styles can upset the opposition's timing. When it comes down to a single game, you go with everything you got. Just like tonight, except it didn't work. There were a million "what ifs." But, not a single one of those "Ifs" could get us another run or change the final score. That's baseball.

Ronnie and I finally retreated to our room. We noticed that the bathroom door was open.

Ronnie entered and saw the girl's door open. They were having a little party. Ronnie came back out and invited me into the girl's room. They had some snacks and some liquor, which they were willing to share.

These two girls are the older sisters of a couple of players on the other team. They fixed us drinks and we sat around talking some about them and about the game. After the third drink it was suggested that we pair up and use the two rooms. Ronnie stayed in the girls' room and I returned with one of the girls to our room. She and I were sitting on the bed sipping highballs.

Suddenly the room door opened and Buzzy stuck in his head. He looked at the girl and me lounging on the bed. For a second, I could see that he didn't know what to say. Finally, he blurted, "You better not be smoking in here" and slammed the door. We laughed hysterically, but if there were any hot thoughts that had the potential to become a fire in this room tonight, his visit extinguished them. The night was over.

# CHAPTER 41

# A NEW ADVENTURE

My parents, Coach West and the Board of Education made an arrangement whereby I could finish my last year at Jefferson. I had my car, so I could drive to school every day. After school I still worked in the car lot. So other than having a different place to eat and sleep, I really hadn't left town.

The senior year in high school is sort of anti-climatic. After years of anticipation, here it is. The next ten months will be spent trying to determine what we are going to do with the rest of our lives. Or, at least people will be trying to help us determine that. The reality of the situation is quite simple. With the uncertainty of the "Police Action" in Korea, the French involved in a civil war in Indo-China, the Jews and Arabs having daily confrontations, and the Russians ready to start an Atomic War, the world right now does not seem like a career oriented place. I can only see where two options exist. The first option is to get into a college and get a deferment. The second option is to either join, or be drafted into the service. There really isn't any middle ground unless you have a disability.

We have people in our class who have no experience at anything. They are making up their minds to go into college and have selected fields where they have no idea in the world what the work entails. Ronnie is like that.

We sit together in English class. One day he asked me, "Lefty, what are you gonna be when you get out of high school?"

"I'm probably still going to be me. Why?"

"No! I mean what professional field are you going to enter?"

"I don't know. What about you?"

"I'm going to be a chemical engineer."

"Is that right? What does a chemical engineer do?"

"He works with chemicals and I like chemistry."

"You've had chemistry class for two weeks and all of a sudden you're gonna be a chemical engineer."

"Yeah, that's right."

"OK. We'll see."

"Well, that's better than what you are going to be."

"What am I going to be that isn't as good as what you are going to be?"

"I don't know, because you don't even know."

"Right. We'll just have to wait 'till I get there, where ever it is and then we can argue."

Ronnie started the year off by trying to put me on the spot with our English teacher, Mrs. Hall. I think he was trying to get back at me for some of the tricks I played this summer.

Mrs. Hall is a tall gray haired lady. Her hair is swept up and tied in a bun on top of her head. She is a pleasant lady and looks and acts like she would be well suited for the part of a fairy godmother, or a good witch in a Judy Garland movie. She has all those mannerisms.

We started the year off studying the works of American poets and authors. A good number of these people came from Massachusetts. Ronnie saw this as an opening to make me the brunt of a joke.

"Mrs. Hall!" Ronnie asked, with a few minutes left in the period.

"Yes Ronald."

"Richard", he said pointing at me. "Played baseball up in Massachusetts all summer and he told me he visited John Greenleaf Whittier's house and Nathaniel Hawthorn's house and Ralph Waldo Emerson's house.

"Oh how wonderful. I'm so glad young men are taking an interest in the cultural things that these travels can offer. Could you tell the class a little bit about these homes, Richard?"

"That Ronnie thinks he has me on the spot" I thought to myself. "I have to turn the tables on this one."

"It would probably take me quite a while to give the class all the details of my visits. But, essentially these are very old homes. When I was there, they were working on John Greenleaf Whittier's house. His house is surrounded by these huge old trees, with big green leaves, Sugar Maples. Squirrels were jumping from these trees to the roof of the house and had done a lot of damage. They didn't let people inside because of all the work going on. It was a little different when I went to Ralph Waldo Emerson's house. They had just finished painting the house. Some lady dressed up in Colonial clothes wouldn't let us sit on any of the furniture. She showed us some of Ralph's clothes. Unfortunately because they were old and didn't get to the cleaners on time, they had some moth holes in them."

"Oh, this sounds so exciting. Did you get a chance to go to Thoreau's cabin on Walden Pond while you were in that area?"

"Oh, yes. I saw his cabin. It's still there, a cabin by the pond. I even went swimming in Walden Pond."

"RRRRRRiiiiiinnnng" The bell sounded ending the English class period.

Saved by the bell.

"I'll tell you some more some other time Mrs. Hall." I said as I hurriedly left the classroom. I hoped that her memory might not be good enough to remember.

Ronnie was waiting out in the hallway for me. "Walden Pond. You went swimming in Walden Pond. Where did you get the idea to go swimming in Walden Pond?"

"Don't you remember, I went over there when you went to take Ralph Waldo Emerson's clothes to the cleaners, or were you getting the squirrels out of John Greenleaf Whittier's attic that day? Why did you tell that woman that stuff? I was never within 50 miles of those places."

"Oh, yes you were. Remember that creek that you were swimming in with the girls? The one near Amesbury? I saw the sign. You parked that station wagon right next to John Greenleaf Whittier's driveway."

"Wow! ...I was right. There are some big trees by his house. Maybe I should tell Mrs. Hall that we were skinny dippin' with some girls in old John Green Leaf's pond. That might get her excited."

I have to give credit where credit is due. Ronnie is a good student. He is conscientious and concerned with getting good grades. I am in the academic program too, but I'm not as concerned as he is. I'm interested in cars and the outdoors. Academic stuff bores me. I do just enough to get by.

Ronnie is also wired into the social life of the school. I play baseball and that is about it.

Most of my interests are outside of school. Whereas school and school work are his things.

One day I got him back for the trick he tried to play on me with Mrs. Hall. It wasn't even planned. It was spontaneous and that is what made it so good.

Mrs. Hall had given us an assignment. We were to write an essay about some unique aspect of American life.

"Have you got your essay ready, Lefty?" Ronnie asked as we sat down at the double desk in Mrs. Hall's English Class.

"What essay?" I responded.

"We had to write an essay about some aspect of American life. I was up until 3 o'clock this morning working on it. I better get a good mark. You didn't do it?"

"I guess I forgot, or I was doing something else."

I could see Ronnie was little annoyed by my cavalier attitude.

After attendance was taken, Mrs. Hall went directly to the assignment and started calling on members of the class to read their work. After three people read their essays and the class made comments, she turned and looked at me with her whimsical smile.

"Richard, let the class hear what you have written."

First Ronnie cringed. Then there was a look of shock and surprise on his face as I stood with a sheet of paper full of doodles and began to make like I was reading from it. On the spot I made up a story about my grandfather's friend, the "Mountaineer Moonshiner," and one of our trips to his well.

From her countenance, I could see she was enjoying the story and it convinced me more than ever that she probably drank something other than tea.

"What a wonderful story and so well written." Mrs. Hall commented when I finished.

"Richard, would you do me a great favor and rewrite that in your best handwriting and give it to me next week. I want to enter that essay in the Columbia University Literary Contest. Everyone else, please drop your papers off on my desk when you leave the classroom."

Ronnie was waiting for me out in the hall. He was livid.

"I stay up to 3 o'clock in the morning and she doesn't even look at my essay. You stand up with nothing and make up a story. Now she wants to send the story you haven't even written into a contest. It's not fair. I should tell her you're a faker."

"OK…and I'll tell everybody that you were so hard up, that you had to climb down a fire escape just to kiss a girl in a phone booth."

He didn't say anything.

Ronnie cooled off quickly, although he never forgot the incident. He would make comments about it every once and while …and he wasn't real happy when I did get a Honorable Mention prize in the literary contest. Hey, it wasn't my fault that he stayed up until 3 o'clock in the morning.

We had Gym class every day. Almost all the boys, who were on athletic teams had seventh period gym class. Those on teams were excused from gym during their team's season. It is a good thing. For example, in baseball season it gave us that extra forty- five minutes a day to travel up to the Park for practice, or to travel out of town for a game. The same applied to all the other sports.

Some of us had extra perks.

Since I was selected All-County and All-State, I didn't take Gym at all. During the fall and winter sports season, I manned the Gym office during the seventh period and handed out basketballs and towels. Because I had a car, I also qualified for another activity which supported the Athletic Department and gave me the opportunity to get sprung from school.

Mr. Webie was responsible for getting tickets or ticket money from whatever other high school was going to our opposition in either a football or basketball game. He didn't have a car, so each year he banked on recruiting some senior to be the runner. I didn't mind. I could get out of school for a while, stop for a soda or a hot dog and just goof off in general. When I was late for another class, the Athletic Department gave me a pass and none of the other teachers questioned it.

My boss at the car lot gave me a case of latex monkeys. All the guys in school wanted a monkey after they saw them hanging in my car. I gave out about half of the case. The rest of the monkeys were compressed and packed into the open box sitting on my back car seat.

One afternoon, Mr. Webie asked me to drive him to Roselle Park high School.

"Do you know where Park Avenue is?" He asked while getting seated in the front.

"Right off Elmora Avenue on the other side of Westfield Avenue."

"Yes. We'll take that to Galloping Hill Road and then I'll show you where to turn for the High School."

Once we were seated, I left Scott Place, in front of Jefferson and headed up Elizabeth Avenue towards Elmora Avenue.

Park Avenue is a residential street with large 1920's vintage houses. The street itself is cobblestone. On this particular day, due to a recent rain, the cobble stones are wet and covered with falling leaves; an ideal situation for some automotive gymnastics.

"Hey, Mr. Webie. Do you want to go for a little spin?"

"Why. Do you know another way?"

"Oh, Yeah! Hang onto your seat and watch this."

Quicky, I down shifted into first, hit the brakes, cut the wheels to the left and punched the gas. The car went into a lazy 360 degree spin. I pulled it out just as it was about to complete one revolution and then I continued on straight down the street like nothing had happened,

"WHAT IN GOD'S NAME ARE YOU DOING?" The white haired gentleman bellowed. "You could get us killed."

"Don't worry. I had it under control. I do this all the time."

"Are you learning to be some sort of a stunt daredevil?" Mr. Webie asked once he got comfortable again in his seat. "I guess when you say spin. You really mean spin."

For the remainder of the trip to Roselle Park, I enthralled Mr. Webie with stories of my automotive exploits. I wanted him to feel confident in my ability to drive the car. I could see that he was quite impressed by the way his eyebrows were lifted almost to the top of his forehead.

Just before we got to Roselle Park High School we had to cross some railroad tracks at a grade crossing. I made a mental note of its location, because it was an ideal type of crossing. The road was ramped up on each side of the single track, an ideal jump situation.

It only took a few minutes for us to conclude the business at the high school and to start our return trip. I could see the grade crossing coming up. It was about a block away when I warned Mr. Webie to hang onto his seat.

"Are we going to spin again?"

"Oh, no." I answered. "This is going to be better."

At what I gauged to be the appropriate distance, I began my run at the grade crossing and the car made an almost effortless leap across the railroad track. The car bounced some on the landing which wasn't too bad considering the age of the car's suspension system. The impact was not as forgiving on the case of monkeys, which was bounced up against the headliner and then slammed back down on the rear seat.

Originally, there were 144 monkeys in the case. I gave out about 30, so a little over 100 remained in the case. The impact jarred the tightly packed monkeys loose and they started to fill up with air and come out of the box.

The incessant squeaking of the moneys, caused by the air rushing into their latex bodies, alarmed Mr. Webie more than the jump. "THE CAR IS FULL OF RATS!" He hollered, after turning to see the activity going on in the back seat. "Pull over quick!"

I obliged. But by then, the disturbance in the back seat had subsided. There were monkeys everywhere and I grabbed one.

"Here, Mr. Webie. It's not a rat. Just a toy monkey."

"By, God, those things looked like they were alive." He said taking the monkey from my hand. "I don't know who is crazier, you …or me for riding with you?"

I thought I was going to get some kind of lecture. Instead, Mr. Webie must have thought about the silliness of the situation, because he began to squeeze the monkey and laugh all the way back to school.

"How was your trip Fred?" Coach West asked when we got back to the Gym office.

"Abner, Let me tell you, it was an experience and more fun than a barrel of monkeys. And, I mean that literally."

I don't know if Mr. Webie ever told anyone about the incident, but I made all the future trips by myself.

Although they didn't know it, The State of New Jersey was building a playground just for me, right in back of my house.

Construction had begun on the Garden State Parkway. A swath of land had been cleared from Centennial Avenue in Cranford to the Lincoln Highway in Woodbridge. Work had also started on a series of over passes and bridges to accommodate local roads, including a bridge across the "Rezy", as the reservoir is known to locals.

A dirt roadbed had been scraped out in the areas between the bridge and overpass construction. These areas became our playground. Right now we had easy access to a mile of dirt roadway from Centennial Ave to the where the bridge was being built over Walnut Avenue.

Robert drove a War surplus Jeep, which his father had at their Westfield gas station. With its four wheel drive, the Jeep could climb over the dirt barriers and gain access to the roadway after dark. We started out by driving up and down the dirt roadway armed with .410 shotguns. The area is loaded with game, particularly rabbits and pheasants. We used the headlights of the Jeep to frame the quarry after they had been startled by the Jeep. The open vehicle provided us with a comfortable shooting platform. The Police can't drive their radio cars onto the roadway without doing damage. There are a couple of places where they can get in close enough to train their spotlights on the road. Once a spotlight is sighted, the lights are put out on the Jeep and we exit the roadway through one of the soil barriers.

Right now the quality of the dirt roadbed is smooth enough for cars. The construction people have built a little yard at the end of New York Avenue, one street over from where I live. From this yard an access road leads out the roadway. Until they find out we're using it; it is a simple thing to drive cars out onto the highway bed.

The road is being built with one northbound roadway and one southbound roadway. A wide grass and treed median separates the North and South bound lanes. To make their jobs easier, the construction people have cut various temporary access drives through the median in order to get equipment from one roadway to the other. These access drives have become the turns for our race track.

With straightaways of about 3/4 of a mile each and the wide turns across the median, the total racing area has to be close to 2 miles.

On most evenings, three or four cars come out to race. But, on Sunday, when the construction workers are off, the place looks like the Indianapolis Motor Speedway for kids. Even though what we were doing is illegal, the kids do have a lot of discipline and obey the track rules, which are simple enough. Go south, turn left, go north, turn left and don't hit someone else's car. So far the police haven't tried to crackdown on us. But, I bet they're watching. I know other people who are.

If Mr. Webie thought the spin on Park Avenue was something, he should ride with me out here. I know that I am pegging the speedometer on the Chevy coming down the straightaway before I broadslide through the turns. This ride would make his white hair whiter.

Our school had some social events during the year. But, I didn't go to any of them. Joanne invited me to a couple of events at her school and I went. They were casual dress affairs, no tuxedos. We went out a few more times over the course of the year for pizza or to somebody's birthday party and that was about it. I am working to save up money for the upcoming baseball season, when I can't work after school. Right now, I really can't keep a steady social calendar. Anyway, I like to do things spontaneously and don't like commitments to hinder my agenda. The summer baseball season did that and I started to resent it. I enjoy fishing in the summer and hunting during the fall and winter. I missed a lot of fishing during the past summer and it bothered me, particularly now that I have a car and can go whenever I have free time. Because I am working, I can only grab a few snatches of time to get out into the woods to hunt. I have made this my priority until we start some indoor baseball training in January.

Fall quickly dissolved into winter. The high school football season ended and the basketball season began. Between the basketball games on Friday night at the Armory and shopping night on Thursday, Broad Street Elizabeth is a busy place. The centers of teen-age activity in the Broad Street area are the Regent Sweet Shoppe, next to the Regent Theatre and Pamel's, further up Broad Street on the other side of East Jersey Street.

I always tried to park the car along Broad Street between the two sweet shops. That way Ronnie and I could monitor the activity at either place and quickly have a car available just in case we met some girls in need of transportation.

Despite wearing varsity sweaters during our parade from one sweet shop to the other, Ronnie and I were not very successful in attracting members of the opposite sex.

"For a change, Ron." I suggested. "Let's go out and make like we're not interested in meeting any girls and see how that works."

"That sounds crazy." He replied.

"Well it sure beats freezing to death. Walking up and down Broad Street with just a sweater on can get us pneumonia. People probably are looking at us and saying, 'look at those two jerks. They're gonna freeze to death.'"

"Alright, we'll try it your way this week"

"Ok. Thursday we'll ignore all the girls. We won't pay any attention to them."

On Thursday night, after parking the car, Ron and I strolled into Pamel's and seated our selves in a booth. Ron sat on the rear seat of the booth, facing the front door and I sat on the opposite side facing the rear of the store. After giving the waitress our order for a couple of milkshakes, Ron said. "This is a good seat. I can see all the girls who come in."

"Yeah. But, remember. We have to ignore 'em." I replied while looking over his left shoulder at a booth towards the rear where three girls were seated.

Two girls were facing me and one girl had her back to me. They were obviously talking about us, because the girl, who had her back to me, made a point of rising up and turning around like she was trying to see something at the front door. I could see the other two girls trying to catch my eye with a wide variety of movements and giggles as they swished their spoons and straws around in their ice cream sodas. But I was ignoring them real good.

"It is really dead in here tonight." Ronnie commented. "Let's finish our drinks and go up to the Regent. All the girls are probably up there."

"Ok. You lead." I answered.

With that, he slid out of his seat and started towards the front door. I followed suit and gave a little wave to the girls in the rear booth. They very coyly answered with a subdued smile and a wiggle of their fingers.

The Regent Sweet Shop was a little more crowded, but Ron and I found a booth. However, this time I sat facing the front door and he sat where he could survey the activity in the other booths.

"Just look, Ron. Remember, you have to ignore all the girls, so that they know they are being ignored. That's the secret of gettin' them to notice you."

"It sounds crazy. I don't know where you got this advice."

"Look, how long have we been paradin' up and down Broad Street?"

"All winter."

"And, what kind of success have we had?"

"None."

"Alright. We've had no success. If we ignore the girls and don't meet any, we will be successful. If we meet girls, when we're ignoring them, we will be unsuccessful. Can you follow that thinking?"

"No. And, you sound confused saying it."

"You just wait and see. I'll bet it works."

The waitress brought over our milkshakes and as she was setting them down on the table, I glanced up to see the three girls from Pamel's coming in the door. They stood up front for a minute surveying the scene, or looking for a booth. A blond haired girl, the smallest of the three pointed over towards our direction and they started to come our way.

I hadn't told Ronnie about the girls in the booth at Pamel's, or the fact that they were now coming in our direction. I was prepared as they approached, but Ronnie was oblivious to the situation and was quite surprised when he heard the female voice honing in over his right shoulder.

"Hi guys." The little blonde chirped. "We know who you are. Have you guys been ignoring us?"

"You know us?" Ronnie answered with a start and eyes big as saucers.

"Of course. We've been watching you guys play baseball for the American Legion Baseball team for the last two years. We live right by the park. We came to all the games."

I could see Ronnie's ego inflating. Then he asked the blonde doing the talking, "You came out just to see us play?"

"Well, not really." She said, sticking a pin in his balloon. "My grandfather belongs to the Legion Post. He is on the committee and we live in the house right behind the field."

Being the gentlemen that we are, we invited the girls to share our booth. I was quite relieved when they only wanted Cherry Cokes, because they had already filled up on ice cream at Pamel's.

The girls all live in Roselle and they come to Broad Street every so often. Most of the time they hang out at a sweet shop on Elmora Avenue. After introductions, we sat around with our drinks and talked about all the kinds of meaningless things that mean so much to teenagers.

The girls were quite interested to hear that I lived in Clark Township, not far from Roselle. The fact that I had to drive through their town twice a day offered some interesting possibilities. We exchanged all the important contact information and naturally I volunteered to drive them home. This was a problem for Ronnie, who lives in North Elizabeth.

"Wait a minute." He said to me. "You are going to drop me off at my house and then you and three girls are going to Roselle. Are you a bigamist or something? Remember, you were out with those two girls in Massachusetts while I had to sit around with those old guys from the Legion. You owe me Lefty. You owe me big."

I relented, even though it meant more driving for me. "That girl's grandfather knows us," I said in a manner meant to caution. "No phone booth stuff with any of these girls. Not tonight."

Ronnie agreed and we delivered our passengers without blemish to their doorsteps.

"You know, Lefty." Ronnie philosophically waxed on the trip back to Elizabeth. "I figured you were crazy. In fact, I know you are crazy. But, that ignoring stuff really works. We have to do more of it. What do you think, were we successful or unsuccessful tonight?"

"Well, we can't even successfully ignore girls." I sarcastically replied.

The beginning of January meant that March and the baseball season weren't far behind.

This year we wanted the best season ever...and Ronnie and I started working out at the Elizabeth YMCA in the evenings. Coach West even made some arrangements for me to go up to the Summit YMCA, where Bob Hooper, a pitcher for Cleveland and Yogi Berra, the Yankee catcher worked out. Mr. Hooper gave me instructions on how to throw an overhand curve ball. He was taught by Hall of Fame Pitcher, Bob Feller, who it is rumored cost the Cleveland Indians a lot of money to be taught by a third man. Whatever the case, I got some of the benefit of that knowledge.

Last year in high school and later during the summer in the Legion Tournament, a lot of baseball scouts were following our progress. Baseball isn't a money making sport for colleges, like football and basketball. Scholarships for baseball are almost unheard of. Ronnie felt our goal should be to impress the professional scouts, who might have connections into some big name colleges. I disagreed.

This is our last Hurrah in high school and we wanted it to be noteworthy.

Before the season began there was pressure on me to improve from last year, when I was named to the All-County first Team and the All-State Team. The newspapers played up our team and all the individual exploits of last season. In reading the newspapers, one would get the impression that we were playing at a level far above high school. This is a hard image to sustain. I was already somewhat jaded by the disappointment I suffered after the final game of the Legion Tournament last summer. I always liked the underdog position; no one expects the under dog to win. When he does, it is a cause celebre'. The favorite on the other hand, is a target for everyone to dethrone. I knew, this season, that I was going to face the best every opposing team had to offer. They are going to be gunning for me.

Any thoughts I may have had about perusing a professional baseball career were pretty much dashed after the Legion tournament. The fun was gone. It became all pressure and disappointment. The pressure is still on, but I'm going to ignore it and have fun.

I approached Spring training with the enthusiasm of a sophomore, who wants to play the game just for the fun of it, rather than using it as a Springboard to something else.

Last year the early Spring was wet and cold, but this year the weather was warmer and drier. With good weather, we were able to take full advantage of our outdoor training in preparation for the opening game in the first week of April.

The girls from Roselle, usually accompanied by a big collie dog, came to watch us work out on a regular basis. We had more girls from Roselle watching us, than girls from Elizabeth. Ronnie is the social secretary and he arranged for our meetings with them. It is a logistical nightmare, complicated by my living in Clark Township and Ronnie in North Elizabeth… Our rendezvous consisted mostly of ice cream sodas on Elmora Avenue and hot dogs, or hamburgers up at the Galloping Hill Inn in Union.

One night for a change, we went to Walt's 42nd Street Bar and Grill on Saint Georges Avenue in Linden, near the Rahway line. Inside of Walt's is a real long bar and next to it is a grill with drive up windows, where they have foot long hot dogs for 20 cents. O'Keefe's Golf Driving Range is next to Walt's and it really lights up the area at night.

I pulled the Chevy into Walt's stone and cinder parking area, on the side of the building by O'Keefe's driving range. After the car was parked, we all walked up to the open outside window and placed our orders.

In short order, the lady behind the window placed our tray with five hot dogs and five Cokes on the counter outside the window. Being the gentlemen that we are, Ronnie and I served the girls. All of us then retired to seats on the running board and fenders of the car to talk and enjoy the feast.

At some point during our repast, I told the girls the story of Mr. Webie and the monkeys.

"You didn't really do that? Did you?" Janet, the little blonde blurted, her eyes becoming as large as streetlights and then quickly closing to a skeptical questioning squint.

"Yeah, I did." I replied without hesitation. Then I proceeded to regale my captive audience with tales of my automotive exploits. The girls seemed to be enthralled with my stories about racing on the unfinished Parkway and the account of my racing debut at Linden Airport. Ronnie, usually the center of attention, was being ignored as the girls hung onto my every word. Finally, he had enough and sought to get back into the limelight.

"I'll bet half of that stuff is made up. Nobody can do those kinds of tricks with a car."

"Is that right." I answered. "Everybody, get off the car and go stand by the building. I'll show you something."

With puzzled looks on their faces, the gang walked over to the building while I climbed into the driver's seat.

The car was facing the building and I wanted to do a reverse 90 degree turn in place so the car ended up facing Saint Georges Avenue. I did this many times and the cinder and stone parking area here at Walt's was a good surface on which to perform the maneuver.

With my passengers out of harms way, I confidently shifted into reverse, cut the wheels, mashed the gas and let out the clutch. The front of the car began a twist to the left and suddenly then there was a loud "Bang." The car jumped and stopped moving. I tried to shift into first gear, but the car still wouldn't move.

Ronnie ran over and hollered through the open window, "You hit the fire hydrant!"

I shut the engine off and then noticed when I opened the door, that the rear of the car was way up in the air and the rear wheels were a couple of inches off the ground.

Three two inch pipes had been planted in the ground around the fire hydrant to protect it from traffic. One of the pipes was bent over and the Chevy rode right up the pipe until the rear bumper got caught on the end of the pipe. The car didn't hit the hydrant, but it was hanging over it.

"That was some trick. What is your next trick?" The feisty Janet commented

"The next trick," I answered. "Is to get this car off this pipe or everybody will be walking home."

I had a bumper jack in the car, but this thing was up too high. I needed to put something under the rear wheels and then have some kind of blocking on which to place the bumper jack to lift the bumper over the pipe. Once that was done, I could slide the car back down the pipe. Looking around, I saw some railroad ties stacked up down along the side of O'Keefe's Driving Range. O'Keefe used the ties as parking bumpers. I guess these were extras.

"Come on, Ron!" I hollered. "Give me a hand carrying some of those railroad ties over here."

He wasn't too happy with the situation, but he had no choice, unless he wanted to walk back to Elizabeth. The girls were much better. While they couldn't help us physically, they did lend moral support and serve as extra eyes when we located the ties under the car. I actually constructed a ramp of railroad ties under the car. The final phase required jacking up the bumper until it just cleared the pipe, at which point the car would have to be moved forward about an inch to be free. With that done, I warned the group.

"Everybody out of the way!" I comanded, while climbing back into the car. "I'm going to drive it off that jack."

I didn't have to move the car far for the jack to kick out. After that, the girls clapped loudly and the Chevy rolled down the railroad tie ramp. We restacked the railroad ties along O'Keefe's property and left the scene.

The girls couldn't be quiet on the way back. For them the experience was great fun. They laughed and made jokes, mostly at me. "What is your next trick in the car going to be? Can we come along for the ride?" They sang continually in a sin-song fashion and then laughed hysterically. It didn't bother me, because I guess it was funny to see.

Ronnie and I wanted this to be a memorable baseball season. I doubt that the girls will remember any of our games. But, I'll bet they will never forget the night the Chevy got stuck on the fire hydrant at Walt's 42nd Street Bar and Grill.

Unlike past seasons, when we lost our first three or four games, this year we came out winning from the start. If anybody tried to write a script for this season, they would have a hard time duplicating what really happened.

In our season opener, we finally beat Columbia High School 6 to 5. The first time in history that Jefferson had accomplished that feat. From that point, we went on to a streak, where only one run was allowed in eight games. We shut out the powerful Montclair High School in both ends of a double header, something that never happened to them.

The newspapers were having a field day reporting our achievements, which continually increased the level of expectation and made me feel like I was living in a fishbowl. Richie Jones and I both pitched no-hit games and a few one hit games. Ray Smith, another junior, joined the rotation and had considerable success. As a team we had 23 wins and two losses going into the final game of the season against Regional High School in Springfield. I didn't start the game, but I probably should have been given credit for the loss.

The game was scheduled for Saturday at 12 o'clock. The previous Saturday we played at 1 o'clock. I had all the equipment in my car and that Saturday morning George and I decided to do some fishing in the Clark Reservoir before the game. For some reason we thought this Saturday's game was at 1 o'clock also. We thought we were on time when we arrived with the equipment and two catfish at 12 o'clock, but it was game time instead of an hour before. Our team wasn't able to take batting practice or infield practice and we lost an extra inning affair. George and I were also stuck with two uncooked catfish.

The season was over and it was a noteworthy one. Five of us made the first team All- County and Ronnie, Richie and I made the first team All-State. I had a lot of personal achievements, like winning 14 straight games over two seasons and ending this season without a loss. It was fun, until the expectations got higher. Now it was over and time to get back to the real world.

We still had a few weeks left before graduation. All the year end social events were squeezed into this period. Joanne had invited me to the Battin High Senior Prom over a month ago and I agreed to go. Recently, Ronnie and I were invited to the Roselle High Prom by our fan club, but it was on the same night as the Battin Prom. I had to decline.

The Senior Letterman's dinner was held at Edison Vocational High School and the school year would end with a boat trip up the Hudson River for the graduating seniors of Elizabeth's high schools.

Last year the baseball scouts were out like bears after honey. This year, despite our great season and all the newspaper stories, they sort of ignored us. Ronnie felt that if we had a good year, we only had to sit back and wait for the offers.

Well, we sat back and nothing happened.

I was contacted by local alumni members of some of the major colleges, but they had nothing to offer me. They were trying to sell me on their school. My folks had just bought property after a lot of years of struggle. They can't afford to send me away to some fancy college.

Ronnie was accepted at Lehigh University. No baseball is involved. He is an only child and his family has been established in the community for a long time. They were not displaced by the War and had the stability my family was now trying to obtain. Finally, one day near the close of the school year, Ronnie and I were summoned to Vice-Principal, Frank Kirkleski's office.

"Boys, Mr. Jacobson, over in City Hall would like to talk to you. Here are passes for you to leave the school. When you come back, just check in at the office."

City Hall is directly across Scott Park from Jefferson High School. Incidentally, Scott Park and Scott Place in front of Jefferson, is named for General Winfield Scott, who came from Elizabeth.

In any event, Irving "Rabbit" Jacobson is the Director of Recreation for the City of Elizabeth. He is also the territorial scout for the Detroit Tigers...and Ronnie and I made our way to his office in the basement of City Hall.

After the usual salutations and small talk, including congratulations on our fine season, the "Rabbit" got down to business.

"Do you boys have any plans after graduation?"

"I got accepted at Lehigh." Ronnie announced.

"Do you expect to play ball up there?"

"I'm going up there to study engineering, Mr. Jacobson. So, I don't know if I'll try out for the team or not."

"How about you, Lefty? Are you ready to go to work?"

"Right now I have a job in a garage. I've been looking for schools that taught automotive subjects, but I haven't found any yet." I was telling the truth. As soon as the season ended I started working at Al's Atlantic Service Station on Elmora Avenue.

"No. I mean going to work playing for the Tigers. I can get you a train ticket for Lakeland, Florida and then the rest is up to you. If they like you, they will send you to one of their farm teams."

"What if they don't like me?"

"Look that's the best I can do right now. You guys are draft bait. This year, or next year you'll be grabbed by the service. The parent club doesn't want to invest in kids who they will have for a short time before the draft gets them...and then the service might send them back as damaged goods. Things were different a few years ago. You guys were good prospects, but now everybody is tight. Why do you think you haven't seen as many scouts around this year?"

I knew the "Rabbit" was telling the truth. A good part of our graduating class is already committed to the military. Some of the guys who want to be plumbers, carpenters, electricians, machinists or any other skilled trade can't get companies to take them as apprentices because of the draft situation.

"'Right now", I replied. "Getting some experience in automobiles might stand me better than gambling on a trip to Florida."

"If you want, I can hook you up with a couple of barnstorming semi-pro teams. No contract. Its good competition and you can make a few bucks."

"That does sound like a better option for now. OK. I'll try that."

Mr. Jacobson took all my information and Ronnie and I left.

"Lefty, it looks like our big bubble got busted."

"Ron, we made the All-State team. That's something thousands of other guys didn't do.

For now I'll take that."

"I guess you're right. I was expecting too much."

After graduation I went to work in the gas station. The semi-pro team played night and weekend games in the tri-state area. I could juggle my work schedule at the gas station to accommodate the baseball games. I only got paid when I pitched. The rate is 5 dollars an inning. I wasn't pitching that bad, but I wasn't getting enough work. I'm a rookie, so I only get an inning, or two in relief once and a while. At least I was making some money in the gas station.

I sold the Chevy for 50 dollars and bought a '39 Plymouth sedan for 100 dollars. The Plymouth had the gear shift on the column, not on the floor like the Chevy. It also had nice comfortable seats that would be good in a Drive-In movie.

I hadn't been able to find an automotive school anywhere around here. I told this to Don, the fellow who originally got me to go to the Prom with Joanne. He stopped for gas one afternoon and we discussed our mutual problems.

"I was talking to the Army," He said. "They gave me a commitment to the Signal Corp School; to learn communication equipment. I'll go into the Army in October. A lot of guys in our class are doing the same thing."

"I think I will check it out. I might just be wasting time around here."

The next day, Friday, I worked in the gas station only in the morning, because this Saturday I was scheduled to work 12 hours until closing. After my Friday morning shift, I drove down to the Post Office on Broad Street. Out there on the sidewalk in front of the Post Office to greet me, was a big sign with Uncle Sam pointing his finger at me saying, "I WANT YOU."

I followed his directions up to the second floor of the Post Office, where an Army Sergeant was seated at a desk, eating his lunch. I asked him for information about the school program, like Don had.

"What are you interested in?" He asked. He then asked several other questions about my education and work experience.

"I want to go to auto mechanics school." I replied. Then I told him about my background with cars in the car lot and the gas station. I told him about my baseball achievements and the fact that I had just graduated from high school.

"The Army really needs mechanics. Along with all your other qualifications, you should do very well in the Army. Do you have any free time this afternoon? I'd like to send you over to take a free physical and a test just to make sure you fit the qualifications."

"I'm free all afternoon."

"Good. Do you think you can get one of your parents to sign this application, so you can take the physical and the test this afternoon?"

"Sure. My father works right across the street in the Elizabeth Journal."

"Go get him to sign this and while your gone, I'll make arrangements for your test and get directions for you to our Newark office."

My father was very busy in the composing room when I entered. I told him what I needed him to sign to get a free physical and he did it. Within 10 minutes, I was back in the recruiting office.

The Sergeant was elated. "Ok. They're waiting for you at 1040 Broad Street, Newark. Here are directions and give these papers to the corporal at the desk on the second floor."

I didn't want to keep the people over in Newark waiting too long, so I buzzed right on over there.

Boy, was the place crowded.

"Sit over there," The corporal said after I gave him my papers. He wasn't anywhere near as nice as the Sergeant in the Post Office. I obeyed and went over and sat down next to about 20 other guys.

One by one, they were called up to the corporal's desk and he sent them off to some other place. When my turn came, he gave me a piece of paper and directed me to a room down the hall. Another soldier gave me a pamphlet and directed me to a vacant desk.

"Write your name on the top line and when I say 'GO' you have 10 minutes to complete the test. Do you understand?"

"Yes" I answered.

"Ok. Go."

I completed the test in about 4 minutes. It had multiple choice questions like; A chicken can lay an (A) Apple (B) Bottle of milk, or (C) Egg. A hammer is used to (A) turn a screw, (B) unlock a door, or (C) drive a nail.

I wonder if anybody ever failed this test.

There must have been about 200 guys in their underwear when I was sent up to the third floor. I had to take off my clothes and get in line. We went from one station to the next, like an assembly line, getting different things checked. A doctor or medic would mark the papers we carried and send us on to the next point. We carried our clothes with us all the way.

"Did you pass?" I asked the guy in front of me, who had only two fingers on one hand.

"Sure" He answered. "They even passed that guy over there, from my group. He has one eye."

"Wow," I thought. That recruiting sergeant wanted to see if I was qualified. Anybody who can breathe and walk is qualified.

After we got dressed, our names were called and we were herded into one room. A captain entered an introduced himself. He then told us to raise our right hand and repeat after him. "I Richard A. Pendell, do solely swear to bear true faith and allegiance to the United States of America...Holy mackerel, I did it! This is the real thing!"

*R. Allen Pender*

"Men, you are now members of the Armed Forces of the United States. Return here at 0800 Monday morning and bring with you 3 sets of underwear, 3 pairs of socks, a towel, a bar of soap, a razor, a tooth brush and a comb. Be here Monday at 0800. That is all."

*Did I do this? Don isn't going 'till October. How come I'm going Monday morning? The Army must really need mechanics bad. Ah! What the heck, I might as well go now. Why delay the inevitable. I have to work tomorrow and help Gramp Sunday morning. Yeah, I can be back here at 8 o'clock. I wonder how much the Army pays anyhow.*

On the way back from Newark, I stopped at the gas station and told Al, the owner, what I did and that tomorrow would be my last day.

"That is somethin'. And, yer still gonna work tomorrow?"

"Yep"

"Ok. I'll make sure you get paid before you go. If I pay you, promise me you won't get in any of those Army card games. Ya Hear!"

My mother wasn't as receptive to the news as Al was. I think she scared the birds out of every tree in Clark Township. "WHAAAT. YOU CAN'T GO. I FORBID IT. I'LL TELL THEM THAT YOU CAN'T GO."

"I got to, Ma. See, I got all the papers. I've already been sworn in. I belong to the government now. I'm on their payroll. It's like a new job."

"New job my foot. Don't you know what the Army does? Right now they have a War on their hands. They fight wars. How did they get you?"

"I just walked in to ask a question. But, I'm not going to be in the part of the Army that fights wars. I'm going to be a mechanic."

This type of dialog went on for about half an hour. Like she didn't already know these things; I brought up the current plight of the youth and how we had become disadvantaged because of the world situation. The fact that we were subject to the Draft and one way or another we are faced with military service. I think I convinced her that I was in control, because right now I had the choice of what I wanted to do. But, once I got drafted, they would put me where they want me.

The kitchen was quiet after my discourse. My mother continued to work on supper preparations and as she readjusted the rope over the refrigerator door, she turned to me and said, "You can go. But, none of this war stuff. You'll have to come right home if they want to send you to a war."

"OK, I'll tell them that."

She was quiet for now, but I knew her tactic. She was waiting to pounce on my father as soon as he entered the door.

"I know." He said. After she jumped all over him when he came in the house. "I signed the paper."

That took me completely by surprise. I didn't think he was paying attention to me when I went to see him in the newspaper, but I guess he was.

Nothing more was said about the Army for the remainder of the evening. I went out after supper to meet Tommy and Robert. We went over to Bowcraft in Scotch Plains to shoot some miniature golf and then afterward to Five Points for hot dogs. I told them about my plans for Monday and they didn't seem too surprised.

"After all that training we did back during the War, you should be well prepared." Tommy quipped.

"Especially if the Army uses sling shots." Robert added.

We spent a while talking about our youthful antics and their applications to military life. We had some good laughs about a lot of those things until we called it a night at around 10:30, because we all had to work the next day.

Saturday was a routine day at the gas station. I told a few people that I was leaving for the Army on Monday. A lot of the customers had served at one time or another, so I got plenty of advice. The typical attitude seemed to indicate that going into the service was as normal as going for a haircut. Around the 10 o'clock closing time, Al came by and took the receipts. He paid me my wages and dispensed some more advice about military life. He should know, his brother is a career Master Sergeant, a Mess Sergeant at Fort Dix., where I think I might be going.

I headed straight home after leaving Al. I had to meet Gramp at the Chester Diner at 5A.M., Sunday morning to deliver free samples of the Star Ledger. He and my cousin Ned had gone up to the camp sometime in the afternoon. That would be too long of a ride for me after closing the station at 10 o'clock, so I arranged to meet them at the diner. I got 5 dollars for a little less than an hours work. If traveling time were counted; it was really closer to 3 hours.

My mother had obviously made some phone calls Saturday. When I got back home in mid- morning on Sunday, she was a blur in the kitchen. In warm weather, it was normal for us to cook over the outside fireplace on Sundays and to eat under the trees. Today my mother had the kitchen oven going to bake a ham and a cake. She was boiling potatoes for salad and was also preparing baked lima beans. In the meantime, my father had gotten beer and soda to complement the already prepared large jug of iced tea.

"Did you tell your grandfather what you did?" Ma asked when I walked into the kitchen.

"Yeah, I did."

"Well, what did he say?"

"Nothin' Ma, Absolutely nothin'."

My relatives began dropping in by mid afternoon. I must have answered the same questions a thousand times. The men weren't that bad because most of them had been through this type of thing themselves. But, the women were something else. I don't think they realized that I wasn't a little boy anymore and the time had come for me to move on.

The little party wound down early in the evening. I was tired from working late on Saturday. Then I was up early this morning to help Gramp. I was happy for my parents that my relatives came to see me off, but right now I needed a goodnight's sleep because I had to get up early again to be in Newark at 8 o'clock.

I packed my gym bag with all the items the Captain told us to bring...and I went to sleep.

I woke up to the sound of my mother rattling around in the kitchen. The smell of coffee and frying bacon wafted up to my room. I could hear my father in the bathroom downstairs as he washed and shaved for work. I had showered last night before bed, so I rose, got dressed and went downstairs.

It was a typical morning, not unlike any morning in the past. I ate breakfast, then went in and washed my face, brushed my teeth and combed my hair. I was set for another day at work. Only this morning, my father was driving me to Elizabeth where I would catch a bus to Newark to a new and different job.

There were no scenes, like they have in the movies. My sisters were still in bed sleeping when my father and I left the house. I kissed my mother good-bye and naturally she had to have the last word.

"Did you bring enough money with you to call us when you get to where you are going?"

"I did Ma. I did."

My father parked his car on the street alongside the Elizabeth Journal and I walked with him to the composing room entrance. It was almost 7 AM., his time to start work. We said a quick goodbye and I walked to the bus stop on the corner. I am sure my father would have driven me to the induction center in Newark if I had wanted that. I learned playing baseball, that when the coach gave me the ball, I had to walk between the lines myself and the game hinged on what I did with that ball. Today was no different and I believe my father was smart enough to know that.

I was standing at the bus stop for only a few minutes, when a black Chevy pulled up at the curb. "Where are you going, Lefty?" The driver hollered out of the open window.

It was "Rabbit" Jacobson. "I'm going to Broad Street, Newark, Mr. Jacobson"

"Hop in. That's where I'm going."

We talked a little about baseball on the drive to Newark. I told him of my disappointment with the semi-pro team. Again, he told me how the world situation had upset professional baseball.

*THE SOJOURNERS*
*Life on the American Homefront During World War II*

We were approaching my stop at 1040 Broad Street, Newark when I told him, "This is where I'm going, Mr. Jacobson. With this new job I won't be draft bait anymore. Thanks for the ride."

One look out the window and he could tell what this building was. It was unmistakable.

Before I could exit the car, the "Rabbit" extended his right hand, which I took and he said. "Good luck and God bless you, soldier."

"Thanks, Mr. Jacobson. I'll see you again."

I was on time. But, I don't know about this Army. I gave in my papers and was told to go sit along the wall. Other guys came in and they were told to sit against the wall. Pretty soon there wasn't enough room along the wall, so they called out some names and moved them to another wall. This went on all morning. I had come here expecting to go on a bus ride to some camp like the World War II bus from Henry's Drug Store. Instead, I've been holding up walls in Newark.

At some point in the early afternoon, the guys on my wall were given these green tickets which we could use at a diner a couple of blocks behind the induction center. We had to be lined up and marched over to this greasy spoon. The counterman took the green ticket and gave us a hamburger and a coke. I think we are in trouble if this cuisine is a barometer of things to come.

Over the course of the afternoon we kept getting moved from wall to wall, but the crowd was slowly getting smaller. I couldn't see where the people were going. But, they were disappearing. My wall had dwindled down to about 20 people by 5 o'clock. Shortly thereafter a corporal appeared with a stack of folders in his hand. He began calling names. Mine among them. We were assembled into a little formation. The stack of folders was given to a guy with previous military experience... College R.O.T.C

It is obvious that his guy didn't successfully complete college, or R.O.T.C. If he did he wouldn't be here.

We were marched to Pennsylvania Station, about a mile away; where we waited some more.

Our leader had one way train tickets for us to Trenton. A bus would meet us in Trenton and take us to the Reception Center at Fort Dix. I didn't know that Fort Dix was near Trenton.

The train ride was nice and I was sitting next to a fellow about my age.

"You been drafted?" He asked.

"No. I enlisted. How about you?"

"I volunteered for the draft."

"What is that?" I asked

"You tell the Draft Board that you want to go. Then, you go in and get it over in two years. Are you Regular Army?"

"I don't know. I enlisted to be a mechanic."

"Let's ask that guy over there if we can see your folder." The draftee suggested.

The R.O.T.C. guy was pretty nice. He showed me my folder and explained everything.

"You enlisted for three years. You are Regular Army, unassigned. That means they can put you where ever they want. You also have a picket fence profile."

"What is a picket fence profile?"

"That means you are in perfect physical shape."

"Well, at least that sounds like something good." I cautiously responded.

"Not exactly," The R.O.T.C. guy answered. "They generally put picket fence profile guys in the infantry, or airborne."

"Does it say any anything in there about me being a mechanic?" I nervously asked him.

"No. But, they will give you a lot of tests in the Reception Center to see what you are best suited for."

I felt a little better knowing that. At least I had a chance on the tests.

The sun was starting to go down when the train pulled into Trenton. We left the train and went out to where the bus was waiting. But, there was no bus. All of us were hungry. That hamburger in Newark didn't go very far. We didn't know if this bus was going to come in five minutes or five hours. Some of the older guys in the crowd wanted to go over to a little greasy spoon by the station and get something. Our leader suggested that one person go and everybody give him money and an order. That way, if the bus came before he got back, we could send someone to get him.

A guy, named Mike, from Jersey City, acted like he knew his way around. He volunteered to go to the luncheonette. It wasn't long before he came back with a box of food and drinks. Somebody from the luncheonette was even helping him carry the stuff.

"This guy never had so much business at one time." He said while passing out the sandwiches and containers of chocolate milk. "I hope everybody likes chocolate milk, because that's all he had."

Darkness was settling in when a bus pulled up at the Station. FORT DIX. The sign on the front read. Our leader went in and talked to the driver. In a second he was back at the door waving us aboard. This was our bus.

Fort Dix is not that close to Trenton. The bus ride seemed longer than the train ride. It was pitch black when we arrived at Fort Dix. We couldn't tell where were. Maybe that's the Army philosophy in case some one wants to run away. They wouldn't know where to run.

# THE SOJOURNERS
## Life on the American Homefront During World War II

A Sergeant was waiting when the bus driver reached his destination. Our leader turned the envelopes over to the Sergeant who formed us up into a column of "ducks" and marched us over to some dark building. We filed inside and a couple of soldiers behind a counter gave us each a foot locker, blankets, sheets and a pillow.

Now carrying all this stuff, the Sergeant marched us to another building. Inside were rows of double decked steel cots. As our names were called off, we were directed to a cot and told where to place our foot locker. This barrack was going to be our home for three days, while we were processed into the Army. Once everyone was assigned a bunk, we were marched up to a huge mess hall for some thing to eat. They had chicken, corn and these little square potato cubes, the likes of which I never saw before.

We had about 15 minutes to eat and then were marched back to the barracks to lean how to make a bed…Army style.

I don't know what time it was when we were finished all these things and were allowed to wash up and go to bed.

I fell asleep right away. The next thing I know I was awakened by someone hollering, banging on the bunks and a whistle blowing. It was still pitch black outside. They couldn't be waking us up already, I just went to sleep. But they were.

"Fall out on the company street in five minutes." This voice was hollering.

"What street?" I thought. I didn't see any company or any street when I arrived here and it is still too dark to see anything. I got dressed and followed the crowd outside. We were lined up again and our names were called. Once they were sure everybody was present and accounted for, we were marched off to some place and told to Halt and Stand at Ease.

Very slowly, I could see what appeared to a lightening of the sky. "That must be the eastern horizon." I thought. As the light increased, the dark areas around me began to take form. They were buildings. Lights came on in the buildings and they were full of people. Suddenly it occurred to me that there were people lined up in front of our group and behind our group. Somebody figured out that we were in the chow line, but we couldn't see the mess hall yet.

We were in a city of yellow buildings filled with men. It was massive. I never saw so many people in one place at one time. I have an idea that this is going to be some adventure.

# CHAPTER 42

# COMPLETING THE WALK

Chicky and I slowly walked through the old one square block neighborhood. With every few paces, one or the other of us would stop to gaze at one of the ancient landmarks. Few words were exchanged as each of us saw an old scene played on the silver screen of our minds. The street was empty. But, we could see and almost touch the fleeting figures of our youth. They all were there and their indelible foot prints of the past marked each step along our way.

Sure, the landscape had changed a lot over the years, but Chicky and I could look beyond those changes and see a different place. The place of our time; where each section of sidewalk had a tale to tell.

As we approached the last of the four apartment buildings, Chicky started laughing.

"R.A., do you remember the redheaded guy who had curlers in his hair when he ran out of that building when he thought everything was blowing up?"

"Yeah, that was George Wheller. He had those metal clamp type hair curlers on his head. That was the night that a barn caught fire over at Juzefyk's livery and he thought the Germans were bombing us."

"He had the funniest look on his face when he realized everyone was looking at him."

Looking at the front door of the building, I couldn't help but chuckle at the thought of old George covering his head with his hands and making a beeline back into the building.

Turning and pointing at the two family house across the street, Chicky said, "That was Chico's house. Do you think his family still lives there?"

"We can look in a phone book and find out. They gotta be pretty old by now. But then, who knows, they still could live here."

"What was the name of the fellow who lived in the brown house next to Chico? I remember him playing baseball out in the big field and then he went into the Army. He hung out with my cousin Sonny and those guys."

"His name was Al Smith, Chick… and, I heard he was captured by the Germans in Europe."

"Oh yeah, I remember now. All of those guys who hung out in the field playing ball; they all went into the service. I can't remember all the names, but I can see the faces. We thought they were old guys then, because they got out of High School and drove junk cars and smoked cigarettes. When we think about it now, God, were they young."

"Sure, before it was all over even those guys we went to the movies with; your cousins; Sonny and Ducky, Breezy's brother, Happy Harrison and Klinky were gone too."

"Hey, R.A., remember that black and white dog that lived in the gray house on the corner of Grove Street? He even went into the Canine Corps and came out a Sergeant."

"I remember the dog. But, I forgot his name. He wore a brown coat with his stripes and campaign ribbons sewed on."

"Breezy's brother brought back that black dog that served on a tanker and they called it "Tanker." That dog didn't like any other dogs, especially Mrs. Harrison's dog, Toby."

The white house next to Al Smith's house was at the corner of Stewart Place and Rosehill Place. In our day the homes on Stewart Place were owned by established Elizabeth residents and we didn't mingle much with them. Except for riding our sleds down the snowy Stewart Place hill in the winter, we only used the street for a crossing to some place else.

"I remember the people that lived on this street were sort of snooty," Chicky intoned as we crossed Rosehill place towards the corner of Stewart Place.

"Most of the people that lived on this street thought they were high class Irish from St. Mary's. That's how the place got the name Quality Hill. Tom Glackin, the bigshot at the Standard Oil and St. Mary's Church lived right here in the second house. Another man named Byrnes lived in the first house. He would always come out of his house when we went by and threaten to call the police if we didn't keep moving. I guess he didn't like the foreigners that moved into the neighborhood."

"Remember the big black car that Mr. Glackin had. He would come up our street at about 5 miles an hour and never once waved to anybody as he went by. He had a daughter, who seemed to be pasted to the back window lookin' out at us. We never saw her outside."

"That was a '38 Buick in mint condition. His daughter's name was Wealthy. At least some one said that was her name. I can't imagine that was a real name. But then again, Mr. Glackin appeared quite taken with himself and his position. I never saw her anyplace, but in the Buick. Maybe she couldn't talk, or she wasn't allowed to associate with people of a lower class; like us. Whatever the case, I often wondered if she was real."

Stewart Place isn't that long of a street and it ended where Lidgerwood Avenue and Edgar road merged into Washington Avenue.

A boy, named Tommy Dwyer, lived in the last house at the corner, by Lidgerwood Avenue. His house was almost on a cliff above the street. As a matter of fact, the garage to that house was entered from Lidgerwood Avenue and it was practically underground.

Chicky and I rounded the corner by Tommy Dwyer's house and started down Lidgerwood Avenue.

Brick garden apartments occupied the big field; the playground of our days. If horses weren't grazing in that field, we were playing baseball, football, digging fox holes, or growing gardens. We also made huge bonfires from discarded Christmas trees.

As we passed Tommy Dwyer's garage, I said, "Chick, remember all the wild cherry trees that grew in through here?"

"Do I? We squeezed those cherries and mixed the juice with water to make soda. Do you remember how we made it fizz?"

"Alka-Seltzer," I replied.

"Ha, ha, we were crazy. Gee R.A., I'm surprised to see the colored people's cottages still standing."

Chicky was referring to three cottages clustered on the opposite side of Lidgerwood Avenue. All of the buildings on that side of the street ... and there were six of them, all very old and weathered; appear to have been part of the large farm that occupied this area years earlier. Just past the last of these six houses was an old barnyard. The front of the barn faced Edgar Road and housed Mr. Ives Welding Shop. The back portion of the barn, within the yard, still had the remnants of stall and shop areas. Tall hedges lined the sidewalk up to the drive next to the large farmhouse on Lidgerwood Avenue.

Colored people lived in the first three houses in from the corner of Edgar Road. Next to the third house was a big garden.

"Oh! I remember when the colored man in the first little house got arrested for making "Moonshine." Didn't he use the plumbing in the house as his still?" Chicky asked.

"Yep. He was makin' "Shine" in the summertime and the smell and the smoke comin' out of the chimney was a dead giveaway."

"Would you look, R.A.! Whoever built those garden apartments left those big Osage Orange trees right where they were. Remember when we used to climb all the way up near the top and heave those "Milk Balls" that grew on the tree into those big cabbages in the colored people's garden."

"Those big cabbages were collard greens. Chick and I used to try to get the milk ball into the big laundry pot in the yard."

"Is that what they used that big pot for - LAUNDRY. My mother told me they made soup out of little white boys in that pot."

"Well, there wasn't enough meat on all our bones to make a good pot of soup. Besides, I don't think we would have tasted too good."

The last house in the group was a little weather beaten cottage surrounded by trees. I sarcastically reminded Chicky about our perception of the house.

"Remember the witch that lived there, Chick?" I said pointing at the little bungalow.

"Oh yeah, The Enchanted Cottage. Balls, or anything that went into that yard never came out. There was a little lady in black clothes that lived there. She must have been a witch. We wouldn't even go near that place on Halloween."

"Aw, she was no witch. She was Klotzey's grandmother. She was a German widow. That's why she spoke funny and wore black clothes."

"Oh man, after all these years my world is shattered. I always thought that old woman was a witch. Ha, Ha, Ha," Chicky laughed. "Boy, did we have some imaginations."

Protruding out of the hedges; just before the drive next to the old farmhouse, was an "Ice House."

The Ice House was really a truck body mounted on some block piers. A crippled man named Jim was the proprietor of the Ice House. Jim lived in the old weathered farm house. I think it was his family that owned the property and the farm that used to be here.

"I guess after the War, the refrigerator put the old ice house out of business," I said to Chicky as we approached the site where it once stood.

"I almost forgot. Jim the Ice Man. It was unbelievable how he used to crawl into the ice house and chop a piece of ice and then slide it out for his customer. Yeah, he sat on the tailgate of that truck body day in and day out. Do you know what happened to his legs?"

"I know that he didn't have use of his legs. How he got that way, I don't know. But, he had good upper body strength from all that crawling in and out of the ice house."

"My Aunt Barbara told me Jim had a girl hanging around the ice house and he got her pregnant. I wonder if it happened in the ice house. It could have been a hot time in the old Ice House."

"I never heard that one," I said. "But, it sure makes a play on words with the name of that Broadway play about an Ice Man."

Although it probably wasn't a funny thing at the time it occurred, we both laughed hysterically at the double entendre the situation had created.

When we wiped the tears of laughter from our eyes, we had completed our circumnavigation of the block. Carl's Tavern was just a few paces away and we went in to find the lunch crowd all almost gone and our table waiting.

"Did you have a nice walk, boys?" asked the friendly bartender as we took our seats.

"Oh yeah," I said. "It's a lot different now, but we saw a lot of sights that rekindled some old memories."

"My friend here promised to write about our times in this neighborhood during World War II."

"That was a little before my time," answered the bartender. "But, I'm sure that if the walls here could talk, they would tell a lot of stories just about this place."

"I knew Jim Cotton, who owned this place and the Hamilton's, who lived upstairs... and I knew all the men that hung out here. This place could probably be a book in itself," I reassuringly answered the bartender.

"From time to time people come in and say they remember this place from years ago. But most of the people are from outside the area and just work around here."

Waving my hand at the walls, I said, "This place had a bar along that wall, a couple of bottles of whiskey on the back bar and served only Briedt's Beer. The place always smelled of stale beer and old cigar smoke. He had a radio for the baseball games and the fights, but beyond some stools and a table for card games, this place was empty. Mr. Cotton would sweep the floor every day, but I doubt that he ever washed the floor, or emptied the spittoons."

"I guess you knew Mr. Cotton pretty good," the bartender answered.

"He did," Chicky replied. "And everybody around here knew us. Only about half the people had telephones and yet our mothers knew just about everything we were up to."

After serving us a couple of cups of decaffeinated coffee, the bartender moved on to take care of a few more customers.

"R.A., Let me tell you... I'm having a great time today. I always wanted to come back and revisit the place, but I had nobody to do it with. I came back one time when my Aunt Barbara and Uncle Jim were moving. That was years ago. Your family and Robert's family had already left. Did you ever come back to visit?"

"Sort of... and it was years ago. Today reminds me of that time, only then I didn't have anyone to share it with."

"What happened?"

"It was my first trip home from the Army in two years and I came through here on my way to Clark. Physically, the area hadn't changed that much, but it was different."

"How so?"

"Well... oh, I don't want to bore you with an old Army story. You most likely have some of your own to tell."

"No, no... go ahead. That's what we're here for today; to reminisce."

"Okay, but stop me if it gets too late."

## CHAPTER 43

## ALL ABOARD FOR NEWARK

It seemed like the winter would never cease. But, in February, in the sand hills of North Carolina, where Ft. Bragg is located, the days began to slowly warm and the signs of Spring were beginning to be displayed at an increased rate each day. The light, the warmth, the smell of the air and yes, even the bugs ... had their therapeutic impact on my recuperation. Finally it was May and I was given orders assigning me back to a regular unit. I liked that. Convalescing in a hospital casual unit wasn't bad duty. But, now my strength and activity level had increased to the point where I needed a challenge and permanent quarters.

"Hey, young sergeant, throw your bag in the back a' this jeep, an let's git back to what this Army pays you to do," shouted the brash jeep driver sent to pick me up.

Corporal Hardwick and I had been together since we attended the Ordnance School up in Aberdeen, Maryland and now have spent the better part of our short military careers in the same unit.

"Wimp," as we called him, was from Arkansas and he stood about 6 foot five inches tall and weighed over 250 pounds. He has been my personal bodyguard ever since I beat him in a boxing match, when I was made corporal before him. That's another story, but basically I was faster in the Ring and he tired before he could lay a glove on me. If he ever did hit me, I probably would have been the first person in orbit.

"I can see the Army sure doesn't care what people they have using their equipment," I retorted.

"Now, that's something. And, coming from the guy who probably wrecked and tore up more equipment than whole Chinese Army did."

"That was my job then. Anyway, where are we headed now?"

"They said to bring you to the RCT Area. Most of the old team is back and we're bunking in our own squad room. There's talk of some new deal coming up once the outfit is back to strength."

"Sounds interesting. I hope I can get some time off before we get involved in any new deals."

"Well, you're the General's boy. If anybody can get the time off, you can."

"I'm not his boy; I just have any easy name to remember."

"Oh sure, he'd just say, 'send Pendell and his team.' The General should've known that there were sixteen other guys on that team and were still corporals."

"Wimp, the next time I talk to the General, I'll mention that."

Wimp and I both laughed at the suggestion, knowing full well such things were out of our control.

"R.A, it's good to have you back, it's good to have everyone back." Wimp dropped me off at the Orderly Room and he proceeded to take my bag up to our barracks.

The Company clerk was alone in the office when I entered.

"The First Sergeant is in with the CO, Sgt. Pendell, he'll be right out. The boys in your old section have already picked up a foot locker, bedding and field equipment for you. After you see the First Sergeant you can go into supply and get your weapon."

As the Clerk was finishing his discourse, the First Sergeant came out of the CO's office. It was Henry Franklin. He had been a Master Sergeant, a platoon Sgt. in our old outfit.

"Hey, Pen, welcome back. The old man wants to see you and then you can get settled in. We got a lot of the old boys in this outfit…almost like the 187 th."

"O.K. Top, what's the CO like?"

"Remember, Lt. Heller, he's a Captain now. Come on in."

After entering the Commanding Officer's office, I came to attention and reported with a sharp salute. Returning my salute, Captain Heller rose from behind his desk and extended his hand in greeting.

"Sergeant, I know your record and I am glad to have you healthy and back with us. However, your primary assignment will be with 18th Corps. Report to Colonel Muldowney at Corps, they will provide your assignment and then notify Sgt. Franklin of your schedule. We are establishing a new concept here … an Army that can be deployed anywhere in the world within 24 hours. We are bringing in specialized people like you as cadre for this new concept. So we all will be working on various elements of the program together. Do you have any questions?"

"Just one, Sir. I haven't had any leave since being in the hospital and I would like to go home for a couple of weeks."

"I am agreeable to anything Colonel Muldowney allows, and I'm sure there isn't going to be any problem. Sgt. Franklin, have Croker prepare the leave papers and we'll put in the dates and make it effective as soon as I get a call from Colonel Muldowney."

"Thank you, Sir," I responded and saluting smartly, I was dismissed.

The First Sergeant instructed the Clerk to type up my leave papers and then he called up to Corps to tell them I was on my way over.

"Get Wimp and his jeep to take you over to see the Colonel and do whatever chores you need to get done. Let me know when you want this leave and I'll have it signed."

*THE SOJOURNERS*
*Life on the American Homefront During World War II*

"Thanks, Sarge," I replied as I exited the Orderly Room and then headed across the parade ground toward the barracks where Wimp parked the jeep.

I was beginning to feel like some kind of celebrity, what with my own driver and with Officers and Senior NCOs greeting me like an equal. This sure didn't seem like the Army I entered two years ago. Back then I was buck private nobody; now I'm treated like some privileged character. But knowing this Army, you don't get something for nothing. There's a price to pay somewhere.

Colonel Muldowney was outside of his office talking with his clerk, Corporal Dietz, when he saw Hardwick and I enter Headquarters.

"You're so tired of convalescing that now you need a two week leave to rest up. Is that the problem, young trooper?"

"Yes Sir, Colonel. I want to go home and get my car."

Wagging his finger and arching his eyebrows, the Colonel responded, "A likely story, I'll bet you got other things planned. Don't worry, Captain Heller already called here. And, we take care of our own. Right Dietz?"

"Yes Sir, Colonel."

"We can give you two weeks, young trooper and then I expect to see you right back here. We got some young replacements coming in and they have got to learn what you and your team know. We are now part of the Strategic Army Command, and you'll learn more about that soon enough. So, get out of here!"

"Yes Sir," I answered with a sharp salute.

"Do you know about any of this stuff, Wimp?" I asked as we walked to the jeep.

"Look, right now I go to the motor pool in the morning. I usually piddle diddle around for a while, then take a jeep and do some driving around, like today. Some of the other boys are painting and fixing up the barracks. It's like we're getting something ready, but I don't know for what."

Right now Wimp was as confused as I was. I sure wasn't going to let it bother me, at least not for two weeks.

When we got back to the Company area, my leave papers were signed. I went up to my new bunk and packed some things into the small bag, I had bought at the PX. Everything else, I squared away in my area, and left my bed rolled up.

I called the train station in Fayetteville. The next train north to Washington, D.C. would arrive at 7:10 P.M. Good, I could eat supper in the Mess Hall and still have plenty of time to get to Fayetteville for that train.

In the meantime, Wimp and I drove over to the Service Club snack bar for Ice Cream sodas and then just cruised around the post to see what was new. We came back to the Motor Pool around 3 o'clock, gave the jeep a bath and parked it for the night.

The Mess hall would open at 5 P.M. So, we just lounged around the barracks until some troops started returning from their daily details. This was a

R. Allen Pender

Headquarters Company, which meant that most of the people billeted here had assignments within the administrative areas of the Corps, or special detachments operating as small units, like us.

With my return to duty our team was now 8 strong. We lost 12 men from the original unit, formed almost a year and a half ago. Wimp was bringing me up to speed on all those details, when some boisterous group started up the stairs. Our squad room was at the rear of the barracks, over the latrine, so with the door open; we could hear all the activity on the stairs.

This group now coming up the stairs would be recognizable anywhere in the world, even in the pitch dark. Vern Ragsley from Alabama, Artie Welker from New York and Clint Hollingstead from Louisiana were part of a tank recovery team. Ragsley's normal speech volume was just slightly below that of a public address system. So, in order for the other two guys to be heard above him, they had to holler all the time. This was the loudest bunch of people I had ever heard, but they were real good guys.

"MY GAWD, WOULD YOU LOOK AT THIS!" exclaimed Ragsley, sticking his head in the squad room door and pointing in my direction.

Hollingstead was next, "There aren't any Russian Tanks around here to steal, or don't they know that yet."

"I am sure glad we're short timers," interjected Welker. "That crazy Colonel is probably cookin' up something like the deals we pulled off for Eighth Army."

"Aw, come on guys, it wasn't all that bad," I chirped. "You never had so much fun, or got fed so well, as when you went on our details."

"FUN... the funniest thing R.A., was you and Lt. Davis after Captain Johnson found out about us eating up all the C Rations," Hollingstead noted.

"YES SIREE. OLD CAPTAIN JOHNSON WAS GONNA BUST R.A. SO LOW, IT WOULD TAKE HIM SEVEN PROMOTIONS TO MAKE PRIVATE," Ragsley informed the world.

The boys whooped it up over the thought of that mission. It wasn't funny then. But, now out of harms way, its funny side emerged and would probably live on in everyone's memory as one of those crazy war stories.

I learned most of my team was out inspecting equipment at various units and they would come directly to the Mess Hall when they returned. In the meantime, different people came in and although I never worked close with most of them, I knew who they were.

I laid out a clean, starched set of Class A sun tans for the train ride home. I also packed a set of tailored TWs in the AWOL bag along with some underwear and that did it. I didn't need much more. I planned on buying some civvies when I got home and then I could just carry everything back in the car.

In small groups, we left the barracks and headed to the Mess Hall.

"I see you finally got here R.A., we figured you were going to make a career in that Casual company," chimed Dale Holton, who was leading a group consisting of Gene Denton, Dave Lexauer, and Roy Markham, up the path to the Mess Hall.

"If I had known what soft duty y'all had over here, I'd a come sooner."

Hardwick joined the conversation with, "This bird just got here and he's already going on leave."

"When?" asked Denton.

"Right after chow, I can catch a train out of Fayetteville at 7:10. All's I need to do is get a ride into the station from the Taxi over at Main Post."

"Who needs a ride into Fayetteville?" inquired Sgt. George Price.

"I do."

"Is it worth a half tank of gas?"

"Tell you what George; I'll make it a flat five bucks. How is that?"

"It's a deal. Let's eat."

The guys made all kinds of comments about my privileged status. It was the typical railing soldiers do. And I didn't pay it any mind. They knew I hadn't been on leave since being shipped back to the hospital at Fort Bragg. Most of us had been through the same situations, it was just a fact that some fared better than others, as the luck of the draw would have it.

After chow, I went back to the barracks, took a quick shower and changed into my sun tans. I had four pairs of jump boots. Two pairs were super spit shined for parades or guard mounts and the others were just super shined for every day use. I also had two pairs of regular issue combat boots polished for work details. I decided to wear my parade boots home and to carry a pair of issue boots in the bag. I was all set to go by 6 P.M.

George Price was in one of the cadre rooms on the first floor of the barracks. When I arrived at his room he had just finished dressing.

"Let's go young sergeant; I got an important date in Robeson County."

That didn't surprise me. George was around thirty years old, a WW II vet, who had served in the submarine service. He joined the Army after the War and was currently a plain Sergeant after rising to the rank of Master Sergeant. George had an affinity for beer, which has been his undoing on more than one occasion. Almost all of the people in our outfit had come from the 82nd and George was no exception. He apparently found a girl friend among the Lumbee Indians over in Robeson County, which would suit George since he was a member of the Sauk and Fox tribe, of the Midwest.

I gave George the five bucks and we moved out across the parade ground toward the parking lot, where his '48 Chevy was parked.

"I'll fill up down on the boulevard at that no brand place and have you at the station in plenty of time."

*R. Allen Pender*

True to his word, George dropped me off at the train station and then he continued down Hay St. towards the highway and his Indian maiden.

I had close to twenty minutes 'till train time, so I parked myself on a seat in front of the station and watched the traffic go by. It felt good to be free with no formations or reveille for a while.

I had thirteen months remaining on this hitch ... if nothing came along to change that. The world situation wasn't too stable. Korea was now a stalemate, with small battles raging back and forth near the 38th parallel. South East Asia, especially Indo-China, looked like a fire ready to burn. China and Formosa appeared to be headed for a showdown, while the Soviet Union was preparing for nuclear warfare. Israel and the Arab nations were constantly probing each other. Anything could happen in the next 13 months and I would wind up like Franklin, Bates, Flowers, Davis and Prince, who came in for WWII and are still here. I sure hoped that isn't my lot.

I was enjoying my relaxing contemplations in the early evening sun, when I was aroused from my musings by the repeated blasts of a Diesel locomotive as it neared Hay St. When the train came to a stop, it began to unload its passengers, mostly young GI's, who appeared to be arriving from basic training centers like Ft. Jackson and Camp Gordon, to the south. I felt like an old man as I watched these troops disembark, although I was probably the same age or younger than most. Several, who saw me waiting to board, didn't know whether to salute or not. It amused me, as they were transfixed by the boots, uniform decorations and military presence. I wondered if any of these boys were the replacements the Colonel was talking about. If they were, I thought, "Boys, when this Airborne unit gets done with you, you'll look the same way. Good luck."

As the last of the recruits moved away from the train, I boarded. The coach was almost empty now, so I had the choice of almost any seat. I picked out one in the middle of the car and prepared for my 12-hour trip up to Washington. This was not any super liner. This train would be picking up and dropping off mail all the way up to Richmond. I wasn't in that much of a hurry, so I could sleep and travel at the same time.

I really enjoyed looking out the window and seeing the North Carolina countryside. As I heard the names of the stops called off; Dunn, Wilson, Rocky Mount, I looked East. Eleven years ago my family and I had left our ancestral home east of Rocky Mount due to the WWII mobilization. Now, my home was 400 plus miles further up this rail line. Isn't it strange how the forces of world circumstances could move us about like little toy figures in a child's play set.

I wondered about David and Pauley. Were they still in the Elizabeth City area? Is our fort still in the cow pasture baseball field? Maybe, one weekend after I come back with my car, I will drive up to the old homestead and look around. Maybe someone will remember me and my family.

After passing Rocky Mount, I made myself comfortable in my seat and decided to catch some sleep.

The train rumbled on into the night and gradually my body got used to its idiosyncrasy and I fell asleep.

Sometime, around 5 A.M., I was awakened by some bumping and banging. When the conductor came by, I asked what was going on.

"Oh, we're in Richmond and their making the train up for Washington. The dining car is coming on now, so pretty soon you can get breakfast, if you desire," the trainman politely explained.

"That sounds real good to me. I would like to have a real train breakfast. The last time I was on a train I was traveling with Army meal tickets and the train had a special meal for GI's. It wasn't bad, but this time I can go first class. I'm payin'."

"Wonderful, I'm sure the dining car boys will take good care of you Sergeant. And I do hope you enjoy your breakfast and trip to Washington."

"Thank you," I replied, thinking that trainman didn't have to be so courteous to me. But he was. Then, I noticed a "ruptured duck" pin on the lapel of his suit. He was a vet, that's why.

There is that common bond we all share. We have paid our debt to those who have served before us and our dues to those who serve in the future. A big unique club.

After about a half hour of jostling around, the train was ready to continue north. I went into the bathroom and rinsed off my face and combed my hair and straightened up my uniform. I then headed for the dining car.

As I headed for the Dining Car, some of the words and melody of that WWII song, "Chattanooga Coo-Coo," buzzed through my head, "Dinner in the diner, nothing could be finer, than to have your Ham and Eggs in North Carolina." The only trouble was... I was going in the opposite direction.

The Stewards were the only people in the Dining Car when I entered. Naturally, I had expected to see Cary Grant, or Bogey or some other leading man type sitting in the Dining Car sipping wine and blowing cigarette smoke at Bette Davis. But, so far I was the only customer.

The Steward, who would wait on me, graciously invited me to be seated and then presented me with the menu of the day. I'm sure he was tipped off by the conductor to the fact that I wasn't a GI on travel orders with a meal ticket. People, like train people, taxi drivers, bus drivers, waitresses, bartenders and others in public service businesses can tell if a serviceman has any money or not. It is a simple matter of reading the uniform. Guys returning from a combat zone have money. Guys traveling on orders don't. And, guys with little baggage are off on pass or leave.

"Would you like me to bring coffee while you make up your mind?" the Steward asked.

"Yes, that would be fine."

The Dining Cars were class places. No matter what your station in life, the elegance of the Dining Car and the gracious staff, made a person feel privileged to be there. At that moment I felt that way. Considering where I'd been and the condition I was in a scant five months ago, I was really privileged to be sitting here.

"I'll have a ham steak with scrambled eggs, pan fried potatoes, toast and orange juice," I spurted as the steward set down a small silver pot of coffee on the table.

"Well it looks like somebody has a good appetite this morning. Enjoy your coffee and we'll get your breakfast."

I was sitting on the north facing side of the table. It was still dark, but a rim of light was beginning to show on the eastern horizon. It was much like that morning in the early months of WWII, when we stopped at Mr. Virgil's filling station on our way north. I had often wondered if his sons had returned home from the war and whether or not his wife used our peaches to make them a cake. Maybe, when I come back with my car, I'll drive up that way and see. I'd like to do that.

"Ham and Eggs with potatoes, juice and toast. Do you need anymore coffee at this time?" The steward said as he placed my breakfast before me and checked my little coffee pot.

"I'll call if I need anything else, thank you."

"Enjoy your meal."

I savored that breakfast. It was seldom, if ever, that I could sit in such grand surroundings, have people wait on me and enjoy a fine breakfast and be able to day dream and think the thoughts I was thinking. This was luxury to me and I would have to return to reality. But not for two weeks.

Some other people had taken seats in the dining car as I was eating and oblivious to the rest of the world. The sun was up and I looked out of the train window, the world was coming to life.

In another hour the train would be approaching Washington, so I had some time to rest on a full stomach. I left my payment and tip on the table and made my way back to the coach.

I knew I had to change trains in Washington for Newark, N.J. But, what kind of connection there was... I didn't know and I would just play it by the seat of my pants.

"Next stop, Union Station, Washington, Union Station," announced the trainman as he came through the coach.

Pulling my ticket stub from the seat, he said, "That's you trooper, have a good trip."

"Thanks, it'll be good to get home for a while."

"Oh, yes! I sure know the feeling," he replied.

"I'll bet you do," I said pointing at the "duck" on his lapel.

"Yes, yes, we both do, don't we?" The trainman said patting me on the shoulder as he moved toward the rear of the car.

Union Station was a bee-hive of activity. Military people of all ranks and branches, along with civilians of every description, were moving across every part of the station.

I stood out in the middle of the main concourse not having any idea which way to go. Out of the corner of my eye I saw a newspaper stand and started walking over in that direction.

When I arrived at the stand the operator was busy taking money and giving change, so I didn't want to disturb him for just questions. I picked up 2 Sportsman chocolate bars and joined the group waving money in front of the harried stand operator.

As the man behind the newspapers reached for the the dollar bill I was holding out as I displayed my purchase, I asked, "Where are ticket windows?"

Without losing any motion, or saying a word, he handed me my change and with a sweep of his arm, pointed up to the right and then took the next customer's money.

I needed these two chocolate bars like I needed another hole in my head. Sticking them into my AWOL bag, I headed off in the direction the newspaper man pointed. In due course I came upon the ticket windows.

"Newark, N.J.," I said.

"Do you have liberty papers?" the man in the window asked.

"Yes, I do," I said as I reached up and unbuttoned my top shirt pocket.

"OK, I can't give you a military fare without papers."

Without looking at my leave papers, the man stamped the ticket, gave me the reduced fare and as he passed my change back, said, "That train leaves in nine minutes from track six, directly across the concourse."

WOW! I had expected to spend a little time in Washington, maybe an hour or two. But, this was quick. I made a bee line for track 6. I didn't want to get lost or tangled up in this crowd and miss the train, or get on the wrong train. As I approached the train now being boarded at Track 6, I must have asked three different people if this was the train to Newark, N.J. Finally, a trainman was standing by the car door. I asked him. "Does this train go to Newark, N.J.?"

"Yes, it does."

Relieved, I hopped aboard and found a seat.

# CHAPTER 44

# THE WELCOME HOME PARADE

This train was much more crowded and traveled faster than the mail train from North Carolina. The train was called the Congressional Limited and it was traveling up the Pennsylvania Railroad mainline, with stops in Baltimore, Philadelphia, Trenton, Newark and New York. We would arrive in Newark around 12 noon. This was great, because it gave me the whole afternoon to get from Newark to Clark Township.

This trip was uneventful. I was either dozing or day dreaming most of the way. I liked to look out the window and try to see places we may have passed through on our way north years back. Each time I thought of something, I made a vow to visit this place or that place, when I was free and had my car with me.

I was starting to get hungry again. I pulled out the two Sportsman chocolate bars when we approached Philadelphia, but I ate only one. I figured we were about an hour from Newark and I could get something good to eat after getting off the train.

I started to get excited as the train came into Rahway. I could see Aunt Hazel's brother Tommy's house. The clock on the Purolator Oil Filter Company sign facing the railroad was at 11:40. Too bad I couldn't jump off the train and walk the two miles to our house. I kept my eyes glued to the window as we passed through Linden and Elizabeth. I was looking to see a familiar face or place, but the train was going too fast for me to stay focused on any one thing for any length of time.

"Newark. Newark, Next stop Newark."

Hearing that alert, I grabbed my AWOL bag and headed for the door. I didn't want to be caught anywhere and not be able to get off the train. The conductor stood at the door and I was right next to him. Within a few minutes I was out on the platform and looking for the exit.

My first act on emerging onto the streets of Newark was to establish some priorities. First was food and second was transportation to Elizabeth. No buses went to Clark, so Elizabeth was the choice. From Elizabeth I could take the 44 jitney bus to Winfield and walk to Clark. Broad Street, Newark was up a couple of blocks from Penn Station, so I headed off in that direction. I crossed McCarter Highway, which ran right along the railroad, and started to walk up Market Street. Right there on the corner of McCarter Highway and Market Street was a place to eat, Neiden's Bar and Grill. Beer was 10 cents a glass and whisky was

25 cents a shot. A window sign advertised Knockwurst and beans for 25 cents a plate. This looked like my kind of place, so in I went.

I sat down at the bar and ordered up the knockwurst and beans and a Birch Beer. They brought me a plate with two fat knockwursts and a little pot of beans and bread and butter. What a lunch, and all for 35 cents, including the Birch Beer. The place was really crowded, which was normal, since it was lunch time in a big city. People were standing behind me and to each side of me with their beers set on the bar. As long as they didn't steal my knockwurst or spill any beer on my sun tans, I didn't care. Amid the din, I sat and ate my meal. When I had finished, I slid 50 cents out on the bar and vacated my seat. Emerging back into the sunlight, I walked up Market Street to Broad Street.

My father once told me that Broad and Market Street in Newark was the busiest four corners in the world. According to him, some sort of statistics backed up that statement. It was busy, no doubt about that. Newark was the major shopping center of the region. Bus and train lines came into Newark from all over the state, disgorging their passengers in the vicinity of Broad and Market Streets. I had to cross to the south side of Broad Street for the bus I wanted. A crowd was forming at the corner, so I stopped there. When the traffic light changed to halt traffic on Broad Street, a policeman walked into the street and blew his whistle and waved his arms at opposing crowds on each side of the street. With those signals the two crowds moved towards each other. I was trying to see which direction we would go as the mob moved across the street. Would my mob stay to the right, or left? Would the other mob do likewise? Neither. Both mobs went straight, so it was a move and dodge thing in the middle of the street. I was worried. Since Broad Street was a very wide street; I wondered if the traffic light provided enough time for the pedestrian interaction that occurred each time the light changed. After reaching the other side, I stopped for a moment to look back across to the street. There weren't any bodies lying out there, so I assumed everyone got across.

Buses were constantly pulling up next to the curb all along the street. Light poles, next to the curb, had little signs listing the numbers of the particular buses that stopped in that location. I wanted the number 50 bus, which went to Elizabeth. I continued to walk south on Broad Street, stopping at each pole as I went. Finally, the sign on one pole listed the 50 bus as one of those stopping at that location. I went no further.

The experienced bus rider seems to instinctively know which bus to get on. On the other hand, people like me, have to check all the destination signs on the bus and still ask some other individual or, the driver if this is the bus to their destination.

When a bus arrived bearing the number 50 designation, I was prepared for that same routine. However, the bus company fooled me. The bus driver had a machine. You told him your destination and he printed up a fare ticket on his machine. Something new. If the bus didn't go where you wanted to go, the driver couldn't print a ticket. Simple.

"Elizabeth," I said. Handing the driver a quarter, I got my ticket and moving to the rear of the bus, I found a seat.

The trip to Elizabeth was around six miles and the bus made frequent stops. I wasn't in any hurry and enjoyed looking out the window at familiar places. I rode the bus through the shopping center of Elizabeth to the end of the line, Caldwell Place and Broad Street. Caldwell Place was named after a Revolutionary War Minister, James Caldwell, who gave torn up hymn books to the Continental Soldiers at the battle of Springfield when they ran out of wadding for their rifles. The colonial style brick building on the corner, housed the N.J. Academy attended by Alexander Hamilton and Aaron Burr, when they were young. That Academy later evolved into Princeton University. The same parcel of property contains a colonial cemetery and the First Presbyterian Church. This is a site of significant historical significance. Next to the Church is the alabaster Union County Court House, an impressive building. Across Rahway Avenue, which runs off Broad Street and along side the Courthouse, stands The Public Library. The 44 bus stopped in front of the Library. My next goal.

It had really turned into a beautiful Spring day. Flowers were blooming in the cemetery and Church yard. The lawn around the Academy building was green and lush. A group of men were sitting in the sun on the low granite wall surrounding the courthouse plaza, next to the flag pole, where our nation's banner waved softly in the warm Spring breeze.

I stepped off the bus and headed down the wide sidewalk towards the Courthouse and my next destination, the bus stop in front of the Library.

As I approached the courthouse, one of the men sitting on the granite wall got up and started towards me. It was Mr. Webie; my high school gym teacher.

Mr. Webie was about 6 inches shorter than my 6 foot height. He was a stocky well-built man with pure white hair. More importantly, he was a fine gentleman.

As I approached, he stood in the middle of the sidewalk with his arms extended and a huge smile on his face.

"Hey, Mr. Webie!" I hollered.

"My boy, Richard," he said as he reached to grab my shoulders. "Praise God, you're back safe."

"Amen, Mr. Webie, Amen. But, never mind me, how are you? What are you doin' on the Courthouse steps?"

"Oh, I'm retired now. And on nice days I like to sit out here and maybe see an old student or two pass by. But, you look good. Have you been discharged yet?"

"No, I have a little more than a year to go. President Truman liked some of us so much he gave us an extra year to keep him company. I've come home for two weeks to get my car and then go back to North Carolina and train troops."

"Will you be going to see the baseball team play while you're home?"

"Oh, sure. I want to get my car running first and then I can travel around a bit."

"How are you getting home from here?"

"I'll keep walking and then take the bus from around Linden. It's a good day and it's good to see familiar things."

"Richard it's so good to see you. I'm glad I was at my post today."

"I'm glad you were too. When I get my car running, I'll come back and take you for a spin. How about that?"

As Mr. Webie thought for a moment probably recalling the trip we took in my car to collect the football and basketball ticket money, he quickly retorted, "I think I had enough of your spins to last a lifetime. I'm still telling people about your crazy driving and all of those rubber monkeys that jumped out of the box when you leaped that car over the grade crossing." Warmly and softly laughing, he said, "That was something. Yes, that was something."

On that note we gave each other a hug, shook hands and then I continued on my way.

I walked past the library and the Sears, Roebuck Store and crossed the bridge over the river, where 10 years ago I wanted to test my World War II Keds on the bridge railing.

Across the street and up on the left was the South Broad Street Playground. A group of black boys were playing basketball. I immediately thought of Scotty and Charles. I stood for a moment and watched, really looking to see if maybe Scotty and Charles would materialize in the group. But, that didn't happen.

I turned on the right oblique and started up Washington Avenue. My fight with Walter Samuel earned me the right to pass through this black neighborhood unobstructed. In my imagination I could see the neighborhood gathering to stand and watch me pass and say, "There goes that Richard that Walter Samuel couldn't beat." That didn't happen either. I guess there wasn't anybody around familiar with my reputation and I moved up the street in total anonymity.

I passed Mary's Spaghetti Bar, Paskow's Drug Store, St. Mary's Church and the Washington Meat Market without seeing one individual I knew. A bus came along, but I decided not to take it. I was going to keep walking until I saw and talked to someone I knew.

Washington Avenue was void of people as I continued to walk. It was early afternoon on mid-week day. Most people were at work or school and there would be few people around until the schools let out and the day shifts ended at the various plants in the area.

Two horses were grazing in St. Mary's Cemetery as I came by. They gave me a quick look and then went back to feeding on the new grass. Washington Avenue ended at that point. The road forked with Edgar Road being the left fork and Lidgerwood Avenue the right fork. I kept on the bus route, which was Edgar Road and walked past the Oasis Tavern, behind which was Juzefek's Livery Stables. Mr. Ives' welding and blacksmith shop was coming up on the right. This shop was located in a barn, which had been part of the Sinnott farm in past years. Mr. Ives did most of his work on the walk in front of the barn door. The building was so full of stuff that there wasn't any room for Mr. Ives to work inside. Even Mr. Ives wasn't working at the shop as I walked by. After walking another 150 feet, I came to the school yard fence. As I walked by the school, I could see children in the classrooms, just like it was on the day I had arrived here. Only today I wouldn't be going in. The little confectionary store across the street had been turned into living quarters. I wonder what happened to the lady who made Ma coffee and me hot chocolate that day 10 years ago.

The little brick building past the school was currently occupied by a rubber products business and next to it, on the corner of Edgar Road and South Elmora Avenue, was Bayway Motors; with the same neon monkeys jumping on the sign.

Up the street one block ahead was another group of stores. Boxes of fruits and vegetables were laid out in front of John's Meat Market. I picked up a juicy looking nectarine from one of the boxes and walked inside.

Old John Cacamo, the owner, was busy cutting meat behind the display case. His nephew and namesake John, along with his son-in-law Tony, were taking care of the 2 customers in the store. Mel Allen, the voice of the N.Y. Yankees, was being blasted out of a small radio set up on the display case, as I approached the counter.

"Hey, Poppa, look who's here," said Tony as he looked up from his duties and saw me at the counter.

"Ritchie Boy," hollered Johnny. "Where did you come from?"

"I'm on my way home for two weeks. I wanted to walk this way and then get the bus."

In the meantime, Old John and Tony had come around the counter to hug me and shake my hand. Young John and Tony were vets. Both had served in the Army in Europe and participated in the Battle of the Bulge. They knew and understood the feelings of a soldier just coming home, just like the trainman on the train to Washington. Not much had to be said or asked.

"Watta you mean, take a da bus. Johnnie can drive'a you home," Old John commanded.

"Thanks, John, but I got all afternoon to get home and I can see the sights along the way."

"Richie is right, Poppa. He wants to visit on the way. Just like we did," interjected Tony, with a smile to sooth his father-in-law's feelings.

My mother and Aunt did business with John ever since we arrived here. We lived in Clark and my Aunt now lived in Hillside. Each week meat and grocery orders were called into John's and either Tony or Johnny would deliver the order and if nobody was home, they would put the food away and leave the bill on the kitchen table. Doors weren't locked in those days and nothing was ever missing.

"You have'a pep-a-see cola with'a that fruit. You give him'a Tony, Ok." commanded Old John.

Dutifully, Tony grabbed a bottle of Pepsi from the cooler and gave it to me after he removed the cap. We made some light conversation as I enjoyed my drink and they went back to their work. When my drink was finished, I thanked the trio for their hospitality and we bid our good-byes.

One block up was the Linden city line where Edgar Road merged with U.S. Route 1. I headed off in that direction and turned in time to see a 44 bus approaching. As I stepped off the curb to flag the bus, I could see Old John Cacamo monitoring my progress from his store front. As I boarded the bus I threw him a wave, which he returned and satisfied that I had my situation under control, he went back into his store.

The little bus started down Route 1, past the White Castle Hamburger Stand, where my friends and I used to buy 5 hamburgers for 20 cents and then after we ate them we would leave of the place walking like penguins. I don't remember who did that first, but it was funny. I probably had a chuckle or a memory for almost every inch the little bus traveled. In my mind, I visited again with all my friends as the bus went past our old haunts. The swamps off Route 1. Wheeler Park and Linden Pool. Wood Avenue. Raritan Road and the Winfield Circle. The Rahway River and the Old Mill. The carefree days of youth were planted as moments in time in these places. Tony was right; I wanted to visit on my way home. I had to visit. Along with all of my contemporaries, I was a part of these places and they of me and we are all linked together by those moments in time and history.

Construction was still underway around the Winfield Circle. The wooden bridge across the river at Raritan Road had been replaced and the river was realigned. A new highway called the Garden State Parkway was being drilled alongside the river and through the woods behind our house. That original section of Parkway, from Union to Woodbridge, would eventually evolve into a road from the northern border of New Jersey to the southern tip of the state in Cape May. Alighting from the bus, I started to walk up Raritan Road.

The Cape Cod and bungalow style houses lining both sides of the street were all dressed for Spring. Green lawns with flowering plants and shrubs welcomed the visitor to this new land, which would ultimately be called suburbia.

R. Allen Pender

    I was less than one mile from home as I walked along to the sound of birds chirping and an occasional dog barking. Squirrels were darting back and forth between the trees along the road and the shrubs in front of the houses.

    I was enjoying my walk and could now see the intersection of Walnut Avenue up ahead. I heard a rooster crowing at Mintel's Chicken Farm as I came to the lane leading to our house. All was quiet as I walked past the neighboring houses towards my family's home. The front door of the house was locked, so I entered the side yard gate. I was greeted by a brown and white dog attached to a long chain. Freckles was part Brittany and part something else, a mid-sized dog that my father had gotten at the pound.

    The dog's main job was to hangout by the kitchen door, which was unlocked. He was familiar with everyone who had reason to be on the premises, including the mailman and the electric meter reader. The garbage collectors even came into the yard for the trash pickups every week. The dog even knew me after almost a two-year absence and put on a display of barking and jumping that I thought was a gala reception. However, my bubble was burst a few minutes later, when my little 7-year old sister came home from school.

    "All he wants is his dog food and he'll quiet down," shouted this little slender strawberry blond girl, who quickly bounded through the kitchen door and then just as quickly returned with a can of Ken-L ration and a can opener, which she presented to me.

    The dog continued to jump at me and around me as I tried to open the can of food. Finally, I got the can open and the contents into the dog's dish after his head and chain fought with me in my effort to get the food in his dish.

    "Does he do this all the time?" I asked my sister Rosemary.

    "Only for Joyce and Daddy. He's very good for Mama and me."

    "Are you supposed to feed him when you come home from school?"

    "Only when nobody is here."

    "Is anyone ever here when you come home from school?"

    "Well, today you were here, so it's your turn. Where did you come from anyhow? Does Mama know you were coming?"

    "No. I just decided yesterday to come and get my car."

    "Joyce will be here soon and Mama will be here at 5 o'clock. She's working in the sewing store in Roselle. And I don't think your car works anymore."

    "How's that?"

    "Well, I know the radio don't play anymore."

    The dog had settled down and was only concerned with his meal, so I entered the kitchen and then headed upstairs to my old room.

    It was a Monday morning, almost two years ago that I left for the Army. I took three pairs of socks and three sets of underwear with me. And now as I entered my old room, everything looked just the same as the day I left. My bed was still unmade and my mother was using it as a storage place for draperies. A few boxes containing glassware had been stored in my room, but beyond that nothing had changed. The clothes in my closet and in my dresser were just as I had left them.

I grabbed a pair of Levi's and a shirt from the closet and quickly changed clothes. I carefully placed my suntans and TW's on hangers and brought them down to my mother's laundry area. The suntans would have to be washed and starched, then pressed with military creases, but the Tropical Worsteds would only have to be pressed.

As I got to the bottom of the stairs, I could hear two girls arguing. My sister Joyce, age 12, had arrived home from school. I don't know what the argument was about, but it stopped when I entered the kitchen.

"What is the phone number for Ma at her job?" I asked. "I want to call and tell her I'm home."

"Oh! We thought you might be going to get your car out of the garage," answered Joyce. "But, Momma's number is on the card by the phone."

I called my mother and told her I was home, after which she gave each of my sisters instructions regarding chores she wanted done. When the phone call was completed, I headed out to the garage.

My 1939 Plymouth was covered with leaves and dirt. The windows were wide open and the interior of the car was littered with candy wrappers, Popsicle sticks and soda pop bottles. It looked like parties were held in the car.

There was no reaction when I inserted the key and tried to start the engine. The battery was stone dead. I opened the garage doors and rolled the car out into the sunlight. I cleaned the car up, both inside and outside. The oil and coolant were fine, but the gas was old and didn't smell too good. The battery case was cracked and all the electrolyte had leaked out. Obviously the battery went dead and then froze in the winter. I needed some fresh gasoline and a new battery for starters and I would have to wait until my mother got home before I would have use of a car.

My first priority was to get some fresh gasoline and a good battery. The gasoline wasn't any problem. Platt's Esso Station at the corner of Walnut Avenue and Raritan Road was within walking distance. I found an empty 5-gallon can in the garage along with a little wagon. After placing the can in the wagon, I set out for the service station.

Jake Platt had two customers at the pumps when I walked up pulling the wagon.

"Hi there young fella, we haven't seen you in a long time."

"I'm in the Army Mr. Platt. First time home in almost two years."

"Two years! Can't be! Well that's what happens when you get old; the days just slip by and fool us old guys."

"I need some gas in the can. And do you have a good battery? Doesn't have to be new. Mine froze and split while I was away."

"I'll fill up the gas and then we can ask Arthur inside about a battery. I'm sure we got something."

Jake filled my 5-gallon can and we walked up to the service bay. Arthur was a township policeman, who worked in the service station during the day. At this moment he was working under a car on the lift.

"Hey, Arthur, do you remember this boy and his '37 Chevy?"

"I'll be darned. I saw Missus Boyd about a month ago and she asked me if I knew what happened to that lunatic who used to come down Valley Road at 11 o'clock each night and scare the daylights out of her and her husband as he broad sided that Chevy around the corner onto Walnut Avenue."

"Well here he is. In the Army for two years and he needs a battery for his car."

"For the old Chevy?"

"No, I traded the Chevy for a '39 Plymouth just before I went in."

"Yeah. I got a couple of good batteries here. How does 4 dollars sound?"

"That sounds real good."

"I'll put one on charge and bring it to your house in about an hour. How's that?"

"Can't ask for much more," I said as I handed Jake Platt a 10 dollar bill and he peeled off 5 singles in change.

"Here, take the jumper battery with you. We can pick it up when we come with the other battery."

"This is good; maybe I can get the car started. Thanks, I'll see you later."

With the transaction completed, I started back to the house.

I poured most of the gasoline into the tank, but left some in the can to prime the carburetor, if need be. I took the old split battery out of its mount and attached the jumper battery to the car's cables. The instant I touched the positive cable to the battery, the car radio started to blast all over the neighborhood. That answered the question of a dead battery. My two sisters had been watching my progress, however after I shut off the radio, they were gone. The evidence was clear, during my absence; they and their friends had been using my car as a hangout. I would be happy if the dead battery was the only problem.

I decided to remove the spark plugs just to check their condition and to put a little oil into each of the cylinders. With the plugs out, I spun the engine over a few times to get the cylinder walls lubricated. I then reassembled every thing; poured a little gas down the throat of the carburetor, turned the key on, pulled the choke and pushed the starter pedal. The engine made two false starts, then finally took hold and kept on running. In a few minutes the engine was running nice and smooth, just the way I left it.

Of course the car registration hadn't been renewed, nor had the car been inspected since I left. I would have to do that tomorrow. I began to go over the car and make a list of things to be done in preparation for the trip back to North Carolina. I would have to take the car to a service station for a grease job, but most of the other work I could do right here in the driveway.

I had things pretty much under control when Arthur arrived with the used battery.

"She sounds good, Rich. Where do you have to take her?"

"Fort Bragg, North Carolina."

"Oh, the airborne outfit."

"That's right, I've been in that outfit for almost two years and I got one more to go."

"My partner and I used to sit up by the ladder company every night waiting for you to wreck that little Chevy. Then all of a sudden, you weren't around any more. We spent more time chasing you and your bunch from the reservoir and other places around town. You boys weren't bad, just public nuisances. But, you guys gave us something to do. This town is really changing. More houses. In a few years it will be all houses. It won't be Toonerville anymore. Boys won't be able to do the things you guys did. No hunting or racing or stuff like that."

"I wonder what it'll be like when that new road is finished?"

"It will bring more people. All the farms west of Central Avenue are going to be cut up for houses. I hope they leave the White Diamond as it is for us "rubes."

"I hope by the time I get discharged, I'll be able to afford living here."

"Yeah, country boys like us are a dyin' breed, Rich. In a few years when you tell people what you did here they won't believe you. Your kids will be in a whole different world."

"I think you're right Arthur. The little I've seen is sure a lot different than just 5 years ago. Ten years from now, who knows?"

As he loaded his battery into the truck, Arthur said, "Don't be a stranger, Rich. If you need anything else, you know where we are."

"Thanks, Arthur, I'll probably be over in a day or so to get the car greased."

"We'll see you then. Take care."

As the service station truck drove off, my mother driving a '50 Ford, rounded the bend in the road. She pulled into the driveway right behind my car. I walked over to greet her as she got out of her car.

"Well look who finally decided he had a home and family. I had to find out from other people that you were home. Why didn't you call?"

I had to give my mother a kiss on the cheek and a hug to stop her from talking. "Ma, I just decided last night to come up, so I didn't bother to call. I figured I would surprise you."

"The boys at John's market told me you were home. They came to my job with a steak for you. That's why I'm home early. Does your father know you are home?"

"No, how could I call anybody while I was riding a train?"

"You should have called," answered my mother... getting in the last word as usual.

"Where are those girls?" She said as she headed for the kitchen door with me right behind.

"Look at this piece of meat John sent. We better get a fire going in the pit out back and cook this on the grill."

"I'll get a fire goin' Ma. Then I want to call some of the boys to see who's around. Is Robert still working for his father in Westfield?"

"I think he's the only one around that isn't in the Army or college," replied Ma.

I walked outside to the rear corner of our yard where we had a brick Bar B-Q pit. I gathered some newspaper and some kindling and built a good wood fire.

In the meantime, I could hear Ma issuing orders to my sisters. Joyce wasn't too bad, but that little one had a question or a comeback for everything my mother said. After hearing them go at it, a body had to wonder; who was the boss?

I had a nice wood coal fire going now and I sprinkled some charcoal down on top of the hot oak embers. Mom came out with some potatoes to be roasted in a tin set upon the grill. She also had a pan of beans, which she set towards the rear of the grill.

"We'll put the steak on when your father gets home. His bus from N.Y. should be coming pretty soon."

My father was now working at the N.Y. Times and he took the first bus of the day, which left from the parking lot of the Clark Rest at Central Avenue and Raritan Road around 6 A.M. He had been taking that bus so long, that the driver picked him up at Walnut Avenue, since he was the only person in town who routinely took the same bus into the city every day. The last stop for the bus coming back from N.Y. was also the Clark Rest. But, the driver would let my father off at Walnut Avenue, since Daddy was usually the last person on the bus.

As I was tending the fire in the cooking pit, I saw my sisters run past the side yard gate. I heard them holler; "Daddy's comin', Daddy's comin'," and then they were out of sight.

Being older, I wasn't that around my sisters enough to know the things which made up their lives and impacted on their behavior. I thought possibly that their racing to meet my father was part of the excitement surrounding my homecoming. That wasn't the case.

These girls had my father wrapped around their little fingers. He would take their side in any issue they had with my mother. Ma was strict and tight with a dollar, so most disagreements occurred about money, clothes, shoes and girl activities. After hearing their complaint, he would plead their case with my mother. I don't recall the issue that they had this particular day. But, some problem generated sufficient cause for them to rush and meet him. The fact that I was home was just an incidental thing.

Within a few minutes, my sisters came skipping through the gate with my father bringing up the rear.

"Hi, Dad. Are you ready for some steak?" I said, as I continued to work at the cooking pit.

"Well you could have called and we could have arranged some sort of party to welcome you home," said my father as he grabbed my hand and forearm. "Your mother called me at work and told me you walked halfway home."

"It wasn't that bad. Besides, I had a good relaxing trip."

"I see you got the car running. Are you going to drive it back?"

"Yeah, I want to do some work on it and get it in good shape. I think some people have been using it as a club house, but there wasn't any harm done."

My father was not surprised by my comment, so I assumed he was aware that the girls had been playing in the car.

Together we walked from the back yard to the kitchen.

"This steak is all ready for the grill," said my mother as we came through the door.

"This is some huge piece of meat!" exclaimed my father. "I'll hang up my coat and then I'll put it on the grill."

"Good," I said. "I want to call Robert. Is he still working for his father in the Westfield Filling Station?"

"Yes, he is," replied my mother. "But, you should call your Grandmother and Grandfather and your uncles first."

"I will, I will!" I exclaimed. "I want to get all the numbers in order first," I said as I walked toward the kitchen counter area where the phone was located.

Naturally, I dialed Robert's fathers' gas station first. I could identify Robert's voice as he answered, "Elm Street Esso."

"Hey, Robert, this is R.A., What are you up to?"

"When did you get home?"

"A few hours ago. What are you up to this evenin'?"

"Nothing' much. I gotta close the place up tonight at nine. Come on over here. I'll get someone to bring over a few beers and we can pitch a few after I close."

"Sounds good, Robert. I'll see you this evenin'."

Quickly, I hung up the phone. Then I dialed my grandmother before my mother caught on to my activities.

"Hi, Gramma, I just got home. I'll be by to see you tomorrow for lunch, O.K. Hey, Ma! Gramma wants to talk to you," I hollered.

Quickly my mother was at my side to take the phone. I was off the hook and out the door towards the steak cooking on the grill.

"Everything is hot and this steak looks done. I think we're ready to eat," my father commented as he inspected the cookin' food.

The girls had set the wooden table located in the opposite corner of the yard and my mother emerged from the house with a salad and some condiments.

"Everybody sit down," she commanded.

"Not you," she said to the dog, which was in the kitchen and was whimpering at the screen door. "You have your own dinner, so let us eat."

My youngest sister said a quick and muttered "Grace" and my father proceeded to cut up the huge steak.

"What are you and Robert planning to do this evenin'?" Ma asked.

"I'm goin' to go over to his station. He has to work tonight."

"Well you be home by 11 o'clock. Nobody comes into this house after 11 o'clock."

"11 o'clock! I don't know. We may be out later than 11 o'clock."

"You make sure your not. You've been pretty sick. You're not ready to stay out late," she scolded.

"Ma, do you see those uniforms hanging in the kitchen and do you see those stripes on those sleeves? They aren't laundry marks. They mean that I'm a Sergeant in the Army, a man of the world."

"Well man of the world, this house belongs to me not the Army. The doors get locked at 11 o'clock and we don't have keys. From what I hear, Robert likes to drink beer. You can't drink beer because your not 21 yet. And don't give me any of that Army Sergeant stuff. You just behave yourself."

The kid sisters were enjoying the exchange between my mother and me. Ma still ruled the roost and wasn't about to give up her authority.

My father continued to eat during the conversation. Finally, he emerged from his plate. "Alice, let him use the car to go over to see Robert. His car has to have the registration renewed."

"Sure, he can use my car. But, he has to be home by 11 o'clock." Like always, Ma had the last word.

All sorts of subjects were discussed at the table as we ate. One would never know that I had been gone almost two years by the type and manner of talk at the table. I wasn't the center of attention and wasn't flooded with questions. It was like I was never gone.

*THE SOJOURNERS*
*Life on the American Homefront During World War II*

I remember when all of those who served came home from World War II. There were no questions. No stories...Just the resumption of life. Almost like turning the page in a book and beginning a new paragraph, there was no ceremony. There doesn't have to be. It is sort of like a rite of passage. Without knowing all the individual details, all those who have served have a common bond. It doesn't have to be articulated, it is known and felt.

When we had finished eating, I called my uncles. Ma was happy that I had completed my family obligations. I would see all of my relatives over the coming weekend. Until then, I could see what my friends were doing and visit a little bit.

The family began to settle down to their normal evening activities. Dad and the dog headed out the back gate towards the old orchard, which was now being converted into the Garden State Parkway. Ma got the girls and their homework organized, before getting back to one of her sewing projects. I reorganized my room upstairs in the converted attic, made the bed up with fresh sheets and took an inventory of available clothes.

I still had a few decent sport shirts and a couple of pairs of slacks hanging in the closet that I could wear for now. But, I needed some new stuff.

To be quite honest, I was getting tired. I don't think Ma had to worry much about my staying out late. The only sleep I had gotten in the past 24 hours was on the train between Fayetteville and Washington. I felt like my battery was starting to run down, but I vowed to go and see Robert and then come home for a good night sleep.

I felt somewhat better after a shower and a little settlement of that big supper. I wasn't used to eating that much food at one sitting, but by seven thirty, I began to feel a little more comfortable and I headed off towards Robert's fathers gas station.

Westfield is the ultimate suburban town, not large, but pretty much built out. Robert's father's gas station was located right in the heart of the center of town shopping area. Clark on the other hand was mostly still farmland. We really didn't have much of a center of town. Our Municipal Building and Police Headquarters were located in a small garage-like building on Westfield Avenue. That road ran from Rahway in the southeast to Westfield in the northwest. Westfield buildings had to conform to a Colonial style of architecture in order to maintain a town standard and theme. Some affluent people lived in Westfield, but I always thought the so-called exclusive reputation of the town was puffed up.

Robert hadn't changed much in the past two years. He and an employee were in the process of cleaning the service bays when I arrived.

"Park by the pumps, R.A.," he hollered as I pulled into the station. "I shut the pumps down. That way nobody will come in while the lights are still on."

## R. Allen Pender

I did as he said and then went into the office.

"Hey, R.A., I heard you were really messed up. You don't look so bad."

"Army life agrees with me, Robert. All I have to do is survive the next year."

"Hey, I might be going in. I just got notice to take a physical. My brother just got out. So now they can call me. I might as well go. Do you think the war will last much longer?"

"I thought it was over a year ago November. But, we got fooled. At least now they're doin' some talking, so who knows how long it will take. But, tell me Robert, where is everybody?"

"Service and College, that's it. Chico and Don are up at Lehigh University. Tommy left the University of Maryland and just went into the Army last week. Richie and Walter went into the Air Force a few months back. Smitty went into the Army. I'm really the only one around, so I might as well go in and get it over with. Chico doesn't come home from college much, but Don does. You know how he liked his beer and poker. That's what we do."

"Wow! I figured you guys were havin' a wild time here at home, Beer, Cars, Girls and makin' money."

"Wild time my foot! My father just opened a second station in Scotch Plains. My brother runs that one. I have to jump in here and then they send me over to the other place...anything but fun and a lot of money."

The gas station was secured for the night. Robert turned off the lights at the pumps as his friend Danny arrived with a paper sack full of bottled beer.

We all agreed that it wasn't going to be a late night. Robert and Danny had to go to work in the morning and I was tired from the trip up.

Over the next hour we shot the breeze over a couple of beers each. I wasn't a great beer drinker, so I'm just as glad we had an early night. By 10 o'clock all of us were done for the day. I told Robert that I would get back to see him before I returned to Ft. Bragg and I headed back to Clark.

"Well the man of the world is home before 11 o'clock," my mother chimed as I walked through the front door. Then she proceeded to bombard me with questions like... "How is his mother and father? Do they still live in Fanwood? Do they know so an' so?" And on and on.

"Ma, I didn't ask Robert about his mother, we just talked about the boys we knew and about things we did. Men of the world stuff. You know."

"O.K. man of the world, I'm ready to put the lights out. Your father has to get that early bus to New York."

"Good night, Ma"

"Good night, Sergeant."

Those clean sheets were luxurious. I was probably asleep before my head hit the pillow.

At some odd hour of the night, I abruptly sat up in my bed. My body was wet with sweat and my nerves were racing at supersonic speed.

I peered out the window and saw a lone light way off in the distance across the fields in front of the house. With urgent reaction, I pulled on my pants and boots and charged downstairs and out the front door.

I stood out in the road in front of the house looking for the rest of my platoon. But I was the only one there. My confusion began to slowly abate as I started to comprehend my surroundings. The countryside was quiet and the great expanse of sky was lit by millions of stars. The moon above me was bright and showed the same face I had seen on the other side of the world. In another 12 hours that moon would be looking down at another night in the Far East and I would be here.

Compared to the moon, I realized how insignificant and small I was standing on that road in the dark. Then I thought of God and how great He is. He made that moon and made this universe. He is bigger than the universe and He can hold us, like grains of sand, in the palm of his hand. The sweating stopped and I was cooled and dried by the night air.

I was home and I was safe. No, there wasn't any homecoming parade with marching bands and cheering crowds...just a normal day, nothing unusual.

Now wide awake, I was embarrassed by my charge into the night. Nothing here had changed. Maybe I was never gone. Was it possible that I was just waking from some wild dream? But then, as I slowly walked back to the house, the night light reflected off the single Silver Star on the banner hanging in the living room window.

# CHAPTER 45

# THE ANSWER

The familiar aroma of bacon frying and coffee brewing roused me from my sleep.

I got dressed and went downstairs.

My father was in the bathroom getting ready for another day in New York. He had to be up at the corner of Walnut Avenue and Raritan Road by 6 AM, to catch that bus to New York.

"How come you're up so early?" My mother asked, as I walked into the kitchen.

"I want to be at Palermo's when they open up, so I can renew the car registration."

"The Motor Vehicle part of the office opens at 8 o'clock." My father said as he came in and took his seat at the kitchen table. He should know; he still sold real estate part-time for Palermo from their Clark office.

"What about you, Ma? What time do you have to be at the sewing store?"

"I usually get there at 9:30. Why?"

"I'd like to use your car to go to Linden. I should be able to get over there and back before you have to go to work. After I get my car registration renewed, I want to go to Elizabeth and get it inspected."

"Why don't you go to the Westfield inspection Station? It's closer and not as crowded as Elizabeth." My father commented between bites of breakfast.

"I want to go to Elizabeth anyway. I want to see Al at the gas station and then go get a haircut at Sal's barber shop."

"Make sure that you make some time to visit all your relatives while you're home." My mother chided.

"I will. I'll be around for 10 days. But, I want to get all my business finished first."

"Don't forget. I know you. You'll get side tracked by something and forget the things you're supposed to do."

"I won't, Ma. I promise. With you around, how can I forget anything?"

After my father left for work, my mother fixed me a breakfast of bacon and eggs. I had eaten, was washed and ready to go by the time my sleepy eyed sisters made their morning appearances.

I felt lucky to be up so early and able to get away from the house. Early in the morning, my mother and sisters resemble two opposing armies engaged in hand to hand combat.

I understand that this is some sort of a daily ritual. They only have to get ready for school, but the girls act like they are being sent to the high altar of the Aztecs for human sacrifice. My mother is a dictator...and she is dictating the dress of the day and is preparing the lunch of the day. They object to everything and become unmovable. My father has left for the day, so they have no avenue of appeal. The tumult continues for quite sometime, but the battle of the wills is won by my mother shortly before the school bus is due to arrive on Walnut Avenue.

Palermo's office on Wood Avenue was still closed when I parked the car in front of the building. I didn't have to wait too long before a lady came along and opened the door to the office. I was inside before she finished turning the lights on.

"Aren't you Joe's son?" She asked when she saw me standing by the counter.

"Yeah, I want to renew my car registration and drivers license. I've been away for almost two years."

"We know. Are you home for good?"

"No, I have to go back. I have one more year to serve."

"Well, let's hope it goes fast. Give me your license and registration."

While we were talking, another elderly lady came in and situated herself behind the counter.

"Florence, this is Joe's son. He's in the service. His license and registration have to be renewed. He's been away for two years. Can we do this right away?" The first lady asked, passing the papers to Florence.

"Sure." She said glancing at the documents. "Here, Richard. Sign the bottom of this application and we'll have you out of here in a few minutes."

Within ten minutes I had my new license and registration. I was home in plenty of time for my mother to get to her job at the sewing store.

"Here are your keys, Ma." I hollered, when I walked into the kitchen. "I'm going to the inspection station now."

"Alright." She answered, from her bedroom, where she was getting dressed to go to business. My mother never had a job. She always told everyone, that she went to business. Why? I don't know. That was her thing. "I'll see you this afternoon. Don't forget what I said about calling your grandmother and Uncle Billy."

"I won't." I said, as I headed out the door to my Plymouth.

I had checked everything on the car yesterday, so there shouldn't be any reason for it to fail inspection. The lights are all working and the brakes are good. But, you can never trust the motor vehicle inspection. Some times they come up with the craziest reasons to fail a car. I have heard of faded tail light lenses and unauthorized license plate holders as reasons for rejections. Improperly adjusted headlights are probably the greatest cause for rejection. Every time a car hits a pot hole the lights go out of adjustment. My car has been in the garage for two years, so the headlight adjustment shouldn't have changed.

When I got to Elizabeth, the inspection line wasn't too long. I have seen days in the past where the line went up Lidgerwood Avenue, down Garden Street across to New York Avenue and then all the way to Grove Street.

When I worked in Al's Gas station, which backs up to the inspection station, the inspectors took their breaks at Al's, where they could get cokes from the machine. The same inspectors are on duty now. I don't know if they recognize me, because they certainly don't show it. It wouldn't do me any good anyway. I think these guys would fail their own mothers without a second thought.

The Plymouth passed. I had my new sticker installed and I pulled out of the station onto New York Avenue. Turning right towards Garden Street, I could see some construction under way. The AMVETS are erecting a Club building on the corner next to Tarzan's Jungle. It looks like the foundation is finished and it appears that they are using the basement as their club house until they get the rest of the building up.

I turned left onto Rosehill Place and parked the car. Something looked different about Harry's store, where I wanted to buy a cold Hires Root Beer. The Union Food Store sign was gone from above the store window. Everything in the store was rearranged from the way I remember it. A lady, who I didn't recognize stood behind the counter.

"Can I help you?" she asked.

"I would like a cold root beer," I said, scanning the store to see where the cooler box was located.

"I'll look and see if I have one in the case over here." She said and walked back to what was Harry's meat case. "I have grape, orange, cherry and Pepsi. No root beer."

"Ok. I'll take a Pepsi. By the way, could you tell me what happened to Harry and his son Seymour, who used to have this store?"

"I didn't know them. They were gone when I came and rented this store."

I asked a few more questions, but I saw that it was fruitless. This lady didn't know anyone around here. I paid for my drink and walked out of the store. I could find out something from Sal the barber, whose shop is next to the store. I needed a nice civilian haircut anyway.

Looking through the shop window, I could see the arms of the white barber jacket belonging to the man reading the newspaper. He was seated in one of the chairs when I entered the shop. At the tinkle of the bell above the door, he dropped the paper to greet me. It wasn't Sal. This man was much younger than Sal.

# THE SOJOURNERS
## Life on the American Homefront During World War II

"You're next!" he said in a joking manner. Of course I was next. I was the only one there.

"Where is Sal?" I asked, taking my seat in the barber chair.

"Sal retired last year. Did you come to Sal?"

I told the barber that I used to live in the neighborhood, that I was in the Army and that my family had moved to Clark Township.

He told me that they were starting to build a garden apartment complex in the big field across the street. He mentioned that Cotton's Tavern was sold and it was going to be renovated by the new owners.

"All new people are moving into this area. Most of my customers when I came here are gone. They moved all over. People from the Port are coming here now. I'll probably have more customers when they finish the apartments." He said, pointing his scissors towards the field across the street.

I did get a little information, but I never did find out what happened to Harry and Seymour.

No one came into the shop while I was there. When he was finished, I paid the man and walked out to survey the old neighborhood from the sidewalk.

Construction equipment was moving earth in the big field up near Chico's house. A couple of ladies were standing on the sidewalk near the building where I had lived. I decided to walk up the street as far as Stewart Place, maybe I would see someone I knew.

Two ladies that I didn't know were talking and rocking their baby carriages in front of the building where my aunt Eileen had lived. She moved to Hillside last year. They didn't pay any attention to me when I walked by. No one else was out. Even the cars parked along the street didn't look familiar. I turned around at Stewart Place and started walking back down the street. This time the two ladies fixed their eyes on me like I was casing the neighborhood, or was planning to steal their babies.

I wanted to holler out, "It's me, the kid who shot out the street light. The kid who flew the airplane off the garage roof. The kid who repelled down the fire escapes. The kid who hid in the trees and shot fat ladies with a pea shooter." But, I didn't. It would have fallen on deaf ears. They wouldn't have known about any of those things. They wouldn't have known anything about this neighborhood, or the people who used to live here... They were new and my old neighbors and I were just sojourners, who were here for a while and then we were gone. We came and went... and just like the circus people, the dust from our tracks has been erased by the wind. The memories may be ours, but it is their place now. We are the strangers.

Al at the gas station and George with the hotdog wagon, gave me a big greeting. George served with the 82nd Airborne Division in Europe during WW II. He was selling hot dogs from a cart out on Elmora Avenue for 15 cents each.

He probably had the best business in the city. The gas station hadn't changed. Al was still busy adjusting headlights on rejects from the inspection station.

We made some small talk about military life while I wolfed down two of George's 15 cent specials with chili and onions. These men were busy running their businesses. It wasn't some sort of a holiday for them because I was home. So, I filled up the tank in the Plymouth with Al's Atlantic Gas and headed back to Clark Township.

The dog was the only one at home when I arrived. Despite having two hot dogs from George's cart, I was still hungry. Suddenly, like the appearance of an apparition, I could smell hamburgers and onions cooking at the White Diamond.

"I'll be right back dog." I said in answer to the bewildered look on the animal's face. Then I quickly turned and went back out the door.

"Two with fried onions. To go." I said to the man behind the counter.

"Ketchup?" He asked in response, while he scratched out my order on a slip of paper.

"Yeah, on both."

The man nodded back as he passed the slip of paper over to the grill man, who looked at the order and then grabbed a handful of chopped meat from a pan next to the grill. Quickly he spread some raw onions out to sizzle on the hot grill. He formed two patties from the chopped meat and slapped them down on the grill. While the meat and onions were sizzling on the grill, he pulled two hard rolls out of a box beneath the grill. The rolls were quickly sliced and lathered with ketchup. Holding the rolls in his left hand, the grill man flipped the burgers with the spatula in his right hand. He pressed the spatula down on the steaming meat, flipped the meat and pressed again; then with one deft movement of the spatula, he gathered a burger, some onions and slid them into the roll. The counterman grabbed the completed hamburgers, wrapped them up and stuffed the order into a bag. Then without losing rhythm, he punched up the total on the old cash register which sat in a niche by the grill.

The dog must have smelled those hamburgers from a mile away, because he was sitting at the door with his tail wagging so fast it looked like it might break off.

"Don't be in such a hurry. I got one for you. But, we have to go into the kitchen. Come on."

I'm sure the animal understood what I had said, because he followed me right to the kitchen table. Talk about impatience, this dog wanted to snatch the hamburger right out of my hand before I could put it in his dish. While he was gorging himself, I went out the back door, so I could eat my hamburger in peace, in the back yard.

The next thing I knew, the dog was looking out at me through the screen door and was barking for more hamburgers.

"That's all you get for now. If you want to make a habit of this, you better get a job and a car." I said in reply to the barked demands. "I have other things to do."

This afternoon I planned on riding over to Warinanco Park to watch the high school baseball team play. I didn't know if they had a game, or were practicing. I just wanted to say hello to Mr. West and anyone else I might know.

The kids, who were sophomores when I was a senior, would now be seniors. They would be the only ones I could possibly recognize, or who would remember me.

"I heard you were back home." Mr. West said in his usual clipped tone. He was leaning on his black fungo bat as I ambled towards the bleachers.

"You must have talked to Mr. Webie. I saw him yesterday up on Broad Street. How are things going here?"

"We're struggling some. We don't have that many experienced players. But, we'll win some ball games. How about you? Are you going to play again? You look a little lighter than when you graduated."

"I gained most of the weight back that I lost. The Army's been trying to fatten me up, but I don't think I'll be able to play any baseball for at least another year. Maybe I'll try again after I get out of the Army."

"Did you ever consider a career in the Army?"

"No way. I had enough Army life. Right now I'm taking some courses at the University of North Carolina. They have an extension school on the Post. I can transfer the credits to another college. I don't know where yet. But, I have the G.I. Bill and that will help a lot."

"How long are you going to be home?"

"I took off for 2 weeks to come up and get my car. I don't know if I'll stay the two weeks, because so far I haven't been able to find anybody to hang out with."

"Most of your class followed you into the service... and then a few like Ronnie and George are away at school. What happened to those girls, who used to come out here every day? I haven't seen them for the past two seasons."

"I don't know. I never kept in touch with them, or anybody else. I went into the Army so fast that I never really told anyone that I was goin'. I felt that everyone is busy with their own lives. What I do isn't important to anybody, but me."

"I know Ronnie and a few others tried to find you. You know how I knew you were in the service?"

"Rabbit Jacobson probably told you. He drove me to Newark the day that I left for the Army."

"That's right. He called me that night to apologize. He felt that the things he said to you discouraged you from continuing on in a baseball career."

437

"No. Playing baseball just wasn't fun anymore. It was time to do something else."

"Ronnie told me you felt that way, when he came to see me during the holiday season that year. I let the Rabbit know and it made him feel better."

"Good."

"I've talked with Buzzy and Jim Devine, and some others...and we feel that maybe we should have taken a more of an interest in the future plans of a lot of you boys. We have a lot of resources, not money or things like that, but contacts to help with schooling and employment. But, we were never asked. Maybe we shouldn't have waited to be asked?"

"Mr. West, you did your job. You taught us and gave us the instructions we needed to play the game. After that we had to go out on the field by ourselves. No one held our hand out there. We're all goin' to sink or swim by our selves. That's the first thing you learn after graduating from high school."

"Do you think your decision in joining the Army was the right one?"

"Believe me; I questioned the wisdom of that decision a lot of times... now I wouldn't trade the experience for anything. But, I wouldn't want to do it again."

"Lefty, you always were an independent individual in school and on the baseball field. I guess that's just your way."

"Yeah, I guess I just have to find out things for myself."

Mr. West and I talked for few more minutes and then I left him to his responsibility of coaching a baseball team.

I drove by the houses where the girls lived in Roselle. But, they weren't around. Next, I pointed the Plymouth in the direction of Clark Township and I drove home.

Over the course of the next few days I made some repeat trips to the old neighborhood and the results were the same. No familiar faces.

I did accomplish a few things. I got some catalogs from Newark College of Engineering. Then I visited my Uncle Billy's auto parts store and machine shop in Belleville. I could possibly go there to work, but I had a year to think about it.

I visited my grandparents and some of my relatives. Then with a week of leave time remaining I decided to take a nice easy ride back to Fort Bragg.

"That," I said to the anxious looking Chicky, sitting on the opposite side of the table. "Was almost 50 years ago." He looked disappointed as I finished my story. Maybe he thought I was going to come out with some earth shaking revelation that would make his day. But, I didn't.

"You know, I didn't know what to expect today. I knew the neighborhood would be changed, but I was surprised by the fact that you came back here and within a few years everybody we knew was gone. When we're young, we think the times and the places as we knew them would go on forever."

"Do you know that old cliche, *you can never go home again*? It's true."

"Oh, I know that. I was just hoping that in seeing and recalling things from the past I might find a clue to that thing that I feel I'm missing in my life. Not that I've had a bad life. I haven't. But, I feel like something is missing. I have a good home life, a nice family and I had a stable career. I never did anything wrong. I've lived a lawful life and never broke any rules. I had a very structured life. Yet, I feel like something is missing.

"I know the feeling. I had it myself about nine years ago."

"You did! You the independent man. The daredevil. How could you be missing anything? It sounds like you did it all; or am I mistaken?"

"I did a lot of things. A lot of them were risky and a lot were beyond the boundary of acceptable social behavior. Like I said earlier, my life was like a roller coaster... up and down real fast. I went off in any direction that piqued my interest, without any concern for the consequences. I quit jobs. Started a business. Closed that business and started another. I had successes, but I kept looking for something else. I had what may have been considered a *charmed life*. I was in all kinds of situations and always came out unscathed. I felt invincible. But, empty. Despite the fact that I had a family and all the trappings. I did everything alone. I didn't permit anyone else to become part of the decision process. I had to be the boss, the one who called all the shots. Finally, everyone just left me to my own devices. I thought that anything I did was destined for success and each venture involved more and more money."

"I'm surprised to hear that you had to do everything by yourself. Years ago, your family seemed like a well oiled machine in the way they all worked together. What happened? How did you drift away from that type of support system?"

"I had accomplished a lot of things... maybe too many things without a setback. I didn't take advice when it was offered. Instead, I took my own counsel and did whatever pleased me. Then, one by one, my supporters became disenchanted with my behavior until I had no supporters left. Within a short time I was in a tailspin and headed for disaster."

"Wow. I didn't realize you had such problems. Is that when you found the key to understanding, fulfillment and peace that you mentioned earlier?"

"I see you remembered that statement."

"Well...yeah. That might be the answer I've been looking for. How do you find it?"

"You don't. The answer finds you when the right time comes."

"I don't understand that!"

"The answer is near us all the time, our entire lives. But, we fail to see it. It has to be revealed to us."

"Is it the same answer for everyone? I don't see how that could be possible."

"It is...and it comes only when we are ready to accept it."

"You really have me confused now. Did the answer come in time to avert the disaster and save the day?

"You make it sound like I had the winning lottery ticket in my pocket, which probably would have been the easy way out of the dilemma, but it wouldn't have changed anything. I had a big money problem alright. I had used my life savings, plus additional money from investors and hocked my 155 acres of land to the bank in order to follow a dream to create the ultimate real estate development. But, I didn't count on the opposition that I encountered, or a declining real estate market that came along as I was waging a two and half year battle against a bunch of so called environmentally conscious citizens at the local zoning board. I was in a predicament alright. The Zoning Board was due to vote on my application. I would be lucky to get one vote, much less the majority needed to approve my plan. The Banks around the country were calling in real estate development loans to protect themselves as a result of the failed Savings and Loan Associations that the government now had to bail out. My bank and my loan were no exception. Once the vote of that Zoning Board was in, I would be lucky if I still had title to my underwear.

My Attorneys and I had put on a marathon presentation with all kinds of experts to prove the soundness of my plan. But, the people didn't care about technology, or improvements to the environment. They just wanted to keep anybody from developing land in their township, regardless of the merits. The Zoning Board vote was due on a Tuesday. I went up to the property on the Sunday before the vote. On the way I picked up a copy of the Sunday New Jersey Herald. Some of the local citizens, who were out campaigning against my project, were on the staff of this publication. Suffice it to say, they used this newspaper to editorialize their views and to print letters to the Editor from people I didn't even know, who cast all kinds of aspersions on my character. After over two years of this treatment, I had developed high blood pressure, was experiencing irregular heart beats and had a couple of mini strokes. I didn't have much fight left in me when I arrived at the property and read the latest attacks on me and my plan.

The property is a beautiful piece of real estate spread out at the foot of the Kitttatinny Mountains. The leaves had just started to change color in their annual journey towards their Fall brilliance. I walked up to a promontory overlooking the 36 acre pond I had been building and scanned the vista across to the Kittatinny Ridge.

Spontaneously, without thought or provocation, from somewhere deep within me, I said aloud, "Lord, I have done all I can do. I'm putting everything in Your hands. Let Your Will be done and I'll accept it." Immediately, I felt like I had lost 100 pounds. I didn't care what the newspaper printed or how the Zoning Board voted. I felt free. When I got back to the car, I turned on the radio to get the latest weather. I picked it up on a local program, which turned out to be coming from a Christian radio station. At the conclusion of the weather, the disk jockey began immediately playing 'How Great Thou Art.' Here I was sitting in the middle of God's creation and listening to a song that described the universe displayed around me. I began to realize how great is the power of God and how weak is the power of man. No sooner had that beautiful piece been concluded when the station began playing 'Amazing Grace.' Yes, I once was lost and now I'm found, was blind and now I see. The song was talking a bout me. I have come through many dangers. toils and snares and it was God who brought me through them, not me. I have been redeemed by the blood of Jesus on the cross at Calvary and saved by His grace. He has been with me all the time and I never realized it until that moment. The missing piece was now in place. I was made complete and now I have started my walk beside Him. God is really something. When He wants your attention, He sure knows how to get it."

"That's the answer?"

"Yep, that's the answer. You only have to believe in him and ask for His forgiveness. Then He comes into your heart and draws you closer to Him."

"Well, did He save your project and your land and prevent a financial disaster?"

"No. But, He gave me the peace and the strength to accept that... and all the consequences that went with it. I dare say my life is better for it."

Chicky, still had a questioning look on his face. I wasn't sure what it was. Maybe he was puzzled by my placing faith in a God, who didn't extricate me from my crisis. But, God did. It wasn't the way I would have done it. But then, I'm not as smart as God. Maybe he didn't understand the nature of God and good news of redemption. He may have a thousand more questions that we can't answer at this time. He may need those answers.

"You know", He said. "When I had that operation on my aorta, I was afraid. I wanted to ask someone to help me get through it. I had never gotten to know about God, or Jesus my whole life and I didn't want to bother Them just at that time. But, I got through it. Then, I began to think, *maybe I should thank somebody.* This bothered me for a long time. When I saw your uncle's death notice, something moved me to go there...and something made me feel good and excited about coming here today. Is that the whole answer? I only have to ask Jesus for forgiveness and he will come into my heart and fill the void? It sounds too simple."

"Yeah. There's nothing to buy except maybe a Bible. Read the word and learn about God. Join a Church or a Fellowship and study the Scriptures. Then, obey His Word.

"You know, this is not real. I came here today to search into my past and maybe find some long lost meaning that would relate, or give me a clue to that something I've been searching for. I never expected such a simple answer... and from you of all people. I don't understand it. After I talked to Police Chaplains and all kinds of doctors; why would God send me here to get the answer?"

"God works in ways we will never understand. He wanted you to hear and He knew the best way for you to get the message. Like I said, Chicky, when He wants your attention...He sure knows how to get it. And, now that He has found you, are you ready to accept Him?"

# ABOUT THE AUTHOR

R. Allen Pender is a retired Engineer and the grandfather of fifteen children. It is this latter circumstance that inspired the U.S. Army veteran in his late sixties to write about his and his family's experiences on the American home front during World War II. He and his peers grew up during a unique time in modern American History. When he entered this world, The United States and rest of the world was buried in the depths of the Great Depression. The world wide economic turmoil which followed the Stock Market crash of 1929 created a political environment which fostered the growth of a variety of nationalistic movements in Europe and Asia. The leaders who rose up from within these movements sought to solve their economic problems by conquering and enslaving neighboring nations. The United States was somewhat isolated from the military operations taking place across the Atlantic and Pacific Oceans. In the late 1930's the United States began assisting England and Russia with war materials as both nations were engaged in repulsing the attacks of Hitler's Germany. Finally, on December 7, 1941; The Japanese Imperial Navy attacked the American Fleet at Pearl Harbor, Hawaii.

And now the U.S. was now thrust officially into the War.

The author was too young to enter military service in the conflict. However, he and his friends became a part of the War effort on the home front. They grew up in an environment beset with shortages and rationing. They shared in the sacrifices, which were imposed on the rest of society. The coming of age through this period has had a lifelong impact on the author and those of his generation. Like many others, he served in the military during the Korean War and then using the G.I. Bill went to college at night. In 1998 he retired after having a successful engineering career with many accomplishments. In his retirement years, Mr. Pender continues to consult with many clients on environmental and construction matters.

Printed in the United States
4616